Challenges of Globalization in the Measurement of National Accounts

Studies in Income and Wealth

NATIONAL BUREAU *of*
ECONOMIC RESEARCH

Volume 81

NBER Challenges of Globalization
NATIONAL BUREAU *of* in the Measurement of
ECONOMIC RESEARCH National Accounts

Edited by Nadim Ahmad, Brent R. Moulton,
J. David Richardson, and
Peter van de Ven

The University of Chicago Press

Chicago and London

The University of Chicago Press, Chicago 60637
The University of Chicago Press, Ltd., London
© 2023 by National Bureau of Economic Research
Published 2023
Printed in the United States of America

32 31 30 29 28 27 26 25 24 23   1 2 3 4 5

ISBN-13: 978-0-226-82589-2 (cloth)

ISBN-13: 978-0-226-82590-8 (e-book)

DOI: https://doi.org/10.7208/chicago/9780226825908.001.0001

Library of Congress Cataloging-in-Publication Data

Names: Aḥmad, Nadim, editor. | Moulton, Brent R. (Brent Richard),
    1954–, editor. | Richardson, J. David, editor. | Ven, Peter van de,
    editor.
Title: Challenges of globalization in the measurement of national
    accounts / edited by Nadim Ahmad, Brent R. Moulton, J. David
    Richardson, and Peter van de Ven.
Other titles: Studies in income and wealth ; v. 81.
Description: Chicago : The University of Chicago Press, 2023. | Series:
    National Bureau of Economic Research studies in income and
    wealth ; vol. 81 | Includes bibliographical references and index.
Identifiers: LCCN 2022053781 | ISBN 9780226825892 (cloth) |
    ISBN 9780226825908 (ebook)
Subjects: LCSH: Gross national product—Measurement. |
    Globalization.
Classification: LCC HC79.I5 C427 2023 | DDC 339.3/1—dc23/
    eng/20230124
LC record available at https://lccn.loc.gov/2022053781

♾ This paper meets the requirements of ANSI/NISO Z39.48-1992
(Permanence of Paper).

Relation of the Directors to the Work and Publications of the NBER

1. The object of the NBER is to ascertain and present to the economics profession, and to the public more generally, important economic facts and their interpretation in a scientific manner without policy recommendations. The Board of Directors is charged with the responsibility of ensuring that the work of the NBER is carried on in strict conformity with this object.

2. The President shall establish an internal review process to ensure that book manuscripts proposed for publication DO NOT contain policy recommendations. This shall apply both to the proceedings of conferences and to manuscripts by a single author or by one or more co-authors but shall not apply to authors of comments at NBER conferences who are not NBER affiliates.

3. No book manuscript reporting research shall be published by the NBER until the President has sent to each member of the Board a notice that a manuscript is recommended for publication and that in the President's opinion it is suitable for publication in accordance with the above principles of the NBER. Such notification will include a table of contents and an abstract or summary of the manuscript's content, a list of contributors if applicable, and a response form for use by Directors who desire a copy of the manuscript for review. Each manuscript shall contain a summary drawing attention to the nature and treatment of the problem studied and the main conclusions reached.

4. No volume shall be published until forty-five days have elapsed from the above notification of intention to publish it. During this period a copy shall be sent to any Director requesting it, and if any Director objects to publication on the grounds that the manuscript contains policy recommendations, the objection will be presented to the author(s) or editor(s). In case of dispute, all members of the Board shall be notified, and the President shall appoint an ad hoc committee of the Board to decide the matter; thirty days additional shall be granted for this purpose.

5. The President shall present annually to the Board a report describing the internal manuscript review process, any objections made by Directors before publication or by anyone after publication, any disputes about such matters, and how they were handled.

6. Publications of the NBER issued for informational purposes concerning the work of the Bureau, or issued to inform the public of the activities at the Bureau, including but not limited to the NBER Digest and Reporter, shall be consistent with the object stated in paragraph 1. They shall contain a specific disclaimer noting that they have not passed through the review procedures required in this resolution. The Executive Committee of the Board is charged with the review of all such publications from time to time.

7. NBER working papers and manuscripts distributed on the Bureau's web site are not deemed to be publications for the purpose of this resolution, but they shall be consistent with the object stated in paragraph 1. Working papers shall contain a specific disclaimer noting that they have not passed through the review procedures required in this resolution. The NBER's web site shall contain a similar disclaimer. The President shall establish an internal review process to ensure that the working papers and the web site do not contain policy recommendations, and shall report annually to the Board on this process and any concerns raised in connection with it.

8. Unless otherwise determined by the Board or exempted by the terms of paragraphs 6 and 7, a copy of this resolution shall be printed in each NBER publication as described in paragraph 2 above.

Contents

III. Globally Intangible Capital

Prefatory Note

This volume contains revised versions of the papers presented at the Conference on Research in Income and Wealth titled "The Challenges of Globalization in the Measurement of National Accounts," held in Bethesda, MD on March 9–10, 2018.

Support for the general activities of the Conference on Research in Income and Wealth is provided by the following agencies: Bureau of Economic Analysis, Bureau of Labor Statistics, the Census Bureau, the Board of Governors of the Federal Reserve System, the Statistics of Income/Internal Revenue Service, and Statistics Canada.

We thank Nadim Ahmad, Brent R. Moulton, J. David Richardson, and Peter van de Ven, who served as conference organizers and as editors of the volume.

Introduction and Overview

Nadim Ahmad, Brent R. Moulton, J. David Richardson,
and Peter van de Ven

The content of this conference volume is in some ways a return to the roots of the Conference for Research in Income and Wealth (CRIW), and in other ways a potential modernization of the national accounting framework that has grown from those roots.

The primal concern of the CRIW in its early years in the late 1930s was measurement:

1. measurement of economic activity within a space and over time, and of how the fruits of economic activity were distributed among groups of workers and resource-owners in that space and time, and

2. measurement of economic activity between spaces and over time periods.

Those measurement concerns remain central today and are reflected in the current international statistical standards, such as *System of National Accounts 2008* (2008 SNA), as well as in the update to these standards that is currently underway (European Commission et al. 2009; United Nations Statistical Commission 2021). But the environment in which measurement

Nadim Ahmad is Deputy Director at the Organisation for Economic Co-operation and Development (OECD) Centre for Entrepreneurship, SMEs, Regions, and Cities.

Brent R. Moulton is former economist at the International Monetary Fund, and former Associate Director for National Economic Accounts at the Bureau of Economic Analysis.

J. David Richardson is Professor Emeritus of Economics and International Relations at Syracuse University, and a research associate of the National Bureau of Economic Research.

Peter van de Ven is the lead editor of the update of the 2008 SNA and former Head of National Accounts at the Organisation for Economic Co-operation and Development.

For acknowledgments, sources of research support, and disclosure of the authors' material financial relationships, if any, please see https://www.nber.org/books-and-chapters/challenges -globalization-measurement-national-accounts/introduction-challenges-globalization -measurement-national-accounts.

concerns are addressed has changed in fundamental ways, many of which relate to varieties of globalization.

The first "environmental" change is that the categories of "space" have expanded to include corporate space as well as geographic space. In some sense, that was always true, but in the modern era corporate and geographic space no longer co-vary or overlap as tightly as they once did. For example, traditional geographic measurement may miss or mismeasure cross-border economic activity when it comes to activities of multinational enterprises (MNEs).[1] Furthermore, it is less and less meaningful to distinguish "our" (domestic) multinational corporate activity from "their" (foreign) multinational corporate activity. Modern MNEs have owners and stakeholders, such as employees and subcontractors, spread around the world.

The second environmental change is that inputs into the production of goods and services are increasingly sourced abroad. While it has long been the case that raw materials have been sourced from around the world, it is more recent that manufacturing processes have become fragmented and specialized with extensive supply chains that combine many components, often supplied from many countries. These fragmented supply chains have rendered some traditional measures of bilateral trade misleading and have led to the development of new ways of summarizing trade flows, such as trade in value added (Ahmad 2015).

The third environmental change is that the long-lived input that we call "capital," which links economic activity over time in a variety of conceptions, has become increasingly intangible (Haskel and Westlake 2018; Corrado et al. 2009). Intangibility, however, is not its most important trait for this conference volume. What really matters in the chapters that follow is that intangible capital is nearly perfectly mobile across space ("footloose"), and that intangible capital is a non-rival collective input to its owner. That is, its use in one of its owner's spaces does *not* heighten its scarcity in other spaces. How to value such non-rival capital—for tax reasons as well as more conventional reasons—has much in common with valuing public goods, such as military security and orderly institutions, that are prototypically non-rival and "owned by everyone."

Intangible capital's mobility correspondingly challenges our ability to conceive and identify its exact location; to what space or country does it "belong"? Perhaps to all spaces in which it is used? If so, then its global value may come close to the sum of the various national values where it is employed on behalf of its global multinational owner.

Modern multinational corporate research and development (R&D) provides an illustration of this third change and its measurement challenges.[2]

---

1. See Baldwin, Lipsey, and Richardson (1998) for an early consideration of issues and for additional citations.

2. Supra-national government-sponsored and owned R&D illustrates in the same way. See chapters 13 and 14 by de Haan and Haynes and by Ker et al. below.

Branstetter et al. (2019a, b) describe the proliferation of US-MNE-owned R&D affiliates abroad, all generating innovation that gets added to the MNE parent's productive-though-intangible capital stock. But it is equally available to the same MNE's affiliate abroad, which is not deprived of it (nor therefore is its country of residence deprived). One of their figures shows a strong and intriguing correlation between a typical affiliate's own patenting—an indicator of its own innovation—and the concentration of the US parent's other affiliates in India, Israel, Japan, and a handful of high-innovation host countries.[3]

All this can render dubious familiar, yet simple-minded, measures of formulary apportionment discussed in several chapters below. It also complicates rules for imputing ownership of MNE intangible capital, and challenges statisticians to creatively consider innovations in methods of apportionment and imputation.

Underlying Measurement Challenges

The first group of chapters focuses on the organization of MNEs, the problems associated with establishing their residence and their economic ownership of intangible assets, and the implications of those problems for economic measurement. The problems are threefold. Over the last three decades, the largest MNEs have grown in size and extent, representing a much larger and more important share of global economic activity than formerly. Digitization has amplified the importance of intangible assets—not only computer software and databases, but also R&D and designs for high-tech products, as well as entertainment and artistic intellectual property that can be easily streamed or otherwise distributed around the globe. And the adaptation of the international statistical standards to these developments, as reflected in the capitalization of most of these newer forms of capital, has resulted in national accounts that are quite sensitive to the residency of MNEs and the assignment of economic ownership to intangible capital.

This volume opens with "Addressing the Challenges of Globalization in National Accounts" by Brent R. Moulton and Peter van de Ven, which provides a broad overview of the measurement challenges associated with globalization. It examines the difficulties associated with applying the concepts of residency and economic ownership to MNEs and their intangible assets. It reexamines long-standing problems with transfer prices within a multinational group when there are no market equivalent prices to which they can be compared. It looks at the financial risks and vulnerabilities that may be disguised by intra-firm financial connections.

---

3. Branstetter et al. (2019b, figure 9, p. 14). Their affiliate-level regression explaining its number of patents controls for its own R&D spending, its specific U.S. parent, and the year of observation.

The chapter concludes with an extensive discussion of possible ways to address the measurement challenges described in the paper. Some of the suggested remedies are available within the current economic guidelines, while others would require going beyond the guidelines of the current 2008 SNA. Most, or all, of these remedies will require the development of new data sources and mechanisms for exchanging individual data on MNEs across countries. These mechanisms will require the development of legal frameworks for exchanging data for statistical purposes. Statistical practices will need to adapt to meet the challenges of the increasingly globalized real economy.

In his discussant comments, Marshall Reinsdorf endorsed the need for more communication and better documentation to enable users to interpret the standards and supplementary data. He also agreed that consideration should be given to possible changes in the SNA that might assign intellectual property assets and profits in a manner that is more reflective of economic activity and less driven by taxation rules. Such changes, however, would "require international cooperation to overcome source data obstacles." He also suggested that, if possible, accounting rules that would pass through retained earnings of corporations to their shareholders should be considered.

European statisticians, policy makers, and data users were taken aback when Ireland reported that its real GDP increased more than 25 percent in 2015, due to the relocation of MNE headquarters and intellectual property product into the country. Silke Stapel-Weber, Paul Konijn, John Verrinder, and Henk Nijmeijer of Eurostat explain how new indicators may be needed to isolate domestic developments in a highly globalized context in their chapter, "Meaningful Information for Domestic Economies in the Light of Globalization: Will Additional Macroeconomic Indicators and Different Presentations Shed Light?" They describe the development of the EuroGroups Register—a statistical register covering 110,000 MNE groups operating in Europe.

To focus the presentation of statistical data on domestic activities, Stapel-Weber et al. suggest that certain existing series such as adjusted disposable income of households may be featured more prominently. They also suggest splitting the nonfinancial corporations sector into subsectors of domestically operating corporations and affiliates of multinational enterprises. They also consider developing an adjusted measure of gross national income that excludes the retained earnings of companies that are mainly owned by foreign investors and the depreciation of foreign-owned capital. An empirical comparison of EU countries shows that while Ireland is an important outlier, these globalization issues also affect the interpretation of national accounts figures of other countries.

"National Accounts for a Global Economy: The Case of Ireland" by John FitzGerald sits prominently as an exemplar of issues not only for Ireland but for the world and for this whole volume. In Ireland, as well as in some other

MNE-friendly countries like the Netherlands, the issues are quantitatively arresting. Elsewhere, the issues are still vital to understanding, using, and comparing national accounts meaningfully across countries, though their quantitative impacts are more modest.

Not only did measured Irish GDP rise by over 25 percent in 2015, but the Irish stock of productive capital rose by 40 percent as non-Irish MNEs moved headquarters and intellectual property capital into the country. In addition, because of the SNA's treatment of global production arrangements, Irish GDP included the value added generated by the production of goods that were the result of Asian contract manufacturing. Irish exports of services associated with the movement of intellectual property capital, through licensing and leasing, were especially large in the pharmaceutical and aircraft industries, causing equally astounding measures of change in the Irish current account.

Following the principle that the most natural constituents for measures of Irish GDP and trade are Irish-resident persons and firm owners not affiliated with foreign MNEs, FitzGerald shows that the impacts on them were far smaller and needed considerable supplementary measurement (denoted with an asterisk, reminiscent of athletic record accomplishments).

FitzGerald's generalization of these findings beyond Ireland is that most users of national accounts data are lost without separate, parallel, comparable, twin measures of economic activity for MNEs and for "strictly domestic" economic activity, illustrated in his table 3.6 for Ireland during 2013–2018, albeit in non-deflated nominal measures. An important takeaway from that discussion is that MNE operations contribute disproportionately more to Irish value added than they do to Irish income (NNI), a provocation for users who fret about trends in inequality.

FitzGerald's chapter is cornucopia as well as exemplar, a cornucopia of essential ingredients for this volume, if not fully refined or blended or digested for countries beyond Ireland.

In his instructive and colorful discussion, Tebrake amplifies and memorably illustrates FitzGerald's main points (e.g., he conjures up an Irish superstar app developer whom the statisticians must track). Toward the end he raises the idea of an Irish-resident-owned aggregate that he calls gross owned product (GOP). Such a measure might be especially useful for countries with disproportionately concentrated ownership of MNEs.

Echoing Stapel-Weber et al. in chapter 2, Tebrake observes that "the bigger issue that needs to be addressed by national statistical offices is consistency in measurement—we need to tell a global story to achieve consistency and cross-national comparability, but we are still using national collection tools and national data. . . . We need a fundamental shift in how we collect data from large MNEs." In contrast, FitzGerald's implicit approach is to encourage a thousand flowers to bloom at the national level to enlighten data users about nationally distinctive issues (e.g., aircraft leasing for Ireland).

Maria Borga and Cecilia Caliandro, in "Eliminating the Pass-Through: Towards FDI Statistics That Better Capture the Financial and Economic Linkages between Countries," focus on a long-standing traditional measure of MNE presence, foreign direct investment (FDI). FDI measures yearly ownership additions of one country's residents in another country's firms, where such additions are in equity that conveys and reflects corporate control. FDI traditionally is an important component of long-term investment by one country in another.

But FDI measures are a far cry from FitzGerald's measures of MNE contributions to a nation's (Ireland's) GDP and current account. Kamran Bilir makes this point right at the beginning of her discussion. And the ensuing general discussion noted that traditional FDI accounting reveals little about characteristics of MNE operations such as shares of value added, payrolls, and capital formation by industry.

FDI accounting can be improved, as Borga and Caliandro demonstrate.[4] Their two interrelated frontiers of FDI measurement are first, how to identify or measure the ultimate owners of cross-border equity by tracing through global chains of holding-company equity to the foundational equity owners and their country of residence, and second, how to distill inter-company financial borrowing and lending along the ownership chains, often through company-owned financial sub-companies called special purpose entities (SPEs). Though the authors provide valuable guidance, its relevance for measuring economic activity in a domestic economy is more distant. For example, though the MNE headquarters that Ireland welcomed in the 2000s are a sort of "headquarters SPE," Borga and Caliandro's focus is on netting them out of traditional FDI measurement, rather than on measuring their effects on national income and product.

The next three chapters of this volume refocus on a key part of national income, corporate profits, as affected by the ownership chains and SPEs of the previous two chapters. In environments with large numbers of MNEs, corporate profits can easily be "shifted"—assigned and reassigned by company accountants to their affiliates abroad or to the MNE parent in response to tax and regulatory incentives. Strategic pricing of intra-company transactions is an obvious way of doing so,[5] but advantageously assigning the residence of an MNE's intangible capital is a growing alternative (see the discussion of chapters 12–14 below).

Jennifer Bruner, Dylan G. Rassier, and Kim J. Ruhl, in "Multinational Profit Shifting and Measures throughout Economic Accounts," focus illustratively on measurement of US MNE corporate operating surplus in 2014. Their measurements of "what might have been" if the MNEs had

---

4. They build on FDI measurement developments pioneered for decades by the Organization for Economic Cooperation and Development (OECD).

5. See Bernard et al. (2006).

allocated their operating surplus differently from their actual arrangements that involved profit shifting are dramatic.[6] Aggregate US operating surplus would have been 3.5 percent higher, and US GDP 1.5 percent higher, than conventionally measured. Consequently, labor income shares would have been correspondingly lower.

Using unpublished firm-by-firm data for US MNEs, the authors reassign operating surplus by a formula that re-weights each affiliate's reported operating surplus by an average of the affiliate's employee compensation and its unaffiliated (non-intra-company) sales, each expressed as a share of the whole MNE's compensation and sales. They essentially force an MNE's profits to reflect its payrolls and sales among the countries in which it operates. They view the specific choice of their two weights as natural, not exclusive, because the weights reflect the concerns of national income and product accounting. They would be open to alternative weights and formulas because their purpose is to show how quantitatively large and misleading is naïve reliance on current MNE corporate accounting, albeit legal from a statutory perspective.

Redding's discussion invites such alternative weights and types of averages, all in the spirit of seeing how robust their quantitative calculations are. He also recommends additional checks of robustness by assessing the computations by industry and affiliate location—do their formulas create the largest differences where we might expect them, e.g., in industries with large amounts of intangible capital and in host countries renowned for being tax havens?

Derrick Jenniges, Raymond Mataloni Jr., Sarah Stutzman, and Yiran Xin, in "Strategic Movement of Intellectual Property within US Multinational Enterprises," focus on US regulations governing parent-affiliate cost-sharing agreements (CSAs).[7] Using a sample of 237 MNEs that are especially dependent on R&D inputs, they confirm that US MNEs relocate and reduce corporate taxes. But, as Jensen observes in his discussion, their ambition is rather narrow—they make no attempt to estimate the aggregate size or impact of CSAs. And, as Jensen noted in the discussion, they leave important measurement questions unanswered: "For example, it would be useful to show that CSAs are more prevalent in R&D-intensive firms and industries, and by how much. Another important fact to document is whether low-tax affiliate jurisdictions are more intensive in MNEs with CSAs than others and, if so, by how much. Last, it would be very helpful to show that the large multinationals with large R&D stocks but with no CSAs are, somehow, unusual outliers."

"The Relationship between Tax Payments and MNE's Patenting Activities and Implications for Real Economic Activity: Evidence from the Neth-

---

6. Redding finds them large in his discussion. They build on similarly large calculations of U.S. productivity effects using the same re-apportionment formula by Guvenen et al. (2017).
7. Sadly, Raymond Mataloni Jr. has passed away since the conference took place.

erlands" by Mark Vancauteren, Michael Polder, and Marcel van den Berg is less about macroeconomic measurement and more about microeconomic forensics. Using a panel of micro-data for Dutch-resident innovating firms, including MNE affiliates, over two subperiods since 2000, they find that firms facing low corporate tax rates to stimulate innovation are marked by two performance premiums. First, they patented more and "better" than other firms. And second, they generally enjoyed better labor- and R&D-productivity[8] performance than other firms. These results are a reminder that even after measurement is refined, many important economic questions remain to be answered. This chapter's specific question is whether policies that lower Dutch taxes on corporate innovation (by both MNEs and local firms) may be justified by the boost to innovation that they generate. If so, and if so for other countries to which MNEs shift profits, then attempts to reign in profit shifting and the MNEs that practice it may discourage economic growth, possibly even global growth.

Global Value Chains for Intermediate Products

The next group of chapters looks at a set of issues around the lengthening of global value chains. A half century ago, it would not have been unusual to think of trade as flows largely consisting of raw agricultural and material commodities on the one hand, and finished products that were destined for use in final consumption or capital formation on the other hand. But with improvements in technology, reduced costs of transport, and opening of trade barriers, the supply chains for manufacturing now often entail a wide variety of intermediate products from many countries reflecting multiple stages of processing. The globalization of supply chains has adversely affected the usefulness of the traditional industry data provided in the national accounts, such as supply and use tables (SUTs). The analysis of input-output relationships based on national statistics necessarily hits a wall when intermediate products are imported or exported. Statistical agencies have made various attempts to provide more information to fill in the blanks—for example, foreign affiliate trade statistics (linking trade to the activities of MNEs) and trade in value added (linking the SUTs of many countries and identifying trade in terms of value added rather than gross flows). While these sources have revealed important information that isn't apparent in traditional trade statistics, they also have their limitations in that traditional SUTs are not designed to identify or highlight the activities of multinational enterprises (MNEs). So additional information is desired to understand the changing relationship between inputs and outputs in the face of globalization.

In "Accounting Frameworks for Global Value Chains: Extended Supply-

---

8. They measure R&D productivity by patents per euro of R&D spending.

Use Tables," Nadim Ahmad observes that the additional information that analysts desire needs to supplement the information from the traditional supply and use tables (SUTs), so he suggests a set of extended SUTs. The first part of his chapter provides an extensive menu of possible extensions, along with explanations of why each extension may be useful. For example, a relatively simple extension is to separately identify goods processing transactions (that is, manufacturing services arrangements in which a processor does not own the material inputs or the output that is being processed) from those not involving processing. Another example is an extension that separates production taking place within a free trade zone from that taking place outside those zones.[9] Ahmad addresses several practical difficulties associated with some of the possible extensions to the SUTs, such as difficulties in blending data from different sources and involving different statistical units. His chapter also provides examples of extended SUTs from several countries, including China, Mexico, the United States, Costa Rica, Canada, and five Nordic countries. While it would not be practical for a statistical agency to pursue all, or even most, of the extensions presented in this chapter, it is nevertheless useful to understand the set of options that might be undertaken in a particular implementation.

A sophisticated and interesting example of this methodology is provided by "Accounting for Firm Heterogeneity within US Industries: Extended Supply-Use Tables and Trade in Value Added Using Enterprise and Establishment Level Data" by James J. Fetzer, Tina Highfill, Kassu W. Hossiso, Thomas F. Howells III, Erich H. Strassner, and Jeffrey A. Young. They estimate extended SUTs for the United States that account for two types of firm heterogeneity: type of ownership (MNEs and non-MNEs) and firm size. Most analytical uses of input-output relationships rely on an assumption of homogeneity in the technical coefficients, but globalization has made homogeneity less common. The chapter shows that accounting for the type of ownership and the firm size is useful for reducing heterogeneity in the value-added share of production, thereby providing more useful estimates. The compilation primarily combines data from the US SUTs with BEA survey data on the activities of multinational enterprises (AMNE); several additional Census Bureau datasets were also utilized. Because the SUTs are based on establishment data, while the AMNE data are compiled for enterprises, adjustments had to be made to convert the enterprise data to an establishment basis. For semiconductors, the estimates used Census of Manufactures microdata that were linked to BEA AMNE surveys—an important proof of concept of the benefits of building the estimates up from the microdata. They found that value added as a share of output is highest for US MNEs and lowest for foreign MNEs. Their results provide

---

9. Saborío and Torres (2018) discuss how to estimate extended SUTs that focus on the role of free trade zones for Costa Rica.

evidence that firm heterogeneity in both ownership and firm size matters in measuring industrial production.

In discussant comments, Susan N. Houseman recommends that caution is needed if the estimates from this chapter are used to compare productivity between MNEs and non-MNE establishments. Implicitly, comparisons of labor productivity across establishments are based on assumptions that production functions are homogeneous—an assumption that is almost certainly incorrect. Just as MNEs and non-MNEs use different imported inputs, they also are different in the stages of production that they engage in. MNEs are more likely to outsource stages of production to non-resident affiliates or producers.

In "The Role of Exporters and Domestic Producers in GVCs: Evidence for Belgium Based on Extended National Supply-and-Use Tables Integrated into a Global Multiregional Input-Output Table" by Bernhard Michel, Caroline Hambÿe, and Bart Hertveldt, heterogeneity is addressed by identifying export-oriented and domestic market firms. The authors combine Belgian SUTs and input-output tables with firm-level data that allow them to disaggregate the tables. In a subsample of larger firms, they identify firms with an export-to-turnover ratio of at least 25 percent as export-oriented. The data are then balanced to ensure consistency with the aggregated data in the standard SUTs. The extended SUT for Belgium are then linked to a global multiregional input-output table for the same year from the World Input-Output Database. They confirm that there is heterogeneity between export-oriented and domestic market firms. Export-oriented firms have a lower ratio of value added to output and a higher share of imported intermediate inputs. Their work also illustrates that for a smaller country, such as Belgium, the sample sizes may sometimes be inadequate to estimate the desired splits at the most detailed industry level.

Bart Los and Marcel P. Timmer, in "Measuring Bilateral Exports of Value Added: A Unified Framework," return to the measurement of trade in value added. The general idea can be illustrated by a production process involving four countries and three stages of production. Country A produces a raw material valued at 1, which it exports to Country B; B produces an intermediate product valued at 2, which it exports to C; and C produces a final product valued at 3, which it exports to D, which consumes it. Countries A, B, and C each produce value added of 1, but only in Country A does that match its gross exports. Country C produces value added of 1 and exports 3. Los and Timmer are looking for measures of value added that are relevant for measuring bilateral trade flows so they can answer questions like, Which countries are most important in demanding the value-added content of a country's exports? They discuss three types of measures, which focus on (a) value added for direct use, (b) value added for the final stage of production, and (c) value added for final consumption. In the example, the Country A's value-added exports are with Country B for the direct use measure, with

Country C for the final stage of production measure, and with Country D for the final consumption measure. They apply these concepts with an empirical example based on data from the World Input-Output Database.

Globally Intangible Capital

"A Portrait of US Factoryless Goods Producers" by Fariha Kamal ties together the concerns about the geographical location of production discussed in the last section with the problem of measuring the role of intangible R&D in production, which will be the focus of this section. The chapter is rooted in firm-level microeconomics with implications for macroeconomic measurement.

It characterizes American factoryless goods producers (FGPs). FGPs are a type of firm in the value chain whose outputs are almost entirely intangible—principally management, design, and coordination of other commercial establishments. In some cases, there are other establishments that reside within the same national boundary as the FGP, but they often reside abroad. These other establishments may or may not be affiliates owned by the FGP.

The macroeconomic significance of such firms is revealed in two comparisons, comparisons that also hold for a less extreme "hybrid" form of manufacturing firm.[10] First of all, FGPs have larger shares of "high-end" employees and of intellectual property (intangible capital) relative to both traditional manufacturing firms and generic services firms. Relative to other firms, they perform more R&D and patent more. Secondly, they are younger and rely more on imports—and implicitly, exports—than other firms do. They are obviously an extreme type of firm born of fragmented value chains that are themselves globalized. But they are just as obviously dynamic contributors to a country's aggregate economic growth and its stock of desirable jobs and globally deployable intangible capital.

Classifying, measuring, and evaluating firms and their respective industry aggregates along globalization and fragmentation continuums is an ongoing challenge for statistical communities and researchers worldwide. The challenges include valuation of a firm's own intangible capital, which can be shared or licensed across national boundaries without depleting the stock that remains, and consistent measurement of the exports and imports of such intangible capital. These are also the concerns of the closing chapters of this volume, as illustrated by R&D.

Mark de Haan and Joseph Haynes, in "R&D Capitalization: Where Did We Go Wrong?" diagnose the central concern of the last group of this volume's chapters, how to measure gross domestic product and national income in a globalized world where a large and growing share of capital and capital

---

10. Hybrid manufacturing firms outsource and offshore many, but not all, manufacturing activities, relative to traditional manufacturers.

formation is intangible—specifically R&D. The diagnosis includes the following challenges:

1. geographically locating such infinitely mobile capital and its ultimate owners;
2. valuing it in cases where its availability to the last user does not diminish its availability to the next (the classic collective-goods trait);
3. employing the answers to 1 and 2 to assign capital services and income measures to the jurisdictions that host the owners and users (sometimes licensees, more often MNE affiliates) of the capital.

The chapter gives few detailed prescriptions for what to do about the diagnostic challenges it so succinctly summarizes. Michael Connolly observes in his discussion that "this is a concept paper, so the practical difficulties associated with the implications of the authors' recommendations are not fully explored." Notwithstanding this lacuna, practical implementation is urgently urged for statistical agencies and communities, since R&D and all intangible capital are growing globally as a share of total capital. And the chapter provides a rich array of illustrative case studies (Samsung, Philips, Apple, Nike, and Google-Ireland/Google-Netherlands/Google-Bermuda), as well as suggestive conceptual parallels. Among the latter, the most important is a comparison of R&D to infrastructure investment and their often-differing capacities for nailing down ownership and corresponding income streams.

In their otherwise comprehensive treatment, the authors spend hardly any time on the mushrooming frequency of MNE R&D that is "public-within-the-firm" and undiminishable to any part of the MNE in its global use/application. A statistician compiling national accounts for a country that hosts such MNE affiliates must decide on what part (none? all? some proportional-yet-arbitrary share?) of the MNE's cumulative R&D "belongs" in the country and its statistics. The measurement challenge almost begs for satellite accounts reflecting alternative coherent approaches. This rich chapter includes much more on related issues, e.g., corporate vs. national accounting differences, how to think about depreciation of R&D capital, national tax policy and MNE corporate tax planning.

"Capturing International R&D Trade and Financing Flows: What Do Available Sources Reveal About the Structure of Knowledge-Based Global Production?" by Daniel Ker, Fernando Galindo-Rueda, Francisco Moris, and John Jankowski extends the previous chapter's discussion. Focusing also on R&D, it uses the so-called Frascati methods described in OECD (2015) to add measurements of its cross-border trade and ownership. These methods complement those in the familiar SNA approaches, but they also, all too frequently, contradict them quantitatively.[11]

Compared with the chapter by de Haan and Haynes, this chapter's scope

---

11. See especially the chapter's discussion of its tables 14.1 and 14.2.

and time coverage is wide. OECD-member data for 1995–2015 on R&D production ("performance"), exports and imports (services trade, licensing), and funding sources are all discussed and presented in tabular cross-country comparisons. The dry term "funding sources" obscures the chapter's interesting detail on MNE R&D compared to aggregate national R&D, on R&D trade among MNE affiliates and arms-length R&D trade, and on patents and ultimate (beneficial) ownership of R&D services. Bilateral nation-to-nation counterparts to all these data are also discussed, showing even larger-than-usual divergences between one country's exports of R&D to another in its own data and the receiving country's corresponding imports of the same.

One of the chapter's most intriguing, though tentative, conclusions is that R&D production is becoming *less* concentrated within countries, leading to a growing decoupling of R&D production and its use and application. This is exactly what we might expect as R&D becomes increasingly "globalized," the phrase the authors use recurrently in their chapter text but not in its title.

Concluding Remarks

During the past decades, the world economy has changed dramatically. Global production arrangements have grown significantly, although the COVID-19 crisis and growing geopolitical tensions may have led to a refocus on international interdependencies and just-in-time deliveries. In addition, the ever-increasing intangible nature of capital has led to capital and related production becoming less tied to geography. MNEs looking for opportunities to minimize their global tax burden can create worldwide fiscally advantageous constructions, including the use of SPEs and transfer pricing, with the result that the allocation of output and value added to countries has become far more challenging. This volume has demonstrated with various examples the challenges that these changes have created and the resulting direct impacts on the measurement of GDP and national income.

The volume includes several proposals to address the measurement challenges. Within the context of the current international standards for compiling national accounts, one can distinguish five ways forward:

- Focus on other indicators in addition to GDP. The tax-motivated allocation of output and value added across countries directly affects GDP, as well as the measurement of capital stocks and services of intangible assets. Other macroeconomic indicators, such as net national income (NNI) and household (adjusted) disposable income, are far less affected by the way in which MNEs have organized their production processes.
- Include further breakdowns in supply and use tables and institutional sector accounts. Here, a delineation of MNE-activities, both foreign and domestic MNEs, may support a better understanding of what exactly drives the domestic economy.

- Invest in arriving at better *international* consistency of data on MNEs. The exponential growth of international interdependencies, including the frequent changes in the global production arrangements, have resulted in numerous inconsistencies in the recording of international flows and stocks. As some examples in this volume have shown, this can even lead to output and value added not being recorded at all. The international inconsistencies can be addressed, at least to a certain degree, by improving international cooperation and coordination, such as the alignment of business register information for MNEs, and the international exchange of information on bilateral flows and stocks, especially in the case of large events such as mergers and acquisitions, relocation of activities, and corporate inversions.
- Invest in arriving at better *national* consistency of data on MNEs. National accounts are based on numerous source data: foreign trade statistics, balance of payments and international investment positions, data on the finances of corporations, production statistics, and the like. Often the information on MNEs that can be derived from these source statistics contain major inconsistencies. In many national statistical offices, so-called Large Cases Units have been set up to arrive at a more aligned recording of MNE activities in the domestic economy.
- Finally, alternative types of analysis can result in an improved understanding of developments in the domestic economy. They may also lead to an improved analysis of productivity and competitiveness of the national economy. An example is trade in value added, which looks at the domestic value added in the context of foreign trade instead of looking at gross trade flows.

However, one may also wonder whether changes in the current international standards could possibly result in improved measures of GDP, which better reflect economic substance, instead of basically following money flows, which are governed by global tax considerations as currently the case. Some of the chapters in this volume include suggestions for possibly modifying the international standards, such as consolidating SPEs or alternatively allocating operating surplus and intangible capital to countries. Notwithstanding the conceptual attractiveness of some of these proposals, the consensus of the participants in this conference appeared to have been very hesitant to introduce such rather dramatic changes in the international standards, first and foremost because of practical problems.

Many proposals would require a massive exchange of individual enterprise data across countries, which is currently impossible because of legal limitations on data sharing. An alternative solution would be to arrive at an internationally centralized collection of data on MNEs, which would then be distributed to the relevant national statistical offices. Whatever the case, it would thus require a paradigm shift in the (international) compilation of national accounts, including the organization of statistical processes across countries. For these reasons, statisticians across the globe tend to focus on the five ways forward presented in the above.

References

Ahmad, Nadim. 2015. "Measuring Trade in Value-Added and Beyond." In *Measuring Globalization: Better Trade Statistics for Better Policy*, Volume 2, edited by Susan N. Houseman and Michael Mandel. Kalamazoo, Michigan: W.E. Upjohn Institute for Employment Research.

Baldwin, R. E., Robert E. Lipsey, and J. David Richardson, eds. 1998. *Geography and Ownership as Bases for Economic Accounting*, Studies in Income and Wealth, Volume 59. Chicago: University of Chicago Press.

Bernard, A. B., J. B. Jensen, and P. K. Schott. 2006. "Transfer Pricing by U.S. Based Multinational Firms." NBER Working Paper No. 12493. Cambridge, MA: National Bureau of Economic Research.

Branstetter, Lee G., Brita Glennon, and J. Bradford Jensen. 2019a. "The IT Revolution and the Globalization of R&D." *Innovation Policy and the Economy* 19: 1–37.

———. 2019b. "The Rise of Global Innovation by US Multinationals Poses Risks and Opportunities." *Policy Brief* 19–9, June. Washington, DC: Peterson Institute for International Economics.

Corrado, Carol, Charles Hulten, and Daniel Sichel. 2009. "Intangible Capital and U.S. Economic Growth." *The Review of Income and Wealth* 55 (3): 661–85.

European Commission, International Monetary Fund, Organisation for Economic Co-operation and Development, United Nations, and World Bank. 2009. *System of National Accounts 2008*. New York, United Nations. https://unstats.un.org /unsd/nationalaccount/sna.asp.

Guvenen, Faith, Raymond J. Mataloni Jr., Dylan G. Rassier, and Kim J. Ruhl. 2017. "Offshore Profit Shifting and Domestic Productivity Measurement." NBER Working Paper No. 23324. Cambridge, MA: National Bureau of Economic Research.

Haskel, Jonathan, and Stian Westlake. 2018. *Capitalism without Capital: The Rise of the Intangible Economy*. Princeton, NJ: Princeton University Press.

Organisation for Economic Co-operation and Development. 2015. *Frascati Manual 2015: Guidelines for Collecting and Reporting Data on Research and Experimental Development*.

Saborío, Gabriela, and Rigoberto Torres. 2018. "Costa Rica: Integrating Foreign Direct Investment Data and Extended Supply and Use Tables into National Accounts." Paper presented at CRIW Conference, "The Challenges of Globalization in the Measurement of National Accounts," March 9–10, 2018, Bethesda, MD. http://conference.nber.org/conf_papers/f100627.pdf.

United Nations Statistical Commission. 2021. "Report of the Intersecretariat Working Group on National Accounts." 52nd session, March 1–3 and 5, 2021, E/ CN.3/2021/8. https://unstats.un.org/unsd/statcom/52nd-session/documents/2021 -8-NationalAccounts-E.pdf.

I

Underlying Measurement
Challenges

1

Addressing the Challenges of
Globalization in National Accounts

Brent R. Moulton and Peter van de Ven

1.1 Introduction—Overview of the Challenges of Globalization

Increased globalization—through increased international trade, capital flows, and the growth of multinational enterprises—is one of the most important developments affecting the world economy during the last 25 years. Globalization grew rapidly over this period, especially during the 15 years leading up to the 2007–2009 economic and financial crisis. Total world trade in goods and services, for example, increased from 41 percent of world GDP in 1993 to 61 percent in 2008, before dropping during the recession and then afterwards rebounding.[1] The growth of foreign direct investment was perhaps even more dramatic. The direct investment asset position for the United States, for example, increased from 14 percent of GDP at year-end 1992 to 40 percent at year-end 2007. Global competition and the deepening of global supply chains have transformed many industries and led to profound economic changes. Globalization has been associated with innovation in business practices as corporations increasingly manage their production and sales activities at a global level.

While we won't attempt to give a full accounting of the reasons for the acceleration in globalization, several factors appear to have played major

Brent R. Moulton is former economist at the International Monetary Fund, and former Associate Director for National Economic Accounts at the Bureau of Economic Analysis.

Peter van de Ven is the lead editor of the update of the 2008 SNA and former Head of National Accounts at the Organisation for Economic Co-operation and Development.

The views expressed in the paper are those of the authors and should not be considered as representing the official views of the OECD or of its member countries. For acknowledgments, sources of research support, and disclosure of the authors' material financial relationships, if any, please see https://www.nber.org/books-and-chapters/challenges-globalization-measurement-national-accounts/addressing-challenges-globalization-national-accounts.

1. Source: World Bank data, https://data.worldbank.org/indicator/NE.TRD.GNFS.ZS.

roles. First, advances in digital information and communication technologies, notably including the introduction of widespread access to the Internet, have enabled enterprises to do things like manage deeper supply chains on a "just in time" basis, manage production and marketing activities in more locations, and utilize intellectual property products on a global scale. Second, economic reforms and investment have allowed developing economies—notably including China and India—to greatly expand their productive capacity and open new markets to trade and investment. Third, the end of the Cold War, along with strengthened international institutions and reductions in trade barriers, has undoubtedly contributed to a more stable economic environment in which enterprises are willing to invest globally.

Our focus, of course, is on economic measurement, and specifically on the impact of globalization on the national accounts. In this chapter we will focus on the interplay between economic activities, which are often not constrained by national boundaries, and national accounting statistics, which are defined in terms of national totals. In particular, we find that the effects of globalization can make national data hard to interpret, and for certain types of analysis may even be considered a distorting influence on the data.

The impact of globalization was one of the driving forces behind the most recent update of the *System of National Accounts* (SNA), the internationally agreed standards for compiling national accounts, in 2008.[2] The updated 2008 SNA addresses many of the challenges in globalization by clarifying fundamental principles such as "residence" (when is an institutional unit considered to be part of a national economy?) and "economic ownership" (when is an institutional unit recognized as the owner of an asset, and when should a change in ownership be recorded?).

The 2008 SNA also acknowledges the growing importance of intellectual property products by recognizing expenditures on research and development as fixed capital formation and the resulting intellectual property product as a fixed asset, joining other intangible intellectual property assets, such as computer software and databases, which were recognized by the SNA in its previous 1993 update. In the globalized context, the fact that intellectual property products are non-rival means that a multinational enterprise can freely use its intellectual property anywhere it operates at zero marginal cost.

While each of these changes in the SNA clarified the concepts and improved the overall coherence of the system, globalization also led to some practical difficulties when these concepts are applied to multinational enterprises that do not operate along national lines. One of the challenges is that multinational enterprises often structure the locations of their operations and legal ownership of their assets in ways that reduce their global tax liabilities or regulatory burdens. Section 1.2 of this chapter looks at some

2. European Commission et al. (2009).

of the challenges that national accountants face when they attempt to apply the concepts of residency and economic ownership more generally, and the ownership of intellectual property products in particular, to multinational enterprises.

The rapid growth of globalization also exposed some new difficulties in the long-standing problems associated with measuring prices and volume changes, which we will discuss in section 1.3. Many international transactions are among affiliated enterprises within a multinational enterprise group, and the valuations assigned to these transactions are considered "transfer prices" because there is often no market equivalent price to which they can be compared. Again, multinational enterprises have incentives to try to set transfer prices to reduce their global tax burden.

In addition to measuring production and generation of income, the SNA also covers financial accounts and balance sheets. In section 1.4 of this chapter, we discuss how globalization may impact these data, and the vulnerabilities that were exposed during the 2007–2009 economic and financial crisis. For example, to understand a nation's financial vulnerabilities, better information is needed on the nature of the relationships with counterparties, whether affiliated or unaffiliated.

Section 1.5 looks at the path forward, examining possible ways to address the measurement challenges described in the earlier sections. Some of the options call for providing supplementary information while staying within the current rules of the SNA. Other options involve possible changes to the standards, which could be considered in a future update of the SNA and related international standards and guidelines. Finally, some options would involve a more fundamental rethinking of the data collection process. Under a new paradigm for data collection, countries would cooperate in the collection and sharing of data on operations of multinationals to more accurately measure the activities of multinational enterprises.

One aspect of the data needs associated with globalization that we will not discuss in detail, but which is well covered at this conference, is producing information on global supply chains for understanding the value added associated with trade. Because gross trade flows by country often have very little to do with where production activities associated with traded goods take place, bilateral trade data are often misinterpreted. Recognizing this problem, the OECD and World Trade Organization developed data on trade in value added, which weights trade flows by the value added associated with a country's contribution to the production of an exported good or service. These estimates rely on global input-output tables developed by the OECD. More recent research, including several papers at this conference, suggests that the estimates can be improved by making various extensions or supplements to the information of the traditional supply and use data used to estimate input-output relationships.

1.2   Multinational Enterprises, Residency, Economic Ownership, and Intellectual Property Products

1.2.1   Concept of Residency in Principle and Practice

One of the core definitions or constructs of the 2008 SNA is the residency criterion.[3] It delineates the units that are part of the national economy, and, at least indirectly, defines all macroeconomic aggregates that can be derived from the system. In § 4.10 of the 2008 SNA, the concept of residence is elaborated as follows: "*The residence of each institutional unit is the economic territory with which it has the strongest connection, in other words, its centre of predominant economic interest.*"[4] § 4.14 subsequently defines an institutional unit as having a center of predominant economic interest "*when there exists, within the economic territory, some location, dwelling, place of production, or other premises on which or from which the unit engages and intends to continue engaging, either indefinitely or over a finite but long period of time, in economic activities and transactions on a significant scale.*" For the period of time, one year is taken as a (somewhat arbitrary) operational definition.

For corporations and nonprofit institutions, the above residency principle means that enterprises have a center of economic interest in the country in which they are legally constituted and registered. Multinational enterprise groups may have centers of economic interest in quite a few countries. In this respect, § 4.15 (c) also explicitly states that when a corporation ". . . *maintains a branch, office or production site in another country in order to engage in production over a long period of time (usually taken to be one year or more) but without creating a subsidiary corporation for the purpose, the branch, office or site is considered to be a quasi-corporation (that is, a separate institutional unit) resident in the country in which it is located.*" So, even in the case in which a legal entity is not created, a unit without separate legal status that engages in substantial economic activities is considered a resident institutional unit.

In § 4.55–4.67, the 2008 SNA also addresses the residency of special purpose entities (SPEs), which are defined as having no employees and no nonfinancial assets; having little physical presence beyond a "brass plate"; always related to another corporation; and often resident in a country other than the country of residence of the related corporation (see § 4.56). Although such legal units would normally not qualify as separate institutional units because they may not perform any activities of economic substance and would be consolidated with the related corporation, if they are resident on

---

3. European Commission et al. (2009).
4. An exception to the rule of each institutional unit only having one country of residence is the existence of so-called multi-territory enterprises, typically involved in cross-border activities such as shipping lines, airlines, pipelines, bridges, tunnels, and undersea cables. The operations of such enterprises are typically prorated into the relevant economic territories.

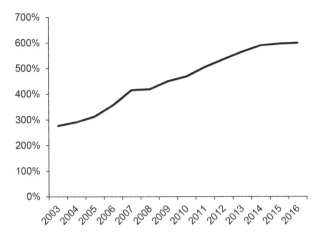

Figure 1.1   Balance sheet totals of "special financial institutions" in the Netherlands, 2003–2016, percentage of GDP
Source: De Nederlandsche Bank (2018).

the economic territory of another country, they are treated, by convention, as separate units. In some countries, this convention can have a massive impact on the system of national accounts. For example, in the Netherlands, a country with a very high presence of SPEs, the total balance sheet value of such units, the main share of which concerns financial assets and liabilities with the rest of the world, amounted to 600 percent of GDP at the end of 2016; see figure 1.1. Also, the related in- and outflows of property income are very substantial, amounting to 20–25 percent of GDP in the years 2010–2016. Flows of imports and exports of services would add another 3–5 percent.

For multinational enterprises, the above residency principles mean that the activities of each group of units belonging to a multinational enterprise that are located on the economic territory of a certain country are to be recorded as part of national economy of that country. This even holds in the case that the relevant unit, or group of units, has physical presence but no separate legal status (e.g., branches), and only performs ancillary activities for the corporation at large, as well as in the case of an SPE with legal status but hardly any physical presence. All these units, if located on the same economic territory as the related corporation, typically would not qualify as an institutional unit.

One may wonder why the above convention has been chosen. Two related reasons are relevant here. First of all, only this treatment would be consistent with the actual cross-border cash flows resulting from economic transactions. The other reason is that a "look-through" recording of SPEs, for example, would require a massive international exchange of individual data between statistical offices, which is not possible given existing legal constraints. However, we note that abandoning this convention and making the international exchange of individual data possible might actually resolve a lot of problems, though by no means all of them, related to the impact of globalized behavior of multinational enterprises on the measurement of national accounts.

The increased international integration of production poses serious challenges to adequately accounting for domestic activities. To arrive at a consistent recording of all transactions of internationally operating enterprises becomes more and more complex, especially in an economic environment that is characterized by quickly changing organizational structures of ever-increasing complexity that also operate across borders. Conceptual differences in recording international trade flows add to the problems, since foreign trade statistics are generally based on goods crossing national borders, whereas national accounts (and business statistics) should be recorded on the basis of change in ownership. In practice, when combining the various source data for individual companies at the national level, one is often faced with major inconsistencies, which may also show up when balancing supply and demand for goods and services at the macro-level in the supply and use tables. One may also be confronted with significant differences between, for example, the transactions recorded in the balance of payments and the source statistics on income and finance of corporations. These consistency problems have triggered various initiatives, such as creating specific units within national statistical offices that are responsible for micro-balancing the transactions and positions of the largest and most complex corporations. Another initiative is the growing international coordination of the allocation of the various parts of multinational enterprises to countries, such as the EuroGroups Register, in which the register information for multinational enterprises in Europe is coordinated across countries.

In addition to the above more practical and source statistics related problems, the activities of multinational enterprises also raise various conceptual or analytical concerns for the compilation of national accounts for national economies. The first and perhaps most prominent issue concerns the allocation of value added to national economies. As discussed in section 1.3, multinationals have substantial intra-group transactions in goods and services that cross the borders of national economies. The valuation of these transactions, often referred to as "transfer pricing," has a direct impact on the allocation of value added and GDP to countries. If, for example, a multinational from the United States arranges the production of its goods in China, and subsequently distributes them to another subsidiary in Europe, a low price for the export from China to Europe will result in lower output, value added, and profits in China, and higher values outside China. Although such prices, according to most national tax legislations, have to be set at market-equivalent prices, there is obviously quite some room to maneuver, especially in the case of goods containing high margins for reasons of knowledge content or brand reputation, or related to corporate and ancillary services, or in the case of goods that are intermediate products which are not marketable, so that it is not possible to apply a true market-equivalent price.

1.2.2 Economic Ownership

Another complication in the recording of cross-border transactions of multinational enterprises, and consequently also in the allocation of economic activities to national economies, concerns the application of the principle of economic ownership. In national accounts, transactions between units are based on the principle of change in economic ownership. In § 3.26 of the 2008 SNA, economic ownership is defined as follows: "*The economic owner of entities such as goods and services, natural resources, financial assets and liabilities is the institutional unit entitled to claim the benefits associated with the use of the entity in question in the course of an economic activity by virtue of accepting the associated risks.*" The change in economic ownership depends, of course, on the delineation of institutional units in the SNA. As noted in the above, an institutional unit, the unit for recording and classifying units in national accounts,[5] is defined as a unit that is capable of owning assets, incurring liabilities, and engaging in economic activities and in transactions with other entities. It is also able to make economic decisions for which it is itself held to be directly responsible and legally accountable. The institutional unit generally consists of a legal unit or a limited group of legal units. Enterprise groups, in which a parent corporation controls several subsidiaries, are not to be considered as a single institutional unit (see § 4.51–4.52 of the 2008 SNA). A change in economic ownership would typically coincide with a financial transaction between two institutional units and would therefore coincide with a change in legal ownership. But there are clear exceptions to this rule.[6]

The principle of economic ownership is not necessarily straightforward within multinational enterprises. All affiliates of an enterprise group are to some degree controlled by their parent, whereby the case of multinational enterprise groups has the added complication of having non-autonomous affiliates which are considered as institutional units by convention, simply because they are resident in an economic territory that is different from the

---

5. Please note that the unit for recording the production process, for example in the supply and use table, is the establishment. "An establishment is an enterprise, or part of an enterprise, that is situated in a single location and in which only one productive activity is carried out or in which the principal productive activity accounts for most of the value added" (§ 5.2 of the 2008 SNA). To be able to compile meaningful statistics on the production process, it must be possible to derive data for establishments on the items included in the production and generation of income account: output, intermediate consumption, compensation of employees, taxes less subsidies on production, etc.

6. An exception relates to, for example, financial leasing. The lessor is the legal owner of the relevant asset (e.g., an airplane), but the lessee is considered to be the economic owner.

parent's. Transactions between units of a multinational enterprise, or the absence of such transactions as recorded in business accounts, may therefore be at odds with the principle of economic ownership. On the other hand, in practice there may be no alternative to following business accounting, unless one performs a detailed and resource-demanding analysis of individual transactions of the relevant enterprise groups. And even in the latter case, one would need to liaise with the statistical offices of other countries to arrive at a consistent recording across countries, which is not an easy task given current confidentiality rules for exchanging micro-data.

1.2.3   Intellectual Property Products (IPPs)

To add yet another layer of complexity, modern economies are more and more knowledge based, in that the competitive edge of an enterprise and a country is often driven by the ownership on intellectual property products (IPPs), the use of which is neither physically nor locally constrained. In the 2008 SNA, four types of produced IPPs are distinguished: (i) research and development; (ii) mineral exploration and evaluation; (iii) computer software and databases; and (iv) entertainment, literary or artistic originals. In addition, some non-produced IPPs are recognized, e.g., contracts, leases, and licenses (e.g., permissions to use natural resources). Also, goodwill and marketing assets are recognized and recorded if evidenced by purchases.[7]

Determining the economic ownership of IPPs, and therefore the allocation of the output and the use of these assets, is already challenging in a more traditional environment of multinational enterprises owning a group of affiliated entities producing goods and services, including corporate or ancillary services. But it gets even more complicated in a world where multinational enterprises set up complex structures to allocate the receipts from IPPs and the payments for using them in the preferred way. For example, SPEs are being established in certain countries to reallocate the collection and distribution of royalties, license fees, or profits more generally, with the purpose of avoiding or minimizing worldwide tax payments. Countries that offer low tax rates or that provide the opportunity of using certain fiscal loopholes are very attractive for the establishment of such conduits. The use of these conduits often gets front-page news coverage once they become publicly known and relate to well-known multinational enterprises. However, it also has become less obvious to exactly pin down the economic ownership of these intangible assets.

The United Nations Economic Commission for Europe (UNECE) *Guide to Measuring Global Production* took up the challenge of trying to come up with a decision tree for determining the economic ownership of IPPs;

---

7. Even when goodwill and marketing assets cannot be recognized and recorded due to the absence of transactions, it should be emphasized that these unmeasured intangible assets may still affect the value of the enterprise and generate operating surplus that may distort the international allocation of income, just as is the case for measured IPPs. The same may be true for organizational capital, such as the services provided by headquarters.

see chapter 4 of UNECE (2015). Looking more closely at the decision tree in this *guide* on how economic ownership is established for units operating within a multinational enterprise, first a distinction is made as to whether a unit is producing the IPP. If the unit is producing the IPP and also uses it in its production process, or receives income from royalties and licenses, the unit is considered to be the economic owner. However, if the unit receives compensation from the parent for the development or the sale of the IPP, the parent is considered the owner. If there is no evidence of compensation at all, it is assumed that the unit is indirectly funded by the parent, and economic ownership is allocated to the producing unit.

On the other hand, if the unit is not the producer of the IPP, and it is using the IPP for the production of other (non-IPP) goods and services, one may distinguish three alternatives: (i) the unit pays royalties and licenses; (ii) the unit made a payment to purchase the IPP; and (iii) no IPP-related payments are being observed. Economic ownership in the first two cases is rather straightforward: in the second case the unit in question is the economic owner, in the first case it is not. In the third case, the default option is not to consider the unit as the economic owner. With respect to the latter case, § 4.36 of the UNECE guide notes the following: *"However, one could also argue that since these units are obtaining the benefits from IPPs, they could alternatively be identified as the actual economic owners inside MNEs. This would argue in favour of imputing the transfer of the IPP original from the parent to the unit and capitalization of this IPP on the balance sheet of the unit under observation. This is not an easy task, and not without risks. The nature, size and timing of these flows are principally unknown. This is why such an approach is not advocated. . . ."* Finally, if the unit is not the producer of the IPP, and its main output is IPP related, we have the case of units created by multinational enterprises with the purpose of taking advantage of low tax jurisdictions. Here, § 4.38 of the UNECE *guide* recommends the following: *"The default solution is assigning economic ownership of the IPP to these units, in correspondence with legal ownership. Rerouting of ownership, and corresponding income flows, from the legal to the economic owner is not recommended."*

For more details on determining economic ownership for a unit that participates in a global production arrangement but not as member of a multinational enterprise, reference is made to the UNECE guide, page 51 ff. More generally, as noted by the guide, it is less problematic to establish the economic ownership in these circumstances, as these are autonomous units and payments for the transfer or use of IPPs can be observed from market transactions.

1.2.4   Effects on GDP, GNI, and Productivity

The above rules clearly can have a significant impact on the allocation of output, value added (GDP), and profits across countries. Reasons related to worldwide tax minimization, instead of "economic substance," often govern decisions at the enterprise level on how to price intra-concern deliveries of goods and services, where to allocate the ownership and returns from IPPs, etc. This may hamper the provision of "meaningful" data on the economic performance of national economies. On the other hand, some would argue that global tax optimization also reflects a macroeconomic reality, albeit not the economic reality one would want to arrive at for more traditional types of economic analysis and policy research. Whatever the case, we do have a problem here, as sufficiently proven by what is commonly referred to as "the Irish case." Ireland noticed a remarkable economic growth of 26.3 percent in 2015, which was mainly driven by international relocations of IPPs and related production activities to Ireland. In response, the Irish government set up an Economic Statistics Review Group (ESRG), under the leadership of Philip Lane, the then governor of the Irish central bank, with among others the goal to arrive at ". . . *supplementary statistics that are more appropriate to the measurement of domestic economic activity . . . that will be comprehensible and stable over time*" (ESRG 2016). More information can also be found in OECD (2016).[8]

Looking closer to the impact on GDP, then transfer pricing will have a direct, one-to-one impact on the levels of GDP across countries. In most cases, the impact on levels of gross national income (GNI)[9] will be far less substantial, as the profit shifting to low tax jurisdictions will be countered by a near equivalent increase of property income received from those countries. Also, in the case that the profits are retained, they will add to the relevant property income receipts in the form of reinvested earnings from foreign direct investment. In the SNA, all profits, including the retained part, of multinational enterprises are recorded as if they were repatriated to the country of the headquarters. To balance the recording of retained earnings as part of property income, the relevant receipts are considered to be directly reinvested into the non-resident affiliate as part of financial investments in shares and other equity. However, it should be noted that in some cases GNI can also be affected significantly—for example, if substantial depreciation costs, which negatively affect profits and retained earnings of affiliates, feed into the equation. But this is another issue, not directly related to the issue of transfer pricing, which will be dealt with below. We also note that net national income (NNI) would not be affected in this latter case. Finally, household disposable income, which is nowadays much more used as an indicator of household material well-being, is invariant for all these transfer pricing mechanisms.

When it comes to multifactor productivity measurement, one should generally be aware of the fact that at the national level one only sees part of

---

8. In this volume, the Irish case is examined in more detail by FitzGerald.

9. GNI is equal to GDP plus primary incomes (property income, compensation of employees, and taxes less subsidies on production and imports) receivable from non-resident units less primary incomes payable to non-resident units.

the elephant. The full production process, including all intermediate inputs, can only be truly analyzed at the global level of the enterprise. Nevertheless, this would not be a major issue if the recording of the national part indeed includes all the implicit intra-concern transactions at fair value. However, as noted before, certain deliveries may be recorded at transfer prices which do not reflect the true value. Furthermore, corporate services, including ancillary services and the use or purchase of IPPs, may not be adequately reflected. Although all of this will have an impact on the description of the inputs that are used in the production process, it is less clear how this will affect the measurement of output, intermediate consumption, and consumption of fixed capital in volume terms, and therefore the measurement of productivity over time. This will be the topic of the next section.

Another problem in arriving at a consistent and exhaustive recording of the worldwide production process concerns the international consistency and exhaustiveness of the various national parts of multinational enterprises. It is not clear what would happen if one could put all these parts of the elephant representing the multinational enterprise together. The different pieces of the puzzle may not fit together, and one may also end up with missing a leg or the trunk. The contribution by de Haan and Haynes in this volume provides an excellent example of potential underreporting of worldwide output.

However, from a point of view of analyzing economic developments of a national economy, changes in the arrangements of the productive activities within the multinational enterprise and international relocation of certain activities may have the most disruptive impact. The UNECE *Guide to Measuring Global Production* provides a nice example in country case study 3.3 on page 37, where a multinational centralized the worldwide purchases of manufactured goods from unaffiliated contract producers, because of which part of the trade margins previously allocated to local distributors ended up being allocated to the country of the headquarters.

Other examples concern the relocation of economic activities from one country to another. It takes some time and significant disinvestments to relocate the physical production of goods in factories. But when it comes to IPPs and other movable assets such as trucks and airplanes, it is far easier to relocate the relevant assets and the related output, only needing the advice of some creative lawyers and business accountants. Such relocations can lead to massive shocks in GDP, especially for smaller economies, such as the Irish example has proven. Certainly, when the relocation cannot be considered as a legal construct without any "economic substance," one is—as was once provocatively expressed by Robin Lynch, the former director of National Accounts at the UK Office for National Statistics—"doomed." At some stage, it was argued that the impact of such relocations could be moderated, or even extinguished, by attributing all IPPs and related returns to the headquarters of the multinational enterprise. But one nowadays also

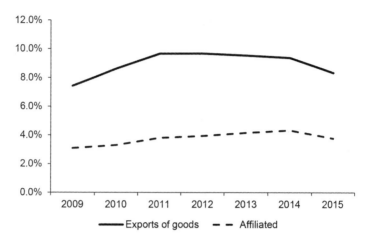

Figure 1.2   Exports of goods, total, and affiliated, United States, 2009–2015, percentage of GDP
Source: Bureau of Economic Analysis.
Note: "Affiliated" is the sum of US exports of goods shipped by US parents to foreign affiliates and US exports of goods shipped by US affiliates.

frequently observes the international relocation of headquarters, thus leaving the national accountant again empty-handed.[10] We will come back to this issue of how to possibly address these adverse impacts on the more traditional economic analysis of domestic productive activities. But at this stage we only would like to add that refocusing on alternative national accounts indicators and looking at the complete framework of national accounts, including further breakdowns of multinational activities versus the activities of national corporations, may become all the more important to understand the performance of a national economy.

1.3   Price and Volume Issues

1.3.1   Transfer Pricing

A large share of international economic transactions, including trade in goods and services, occurs within multinational enterprise groups. The United States reports data on the trade by US multinational enterprises with their affiliates (both US parents and US affiliates of foreign parents). As seen in figure 1.2, goods exports to affiliated entities ranged from 38–46

---

10. Corporate inversion is an increasingly common practice that uses strategic mergers to relocate the headquarters of a corporation to a lower tax country. According to Congressional Budget Office (2017), in 2014 U.S. corporations with combined assets of $390 billion announced plans to invert that year.

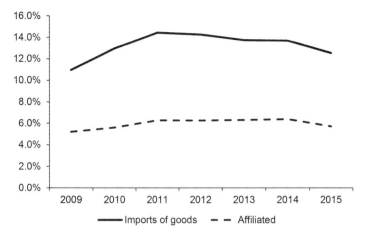

Figure 1.3   Imports of goods, total, and affiliated, United States, 2009–2015, percentage of GDP
Source: Bureau of Economic Analysis.
Note: "Affiliated" is the sum of US exports of goods shipped by US parents to foreign affiliates and US exports of goods shipped by US affiliates.

percent of total exports of goods. Figure 1.3 shows that goods imports from affiliated entities ranged from 43–48 percent of total imports of goods. How does trade among affiliated parties differ from unaffiliated trade?

For transactions among members of a multinational enterprise group, the multinational has a great deal of discretion in structuring the transactions and setting the internal trading terms, or "transfer prices," at which goods and services are exchanged between affiliates. Because the intra-group transactions often consist of specialized components that are unique to the multinational enterprise and thus not directly comparable to transactions by unrelated parties, it can be difficult to establish a market price, and the multinational has an incentive to set a transfer price that lowers its global tax burden.

Transfer pricing rules used by tax administrations in most countries require multinational enterprises to set prices for tax purposes according to the "arm's length principle"—that is, to value the transactions and calculate profits as if the transactions had been between independent businesses. The use of the arm's length principle represents an attempt to provide a consistent basis for profit allocation and helps prevent multinationals from experiencing double taxation. But as globalization has increased, transfer pricing arrangements have become more complex and important, while management of multinational enterprises has become more integrated and sophisticated. These changes have given multinationals more latitude to set business arrangements and transfer prices to reduce tax burden and have been a challenge to national tax administrations, which often lack the specialist industry expertise that is possessed by the multinationals. Thus, it is reasonable to assume that the effects of transfer pricing have increased over time.

To the extent that multinational enterprises are successful in booking transfer prices that overstate or understate the appropriate economic value of a transaction, GDP will be misstated as well. If transfer prices are reported consistently in the enterprise's books and those book values are the source of national statistical data, then all three approaches to measuring GDP (the production, expenditure, and income approach) will reflect the misstatement. However, because the 2008 SNA treats the reinvested earnings on foreign direct investment as if they were distributed to the owners, GNI should be less affected by the use of misleading transfer prices (UNECE 2011, § 2.21).

While the 2008 SNA recommends that prices should be adjusted to a market-equivalent price when values do not represent market prices, especially when distortions are large, it also recognizes that this may not be practical. Because exchanges between affiliated enterprises often do not have any near market equivalents, ". . . *compilers may have no choice other than to accept valuations based on explicit costs incurred in production or any other values assigned by the enterprise*" (2008 SNA, § 3.131–33). Statisticians thus have to rely on data reported by enterprises that follow tax and legal requirements, and the best prospect for addressing transfer pricing problems is likely to come from reforms to international tax rules.

The overall effect of transfer pricing and other profit shifting strategies is probably quite large. For example, the OECD estimated that for 2014, the broad strategies known as Base Erosion and Profit Shifting (see below), which include transfer pricing as well as other tax avoidance strategies, reduced global corporate income tax liabilities by $100 billion to $240 billion, or 4–10 percent of total corporate income taxes (OECD, 2015b). While most estimates are in terms of foregone tax revenues rather than the effects on GDP, Guvenen et al. (2017) conclude that reattributing earnings of US multinationals would raise US GDP by about $280 billion, or 1.7 percent, for 2012.[11] This reattribution would be offset by lower GDP in other countries if the income has been attributed to those other countries. Although their data couldn't be used to measure the full effect of earnings reattribution on the GDP of other countries, it is likely that for some countries—especially for tax havens—the effect as a percentage of GDP may be quite large.

While transfer pricing affects the value of GDP in current prices, if the transfer prices are reported on a consistent basis over time, the use of

---

11. Clausing (2016), using a somewhat different methodology, derives a similar estimate of the overall effect for the United States: $258 billion for 2012. Bruner, Rassier, and Ruhl (in this volume) examine the effects with a fully articulated set of economic accounts.

transfer prices may not necessarily bias the price indices used for deflation, and consequently for the volume measurement of economic growth. For example, if the price of an exported component is consistently undervalued by 25 percent, the bias in the price level would not necessarily bias the measure of price change. But if deflation is used and the level of the bias of GDP in current prices changes, the latter biases will also be reflected in GDP volume changes and the resulting productivity statistics. That is why Guvenen et al. (2017) report biases in US productivity growth due to profit shifting.[12]

Beginning in 2013, the OECD and the G20 governments embarked on a major project, the Base Erosion and Profit Shifting (BEPS) initiative, to update the international tax rules to align with developments in the world economy and to ensure that profits are taxed where economic activity takes place and value is created. A set of major recommendations was published in 2015. There is new guidance on transfer pricing that reinforces the arm's length principle and requires multinational enterprises to report information on their global business operations and pricing policies to help ensure compliance. Tax treaty provisions are strengthened, and measures are introduced that should eliminate or reduce tax regimes that attract paper income rather than substantial business activities. Model rules are introduced to improve consistency in domestic tax laws. The BEPS measures focus especially on the digital economy, associating income more closely with the value-added activities of the business (OECD 2015a).

Despite some initial uncertainty about how effective the BEPS initiative would be when it comes to country compliance, the project now appears to be moving forward quite successfully. In 2016, the European Commission adopted the Anti-Tax Avoidance Directive, which directly addresses several of the BEPS recommendations. Furthermore, the EU member states adopted the BEPS multilateral instrument, which improves dispute resolution methods. In the United States, the 2017 Tax Cut and Jobs Act also implemented many BEPS recommendations, including its underlying single tax principle. Reuven Avi-Yonah of the University of Michigan has described the US tax act as "the triumph of BEPS." In July 2021, 130 countries[13] that were participating in the BEPS Inclusive Framework agreed to a two-pillar solution in which a portion of the taxing rights on the largest MNEs would be reallocated to the jurisdictions where the customers and users are located, and a global minimum tax rate of 15 percent on large MNEs would be adopted (OECD 2021). The implementation of these pil-

12. Biases in price indices for imported and exported goods and services can also have large effects in measures of GDP volume change and productivity. For example, Houseman et al. (2011), focusing on U.S. manufacturing, find that the price indices for manufacturing inputs failed to pick up the full price saving from switching from domestic to foreign suppliers. They estimate that manufacturing real value added was overstated by about 0.2 to 0.5 percentage point per year from 1997 to 2007.

13. By November 4, the number of countries agreeing to the two-pillar solution had increased to 137, though several members of the framework had not yet agreed to it.

lars remains somewhat tentative and provisional, however, as many details remain to be worked out and rules need to be adopted. The BEPS project is not a panacea. We can expect countries to continue to try to enhance their tax competitiveness and multinational enterprises to take advantage of these opportunities. Nevertheless, based on what has already been accomplished, the BEPS initiative has already been a turning point in improved international tax cooperation and compliance that should ultimately improve the quality of national and international data. However, in the transition period, statisticians may be faced with discontinuities in the source data they collect, potentially having an adverse impact on the measurement of economic growth and productivity.

1.4   Financial Vulnerabilities/Balance Sheets

The previous sections mainly dealt with the impact of globalization on the recording of production and income-generating activities. However, globalization also has significant consequences for the recording and interpretation of financial transactions and positions. No one doubts that financial frictions and failures affect the cost of capital and other inputs to production and income-generating activities that are the dominant concern of this volume.

This short intermezzo discusses some of the issues related to foreign direct investment (FDI) statistics and the monitoring of financial risks and vulnerabilities through financial exposures to the rest of the world. The latter challenges were exposed during the 2007–2009 economic and financial crisis, when many countries were surprised by their vulnerability to collateralized securities and other risky instruments. While the G20 Data Gaps Initiative (see, e.g., Heath 2013) has made progress toward filling data gaps and providing better statistical data for dealing with possible future crises, continued work is needed to reach goals for comprehensive and transparent financial data, including FDI and exposures related to portfolio investment. One of the problems in appropriately monitoring these financial risks and vulnerabilities is related to the difference in financial exposure of intra-firm financial connections versus true financial positions between autonomous firms at arm's length.

It is clear that globalization and the setting up of complicated organizational structures using SPEs complicates the economic analysis of FDI. Multinationals not only set up SPEs to arrange worldwide borrowing and lending activities but they also establish SPEs that "intermediate" between the ultimate controlling unit (the parent of the multinational) and the ultimate beneficiary of the investments to minimize the global tax burden or other reasons. Countries like Ireland, Luxembourg, and the Netherlands are very popular destinations for such intermediate SPEs. The direct consequence is that FDI statistics often show these countries as the country of destination and origin of direct investments, while they only have an intermediating role from an economic substance point of view. This has led to compiling more granular FDI statistics, separating out transactions and positions which are related to SPEs. In addition, guidance on the compilation of FDI statistics, such as the OECD *Benchmark Definition of Foreign Direct Investment* (BMD4), recognizes the need for having alternative numbers looking, for outward investments, to the ultimate host country (UHC); and for inward investments to the ultimate investing country (UIC). However, although recommendations on how to define and compile data according to UIC have been put forward, it was not yet possible to provide methodology for monitoring outward FDI according to UHC, as a consequence of which it has been put on the research agenda.

More generally, when assessing the foreign exposures, and therefore the financial risks and vulnerabilities, of a national economy, it makes quite a difference whether the counterparty of financial assets and liabilities is an affiliated enterprise or nonaffiliated enterprise. Especially in the case of large financial conglomerates, the impact can be quite substantial. For example, the Bank for International Settlements (BIS) produces banking statistics not only on a locational basis, i.e., applying the residence principles of the 2008 SNA and BPM6, but also from a so-called nationality perspective. In the latter statistics, they consolidate the positions of global financial conglomerates, and allocate all financial assets and liabilities of the relevant multinational enterprise to the home country of the parent. In this way, they manage to arrive at statistics showing the link between the controlling unit and the ultimate borrower or lender from the perspective of the conglomerate bank. One thus arrives at a different perspective of foreign exposures, according to which, for example, positions of resident affiliates of foreign multinationals are excluded, while positions of foreign affiliates of resident multinationals are included. McCauley et al. (2017) include a nice example of how this alternative perspective provides a different view on the declining trend since the 2007–2009 economic and financial crisis of banks' cross-border claims.

The above nationality perspective basically comes down to using the enterprise group as a single institutional unit. Inasmuch as the parent is indeed the ultimate bearer of all the risks and rewards, this certainly makes sense from an economic substance point of view. It is also clear that international intra-concern financial positions are different from other foreign exposures. This is not only true for financial conglomerates but also for multinational enterprises producing nonfinancial goods and services. The attempts made to have alternative presentations for FDI according to the UIC- and UHC-principles basically go in the same direction. However, it may not always be that clear-cut who bears the ultimate risks. A foreign affiliate may go bankrupt, and the parent may lose the money invested, but that does not necessarily mean that they will have to pay for all the claims toward the foreign affiliate. Indeed, a separate legal unit may be created for the purpose, among others, of minimizing liabilities in the event of bankruptcy. Furthermore, such a consolidated perspective may be less suitable when it comes to production and income-generating activities. We will come back to that in the next section.

1.5   International Standards and Guidelines—The Path Forward

As noted before, the allocation of value added generated by multinational enterprises is, for a large part, driven by tax and regulatory considerations. Typical routes of minimizing the worldwide tax burden consist of transfer pricing and the allocation of the use of intellectual property products and various services within the enterprise group. The establishment of SPEs further complicates the picture. Even more disruptive to the traditional analysis and interpretation of GDP is the sudden relocation of economic activities, significantly facilitated by the lack of physical and local constraints on movement of intangible assets and related income from one country to another. Also, relatively minor reorganizations within multinational operations can have quite severe impacts on the allocation of output and value added to countries. So, the key question is how to solve these issues to arrive at a more meaningful framework from a user's perspective. In the following, a distinction is made between possible ways forward that would stay within the conceptual boundaries of the current international standards for compiling national accounts (the 2008 SNA), and possible alternatives that would require a change in the current conceptual framework of national accounts.

1.5.1   Staying within the Boundaries of the Current Conceptual Framework: Providing Supplementary Information

Staying within the boundaries of the current concepts and definitions, one can distinguish three options, in addition to more advanced types of analysis such as looking at trade in value added, as discussed in other papers presented in this volume: (i) better use of available data within the framework of national accounts; (ii) provision of additional details on activities of multinationals; and (iii) definition of alternative indicators that can be derived from the current set of national accounts data.[14]

Although the first option is not truly a solution to the problems caused by the allocation of value added to national economies by multinational enterprises, we think it is important to acknowledge that the system of national accounts is a complete and comprehensive framework from which a variety of indicators can be derived, which can provide lots of information on what actually is going on in the economy. All too often, users, policy makers,

---

14. Further discussion of additional indicators and presentations is provided by Stapel-Weber et al. (in this volume).

and researchers seem to focus solely on GDP as the ultimate yardstick for monitoring economic progress. Sudden shocks in GDP due to substantial relocations of economic activity that are difficult to interpret, such as the Irish case, are then used to disqualify the whole system and to ridicule the current international standards as not being able to keep up to its task. However, as noted before, there are other indicators like GNI/NNI, which are much less affected by relocations of activities without requiring substantial physical presence on the geographical territory. In this respect, it came a bit as a surprise that GNI (but not NNI) had a massive impact from the relocation to Ireland. The reason for this impact on GNI was related to the fact that the relocation was accompanied by a substantial shift of IPPs, as a consequence of which the depreciation of these IPPs led to less reinvested earnings on foreign direct investment, which normally would counterbalance the upward shift of GDP. In this respect, it may be useful to reiterate the point made in § 2.142 of the 2008 SNA: "... *GDP is broadly used even if it is, on a conceptual basis, economically inferior to NDP [net domestic product]*." One of the reasons for not using net concepts, as explained in the 2008 SNA, is lack of internationally comparable data on depreciation or, in SNA terminology, consumption of fixed capital. However, one may wonder whether this reason still holds nowadays. It may well be that there simply is a significant amount of reluctance by both producers and users to change the tradition of focusing on the volume growth of GDP. As we see it, the margins of error in adjusting for price changes may well go beyond the margins of error in adjusting for depreciation.

In addition to the above discussion on GDP/NDP and GNI/NNI, it is important to keep on reminding users that GDP is not the appropriate measure of the economic well-being of households. For the latter, the SNA provides significantly superior indicators such as household (adjusted) disposable income. And, as the Irish case has shown, this indicator is only affected by the relocation of economic activities to Ireland in 2015 to the extent that it concerns true physical presence in the form of additional employment and compensation of employees for households.

The second option is to provide more granularity in the system of national accounts. For example, as part of further improving and enriching the analysis on trade in value added, extended supply and use tables are being defined, in which relevant industries are broken down into enterprises operating domestically, enterprises controlled by domestic multinationals, and foreign-controlled affiliates of multinational enterprises. To improve the information content of national accounts, Rassier (2017) proposes a separate identification of transactions and positions of SPEs, different from "operating activities," in the recording of domestic economic activities as well as in the accounts for the rest of the world.

The above breakdowns may indeed be very illustrative in explaining what's happening in the national economy. As part of the previously mentioned

G20 Data Gaps initiative (G20 DGI), the templates for collecting national data on institutional sector accounts are being reconsidered. One of the proposals in this context consists of having a breakdown of the sectors' non-financial corporations and financial corporations along the lines proposed for the extended supply and use tables. Similar to what has been proposed by Rassier (2017), one could also consider a separate identification of SPEs within the subsector foreign-controlled financial corporations. However, all of this is not a straightforward exercise from a practical point of view, as a consequence of which the breakdown according to the extended supply and use tables has only been included on a voluntary basis. Notwithstanding this voluntary basis, many countries—as some of the other chapters in this volume show—are beginning to incorporate these breakdowns, because (i) they provide improved insights on the impact of globalization on the domestic economy; (ii) they usually do not require new data collections; and (iii) they improve the overall quality of national accounts. At the international level, no provision has yet been made for a separate identification of SPEs, although in some countries' national accounts, data (e.g., for financial corporations and the rest of the world) are already being produced with and without SPEs, simply because the sheer magnitude of the transactions and positions of these SPEs completely blurs the overall picture of the national economy.

The third option within the boundaries of the current conceptual framework concerns the definition of alternative indicators that can be derived from the system of national accounts. Some may argue that this option is not truly in line with the 2008 SNA. On the other hand, it does leave the recording of transactions and positions unchanged as compared to the current international standards, as it merely rearranges some transactions to arrive at an alternative headline indicator. Perhaps it may not be feasible to agree on the definition of such an alternative at the international level. For example, one may end up with an indicator that does not add up to an exhaustive worldwide estimate, and for that reason the indicator could be considered as less suitable from a conceptual point of view. But applying this option at the national level could be a viable way out, and this is exactly what Ireland has done in response to the extraordinary circumstances caused by the international relocations in 2015.

As mentioned before, after the 2015 jump in the level of GDP, leading to a concomitant economic growth of 26.3 percent, the Irish government decided to set up an Economic Statistics Review Group (ESRG), with the objective ". . . *to provide recommendations for the Central Statistics Office (CSO) on how best to meet user needs for greater insight into Irish economic activity, taking account of the measurement challenges inherent in providing a comprehensive picture of the highly-globalised Irish economy*" (ESRG, 2016). As it was considered ". . . *essential to have a reliable level indicator of the size of the economy . . . for private-sector decision making, fiscal planning* *and the sustainability of public and private debt stocks"* (ESRG, 2016), one of the most important recommendations concerned the development of an adjusted level indicator, in addition to developing cyclical indicators of ". . . *underlying investment and underlying domestic demand measures that take account of the impact of intellectual property relocations, contact manufacturing, aircraft leasing and re-domiciled firms"* (ESRG, 2016). As it has long been recognized that GNI is superior to GDP in measuring the size of the Irish economy, an alternative GNI measure, GNI*, has been put forward by the review group.

GNI* is defined as GNI *minus* retained earnings of re-domiciled firms *minus* depreciation of categories of foreign-owned domestic capital assets such as intellectual property. The main reason for the first adjustment is that they prefer to align the treatment of FDI enterprises and portfolio investments, in the sense that in both cases only distributed profits are recorded, whereas GNI treats non-distributed profits of FDI-type affiliates as if they were distributed, in the form of reinvested earnings on foreign direct investment, and subsequently reinvested in the equity of the affiliates. One may indeed dispute this difference in treatment, although there are good reasons for it—for example, in direct investment relationships the owner has a direct influence on whether or not the profits are actually distributed, while this is less so for portfolio shareholders[15]—but it is somewhat peculiar that this change is limited to the inward flows of retained earnings and not extended to outward flows as well. This may, however, be related to the second deduction, the exclusion of depreciation of foreign-controlled IPPs. Here, the ESRG (2016) states that this depreciation is borne by foreign investors and therefore ". . . *should not affect a measure that is intended to capture the resources accruing to domestic residents."* Here, one could argue that not only depreciation but also the profits related to these IPPs, i.e., the total of capital services from foreign-controlled IPPs, are to be excluded, and that may be the reason for not excluding outward reinvested earnings. Whatever the case, it is clear that calculating and summing up GNI* would not lead to a consistent worldwide aggregate, a property that would be considered essential if it were to be considered as part of the international standards. Furthermore, although it may work at the national level in dealing with some of the adverse impacts of globalization on the measurement of GDP under the 2008 SNA, one wonders whether it would be suitable in addressing other possibly emerging cases. Here, one could think of the example of the real-

---

15. As stated in §7.138 of the 2008 SNA: *"The rationale behind this treatment is that since a foreign direct investment enterprise is, by definition, subject to control, or influence, by a foreign direct investor or investors, the decision to retain some of its earnings within the enterprise must represent a deliberate investment decision on the part of the foreign direct investor(s). In practice, the great majority of direct investment enterprises are subsidiaries of foreign corporations or the unincorporated branches of foreign enterprises, which are completely controlled by their parent corporations or owners."*

location of headquarters, instead of affiliates, with considerable amounts of IPPs. All in all, one would like to look at other solutions that are more sustainable, and arguably better from a conceptual point of view. This is the subject of the following subsection.

Another option to arrive at macroeconomic indicators for certain types of analysis is to decompose (volume growth) of GDP into the production factors that have contributed to it. By separating out the contributions of IPPs and other easily movable capital assets, one could arrive at a measure that better reflects, for some types of analysis, those parts of growth in GDP that can be attributed to a certain geographical territory. However, it's not that straightforward to allocate the remaining multifactor productivity—or in the case of level estimates in current prices, the net operating surplus— to the various inputs. In volume terms, one could think of a proportional allocation of the resulting multifactor productivity. For the measurement of an adjusted level estimate for GDP, one may consider calculating capital services using an exogenous rate of return on invested capital.

To realize these efforts to better use existing data, provide enhanced granularity, and provide alternative indicators within the international standards, national statistical offices and international organizations will need to communicate how to interpret the standard, alternative, and supplementary data. They will also need to develop additional documentation and provide examples of enhanced analysis.

1.5.2   Going beyond the 2008 SNA: Possible Methods for Dealing with Distortions

The main discomfort with the current international standards is related to the fact that the allocation of multinational activities to national economies is not governed by economic substance, but that legal considerations, often related to the avoidance of regulatory burden and the minimization of the global tax burden, directly affect the macroeconomic statistics, including the indicators derived from them.[16] It may not only have quite disruptive impacts on the measurement of economic growth, but it can also significantly hamper an "appropriate" analysis of economic developments. As we've seen, the main problems are caused by transfer pricing and by the international allocation of IPPs and related income, with or without the involvement of SPEs. In this section, a number of options going beyond the 2008 SNA will be discussed, gradually departing more and more from the current conceptual framework. Practical issues may seriously affect the current possibilities

16. Regulatory arbitrage can affect the locational decisions that are made by MNEs in ways that have little to do with the underlying economic conditions. An example of regulatory arbitrage are the tax credits and subsidies that Vancauteren, Polder, and van den Berg (this volume) examine in the case of the Netherlands. Other examples might be lack of laws, or enforcement of laws, for worker safety or environmental pollution. While we mostly focus in this chapter on tax arbitrage, regulatory arbitrage should also be a consideration.

to apply these alternative concepts. These practicalities will be addressed separately in the next subsection.

The first issue to address concerns the treatment of the SPEs. It is apparent from the start that these SPEs are only considered as separate institutional units because they are resident in an economy different from their parents and/or affiliates. Were this not the case, they would be consolidated into the rest of the multinational enterprise. Similarly, assigning economic ownership of IPPs to these brass plate companies is a matter of practicality or legality, not a way of approximating economic substance. Therefore, as also proposed by Rassier (2017), a first suggestion to be considered in the future international standards for compiling national accounts is the consolidation of SPEs with their ultimate owners. As a consequence, all returns, outlays, financial stocks, and positions of these SPEs would directly end up in the accounts of the country where the headquarters of the multinational are located. The only relationship of the multinational with the economy in which the SPE is located would consist of payment of corporate taxes, payments for administrative services, and potentially a rather negligible amount of wages and salaries, which would need to be recorded as cross-border transactions.

One may also argue that affiliates providing ancillary services to the rest of the multinational do not qualify as separate institutional units. Indeed, § 4.66 of the 2008 SNA states the following: "*Units undertaking only ancillary activities will in general not satisfy the conditions of being an institutional unit (for the same sort of reason as artificial subsidiaries do not) but they may sometimes be treated as a separate establishment of the enterprise if this is analytically useful.*" However, given that these establishments usually have a physical presence on the economic territory, by employing paid staff which needs to be accommodated in office buildings, it makes sense to consider them as separate resident entities. The same line of reasoning holds for artificial subsidiaries.

This brings us to the point of how to deal with the relocation of affiliates with high volumes of IPPs and related value added, which have a true physical presence and also economic ownership of the IPPs, such as in the Irish case. Some have argued in favor of defining a "Gross International Product," according to which the multinational is treated as one single institutional unit, basically putting the institutional unit on a par with the enterprise group without giving any consideration to the physical allocation. All output and value added generated worldwide by the multinational enterprise would thus be allocated to the country of the ultimate parent, a treatment that resembles the treatment of embassies of foreign governments, although in this case the location of the embassy is not considered part of the economic territory of a country. In the case of multinational enterprises, this looks overdone. As previously stated in the context of ancillary services and artificial subsidiaries, there is true physical presence on the economic territory of the countries where these operational affiliates are located. It thus feels unjustified to exclude the value added generated by these affiliates, or at least the part of value added that is physically located at the economic territory, from the GDP of the relevant countries.

The problem of allocating output and value added of multinational enterprises to national economies first and foremost concerns the parts that are neither physically nor locally constrained, so that it is relatively easy to relocate these assets and the related income. A logical alternative to allocating all output and value added to the country of the ultimate parent is to limit this reallocation to the IPPs and the global profits of the multinational enterprise, and attribute the part of value added with a physical presence, i.e., compensation of employees and depreciation of non-IPP assets, possibly including a return on the investment, to the countries in which the affiliates are located.[17] From a conceptual point of view, this treatment is justified, as the ultimate parent is indeed the true economic owner of the IPPs and the profits generated worldwide, and also because it is practically impossible to find a good rationale for allocating these assets and profits to certain parts of the worldwide production process. Leaving apart the relocation of IPPs and related depreciation, in a sense it would also come down to an "upward shift" of distributed and reinvested earnings from GNI to GDP.

As an alternative to the above allocation of IPPs and profits to the headquarters, it has been proposed, e.g., by Rassier (2017), to apply a formulary apportionment of IPPs and profits: "*Under formulary apportionment, company accounting records are consolidated and measures are attributed to economic territories on factors that reflect where economic activity takes place—such as compensation, tangible property, and sales—which are also available in company accounting records.*" From a conceptual point of view, this alternative seems less attractive, as one would, for example, also allocate IPPs and related income to production facilities in China, let's say, though we know that the economic activities taking place there may be low-skilled labor assembling a final product. As a consequence, the knowledge-intensity of the Chinese economy would increase, while it is fully apparent that this knowledge has been created elsewhere and that the low-skilled operations, as such, do not add to the value added of the goods and services produced. More generally, one can question the economic validity of apportioning IPPs and profits, and consequently value added, to countries. Allocating value added to regional operations in this way is a kind of illusion from the perspective of economic substance. It is in fact very similar to imputing profits on the basis of tax considerations by the relevant enterprises. It says little, if anything at all, about, for example, the economic competitiveness

---

17. Please note that, for reasons of simplification, we do not dwell upon the treatment of borrowing and lending of multinational enterprises including the related Financial Intermediation Services Indirectly Measured (FISIM) and the payments and receipts of interest.

of a certain country or the productivity of a certain part of a multinational enterprise.

Although the above solution of apportioning IPPs and profits may be less attractive from a conceptual point of view, it has the clear advantage that a relocation of headquarters does not have a major impact on the level of GDP. Allocating IPPs and profits to the country of the ultimate owner may bear this risk, as the relocation of headquarters would be accompanied by a massive transfer of value added and IPPs from one country to another. This brings us to yet another alternative, i.e., to treat IPPs and profits of multinational enterprises as being a supranational phenomenon, for which it is simply impossible to arrive at an economically meaningful allocation to countries. It would also mean that total value added of countries does not add up to world GDP, similar to the exclusion of international organizations from national estimates. From a certain perspective, such a recording could be interpreted as "the funeral of GDP," as a major part of value added will be allocated to a supranational "country" of multinationals, and consequently not to the "real" countries. GNI would be less affected though, as this aggregate will keep on including the distributed profits in the form of dividends. Further down, national savings would still be affected by the exclusion of retained earnings of multinationals.

The latter element, the exclusion of retained earnings of multinationals from national savings, but also the "illusionary" nature of allocating profits of multinationals to countries more generally, leads to the consideration of extending the treatment of reinvested earnings to the owners of the corporations, as proposed, for example, by Reinsdorf et al. (2017). This idea, put forward in a more general context of accounting on an accrual basis, is also included in the SNA research agenda; see SNA 2008, § A4.28–29. As stated in § A4.29: "*This would mean that distribution of earnings from corporations was measured on a strict accrual basis but would also mean that the saving of corporations would always be zero. Such a change would have serious implications for the interpretation of the accounts since it would be built on a different paradigm from the current treatment of dividends and corporate saving.*"

We would like to make one final point here. In all circumstances, looking at the national part of a globally operating enterprise with internationally fragmented production processes may be somewhat similar to looking at the trunk or the left leg of an elephant, and pretending to analyze these parts as if one is dealing with a complete animal. One starts to wonder whether the framework of national accounts should not include as a future objective the compilation of an image of the complete animal. We need to think about compiling international or supranational accounts for multinational enterprises, in which all the national parts are consolidated, both for describing the process of producing goods and services, and for transactions and positions related to income and finance, similar to what is being done by the BIS in compiling banking statistics based on the "nationality" perspective.

All of this could be done in a set of supplementary tables, in addition to the traditional core set of national accounts data, with or without including the above amendments to the international standard

1.5.3 "In between Dream and Act There Are Hindering Laws and Practical Issues"[18]

A serious complication in the application of the above options or solutions for dealing with the impact of globalization on the compilation of GDP, and national accounts more generally, is the availability of relevant data. When it comes to the options suggested within the boundaries of the 2008 SNA, putting more emphasis on alternative indicators within the framework of national accounts can be implemented immediately, although it may be hard to get away from the traditional analysis of economic growth, based on volume growth of GDP. Furthermore, not all countries may be able to provide results for the net concepts (NDP/NNI), but for advanced economies this should not pose any major problems.

It gets somewhat more difficult to implement the option of providing more breakdowns of industries in the supply and use tables and of the corporations' sectors in the institutional sector accounts. Leaving apart problems related to resources, knowledge, and time to implement them, countries should be able to provide these additional breakdowns if the source data provide the necessary granularity. But it may not be that straightforward to arrive at a set of more granular data that are fully consistent with the current set of national accounts data. It may require a redesign of the production system in which the required granularity is included from the start of the compilation process. The same holds, but to a significantly lesser extent, for the third option, i.e., the definition of alternative macroeconomic concept such as GNI* in Ireland.

The above assumes that the national source data are fully correct. But we all know that this is not true if one takes a look at the inconsistencies at the international level.[19] Whether it concerns data on foreign trade, foreign direct investment or any other statistics on cross-country transactions and positions, serious inconsistencies exist between the worldwide totals of receipts/stocks of financial assets and the worldwide totals of payments/stocks of liabilities. One may also wonder whether the summation of the parts of a multinational enterprise recorded at the national level actually add up to the complete group. It is highly probable that there may be cases of double counting or missing information, which is why it is important to

18. Quote from the poem "The Marriage" by Willem Elsschot (Flemish author).
19. The update of the SNA and *Balance of Payments and International Investment Position Manual* that is currently underway includes several proposals that should improve the overall quality of data on MNEs and international transactions. At this point, the proposed changes to the standards should provide detail to support some of the analyses presented in this volume, such as extended supply and use tables, but will not fundamentally change the accounting rules for the flows of MNEs. For information on the SNA update, see https://unstats.un.org/unsd /nationalaccount/aeg.asp.

liaise internationally, to work together across borders in profiling multinational enterprises, and to agree upon the national allocation of the various units comprising the enterprise group. The initiatives at the European level to create and maintain an internationally agreed EuroGroups Register is a good example.[20]

Now addressing the options which go beyond the 2008 SNA, it is clear that all of them require, at least to some extent, the exchange of individual data on multinational enterprises across countries. In the current legal circumstances, this is a major issue that would need to be resolved rather urgently. Two possible ways forward can be distinguished: (i) a top-down approach according to which data on multinational enterprises are collected at the international level, with a subsequent provision of data on the national parts of the multinational enterprises to the countries; and (ii) a bottom-up approach according to which each country collects data on the national parts of the multinational enterprises, which are subsequently exchanged and verified across countries. Given current circumstances, both ways forward require a paradigm shift in allowing for international exchange of individual data within the statistical community and, in the case of the top-down approach, in collecting statistical data and compiling national accounts data. One possible step would be the reuse of the data that will become available from the OECD BEPS initiative.[21] Action 13 of this initiative requires multinational enterprises to provide much more detailed country-by-country reporting on their worldwide business, with more detailed information requested for large multinationals. But it remains unclear whether this data becomes available for statistical purposes as well.

Another layer of complexity is added when one would want to allocate profits to the ultimate owner of the shares. In this chapter, it has not yet been well thought through in all its consequences. It is probably also a bit too far-fetched for the time being.[22] One would definitely need very detailed data on the ultimate holdings of securities. On the positive side, it can be noted that in recent years, as part of the G20 Data Gaps Initiative, much progress has been made in compiling "securities databases" containing very granular data on the issuance and the holdings of publicly traded securities.

Finally, on creating supplementary tables with worldwide accounts for multinational enterprises, several initiatives, including one at the OECD, are underway to set up such databases for multinationals using existing information from public and private sources. The initiative of the EuroGroups Register within the European Union has already been mentioned. Here, the

20. Stapel-Weber et al. (this volume) describe the EuroGroups Register and efforts underway within the European Union to improve profiling of MNEs. They also suggest the use of some new indicators and aggregations.

21. See http://www.oecd.org/ctp/aggressive/beps-2015-final-reports.htm.

22. Ahmad (this volume) suggests the possibility of extending the SNA to provide breakdowns of the distribution of income account, including primary incomes, by industrial activity. Currently, the SNA only calls for providing the information by institutional sector, which may limit the potential analyses of relevant international income flows related to production.

development and implementation of a unique system of Global Legal Entity Identifiers (LEI) may provide huge value added in compiling consistent sets of data on multinational enterprises.

To arrive at a legal framework that would allow for the international exchange of individual data for statistical purposes is most probably a bridge too far for the near future. It would require very tedious legalistic negotiations with a highly uncertain outcome, taking many years, if not decades, to find adequate solutions. That should not prevent statisticians from making maximum use of publicly available information, if only to improve the international consistency. All too often statisticians treat all individual data as being confidential, not taking into consideration that the relevant information is already out there. The development of databases on MNEs may add another useful layer of information, certainly if one would be able to arrive at an appropriate monitoring of the group structures, for example by a wider application of the Legal Entity Identifier (LEI). Whether such information would actually enable alternative recordings of activities of MNEs remains to be seen.

1.6   Concluding Comments

We have seen that effects of globalization can impact both the levels and rates of change of major aggregates such as GDP and GNI. These effects arise for various reasons, but many of them reflect how multinational enterprises respond to tax incentives in allocating their assets and locating their activities. And, as seen in the Irish case, the effects can include large changes to GDP and/or GNI that have little relation to other variables that are traditionally associated with production, such as employment and compensation of employees. Some data users feel that the effects of globalization have diminished the usefulness of national accounts data.

We have suggested several options for moving forward. Although we might wish for a world in which national accounts fit into traditional narratives about domestic production using capital and labor, the way forward involves recognizing that the world has become more complex. While we can supplement the standard SNA to help in the analysis of a globalized economy, in the long term we will need to adapt our data collection and compilation strategies to come up with innovative ways to measure global entities that are engaged in production that is not limited by national boundaries.

References

Ahmad, Nadim. 2022. "Accounting Frameworks for Global Value Chains: Extended Supply-Use Tables." In *Challenges of Globalization in the Measurement of National*

Accounts, Studies in Income and Wealth, volume 81, edited by Nadim Ahmad, Brent R. Moulton, J. David Richardson, and Peter van de Ven. Chicago, IL: University of Chicago Press. This volume.

Avi-Yonah, Reuven S. 2017. "The Triumph of BEPS: US Tax Reform and the Single Tax Principle." University of Michigan Public Law Research Paper no. 579. https://ssrn.com/abstract=3081523.

Bruner, Jennifer, Dylan G. Rassier, and Kim J. Ruhl. 2022. "Multinational Profit Shifting and Measures throughout Economic Accounts." In *Challenges of Globalization in the Measurement of National Accounts*, Studies in Income and Wealth, volume 81, edited by Nadim Ahmad, Brent R. Moulton, J. David Richardson, and Peter van de Ven. Chicago, IL: University of Chicago Press. This volume.

Clausing, Kimberly A. 2016. "The Effect of Profit Shifting on the Corporate Tax Base in the United States and Beyond." *National Tax Journal* 69 (4): 905–34.

Congressional Budget Office. 2017. "An Analysis of Corporate Inversions." November. https://www.cbo.gov/system/files/115th-congress-2017-2018/reports/53093 -inversions.pdf.

De Nederlandsche Bank. 2018. Data on Balance Sheets of Special Financial Institutions. https://statistiek.dnb.nl/en/downloads/index.aspx#/details/special-financial -institutions-balance-sheet/dataset/b9514410-3b36-4812-9013-3d3862a098d2 /resource/efbc3c99-f381-411f-b9dd-b1ded6549e16.

ESRG. 2016. "Report of the Economic Statistics Review Group (ESRG)." Dublin, Ireland, December. http://www.cso.ie/en/media/csoie/newsevents/documents /reportoftheeconomicstatisticsreviewgroup/Economic_Statistics_Review _(ESRG)_Report_Dec_2016.pdf.

Central Statistics Office (CSO). 2017. "Central Statistics Office (CSO) Response to the Main Recommendations of the Economic Statistics Review Group (ESRG)." Dublin, Ireland: Central Statistics Office (CSO) Ireland. February 3. http://www .cso.ie/en/media/csoie/newsevents/documents/reportoftheeconomicstatistics reviewgroup/ESRG_CSO_response_3_Feb_2017.pdf.

European Commission, International Monetary Fund, Organisation for Economic Co-operation and Development, United Nations, and World Bank. 2009. *System of National Accounts 2008*, New York: United Nations. https://unstats.un.org /unsd/nationalaccount/sna.asp.

FitzGerald, John. 2022. "National Accounts for a Global Economy: The Case of Ireland." In *Challenges of Globalization in the Measurement of National Accounts*, Studies in Income and Wealth, volume 81, edited by Nadim Ahmad, Brent R. Moulton, J. David Richardson, and Peter van de Ven. Chicago, IL: University of Chicago Press. This volume.

Guvenen, Fatih, Raymond J. Mataloni, Jr., Dylan G. Rassier, and Kim J. Ruhl. 2017. "Offshore Profit Shifting and Domestic Productivity Measurement." BEA Working Paper WP2017–2. https://www.bea.gov/papers/pdf/GMRR-2017.pdf.

Heath, Robert. 2013. "Why Are the G-20 Data Gaps Initiative and the SDDS Plus Relevant for Financial Stability Analysis?" IMF Working Paper WP/13/6. Washington DC: International Monetary Fund. January. http://www.imf.org/external /pubs/ft/wp/2013/wp1306.pdf.

Houseman, Susan, Christopher Kurz, Paul Lengermann, and Benjamin Mandel. 2011. "Offshoring Bias in U.S. Manufacturing." *Journal of Economic Perspectives* 25 (2): 111–32. https://www.aeaweb.org/articles?id=10.1257/jep.25.2.111.

McCauley, Robert N., Agustín S. Bénétrix, Patrick M. McGuire, and Goetz von Peter. 2017. "Financial Deglobalisation in Banking?" BIS Working Papers, No. 650. Basel, Switzerland: Bank for International Settlements. https://www.bis.org /publ/work650.pdf.

OECD. 2008. *OECD Benchmark Definition of Foreign Direct Investment, 4th edition.* Paris, France: OECD. http://www.oecd.org/investment/fdibenchmarkdefinition.htm.

OECD. 2015a. "Information Brief." OECD/G20 Base Erosion and Profit Shifting Project: 2015 Final Reports. Paris, France: OECD. http://www.oecd.org/ctp/beps-reports-2015-information-brief.pdf.

OECD. 2015b. "Measuring and Monitoring BEPS, Action 11—2015 Final Report." OECD/G20 Base Erosion and Profit Shifting Project. Paris, France: OECD Publishing. http://dx.doi.org/10.1787/9789264241343-en.

OECD. 2016. "Are the Irish 26.3% Better Off?" OECD Insights Blog. Paris, France: OECD Publishing. http://oecdinsights.org/2016/10/05/are-the-irish-26-3-better-off/.

OECD. 2021. "Two-Pillar Solution to Address the Tax Challenges Arising from the Digitalisation of the Economy." OECD/G20 Base Erosion and Profit Shifting Project. Paris, France: OECD. https://www.oecd.org/tax/beps/brochure-two-pillar-solution-to-address-the-tax-challenges-arising-from-the-digitalisation-of-the-economy-october-2021.pdf.

Rassier, Dylan. 2017. "Improving the *SNA* Treatment of Multinational Enterprises." *Review of Income and Wealth* 63 (s1): s287-s320. http://onlinelibrary.wiley.com/doi/10.1111/roiw.12323/abstract.

Reinsdorf, Marshall, Dominique Durant, Kyle Hood, and Leonard Nakamura. 2017. "Improving the Treatment of Holding Gains and Default Losses in National Accounts." *Review of Income and Wealth* 63 (s1): s321-s354.

Stapel-Weber, Silke, Paul Konijn, John Verrinder, and Henk Nijmeijer. 2022. "Meaningful Information for Domestic Economies in the Light of Globalization—Will Additional Macroeconomic Indicators and Different Presentations Shed Light?" In *Challenges of Globalization in the Measurement of National Accounts*, Studies in Income and Wealth, volume 81, edited by Nadim Ahmad, Brent R. Moulton, J. David Richardson, and Peter van de Ven. Chicago, IL: University of Chicago Press. This volume.

United Nations Economic Commission for Europe. 2011. *The Impact of Globalization on National Accounts.* New York and Geneva: United Nations. http://www.unece.org/index.php?id=28890.

United Nations Economic Commission for Europe. 2015. *Guide to Measuring Global Production.* New York and Geneva: United Nations, http://www.unece.org/index.php?id=42106.

Vancauteren, Mark, Michael Polder, and Marcel van den Berg. 2022. "The Relationship Between Tax Payments and MNE's Patenting Activities and Implications for Real Economic Activity: Evidence from the Netherlands." In *Challenges of Globalization in the Measurement of National Accounts*, Studies in Income and Wealth, volume 81, edited by Nadim Ahmad, Brent R. Moulton, J. David Richardson, and Peter van de Ven. Chicago, IL: University of Chicago Press. This volume.

2

Meaningful Information for Domestic Economies in the Light of Globalization
Will Additional Macroeconomic Indicators and Different Presentations Shed Light?

Silke Stapel-Weber, Paul Konijn, John Verrinder, and Henk Nijmeijer

2.1 Introduction

Globalization is a historic process of increasing interaction between national economies on a worldwide scale. While not new, interconnectedness has accelerated in recent years as it is closely related to activities by multinational enterprises (MNEs). Fragmented production processes span the world, exploiting comparative production advantages and tax competition between nations. This is also helped by the fact that increasingly a main component of many (particularly high-tech) products is intellectual property. These intangible assets of an MNE, however, are extremely mobile and often huge.

In methodological terms, in the most recent releases of the international standards for National Accounts and BOP (2008 SNA, ESA 2010, BPM6), globalization phenomena such as "goods sent abroad for processing" and "merchanting," "special purpose entities" or "other captive institutions"

Silke Stapel-Weber has been Director General for Statistics and Chief Data Officer at the European Central Bank since February 2019.

Paul Konijn is Head of Unit Price Statistics, Purchasing Power Parities, and Real Estate Statistics at Eurostat.

John Verrinder is Head of Unit National Accounts Methodology; Standards and Indicators at Eurostat.

Henk Nijmeijer is a former statistician at the Central Bureau of Statistics in the Netherlands. He co-authored this paper while on secondment to Eurostat.

The views expressed in this paper are those of the authors, not necessarily those of Eurostat. The authors would like to thank Eurostat colleagues, and notably August Götzfried, Karin Isaksson, Merja Rantala, and Veijo Ritola for their helpful comments. For acknowledgments, sources of research support, and disclosure of the authors' material financial relationships, if any, please see https://www.nber.org/books-and-chapters/challenges-globalization -measurement-national-accounts/meaningful-information-domestic-economies-light -globalization-will-additional-macroeconomic.

have been given more attention, and subsequently more detailed guidance has been developed. Various tools have already been developed by statisticians, and initiatives have been taken to go "beyond GDP."

We have, however, to admit that we are only at the very beginning of getting a grip on properly measuring globalization in a systematic cross-country way in practice. Which parts of the production activities of MNEs are actually "taking place" on the domestic territory of any given country? Or, in other words, how can we distinguish between movements in GDP or its components which are relevant for the domestic economy and those which are driven by the worldwide activities of multinational companies?

Efforts to single out globalization activities and present them alongside purely domestic developments are very challenging, given that they require statisticians to isolate in balance sheets and flow accounts those positions and flows relating to the rerouting of revenues and profits. This may require infra-MNE information and raises sensitive questions concerning enhanced cross-border cooperation among statistical authorities.

Nevertheless, the price for not addressing them would be increasing irrelevance of our statistical products and persistent/growing bias and asymmetries between countries. Users of statistics need to understand clearly how (and how much) globalization phenomena impact on those statistics, and which statistics are useful for which analytical purpose. This is particularly important for users, who focus on one or a few aggregates for their needs, and where statistics are used for direct administrative purposes.[1]

2.2 Current and Future Policy Developments Impacting on Macroeconomic Data

The impacts of globalization can be seen in longer-term trends driven by economic fundamentals[2] but also—and particularly for smaller countries—in discrete MNE business model restructuring events, often triggered by policy developments that change the "rules of the game."

Over recent years, as a response to popular concerns about the impacts of globalization (and apparent impunity with which MNEs can "offshore"), we have seen an acceleration in coordinated policy developments that are designed to further regulate MNEs and, at least, improve the transparency of their financial affairs.

The best known of these initiatives at international level is the Base Erosion and Profit Shifting (BEPS) project led by the OECD. The recommendations of the project, agreed and published in 2015, have led to implementation of

1. For example in Europe in setting contributions to the EU budget (GNI) or for fiscal policy (government deficit and debt/GDP).
2. For example, see the article "The retreat of the global company" in the *Economist*, January 28, 2017.

new requirements for MNE financial reporting across many jurisdictions worldwide, and in particular for "country-by-country" reporting requirements by 2020.[3] This improves the transparency of MNE operations, which would have previously been brought together only in high-level consolidated company accounts and tax returns.

In Europe, one of the major impacts of the initiative has been the end of certain tax structures which were widely used by non-European (and often US-owned) MNEs, such as the "Double Irish" and the "Dutch sandwich," to be replaced by a focus on the tax treatment of intellectual property ("Patent boxes," accelerated depreciation) and the need for MNEs to demonstrate "substance" in an economy in order to benefit from local tax rules. This has already been observed to have impacts on some MNEs' business structures, with movements of intellectual property and increased specification of decision-making functions.

It is also evident in Europe that other policy initiatives are closely accompanying the taxation agenda. For example, successive state aid cases (for example for Apple in Ireland, Amazon in Luxembourg, Starbucks in the Netherlands) have shown the willingness of the European Commission to challenge the selective tax treatment of some MNEs.

Looking forward, one can see that recently agreed reforms, or those under discussion, could bring further triggers for changes to MNE business models. There is a widespread anticipation that the latest round of corporate tax reforms in the United States will provide an incentive for US-owned MNEs to repatriate (at least some of) their accumulated profits so far held abroad,[4] and to relocate some of their physical operations to the United States (or at least favor the United States in future developments).

There are also ongoing developments in Europe. In 2017 the European Commission released a communication on the taxation of the digital economy.[5] This underlined the principle that taxation should take place "where profits and value are generated," and has been interpreted as a push to tax the operations of digital enterprises based on the location of the source of revenues that they generate (whether from consumers or businesses).[6]

3. For more details, see http://www.oecd.org/tax/beps.

4. Exactly how this might be done is still unclear, though one might expect the use of (one-off) dividends or flows relating to intellectual property (royalties). One of the tax reform's major, but less reported, features is that MNEs would be taxed on use of intellectual property wherever it is located (thereby removing some of the incentive to locate intellectual property "offshore" or in low-tax jurisdictions), though the reform does not provide a low-cost way to relocate existing intellectual property to the United States.

5. See https://ec.europa.eu/taxation_customs/business/company-tax/fair-taxation -digital-economy_en.

6. It is interesting to see that Facebook is somehow anticipating these developments by moving to a model of declaring its advertising revenues in the countries where they are generated (though no doubt to be offset by attributed costs from intellectual property and other "central" costs).

Broader political developments may also bring pressures for MNE restructuring. Depending on the eventual way in which Brexit is implemented, one might also expect a significant reorganization of MNEs with substantial UK operations. This might range from the establishment of (small or even token) branches in EU27 countries, through to the physical relocation of operations and staff.

Thus, aside from the longer-term trends in the impacts of globalization arising from developments in economic fundamentals, we have seen a rise in MNE restructuring and can anticipate that this may even accelerate in the future. Given the potential impacts on macroeconomic statistics across countries, and the adverse reaction of users to "surprises" in data, this presents a major challenge to official statisticians. Addressing that challenge will need coordinated development of the "statistical infrastructure" (broadly defined, see section 2.3 below) and improved communication to users, including extended data availability (see sections 2.4 and 2.5 below).

2.3   Improving EU Statistical Infrastructure to Capture Globalization

To ensure high-quality, consistent, and complete micro- and macroeconomic statistics, it will be necessary to upgrade our statistical infrastructure, in particular as regards the data production on MNE groups (MNEs). Countries' statistical offices will have to cooperate much more closely than is the case today to make sure that the recording of flows and stocks belonging to MNEs are consistent across countries. Whereas "balancing the national accounts" used to mean integrating data sources on the three approaches to GDP (whether or not in a supply/use framework) at national level, in the future the balancing should also take place at the international level. Asymmetries in balance of payments data could, for example, be indicators of inconsistent treatment of MNEs.

At national level, a trend is observed in several EU countries for the balancing of data sources to be undertaken upstream, i.e., at the national data collection point. Several countries have established, and others are in the process of establishing, so-called Large Cases Units (LCUs) to ensure a consistent treatment of MNEs in national statistics. Depending on the business model chosen, these units collect centrally all data from the largest MNEs in a country, coordinate national data collections, and/or ensure their consistency before processing for the various statistical outputs. They often provide a single point of contact between the statistical office and the MNE.

While these LCUs are very important tools for the NSIs, they still focus on consistency at national level only. As said above, to tackle globalization challenges, NSIs will also have to work more closely together than in the past.

A lot of groundwork for this is already being undertaken in Europe. For example, the EuroGroups Register (EGR) is the statistical register of the

EU on MNEs. For 2016, the EGR covers around 110 000 multinational enterprise groups active in the EU (i.e., having at least one legal unit in the EU).[7] The EGR requires a close cooperation between the EU countries and Eurostat; the exchange of data is regulated with legal acts.[8] EU statistical institutes and Eurostat are continuously working on the EGR to improve its quality. This has been achieved from year to year with the best coverage so far for the 2016 reference year.

The EGR contains information on the following units and characteristics:

- **legal units**: identification, demographic, control and ownership characteristics;
- **enterprises**: identification and demographic characteristics, main activity code (NACE), number of persons employed, turnover, institutional sector;
- **enterprise groups**: identification characteristics, the structure of the group, the group head, the country of global decision center, main activity code (NACE), consolidated employment and turnover of the group.

Hence, the EGR compiles all above units within multinational enterprise groups (including the ownership structures and relationships). It is important to underline: the MNE structures are obtained by collecting and combining national business register information from all countries in which the MNE has a legal unit.

This information is a crucial input for the next stage: European profiling of MNEs. Profiling is defined as "a method to analyse the legal, operational and accounting structure of an enterprise group at national and world level, in order to establish the statistical units within that group, their links, and the most efficient structures for the collection of statistical data." Thus, the focus is shifted from legal units in the business register to statistical units from which data can be collected. The statistical units can be groups of legal units (forming an enterprise). Profiling is an activity that is carried out by business statisticians, often within the LCUs mentioned above, at national level. European profiling brings the countries concerned by one enterprise group together with the aim to agree on the structure, the perimeter, and the global decision center of the group and to describe its activities—across countries—in an economically meaningful way. Profiling of the largest groups is done in consultation with the MNE itself and is a crucial step in getting an up-to-date understanding of MNE structures and ensuring their consistent recording across countries. So far, about 300 MNEs (most of them with European headquarters) have been profiled at European level. The benefits from profiling are integrated into the national statistical busi-

---

7. For some experimental statistics based on the EGR, see http://ec.europa.eu/eurostat /statistics- explained/index.php?title=Structure_of_multinational_enterprise_groups_in _the_EU.
8. E.g., Regulation 177/2008.

ness registers and thus improve their quality. There is also the intention to integrate the profiling results into the EGR in a more automated way in the future.

Learning from the 2016 "Irish case," and in parallel to the above projects, Eurostat and the NSIs have also set up an Early Warning System, which aims at the early detection of important restructuring of MNEs; as described above, these restructuring events often impact macroeconomic or business statistics. The early reception of such information allows discussion and agreement on the statistical treatment of these events before they have to be included in published statistics, and thereby ensure consistency, and, if needed, a timely and coordinated communication to users.

The above listed developments will require a change of approach from NSIs: it will no longer suffice to focus on what happens within national borders. For the quality and relevance of *national* statistics, cooperation and exchange of information at *international* level will be essential to correctly reflect the activities of MNEs.

2.4   Presenting and/or Extending National Accounts Data[9] in Times of Globalization?

2.4.1   Alternative Existing Indicators

GDP is a measure of (net) output of an economy. The income side of GDP reflects the income generated in production processes resident in the economy, which is not the same as the income accruing to its citizens. National accountants know very well that there is a multitude of alternative indicators produced within the national accounts that are better measures of income, such as:

- Gross National Income (GNI): a measure of the gross primary income earned by residents of a country. The difference with GDP consists of the net flows of primary income with the rest of the world. Hence, it is less sensitive to globalization, as any profits earned by foreign companies are not included. However, it is still a gross measure, i.e., including consumption of fixed capital, and thus not a measure of income as finally received by residents.
- Net National Income (NNI): derived from GNI by taking out consumption of fixed capital. It is thereby a step closer to a pure income measure for the economy as a whole.
- Gross or Net National Disposable Income (NDI): derived from GNI or NNI, respectively, by adjusting for net flows of current transfers with

9. Of course one can also consider alternative presentation for other macroeconomic indicators, notably Balance of Payments. This chapter does not do so in this and following sections, concentrating on national accounts, however an important issue to consider is if alternative indicators across different macroeconomic data sets should also be consistent with each other.

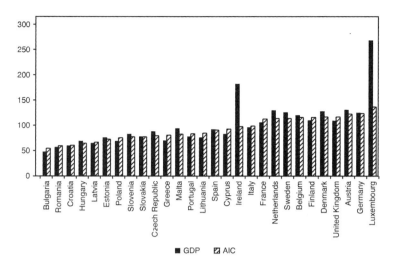

Figure 2.1   Volume of GDP and AIC per capita in PPS, EU28=100, 2015

the rest of the world. This is finally what is available to the economy for consumption or saving.

• Disposable income, however, is more commonly used for households only. Gross or net household disposable income is the share of NDI that accrues to households. Adjusting for social transfers in kind finally gives Adjusted (gross or net) Disposable Income of Households.

All of these indicators are income measures and thus potentially useful as indicators for increased or decreased material welfare of residents of the economy.

Another indicator that is closely related to Adjusted Disposable Income of Households is Actual Individual Consumption, which aggregates the final consumption expenditure of households and NPISHs with the final individual consumption expenditure of general government. This is conceptually a very comparable measure across countries. It is, on average in the EU, about 70 percent of GDP and is not affected by globalization, as it excludes GFCF and net exports. This indicator may deserve more attention in national publications than it currently gets.

Figure 2.1 shows a comparison of GDP and AIC per capita (in PPP terms). It shows they are mostly highly correlated except for two countries strongly affected by globalization: Luxembourg and Ireland. The high GDP per capita in Luxembourg is partly due to the country's large share of cross-border workers in total employment. While contributing to GDP, these workers are not taken into consideration as part of the resident population, which is used to calculate GDP per capita. Luxembourg still has the EU's most affluent residents as measured by AIC per capita. Eurostat has since long caveated the GDP level of Luxembourg in its news releases; in that

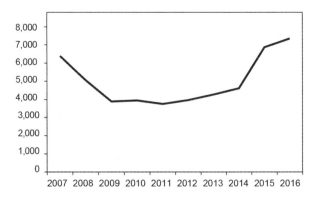

Figure 2.2   Taxes on the income or profits of corporations in Ireland, million euros

sense, it is not "news" that GDP can be distorted by globalization (albeit globalization on a more regional scale).

Since 2016, Eurostat has also provided footnotes on the level of Irish GDP for years after 2015 in these cross-country comparisons, describing it as being "substantially affected by the relocation from outside the EU to Ireland of balance sheets of large multinational enterprises." Indeed, where Ireland's GDP per capita stands at more than 80 percent above EU average, its AIC per capita is just below the corresponding EU average. It is clear that AIC gives a more realistic picture of the material living standards of Irish residents than GDP.

For some years now, Eurostat's news releases with cross-country comparisons in PPP terms no longer use GDP per capita in its headline but AIC per capita.[10]

2.4.2   Follow the Money

With respect to a common underlying question—what actually arrives at the domestic population in terms of improved material conditions as result of globalization—it is also interesting to have a look at the tax income of the government. Figure 2.2 shows by means of example the income from corporate tax in Ireland from 2007 to 2016. There is a noticeable increase between 2014 and 2015, which coincides with the relocation of the balance sheets of a small number of large MNEs to Ireland in 2015. Whether this will contribute to better material welfare of the domestic Irish population depends on what use this increased tax income will be made of now and in the years to come. One can, however, not say that the increased GNI in Ire-

10. See, e.g., http://ec.europa.eu/eurostat/documents/2995521/8536114/2–14122017-BP-EN .pdf/0c8f87ee- 42e8–4474-b7c6–724515917ea5. It should be noted that media attention has waned somewhat since Eurostat dropped GDP from the headline.

land is a pure statistical fantasy and nothing happens in the "real economy." Follow the money. . . .

2.4.3   But What about Growth Rates?

The most high-profile national accounts indicator is not the level of GDP but the volume growth of GDP. What alternatives exist for that?

The national and disposable income measures mentioned above do not have a natural volume component. Deflation of income is about finding an appropriate measure of price change that reflects changes in the purchasing power of that income. OECD publishes income measures at constant prices using the implicit deflator for domestic demand (total consumption plus total capital formation).[11]

Eurostat publishes—for EU members and European aggregates—the real growth of adjusted GDI of households per capita, together with real AIC per capita, using the price index of AIC as a deflator for both.

For communication purposes, the international statistical community could agree on an (existing) measure of income growth to promote instead of, or in addition to, GDP growth. This would also include agreement on deflators to use to measure real income.

Nevertheless, GDP is also seen by users as a measure of "economic power." For that purpose, it is hard to replace.

2.4.4   Additional Breakdowns

Additional detailed data on globalization will help users better understand economic developments. In the wake of the large revision to Ireland's GDP in 2016, the Economic Statistics Review Group (ESRG) produced recommendations to the Irish CSO on how to meet user needs for greater insight into Irish economic activity. Even if written for the specific Irish situation, their report[12] provides a useful starting point for a discussion on additional data and breakdowns.

The main recommendation is to split the accounts for the nonfinancial sector in a part related to the largest MNEs and the rest. One could also consider breakdowns according to other dimensions, such as foreign control (see below) or size, or of other parts of the accounts, such as the supply and use tables. Each dimension will tell a different story but essentially provides information on the phenomenon of globalization as such.

A breakdown of sector S11 Non-financial enterprises by ownership is already foreseen in ESA 2010, although Eurostat collects no data for this from the EU member states.

Work in this direction is also being undertaken in the context of extended

---

11. OECD also includes measures in PPP terms using the PPPs for GDP.

12. http://www.cso.ie/en/media/csoie/newsevents/documents/reportoftheeconomic statisticsreviewgroup/Economic_Statistics_Review_%28ESRG%29_Report_Dec_2016 .pdf.

supply and use tables that are being promoted by OECD as part of the Trade in Value Added project. Several EU member states are already working on this.

Another recommendation from the ESRG is to provide users with information on the impact of globalization on the economic data, for example to provide the transition from international trade in goods data to national accounts and balance of payments data on exports and imports, i.e., by showing explicitly the adjustments made for goods for processing and merchanting (at product level).

One could also imagine data that show how much production abroad is allocated to the domestic economy following the principle of economic ownership. Such a "building blocks" approach was proposed in the article of Silke Stapel-Weber and John Verrinder in EURONA 2/2016.[13]

2.4.5   New Indicators?

The above-mentioned report of the ESRG also recommended producing and disseminating an adjusted level indicator. To meet the analytical needs identified by national users, the ESRG recommended the development of a modified version of GNI (named GNI*) with the effects of certain globalization activities excluded.

For many purposes it is important to generate reliable measures of the aggregate size of the economy. The ESRG states that it has long been recognized that GDP is an inadequate indicator for Ireland, given the size of measured factor income accruing to the foreign owners of multinational enterprises (MNEs) operating in Ireland. For this reason, GNI has been widely employed as an alternative indicator, since GNI strips out net international factor income flows.

Already prior to the 2016 "events" it was suggested by users that even GNI is no longer a sufficiently useful alternative indicator. The impacts of entities moving their global headquarters into or out of Ireland have always caused difficulties for users of Irish statistics.

The ESRG proposes to compile an adjusted measure of GNI, named GNI*, excluding the retained earnings of companies that are predominantly owned by foreign portfolio investors. By extension, an equally adjusted measure of the current account should be published.

In addition, due to the strong increase of the foreign-owned domestic capital stock from the relocation of foreign-owned IPP assets into Ireland, an adjustment of the capital stock and thus of the associated consumption of fixed capital is proposed. The ESRG recommends that GNI* should exclude the depreciation of foreign-owned domestic capital.

There are pros and cons to developing alternative, special-purpose, indicators like the proposed GNI*. Clearly, at a national level, they may serve

13. http://ec.europa.eu/eurostat/cros/system/files/euronaissue2-2016-art2.pdf

an important purpose or satisfy certain users. But it is not clear whether the same indicator would be relevant for other countries too, or even be useful in one country over time (when different forms of restructuring may have different impacts). It would also be confusing to users (and a step back in time) if different countries would start using different, incomparable, headline indicators for their economies.

2.5   Some Experimental Data

In this section, we present experimental data, which demonstrate that it is possible to describe effects of globalization on the national economies within the existing indicator framework, by combining available information.

What remains is to develop these experimental indicators into parts of future standard releases on NA and work with users to enable them to make use of the additional information provided.

2.5.1   Combining FATS and NA—Value Added in the EU Generated by Foreign-Controlled Enterprises

As a first example, figure 2.3 combines data from the inward Foreign Affiliates statistics (FATS) and national accounts[14] to show the share of total economy value added created by foreign-controlled enterprises in 2014, broken down into control by intra-EU and by extra-EU units.

Not surprisingly, Ireland is the country with the highest share of foreign-controlled value added created in the EU (36 percent).[15] More than 80 percent of this value added is produced by enterprises with mother companies outside the EU. Slightly more surprising is the high position of five central and Eastern European countries (Hungary 35 percent, Czech Republic 30 percent, Slovakia 30 percent, Romania 29 percent, and Estonia 29 percent), for which intra-EU relations play the dominant role.

On the lower end of the scale, we find mostly southern European countries, but also France, Denmark, and Finland. The EU28 average is 14 percent, nearly half of which is controlled by countries outside the EU.

Figure 2.4 breaks down the intra-EU shares given above into the shares of the most relevant countries in this context. German companies play an important role in the central and Eastern European countries. Estonia has high shares of control by Finland and Sweden.

Figure 2.5 breaks down the extra-EU shares given in figure 2.2 into the shares of the United States and other countries. In Ireland, nearly 90 percent

---

14. FATS data provide the share of foreign affiliates' value added in the total business economy. This share has been multiplied by the share of the business economy in the total economy according to the national accounts, thereby (for example) assuming that the government is not foreign controlled.
15. In 2015, the corresponding share was 44 percent.

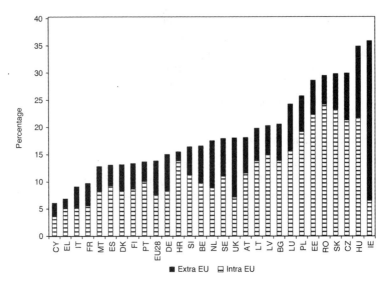

Figure 2.3 **Share of total economy value added created by foreign-controlled enterprises, by region of foreign control, 2014**

of extra-EU-controlled value added is created by US-controlled companies. In the EU as a whole, US units generate around 50 percent of all value added of extra-EU-controlled enterprises.

Whereas the share of US-controlled production in Ireland is very high compared to other countries, the level of value added (in euro) in this country is modest compared to some of the bigger countries of the EU. Figure 2.6 shows in which countries non-EU-controlled enterprises create the most value added. It shows that 26 percent of the total value added creation in the EU by extra-EU-controlled enterprises takes place in the UK and 21 percent in Germany.

2.5.2   Combining FATS and NA—Employment Controlled by EU Enterprises in the Rest of the World

As a second example, we have asked the question the opposite way around—how about EU enterprises having affiliates outside the EU and what do they control? Unfortunately, outward FATS statistics do not provide data on value added. Instead, we will use employment data. According to the FATS statistics, in 2014, foreign affiliates of EU enterprises employed around 14.4 million persons outside the EU (for comparison: the total number of employees in the EU was about 135.5 million). Figure 2.7 shows that France has the highest share (25 percent) in that number. France, the UK, and Germany together are responsible for nearly two-thirds.

Figure 2.8 shows in which continents the employees of these affiliates of EU enterprises were working. The largest share of employees is in (North, Central and South) America, half of which is in the United States.

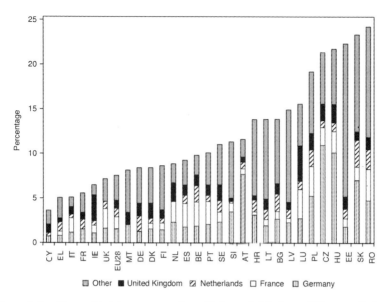

Figure 2.4   Share of total economy value added created by intra-EU-controlled enterprises, by country of foreign control, 2014

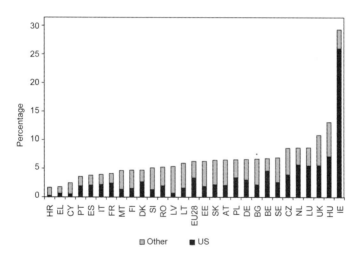

Figure 2.5   Share of total economy value added created by extra-EU28-controlled enterprises, by country of foreign control, 2014

2.5.3   Exposure to Globalization of the EU Member States

The inward FATS statistics also provide insight in foreign-controlled employment in the EU. The shares of foreign-controlled employment can be quite different in some cases from the shares of foreign-controlled value added that were presented above. Figure 2.9 plots these shares against each

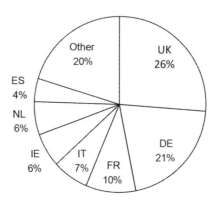

Figure 2.6   Share of total EU28 value added created by extra-EU28-controlled enterprises in EU countries, 2014

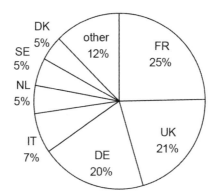

Figure 2.7   Share of total employment in extra-EU affiliates of EU enterprises, by country, 2014

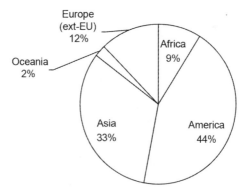

Figure 2.8   Share of total employment in extra-EU affiliates of EU enterprises, by continent, 2014

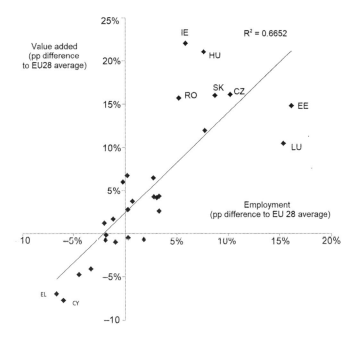

Figure 2.9   Foreign-controlled value added shares versus foreign-controlled employment shares, 2014

other, in relation to the EU28 averages for each indicator.[16] It gives a picture of the different exposure to globalization experienced in different countries.

While there is an (expected) correlation between the two indicators, there are some interesting outliers. For example, Ireland and Hungary score much less high on employment than on value added, while the opposite is true for Estonia and Luxembourg. Romania, Slovakia, and Czech Republic are also more exposed to foreign control of value added than of employment. It should, therefore, not come as a surprise if future globalization events involving relocations out of the countries would affect those countries mentioned much more than others in terms of shocks to local production and employment.

Greece and Cyprus are the countries that are currently least exposed to foreign control, on both dimensions. This is interesting in the case of Cyprus, since it is well known that many non-Cypriot enterprises maintain special purpose entities there; however, these do not generate significant additions to either employment or value added.

16. For the employment data, we used the same grossing-up technique to national accounts as outlined in footnote 14 for value added.

2.6   A New Initiative in European National Accounts

Building on the profiling work described in section 2.3 above, a new EU pilot project has started in 2018 to assess the treatment of a small number of (profiled) MNEs in the national accounts of the countries concerned. The initial focus will be on the allocation of value added for these companies across countries. The selection of companies is based, among other criteria, on significance for GNI at national level.

The primary reason behind this is the administrative use of GNI as base of the biggest so- called own resources of the EU budget. However, it has also utmost importance for piloting how the exhaustiveness and consistency of the national accounts and balance of payments aggregates across Europe can be ensured in the future under conditions of globalization. The allocation of R&D by country will play an important role in this exercise.

The time horizon of this piloting exercise is until 2019, which coincides with the next NA benchmark revision in most EU member states. If the pilot is successful, it may provide a blueprint for a systematic, consistent, and exhaustive approach to the recording of MNEs in national accounts and balance of payments in the future.

The full fruits of a possible new approach involving systematic cross-country collaboration of statistical compilers will, however, most likely stretch until the following common benchmark revision in all EU member states, agreed for 2024.

3

National Accounts for a
Global Economy
The Case of Ireland

John FitzGerald

3.1 Introduction

This chapter considers some of the problems for users of the current system of national accounts due to the globalization process. While this chapter concentrates on the problems using data for Ireland, many of the same problems affect users of national accounts for other economies, albeit to a lesser extent (Avdjiev et al. 2018).

In the case of Ireland, the problems with the national accounts have manifested themselves in a particularly remarkable way, giving rise to a growth in real GDP in 2015 of over 25 percent, which was clearly incredible. The fact that it was incredible reflects limitations in the underlying accounting framework, not with a failure to apply the accounting standards. Because of the nature of the globalization of the Irish economy, the accounting framework, as it stands, gives an incomplete representation of substantial developments in the domestic economy that affect the economic welfare of those living in Ireland. As a result, the existing accounts need to be supplemented with significant additional data to provide appropriate information for policy makers.

John FitzGerald is an adjunct professor of economics at Trinity College Dublin.

The author would like to thank Seamus Coffey, Patrick Honohan, James Tebrake, formerly Statistics Canada, Michael Connolly, Central Statistics Office and Peter van de Ven, OECD and the participants at the Conference on Research on Income and Wealth workshop in Washington in March 2018 for helpful comments and suggestions. It has been revised to take account of recent development of the Irish national accounts. An earlier version of the chapter was published at https://www.esri.ie/publications/national-accounts-for-a-global-economy-the -case-of-ireland. For acknowledgments, sources of research support, and disclosure of the author's material financial relationships, if any, please see https://www.nber.org/books-and -chapters/challenges-globalization-measurement-national-accounts/national-accounts -global-economy-case-ireland.

National accounts were developed to meet a range of needs of policy makers in managing a modern economy. For example, national accounting data are required by those responsible for fiscal policy to understand what is happening on the domestic labor market and the level of utilization of capital located in Ireland. They also need to know how much of the output in Ireland represents a benefit to Irish residents. Increasingly national accounting data are used to understand the drivers of emissions of greenhouse gases within an economy.

A very important aggregate in the Irish national accounts has been the development of net factor income from abroad (or paid abroad). Since the early 1980s this includes the accrued profits of foreign multinational enterprises (MNEs) operating in Ireland. When this outflow of profits (and the other items in net factor income) is deducted from gross domestic product (GDP), the resulting aggregate, gross national income (GNI), has, until recent years, satisfactorily represented the income generated in Ireland that is available to benefit those living in Ireland. However, recent developments have made even this key aggregate a less reliable indicator of what is happening to the income of those living in Ireland. Domestic policy makers now require additional information on the economy to understand what is driving change and what is the appropriate stance of domestic economic policy.[1]

While most significant developed countries have standardized on SNA 2008 (ESA 2010), the failure to implement it globally across all economies may give rise to a mismeasurement of global GDP: the movement of major economic activity to Ireland in 2015, as measured by SNA 2008, does not appear to have been counterbalanced by a corresponding fall elsewhere. This probably reflects under-reporting in the accounts of economies from which the activity has moved to Ireland.[2]

There are also special problems in interpreting the current account of the balance of payments as a result of the unfolding of the globalization process. The current account of the balance of payments is a key indicator of the financial sustainability of the current level of economic activity in an economy, but the standard treatment under SNA 2008 renders it totally ineffective as an indicator for a country such as Ireland. As a result, the Irish Central Statistics Office has developed an alternative measure of the current

1. The economic welfare of domestic residents includes not just the income and current final consumption of residents but also the use of the capital stock, as enhanced by investment. That logic underpinned the original closed-economy definition of GDP as the sum of private and public consumption and investment. Following this logic, indicators such as household disposable income and household final consumption are considered as a partial measure of domestic economic welfare. The Irish CSO have developed an adjusted GNI aggregate, commonly referred to as GNI*, to provide a measure of the economic welfare of residents that can be used by domestic policy makers. This measure is discussed in more detail later.
2. These are probably small economies outside the OECD, whose national accounts are not as well developed as those of OECD members.

account of the balance of payments, which should give a much better measure of domestic balance or imbalance.

In seeking a solution to the Irish accounting problems, the best approach would be to modify the ESA / SNA to ensure that it provided appropriate data for policy makers in all jurisdictions. However, this will require a lot of work at an international level,[3] and it may take some considerable time to be fully reflected in an update to the standards for national accounts. Instead Ireland and other countries affected in a similar manner will have to persevere in producing an appropriate supplementary framework of accounts that provides a more sensible depiction of what is happening in the domestic economy from an economic substance point of view. This development work may help inform future improvements at the level of the United Nations.

While most external users will continue to use GDP for international comparisons, if suitably explained, an alternative domestic framework providing more appropriate indicators of domestic economic activity could be used by those interested in economic policy in Ireland. The gains would be even larger if a similar supplementary framework of accounts was adopted by any other countries affected by some of the problems discussed in this chapter. Thus, there is a role for Eurostat and the OECD to help coordinate this development work.

Where problems will arise will be with EU aggregates, such as Euro area GDP, which is affected by the discontinuities in the accounts for Ireland. In 2015 the exceptional growth in Irish GDP added 0.5 percentage points to the euro area growth rate. International agencies such as the ECB, DG Ecfin, the OECD, the IMF, etc., will need to make allowances for such discontinuities in their economic analysis.

Section 3.2 discusses the needs of major users of national accounts. Section 3.3 considers how we model output in a global world. Section 3.4 describes the national accounting significance of the legal structures used by MNEs when operating in different economies. Section 5 describes how globalization has affected the Irish national accounts and Section 6 sets out some possible solutions to the problems identified. Conclusions are reached in Section 7.

3.2   What Is the Purpose of Collecting National Accounts?

The national accounts are designed to present a picture of an economy that can be useful to those managing that economy or working in an economy. The way the accounts are defined and presented should take account of the needs of users and the purpose for which they will be used.

---

3. See Moulton and van de Ven 2018, http://conference.nber.org/conf_papers/f100570.pdf and de Haan and Haynes 2018, http://conference.nber.org/conf_papers/f92462.pdf.

3.2.1   Fiscal and Monetary Policy

Since the national accounting framework was first developed, the national accounts, especially the key aggregates, have been an essential tool for those responsible for fiscal and monetary policy who need to understand the state of the economic cycle.

In addition, in preparing a budget, governments need to understand not just the overall level of output but also what is happening on a range of other important national accounting aggregates. This is essential in assessing tax revenue for the coming year, and in understanding the pressures on expenditure.

Both for fiscal and monetary policy it is, therefore, necessary to have at least one or two key aggregates that reflect the trend of "real" activity in the domestic economy—the economy for which the policy makers are responsible.

Fiscal rules, such as the ones used in the Stability and Growth Pact and its successor,[4] depend on GDP being a meaningful indicator of domestic activity. For countries such as Ireland, an alternative set of measures is needed on which to base fiscal rules.

In managing monetary policy, the behavior of central banks is often characterized using a Taylor rule. Under such a rule monetary policy is tightened as actual output rises above potential output. However, such a rule depends on the availability of reliable measures of domestic output.

To fulfill its policy role, the national accounting aggregate (or aggregates) must provide a consistent picture of what is happening in the domestic economy over time.[5] Discontinuities, such as that which occurred in the Irish GDP series in 2015, make it impossible to determine the growth rate at the point of discontinuity. In addition, to understand the behavior of the economy and to calibrate policy interventions correctly, it is essential to have consistent time series for the important features of the domestic economy that can be used for research and related modeling.

A second requirement for the national accounts aggregates is that they reflect the level of physical activity in the economy being regulated by the fiscal or monetary policy authorities. Production undertaken in another economy, on contract, for firms located in Ireland using IP located in Ireland, does not put pressure on the domestic labor and physical capital markets.[6] As a result, this activity does not have implications for domestic

---

4. The Stability and Growth Pact is a set of EU rules that determine the appropriate stance of domestic fiscal policy in individual countries.

5. Here the term *domestic* is used to reflect economically substantial developments in an economy, for example, to distinguish activity involving domestic labor and capital from activity undertaken abroad on contract for Irish firms using physical capital and labor located abroad, albeit activity using intellectual property owned in Ireland.

6. IP is generally infinitely scalable so that the level of production using that IP, whether in Ireland or abroad, does not have inflationary implications and, as a result, is of lesser concern for domestic policy makers.

inflation and is not of concern for domestic fiscal or monetary policy. The data could well prove misleading if they cover physical activity that takes place in other economies, albeit using intellectual property owned by firms located in Ireland.

This approach means that in analyzing the appropriate stance of fiscal and monetary policy, the "real" activity of subsidiaries of domestic multinationals should be included in the output of the economies where the subsidiaries employ labor and physical capital. In turn, domestic activity for Ireland should include the "real" activity of subsidiaries of foreign-owned multinationals that takes place in Ireland.

3.2.2 Broader Economic Policies

A second major role for the national accounts is to provide appropriate information to governments on how an economy is behaving, where growth is coming from, where output is being sold, and what is driving emissions of greenhouse gases, etc. This information is needed to support governments in developing policy across a wide range of fields.

Policy makers in Ireland are primarily concerned with output and economic activity that benefits domestic residents. For example, if a significant part of the output in the industrial sector reflects profits on contract manufacturing in Asia, using IP owned by foreign MNEs located in Ireland, this activity does not directly benefit Irish residents and it will be of little concern to domestic policy makers. The profits on the foreign-owned IP flow back out of Ireland to the ultimate owners of the IP. The benefit to those living in Ireland arises from the tax paid on the profits located in Ireland.

Also, greenhouse gas emissions are intimately connected with where physical production takes place, not where the IP used in the production process is owned. It is only insofar as the activities of such businesses directly affect those who are living in the country for which the accounts are prepared that the accounts will be useful.

As discussed later, the accounts for Ireland, prepared under SNA 2008 / ESA 2010, do not meet either of these two needs of policy makers. In Ireland the problem arises in trying to identify what part of the activity being measured in the accounts directly benefits those living in Ireland.[7]

In principle, GNI should meet this need. However, in practice it suffers from a range of defects.

- While GNI provides an appropriate single measure of economic activity, much more information is needed by policy makers to understand

---

7. While much of the analysis underpinning fiscal and monetary policy relies on trends in key aggregates on the expenditure side of the national accounts, modeling long-term growth in an economy also relies on data from the income and the output side of the accounts. The major discontinuity in 2015 in the industrial output series for Ireland also poses major problems in understanding trends in greenhouse gas emissions from the sector.

what is driving change in this aggregate. Since the 1970s, with a large amount of activity by foreign MNEs, it has become increasingly difficult to understand which sectors are contributing to the growth in economic welfare of those living in Ireland.

• While the inclusion of intellectual property (IP) in the capital stock provides a much more appropriate measure of capital, because of the fact that it can be owned in one country and used to produce output in another, it has had some very unexpected effects on key Irish national accounting aggregates. For example, the relocation of intellectual property to Ireland by foreign MNEs in 2015 caused a big rise in GDP. While the profits of the foreign MNEs that owned the IP flowed back out of the economy, there was still a major discontinuity in GNI, due to the rise in depreciation on the large stock of IP that had relocated to Ireland. This depreciation reflected a reduction in the value of the foreign-owned IP, and it had no effect on the welfare of Irish residents. If NNI were used by policy makers instead of GNI, this problem would not arise.

• As discussed later in 3.5.4, there is a problem because of the way that the profits of certain MNEs engaged in financial activity (redomiciled PLCs) are treated in the national accounts. These firms do not do any business in Ireland but just receive profits, including retained earnings, on their portfolios of foreign direct investments in the rest of the world. On the other hand, the retained profits of the redomiciled PLC itself are not treated as being paid out to the beneficial owners resident abroad and thus they do not flow back out as factor income.[8] This distorts both the GNI figure and the current account of the balance of payments, so that GNI does not appropriately reflect the economic welfare of those living in Ireland. The retained profits only appear as an increase in foreign-owned assets on the financial account of the balance of payments.

There is, thus, a need to separate the activity that is beneficial for those living in Ireland from the activity that benefits the owners of the foreign MNEs operating in Ireland. The accounts must elucidate what is physically happening in an individual economy as well as what is happening to companies located in that country.

To understand what is driving growth in an economy, it is essential to have data on trends in growth and productivity at a sufficiently detailed industry level[9] to provide real understanding of the sectors where growth is, or is not, occurring.

The current account of the balance of payments should have been a key indicator showing that the growth in economic activity in Ireland (and some

8. https://www.cso.ie/en/releasesandpublications/in/rpibp/redomiciledplcsintheirish balanceofpayments2018/.
9. E.g., agriculture, manufacturing, construction, etc.

other EU economies) was unsustainable in the last decade. However, because of the effects of globalization on the accounts, the danger signal provided by the balance of payments was much less clear than it should have been. This problem has gotten even worse, so that today the current account of the balance of payments for Ireland no longer signals the gap between savings and investment of Irish agents. However, the Irish Central Statistics Office (CSO) has published a modified indicator, which goes back before the crisis.[10] This provides the kind of information that policy makers need for the safe management of a modern economy. It is a good example of how the provision of suitable additional information, together with new ways of presenting that information, can deal with some of the problems identified in this chapter.

3.2.3   Informing Citizens and Companies in the Economy about What Is Happening

The considerations here are very similar to those for other policy makers. Citizens and companies need information on what is happening in an economy insofar as it will affect them. In an economy with large foreign MNE activity this means that the attention should be more focused on GNI and net national income (NNI) than on GDP.

For this broader audience it is even more important that the development of the economy, as manifested in the accounts, is clearly explained. There will also be a need to concentrate on one or two key aggregates when communicating with a very wide audience.

3.2.4   Tax Base

The national accounts data, especially GNI, is used as a tax base in calculating budgetary contributions to the EU. For this purpose, it should include activity that benefits those living in a country, even if much of the related activity does not take place in that country. Because Ireland benefits from the corporation tax paid by foreign MNEs operating in Ireland, it is appropriate that their profits, on which Irish corporation tax is paid, are included in the base for EU taxation. This should inform the choice of the appropriate national aggregate to form the tax base. It also means that the income of MNEs needs to be presented separately from that for the rest of the economy.

3.2.5   International Comparability

A further very important use of national accounts data is to provide comparisons between economies. For this purpose, it is essential that the data are prepared on the same accounting basis across countries. Currently

10. https://www.cso.ie/en/releasesandpublications/in/acabi/amodifiedcurrentaccount balanceforireland2008-2018/.

all EU countries use SNA 2008 / ESA 2010, which facilitates comparisons within the EU. However, because countries are affected in different ways by the process of globalization, if there are anomalies in how the accounting standards treat certain items, it may affect the usefulness of the data for comparative purposes.

Where the inadequacies of SNA 2008 require the development of satellite accounts, as discussed in this chapter, it would be better that they were done on a consistent basis across countries. If each country develops its own system of satellite accounts, policy making at an international level would be less transparent. To the extent that SNA 2008 is not fully implemented in some non-OECD countries this makes international comparisons with some non-OECD countries more difficult.

3.3   Modeling Output

When national accounts were first developed in the 1930s, it was not unreasonable to consider the world as being made up of a series of national economies that undertook limited trade in final goods. However, since the Second World War, a series of major changes in the world economy, especially the freeing of trade and improvements in communications and logistics, has changed this situation so that for some purposes national economies, in the sense of the 1930s, have been transformed into subsectors of a global economy.

It can be useful to consider these and other changes within an encompassing model of world production. In this model the choice of the location for production by a stylized world firm (or myriad of firms) is made to minimize the world firm's cost of production. In the 1930s each firm chose capital, labor, and materials in each separate national economy to minimize the cost of production of national output. Domestic production was primarily directed at satisfying domestic demand.

However, with the freeing of trade, the world firm(s) can choose to locate some of the production process of a good in one country and then combine the components produced in one country with labor and capital in another location to produce a final good. In this case the production of the final good in a relevant country will be undertaken using domestic capital and labor, combined with materials for further production that are produced in another location. Where final products consist of components from many countries, the cost of production in an individual country can influence domestic value added (GDP) in two ways:

First the relative cost of production in one country compared to the rest of the world will affect the location where the final good will be produced, hence affecting domestic value added (GDP).

Secondly, changes in relative factor prices within a country can also affect domestic value added by causing the world firm to produce more or less of that final good in the relevant country by varying the share of material inputs, many of which may be imported—the substitution effect of changes in relative prices.

Thus, this model encompasses behavior such as outsourcing, modeling it as a function of the changes in the cost of domestic inputs relative to the cost of materials produced abroad. As a result, as discussed below, the effect of changes in the relative cost of domestic inputs on domestic value added must include both the substitution of gross output in a particular economy for similar output elsewhere, and also the substitution of domestic inputs (labor and capital) by material inputs, which are generally imported.

(1) $C_w = f(c_I, c_R, t)$

The approach taken in the traditional national accounts of the 1930s assumed a model where the production of goods on a worldwide scale could be characterized by a cost function, where (1) the cost of world output, C_w, is a function of the unit cost of production in an individual country c_I relative to the rest of the world, c_R, and technical progress, t.[11] Then (2) the share of world output Q_W that is located in the individual country i, Q_I, is a function of the unit cost of production in country i, c_I, relative to the unit cost of production in the rest of the world, c_R, and technical progress, t.

(2) $$\frac{Q_I}{Q_W} = f\left(\frac{c_I}{c_R}, t\right)$$

(3) $$c_i = \frac{C_i}{Q_i} = f(p_l, p_k, p_m, t)$$

The unit cost of production in country i is defined in equation (3) as a function of the price of labor, p_l, the cost of capital, p_k, the price of inputs of goods and services, p_m, and technical progress, t. From this equation the share of each of the factors of production—labor, capital and materials—in domestic output can be determined. For this model to be a valid representation of the economy of country i, a number of assumptions are necessary, including the assumption of constant returns to scale.

For a national output aggregate to be valid for any country it must be weakly homothetically separable from output in all other countries (Denny and Fuss 1977, and Pindyck 1979). This allows a two-stage optimization procedure, where firms in individual countries choose the optimal mix of inputs to use to produce national output. Then the share of world output to be produced in country i is a function of the unit cost of production in country i relative to the unit cost of production in all other countries.

The assumption of weak homothetic separability means that changes in relative prices of factors of production within one country, which do

11. The exposition here is based on Bradley and FitzGerald, 1988.

not affect the overall cost of production in that country, will not affect the mix of inputs used to produce a good in another country. In other words, in producing a good or service it is not possible to freely mix factor inputs from different countries in different proportions to produce a final good or service. This is a world where the supply chain does not spread across different countries but all inputs, including materials and services, are sourced nationally. While this restriction may have seemed realistic in the 1930s, in a modern world the restrictions are no longer valid.

The freeing of trade in the postwar world saw trade expanding rapidly, not just in final goods and services but also in inputs used in the production process. This has gradually resulted in the complex supply chains that underpin modern production. This change gives rise to many of the problems with the national accounts for countries such as Ireland, which are small but fully integrated into the global supply chain.

Because of the ability to shift production between countries, the effects of reaching full employment or full utilization of fixed capital in a particular economy can be rather different from that in a closed economy world. Instead of factor prices rising rapidly in the face of high levels of capacity utilization, it is possible to shift some of the production process elsewhere. This has implications for fiscal and monetary policy.

A second assumption of the standard production model is that capital is located in a particular country and used for production in that country. It also assumes that the marginal product of capital (and of other factors) is diminishing. However, intellectual property, which is now, appropriately, included as an element of the capital stock, has rather different characteristics. It may be technically located in one country (and receive its returns in that country), while it may be used to produce output worldwide. As Haskel and Westlake (2017) emphasize, intellectual property (IP) is highly scalable: the same IP can be used to produce a million or a billion smartphones. As a result, this type of capital does not fit easily into the traditional model of production or into the traditional national accounts framework; the marginal product of IP is not diminishing. Also, it can be used simultaneously across many different countries.

(4) $$C = f(K_p, p_{il}, p_{ik}, p_{jl}p_{jk} \cdots p_r, t)$$

Today the choice facing the world firm(s) may be better represented by equation 4, which relaxes the assumption of weak homothetic separability between factors in individual countries. Instead the world firm(s) can choose to mix the factors from different countries i, j, etc. in a complicated supply chain. Raw materials p_r are located independently of where the production takes place. Also, in the modern world the stock of IP, K_p is increasingly separable from all other factors of production. It can be located anywhere in the world.

The returns on IP are separable from the returns to the other factors.

This means that the inclusion of the returns to IP in an economy may not reflect the returns to that factor as used in that economy. National output, as understood when the national accounts were first developed, no longer exists as a separable aggregate. The attribution to Ireland of the returns to IP owned by foreign MNEs in Ireland is very seriously distorting the traditional measure of national output. That is because much of the returns to IP arise from the use of the IP to produce goods in Asia, not Ireland.

However, while such a model better represents a global world, it has been necessary to impose significant restrictions to make it tractable for economic analysis. Nonetheless, it is important that the data provided by the national accounts reflect the complex decision-making process that determines the global location of output and the utilization of factors in individual countries.

3.4   Legal Distinctions Matter

Two legal issues may have a significant effect on how the operations of MNEs are reflected in national accounts. The first concerns the legal form used by an MNE operating in a country other than its home location. The second is how the company is affected by tax law, especially how US companies are affected by US tax law.

3.4.1   Legal Structure

For over a century many companies have moved from operating on a purely national scale to operating in two or more different countries. This "globalization" can occur in different ways. Initially a company may buy services or inputs from firms in other countries. A second stage may involve the establishment of a subsidiary in one or more foreign countries, making the company a multinational enterprise (MNE). A third approach, which has become more popular in recent decades, is to contract with foreign firms to manufacture goods on behalf of the MNE in factories owned by independent companies in foreign locations.

Where firms buy goods or services abroad this appears in the national accounts as imports and exports in a straightforward manner. The output in the foreign location is included in that country's GDP.

Before the freeing of trade, the establishment of a foreign subsidiary was often the only way to move into a new market, bypassing tariff barriers. It allowed companies to exploit their intellectual property on a wider scale in the face of major restrictions on trade. However, the reduction or abolition of barriers to trade and the development of communications and logistics have made possible complex supply chains. Whereas initially the production process may have been replicated in different locations to avoid tariffs, today the different stages in the supply chain may be undertaken by subsidiaries located in different countries around the world to minimize the world cost of production.

Very often, in setting up a subsidiary in a country, an MNE establishes a legal presence there.[12] The physical capital and labor used by the subsidiary are clearly part of the stock of physical capital and labor force in the country where the subsidiary is located. As a result, the activity of the subsidiary is recorded as part of the activity in the country where it is located: the GVA, physical investment, employment, wage bill, profit, and depreciation are all included in the detailed national accounts for the country where the subsidiary resides.

The relationship of a subsidiary in another country with the parent MNE, wherever it is located, is reflected in a transfer of the after-tax profits earned by the subsidiary to the parent, flows of factor income which represent a wedge between GDP and GNI. Even if temporarily retained in the origin country, this payment is treated as being accrued to the MNE parent. There may also be other intra-company transfers that affect the national accounts. For example, royalties may be paid for use of the parent company's IP. Also, parts or services may pass from one subsidiary to another appearing as exports and imports.

A third approach to operating on a global scale involves an MNE contracting with a company in another country to have goods or services produced for it. This approach has been adopted by some large MNEs operating in Ireland where they hold their IP. In this case the MNE provides the IP but the local company owns the physical capital and employs local labor. Because the work is done on contract for the MNE, the goods or services produced by the local company are owned by the MNE from the initiation of the production process.[13] The value added of the contract manufacturer appears as an import in the country where the MNE owner resides. Then the goods (or services) are recorded as an export from the country where the MNE that owns the goods resides, not from the country where they were manufactured. Also imported inputs used in the process are recorded as imports in the country where the MNE that owns the goods resides. The operating surplus, over and above the payments to the local producer, is recorded as output in the country where the MNE that owns the IP is located.[14]

12. For example, German car manufacturers have established subsidiaries in Hungary and Slovakia to make their cars or car parts.
13. For example, while small relative to the total output of the Irish pharmaceutical sector, there has been contract manufacturing work done in Ireland for foreign pharmaceutical companies. In this case the drug is shipped in powder form to an Irish company to be pressed into tablet form. The powdered drug is, at all times, owned by the foreign company contracting with the Irish company so that it is not considered as being produced in Ireland. Rather, for national accounting purposes, only the payment to the Irish company for the services is included in Irish exports. Meanwhile, the gross flows of the drug are included in the trade statistics.
14. Thus, the operating surplus on manufacturing Donald Trump ties in China in 2015 would have been treated as U.S. GDP, in spite of the fact that they were manufactured in China on contract.

Thus, there can be a very different national accounting treatment for goods or services physically produced in a country depending on the organizational arrangements between the MNE and the local company. The decision by MNEs to go the contract manufacturing route may be due to uncertainty about how well a subsidiary company may be treated in the host country's legal system or by its administration.[15] Local entrepreneurs may be favored in many ways. Also, the MNE may be concerned that, if IP is transferred to a subsidiary, it might not be protected by the host country legal system.

For whatever reason, contract manufacturing tends to be used by IT companies with large IP having goods manufactured in countries such as China. The subsidiary route is favored in cross-border activities by MNEs, such as German or Japanese MNEs, especially where the subsidiaries are located in OECD countries.

The fact that, as described in the above, the distinction between manufacture by a subsidiary and manufacture on contract may make a big difference to the national accounting treatment of MNE activity leaves open the possibility of future big discontinuities in the national accounts for individual countries. If the legal or organizational framework changed to make establishing a subsidiary preferable in certain major Asian economies, such as China, the MNEs currently operating contract arrangements could suddenly change their production arrangements. This could result in a large amount of what is treated as output in Ireland, or elsewhere, suddenly being included in the national accounts for the Asian country where the physical manufacturing takes place. The relocation of output in the accounts would be replaced by a transfer to the MNE, wherever it is headquartered, of after-tax profits as part of factor income. Similarly, a shift of production from China to a country such as India, where the establishment of subsidiaries is preferred, could also see a major change in output in the country where the MNE's head office is located, such as Ireland. While these cases would give rise to significant discontinuities in GDP, they should not affect GNI. Instead of the profit on the IP used in contract manufacturing abroad appearing as output in Ireland, the profit of the foreign subsidiary would be remitted to Ireland as factor income, leaving GNI unchanged.

While the current approach to recording activity in SNA 2008, if applied across the world, will consistently record world GDP, it poses many problems for the key users of the data. It means that GDP and also, as is outlined later, GNI may not provide a good guide for policy makers. In addition, if the SNA is not correctly applied in all countries by their national accounting authorities, world GDP and GNI may be incorrect and subject to discontinuities as MNEs change their legal structure.

---

15. For example, foreigners may be subject to arbitrary charges.

Table 3.1   Share of gross operating surplus in Irish GVA, by country of ownership, %

	2008	2009	2010	2011	2012	2013	2014	2015
Germany	34.4	31.8	41.6	40.5	53.4	NA	59.2	36.3
France	53.3	42.0	56.0	71.5	47.1	NA	60.3	58.7
UK	38.1	34.1	32.9	46.6	43.4	NA	49.3	38.2
US	79.8	80.1	81.1	82.6	82.8	NA	85.6	94.4
Japan	62.8	69.3	62.6	74.5	70.9	NA	82.7	84.0
Other foreign	58.3	54.9	62.2	63.3	66.6	NA	54.5	80.2
Ireland	28.1	31.2	32.6	35.4	35.4	NA	37.9	44.7

Source: Eurostat Structural Business Statistics.

3.4.2   Tax Law

Some of the problems with the Irish national accounts arise from how US tax law affects the behavior of US MNEs (Barry 2019). The problems are much fewer in dealing with MNEs originating in other countries such as Germany, France, or the UK. The key difference is that, until now, US tax law meant that all profits of US firms, wherever earned, were taxable eventually in the United States. However, until now, US firms could defer repatriating profits and so "temporarily" avoid paying the US tax liability. This has proved especially important for firms with large IP, such as firms in the IT sector.

The changes in US tax law in 2017 are significant and may lead to further movement, especially changes in the country where firms locate their IP. The requirement that the US owners of IP held abroad pay a minimum tax rate of 10 percent could see further major relocation of such IP, possibly to Ireland, where the rate is 12.5 percent. However, this chapter does not consider how the recent US changes in tax law may affect the national accounts in the future in any detail.

Since 1956 Ireland has operated a low rate of corporation tax, which was gradually extended to cover all activity undertaken in Ireland.[16] This has made it attractive for some MNEs to adjust their global structure so that a larger share of their global profits are earned in Ireland and subject to Irish corporation tax (Conroy, Honohan, and Maître 1998). Such a transfer of profits is reflected in the gross operating surplus of firms, so that it represents a high share of their value added in Ireland.

Table 3.1 shows the gross operating surplus (GOS) of subsidiaries of foreign MNEs operating in Ireland as a share of gross value added (GVA), and a comparable figure for Irish firms. The shares for German, UK, and

16. In 1956 the law was changed to exempt profits earned from exporting from corporation tax. In 1980 this exemption was replaced by a 10 percent rate of tax on all manufacturing firms. In the 1990s a 12.5 percent rate was gradually applied to all sectors of the economy, being fully implemented by 2003.

Irish firms are rather similar. The share for French subsidiaries in Ireland is a bit higher. However, the profit share for US firms is exceptionally high, and also very high for other non-EU firms, including Japanese firms. After the relocation to Ireland of IP by US-owned MNEs in 2015, the profit share of these firms approached 95 percent of value added.

These data suggest that for MNEs owned in the EU, domestic tax law in the country where the MNEs are resident makes shifting of profits to an offshore location, such as Ireland, difficult. Alternatively, the nature of their business may also make the separation of the returns to IP (which can be relocated) from other profits difficult.

After the relocation to Ireland of IP in 2015 by one or more US firms, two-thirds of the gross operating surplus arising in the Irish economy was attributable to US firms and under 10 percent to firms from other foreign countries. By contrast, only 6 percent of employment in Ireland was in US owned companies.

The obvious conclusion from table 3.1 is that US tax law has resulted in US companies transferring substantial profits to Ireland, whereas MNEs from other countries that account for the bulk of employment by MNEs in Ireland have not transferred much of their global profits to Ireland because of the nature of their business or because of the way the domestic tax law is implemented in the country where the MNEs are headquartered.

3.5   Irish National Accounting Issues

Ireland joined the EU in 1973, and, since that date, the economy has become increasingly globalized. There has been a series of additional important developments as a result of globalization, which has affected the portrayal of the economy in the national accounts over the subsequent 45 years.

The first development was the important role played by the low rate of corporation tax in attracting foreign MNEs to establish subsidiaries in Ireland. In turn, they tended to be highly profitable with some firms, especially from the United States, transferring profits to Ireland.

Initially the profits of such MNEs were only reflected in factor outflows when the profits were actually remitted to their parent. With substantial deferral of payments, especially by US companies, this led to an underestimate of the true outflow and an overestimate of GNI. The recognition of the importance of including the profits of MNEs on an accruals basis, rather than on the basis of actual remittances, only occurred in the early 1980s (Honohan 1984).

More recently the national accounts for Ireland have been significantly affected by a range of other factors arising from globalization: the growth of a large aircraft leasing sector; changes in patents of pharmaceutical companies; the growth in activity by redomiciled PLCs; and, finally, the inclusion of IP in investment, interacting with changes in ownership of this IP (de Haan and Haynes 2018). National accounting rules have significantly affected how these developments are represented in the national accounts: in some cases, their treatment in the accounts means that GNI, rather than GDP, provides a more appropriate reflection of the income of those living in Ireland. However, the effect of the growth of redomiciled PLCs, and of the ownership of IP by MNEs located in Ireland, has, in more recent years, also seriously affected the usefulness of GNI for the purposes for which national accounts are used by policy makers.

3.5.1   Accrued Profits of MNEs

The direct benefit for people living in Ireland from the activity of foreign-owned MNEs is the wage bill and the corporation tax paid in Ireland. The profits flow back to the foreign owners of MNE subsidiaries in Ireland. Thus GDP, which includes the profits of the MNEs, is not as good a measure of the income flowing, directly and indirectly, to those living in Ireland as GNI, which excludes the profits of foreign MNES.

By the end of the 1970s there was very substantial manufacturing activity undertaken in Ireland by foreign-owned MNEs. The attraction of Ireland for MNEs derived from their ready access to the wider EU market, the fact that labor costs were significantly lower than elsewhere in the EU, a stable business environment, and a low corporate tax rate.[17] As a result of the low corporate tax rate there was a significant incentive for MNEs to move profits to Ireland through transfer pricing (Conroy, Honohan, and Maître 1998). The result was that the profits earned by MNEs have represented an increasing share of GDP over time, driving a growing wedge between GDP and GNI.

As shown in figure 3.1, whereas in the early 1970s GNI was higher than GDP, by 1980 GNI was 5 percent less than GDP as a result of the outflow of profits of MNEs. This gap between the two has widened over time, and, since 2009, GNI has generally been less than 85 percent of GDP.

In the 1970s the profits recorded as flowing out of the country were actual remittances, but there was a growing buildup of accrued profits, especially among US MNEs. This was not recognized in the national accounts till 1984, when the profit outflows were shown on an accruals basis for the first time. This resulted in a substantial upward revision in the deficit on the current account of the balance payments. (The deficit on the current account of the balance of payments was revised upwards from 12.5 percent of GDP to over 15 percent for 1981).

3.5.2   The Patent Cliff

The pharmaceutical sector has grown in importance in the economy since the 1990s with the vast bulk of the output coming from foreign-owned

---

17. Up to 1980 a zero rate of corporate tax rate applied to profits deriving from exports.

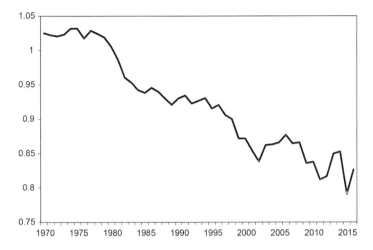

Figure 3.1   Ratio of GNI to GNP, current prices
Source: CSO National Income and Expenditure, 2016 and CSO Historical National Accounts.

MNEs. By 2010 the sector accounted for almost 10 percent of GDP. These firms are generally highly profitable, reflecting the huge IP involved in developing their products. This IP is protected by patents that have a limited life.

While the pharmaceutical sector involves significant employment, the actual impact of the sector on GNI is much more limited than the gross value added (GVA) figures would suggest. This is because the profits of the relevant firms located in Ireland, with the exception of the corporation tax paid in Ireland, accrue to their foreign parents. Thus, the eventual impact of the activity in these firms on Irish GNI depends on the size of the wage bill and the corporation tax paid on their profits in Ireland, and any reduction in profitability as patents lapse has no effect.

At the end of 2011 and through 2012 a number of major drugs produced in Ireland fell out of patent. In particular Lipitor, produced by Pfizer in Ireland, went off patent first in the United States and then in Europe and Japan between the end of 2011 and the end of 2012 (FitzGerald 2013a). This resulted in a reduction in revenue for the company of around US$5.5 billion (around 2.5 percent of Irish GDP). In turn, this reduction in revenue was reflected in a reduction in Irish exports. To the extent that the patented drug was replaced by an unpatented generic drug,[18] this was treated as a fall in volume rather than a fall in price. This had a significant impact on GVA, reducing its growth rate by over 0.5 percentage points a year over the two years. As there was no loss of employment, the only loss to Irish national income was a reduction in corporation tax receipts amounting to something

18. It was the same drug manufactured in the same plant but with different packaging.

Table 3.2   Aircraft leasing share for key national accounts aggregates, 2016, % of national total

Wage Bill	0.3
Gross operating surplus	4.7
Corporation Tax	2.5
GDP	3.0
GNI*[a]	0.2
Depreciation	8.1
Capital Stock, 2014	15.6

Source: http://www.cso.ie/en/releasesandpublications/ep/p-ali/aircraftleasinginireland2007-2016./

[a] This is "adjusted" national income, excluding depreciation on foreign capital. See section 5.5.

over 0.1 percentage points of GVA each year. The impact of the fall in output on GDP was almost entirely offset by the fall in profits flowing back to the MNE, leaving very little impact on GNI.

3.5.3   Aircraft Leasing

Over the last fifteen years aircraft leasing has expanded dramatically in Ireland, with most of the major MNEs engaging in this business having subsidiaries in Ireland (FitzGerald 2015). The Irish Central Statistics Office (CSO) has recently published detailed data on the operation of the sector over the last decade. It shows the value of the stock of aircraft owned in Ireland in 2014[19] at €77 billion, representing approximately 10 percent of the stock of civilian aircraft in the world.[20] This also represented 16 percent of the capital stock for the country as a whole. As a result of the large stock of capital, the sector also accounted for around 8 percent of the depreciation in the economy in 2016. The large purchase of aircraft each year also seriously distorts the figures for investment, and it has a corresponding effect on imports.

As shown in table 3.2, while aircraft leasing has a major impact on some aggregates in the national accounts, its impact on GNI* is actually very small at 0.2 percent in 2016. This reflects the fact that the sector's wage bill is only 0.3 percent of that for the economy as a whole, while corporation tax paid by the sector accounts for 2.5 percent of the national total. While a big global player, the ultimate impact of the sector's activities on the income of those living in Ireland, measured by GNI, is actually very small.

3.5.4   Redomiciled PLCs

Over the last few years a number of companies have relocated their headquarters to Ireland without generating any real activity in the economy in

19. This is the latest year for which data on the capital stock of the sector are available.
20. According to avolon.aero/wp/wp-content/uploads/2014/09/WFF_2014.pdf there were 21,000 civilian aircraft in 2013. If the aircraft are valued at an average of €40 million each, the value of the world stock of aircraft would be €840 billion.

Table 3.3				Net income of redomiciled PLCs, as % of GNI						
2008	2009	2010	2011	2012	2013	2014	2015	2016	2017	2018
0.2	1.1	3.7	4.0	5.0	4.3	4.2	2.3	2.6	1.9	2.0

Source: https://www.cso.ie/en/releasesandpublications/in/rpibp/redomiciledplcsintheirish
balanceofpayments2018/.

terms of employment or purchases of domestic inputs (FitzGerald 2013b). The issues that arise with this activity are clearly explained in Avdjiev et al. (2018).

These companies, referred to technically as redomiciled PLCs, manage large investments elsewhere in the world. However, while they have established a legal presence in Ireland, they undertake no real activity in the country and they are resident elsewhere for tax purposes.[21] While they receive large profits in Ireland, they pay out only 30 percent of the profits as dividends to their shareholders abroad.

The retained earnings in Ireland enhance the value of the companies. As a result, the recorded inflows into the economy that these firms generate are much larger than the recorded outflows on the current account of the balance of payments. However, the benefits of the retained profits of redomiciled PLCs are attributable to their foreign owners—there is no benefit to the Irish economy. Nonetheless, using the standard SNA / ESA accounting procedures, this has the effect of raising the measured current account surplus in the balance of payments and increasing the level of nominal GNI arising in Ireland.

Because the equity of these redomiciled PLCs is treated as portfolio investment, the distributed income is treated differently in the national accounts than the profits on foreign direct investment by MNEs. For the Irish subsidiaries of foreign MNEs producing goods and services, their profits, whether or not they are remitted to their parent, are accrued as an outflow of factor income in the national accounts (and in the current account of the balance of payments), whereas the distributed income of the redomiciled PLCs is only treated as a factor outflow if they actually pay dividends to their foreign shareholders.

Redomiciled PLCs grew very rapidly from a very low level in 2008, so that, as shown in table 3.3, their retained earnings reached 5 percent of GNI in 2012. Since 2008, their activity has had a significant impact on the Irish national accounts and on the current account of the balance of payments. Having risen rapidly in the period 2009–2012, expressed as a share of GNI their retained earnings had fallen back by 2015.

To get a picture of what is happening to the income of those living in

---

21. Initially they were predominantly UK firms, but the bulk of the retained profits now belong to U.S. firms, some of which redomiciled to Ireland from Bermuda. They now include the treasury operations of a number of MNEs.

Ireland, national income needs to be adjusted to exclude these retained earnings. This makes a significant difference to the growth rate in GNI over the period of the economic crisis. It also substantially alters the path of the current account deficit/surplus on the balance of payments, making a difference to how one understands the recent development of the Irish economy.

Ireland is not unique in having this problem with headquartered companies that have little economic presence, boosting the current account surplus. The Netherlands also has problems with how the operations of foreign firms are reflected in their accounts, though there it does not seem to have as much impact on the current account of the balance of payments (Rojas-Romagosa and van der Horst 2015).

3.5.5   IP and Contract Manufacturing

The scalability of the IP capital means that it can be, and has been, used to produce very large output of phones and computers. A second aspect of the IP capital is that it can be exploited by workers (and physical capital) located in different jurisdictions than where the IP capital is itself located; it is separable from the other factors of production. This is very different from other capital, where the equipment must be physically present in the country where the production takes place.

While IP plays a very important role in many industries, the IT sector is unusual in the extent to which the IP is separated in terms of geographical jurisdiction from the related physical production. The pharmaceuticals sector, which is also an important part of the Irish economy, and where production is dominated by foreign MNEs, uses very extensive IP in producing its output. The IP is either located in Ireland, where the production takes place, or is licensed by the Irish subsidiary from the parent MNE, appearing as an import of services. Thus, the IP in pharmaceuticals is more closely associated with where the goods themselves are actually produced.

In the case of some key IT sector firms in Ireland, they have used contract manufacturing to undertake the manufacture of their products, such as smartphones and computers. This contract manufacturing does not involve the transfer of the IP or the licensing of the IP to the contract manufacturer.

Since the early 2000s, there has been extensive investment in intellectual property by foreign MNEs. Figure 3.2 shows investment in IP as a percentage of GDP for Ireland and the other EU countries where it is also important. In the case of Ireland, this investment represented between 3 percent and 4 percent of GDP for much of the 2000s, rising to 5 percent in 2009. The vast bulk of this investment was not produced in Ireland but was imported. The investment in IP is being undertaken by foreign MNEs who choose to operate in Ireland through subsidiaries of their parent companies.

The biggest shock to the Irish national accounts in recent years has come from the one-off movement to Ireland in 2015 of IP owned by foreign MNEs.

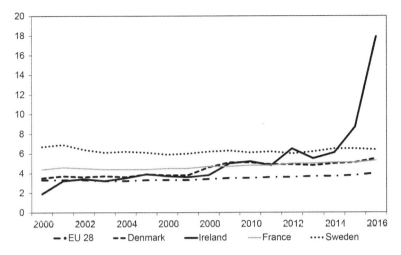

Figure 3.2   Investment in intellectual property as a percentage of GDP
Source: Eurostat.

Because it was a relocation of firms, it did not show up in investment; instead the transfer shows up in the financial account of the balance of payments. This transfer of IP capital amounted to between €250 billion and €300 billion, increasing the domestic capital stock of the economy by 40 percent in that year. The increase in the capital stock also amounted to over 50 percent of Irish GNI.[22] In addition to the transfer of ownership of IP, there has been major additional investment in IP in 2015 (10 percent of GNI) and in 2016 (21 percent of GNI) as well (see figure 3.2), which is also reflected in services imports of IP. As a result, the capital stock rose by another 10 percent in 2016.

This movement of firms and their IP to Ireland was also associated with dramatic changes in the output recorded in the Irish national accounts. The newly relocated firms used their IP, located in Ireland, to produce IT products, such as smartphones and computers, in Asia. These operations were undertaken in the third countries on contract. The Asian firms undertaking the manufacture were paid a fee for the manufacture, which covered the cost of the physical capital and the labor used in the production process. The difference between this payment to the firm manufacturing the goods and the value of the product produced (the profit on the goods), which embodied the parent firm's IP, is then considered as output in Ireland.

The fact that the actual manufacture took place in a third country and that the goods produced never passed through Ireland is irrelevant from the point

22. It also represented over 2 percent of U.S. GNI.

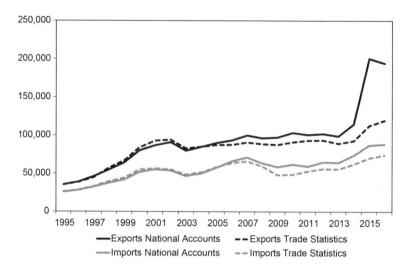

Figure 3.3   Trade on a national accounts and trade statistics basis, € million CSO: national income and expenditure and quarterly national accounts and trade statistics

of view of the national accounts. What is crucial in determining where this output is located in the accounts is the ownership of the goods produced.

The profit of the company owning the IP, which is the "pure" return on the firms' IP, is treated as output in Ireland, and the full value of the goods produced in the third country is treated as an export from Ireland in the national accounts. (The value added arising in the country where the goods are manufactured is treated as an import into Ireland.) This has seen a huge difference open up between the merchandise export figures on a trade statistics basis and the same item in the national accounts (figure 3.3).

In the national accounts the relocation of these firms to Ireland accounted for much of the very large increase in real GDP in 2015 of 26 percent. Obviously, this increase in the output of the foreign MNEs, which is primarily reflected in an increase in their profits, only benefits those living in Ireland to the extent that corporation tax is paid in Ireland on those profits.[23]

GNI is arrived at by deducting the profits of the MNEs, after depreciation, as they are treated as being accrued to the foreign parent whether or not they are actually remitted in the year in question. However, because of the presence of these MNEs' very large stock of IP in Ireland, from 2015 depreciation accounted for by large foreign MNEs jumped from under €6 billion in 2014 to €30 billion in 2015 and rising to €46 billion in 2018.[24] This

23. Because Ireland's contribution to the EU budget is based on GNI, part of the increase in corporation tax was offset by an increase in the EU budgetary contribution.
24. http://www.cso.ie/en/media/csoie/newsevents/documents/seminars/globalisationinireland/Multinationals_in_the_Institutional_Sector_Accounts_-_Peter_Culhane,_CSO.pdf.

massive rise in depreciation in 2015 accounted for much of the increase in GNI of around 16 percent in that year. Because the depreciation on the capital stock of foreign-owned MNEs does not benefit domestic residents, the resulting growth in GNI in no way reflects the change in income, directly or indirectly, of Irish residents.

GNI was used by policy makers as a good indicator of what was happening to domestic economic activity over the last 30 years. However, as a result of these changes, it is no longer fit for the needs of domestic policy makers.

As discussed later, to deal with this problem, the Irish Central Statistics Office (CSO) has introduced an "adjusted" GNI, referred to as GNI*, which excludes the depreciation on foreign-owned IP and leased aircraft, and also makes an adjustment for the profits of redomiciled PLCs (CSO 2017). Alternatively, net national income, which grew in nominal terms by around 10 percent in 2015, would be an appropriate variable for domestic policy makers to target if it were also adjusted for the profits of redomiciled PLCs. However, in the case of NNI the CSO has not yet developed this series on a constant price basis. They have, however, published constant price data for GNI* on an experimental basis for the years 2013 to 2018.[25]

While the effects of the large IP-related activity of foreign MNEs on the output side of the national accounts is confined to gross operating surplus in the sectors where these companies operate, the effects on the expenditure side of the account are more complex.

Investment in IP and aircraft for leasing accounts for a substantial share of total investment. The CSO publishes a figure for modified total domestic demand, which excludes these components of investment. It gives a better picture of domestic demand of Irish residents.

However, it can be very difficult to unscramble what is happening on trade. It is affected by the import of the IP and aircraft for leasing that are included in investment. There are also large amounts of contract manufacturing affecting both imports and exports. There are substantial services imports and exports in respect of the licensing of IP, and there is the repatriation of profits by foreign MNEs and the profits of redomiciled PLCs. This has made it very difficult to determine the contribution from trade with the outside world to domestic income.

Because of the complexity of the relationship between the domestic economy and the rest of the world, much of which arises from the effects of a large foreign MNE presence, it is also difficult to interpret the current account of the balance of payments.

As discussed already, the activities of redomiciled PLCs has served to artificially boost the surplus (reduce the deficit) on the current account of the balance of payments in recent years. The massive increase in depreciation in 2015 on the IP of foreign MNEs in Ireland also greatly magnified the sur-

25. https://www.cso.ie/en/releasesandpublications/in/nie/in-mgnicp/.

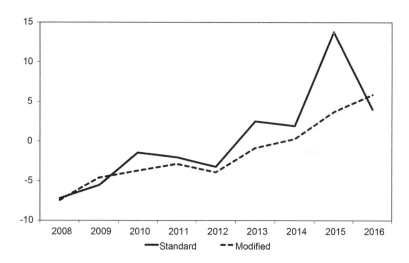

Figure 3.4   Current account of the balance of payments, % of GNI

Source: http://www.cso.ie/en/releasesandpublications/in/acabi/amodifiedcurrentaccount
balanceforireland1998-2016/.

plus. The gross operating surplus of these foreign MNEs includes the depreciation. While the net operating surplus, after tax, flows back out in factor income, this is not the case for the depreciation. Instead the write down in the value of the assets in Ireland is reflected in the financial accounts of the balance of payments. As shown in figure 3.4, the effect of this relocation in 2015 was to produce a massive surplus on the current account reflecting the depreciation on the IP that was relocated to Ireland. This makes the balance on the unadjusted current account less useful for monitoring internal pressures in the Irish economy.

To deal with this problem the CSO has issued an adjusted current account balance as shown in figure 3.4. This excludes imports of aircraft for leasing, imports of IP, depreciation on these two items, and the profits of redomiciled PLCs. This provides a more realistic picture of the balance between savings and investment in the Irish economy.

3.5.6   Problem for Policy Makers

The wide-ranging and complex effects of globalization on the Irish national accounts have made it very difficult for policy makers to understand what is really going on in the economy. During the economic crisis, the headline indicators of GDP and GNI, which are normally targeted by policy makers, were seriously distorted by the changing effects of globalization on the economy. Today there are concerns as to how rapidly the economy may be approaching capacity. However, the problems related to the interpreta-

able 3.4	Key national accounts aggregates, growth rate nominal and real, %											
	2007	2008	2009	2010	2011	2012	2013	2014	2015	2016	2017	2018
urrent Prices												
GDP	6.6	−4.8	−9.4	−1.4	1.8	2.5	2.6	8.4	34.9	3.4	9.4	9.1
GNI	5.1	−4.6	−12.5	−1.2	−1.5	1.9	7.4	8.5	22.9	9.7	6.5	7.7
GNI*	4.9	−5.2	−14.1	−4.4	−2.0	0.1	8.3	8.6	9.4	8.0	4.7	7.3
onstant Prices												
GDP	5.3	−4.5	−5.1	1.8	0.3	0.2	1.4	8.6	25.2	3.7	8.1	8.2
GNI	3.6	−3.9	−8.3	3.2	−3.4	0.0	5.6	8.7	13.7	9.7	5.1	6.5
GNI* (experimental)								8.8	−0.4	8.7	3.7	6.3

ource: CSO National Income and Expenditure, 2018.

tion of available national accounting data make it very difficult to assess the urgency with which corrective action should be taken.

Table 3.4 shows the growth rate from 2007 for certain key aggregates in current and constant prices. The constant price series for GNI* are produced on an experimental basis.

As shown in the table, GNI* at current prices shows a markedly different path than GNI or GDP from 2010 onwards. At the height of the crisis in 2010 it suggests that the economy was performing worse than would have been understood using GNI. It also suggests that the robust recovery might have begun in 2013 rather than in the second half of 2012. Finally, it provides a picture of a more stable, but still very rapid, rate of growth in 2014 to 2018, in contrast to the extraordinary picture from GDP and GNI. However, the growth rate in 2015 in the experimental GNI* at constant prices series does not fit in with any of the other information we have on the economy for that year. There is still further work needed.

3.5.7   Wider Implications of Developments in Ireland

Obviously, the problems in interpreting the national accounts for Ireland, identified in this section, are of primary concern to Irish policy makers. However, some of the changes in 2015 are big enough to even have a noticeable impact on the accounts for other larger economies, such as the United States'. Guvenen et al. (2017) have considered how US output may be under-recorded as a result of the operations of US MNEs that own large IP. Given the size of the relocation to Ireland in 2015, and the fact that the companies involved were almost certainly ultimately US-owned, the changes in key Irish aggregates can also usefully be considered in terms of how the US national accounts might have been affected if the relocation had been to the United States.

Table 3.5 gives an estimate of the change in Ireland in 2015 of nominal GDP, exports, and depreciation as a result of the movement of the reloca-

Table 3.5   Changes in some key Irish national accounts aggregates, % of Irish and US GDP

	Ireland 2015, Change, € M	Ireland 2014 € M	US 2014 € M	Change in Ireland as % of Ireland	US
GDP	50,000	194,537	131,18,250	25.7	0.4
Exports	66,075	219,786	1,786,676	30.1	3.7
Depreciation	23,861	29,486	2,068,497	80.9	1.2

Source: Author's estimates.

tion of companies with very large IP. The increase in output attributed to Ireland added almost 26 percent to nominal GDP. This output was produced on contract in Asia for subsidiaries of US firms located in Ireland. If the subsidiaries relocating to Ireland had instead relocated to the United States, it would have added 0.4 percent to US GDP.

Similarly, the increase in exports of goods, produced on contract in Asia, amounted to 30 percent of Irish exports and would have amounted to almost 4 percent of US exports. Finally, the increase in depreciation added around 80 percent to the Irish aggregate, and the change was equivalent to 1.2 percent of the relevant US aggregate.

3.6   Possible Solutions

The difficulties caused by the process of globalization for national accounting obviously differ from one country to another. However, many of the problems faced in accounting for the Irish economy are faced by other economies, albeit generally to a lesser extent. To meet the needs of users of national accounts, significant additions are needed to the current standard accounting framework.

Both Eurostat and the CSO will, as the law requires, continue to produce the national accounts on the SNA 2008 / ESA 2010 basis. This means that the headline GDP figure will not be amended but will continue to be affected by the actions of MNEs that are resident in Ireland. However, while the law requires accounts to be produced on this basis, and these accounts must be used for certain administrative purposes in the EU, there is no restriction on the Irish CSO (or Eurostat) from producing additional "satellite" accounts, which could better meet the needs of most users of national accounting data.

In the case of Ireland, the Central Statistics Office has already introduced a number of innovations dealing with some of the problems identified earlier in this chapter. In 2019 they produced important additional data in the institutional sector accounts that will allow a comprehensive framework of supplementary accounts to be developed to deal with the aspects of the globalization process that have already been identified as problematic for the standard accounting presentation. A range of suggestions were made in CSO (2017 and many of them have now been delivered). The supplementary accounts that are needed should have a number of characteristics:

- Ideally, they should be developed to meet the needs of all economies, to ensure transparency.
- They should provide a treatment of economic activity over time that does not have serious discontinuities due to special factors, such as those discussed in this chapter. Serious discontinuities, such as that in the Irish growth rate of GNI in 2015, can pose major problems for policy makers.
- They should provide a good representation of the economic welfare of those living in a country.
- It is important that they are publishable without infringing on the confidentiality of data on individual companies (and households). This is a problem for small economies like Ireland. The supplementary accounts need to be robust: possible future changes in location by MNEs (or domestic firms) should not prevent the continuing publication of the series on confidentiality grounds.
- They should not be affected by changes by MNEs in the legal and organizational arrangements used in the country where their goods or services are physically produced.
- The supplementary accounts need to deal with the problems affecting both the national accounts and the balance of payments.

There is unlikely to be a single framework of supplementary accounts that will meet all these requirements. As the process of globalization evolves, new problems will arise and new solutions will be needed.

This chapter first considers three minor adaptations of the existing framework that would be helpful. It then sets out a simple set of indicators that could be developed to provide additional information for users. Finally, it considers features of a more detailed disaggregation of the SNA 2008 accounts that can provide a useful framework for understanding the Irish economy.

3.6.1 Adapting the Current Accounts

As outlined above, the very extensive aircraft leasing business, which makes a small contribution to Irish GNI, greatly complicates some aspects of the national accounts due to very large gross flows it generates. It is likely that the standard financial accounting treatment of this business may change in the coming years, with implications for the national accounts. This would involve essentially treating this business as a financial corporation.

In the aircraft leasing business planes are provided to airlines under a range of different legal agreements. In some cases the lease of the aircraft includes the staff to operate the plane. More frequently the lease may be closer to a pure financial arrangement, with the lessee providing crew, maintenance, etc.

The planes are largely financed by loans, with the planes themselves as collateral. As shown by the Irish CSO,[26] because the leasing companies, i.e., the lessors, are generally foreign-controlled subsidiaries, the profits and interest payments in respect of the financing of the aircraft flows back out of Ireland as a factor flow. Thus, the effect on NNI from the activity and the large capital stock is very limited.

The possible change in business accounting would see the aircraft recorded as the asset of the airline that is the lessee, and the relationship with the leasing company would then be treated as a purely financial relationship. Some of the fees received by the leasing company would be recorded as value added generated in Ireland and as a service export to the country where the lessee resides, but most of the fees would be recorded as interest payments and as down payments of the (implicit) loan. It would eliminate the large investment, capital stock, and depreciation from the Irish accounts.

In the case of foreign MNEs that produce goods or services in Ireland, their after-tax net operating surplus is accrued as a factor outflow in the year in which it is earned, irrespective of whether a dividend is paid to the parent company. If a similar treatment were applied to the income on portfolio investment, the retained profits of redomiciled PLCs would also be accrued as a factor outflow, thus removing another complication related to globalization from the Irish national accounts.

Connolly (2018) suggests that some of the problems arising from the relocation of firms with a major stock of IP could be better handled in the long run if they were treated as financial enterprises: the ownership of the IP has been separated from its use, and the owner in Ireland receives income in respect of this asset, just as an investment company receives income from its assets. As with a change in the treatment of the aircraft leasing companies, this could greatly simplify the national accounts, especially of smaller economies such as Ireland where substantial IP is located. However, the downside is that at a global level it might not adequately capture the key role that such IP plays in the global production process. It is a stock of capital that has been produced and must be located in some jurisdiction to be included in global measures.

3.6.2   Limited Set of Additional Indicators

The CSO, as recommended in CSO (2017), has introduced an adjusted GNI figure, referred to as GNI*, in its latest set of national accounts. This

---

26. https://www.cso.ie/en/releasesandpublications/ep/p-ali/aircraftleasinginireland2007 -2016/.

measure adjusts GNI to exclude the depreciation of IP and leased aircraft and the retained profits of redomiciled PLCs.

While this indicator is potentially more useful than GNI, it could need further changes if globalization affected the economy in new ways. For example, if the pharmaceutical sector were to fully separate its IP capital from production, and locate such IP in Ireland, this would need a further change in GNI*.

GNI* is designed to mimic GNI as it is measured in many other countries. This should facilitate its use in Ireland for international comparisons. However, as it is a measure only used in Ireland, it will not be universally understood. Thus, the measure currently lacks transparency for international users.

Even within the current ESA 2010 data, net national income, NNI, is less affected than GNI by the problems that surfaced with the Irish national accounts for 2015. The bulk of the activity of the MNEs that shifted to Ireland is effectively excluded from this aggregate, including the huge effect on depreciation. This may make it more useful than GNI*, which only excludes some of the depreciation of foreign MNEs.

However, NNI has, until now, only been available on a current price basis for Ireland, though the CSO plans to address this problem in future publications. In addition, it still includes the retained profits of redomiciled PLCs. The exclusion of this latter item would produce a very useful variable for Ireland but, like GNI*, it would also not be well understood internationally.

The other problem with NNI is that while it is included in the standard framework of national accounts, little attention is given to it internationally, making it much less useful for the purpose of international comparisons.

A second essential indicator that is required is one for the current account balance of the balance of payments. The two issues causing problems for the interpretation of the current measure for Ireland relate to the treatment of depreciation by foreign MNEs and the treatment of redomiciled PLCs' retained profits. The CSO is now publishing an adjusted current account figure for the balance of payments, which deals with many of these problems. However, further work may be needed on this measure. In particular, if depreciation of some major foreign-owned MNEs is excluded, should depreciation of all other foreign MNEs be similarly treated?

3.6.3   Supplementary Accounts

The effects of globalization on the Irish economy permeate many of the items of the national accounts. This makes it very difficult to understand developments in the income and economic welfare of those living in Ireland or to establish the productive capacity of the Irish economy. Even if one or two high-level indicators of growth are used, such as GNI* or NNI, it is still exceptionally difficult to understand where this growth is occurring in the economy. Detailed knowledge of what is happening in the economy is vital for economic policy; it was part of the original justification for developing national accounts.

Even before the latest difficulties with the Irish data, related to the relocation of IP, there were increasing problems in identifying where growth was arising in the Irish economy. While the foreign-owned MNE sector contributes hugely to exports and industrial output, the sector also has massive imports, and the very large profits from the sector flow back out of the economy. Thus, while the contribution of the MNE sector to the economy is undoubtedly very positive, it is difficult to identify just how much of the economic growth in recent years has come from this sector and how much has come from domestic firms.

It is essential for economic policy that a range of supplementary data are provided in the national accounts identifying the contribution of foreign MNEs and domestic firms to growth. Here the focus is on the additional information needed on the output and income side of the accounts.

Any new presentation of national accounting data must also ensure that confidential information on individual companies is not disclosed. This constraint is important in determining the appropriate level of detail by industry to present. If the breakdown is too fine, then individual large companies may be easily identified. However, if there is inadequate detail by industry, it will be very difficult to understand what is driving change in the economy. While a particular level of disaggregation by industry may be possible today without disclosing confidential information, new companies, or closure of existing companies, may make such a level of detail impossible in the future. Thus, in choosing the appropriate level of disaggregation by industry to use, it should be robust to movement of companies in the future.

In recent years, the CSO has also published data at current and constant prices on GVA generated by much of the foreign-owned MNE sector and the rest of the economy at an aggregate level.[27]

In the latest release of their institutional sector accounts, the CSO gives separate details for foreign MNE firms. This is a major step forward, and it may potentially deal with many of the problems discussed in this chapter. The additional data show the contribution of these firms to NNI—their wage bill and the corporation tax they pay. It also shows their depreciation and operating surplus. Also, the latest release of the institutional sector accounts gives details of GVA, compensation of employees and gross operating surplus, by industry, broken down by foreign MNEs and the rest of the economy. This release of additional information gives a much better picture of where output that contributes to NNI is arising in the economy.

27. http://www.cso.ie/en/releasesandpublications/er/gvafm/grossvalueaddedforforeign -ownedmultinationalenterprisesandothersectorsannualresultsfor2016/. However, the coverage of MNEs is not complete, so there may be some mismatch with the firms covered by the Large Cases Unit.

Set out in table 3.6 is a summary of the results from the latest release of the institutional sector accounts. Here the aggregates for the foreign-owned financial and nonfinancial corporations are summarized in the first panel. The second panel shows the aggregates for the rest of the economy—the domestic corporations, the government, and households. The third panel shows the totals for the economy as a whole, and the fourth panel shows net national income (net primary income) at factor cost after excluding the factor income received by the redomiciled PLCs. NNI is probably the best representation of the income available to those living in Ireland, a key focus of attention for domestic policy makers.

The table includes details of the corporation tax paid by the sectors. In the case of foreign-owned MNE sector, the contribution to NNI is ultimately equal to the wage bill in the sector plus the corporation tax paid. The rest of the net operating surplus flows back out of the economy to the foreign owners of the MNEs. This profit outflow is shown as a memo item at the bottom of the panel. The factor flows for the foreign-owned MNE sector includes this outflow of profits, in addition to other net factor flows from/ to the sector. However, as can be seen in the table, the two items are rather similar in magnitude, showing that the bulk of the factor outflows are related to the after-tax profits of the sector.

The final panel of table 3.6 shows that the contribution of the foreign-owned MNE sector to NNI ranged between 20 percent and 25 percent between 2013 and 2018. However, the contribution of the sector to GVA ranged between 43 percent and 56 percent over the period.

The new detail available from the institutional sector accounts is important, as it shows that for policy purposes, the contribution of the foreign-owned MNE sector to the income of those living in Ireland is much less than the headline figures would suggest. The trend over 2013 to 2018 also suggests that while there has been very rapid growth in the headline numbers for the foreign-owned MNE sector, the contribution to growth from the domestic sector over the same period has been of much greater importance in absolute terms.

While not presented here, the newly available data also allow a similar breakdown to that of table 3.6 to be done for each of the main economic activities in the economy.[28] This allows policy makers to identify which sectors of the economy are contributing to the growth in the income of those living in Ireland. For example, this is particularly important in understanding the contribution to growth in the economy from the information and communications industry. The sector includes a range of major global players such as Google and Facebook, giving rise to a very large GVA. However,

---

28. There is still a need to do some limited imputation of corporation tax and depreciation to some of the industrial sectors. Hopefully, the CSO will be able to fill in some of these minor gaps in the data in the coming years.

Table 3.6   Derivation of GVA and NNI, distinguishing foreign and domestic sectors, € million

Foreign-Owned Corporations	2013	2014	2015	2016	2017	2018
1. Compensation of employees	18,059	18,848	20,201	21,091	22,372	23,306
2. Gross operating surplus/mixed income	52,074	58,868	116,965	117,356	130,576	144,925
3. Consumption of fixed capital	14,710	16,135	42,730	49,244	57,244	62,279
4. (2−3) Net operating surplus	37,364	42,733	74,235	68,112	73,332	82,646
5. (1+2) Gross value added (factor costs)	70,133	77,716	137,166	138,447	152,948	168,231
6. (5−3) Net value added (factor costs)	55,423	61,581	94,436	89,203	95,704	105,952
7. Corporate taxes	3,329	3,427	5,202	5,615	6,258	7,936
8. Factor flows (allocation of primary income flows)	−32,992	−36,230	−64,932	−56,213	−66,755	−76,754
9. (6+8) Net primary income (factor costs)	22,431	25,351	29,504	32,990	28,949	29,198
10. (4−7) Memo item	34,035	39,306	69,033	62,497	67,074	74,710

Domestic	2013	2014	2015	2016	2017	2018
1. Compensation of employees	52,587	54,251	57,589	61,582	65,781	69,986
2. Gross operating surplus/mixed income	41,564	45,831	49,058	53,258	57,664	63,895
3. Consumption of fixed capital	11,829	12,548	13,603	14,512	15,832	16,989
4. (2−3) Net operating surplus	29,735	33,283	35,455	38,746	41,832	46,906
5. (1+2) Gross value added (factor costs)	94,151	100,082	106,647	114,840	123,445	133,881
6. (5−3) Net value added (factor costs)	82,322	87,534	93,044	100,328	107,613	116,892

	2013	2014	2015	2016	2017	2018
7. Corporate taxes	955	1,206	1,689	1,758	1,959	2,485
8. Factor flows (allocation of primary income flows)	3,847	4,980	2,979	5,236	4,617	5,861
9. (6 + 8) Net primary income (factor costs)	86,169	92,514	96,023	105,564	112,230	122,753
10. (4 − 7) Memo item	28,780	32,077	33,766	36,988	39,873	44,421
Total	2013	2014	2015	2016	2017	2018
1. Compensation of employees	70,646	73,099	77,790	82,673	88,153	93,292
2. Gross operating surplus/mixed income	93,638	104,699	166,023	170,614	188,240	208,820
3. Consumption of fixed capital	26,539	28,683	56,333	63,756	73,076	79,268
4. (2 − 3) Net operating surplus	67,099	76,016	109,690	106,858	115,164	129,552
5. (1 + 2) Gross value added (factor costs)	164,284	177,798	243,813	253,287	276,393	302,112
6. (5 − 3) Net value added (factor costs)	137,745	149,115	187,480	189,531	203,317	222,844
7. Corporate taxes	4,284	4,633	6,891	7,373	8,217	10,421
8. Factor flows (excluding PLCs)	−29,145	−31,250	−61,953	−50,977	−6,2138	−70,893
9. (6 + 8) Net primary income (factor costs)	108,600	117,865	125,527	138,554	14,1179	151,951
10. NNI, excluding Redomiciled PLCs (Factor costs)	102,108	111,013	120,865	132,773	13,6721	146,949
Foreign MNEs % of GVA	43	44	56	55	55	56
Foreign MNEs % of NNI	22	23	24	25	21	20

Source: CSO: Institutional Sector Accounts.

while the foreign-owned MNEs in the industry account for 85 percent of the GVA, they only account for just over 50 percent of the contribution of the sector to NNI.

One issue, which has not been discussed earlier, is the treatment of factor inflows. Where there are large Irish MNEs with operations abroad, the profits of these MNEs are included in factor income at the level of the economy as a whole. This treats the activity abroad by MNEs as a financial investment that is not related to its domestic output. While this may be appropriate for some MNEs, for MNEs that have developed substantial IP, using it to produce goods or services abroad, it may be appropriate to include the factor flows in deriving the domestic value added for the relevant industry. This latter approach has been adopted in table 3.6. The profits from operations abroad and other factor income is included in domestic output on the assumption that these profits arise largely from the exploitation of the home country MNEs' IP. Guvenen et al. (2017) attempt such an exercise for the United States. However, it is difficult for most businesses to separate out the return on IP from profit reflecting the return on the use of physical capital.

A further future improvement that will be of importance to policy makers will be to develop appropriate deflators for the output of foreign MNEs and the domestic sectors for each industry. This would allow a more robust and useful measure of the trend in output in real terms.

3.6.4   Alternative Approaches to the Expenditure Side of the National Accounts

The CSO currently produces a measure of "modified" domestic demand, which excludes investment in IP and aircraft for leasing. These forms of capital are excluded because they are less relevant for monitoring the Irish economy. The modified variable therefore provides a better picture of what is happening on domestic demand.

However, to date, a suitable approach to the trade and factor flows separating out the role of foreign MNEs and domestic firms has not yet been established. Without such a separation between the activities of these two types of firms it is very difficult, using the expenditure side of the national accounts, to establish the effects of trade on the income of those living in Ireland.

As a result of globalization, foreign MNEs affect the external sector of the economy through a multiplicity of different channels. They may simultaneously export goods and import materials for use in domestic production; license IP for use abroad; purchase IP abroad; provide services abroad; receive profits from subsidiaries abroad; and remit profits to their head offices. While for the larger foreign MNEs the Irish CSO captures good data on these transactions, it is a much more complex task to derive appropriate deflators and maintain consistency with the available data on output.

In the past, much of the attention of those forecasting the economy has gone on the components of the expenditure side of the national accounts. Thus, the problems in interpreting what is happening on the expenditure side of the accounts are particularly difficult for policy makers. For example, both the Central Bank of Ireland and the Irish Department of Finance only provide detailed estimates of current and expected future economic activity on an expenditure basis.

A further problem with the trade data is that there are massive gross flows. In recent decades globalization has seen production processes being broken up into multiple stages occurring in many countries. Thus, the exports associated with the production of a car or a computer (including exports of parts) could end up being a multiple of the value of the final product. We have seen in the Irish input-output tables how the true domestic value added associated with exports, especially of services, has fallen over time.

This is not just an Irish problem. Work by OECD developing data on trade on a value-added basis is an important way of dealing with this problem (Ahmad 2019), providing a more meaningful presentation of trade flows in so far as they affect individual economies. Koopman, Wang, and Wei (2014), Rojas-Romagosa and van der Horst (2015), and Los, Timmer, and de Vries (2016) use input-output information to derive the domestic value added content in gross exports. If the data were readily available on a timely basis, this might be a useful approach.

If implemented, it would involve using the latest available data to undertake the analysis, but these would, inevitably, be out of date. As we have seen in Ireland, there have been very rapid changes in the structure of the economy over time, which could render such an approach unreliable.

3.7 Conclusions

Globalization has changed the model that traditionally underpinned the national accounts. Economic activity in one country is now linked to activity in other countries through many different channels. This interdependency of economic activity in different countries makes it difficult to separate out the output of one country and to measure it appropriately.

The revisions to the System of National Accounts (SNA 2008) have tried to capture the effects of this globalization process. The inclusion of IP in the capital stock has a strong basis in economic theory. However, more effort is needed to capture other important consequences of globalization for the national accounts. As they stand today, the headline national accounting indicators, such as GDP, do not provide a useful guide for policy makers in countries such as Ireland.

In recent decades the growth of MNEs spanning the globe has driven a growing wedge between the output attributed to a country such as Ireland, measured by GDP, and the income of those living in a country, previously measured by GNI. While in the past GNI provided a good guide to the output and income available to those living in a country, this is no longer the case for Ireland because of the way globalization has affected the behavior of MNEs. The traditional indicators need to be supplemented by satellite accounts giving more detailed information.

Probably the biggest distortion to the Irish national accounts has arisen as a result of the movements in the stock of foreign-owned IP in the domestic capital stock. The relocation to Ireland in 2015 of companies with large IP had a dramatic effect on the national accounts. The fact that IP capital is scalable, in the sense that it can be used to produce unlimited output, and the fact that it is separable from all the other factors of production and can be combined with physical capital and labor in many countries to produce output, means that it does not fit well into the framework of national accounts for a single country.

Also, the fact that the national accounts can treat activity undertaken by MNEs in third countries very differently, depending on their legal and organizational structure in the third countries, could give rise to serious discontinuities if firms change that structure.

To deal with these problems one approach is to develop satellite accounts that separate out the activities of MNEs in each sector and industry of the economy. This will allow policy makers to identify where growth is occurring in the economy and the contribution to growth that is coming from different industries.

While the Irish CSO has developed a headline indicator for the income and economic welfare of domestic residents, referred to as adjusted GNI or GNI*, this indicator could need further development if there is a significant change in the population of foreign MNEs in Ireland.

While developing national solutions to these problems can meet the needs of domestic policy makers, this is not ideal: it lacks transparency at an international level. Because the national accounting problems discussed in this chapter are not unique to Ireland, further discussion on the most appropriate way of recording in the international standards, and/or a coordinated international action on the development of the necessary satellite accounts, are needed to understand how individual economies are really behaving.

References

Ahmad, Nadim. 2022. "Accounting Frameworks for Global Value Chains: Extended Supply-Use Tables." In *Challenges of Globalization in the Measurement of National Accounts*, Studies in Income and Wealth, volume 81, edited by Nadim Ahmad, Brent R. Moulton, J. David Richardson, and Peter van de Ven. Chicago, IL: University of Chicago Press. This volume.

Avdjiev, S., M. Everett, P. Lane, and H. Song Shin. 2018. "Tracking the International Footprints of Global Firms." *BIS Quarterly Review* (March).
Barry, Frank. 2019. "Aggressive Tax Planning Practices and Inward-FDI Implications for Ireland of the New US Corporate Tax Regime." *The Economic and Social Review* 50 (2): 325–40.
Bradley, J., and J. FitzGerald, 1988. "Industrial Output and Factor Input Determination in an Econometric Model of a Small Open Economy." *European Economic Review* 32: 1227–41.
Connolly, M. 2018. "The Expected and Unexpected Consequences of ESA 2010— An Irish Perspective." *Journal of the Statistical and Social Inquiry Society of Ireland* 47 (2017–18): 39–70.
Conroy, C., P. Honohan, and B. Maître. 1998. "Invisible Entrepôt Activity in Irish Manufacturing." *Irish Banking Review* (Summer): 22–38.
Central Statistics Office. 2017. "Economic Statistics Review Report." http://www.cso.ie/en/media/csoie/newsevents/documents/reportoftheeconomicstatisticsreviewgroup/Economic_Statistics_Review_(ESRG)_Report_Dec_2016.pdf.
De Haan, M., and J. Haynes. 2018. "R&D Capitalisation: Where Did We Go Wrong?" Conference on Research in Income and Wealth, Challenges of Globalisation in the Measurement of National Accounts, Bethesda, MD, March 9–10. http://papers.nber.org/sched/CRIWs18?show_participants=1.
Denny, M., and M. Fuss. 1977. "The Use of Approximation Analysis to Test for Separability and the Existence of Consistent Aggregates." *American Economic Review* 67: 404–18.
Eurostat. 2013. European System of Accounts: ESA 2010. Eurostat: Luxembourg.
FitzGerald, J. 2013a. "The Effect on Major National Accounting Aggregates of the Ending of Pharmaceutical Patents." QEC Research Note 2013/2/1. Dublin: ESRI.
FitzGerald, J. 2013b. "The Effect of Redomiciled plcs on GNP and the Irish Balance of Payments." Quarterly Economic Commentary, Summer. Dublin: ESRI.
FitzGerald, J. 2015. "Problems Interpreting National Accounts in a Globalised Economy—Ireland." ESRI *Quarterly Economic Commentary* (Summer).
Guvenen, F., R. Mataloni, D. Rassier, and K. Ruhl. 2017. "Offshore Profit Shifting and Domestic Productivity Measurement." NBER Working Paper 23324. Cambridge, MA: National Bureau of Economic Research.
Haskel, J., and S. Westlake. 2017. *Capitalism without Capital. The Rise of the Intangible Economy.* Princeton, NJ: Princeton University Press.
Honohan, P. 1984. "Transfer Pricing in Ireland—A Cautionary Note." Central Bank of Ireland Research Paper 2/R/84.
Jacobson, David. 1977. "The Political Economy of Industrial Location: The Ford Motor Company at Cork 1912–26." In *Irish Economic and Social History*, vol. 4, 36–55. London: Sage Publications, Inc.
Koopman, Robert, Zhi Wang, and Shang-Jin Wei. 2014. "Tracing Value-Added and Double Counting in Gross Exports." *American Economic Review* 104 (2): 459–94.
Los, Bart, Marcel P. Timmer, and Gaaitzen J. de Vries. 2016. "Tracing Value-Added and Double Counting in Gross Exports: Comment." *American Economic Review* 106 (7): 1958–66.
Pindyck, R. 1979. "Interfuel Substitution and the Industrial Demand for Energy." *Review of Economics and Statistics* (May): 169–79.
Rojas-Romagosa, H., and A. van der Horst. "Causes and Policy Implications of the Dutch Current Account Surplus." Netherland Central Planning Bureau, Policy Brief 2015/05.

4

Eliminating the Pass-Through
Towards FDI Statistics That
Better Capture the Financial
and Economic Linkages
between Countries

Maria Borga and Cecilia Caliandro

4.1 Introduction

Foreign direct investment (FDI) has been and remains a key aspect and driver of globalization. Multinational enterprises (MNEs) access markets and key inputs, such as natural resources and human capital, and locate stages of production in countries to take advantage of factor cost differences through their foreign investments. These foreign investments have facilitated the creation of complex global production chains managed by MNEs that support employment and generate income in the host economies. FDI statistics seek to measure these long-term investments. However, other factors, in particular fiscal optimization, have also played a role in the shape and depth of these chains. When the FDI flows are related to purely financial flows engineered to minimize tax payments or overcome regulatory barriers, there is little direct impact on the host economy, at least in a traditional production sense. This latter form of FDI often involves MNEs channelling investments

Maria Borga is currently the Deputy Head of the Balance of Payments Division at the International Monetary Fund, and was a senior statistician at the Organisation for Economic Co-operation and Development when this chapter was written.

Cecilia Caliandro is an associate with Analysis Group.

The views expressed in this paper are those of the authors and should not be considered as representing the official views of the OECD or its member countries. The authors wish to thank Nadim Ahmad, Caroline Mehigan, Joachim Pohl, Kamran Bilir and participants at the NBER-CRIW Conference on the Challenges of Globalization in the Measurement of National Accounts, delegates to the OECD Working Group on International Investment Statistics, and colleagues in the OECD Investment Division for valuable comments, and Emilie Kothe and Perla Ibarlucea Flores for their useful statistical assistance. For acknowledgments, sources of research support, and disclosure of the author's or authors' material financial relationships, if any, please see https://www.nber.org/books-and-chapters/challenges-globalization -measurement-national-accounts/eliminating-pass-through-towards-fdi-statistics-better -capture-financial-and-economic-linkages.

through several countries, "inflating" FDI flows and positions, as each flow into and out of each country is counted even if the capital, or income, is just passing through. This can make it difficult to interpret FDI statistics in the sense that they are not "real" and provide little in the way of "long-term" investments in the host economy. In essence, the financial structure of the MNE as captured in FDI statistics does not match the operational structure of the MNE, which reflects the organization of its operations across countries. Indeed, in some countries such as Hungary, so significant is the perceived scale of "pass-through" capital that the policy focus now looks in large part at net rather than gross flows of FDI to determine the amount of inward FDI that remains in the host economy; however, while this approach provides a better metric for Hungary than traditional FDI statistics, it is far from ideal for countries with significant amounts of outward investment that originate from their economies. Moreover, this approach cannot provide information on the ultimate sources and destinations of FDI when the statistics are compiled by immediate partner country.

The main goal of this chapter is to propose a definition of pass-through capital, together with experimental estimates, based on the ultimate ownership and location of the assets that can be used as the basis for techniques to consolidate FDI statistics to remove these "distortionary" flows, and in turn reallocate FDI positions and income flows from immediate to ultimate partner economies. The statistics, therefore, take a nationality approach to classification by reflecting the entity that ultimately influences or controls the FDI units and, thus, could contribute to further developing nationality-based statistics to better analyze globalization.

However, this is not the only area where FDI data, on their own, may fail to create a complete picture of the overall scale of the impact of investment within an economy. Because MNEs can leverage their direct investments, parent enterprises can control assets in the host country that are many multiples of their initial investment. As discussed further below, the framework proposed in the chapter to consolidate FDI statistics can be extended to capture the full financing of the MNE, providing a more complete picture of the economic involvement of the MNE in the host and home economies.

The methodology proposed in this chapter would produce statistics that are designed to address some important policy issues surrounding FDI. For example, they would provide better measures of financial integration between economies by stripping out the financial intermediation activities within MNEs. The statistics could be linked to other statistics capturing the operations of MNEs to analyze the links between FDI and trade as well as provide information on the alignment between where economic activity occurs and where the MNE attributes its income. Finally, they could provide a more complete picture of the involvement of the MNE in the economy as well as its cross-border and local exposures.

The first section of this chapter gives some examples of the ways MNEs pass capital along their ownership structures and establishes the connection between pass-through capital and ultimate partner country. The second section defines what we mean by pass-through capital in terms of direct investment positions. From this, the related definition of pass-through income is derived. Then, the chapter defines the concepts of ultimate investing country, based on the nationality of the ultimate investor, and of ultimate host country, based on the objective of producing symmetric statistics. The third section provides experimental estimates for some European members of the OECD to provide order of magnitude estimates of their importance and potential "distortionary" impact on current FDI statistics. The fourth section considers the relationship of the proposed consolidated FDI statistics to other sets of economic statistics as well as some unresolved issues. The fifth section discusses potential policy uses for the proposed statistics. The final section concludes and provides some recommendations for ways forward.

4.2 Pass-Through Capital: Issues and Examples

Interpretability challenges presented by measurement issues with FDI statistics are not new (see box 4.1), but the spotlight has intensified in recent years, particularly with regard to pass-through capital. Put simply, pass-through capital is capital that flows into one economy and that is subsequently invested in another economy. In a 2016 report, Blanchard and Acalin concluded that a large proportion of measured FDI flows consisted of flows going into and out of countries on their way to their final destinations (passing through) and moreover that these flows were, in effect, driven by changes in tax regimes and short-run movements in US monetary policy to a much greater extent than would have been expected if the flows had actually been in relation to the long-run "bricks and mortar" type of investment that analysts typically infer from FDI statistics. Lane and Milesi-Ferretti (2017) drew similar conclusions, finding that measured FDI flows inhibited the post-crisis analysis of international financial integration as they show that much of the expansion in FDI flows was with financial centers, suggesting that it was driven by the increasing complexity of corporate structures rather than by "genuine" FDI flows.

MNEs can access financial systems in many different countries to optimize their capital structures, so there are several different forms that pass-through capital can take. This is, of course, not a new phenomenon, although it is growing, and the latest international standards (BMD4)[1] began to address

---

1. The OECD's *Benchmark Definition of Foreign Direct Investment*, 4th edition (BMD4) was published in 2008. It provides the most complete and detailed guidance on the coverage, collection, compilation, and dissemination of FDI statistics. In addition to providing guidance on the collection of aggregate FDI statistics, it is aligned with the IMF's *Balance of Payments and International Investment Positions Manual*, 6th edition (BPM6) but also offers guidance on compilation of supplemental FDI series that enhance the usefulness and relevance of FDI statistics.

Box 4.1   OECD *Benchmark Definition of Foreign Direct Investment,* **4th edition: Recommendations Related to Pass-Through Capital**

The 4th edition of the OECD's *Benchmark Definition of Foreign Direct Investment* (BMD4) took an important step toward improving the measurement of FDI statistics by addressing some of the challenges raised by pass-through capital. BMD4 recommended that FDI associated with resident special purpose entities (SPEs) be separately compiled so that FDI statistics excluding resident SPEs could be derived. SPEs are entities whose role is to facilitate the internal financing of the MNE but that have little or no physical presence in an economy. By excluding such entities from their FDI statistics, countries have a better measure of the FDI into their country that is having a "real" impact on their economy. In addition, BMD4 also recommended use of the *extended directional principle* to better capture the direction and degree of influence of the investment and to remove some double-counting in the FDI statistics when debt passes through affiliated entities, called fellow enterprises (BMD4, page 29-31). Under the extended directional principle, if the fellow enterprise in the reporting economy makes a loan to a fellow in another country, it is treated as a reduction in inward investment in the reporting economy if the common direct investor is non-resident because the funds that flowed into the reporting economy from the foreign direct investor have now flowed to another country, reducing the amount of foreign investment in the reporting economy. Previously, such loans were usually treated as outward investment by the resident fellow but should not have been because it is their common direct investor that retains the influence.

Additionally, to look through complex corporate structures to see the ultimate source of investment, BMD4 recommended that countries compile inward investment positions according to the ultimate investing country (UIC) to identify the country of the investor that actually controls the investments in their country. Although not directly related to the "pass-through" problem, the ability to identify FDI flows on a UIC basis can be an important part of a comprehensive solution to the measurement issues in FDI statistics.

Nevertheless, BMD4 recognized that these were only partial solutions. As such, it included a research agenda that included items related to pass-through capital, including through operating affiliates, and to further develop the presentation by ultimate partner country, especially by ultimate host country (BMD4, page 223 to 225).

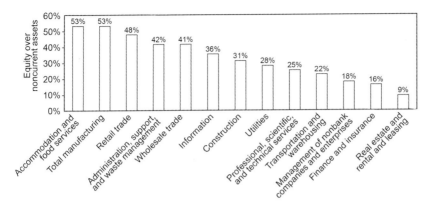

Figure 4.1   Shares of equity in other foreign affiliates in affiliates' total noncurrent assets by major sector of the parent, 2014

Source: US Bureau of Economic Analysis.

Note: Not all sectors could be shown due to data confidentiality.

this issue through the recommendation that entities that have pass-through capital activities as their only, or main, activity and that have little or no physical presence in an economy are separately identified. Excluding FDI associated with these entities, called special purpose entities (SPEs), yields better measures of the inward FDI that is having a real impact on their economy and of the outward FDI that originates in their economy. However, BMD4 acknowledged that while SPEs are an important channel for pass-through capital, they are not the only one. As such, it included developing guidance on the identification of capital passing through operating affiliates on its research agenda.

Fully capturing pass-through capital necessarily requires a basic framework for identifying pass-through capital in all its forms. Evidence from the US Bureau of Economic Analysis on the balance sheets of US-owned affiliates shows that pass-through capital is extensive but also that it varies significantly across different sectors. Figure 4.1 shows the shares of equity investment in other foreign affiliates in the total non-current assets of US-owned affiliates abroad by major sector of the US parent. This variation indicates that pass-through capital could serve several purposes and provide more benefits to enterprises in some sectors than in others.

The discussion below begins to develop a framework through a taxonomy of the motivations for pass-through capital, the characteristics of the countries that attract that type of pass-through, and the likely impacts on the host economy. The taxonomy illustrates the particular difficulties in identifying capital passing though operating affiliates: while the issue of pass-through capital focuses on the distortions between the financial and operational structures of MNEs caused by the fiscal and financial optimization activities within the firm, some forms of pass-through capital in operating affiliates facilitate the operational structure, making it difficult to distinguish the pass-through capital. At the highest level, the framework divides pass-through activities into those that occur completely within the firm and so only involve FDI and those that involve financing from sources other than FDI; this latter type would have to extend the identification of pass-through capital to other forms of international investment, such as portfolio and other investment, to fully address them in the International Investment Position (IIP) statistics. Much of this discussion draws on Lewellen and Robinson (2013).

4.2.1   Pass-Through Capital within the Firm

Pass-through capital within the firm can take different forms and serve different purposes. Five major reasons for pass-through capital are discussed below.

1) *Tax avoidance*. This is probably the most cited motivation for pass-through capital. MNEs can channel funds through affiliates in different countries to both shift income and take advantage of opportunities to defer taxes on income (see Desai, Foley, and Hines 2003 for a discussion of the use of indirect ownership to avoid and defer taxes). This activity can be done through both SPEs and operating affiliates. Somewhat paradoxically, recent initiatives to encourage MNEs to better align where they report income with where they have economic activities[2] may have exacerbated measurement challenges by encouraging firms to record pass-through capital in affiliates with a small, but real, presence in the host economy (IMF, 2017 Task Force on SPEs report). The capital passing through these "near SPEs" is not captured in the current statistics of resident SPEs because these entities do not meet all of the criteria, especially little or no employment or physical presence in the host economy.

Pass-through capital due to tax avoidance would be associated with countries that offered tax advantages, including special tax treatments for intellectual property (IP). These countries typically offer not only low tax rates but also networks of double taxation treaties. Pass-through capital associated with tax avoidance is likely to result in significant FDI positions for the countries involved but have less direct impact on the economy (that is, lower levels of employment, value added, and tangible capital at the foreign-owned entities). This type of pass-through capital would be characterized by high asset to employment ratios as well as significant royalty and license fee income at the entity involved in the pass-through. It could also be associated with certain industries, such as holding companies. While it might not have significant direct impacts, it can have considerable indirect impacts on the host economy by supporting industries offering services to foreign investors

---

2. Such as the G20/OECD framework to address base erosion and profit shifting (BEPS).

such as financial services and tax planning industries; these indirect impacts can be particularly important in small economies.

2) *Expropriation or other risks to the value of their investment.* MNEs that seek to limit their exposure to "political" risk or wish to benefit from an advantageous investor protection regime could structure an investment through a country that offers the desired treaty-based protections. For example, if the investor's home country does not have a bilateral investment treaty or equivalent arrangement with the host country, it may choose to hold the investment indirectly through one of its affiliates in a country that does have such a treaty with the host country of the investment. An examination of disputes records and law firms' client advisory services shows that, for example, subsidiaries in the Netherlands are often recommended and used by investors that are ultimately controlled by non-Dutch parents to bring claims under Dutch IIAs (Van Os and Knottnerus 2011).[3] Because treaties are often interpreted as to enable indirect shareholders to obtain compensation for losses, in the event that host government measures affect the operating company (if there is a treaty in force between their country of nationality and the host country), complex ownership structures may actually be advantageous because they offer options for additional shareholder claims (Gaukrodger 2013).[4] As a result, this type of pass-through capital would be more likely to occur in host countries with a large network of bilateral investment treaties or in countries that have treaties with unusual partners. It would also likely have limited direct impacts on the host economy but possibly could have indirect impacts by supporting an industry offering services to foreign investors.

3) *Reduction in transaction costs.* Affiliates in the MNE's production network that have a significant amount of interactions may find closer ownership links reduce transaction costs and facilitate these interactions. For example, an MNE investing in the United States may invest in Mexico and Canada through their US operation, forming an integrated, regional operation. While the motivation for this pass-through capital clearly differs from those described above, it remains the case that the US operation is still facilitating pass-through capital for the ultimate parent.

This type of arrangement would be more likely to happen between affiliates with strong commercial links or with more complex production processes and products, where the transaction costs would be expected to be higher. Thus, it is more likely to happen between affiliates in countries that share strong commercial ties as evidenced by significant trade flows and

3. Of the 41 claims that had been brought under Dutch IIAs and were known as of June 2011, in 29 of them, the ultimate controlling parent was not Dutch, and 25 of the claimants had no staff in the Netherlands.

4. For a review of the role that complex ownership structures can play in obtaining investor protections, see Pohl (2018).

that share preferential trade agreements. It would also be more common in countries that are physically or culturally close.

With this type of pass-through capital, the financial structure overlaps with the reporting and operational structure within the MNE. As such, there is likely to be more direct impacts in the host economy as these pass-through entities may have significant employment, value added, R&D, and trade in both goods and services; they are also likely to have indirect impacts in the host economy in a number of areas, including by integrating domestic suppliers into the production networks they coordinate.

4) *Inherited ownership links.* When an MNE acquires an existing MNE, it also acquires the ownership structure. In these cases, the amount paid by the acquiring MNE covers not just the assets in the reporting economy where the acquired MNE was headquartered, but also assets in other economies where the acquired MNE's foreign affiliates were located; there will not be any FDI transactions recorded in the countries of these foreign affiliates, since they were already foreign owned. The acquiring MNE may choose not to change the ownership structure, in which case the acquisition creates an ownership chain and the position in the reporting economy reflects not just the value of the assets held in that economy but also the assets in the subsequent economies along the chain. In this form of pass-through capital, the financial structure and operational structure could overlap, and, so, as for the case of the reduction in transaction costs discussed above, the motivation may not represent what is usually associated with pass-through capital but, nevertheless, the acquired MNE is now serving as a pass-through entity for its new parent.[5]

This form of pass-through would be more likely to occur in countries where more of the inward FDI transactions were the result of M&A than of greenfield investment and, more specifically, that are home to MNEs that have since been acquired. It is hard to assess the impacts of this type of pass-through capital on the host economy. While it may be expected that there would be a drop in employment and value added at the former head of the MNE, it may still maintain significant operations there.

5) *Protection of the parent from claims against the affiliate.* If the parent is concerned that the affiliate is exposing them to financial claims, they may be more likely to own it indirectly to limit those claims. This might be the case, for example, with joint ventures or other cases of shared ownership. This might be more likely to happen in host countries that provide greater protections to investors as discussed above. It is hard to assess the impacts

---

5. The acquiring MNE could choose to change the ownership structure and hold these foreign affiliates directly, in which case the FDI positions would be reclassified from the economy of the former parent to the economies of the foreign affiliates. In this case, there would be no pass-through capital and the FDI statistics would accurately reflect both the value and ultimate origin and destinations of the FDI.

of this type of pass-through capital on the host economy. On the one hand, it might be more associated with indirect impacts in the host economy if it is driven by investor protection, but, on the other hand, enterprises that are joint ventures or in which the foreign investor holds a minority stake could have significant employment, value added, and so on.

4.2.2   Pass-Through Capital outside the Firm

1) *External financing.* MNEs can raise financing outside the firm and may do this through their foreign affiliates. For example, MNEs can use their foreign affiliates to raise capital by issuing debt securities and then channel the funds raised to other parts of the MNE, including back to the parent. The first part of this transaction is either domestic or portfolio investment, but the second part is an FDI transaction. There is evidence that this activity is increasing, particularly for MNEs from emerging market economies (Tarashev, Avdjiev, and Cohen 2016), and that it is tied to the presence of capital controls (Caballero, Panizza, and Powell 2015). In this case, pass-through capital goes beyond FDI to include the other functional categories of international investment, and, so, the concept of pass-through capital would need to be broadened beyond FDI to address it.

This form of pass-through capital would be more likely in countries with deep capital markets, strong investor protections, and sophisticated financial services. It would not have significant direct impacts in the economy but could have significant indirect impacts in the financial services sector.

2) *Financial conduits.* A private investor may establish an affiliate in a foreign country for the purpose of engaging in portfolio investment from the host economy. It is the first leg of this case that brings the transaction within the scope of FDI, while the other leg would either be in domestic investment or in the other functional categories of international investment. This kind of pass-through capital would be more likely in countries that offer offshore or sophisticated financial services or secrecy. The home country would likely be one with higher tax rates and stronger controls on outflows of portfolio capital than on direct investment. It would not have significant direct impacts in the host economy but could have significant indirect impacts in the financial services sector.

3) *Corporate redomiciliations.* In a corporate redomiciliation, the headquarters of the company move to another country. While they can take many forms, corporate redomiciliations often involve substantial FDI flows that are almost completely, if not completely, offset by portfolio investment flows. It is possible that these kinds of transactions, when they result in offsetting flows, could be treated as a form of pass-through capital because the capital that has flowed into the reporting economy flows out to other economies. In this case, the characteristics that would make a country likely to host a redomiciliation would be those offering relative tax, regulatory, and other

benefits to foreign investors. The extent of impacts on the host economy would depend on the extent to which the redomiciled company actually shifted operations to its new headquarters country.

4.3   Defining Pass-Through Capital and the Ultimate Partner Country

The section begins with the definition of pass-through capital and ultimate partner country in FDI positions. It then examines how these concepts could be extended to FDI income. Next, it discusses implications for measuring pass-through capital in financial flows and for producing these statistics.

4.3.1   Pass-Through Capital in FDI Positions

This section begins with the definition of pass-through capital in FDI positions illustrated by two examples. It then discusses the conventions applied in these examples, and next it presents a nationality-based consolidation that captures the entire financing of the MNE.

4.3.1.1   Pass-Through Capital and Ultimate Partner Country

The concept of pass-through capital is straightforward: *capital flowing into the host economy that is then invested in a subsequent economy.* However, identifying these flows in practice is more complicated. Entities receive financing from a variety of sources and use it in a variety of ways, especially operating affiliates, which can blur the relationship between inward and outward flows. As a result, assumptions necessarily have to be made about the relationship between the financing and its eventual use.[6]

The definition in this chapter is derived from the position data and is based on the concept of ultimate ownership of the FDI assets. In FDI statistics, the inward position in a country reflects not just the claims on the direct investment enterprise in that country but may also reflect foreign direct investments that enterprise may have. This necessarily means that the outward investment position of a country reflects investments made by entities headquartered in that country but also by enterprises that are ultimately owned by investors in another country. Therefore, any reasonable definition of the UHC would have to, in effect, remove the multiple-counting that results from pass-through capital (Mahoney 2007). The removal of pass-through capital also has implications for statistics by UIC because, ideally, statistics by UIC and UHC would be symmetric. Indeed, eliminating

---

6. As a result of these difficulties, BMD4 chose to identify entities associated with pass-through capital rather than to identify the flows themselves because it was thought to be more feasible. The criteria listed in BMD4 to identify SPEs—including little or no physical presence, foreign ownership, and almost all assets and liabilities of the enterprise representing investments in or from other countries—were designed to identify entities for which almost all of the FDI into and out of SPEs qualified as pass-through capital.

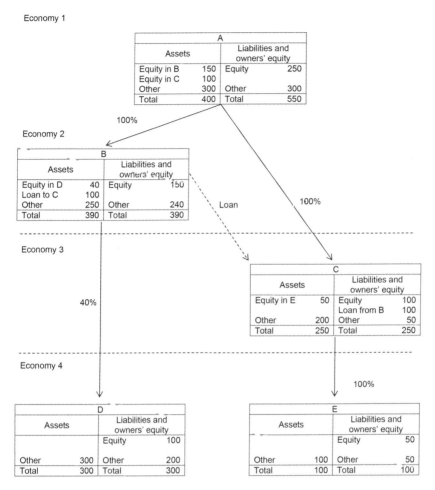

Figure 4.2   Pass-through capital in a simple example of an MNE ownership structure

multiple-counting of pass-through capital in constructing UIC statistics is preferable from a policy perspective, as the ultimate goal of the statistics is to identify the country of the investor influencing the investment in the host country. However, as before, that influence is overstated if part of that investment is capital passing through the host economy. In other words, the two ideas—pass-through capital and ultimate partner economy—are ultimately and inextricably linked and should be considered together in order to produce complementary FDI statistics that are more analytically meaningful.

Figure 4.2 illustrates some of the challenges presented by pass-through capital in current FDI statistics compilation, and how interpretability could be improved using the concept of UIC. It presents the ownership diagram of a simple MNE structure consisting of five different enterprises in four different economies; A (in Economy 1, the UIC) is the ultimate controlling parent (UCP), and it owns B and C directly and D and E indirectly. For each entity and country, the figure shows an abridged balance sheet consisting of total assets, with the equity investments in foreign affiliates broken out; total liabilities; and owners' equity. The figure also shows the ownership chains and the percentage of ownership.

Table 4.1 shows the inward and outward FDI positions that would be recorded under the extended directional principle. Outward positions are allocated to the immediate partner country, but inward positions are recorded on both the immediate country and UIC basis as recommended in BMD4.[7]

Table 4.1 shows that the inward and outward positions are globally additive, each summing to 340. But the reallocation of inward positions to economy 1, the UIC, results in a total of 340 being recorded by economies 2, 3, and 4 as inward investment from economy 1, exceeding 1's total outward FDI of 250 due to pass-through capital. Moreover, under the extended directional principle, the loan between fellow enterprises B and C is treated as a reduction in inward investment in B, as the funds that flowed into economy 2 from the fellow enterprises' common direct investor (enterprise A) have flowed to another country (economy 3). This loan does not give B any influence over the operations of C, and, so, should not be recorded as an outward investment. However, because it is recorded against the immediate partner economy, it does lead to an asymmetry in the bilateral inward and outward FDI positions reported by the two countries.

Table 4.2 presents the results for the consolidated FDI statistics in which pass-through capital has been netted out and positions reallocated to ultimate partner country.

If the positions were also reallocated to the ultimate investing country, then economy 1 would still report outward investment of 250 but, now, economy 2 would recognize that both the loan of 100 to C and the equity investment in D of 40 are pass-through capital and would net these from its inward and outward investment, and the remaining inward investment would remain allocated to economy 1, the economy of the ultimate investor A. Economy 3 would also recognize that the equity investment of 50 in E is pass-through capital and net it from its inward and outward investment, and the remaining inward investment would be reallocated to economy 1. Economy 4 does not have pass-through capital and would reallocate its inward position to economy 1. In this case, the only country with outward

7. BMD4 recommends that the UIC be identified by proceeding up the ownership chain of the immediate direct investor until a unit that is not controlled by any other unit is reached.

Table 4.1   Inward and outward FDI positions under the extended directional principle

Reporting economy

Partner country	Economy 1 Immediate Outward	Inward	UIC	Economy 2 Immediate Outward	Inward	UIC	Economy 3 Immediate Outward	Inward	UIC	Economy 4 Immediate Outward	Inward	UIC
1	0	0	0	0	150	50	0	100	200	0	0	90
2	150	0	0	0	0	0	0	100	0	0	40	0
3	100	0	0	0	−100	0	0	0	0	0	50	0
4	0	0	0	40	0	0	50	0	0	0	0	0
Total	250	0	0	40	50	50	50	200	200	0	90	90

Table 4.2   Inward and outward positions under consolidated FDI statistics by ultimate partner country

	Reporting economy							
Partner country	Economy 1		Economy 2		Economy 3		Economy 4	
	Outward	Inward	Outward	Inward	Outward	Inward	Outward	Inward
1	0	0	0	10	0	150	0	90
2	10	0	0	0	0	0	0	0
3	150	0	0	0	0	0	0	0
4	90	0	0	0	0	0	0	0
Total	250	0	0	10	0	150	0	90

investment is economy 1, since that is the economy of the domestic parent of the MNE; economies 2 and 3 no longer have outward investment, since all of their outward investment was from A, the foreign and ultimate controlling parent. As before, the statistics are globally additive but now the amount of inward FDI attributed to economy 1 (the UIC) is the same as its outward investment (250), reflecting the elimination of pass-through capital.

While BMD4 recommended a supplemental presentation of inward FDI positions by UIC, it also included an item on the BMD4 research agenda to develop a presentation by ultimate host country (UHC) as the natural counterpart of the presentation by UIC. If we define the UHC as the country where the foreign-owned assets are ultimately located and that the reallocation to UHC should be based on the total intra-group funding that each foreign affiliate receives net of any intra-group funding it provides to fellow enterprises or its subsidiaries, then the FDI positions by UHC can be derived from the inward statistics by using mirror relationships.

Of course, ownership structures can be more complicated than presented in figure 4.2. The first complication is that FDI statistics cover influence as well as control relationships and, so, can include multiple direct investors. The second difficulty is that FDI positions can be negative. Negative positions usually result when the loans from the affiliate to its foreign parent group exceed the loans and equity capital it has received.[8] The final difficulty is that MNEs can raise financing from outside the group. Figure 4.3 presents a more complicated ownership structure including these aspects. Each case will be discussed more completely below, as well as the measurement and identification challenges that they raise.

In figure 4.3, there are two direct investors in enterprise E in economy 4, both from economy 3. Under the recommendations in BMD4 for the UIC,

---

8. Negative positions could also occur if the distributed earnings exceeded total earnings or the affiliate operated at a loss, resulting in negative reinvested earnings.

Economy 1

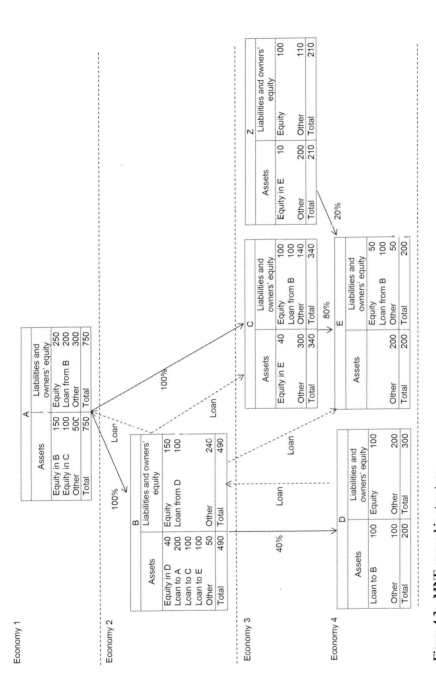

Figure 4.3   MNE ownership structure

Table 4.3   **Standard and consolidated FDI positions from figure 4.2**

Partner country	Reporting economy							
	1		2		3		4	
	Inward	Outward	Inward	Outward	Inward	Outward	Inward	Outward
1	0	0	−50	0	100	0	0	0
2	0	−50	0	0	100	0	40	0
3	0	100	−100	0	0	0	50	0
4	0	0	−100	−60	0	50	0	0
Total	0	50	−250	−60	200	50	90	0
	Consolidated FDI statistics							
1	0	0	−190	0	160	0	80	0
2	0	−190	0	0	0	0	0	0
3	0	160	0	0	0	0	10	0
4	0	80	0	0	0	10	0	0
Total	0	50	−190	0	160	0	90	0

the 20 percent of equity held by enterprise Z would be attributed to economy 3, while the equity investment held by C would be reallocated to country 1, as would the loan from enterprise B in economy 2. An alternative way to reallocate the FDI positions to the UIC is based on who controls the enterprise rather than who owns the investment. The implications for this change in identifying the ultimate investor will be discussed below. Enterprise B in economy 2 has a minority ownership interest in enterprise D in economy 4, but, in this case, it is assumed that no other investor owns more than 10 percent of the voting power, so there are no other direct investors. Enterprise B plays an important role in the MNE's financing structure, borrowing money from some parts of the MNE, as well as from outside the group and lending money to other parts of the MNE.

Table 4.3 presents the standard FDI statistics in the upper panel that would result from this ownership structure, and there is a negative inward position in economy 2 from economies 1, 3, and 4 under the extended directional principle resulting from the role that enterprise B plays in the internal financing of the MNE. So under what circumstances does pass-through capital occur in the case of negative positions? There are three possible cases to consider. First, if the inward position of enterprise B is negative and its outward position is negative, then there has been pass-through capital, but it has gone in the opposite direction. This is the case shown in figure 4.3; in this case, enterprise B has borrowed more from its affiliate (enterprise D) than it invested and some of this financing contributes to the financing that it provides to other parts of the MNE, including the parent. In the other two cases, there is no pass-through capital. If the inward position in enterprise B is negative but its outward position is positive, then the financing for the outward investment must have come from extra-group sources. This would be the case, for example, if there had been no loan from enterprise D to B in figure 4.3. Similarly, if the inward position in enterprise B had been positive but its outward position in D is negative, then there has been no pass-through capital; in this case, the funding received by B from its parent has not gone to its subsidiary, enterprise D.

To formalize, the amount of pass-through funding, PT, for each enterprise j in period t, is:

(1) $PT_{j,t} = \min(I_{j,t}, O_{j,t})$ if the $I_{j,t} > 0$ and $O_{j,t} \geq 0$

(2) $= \max(I_{j,t}, O_{j,t})$ if the $I_{j,t} < 0$ and $O_{j,t} < 0$

(3) $= 0$, otherwise

where $I_{j,t}$ and $O_{j,t}$ represent the inward and outward positions of the direct investment enterprise j in period t, respectively. Looking from the inward FDI perspective, a foreign-owned enterprise with no subsidiaries would have no pass-through capital ($O_{j,t} = 0$ under (1)). If it did have a foreign subsidiary, the amount of pass-through capital is the smaller of the inward and outward positions of the foreign-owned enterprise if both its positions are positive (under (1)) or negative (under (2)), and it is zero otherwise. Looking from the outward FDI perspective, the same amount of pass-through would be identified for direct investors in the economy. The total pass-through capital in the economy would be found by either summing the pass-through capital across the direct investment enterprises or across the direct investors in the economy. This follows one of the methods described in Leino and Ali-Yrkkö (2014).

The bottom panel of table 4.3 shows the consolidated FDI statistics that would result from applying this definition and reallocating positions to the ultimate partner country. Starting with economy 4, the inward positions from B in economy 2 (the –60 in D resulting by netting the loan of 100 from the equity investment of 40 plus the loan of 100 to E) and from C in economy 3 (equity investment of 40) are reallocated to A in economy 1, but the investment from Z in economy 3 remains allocated to economy 3 because Z is not controlled by another entity. For economy 3, the pass-through capital from C to E is deducted from its inward investment from A (100–40) and, along with the loan from B (100), is reallocated to A; the outward investment from Z to E (10) remains as outward investment from economy 3 to economy 4. For economy 2, the negative outward investment to D (–60) is identified as pass-through capital and is netted from the inward positions from A, C, and E (–250), for a total inward position of –190 allocated to A. For economy

1, there is no inward investment, but its outward investment identifies the ultimate destination for its direct investment as well as the fact that enterprise A controls B and uses it as a source of funding to the rest of the MNE.

Another complication arises if the MNE raises financing from outside the group. This could include any minority ownership interests from the reporting economy, as depicted by enterprise Z in economy 3, and funds raised from third parties that are then lent to other parts of the MNE group, as depicted in the case of enterprise B.

4.3.1.2 Conventions in the Recording

There are conventions used in the method discussed above to compile the consolidated FDI positions. Enterprises can receive financing from a number of different sources and can use that financing in a number of different ways. Due to the fungible nature of capital, it is not possible to trace the source to the use. As a result, it is necessary to make assumptions about how much of the FDI received by the enterprise is used in local production and how much passes through. This is much more difficult for operating affiliates than for SPEs.

Some proposed definitions have focused on applying shares of intra-group financing in total financing. For example, one proposed definition of pass-through capital in Mahoney (2007) used the proportion of the total liabilities (including shareholder's equity) of an enterprise that are equity liabilities to a direct investor to determine the amount of its equity assets that should be deemed pass-through capital; so, if one-third of the total liabilities of the enterprise were equity liabilities to its direct investor, then one-third of its direct investment equity assets were deemed to be pass-through capital. Other definitions have included debt liabilities as well as equity (OECD 2006). The assumption in these definitions is that all sources of funding are used equally in all uses. In contrast, the assumption used in this chapter is that the intra-group financing is the primary source of funding for intra-group investments.

It is important to note that whichever of the estimation approaches is used, the use of conventions is required. The preference for the approach (and underlying assumption) used in this chapter largely reflects practical reasons. First, it requires less information than those approaches that require information on the full funding of the enterprise. Economies with entities lower in the chain would only need to know details on the ownership shares and investments to and from the entities in their economy; only the country of the UCP would need to have information on the complete chain. Second, basing the amount of pass-through capital on the share of total financing could result in volatility, as the share changes due to increases or decreases in the amount of total financing needed by the enterprise but with no change in the underlying intra-firm financing. Potentially introducing such volatility in measured FDI is arguably contrary to the goal of measuring stable,

Table 4.4   **Consolidated FDI positions from figure 4.2: only control relationships**

	Reporting economy							
	1		2		3		4	
Partner country	Inward	Outward	Inward	Outward	Inward	Outward	Inward	Outward
1	0	0	-250	0	160	0	140	0
2	0	-250	0	0	0	0	0	0
3	0	160	0	0	0	0	0	0
4	0	140	0	0	0	0	0	0
Total	0	50	-250	0	160	0	140	0

long-term financing. Finally, it is in keeping with the extended directional principle in which the full amount of the loan between fellow enterprises is netted from the inward investment of fellows making the loan. The result of the assumption that intra-group financing is the primary source of funding for intra-group investments is that more of the direct investment positions are reallocated to the entities at the end of the chain compared to the assumption that all sources of funding contribute to the intra-group lending.

The second convention that has been used is that the reallocation to the UIC is based on the country of the entity that controls the immediate direct investor; alternatively, it could be based on who controls the direct investment enterprise. When moving to focusing on control of the direct investment enterprises, it makes sense to move to examining only control relationships in the consolidation of the financing structure of the MNE; that is, the definition of FDI covering both influence and control relationships would need to be changed to only control relationships. Table 4.4 presents the results of the consolidated FDI statistics with only control relationships.

One change is that the investment from Z in economy 3 to E in economy 4 is no longer shown because it is not a control relationship. Similarly, the investment by B in economy 2 in D in economy 4 and the loan from D to B are not included because it is not a control relationship. One thing this highlights is the trade-off in focusing only on control of the enterprise—the information on minority investors is no longer captured in the data.

4.3.1.3   Expanding Consolidated FDI Statistics to Capture the Full Financing of the MNE

It is instructive to note that consolidated FDI statistics by UIC fits in with the broader thrust toward, and greater interest in, the use of nationality-based statistics for understanding globalization across a number of statistical areas, such as recommendations included in the G20 Data Gaps Initiative for more nationality-based statistics to better understand financial integration and monitor financial stability (Bank for International Settlements

2015, and Tissot 2016). In addition a full nationality-based approach could allow the statistics to be expanded to capture other sources of financing to better represent the full economic involvement of the foreign investor in the host economy. Indeed, the framework for consolidated FDI statistics discussed here can be extended to the total assets and liabilities of the MNE. This expansion goes beyond FDI statistics by capturing the cross-border assets and liabilities from other functional categories, especially portfolio and other investments, but also beyond the international accounts by capturing domestic assets and liabilities. Nevertheless, it can be underpinned by the Framework for Direct Investment Relationships (FDIR) to identify the relevant units to be consolidated, as well as the ultimate investor.

The expansion would reveal the extent to which MNEs have leveraged their direct investment to control more assets in the host economy. The difference between the direct investment figures (positions) and the actual value of assets the foreign parent firm controls in the host economy can measure the extent of this leverage. The framework can also be harmonized with the concepts underlying the Activity of Multinational Enterprise statistics (AMNE) or Foreign Affiliates Statistics (FATS) so that the two data sets can be linked to analyze the relationship between the operations of MNEs and their financing. These statistics could also be linked to data sets developed to explore the competitiveness of economies by allocating value added not by location but instead by ownership of the firms and of the factors involved in production (Federico 2015). Such a linking would shed light on the role that FDI plays in the competitiveness of economies.

The Working Group on International Investment Statistics (WGIIS) developed a framework for harmonizing the concepts and definitions used in FDI and FATS statistics, as well as to capture the full financing of the MNE. Called the MNE framework, it focuses on control relationships and uses rules like the consolidation rules used in international accounting standards to identify intra-group assets. The MNE framework recommended expanding the coverage of financial variables to total assets and liabilities. So, these statistics would include FDI but would go beyond it to include purely domestic sources of financing and cross-border sources other than FDI. This expansion recognizes that all of the funding received by the enterprise, not just FDI, affects its operations.

Next, the MNE framework made use of the ultimate controlling parent (UCP) concept from the FDIR to classify investment and to define the entities to be covered. The UCP is the entity on top of the ownership chain and which is not controlled by another entity. For inward investment, the MNE framework recommended allocating all variables to the country of the UCP. Not only does this align with the recommendation for a supplemental presentation of FDI statistics by UIC, but it also aligns with the recommendations for compiling AMNE/FATS statistics. For outward investment, it recommends that the entities covered include only non-resident subsidiaries

Table 4.5   Assets controlled by A in each country

| | Total assets | Intra-group assets | Consolidated assets controlled by A | FDI positions by UHC | Extra-group financing | | |
| | | | | | Total | Equity | Debt |
Economy	(1)	(2)	(3) = (1) − (2)	(4)	(5)	(6)	(7)
1	750	250	500	0	500	200	300
2	490	400	90	−250	340	0	340
3	340	40	300	160	140	0	140
4	200	0	200	140	60	10	50
Total	1,780	690	1,090	50	1,040	210	830

that are controlled by UCPs resident in the reporting economy. That is, it removes from the outward investment of a country investments made by entities that are resident in the economy and that are in turn themselves foreign controlled. This prevents overestimation of the amount of overseas assets under control.

Finally, the MNE framework recommended that the financial measures be consolidated for the group to eliminate the double-counting of funds in transit or round-tripping. This consolidation is done by netting investments between the affiliates of the group from the group's total assets and is equivalent to the methods discussed above. This consolidation not only removes fund that go into and out of subsidiaries simultaneously (funds-in-transit) but also removes funds that have been invested by subsidiaries in other affiliated enterprises on behalf of the UCP; the funds removed correspond to the definition of pass-through capital proposed in this chapter. For a complete description of the method, see OECD (2011) and OECD (2015).

The results of expanding the presentation to the full financing of the MNE are presented in table 4.5. Table 4.5 presents the assets that enterprise A controls in each economy. The amount of total assets in column 1 overstates the total assets controlled by A due to intra-group positions, so column (2) identifies the amount of intra-group assets, and column (3) identifies the consolidated assets of A by netting these intra-group positions from the total assets.

The total financing reveals the extent to which A has leveraged its direct investment (in column (4)) to control a much larger amount of assets. It also reveals the extent to which it relies on extra-group financing (column (5), broken out between equity (6) and debt (7)). This includes both the equity in A itself as well as the equity investment that enterprise Z has in enterprise E. It also reveals the extent of debt at A's foreign subsidiaries, particularly the reliance on extra-group financing through its subsidiary B.

It is important to note that the nationality/group consolidated statistics are not a substitute for, but rather a complement to, the residency-based financial statistics. The residency-based FDI statistics capture cross-border intra-group financing and are a starting point to analyzing the international exposures of MNEs. However, it is not a complete picture, because the MNE parent controls assets and incurs liabilities through its foreign affiliates. Residency-based financial statistics are useful to know where financial claims and liabilities are created and held. However, to know who makes the underlying decisions, who reaps the benefits, and who takes on the risk and needs to hold sufficient capital to cover potential losses, data are needed on a nationality basis.

4.3.2   Income-in-Transit

Just as capital can flow down an MNE ownership structure, income can flow up it. The same concept of pass-through capital used for positions can be used for FDI income: income-in-transit is the FDI income a foreign-owned parent receives from its foreign affiliates. In the same way therefore, bilateral income-in-transit flows can exaggerate the degree of interdependence between partners and give a misleading picture of the importance that productive activity (in particular with respect to GDP) in one country (and its resident affiliates) makes to the generation of income in another (especially the parent). In addition it blurs the ability to identify where the income was generated within an MNE, and so, in turn, hampers analyses of GVCs and also our understanding of potential income shifting occurring under BEPS.

But by netting flows between affiliated enterprises it is possible to derive a meaningful estimate of the actual FDI income generated within the host economy (as opposed to the total income passing through). Figure 4.4 presents a simple example of an MNE ownership structure with three economies to illustrate this. For each entity, an abridged income statement showing their total income, total costs, and net income is shown; additionally, under the total income, the amount of that income that represents income resulting from their equity investments in other parts of the MNE, called "income from foreign affiliates," is shown. Table 4.6 shows the FDI income that would be reported by immediate partner country in standard FDI statistics and the consolidated FDI statistics by ultimate partner country.

As with the positions, the total amount of income recorded in the consolidated statistics is equal to the earnings of the MNE from its foreign operations, and, so, the double-counting resulting from income-in-transit has been removed. The amounts shown for income payments for economies 2 and 3 represent the income generated within their economies and are allocated to economy 1, which ultimately has the claim on the earnings.

4.3.3   Pass-Through Capital in Financial Flows

Another method that FDI statisticians have used to produce estimates of pass-through capital in response to the concerns expressed by data users is

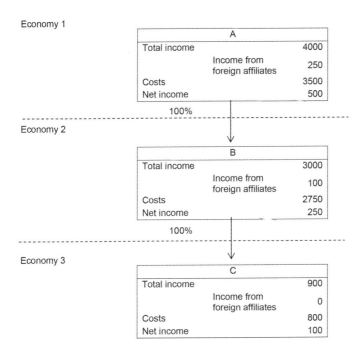

Economy 1

Economy 2

Economy 3

Figure 4.4   Income in transit through a simple MNE structure

Table 4.6   FDI income by immediate partner country and consolidated income by ultimate partner country

	Reporting economy											
	Standard FDI statistics by immediate partner						Consolidated FDI statistics by ultimate partner					
	Economy 1		Economy 2		Economy 3		Economy 1		Economy 2		Economy 3	
Partner country	Out	In	Out	In	Out	In	Out	In	Out	In	Out	In
1	0	0	0	250	0	0	0	0	0	150	0	100
2	250	0	0	0	0	100	150	0	0	0	0	0
3	0	0	100	0	0	0	100	0	0	0	0	0
Total	250	0	100	250	0	100	250	0	0	150	0	100

to identify the capital coming into and passing out of a direct investment enterprise in the same period (Kocerka and Makowski 2017, and Montvai 2016). As Blanchard and Acalin (2016) noted, these estimates do not appear to completely resolve the problem of pass-through capital. An important issue that arises when trying to identify capital coming into and going out of the same enterprise is timing. As the Swiss National Bank (2017) noted in its analysis of pass-through capital, it can be a gradual process.

Another issue is that the method of identifying flows going in and out will not identify pass-through capital resulting from the acquisition of domestic MNEs (as discussed above). The acquisition of a domestic MNE can involve a significant inward FDI flow, but much of this could represent funds to purchase assets in other countries that are part of the MNE; since they are already owned by the domestic parent, there would be no subsequent outflows to those foreign affiliates associated with this transaction. For example, in 2016, when Anheuser-Busch InBev acquired SAB Miller for US$103 billion, there was a large inflow to the United Kingdom, where SAB Miller was headquartered, but much of those funds were payment for the operations of SAB Miller outside the United Kingdom; there were no outflows from the United Kingdom or inflows to those countries because the assets were already foreign owned. Defining pass-through capital as is done in this chapter would recognize that a substantial portion of that inward flow was for foreign assets and would produce a smaller estimate of genuine FDI to the United Kingdom from that transaction. Leino and Ali-Yrkkö (2014) provide a good example of the impact this can have on measures of pass-through capital, as they measure pass-through capital based on positions[9] as well as according to the difference between inflows and outflows to direct investment enterprises in a given year. They find that between 2002 and 2011, the accumulated pass-through flows were €5.7 billion, but the increase in the stock of pass-through investments was almost €12 billion. They attribute this difference to the acquisitions of Finnish MNEs by foreign investors.

In theory, the definition of pass-through capital in financial flows can be derived from the pass-through positions because the change in these positions between two periods would be the result of valuation changes and pass-through financial flows. However, the interpretation of these flows would be complicated, because there would not necessarily be any flows recorded in the standard FDI statistics due to differences in timing.

4.3.4   Producing Consolidated FDI Statistics

The statistics separately identifying pass-through capital could be produced by FDI statisticians by linking the inward and outward FDI position and income statistics at the micro level. The compilers would then be able to see the outward positions and income receipts and inward positions and income payments for foreign-owned parents and to calculate how much of the position is located and income is generated within the economy rather than passing through. As a first step, and subject to the usual confidentiality restrictions, countries could identify the FDI outward position and income

---

9. Their preferred measure of pass-through capital adjusts for the source of funding by using the portion of FDI liabilities in total liabilities to determine the amount of pass-through capital.

receipts of all foreign-owned parents, and not just SPEs, in their outward investment statistics. Then, data users interested in identifying the pass-through capital and income in transit could use this published information. The Austrian Central Bank and the Swiss National Bank already publish such statistics.

4.3.4.1   Differentiating Different Types of Pass-Through Capital

The definition of pass-through capital proposed here would cover all of the types of pass-through capital within the firm discussed in the taxonomy discussed above (section 1.1). However, some of those types can have significant impacts on the host economy while others will not. Therefore, it could be useful to differentiate between these different types. However, it is not possible for the statistician to ask the motivation behind the pass-through capital to determine what type it is. It is also possible that pass-through capital serves several purposes within the MNE structure at the same time. As such, it may not be possible to completely differentiate between all of the different types. Given the motivation for separately identifying pass-through capital is to derive better measures to understand the impact of FDI on an economy, the total pass-through capital within the firm could be divided into two categories. The first category has little direct impact on the host economy but could have significant indirect impacts on specific sectors of the economy, including financial, legal, and tax planning services. This category would include FDI for tax avoidance, expropriation or "political" risk, and protection from claims against the parent. The second category is that which is likely to involve more real economic activity in the host economy and would include pass-through capital associated with reducing transactions costs and inherited ownership structures.

Distinguishing between these two broad categories would involve looking at some characteristics of the enterprises involved to gauge the importance of real versus financial activity in the enterprise, such as assets per employee, tangible assets per employee, importance of royalties and license fee income in total income, and economic activity. It would also be possible to look at the characteristics of the country involved, such as whether it offers preferential tax rates; protections to foreign investors, such as through investment treaties or equivalent arrangements; and whether it has deep capital markets and a large financial services sector. Because these forms of pass-through capital take place within the firm, they could be addressed solely within FDI statistics.

For pass-through capital that goes outside the firm (section 1.2), there is a need to look beyond the intrafirm transactions to other functional categories to define pass-through capital. Such a definition is beyond the scope of this chapter. However, as a first step, it is possible to think about a set of statistics that captures the full financing of the MNE, both internal and external, that could be the basis for considering pass-through capital that comes from outside the firm. The concepts and definitions of such a set of statistics are discussed further below.

4.3.4.2   Attribution to the Ultimate Partner Country

To compile the statistics by UIC, the inward positions (with pass-through capital removed) could be reallocated as recommended in BMD4 for traditional FDI statistics. BMD4 recommends that the UIC be determined by the country of the entity that ultimately controls the investment by proceeding up the direct investor's ownership chain, until an entity that is not controlled by another entity is reached. This is akin to the ultimate beneficial owner (UBO) of the investment, and the UBO is generally considered to be the best concept for use with financial statistics. However, there are alternative concepts. One of the most well-known is the ultimate controlling investor used in AMNE/FATS statistics. The ultimate controlling investor is the entity that controls the direct investment enterprise. For some countries, the information on the country of the ultimate controlling investor is available and can be used relatively easily to generate FDI statistics by ultimate investor. However, because the ultimate controlling investor is only available for majority-controlled enterprises, it cannot be used for attributing minority investments to the ultimate investor.

The determination of the nationality of MNEs is becoming more difficult as more and more companies separate their global headquarters from their operational headquarters. For example, Shire Plc, a large pharmaceutical firm, has its group headquarters in Ireland, its international operational headquarters in Switzerland, and its registered office in Jersey.[10] The global group headquarters generally follow the ownership structure and may be chosen for fiscal optimization or other benefits. On the other hand, the operational headquarters would reflect where the decisions are made. The EuroGroups Register includes these two concepts: the global group head is defined as a "parent legal unit, which is not controlled by any other legal unit . . . the global group head is the group head of the multinational enterprise group," and the global decision center is defined as "the unit where the strategic decisions referring to an enterprise group are taken" (Eurostat 2012).

Unlike the case for determining the UIC, where countries only need to collect information on the ultimate parent, the presentation by UHC is more problematic, as it would require additional information on how flows/positions are channelled through countries, requiring some form of cross-border statistical collaboration or data collection for the MNE and all of its affiliates in the compiling country. Very few countries currently collect these data as either part of their FDI or FATS data collections. However, initiatives

10. Information extracted from: https://www.shire.com/contact-us. Last accessed: August 31st 2018.

by international organizations, such as the EuroGroups Register, the U.N. Global Group Register, the Eurostat initiative on profiling large and complex MNEs, and the forthcoming OECD ADIMA database (OECD 2018), could provide important information to compilers to help them reallocate their outward positions to the UHC, as well as to reallocate inward positions to the UIC. The use of common registers would also help to ensure that all countries are using the same information when doing the reallocation.

The presentation of consolidated FDI positions by ultimate partner country could be extended to the related FDI income receipts and payments. This would be very useful information for the analysis of where income is generated along GVCs and where it accrues.

4.4   Estimates of Pass-Through Capital and Its Key Characteristics

4.4.1   Estimates of the Prevalence of Pass-Through Capital

To assess the importance of pass-through capital through operating affiliates, one needs good-quality, firm-level micro-data. Such information, covering the entire activity of an MNE and its affiliates across borders, is not typically available or publishable by national statistics authorities. However, Bureau van Dijk's Orbis database provides financial information on enterprises in 158 countries and also includes detailed information on their ownership structure. It is possible to use these data to derive broad estimates of the extent of pass-through capital using the methods described above.

For this exercise, Orbis data for some of the European members of the OECD were examined to assess the extent of capital passing through "operating entities" (as opposed to SPEs), as most of these countries already produce FDI statistics that separately identify the FDI associated with SPEs.[11] The data appendix provides detail on the data from Orbis and how it was used to identify non-SPE entities potentially used to pass capital to other parts of the MNE.

To estimate the importance of pass-through capital, the first step is to identify all of the direct investors in Orbis from a country and to calculate the total amount of shareholders' funds these direct investors hold in their foreign subsidiaries; entities that appear to be SPEs are dropped from the Orbis sample to focus on capital passing through operating affiliates. Once all of the enterprises with foreign subsidiaries were identified, their ownership percentage in their foreign subsidiaries was multiplied by the shareholders' funds to estimate the equity claim the direct investors had on

11. It was decided to focus on European countries as they are generally considered to have among the best coverage in Orbis. Data were used for the following countries: Austria, Belgium, Czech Republic, Denmark, Estonia, Finland, France, Germany, Hungary, Iceland, Ireland, Italy, Luxembourg, Netherlands, Norway, Poland, Portugal, Slovak Republic, Slovenia, Spain, Sweden, Switzerland, and the United Kingdom.

the subsidiaries. Then, equity claims tied to the same enterprise group were aggregated at the shareholder level.

The next step is to use the information on the global ultimate owner (GUO) included in Orbis to identify the direct investors in the country that are, in fact, ultimately controlled by an investor in another country. For these foreign-owned parents, the different options for the direction of pass-through (or zero-pass-through) were evaluated as in equations (1) to (3). Data was summed across firms for each country, and the ratio of pass-through equity over total equity for its resident direct investors was derived. Then, this ratio (calculated from the Orbis data) is applied to the official outward FDI statistics of the country to develop an estimate of the total amount of pass-through capital in the economy. The official FDI statistics used exclude resident SPEs to focus on the pass-through capital through operating affiliates.

This provides a broad estimate of the amount of pass-through capital in the economy. These estimates are broad partly because they rely on certain assumptions as highlighted above but also for other reasons. First, they only consider equity and not debt because the Orbis data do not provide information on intra-group lending. As such, the estimates assume that debt financing follows the same pass-through pattern as equity financing. Second, the method used to drop possible SPEs from the Orbis data was based only on industry codes and, thus, likely captured some non-SPEs while also missing some SPEs in other cases. Finally, it is not known how representative the samples are for each country. Overall, the sample from Orbis covered about one-quarter of the outward positions of the countries examined. The coverage of outward investment by region varied, reflecting differences in country coverage in Orbis; the coverage of outward investment to the European region tended to be higher than other regions. The data appendix provides information on coverage by country. Nevertheless, the goal was only to give an indication of how important the phenomenon of pass-through capital is.

Table 4.7 presents evidence for 2015 on the importance of pass-through capital for each country. The first column is the estimate of pass-through capital through operating affiliates estimated as described above; it is presented as a share of the total inward position in the country excluding resident SPEs. To compare to the importance of pass-through capital through SPEs, the last column shows the share of SPEs in the total inward investment position of each country as reported in their official statistics.[12]

Only a few countries have published information that can serve as a basis for comparison to these estimates. Switzerland is the most problematic, as

12. Countries with 0 percent of outward investment accounted for by SPEs either do not host SPEs or they are insignificant. Data on SPEs are currently not available for Ireland; the United Kingdom publishes FDI statistics on SPEs with its annual detailed statistics but not the aggregate statistics, making it difficult to reconcile the data when there are differences in vintages between the two sets of statistics.

Table 4.7   **Importance of pass-through entities 2015**

Reporting country	Share of pass-through capital in inward positions, excluding resident SPEs	Share of SPEs in inward investment positions
Austria	51%	32%
Belgium	54%	5%
Czech Republic	6%	0%
Denmark	59%	19%
Estonia	14%	3%
Finland	13%	0%
France	18%	0%
Germany	9%	0%
Greece	43%	0%
Hungary	27%	57%
Iceland	7%	30%
Ireland	31%	n.a.
Italy	23%	0%
Latvia	6%	0%
Luxembourg	55%	94%
Netherlands	65%	82%
Norway	23%	1%
Poland	3%	1%
Portugal	15%	11%
Slovakia	2%	0%
Slovenia	10%	0%
Spain	14%	5%
Sweden	23%	7%
Switzerland	2%	14%
United Kingdom	21%	n.a.

n.a. Not available.
Source: OECD FDI statistics database and author calculations based on Orbis.

the Swiss National Bank estimates that 53 percent of the inward position in 2016 is pass-through capital under a broad definition that captures both SPEs and operating affiliates (Swiss National Bank 2017). This could be because the coverage of Swiss companies in Orbis is not representative. For Austria, the estimates look reasonable, as the Austria Central Bank estimated that about half of the inward FDI position, excluding SPEs, represented pass-through capital in 2012 (Austria Central Bank 2015). This could reflect Austria's role as a gateway to investment in central and Eastern Europe (Cernohous 2017). As mentioned above, Leino and Ali-Yrkkö (2014) estimate that about 28 percent of the inward investment position is pass-through, so the estimate here looks a little low. For Ireland, the Central Statistics Office estimates that foreign-owned direct investors accounted for about two-thirds of FDI liabilities in 2014 (Lane 2015). The estimate in table 4.7 is lower, but it should be noted that their estimate includes liabilities in

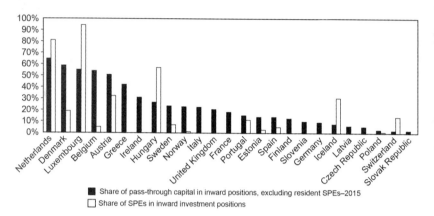

■ Share of pass-through capital in inward positions, excluding resident SPEs–2015
□ Share of SPEs in inward investment positions

Figure 4.5   Comparing pass-through capital in SPEs and operating affiliates, 2015
Source: OECD FDI Statistics database and author calculations based on Orbis.

Ireland as well as pass-through liabilities. In addition, the estimated share from Orbis excluded SPEs but the FDI position includes resident SPEs, so pass-through via SPEs may not be accounted for in the estimate.

The extent of pass-through capital varies significantly across countries. Figure 4.5 plots the values in table 4.7 sorted by the share of resident SPEs in the inward position of countries. Some countries with significant presence of SPEs, such as Luxembourg, Hungary, and the Netherlands, also have high rates of capital passing through operating affiliates as MNEs find it beneficial to take advantage of the benefits that these countries offer through their operating affiliates as well as by establishing SPEs. For other countries, including Austria, Denmark, and Belgium, we estimate a greater amount of pass-through in operating affiliates than in SPEs. Some countries with little or no presence of SPEs have significant pass-through capital through operating affiliates, including Greece, Italy, and France.

Figure 4.6 presents the total inward FDI positions for these countries between 2007 and 2015; the black bars represent the standard inward FDI positions excluding resident SPEs as reported to the OECD. The white bars represent the consolidated FDI positions as estimated in this chapter. Overall, the consolidated positions are about one-quarter lower than the standard positions. They also grew less over the period: the 2015 consolidated position is 51 percent higher than the 2007 position, while the 2015 standard FDI position is 58 percent higher than the 2007 position, indicating that pass-through capital could have been growing faster than "real" FDI.

4.4.2   Key Features of Pass-Through Entities

One conclusion from section 1 is that pass-through entities may differ from their purely domestic counterparts, especially in terms of the size of their balance sheets, as their pass-through activities would tend to increase

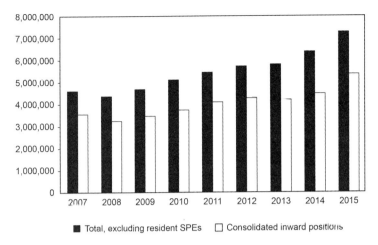

Figure 4.6   Inward FDI positions excluding SPEs and consolidated positions, 2007–2015 (millions of euros)
Source: OECD FDI Statistics database and author calculations based on Orbis.

the size of their financial assets and liabilities. In addition, given the different motivations for pass-through, MNEs from some countries may be more likely to employ complex ownership structures than from other countries. Data from Orbis can shed light on these issues by describing patterns in the types of entities involved in pass-through as well as the origin of pass-through countries globally.

In the Orbis sample, it is possible to compare the pass-through entities (that is, foreign-owned parents) to the purely domestic parents. As figure 4.7 shows, pass-through entities had about 50 percent higher fixed assets per employee than purely domestic parent companies, but their total assets per employee were more than two times higher in 2015. This is consistent with these entities having much larger financial assets. When examining the data by country, this pattern held in only half of the countries in the sample, but the results are not shown, given concerns about the small sample sizes for some countries due to missing employment data in Orbis.

The data in Orbis can also provide information on the country of the ultimate investor of the MNE group. An examination of these data reveals that US MNEs appear to be more involved in pass-through activity than MNEs from other countries. For example, in 2015, US-owned MNEs accounted for about 25 percent of all pass-through firms in the countries examined and for about 32 percent of capital (figure 4.8). This is not surprising given the complexity of the ownership structures of some US MNEs. The practical impact of this is that while FDI statistics by immediate partner country would understate the importance of the United States as an investor, the reallocation of the inward position to the UIC would overstate the importance of the United States because some of that position represents funds passing

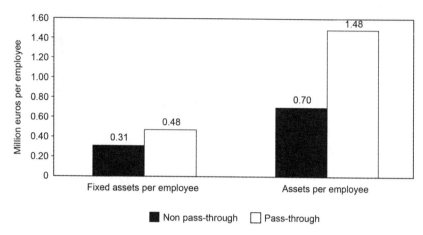

Figure 4.7   Size and profitability metrics for pass-through and non-pass-through firms, 2015

Source: Author calculations based on Orbis.

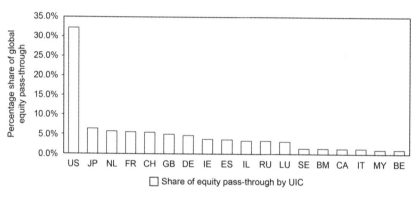

Figure 4.8   Composition of equity pass-through by ultimate investing country, 2015

Source: Author calculations based on Orbis.

Note: Only UIC countries with share >1% are shown; full data on UIC shares of equity and of number of entities are available in the appendix.

through the economy. Japan, the Netherlands, and other large economies in Europe are the next most significant sources of pass-through capital. Looking at the earlier years (see the appendix), the composition and shares of UICs have stayed largely unchanged, with the exception of the United Kingdom, which had a more marked presence in 2007 (17 percent) than it had in 2015 (5 percent).[13]

13. It should be remarked that while the UK share in equity pass-through drops substantially from 2007 to 2015, the percentage of direct investment enterprises that the country ultimately controls in the sample does not vary in the same way (6.6 percent in 2007 and 6.7 percent in 2015, as shown in section 4A.3 of the appendix).

4.5   Related Statistics and Measurement Issues

This section begins by examining some related sets of statistics, including consolidated statistics as well as those on the operations of MNEs and on international investment. Then, it will examine some measurement issues that are relevant to consolidated FDI statistics but also more broadly, including determining the value and location of intangible assets.

4.5.1   Related Statistics

The Bank for International Settlements (BIS) publishes two sets of nationality-based statistics. The first of these is the consolidated banking statistics (CBS). The CBS are collected by the country where the international bank is headquartered. While the consolidation practices vary across countries, the CBS include claims of the bank's foreign affiliates but remove the intra-group positions. The statistics are presented on both an immediate counterparty basis as well as on an ultimate risk basis. For example, if a German bank makes a loan to a Canadian company that was guaranteed by a United States entity, then Canada would be the immediate counterparty, while the United States would be the country of ultimate risk. The BIS also compiles the international debt securities on a nationality basis so that debt securities of foreign affiliates are attributed to the country where the MNE is headquartered. These statistics demonstrate the contribution of nationality-based and consolidated statistics to the analysis and monitoring of financial developments.

Statistics on the activities of MNEs (AMNE/FATS statistics) are closely related to FDI statistics. To determine if the consolidating FDI statistics provided better measures of the FDI into an economy that is having a real impact on the host economy, the correlations between the inward FDI positions excluding resident SPEs and key measures of the activities of MNEs—employment, turnover, and value added—were compared to the correlations with the consolidated FDI statistics. Overall, consolidating the FDI positions yields better alignment with activity measures. Considering employment data from AMNE/FATS, for example, the R-squared with FDI positions improves from 0.73 to 0.86 after consolidation (see figure 4.9). Improvements in the correlation are particularly large in Belgium, Finland, Germany, Portugal, and Sweden. In contrast, in the Netherlands, Ireland, and, to a lesser extent, Hungary and Luxembourg, the relationship between employment and FDI positions loses strength when taking pass-through into consideration.

Similarly, the analysis of FDI positions against turnover and value added data from AMNE/FATS also shows increased alignment. For turnover (top panel of figure 4.10), the R-squared shows only a slight improvement, from 0.86 to 0.89, after consolidating, while for value added (bottom panel), the relationship improves from 0.80 to 0.88. Once again, the improvement in correlation was substantial in some countries. For turnover, consolidation

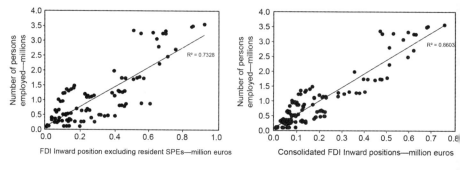

Figure 4.9   Correlation between employment (AMNE/FATS) and FDI inward positions—before and after consolidation

Source: OECD FDI Statistics database, OECD AMNE Statistics database, and author calculations based on Orbis.

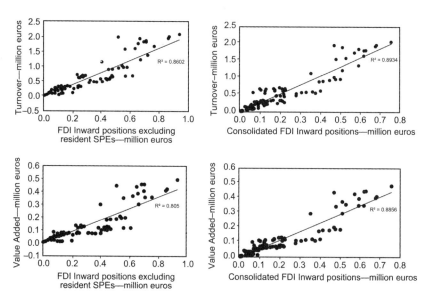

Figure 4.10   Correlation between turnover (AMNE/FATS), value added (AMNE/FATS), and FDI inward positions—before and after consolidation

Source: OECD FDI Statistics database, OECD AMNE Statistics database, and author calculations based on Orbis.

increased the R-squared for Estonia and Spain, while for value added, Denmark and Hungary both show a particularly stronger alignment with FATS. The correlations between changes in the positions and changes in the activity measures were also examined to determine if changes in the consolidated statistics could provide a better indication than the traditional FDI statistics of where MNE activity is increasing or decreasing. However, the correlations were very weak with both sets of FDI statistics, and the results were mixed. This could be because changes in FDI positions reflect not only investment flows that could be associated with changes in MNE activities but also changes in valuation.

As noted in section 2.1.3, the WGIIS developed a framework to harmonize and align the definitions, concepts, and classifications used for FDI and AMNE/FATS statistics so that they could be used together. Use of this framework would likely further enhance the alignment between the two sets of statistics by not only focusing on the same populations but also by providing better measures of the full involvement of the MNE in the host economy.

Trade in value added (TiVA) statistics were developed in response to the growth of global value chains (GVCs) and increased globalization. These statistics focus on the value added in each country in the production of goods and services that are traded. TiVA statistics identify the domestic value added of a country that ends up in foreign final demand as well as the ultimate destination for that domestic value added; similarly, they identify the foreign value added in domestic final demand as well as the ultimate source of that value added. These statistics have provided important insights into the economic relations between countries that could be obscured by the increasing complexity and globalization of economic production (OECD and World Trade Organization 2015).

The OECD has been developing a methodology to integrate FDI income statistics into the TiVA framework to understand where the income is generated along GVCs and where that income accrues (OECD 2016). This work highlighted the limitations in FDI statistics that inhibited their use for such globalization analysis, including income-in-transit and the presentation by immediate rather than ultimate partner country. The consolidated FDI statistics proposed in this chapter address these issues and should enhance the integration of FDI statistics into TiVA and the ensuing analysis.

4.5.2   Some Remaining Measurement Issues

The methodology proposed in this chapter relies on being able to identify where the assets of the MNE are located so that the consolidated view of the MNE can be attributed to specific economies. While this is usually straightforward for tangible assets with some exceptions, it is much more difficult for intangible assets. MNEs can move their intangible assets to economies that offer advantages, such as concessional tax rates, while continuing to use these assets in their production in other countries. The determination of the location of intangible assets within MNEs is not straightforward (UNECE 2015). Improved guidance on determining the location of intangible assets using economic rather than legal ownership would enable better recording of transactions and positions in intangible assets in FDI statistics. In addition, the framework developed here could be used to present the recording of intangible assets on an ownership, or nationality, basis rather than residency basis.

The value of intangible assets also poses difficulties for FDI statisticians.

Market values are considered to be the appropriate valuation for FDI positions. However, in practice, market values are only available for a small portion of FDI positions because most of the equity of direct investment enterprises is not listed. As such, it is necessary for FDI statisticians to estimate market values. The international guidelines offer several methods for doing this (see annex 10 in OECD 2008), but most of these methods exclude intangible assets from these market value estimates. For example, the most common method used, Own Funds at Book Value, relies on the accounting records of the direct investment enterprise kept according to International Financial Reporting Standards. These standards do not include the revaluation of intangible assets. Better methods to estimate market values of FDI positions would improve the comparability across functional categories in the BOP and IIP statistics as well as better reflect the important contribution of intangibles to the value of corporations, particularly MNEs, and to global production arrangements.

Another phenomenon that has affected FDI statistics is the decision by MNEs to move their headquarters to new countries to take advantage of benefits from the relocation, such as lower taxes. This phenomenon, sometimes called redomiciliation, can result in significant FDI flows that are almost completely offset by portfolio investment flows (Irish Central Statistics Office 2016); in addition, there is likely very little change in the actual operations of the MNE. It is possible that the methods used here to identify pass-through capital in FDI could be extended to portfolio investment to encompass these transactions. By doing so, the flows and positions associated with these transactions could be eliminated from the consolidated FDI statistics to reflect their limited impact on the economies involved.

4.6   Potential Policy Issues

Consolidated FDI statistics by ultimate partner economy would have many uses. First, they would provide better measures of financial integration between economies. By eliminating pass-through capital, the statistics would represent true financial integration and not financial intermediation between countries. In addition, the statistics by ultimate partner would provide better bilateral statistics for understanding the financial linkages between specific countries. These statistics could be used to analyze how a wide range of policies, such as trade and investment agreements and tax policies, are related to pass-through FDI or to true financial integration between countries and would help us better understand the financial interdependencies between countries.

Second, to the extent that pass-through capital responds to tax considerations, changes in tax policy can have significant impacts on FDI flows and positions, but these changes may not be associated with any real changes in their operations, as they only affect the ownership structure and not their actual operations (Foley, Dharmapala, and Forbes 2011). With recent or forthcoming tax policy changes in several countries, including the United States, these statistics would allow for the analysis of trends in genuine FDI separately from those related to fiscal optimization by MNEs. In broader terms, these statistics would enable a better analysis of the factors that attract FDI. Economists usually distinguish the factors that drive FDI, such as market-seeking behavior or factor cost differences, from those that drive portfolio investment, such as monetary policy or the business cycle. Yet, Blanchard and Acalin (2016) found that the factors usually considered drivers of portfolio investment flows were more highly correlated with FDI flows to emerging markets than to portfolio investment flows to those markets. They hypothesized that this was due to pass-through capital, so consolidated FDI statistics, from which the pass-through capital has been eliminated, should enable a better analysis of the drivers of FDI.

Third, these statistics would allow for better monitoring of commitments made under international agreements, such as free trade agreements, in the area of investment by enabling the monitoring of changes in the amount of assets in the reference economy owned by the partner country. In addition, they could also be used to monitor the contribution of FDI from advanced economies to financing other international initiatives, including the Sustainable Development Goals (SDGs), the transition to a carbon neutral economy, and official development assistance. In particular, having FDI statistics that reflect the extent of FDI in the ultimate host country would allow us to better link FDI with outcomes on the SDGs, such as job creation or gender equality.

Fourth, the statistics would enable better analyses of the impact of globalization on an economy. A key use of the statistics, for example, could be to integrate them into the extension of the trade in value added (TiVA) framework that incorporates primary income flows. Because the new statistics would more accurately measure the "real" FDI income generated within an economy and the ultimate destination of that income, they are better related to the underlying value added generated within a given period and so are better equipped to identifying where income is generated in a global value chain (GVC) and where it ultimately accrues. Moreover, by distinguishing outward FDI positions between purely domestic parent companies and foreign-owned parent companies, the statistics would provide essential information to quantifying the benefits to home countries of their ownership of foreign production facilities.

The expanded statistics that capture intra-group as well as extra-group financing and that reflect the nationality of the firms would also have several uses. For example, these statistics could be linked to AMNE/FATS statistics to analyze the relationship between MNEs' operations and their financing; this would be especially valuable if the statistics are expanded to capture the total financing of the MNE. Such linked statistics could show, for example, if foreign-owned firms can tap into intra-group financing in times of financial crises in the host countries, thus contributing to the resilience of these economies. Similarly, it could show how crises in the home countries affect the operations of their foreign affiliates. It could also show how well aligned MNEs' activities are with where they attribute the income, shedding light on profit shifting.

Finally, these statistics would help to monitor the cross-border exposure of MNEs. A true nationality, or ownership-based approach, to measuring the cross-border exposures of MNEs would include borrowing by the foreign subsidiaries of MNEs from unaffiliated parties, either domestic or foreign. Expanding the measures beyond FDI to capture the total assets of the group would provide a more complete picture of the economic involvement of the group as well as its cross-border and local exposures. The nationality approach recognizes that the headquarters control many of the decisions taken by the firm. This means that some aspects of the operations of the foreign-owned firm may respond more to home country policies than host country policies. Differentiating between domestic and foreign-owned entities is necessary to understand who ultimately bears the risk (Lane 2015). Consolidation would also be a step to developing a consolidated measure of the wealth of nations for their nonfinancial corporations.

4.7   Conclusion and Next Steps

MNEs play a central role in the creation and management of complex production networks. However, FDI statistics reflect not just the FDI associated with these networks but also other factors, such as fiscal optimization to reduce tax burdens and the increasing sophistication in MNEs' capital structures. This can make it difficult to interpret FDI statistics in the sense that they are not real and provide little in the way of long-term investments in a country. When MNEs channel investments through several countries, FDI flows and positions may be inflated because each flow into and out of each country is counted even if the capital, or income, is just passing through. Moreover, this behavior can further obscure the ultimate source and destination of FDI when the statistics are compiled by immediate partner country.

This chapter proposed a method to compile consolidated FDI statistics that removes pass-through capital. Estimates of the amount of pass-through capital in operating affiliates for a selection of European members of the OECD were derived using data from the Orbis database. These estimates indicate that the amount of pass-through capital in operating affiliates, rather than in SPEs, is quite extensive, accounting for about one-quarter of the inward FDI positions excluding resident SPEs in a selection of European countries. It also appears that pass-through capital is growing faster than the real FDI.

Future research will focus first on estimating pass-through capital for a greater number of countries. In addition, the possibility that information on the nationality of the MNE group could be introduced into the estimates will also be explored. These nationality-based statistics would be a complement to the residency-based FDI statistics. While residency-based financial statistics are useful to know where financial claims and liabilities are created and held, nationality-based statistics provide information on who makes the underlying decisions, reaps the benefits, and takes on the risk and needs to hold sufficient capital to cover potential losses. These statistics would be useful for better measuring financial integration and the links between economies as well as possibly being used in conjunction with statistics on the operations of MNEs to analyze the relationship between the financing of MNEs and their operations. Whether it is possible to differentiate pass-through capital that has little direct impact on the host economy, such as that related to tax avoidance, from pass-through capital that does have a direct impact on the host economy, such as from reducing transactions costs, will also be explored. Finally, it would be useful to use additional information from the balance sheets included in Orbis to develop some estimates of the total assets controlled by the foreign investor in the host economies.

Nevertheless, the estimates in this chapter will continue to rely on the availability of detailed micro-data that include ownership information. It would obviously be preferable for the estimated to be based on data collected for the production of official FDI statistics. As a first step, countries could publish a limited set of data based on the nationality of the ultimate investor; that is, identifying the outward investment positions of a country accounted for by direct investors in the reporting country that are in fact foreign owned. Ultimately, it would be useful to have countries attempt to use these methods. This could identify additional complexities in the financial structure of MNEs that need to be addressed and could also give an indication of the feasibility of these methods.

Appendix
Data Annex

To produce the estimates of pass-through capital, two data sets were used: micro-level data from Bureau van Dijk's Orbis database and aggregate FDI positions from the OECD FDI Statistics Database.

4A.1   Micro-data

The source database for this analysis is Orbis by Bureau van Dijk. This is a cross-country, firm-level database containing ownership link information connecting subsidiaries through their direct owners to their ultimate (global) owners. These data are sourced from a variety of documents (company reports and accounts, stock exchange filings, and regulatory records) and includes ownership percentages, types of relationships (such as global or domestic ultimate owner) and dates related to each relationship.

The data set was created by pooling cross sections of linkages for years 2007 to 2015. For each linkage, the variables examined were:

- Subsidiary identifier and country;[14]
- Shareholder identifier and country;[15]
- Global ultimate owner (ownership above 50 percent) and country;[16]
- Percentages of ownership (direct and total).

To be included in each cross section, the linkages had to be active in the year, and entities at shareholder level (hence, the country of pass-through) were limited to be European Union and EEA countries. This was done to ensure maximum quality and timeliness of data (the higher European coverage is a well-known feature of Orbis). Subsidiaries and ultimate owners were, however, unconstrained in terms of geographic location. The cases in which the entire ownership chain was located in the same country were removed.

Subsequently foreign-owned investors and their affiliates were identified. These are the instances of pass-through linkages. Foreign-owned investors were found using the GUO50 variable. Orbis identifies the GUO by following the ownership chain of the enterprise through control relationships until an entity that is not controlled by another entity is reached.

In addition, to focus on pass-through capital through operating affiliates rather than SPEs, enterprises with NACE codes 6420 and 6430 were dropped from the sample. This was a rough definition of SPE[17] because it only considered the industry code and not other factors, such as the amount of employment or share of foreign assets or liabilities on their balance sheets. Financial accounts data on shareholder funds and income were then added to the database via the respective identifiers. Preference was given for subsidiaries to the unconsolidated financial statements. For the shareholders and the GUOs, priority was given to unconsolidated accounts, but where the shareholder funds variable was not available, consolidated data were retained.

14. Country was based on the two-letter ISO code prefix contained in the entity identifier. This reflects the country of registration of the firm.
15. Ibid.
16. Ibid.
17. For further details, please consider, for example, the Eurostat NACE Rev.2 Introductory guidelines. Units classified in these two classes do not have any revenue from the sale of products, and usually do not employ staff (except possibly one or a few persons acting as legal representatives). Sometimes these units are called "brass plates," or "post boxes" or "empty boxes," or "special purpose entities—SPE," as they just have a name and an address.

4A.1.1   Treatment of Outliers and Missing Values

Each cross section of data was scrutinized in order to prevent individual outliers from driving pass-through estimates. Maxima and minima by country and year were removed; in addition, data points ranked second within country-year distributions, where the ratio of the data point to the maximum or minimum exceeded 75 percent, were also dropped.

In cases where the total ownership percentage—both direct and indirect—was missing, the direct ownership percentage was used. This means that the estimates are likely a lower bound on the amount of pass-through capital.

4A.1.2   Coverage of FDI Statistics

Orbis outward equity stock by country of immediate investor was compared to official FDI equity positions (excluding SPEs) to assess the coverage of the sample (table 4A.1).

This comparison is rough, as differences in valuation can result in significant asymmetries in FDI statistics (Angulo and Hierro 2017), and there is no way to determine how the valuations of total equity in Orbis compare to the valuations in the source data countries use in compiling their FDI statistics. As a result, this comparison should be taken only as indicative of the coverage the Orbis data provide. The coverage varies across countries and over time. There is a general trend upward in coverage, reflecting the improved country coverage in Orbis in terms of both the number of countries covered and the coverage within countries. Because the European region is generally better covered in Orbis, countries with a higher share of outward investment in Europe would be expected to have higher coverage than other countries. The figures for Luxembourg likely exceed the total outward investment because the procedure for removing SPEs from Orbis did not capture all of the entities identified as SPEs by Luxembourg. The negative value for the Czech Republic in 2011 reflected a large negative value for equity in a subsidiary that was subsequently dropped in treating the data for outliers.

4A.1.3   Computation of Pass-Through Capital

The computation of pass-through capital was done in two steps:

1) Once all of the enterprises with foreign subsidiaries were identified, their ownership percentage in their foreign subsidiaries was multiplied by the shareholders' funds to estimate the equity claim the direct investors had on the subsidiaries. Then, equity claims tied to the same enterprise group were aggregated at the shareholder level.

2) The different options for the direction of pass-through (or zero-pass-through) were evaluated as outlined in 2.1.1 Data were summed by direct investor country, and the share of pass-through was than calculated by tak-

Table 4A.1   Outward equity stock as calculated from Orbis data as share of aggregate outward FDI equity positions excluding SPEs, 2007–2015

Reporting country	2007	2008	2009	2010	2011	2012	2013	2014	2015
Austria	17%	18%	16%	15%	15%	15%	22%	19%	50%
Belgium	12%	19%	22%	25%	29%	28%	37%	30%	17%
Switzerland	23%	15%	14%	14%	18%	15%	14%	13%	13%
Czech Republic	19%	10%	29%	7%	−137%	9%	11%	10%	
Germany	21%	20%	21%	28%	23%	21%	22%	20%	23%
Denmark	13%	13%	10%	9%	12%	8%			
Estonia	5%	7%	5%	12%	18%	16%	16%	8%	9%
Spain	17%	12%	15%	16%	18%	19%	19%	17%	15%
Finland	27%	18%	18%	35%	31%	21%	29%	23%	35%
France	21%	27%	21%	21%	30%	21%	26%	17%	20%
United Kingdom	64%	59%	72%	80%	87%	65%			
Hungary	6%	5%	8%	17%	3%	4%	16%	8%	14%
Ireland	25%	17%	21%	22%	24%	20%	10%	10%	11%
Iceland	26%	7%	30%	34%	32%	16%	14%	10%	0%
Italy	7%	18%	11%	17%	9%	16%	20%	13%	17%
Luxembourg	123%	92%	129%	120%	169%	199%			
Netherlands	29%	24%	29%	23%	22%	21%			
Norway	14%	16%	11%	17%	24%	29%	38%	39%	23%
Poland	2%	4%	6%	8%	8%	10%	8%	11%	12%
Portugal	15%	24%	18%	30%	31%	38%	19%	27%	25%
Sweden	35%	27%	41%	24%	27%	28%	48%	46%	31%
Slovenia	8%	21%	15%	26%	30%	22%	29%	31%	16%
Slovak Republic	26%	47%	43%	23%	45%	32%	30%	56%	48%

Note: Data for Austria, Hungary, the Netherlands, Iceland, and Luxembourg exclude resident SPEs for the whole time series, 2007–2015. Data for Belgium, Denmark, Norway, Poland, Portugal, and Switzerland exclude resident SPEs for BMD4 data only. Empty cells denote confidential data or no available instrument breakdown.

ing the ratio of pass-through equity over total outward equity positions by country.

4A.2   FDI Positions

A time series of inward and outward FDI positions from 2007 to 2015 was constructed from the OECD FDI statistics database. Statistics excluding resident SPEs were used when available. For countries that did not separately identify the FDI to and from resident SPEs in earlier years, the share of resident SPEs in the total positions for the first year the data were reported was carried back to 2007. No other adjustments were made for the implementation of BMD4, so there might be other breaks in series.

The United Kingdom reports SPEs for detailed annual statistics but not for the aggregate statistics, resulting in differences in vintage that make it difficult to construct a time series.

Table 4A.2   Composition of pass-through (equity and number of entities) by ultimate investing country, 2007 and 2015

	2007			2015	
Country of ultimate investor	Share of pass through by UIC	Share of pass through entities by UIC	Country of ultimate investor	Share of pass through by UIC	Share of pass through entities by UIC
United States	25.9%	28.1%	United States	32.2%	25.6%
United Kingdom	17.3%	6.6%	Japan	6.5%	4.9%
France	9.4%	6.1%	Netherlands	5.8%	4.9%
Netherlands	5.8%	4.4%	France	5.6%	4.8%
Germany	5.7%	8.7%	Switzerland	5.4%	4.3%
Japan	5.7%	5.0%	United Kingdom	5.0%	6.7%
Italy	4.1%	3.0%	Germany	4.8%	7.2%
Ireland	3.2%	0.8%	Ireland	3.7%	1.1%
Spain	3.0%	1.0%	Spain	3.6%	0.9%
Cayman Islands	2.8%	0.8%	Israel	3.4%	0.6%
Luxembourg	2.1%	4.2%	Russian Federation	3.4%	0.9%
Switzerland	1.9%	3.8%	Luxembourg	3.1%	5.7%
Australia	1.8%	1.3%	Sweden	1.5%	2.6%
Sweden	1.8%	3.5%	Bermuda	1.4%	0.8%
Finland	1.4%	1.5%	Canada	1.3%	1.7%
Bermuda	0.8%	1.2%	Italy	1.3%	3.1%
Norway	0.8%	1.4%	Malaysia	1.0%	0.2%
Belgium	0.8%	2.5%	Belgium	1.0%	2.0%
Canada	0.6%	1.1%	Saudi Arabia	0.8%	0.1%
Virgin Islands (British)	0.6%	0.7%	Singapore	0.7%	0.4%
Cyprus	0.4%	1.0%	Curaçao	0.7%	0.7%
Curaçao	0.3%	1.3%	Australia	0.6%	0.8%
Mexico	0.3%	0.1%	Cayman Islands	0.6%	1.5%
South Africa	0.3%	0.4%	Portugal	0.5%	0.8%

(continued)

Table 4A.2 (continued)

	2007			2015	
Country of ultimate investor	Share of pass through by UIC	Share of pass through entities by UIC	Country of ultimate investor	Share of pass through by UIC	Share of pass through entities by UIC
Greece	0.3%	0.2%	Norway	0.5%	1.6%
United Arab Emirates	0.3%	0.1%	Mexico	0.5%	0.2%
Singapore	0.3%	0.4%	China	0.5%	0.9%
Austria	0.3%	1.4%	Cyprus	0.3%	1.5%
Bahamas	0.2%	0.4%	United Arab Emirates	0.3%	0.3%
Denmark	0.2%	1.4%	Poland	0.3%	0.3%
Israel	0.2%	0.6%	Brazil	0.3%	0.3%
Liechtenstein	0.2%	0.6%	Liechtenstein	0.3%	0.5%
Iceland	0.2%	0.4%	India	0.2%	0.8%
Russian Federation	0.1%	0.5%	Qatar	0.2%	0.1%
Lebanon	0.1%	0.2%	Monaco	0.2%	0.2%
Hong Kong	0.1%	0.2%	Virgin Islands (British)	0.2%	1.2%
Korea, Republic of	0.1%	0.2%	Denmark	0.2%	1.0%
India	0.1%	0.6%	Korea, Republic of	0.2%	0.2%
Saudi Arabia	0.1%	0.1%	Austria	0.2%	1.6%
Hungary	0.1%	0.1%	Lithuania	0.2%	0.1%
Malta	0.1%	0.2%	Thailand	0.1%	0.1%
Czech Republic	(*)	0.1%	Bahamas	0.1%	0.3%
Taiwan	(*)	0.3%	South Africa	0.1%	0.3%
China	(*)	0.2%	Egypt	0.1%	0.1%
Cote D'Ivoire	(*)	(*)	Hungary	0.1%	0.2%
Kuwait	(*)	0.3%	Turkey	0.1%	0.2%
Malaysia	(*)	0.1%	Venezuela	0.1%	(*)
Portugal	(*)	0.4%	Taiwan	0.1%	0.3%
Slovakia	(*)	0.2%	Hong Kong	0.1%	0.4%

Poland	(*)	0._%	Finland	0.1%	0.8%
Turkey	(*)	0.1%	Panama	0.1%	0.3%
Lithuania	(*)	(*)	Lebanon	0.1%	0.2%
Slovenia	(*)	0.1%	Libyan Arab Jamahiriya	0.1%	(*)
Brazil	(*)	0.1%	Malta	(*)	0.3%
Mauritius	(*)	0.1%	Gibraltar	(*)	0.1%
Saint Kitts and Nevis	(*)	0.1%	Ukraine	(*)	0.2%
Barbados	(*)	0.1%	Croatia	(*)	0.2%
Monaco	(*)	C.1%	Cote D'Ivoire	(*)	(*)
Colombia	(*)	0.1%	New Zealand	(*)	0.2%
Panama	(*)	0.5%	Colombia	(*)	0.1%
Croatia	(*)	0.1%	Greece	(*)	0.1%
Estonia	(*)	0.1%	Czech Republic	(*)	0.5%
Chile	(*)	(*)	Slovenia	(*)	0.1%
Belize	(*)	0.3%	Philippines	(*)	(*)
Ukraine	(*)	(*)	Kuwait	(*)	0.1%
Seychelles	(*)	0.1%	Iceland	(*)	0.2%
New Zealand	(*)	0.1%	Slovakia	(*)	0.4%
Trinidad and Tobago	(*)	(*)	Congo, Republic of	(*)	(*)
Liberia	(*)	0.1%	Brunei Darussalam	(*)	(*)
Gibraltar	(*)	0.2%	Belize	(*)	0.1%
Uzbekistan	(*)	(*)	Latvia	(*)	0.2%
Iran (Islamic Republic of)	(*)	(*)	Saint Vincent and the Grenadines	(*)	(*)
Moldova, Republic of	(*)	(*)	Seychelles	(*)	0.1%
Bulgaria	(*)	0.1%	Bulgaria	(*)	0.1%
Namibia	(*)	(*)	Bosnia and Herzegowina	(*)	(*)
Kazakhstan	(*)	(*)	Romania	(*)	0.2%
Bahrain	(*)	(*)	Belarus	(*)	0.1%
Romania	(*)	0.1%	Algeria	(*)	(*)
Vanuatu	(*)	(*)	Mauritius	(*)	0.1%
Thailand	(*)	(*)	Morocco	(*)	(*)

(continued)

Table 4A.2 (continued)

2007			2015		
Country of ultimate investor	Share of pass through by UIC	Share of pass through entities by UIC	Country of ultimate investor	Share of pass through by UIC	Share of pass through entities by UIC
			Angola	(*)	(*)
			Kazakhstan	(*)	(*)
			Viet Nam	(*)	(*)
			Oman	(*)	(*)
			Indonesia	(*)	(*)
			Chile	(*)	(*)
			Iran (Islamic Republic of)	(*)	(*)
			Estonia	(*)	0.1%
			Sri Lanka	(*)	(*)
			Bahrain	(*)	(*)
			San Marino	(*)	(*)
			Dominica	(*)	(*)
			Saint Kitts and Nevis	(*)	(*)
			Moldova, Republic of	(*)	(*)
			Vanuatu	(*)	(*)
			Marshall Islands	(*)	(*)
			Andorra	(*)	(*)
			Costa Rica	(*)	(*)
			Kenya	(*)	(*)

(*) greater than zero but less than 0.05%.

4A.3   Additional Descriptive Statistics for Ultimate Investing Country

Table 4A.2 provides information on all countries identified as UICs of pass-through entities and their respective shares of the equity and number of entities they account for in 2007 and 2015.

References

Angulo, Emma, and Alicia Hierro. 2017. "Asymmetries in the Coordinated Direct Investment Survey: What Lies Behind?" IMF Working Paper 17/261. Washington, DC: International Monetary Fund.

Antràs, Pol, Mihir Desai, and Fritz Foley. 2009. "Multinational Firms, FDI Flows and Imperfect Capital Markets." *Quarterly Journal of Economics* 124 (3): 1171–219.

Austria Central Bank. 2015. "Who is the Investor? A Simple Question that May Improve FDI Statistics." Presentation to the WGIIS, March 18.

Bank for International Settlements. 2015. "Consolidation and Corporate Groups: An Overview of Methodological and Practical Issues." Inter-Agency Group on Economic and Financial Statistics (IAG), IAG reference documents.

Blanchard, Olivier, and Julien Acalin. 2016. "What Does Measured FDI Actually Measure?" Peterson Institute for International Economics, PB16–17, October.

Caballero, Julian, Ugo Panizza, and Andrew Powell. 2015. "The Second Wave of Global Liquidity: Why Are Firms Acting Like Financial Intermediaries?" Graduate Institute of International and Development Studies, International Economics Department, Working Paper HEIDWP21–2015.

Central Statistics Office of Ireland. 2016. "The Impact of Redomiciled Companies on the Balance of Payments and International Investment Position."

Cernohous, Thomas. 2017. "FATS and FDI Statistics: Close Connections, Different Focus." *Focus on External Trade 2016/2017: Foreign Direct Investment and Trends, Drivers Limiting Factors*, Austria Central Bank.

Desai, Mihir A., Fritz Foley, and James R. Hines. 2003. "Chains of Ownership, Regional Tax Competition, and Foreign Direct Investment." In *Foreign Direct Investment in the Real and Financial Sector of Industrial Countries*, edited by Heinz Herrmann and Robert Lipsey, 61–98. Heidelberg: Springer Verlag.

Desai, Mihir, Fritz Foley, and James R. Hines. 2006. "The Demand for Tax Haven Operations." *Journal of Public Economics* 90: 513–31.

Eggelte, Juriaan, Melle Bijlsma, and Krit Cartier. 2016. "What Shall We Do with Pass-through? DNB's Experiences with Special Financial Institutions." Mimeo, Dutch National Bank.

Eurostat. 2012. *Foreign Affiliates Statistics (FATS) Recommendations Manual.* Luxembourg.

Federico, Stefano. 2015. "How Does Multinational Production Affect the Measurement of Competitiveness?" Presentation to the March 2015 WGIIS meeting, Paris, France. [DAF/INV/STAT/WD(2015)5].

Foley, Fritz C., Dhammika Dharmapala, and Kristin J. Forbes. 2011. "Watch What I Do, Not What I Say: The Unintended Consequences of the Homeland Investment Act." *Journal of Finance* 66 (3): 753–88.

Gaukrodger, D. 2013. "Investment Treaties as Corporate Law: Shareholder Claims and Issues of Consistency." *OECD Working Papers on International Investment, 2013/03*. Paris: OECD Publishing.

International Monetary Fund. 2017. "Preliminary Report of the Task Force in Special Purpose Entities." Balance of Payments Committee Meeting, BOPCOM-17/05.

International Monetary Fund. 2008. *Balance of Payments and International Investment Positions Manual, 6th edition*. Washington, DC.

International Monetary Fund and the Financial Stability Board. 2009. "The Financial Crisis and Information Gaps." Washington, DC.

Irish Central Statistics Office. 2016. "Redomiciled PLCs in the Irish Balance of Payments." http://www.cso.ie/en/media/csoie/methods/balanceofinternational payments/RedomiciledPLCs.pdf.

Kocerka, Jacek, and Krzysztof Makowski. 2017. "Does Pass-thru Funds Require Their Own Functional Category?" ISI World Statistics Congress.

Lane, Philip R. 2015. "Cross-Border Financial Linkages: Identifying and Measuring Vulnerabilities." Mimeo, Trinity College Dublin and CEPR.

Lane, Philip R., and Gian Milesi-Ferretti. 2017. "International Financial Integration in the Aftermath of the Global Financial Crisis." International Monetary Fund, WP/17/115, May.

Leino, Topias, and Jyrki Ali-Yrkkö. 2014. "How Well Does Foreign Direct Investment Measure Real Investment by Foreign-Owned Companies?" Bank of Finland, Bank of Finland Research Discussion Paper No. 12/2014, May.

Lewellen, Katharina, and Leslie Robinson. 2013. "Internal Ownership Structures of US Multinational Firms." https://ssrn.com/abstract=2273553 or http://dx.doi .org/10.2139/ssrn.2273553.

Mahoney, Paul. 2007. "Developing a Consolidated Approach to Identifying Pass-through Capital and Reallocating Positions to Ultimate Investors and Ultimate Investees." Paper of the Research Agenda of the OECD Workshop on International Investment Statistics, mimeo, October.

Montvai, Beata. 2016. "Towards Interpretable FDI Data in External Sector." Hungarian Central Bank. www.ksh.hu/cess2016/prezi/cess2016_b6_beata_montvai .pptx.

Organisation for Economic Co-operation and Development. 2006. "A Method for Allocating the US Direct Investment Position Abroad to the Country and Industry of Ultimate Destination." Note by the United States, Paris, France.

Organisation for Economic Co-operation and Development. 2008. *Benchmark Definition of Foreign Direct Investment, 4th edition*. Paris, France.

Organisation for Economic Co-operation and Development. 2011. "Harmonising FDI and Activities of MNE Statistics." Paris, France.

Organisation for Economic Co-operation and Development. 2015. "Harmonising FDI and Activities of MNE Statistics: Feasibility of and Priorities for Compilation." Paris, France.

Organisation for Economic Co-operation and Development. 2016. "Integration of FDI Statistics in TiVA: Results and Data Challenges." Paris, France.

Organisation for Economic Co-operation and Development. 2018. "Measuring MNEs Using Big Data: The OECD Analytical Database on Individual Multinationals and their Affiliates (ADIMA)." Paris, France.

Organisation for Economic Co-operation and Development and World Trade Organization. 2015. "Trade in Value Added." Paris, France. http://www.oecd.org/sti /ind/measuringtradeinvalue-addedanoecd-wtojointinitiative.htm.

Pohl, J. 2018. "Societal Benefits and Costs of International Investment Agreements:

A Critical Review of Aspects and Available Empirical Evidence." *OECD Working Papers on International Investment*, No. 2018/01. Paris: OECD Publishing.

Swiss National Bank. 2017. *Direct Investment 2016*, Volume 17.

Tarashev, Nikola, Stefan Avdjiev, and Ben Cohen. 2016. "International Capital Flows and Financial Vulnerabilities in Emerging Market Economies: Analysis and Data Gaps." Note submitted to the G20 International Financial Architecture Working Group, Bank for International Settlements.

Tissot, Bruno. 2016. "Globalisation and Financial Stability Risks: Is the Residency-based Approach of the National Accounts Old-Fashioned?" BIS Working Paper No. 587.

United Nations Economic Commission for Europe. 2015. *Guide to Measuring Global Production*. "Ownership of Intellectual Property Products inside Global Production," New York and Geneva.

Van Os, R., and R. Knottnerus. 2011. "Dutch Bilateral Investment Treaties: A gateway to 'treaty shopping' for investment protection by multinational companies." SSRN Electronic Journal. 10.2139/ssrn.1974431.

5

Multinational Profit Shifting and Measures throughout Economic Accounts

Jennifer Bruner, Dylan G. Rassier, Kim J. Ruhl

5.1 Introduction

Economic accounts offer a comprehensive summary of stocks and flows for a given economy. To promote consistency and comparability of economic accounting measures across economies and time, economic accounts are based on internationally agreed principles that reflect organizing conventions from business accounting and definitions and concepts from economic theory. The primary sources of guidance on economic accounts are the *System of National Accounts* (*SNA*) (European Commission et al. 2009) and the *Balance of Payments and International Investment Position Manual* (*BPM*) (International Monetary Fund 2009). The *SNA* framework is designed with a set of interrelated balanced accounts for five domestic institutional sectors and an additional account for transactions and positions with the rest of

Jennifer Bruner is a senior research economist at the Bureau of Economic Analysis.

Dylan G. Rassier is former Chief of National Accounts Research and Analysis at the Bureau of Economic Analysis.

Kim J. Ruhl holds the Mary Sue and Mike Shannon Distinguished Chair in Economics and is professor of economics at the University of Wisconsin–Madison, and is a research associate of the National Bureau of Economic Research.

For comments and helpful questions, we thank Ray Mataloni, Brent Moulton, Marshall Reinsdorf, Peter van de Ven, Dan Yorgason, and especially our discussant, Steve Redding. The statistical analysis of firm-level data on US multinational companies and companies engaged in international transactions was conducted at the Bureau of Economic Analysis, US Department of Commerce, under arrangements that maintain legal confidentiality requirements. The views expressed in this paper are solely those of the authors and not necessarily those of the US Department of Commerce or the Bureau of Economic Analysis. For acknowledgments, sources of research support, and disclosure of the authors' material financial relationships, if any, please see https://www.nber.org/books-and-chapters/challenges-globalization -measurement-national-accounts/multinational-profit-shifting-and-measures-throughout -economic-accounts.

world. The *BPM* framework is also designed with a set of interrelated balanced accounts that provide more detail on the *SNA* rest of world account. The *SNA* and *BPM* frameworks are intentionally harmonized to ensure a consistent treatment of rest of world transactions, other flows, and positions in each framework.

Under *SNA* and *BPM* recommendations, rest of world transactions are attributable to economies based on the residences of transacting entities. Under this treatment, affiliates within multinational enterprises (MNEs) are considered resident in the economies in which they are located. While the residence of an entity is generally the economy in which the entity is physically located, an entity with few or no attributes of physical presence—such as a holding company or a special purpose entity—is considered resident in its economy of legal incorporation or registration. In this case, the entity is not consolidated with its parent unless the entity is resident in the same economy as its parent. As a result, economic accounts for a given economy reflect transactions, other flows, and positions that are recorded in each resident entity's separate accounting records—known as the method of separate accounting.

A trend in the last couple of decades is MNEs that are structured with holding companies or special purpose entities that are created for purposes other than production. In particular, MNEs have access to countries that vary widely in corporate tax rates, which enables profit-maximizing MNEs to legally take advantage of differences in national tax regimes and shift profits from high tax countries to low tax countries through transfer pricing and complex global structuring that generally includes holding companies or special purpose entities. Sanchirico (2015) describes these strategies as "unsoundably elaborate and only rarely publicly visible" (page 210), and they have generated concern among official statistics compilers and users of official statistics regarding the *SNA* and *BPM* treatment of transactions within MNEs and their effects on economic accounting measures.[1]

In the US economic accounts, the treatment of transactions within MNEs under the residence concept is generally consistent with *SNA* and *BPM* recommendations. As a result, Guvenen et al. (2017) study offshore profit shifting within MNEs as a source of the measured slowdown in US productivity growth.[2] Under the international guidelines, profits shifted out of the United States may generate low measures of domestic real value-added growth in official statistics, yielding a slowdown in related measured productivity growth. In contrast to the method of separate accounting, the authors construct an adjusted time series of business sector real value added that is based on a measurement methodology known as formulary apportion-

---

1. See, for example, Lipsey (2010), Rassier (2017), and United Nations et al. (2011).
2. Other studies that consider possible measurement explanations for the recent productivity slowdown include Brynjolfsson and McAfee (2011), Byrne, Fernald, and Reinsdorf (2016), Byrne, Oliner and Sichel (2015), Mokyr (2014), and Syverson (2017).

ment. Under formulary apportionment, the total worldwide earnings of MNEs are attributed to locations based on apportionment factors such as compensation and sales that aim to capture the true location of economic activity. Since earnings by US MNEs are disproportionately booked to low tax jurisdictions in which little real economic activity occurs, the result is a net reattribution of earnings on US direct investment abroad (USDIA) from tax-advantaged locations to US parents. Holding prices constant, the reattribution generates an implied increase in measured domestic business sector real value added and related measured labor productivity growth.[3] In this chapter, we use the same adjustments of profit shifting by US MNEs calculated in Guvenen et al. (2017) for value added in the production account to empirically demonstrate how "offshore profit shifting"—profit shifting accomplished through rest of world transactions—affects other key economic accounting measures throughout the *SNA* and *BPM* frameworks for the United States in 2014. We limit the scope of adjustments to US MNEs because complete data are not available for foreign MNEs operating in the United States. Consistent with Guvenen et al. (2017), we determine offshore profit shifting as the difference between measures derived under formulary apportionment and measures derived under separate accounting. We then apply the aggregate adjustments to relevant published aggregates in each of the *SNA* and *BPM* frameworks. We focus on the effects of our adjustments on nominal measures and do not attempt to split the adjustments into volume and price effects. In addition to effects on key economic accounting measures, we present implications for common analytic uses of the US economic accounts, including the labor share of income, national saving rates, returns on domestic nonfinancial business, returns on foreign direct investment, and external balances.

For 2014, we find notable changes in key economic accounting measures throughout the US economic accounts, which may have significant implications for their analytic uses. Our adjustments yield a 3.5 percent increase in US operating surplus, which generates a 1.5 percent increase in US gross domestic product (GDP) as a result of an implied increase in output that is used as services exports. Likewise, we find a 33.5 percent decrease in US income receivable from the rest of world, which is overwhelmingly attributable to a decrease in earnings on USDIA with a small amount attributable to net interest receivable on USDIA. In dollar amounts, the increase in operating surplus is offset by a larger decrease in income receivable from the rest of

---

3. Guvenen et al. (2017) do not adjust price indices for any effects that may be caused by transfer pricing. The authors apply their nominal adjustment series to nominal value added and deflate the adjusted measures of value added using existing price indices—both aggregate and industry-level indices. Thus, the authors make an implicit assumption that profit shifting made possible by global structuring primarily affects volume measures rather than price measures. If transfer prices are consistent over time or reflect arm's length values, this assumption is reasonable.   .

world. As a result of these offsetting effects, US gross national income (GNI) and gross national disposable income decrease by 0.1 percent, while gross national saving decreases by 0.8 percent and national borrowing increases by 6.9 percent. Finally, net worth in the balance sheet decreases by 0.3 percent.

The results for analytic uses include a decrease for the labor share of income of 1.4 to 2.4 percentage points because the additional domestic income accrues to capital rather than labor and includes a decrease for the return on USDIA of 5.0 percentage points because the adjusted income on USDIA decreases proportionally more than the decrease in the stock of direct investment assets. The results for analytic uses also include an increase for the trade in services balance as a percentage of GDP of 1.4 percentage points because the additional services exports are proportionally higher than the increase in GDP and include an increase for the return on domestic nonfinancial business of 1.3 percentage points, assuming no change in the stock of produced assets. Changes for the national saving rate and the current account balance as a percentage of GDP are negligible.

The rest of the chapter is organized as follows. The next section describes related tax literature and measurement literature. Section 5.3 outlines the *SNA* and *BPM* frameworks. Section 5.4 explains our empirical approach and the data. Section 5.5 presents results and a related discussion. Section 5.6 summarizes our conclusions.

5.2   Related Literature

Most of the evidence on MNE profit shifting comes from cross-country regressions of MNE profits on tax rates, which generally find a strong relationship between differential tax rates and income attribution. Dharmapala (2014) provides a comprehensive survey of the profit shifting literature. In early work, Hines and Rice (1994) use cross-country regressions to study profit shifting behavior of US MNEs in 1982. They find that US MNEs report high profit rates in tax havens and that the revenue-maximizing tax rate for a typical haven is between 5 and 8 percent. Clausing (2016) uses estimates of the elasticity of MNE income to tax rates to compute the cross-country distribution of MNE income and determine foregone US tax revenue. She finds that profit shifting amounts to about $258 billion in 2012. Dowd, Landefeld, and Moore (2017) also compute elasticities to determine how MNEs alter the global allocation of profits in response to changes in tax rates. They find that log-linear specifications may understate the sensitivity of profits in low-tax jurisdictions with the opposite effect in high-tax jurisdictions. In addition to these academic studies, country-level indicators of base erosion and profit shifting are offered by the Organisation for Economic Co-operation and Development (2015a).

Measurement challenges imposed on economic accountants by MNE profit shifting are widely addressed in the literature. Under separate accounting, profit shifting has been shown empirically to generate questionable outcomes for some published supplemental income-based value-added measures on US MNEs (Lipsey 2010; Rassier and Koncz-Bruner 2015). However, no empirical study comprehensively traces the effects of profit shifting throughout the *SNA* and *BPM* frameworks. Three papers in United Nations et al. (2011) are dedicated to identifying and explaining challenges associated with allocating production of MNEs and special purpose entities to national economies. In addition, Lipsey (2010) concludes that some US supplemental statistics on financial and operating activities of foreign affiliates of US MNEs are affected by global structuring and the mobility of some factors of production such as intangible assets. Lipsey (2010) suggests, but does not develop, an alternative to separate accounting for measuring transactions in services and intellectual property. Early work by Baldwin and Kimura (1998) and Kimura and Baldwin (1998) also suggests supplemental concepts for organizing foreign direct investment and trade statistics based on ownership. Landefeld, Wichard, and Lowe (1993) evaluate ownership-based trade measures and propose an alternative residence-based trade measure.

Formulary apportionment has been primarily applied in multijurisdictional tax practice. The treatment of global income under formulary apportionment is explored in multidisciplinary research (Gordon and Wilson 1986; Clausing and Avi-Yonah 2007), and formulary apportionment has been proposed as an alternative to the complexity and subjectivity of transfer pricing for the allocation of international tax obligations within multinationals in studies such as Avi-Yonah (2010) and Fuest, Hemmelgarn, and Ramb (2007). However, formulary apportionment also presents challenges from a tax policy perspective, which is demonstrated in Altshuler and Grubert (2010) and Hines (2010). Because firm-level data collected on statistical surveys may only be used for statistical purposes and not for the purpose of taxation or regulation, formulary apportionment applied in economic accounting faces fewer challenges compared to its use in international taxation.

5.3   Accounting Frameworks

Offshore profit shifting imposes two challenges for the treatment of MNEs in the *SNA* and *BPM* frameworks. First, transactions within MNEs are valued using transfer pricing methods that may fail to resemble market outcomes, which is the preferred basis for all transactions recognized in the *SNA* and *BPM*. Second, MNEs are structured with holding companies and special purpose entities that may not engage in actual production because such structuring simply facilitates the strategic location of intangible productive assets and related income, as well as the artificial characterization of financial claims and liabilities.

One common arrangement among MNEs is a series of sublicensing trans-actions on intellectual property that results when the intellectual property is legally owned, in whole or in part, by a holding company in a low-tax juris-diction. In economic accounts, these arrangements can affect production and related income measures such as GDP and operating surplus because legal ownership of intellectual property is often used as a practical solution to determine economic ownership. Another common arrangement is the characterization of a financial instrument as debt in one jurisdiction and as equity in another jurisdiction to take advantage of differences in tax-ability of interest and dividend flows. In this case, economic accounting mea-sures such as GNI can be affected as a result of interest and dividend flows. The consequences of these and similar arrangements is a wedge between the location of production, the location of underlying factors of produc-tion, and the location of means for financing production, which affects the interpretability of key economic accounting measures in the *SNA* and *BPM* frameworks.

5.3.1   Overview of the SNA and BPM Frameworks

The *SNA* framework is divided into five domestic institutional sectors that include financial corporations, nonfinancial corporations, general govern-ment, households, and nonprofit institutions serving households. For each sector, the *SNA* groups accounts according to whether they include current transactions or transactions and flows in the accumulation of assets and liabilities. The "current accounts" include a production account and multiple income accounts that reflect the generation, distribution, redistribution, and use of income. The "accumulation accounts" include a capital account that records transactions in nonfinancial assets and a financial account that records transactions in financial assets and liabilities. The accumulation accounts also include accounts for other changes in assets and liabilities that are not a result of transactions. In addition to the current accounts and the accumulation accounts, the *SNA* framework includes a balance sheet that records opening and closing stocks as well as changes between them for nonfinancial assets, financial assets, liabilities, and resulting net worth.

The balanced structure of the *SNA* is made possible by the inclusion of a goods and services account and by balancing items or residuals in each account. The goods and services account supports the fundamental accounting identity that the supply of goods and services from domestic output and imports must equal the uses of goods and services for intermedi-ate consumption, final consumption, capital formation, and exports. The balancing items link one account to the next in a sequence of accounts that includes the production account, income accounts, capital account, and financial account. The *SNA* balancing items are generally considered key measures in the *SNA* framework because they help guide macroeconomic policy—they include items such as value added, operating surplus, national income, disposable income, saving, net lending/borrowing, and net worth. In addition to the five domestic institutional sectors, the *SNA* framework includes a set of accounts for transactions and positions with the rest of world, which are also included with more detail in the *BPM* framework. Like the *SNA* framework, the *BPM* framework is a sequence of accounts with balancing items or residuals. In addition, concepts and definitions are intentionally harmonized between the *SNA* and *BPM*. There are, however, two notable differences in scope and two notable organizational differences between the two frameworks.

One difference in scope is that the *SNA* framework includes three core accounts that are not necessary in the *BPM* framework: production account, generation of income account, and use of income account. The second difference in scope is that every transaction in the *SNA* framework is recorded from the perspective of each institutional sector to the transaction, which requires a quadruple entry accounting system with a debit and a credit for each sector. As a result, rest of world transactions in the *SNA* framework are recorded from the perspective of the rest of world. In contrast, each transaction in the *BPM* framework is recorded only from the perspective of resident institutional sectors, which allows for a more traditional double entry accounting system.

One organizational difference is that the *BPM* groups accounts according to whether they contribute to the balance of payments or the international investment position. The "balance of payments" consists of a current account, a capital account, and a financial account. The current account in the balance of payments includes a goods and services account and two income accounts. Entries in the current account generally capture current transactions, which is akin to the current accounts of the *SNA*. The "international investment position" records beginning and ending positions as well as changes between them for financial assets (i.e., claims of residents on non-residents or reserves) and liabilities (i.e., claims of non-residents on residents), which is akin to the balance sheet of the *SNA*. Changes between beginning and ending positions are attributable to financial account transactions and other changes in financial assets and liabilities that are not a result of transactions.

The second organizational difference between the *SNA* and *BPM* frameworks is classification of financial assets and liabilities. The *SNA* classifies financial assets and liabilities by type of instrument (e.g., currency, debt, equity, etc.). In addition to instrument classification, the *BPM* classifies financial assets and liabilities by functional category (e.g., direct investment, portfolio investment, reserve assets, etc.). Transactions among MNE parents and affiliates are included in the direct investment category.

Like balancing items in the *SNA* framework, balancing items in the *BPM* framework are generally considered key measures because they have implica-

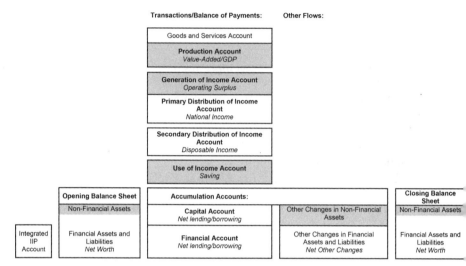

Figure 5.1   Overview of the SNA and BPM frameworks

Note: The figure is adapted from *BPM*, 6th edition, figure 2.1. Account names are shown in bold, and *SNA* balancing items are shown in italics. Shaded areas do not appear in the BPM framework.

tions for macroeconomic policy—they include items such as the balance on goods and services, the current account balance, net lending/borrowing, and the net international investment position. Figure 5.1 provides an overview of the *SNA* and *BPM* frameworks.

5.3.2   Institutional Units and Residence

The most basic unit of observation in the *SNA* and *BPM* is an institutional unit, which satisfies four criteria including the right to own assets and incur liabilities, the ability to make economic decisions and to be held legally accountable for the decisions, and the existence of a complete set of financial accounting records for the unit (or the feasibility of compiling a complete set). The *SNA* and *BPM* attribute stocks of assets and liabilities and related flows to an economy based on the residence of the institutional unit. Residence is the economic territory in which an institutional unit has a center of predominant economic interest, which is generally defined in the *SNA* and *BPM* as a physical location from which the unit engages in economic activity and transactions. An economic territory in the *SNA* and *BPM* is defined as the legal jurisdiction to which an institutional unit is subject. The *SNA* and *BPM* concepts of economic territory and residence are designed to attribute the stocks and flows of an institutional unit based on residence in a single economic territory, including stocks and flows within MNEs.

In the case of an MNE structured with a holding company or a special purpose entity that lacks physical presence, residence for the holding company or special purpose entity is determined in the *SNA* and *BPM* as the economic territory under whose legal jurisdiction the unit is incorporated or registered. If the unit is legally located in the same economy as its parent, the unit is consolidated with the parent and not recognized as a separate institutional unit because it does not satisfy the four *SNA* and *BPM* criteria for an institutional unit. However, if the unit is legally located in an economy different from its parent, the unit is recognized as a separate institutional unit. As a result, the *SNA* and *BPM* frameworks include stocks and flows within MNEs regardless of any physical economic activity.

The *SNA* and *BPM* recommendations to recognize an institutional unit based on *legal* registration or incorporation of holding companies and special purpose entities introduces an exception to the recommendation for determining residence based on predominant *economic* interest. The recommendation raises concerns for effects on "real" economic accounting measures such as GDP and GNI, since holding companies and special purpose entities are used by MNEs for transactions in intellectual property and other services. However, the recommendation is important to users of economic accounts such as central banks and other institutions responsible for supervising financial markets, since holding companies and special purpose entities are also used by MNEs to facilitate financing arrangements and to channel funds in a way that can expose MNEs and compiling economies to global financial risks.

5.3.3   Accounting Identities and Relationships

Based on the formulary methodology that we outline in section 5.4, we will be making adjustments to three measures: operating surplus, earnings on USDIA, and net interest receivable on USDIA. Before we make our adjustments, we first outline the relationships among the measures. We focus on production and primary income measures because we do not make adjustments to secondary income measures or measures of capital formation.

The most fundamental accounting identity in the *SNA* framework is the supply-use identity, which is embodied in the goods and services account. The intuition of the supply-use identity is that the total amount of goods and services available for use in an economy for a given period must be supplied by either domestic output (Q) or imports (M). The uses of goods and services include intermediate consumption (Z), final consumption (C), capital formation (I), and exports (X). The following equation summarizes the supply-use identity:

(1) $$Q + M = Z + C + I + X.$$

If we rearrange equation (1) as follows, the result yields two familiar approaches to measuring GDP:

(2) $Q - Z = C + I + X - M.$

The left side of equation (2) yields the production approach, and the right side yields the expenditure approach—both government expenditures and private expenditures are included in C and I.

An additional approach to measuring GDP is the income approach, which is a matter of summing the incomes generated through production. Incomes generated through production include compensation of employees (W), taxes (T) less subsidies (S) on production and imports, and operating surplus (O).[4] Each of the approaches to GDP can be summarized as follows:

(3)   GDP = $\underbrace{Q - X}_{\text{Production Approach}}$ = $\underbrace{C + I + X - M}_{\text{Expenditure Approach}}$ = $\underbrace{W + T - S + O}_{\text{Income Approach}}$.

In the *SNA* sequence of accounts, the production account reflects the production approach to measuring GDP. In addition, the generation of income account reflects the income approach, and the goods and services account reflects the expenditure approach.

5.3.3.1   Operating Surplus

In the *SNA* framework, operating surplus is a domestic measure—i.e., it is not calculated in the rest of world account and it is not included in the *BPM* framework. To better understand operating surplus, we start with a simplified version of net income (π) for a domestic firm (either MNE or non-MNE), which is the difference between total income and total expenditures.[5] Total income includes sales of output (q), holding gains (h), earnings on equity (d), and interest receivable (i_r).[6] Total expenditures include intermediate inputs (z), payments for labor (w), income taxes payable (t), and interest payable (i_p). Net income for the firm can be written as follows:

(4) $\pi = \underbrace{(q + h + d + i_r)}_{\text{Total Income}} - \underbrace{(z + w + t + i_p)}_{\text{Total Expenditures}}.$

Note that earnings on equity and interest flows may include transactions with directly held foreign affiliates when the domestic firm is an MNE.

To derive a measure of operating surplus, equation (4) is adjusted to exclude all components that do not result directly from current production,

---

4. Operating surplus may either be measured as a residual or measured directly, in which case the primary components include entrepreneurial income of enterprises and rental income on owner-occupied housing.

5. In this simplified version, we ignore taxes and subsidies on production and imports, economic depreciation on property, plant and equipment, rents on natural resources, and other income and expenditures, such as transfers, that are not explicitly included. We also assume the domestic firm has no indirect holdings in foreign affiliates.

6. For economic accounting purposes, the scope of sales (q) may include explicit sales of products to customers or may include implicit sales of output such as own-account software.

including holding gains, earnings on equity, interest receivable, income taxes payable, and interest payable. The result is as follows:

(5) $Operating\ Surplus = q - z - w.$

The first two terms in equation (5) (i.e., q minus z) reflect a measure of value added, and the last term (i.e., w) is a measure of compensation, which reflects labor's contribution to value added. Thus, operating surplus is invariant to all flows that do not result directly from current production.[7]

5.3.3.2   Income on Foreign Direct Investment

In the *SNA* and *BPM* frameworks, foreign direct investment by a domestic firm is treated as a financial asset, and income on foreign direct investment reflects a return on that asset. Income on foreign direct investment includes two components: earnings and net interest receivable. Earnings on foreign direct investment include the domestic firm's share of a foreign affiliate's earnings, whether distributed or reinvested. Since they reflect a return on a financial asset, earnings on foreign direct investment are derived by adjusting net income from equation (4) for the foreign affiliate to exclude holding gains only.[8] The calculation of earnings on direct investment in a wholly owned foreign affiliate (f) is as follows:[9]

(6) $Earnings\ on\ FDI = q^f - z^f - w^{f\cdot} + d^f + i_r^f - i_p^f - t^f.$

Foreign income taxes payable directly by the foreign affiliate are included in equation (6) because they reduce the domestic firm's return.

Net interest receivable on foreign direct investment includes interest receivable by the domestic firm from the foreign affiliate less interest payable by the domestic firm to the foreign affiliate. Net interest receivable by the domestic firm from the foreign affiliate is exactly equal to net interest payable by the foreign affiliate to the domestic firm, which if all interest flows in equation (6) are between the domestic firm and the foreign affiliate, can be calculated as follows:

---

7. Operating surplus is measured for all institutional sectors except the rest of world in the *SNA* framework. In contrast, entrepreneurial income is only measured for the nonfinancial and financial corporations sectors. To derive a measure of entrepreneurial income, operating surplus in equation (5) is adjusted to include earnings on equity, interest receivable, and interest payable. Thus, entrepreneurial income is only invariant to holding gains and income taxes payable. We do not articulate a measure of entrepreneurial income separate from operating surplus in this paper because we present all sectors as one total economy.

8. Since holding gains reflect changes in prices rather than production, they are not included in *SNA* and *BPM* measures of income. They are instead reflected in the *SNA* and *BPM* revaluation accounts, which contribute to changes in net worth and the international investment position.

9. For a majority-owned foreign affiliate that is not 100 percent owned, equation (6) would need to include the parent firm's ownership share in the foreign affiliate.

(7) $Net\ Interest\ Receivable\ on\ \mathrm{FDI} = i_p^f - i_r^f$.

Adding equations (6) and (7) yields the following equation for income on foreign direct investment:

(8) $Income\ on\ \mathrm{FDI} = q^f - z^f - w^f + d^f - t^f$.

Note that equation (6) can be subtracted from equation (8) to obtain a measure of net interest receivable on foreign direct investment as shown in equation (7)—this is the approach we take in computing the adjustment for net interest receivable. Since equation (7) assumes that all interest flows are between the domestic firm and the foreign affiliate, equation (8) includes no interest flows. However, interest flows may likely exist between the foreign affiliate and unrelated firms.

Intuitively, income on foreign direct investment reflects "actual" income after the elimination of intra-firm interest flows, and earnings on foreign direct investment reflect amounts booked to each part of the firm. Measures comparable to equations (6) and (8) for the foreign affiliate can also be calculated for the domestic firm in order to generate consolidated measures of earnings and income for the entire MNE.

5.3.3.3   Gross National Income

The difference between GDP and GNI in the *SNA* framework is income receivable from and payable to the rest of world, which can be summarized as follows:

(9)   GNI = GDP + *Income Receivable from Ro W – Income Payable*

        to Ro W.[10]

Income receivable from and payable to the rest of world includes income on foreign direct investment, income on portfolio investment, income on other investment, and income on reserve assets. Offshore profit shifting may affect each of the right-side components of equation (9). However, we only calculate adjustments for GDP and income receivable from the rest of world due to limited data on foreign MNEs that would be required to adjust income payable to rest of world.

5.4   Empirical Approach and Data

Our objective is to demonstrate the effects of offshore profit shifting on key US economic accounting measures that are compiled under a method of separate accounting. As explained in section 5.3, profit shifting within

10. GNI is an *SNA* term for income earned by domestic-owned factors of production anywhere in the world. In the United States, the equivalent of GNI is gross national product (GNP), which is derived from expenditure-based GDP by adding income receivable from the rest of world and subtracting income payable to the rest of world.

MNEs is generally accomplished under separate accounting through transfer pricing and global structuring that includes the use of holding companies or special purpose entities with very little physical presence and very little economic activity. While the identification of a typical institutional unit under the *SNA* and *BPM* recommendations depends on the four criteria that generally reflect economic substance, the *SNA* and *BPM* make an exception for holding companies and special purpose entities that are located in economies other than their parents or other affiliated entities. As a result, key measures throughout the *SNA* and *BPM* frameworks may not adequately capture the economic activity of some MNE entities. Thus, we follow Guvenen et al. (2017) and design an empirical framework to attribute economic accounting measures based on physical presence and other attributes of economic activity within MNEs. In particular, we use formulary apportionment to reattribute operating surplus, earnings, and net interest received by US parents from their foreign affiliates.

Formulary apportionment attributes measures to locations based on apportionment factors intended to reflect economic activity of each entity in an MNE—the essence of the *SNA* and *BPM* concepts of institutional unit and residence. For our apportionment factors, we use compensation and sales to unaffiliated parties. Compensation reflects labor's contribution to production. In contrast to employment, which only captures number of employees, compensation captures variation in returns to labor across entities located in different countries and industries, assuming workers are paid their marginal products. Likewise, the market presence of each entity is captured by the sales measure, and restricting sales to unaffiliated parties mitigates problems with transfer pricing and global structuring. Under each factor, formulary apportionment allocates less economic activity (e.g., operating surplus) to locations with low-paid workers and low market presence than to locations with high-paid workers and high market presence.[11]

In addition to the conceptual basis of our chosen apportionment factors, there are two practical considerations that support formulary apportionment as a reasonable alternative to separate accounting. First, formulary apportionment is suggested in the *SNA* as a potential alternative to allocate the market value of global firms in the balance sheet. As a result, formulary apportionment should also be a reasonable potential alternative to allocate production and income measures. Second, in contrast to the opacity of separate accounting under complex global structuring, formulary apportionment promotes transparency because it is easy to understand and easy to apply if appropriate data are available.

In lieu of formulary apportionment, another option for allocating mea-

---

11. Under country-by-country reporting, the Organisation for Economic Co-operation and Development (2015b) asserts that indicators such as profits, income taxes paid, revenue, number of employees, and tangible assets of individual MNE entities should help tax administrations determine the location of economic activity and evaluate the presence of audit risk.

sures on holding companies and special purpose entities is a treatment that either consolidates them entirely with their parents or considers them supranational entities with no location, as suggested for intellectual property products in Moulton and van de Ven (2018). If the apportionment factors for a holding company or special purpose entity reflect no economic activity (e.g., no compensation and no unaffiliated sales), then formulary apportionment allocates measures away entirely from the holding company or special purpose entity and toward other entities within the firm where economic activity is evident. The measures are split between the parent and other entities based on their own proportionate shares of economic activity reflected in the apportionment factors. As a result, formulary apportionment strikes a balance between the current treatment of holding companies and special purpose entities as completely separate institutional units and a treatment that either consolidates them entirely with their parents or considers them supranational entities with no location.

Despite the strengths associated with formulary apportionment as a measurement tool, note that we are not proposing formulary apportionment as a replacement for separate accounting in the *SNA* and *BPM* but rather using it to generate a point of reference to estimate the effects of profit shifting under a method of separate accounting.

5.4.1   Formulary Apportionment

Consider an MNE (m) that is composed of one domestic parent and at least one foreign affiliate. Let ψ denote operating surplus, earnings, or income determined under a method of separate accounting for each entity (n) (i.e., parent and foreign affiliates). Following Guvenen et al. (2017), we construct for each entity in the MNE an apportionment weight (ω_n) that reflects the entity's share of the total apportionment factors. Weighting unaffiliated sales and compensation equally yields the following apportionment weights for each entity within the MNE:

(10)
$$\omega_n = \underbrace{\left(\frac{1}{2} \times \frac{w_i l_i}{\sum_i w_i l_i} \right)}_{\text{Compensation}} + \underbrace{\left(\frac{1}{2} \times \frac{p_i y_i}{\sum_i p_i y_i} \right)}_{\text{Unaffiliated Sales}} \quad \forall n \in m .^{12}$$

Under formulary apportionment, measured operating surplus, earnings, or income (F) attributable to each entity n within MNE m is calculated as follows:

(11)
$$\bar{\psi}_n = \omega_n \sum_i \psi_i \quad \forall n \in m .$$

---

12. Results will be affected by the chosen apportionment factors, and papers such as Runkel and Schjelderup (2011) contribute to a body of literature that focuses solely on the choice of apportionment factors. Guvenen et al. (2017) present alternative results under different weights on the apportionment factors—weighting compensation 100 percent and unaffiliated sales 100 percent in separate calculations—and find that their results are robust to the alternative weighting schemes. They ultimately settle on a simple average for their core results.

The measure attributable to each entity under formulary apportionment is a weighted average of the consolidated measure determined for the MNE (i.e., parent and foreign affiliates) under separate accounting. Thus, measured operating surplus, earnings, or income attributable to each entity is proportionate to the entity's economic activity embodied by the chosen apportionment factors.

The formulary adjustment for each entity is calculated by subtracting the measure determined under separate accounting from the measure determined under formulary apportionment as follows:

$$(12) \qquad \varepsilon_n = \bar{\psi}_n - \psi_n \ \forall n \in m.$$

The formulary adjustment for each entity reflects an amount of operating surplus, earnings, or income to be added to or subtracted from each entity, depending on whether the adjustment is positive or negative. The aggregate formulary adjustment for US parents is exactly equal (with an opposite sign) to the aggregate formulary adjustment for their foreign affiliates.

5.4.2   Data

We use unpublished firm-level survey data collected by the Bureau of Economic Analysis (BEA) on the financial and operating activities of US MNEs—referred to as the activities of multinational enterprise (AMNE) data—and on the direct investment income transactions of US MNEs for 2014.[13] The AMNE data cover the worldwide operations of US MNEs and contain balance sheet information and income statement information for US parents and their foreign affiliates. For each US parent and foreign affiliate, the data include information on net income and the components of total income and total expenditures consistent with equation (4) under separate accounting. In addition, the data include compensation and unaffiliated sales for each US parent and foreign affiliate necessary for the apportionment weights in equation (10). Moreover, the AMNE data include information necessary to construct measures of operating surplus, earnings, and income equivalent to equations (5), (6), and (8) for each US parent and foreign affiliate. The direct investment income transactions data include data on earnings of foreign affiliates and interest flows between US parents and foreign affiliates.[14]

In addition to the firm-level survey data, we use published data for 2014

13. The financial and operating data are reported on the Benchmark Survey of U.S. Direct Investment Abroad (form BE-10) for all U.S. parents and all foreign affiliates. The income transactions data are reported on the Quarterly Survey of U.S. Direct Investment Abroad Direct Transactions of U.S. Reporter with Foreign Affiliates (form BE-577) subject to thresholds for assets, sales, and net income.
14. The income transactions data do not include information on operations that are needed to construct the apportionment factors. Likewise, the data do not include information on U.S. parents. In order to get a complete picture of each U.S. MNE, we use the AMNE data to generate proxies for earnings and income.

from the US National Income and Product Accounts (NIPAs), the US Industry Economic Accounts (IEAs), the US Integrated Macroeconomic Accounts (IMAs), the US International Transactions Accounts (ITAs), and the US International Investment Position (IIP) accounts. We use the NIPA data and the IEA data to compile the *SNA* current accounts, and we use the IMA data to compile the *SNA* accumulation accounts and balance sheets. We use the ITA data to compile the *BPM* balance of payments, and we use the IIP data to compile the *BPM* international investment position.[15]

5.4.3   Adjustments

We calculate formulary adjustments as shown in equation (12) using the measures constructed from the BEA survey data—operating surplus, earnings, and income—for each US parent and each foreign affiliate. We then tabulate the formulary adjustments for each measure to derive an aggregate adjustment for domestic operating surplus, earnings on USDIA, and income on USDIA. To derive an aggregate formulary adjustment for net interest receivable on USDIA consistent with equation (7), we subtract the aggregate adjustment for earnings on USDIA from the aggregate adjustment for income on USDIA.

Since the scope of our adjustments is limited to US MNEs due to data limitations, we can rewrite equation (9) to focus exclusively on incomes receivable on USDIA as follows:

(13)   GNI = GDP + *Earnings on* USDIA + *Net Interest Receivable on*

USDIA ± ⋯.

The ellipsis in equation (13) denotes all omitted incomes receivable and payable that account for differences between GDP and GNI. We apply our aggregate formulary adjustments constructed with the unpublished survey data to the relevant published aggregates in each of the *SNA* and *BPM* frameworks. In particular, we apply our aggregate adjustment for operating surplus to US GDP. Likewise, we apply our aggregate adjustment for earnings on USDIA to the portion of earnings on USDIA that is calculated as reinvested, since dividends reflect an actual payment. Finally, we apply our aggregate adjustment for net interest receivable on USDIA to the interest portion of income on USDIA.

5.5   Results

Our formulary adjustment for operating surplus in equation (5) amounts to a $255.5 billion increase in US operating surplus in 2014, which implies that

---

15. In practice, there are statistical discrepancies between key measures for the U.S.—such as net lending/borrowing and trade balances—in the NIPAs, IMAs, ITAs, and IIP as a result of different source data and measurement methodologies. We do not attempt to reconcile the discrepancies but rather use data as published in each of the accounts.

level of value added attributable to foreign affiliates of US MNEs under a method of separate accounting is instead attributable to US parents under a method of formulary apportionment. Likewise, our adjustment for earnings on USDIA in equation (6) amounts to a $273.1 billion decrease in earnings on USDIA, which reflects earnings attributable to foreign operations of US-owned firms under separate accounting that are no longer attributable under formulary apportionment because they are accrued domestically. In addition, the adjustment for net interest receivable on USDIA amounts to an $8.7 billion decrease, which is the difference between the adjustment for income on USDIA of $281.8 billion calculated with equation (8) and the adjustment for earnings on USDIA of $273.1 billion. The adjustment for net interest suggests that financing arrangements between US parents and foreign affiliates also raise the measure of income on USDIA under the *SNA* and *BPM* recommendations for separate accounting. For each of the adjustments, about 75 percent of the adjustment is attributable to foreign affiliates classified as holding companies, which is consistent with profit shifting accomplished through the use of holding companies and special purpose entities.

We present three sets of adjusted and unadjusted (i.e., published) measures. The first set (tables 5.1–5.4) shows adjusted and unadjusted measures for the United States in the *BPM* framework. The second set (tables 5.5–5.10) shows adjusted and unadjusted measures for the United States in the *SNA* framework. The *SNA* and *BPM* sets of results demonstrate the effects of offshore profit shifting on the key measures in each framework. The initial entries for our adjustments are outlined in boxes in our presentation of the *SNA* and *BPM* accounts. In addition, the adjustments are shown separately by type: operating surplus, earnings on USDIA, and net interest received on USDIA.[16] The third set of results includes figures to demonstrate implications for five common analytic uses of the US economic accounts: labor share of income, national saving rates, returns on domestic nonfinancial business, returns on foreign direct investment, and external balances.

5.5.1   BPM Measures

The *BPM* balance of payments is presented in table 5.1. In the goods and services account, we apply the $255.5 billion adjustment for operating sur-

---

16. Although the standard presentation of BEA statistics on direct investment transactions, positions, and associated income is on an asset-liability basis in accordance with international guidelines, we use a directional basis in tables 5.1 to 5.2 and 5.5 to 5.10. For our purposes, the directional basis is more analytically useful, and it is consistent with the recording of direct investment in the U.S. IMAs. For equity, there is no difference between a directional basis and an asset-liability basis. However, there is a difference for debt. Measures of direct investment transactions and earnings are shown with current cost adjustment in tables 5.1 to 5.2 and 5.5 to 5.10. Direct investment positions are shown at market value in tables 5.3 and 5.4. We provide a reconciliation of the direct investment position on a directional basis with current cost adjustment and the direct investment position on an asset-liability basis at market value in appendix table 5A.1.

Table 5.1   *BPM* balance of payments current account and capital account for the United States

Line	Credits Published (1)	Op. surplus (2)	Earnings (3)	Net interest (4)	Adjusted (5)	BPM code	SNA code		Debits Published (6)	Op. surplus (7)	Earnings (8)	Net interest (9)	Adjusted (10)
1							B12	Current account balance	−373.8	255.5	−273.1	−8.7	−400.2
								Goods and Services Account					
2	2,375.9	255.5			2,631.4	1.A	P6/P7	Transactions in goods and services	2,866.2				2,866.2
3							B11	Balance on goods and services	−490.3	255.5			−234.9
4	1,634.0				1,634.0	1.A.a	P61/P71	Goods	2,385.5				2,385.5
5								Balance on trade in goods	−751.5				−751.5
6	1,611.0				1,611.0	1.A.a.1		General merchandise	2,370.0				2,370.0
7	0.3				0.3	1.A.a.2		Net exports of goods under merchanting					
8	22.7				22.7	1.A.a.3		Nonmonetary gold	15.5				15.5
9	741.9	255.5			997.4	1.A.b	P72/P82	Services	480.8				480.8
10								Balance on trade in services	261.2	255.5			516.6
11	21.1				21.1	1.A.b.2		Maintenance and repair	7.5				7.5
12	282.6				282.6	1.A.b.3-4		Transport and travel	199.9				199.9
13	124.3				124.3	1.A.b.6-7		Insurance and finance	75.9				75.9
14	129.7	255.5			385.2	1.A.b.8		Charges for the use of intellectual property	42.0				42.0
15	34.7				34.7	1.A.b.9		Telecommunications and information	36.5				36.5

#	Value	−273.1	−8.7	Code	Value	Item	Value	Adj	Value
16	128.9			1.A.b.10	128.9	Other business services	94.8		94.8
17	20.5			1.A.b.12	20.5	Government goods and services	24.2		24.2
						Primary Income Account			
18	807.1	−273.1	−8.7	1.B	525.3	Transactions in primary income	596.4		596.4
19						Balance on primary income	210.8	−273.1 / −8.7	−71.1
20	6.5			1.B.1 — D1	6.5	Compensation of employees	17.1		17.1
21	800.6	−273.1	−8.7	1.B.2	518.8	Investment income	579.3		579.3
22	464.6	−273.1	−8.7	1.B.2.1 — D4D	182.7	Direct investment	187.9		187.9
23	455.6	−273.1		1.B.2.1.1	182.5	Income on equity	162.4		162.4
24	144.0			1.B.2.1.1.1 — D42D	144.0	Dividends and withdrawals	67.6		67.6
25	311.6	−273.1 (boxed)		1.B.2.1.1.2 — D43D	38.5	Reinvested earnings	94.8		94.8
26	9.0		−8.7	1.B.2.1.2 — D41D	0.3	Interest	25.4		25.4
27	305.0			1.B.2.2 — D4P	305.0	Portfolio investment	377.5		377.5
28	30.7			1.B.2.3 — D4O	30.7	Other investment	13.9		13.9
29	0.3			1.B.2.4 — D4R	0.3	Reserve assets			
						Secondary Income Account			
30	140.1			1.C	140.1	Transactions in secondary income	234.3		234.3
31						Balance on secondary income	−94.2		−94.2
						Capital Account			
32				2		Capital account balance	0.0		0.0
33				2.1 — N2		Gross acquisitions			
34	0.0			2.2 — D9	0.0	Capital transfers	0.0		0.0
35	0.0			B9	0.0	Net lending/borrowing (current and capital account)	−373.8	255.5 −273.1 −8.7	−400.2

plus as an implied increase in charges for the use of intellectual property (row 14) by foreign affiliates. The increase in measured exports of goods and services is 10.8 percent, which is a result of the increase in US exports of services with no change for trade in goods.

The treatment of the adjustment as charges for the use of intellectual property is consistent with a simple model outlined in Guvenen et al. (2017) that attributes profit shifting made possible by the mobility of intangible capital. Likewise, the treatment is consistent with literature that focuses on intangible capital as an explanation for higher rates of return earned by US MNEs on their direct investments abroad compared with rates of return earned by foreign MNEs on their direct investments in the United States (McGrattan and Prescott 2010; Bridgman 2014). Intangible capital may result from research and development (R&D) efforts, which are generally embodied in observable measures such as patents or formulas in addition to a firm's profits. Intangible capital may also result from efforts other than R&D such as brand and trademark development, management consulting, and workforce training, which are generally less observable but still reflected in the firm's profits. Corrado, Hulten, and Sichel (2009) refer to the latter form of intangible capital as "economic competencies," and subsequent authors have referred to it as "organization capital" (e.g., Eisfeldt and Papanikolaou 2013). We consider transactions (explicit and implicit) in both forms of intangible capital to be candidates for charges for the use of intellectual property.

In the primary income account in table 5.1, we apply the $273.1 billion adjustment for earnings on USDIA as a decrease in reinvested earnings (row 25). Likewise, we apply the $8.7 billion adjustment for net interest received on USDIA as a decrease in interest flows (row 26), which we consider a change in the price of intra-firm lending (i.e., arm's length interest rates) rather than a change in the underlying stocks of intra-firm debt.[17] In addition, the adjustment for net interest implies either a decrease in interest received by US parents from their foreign affiliates or an increase in inter-

17. This treatment means we do not adjust the underlying stocks of intra-firm debt. In reality, the result may suggest changes in both the price of intra-firm lending and stocks of intra-firm debt. In either case, the result is counterintuitive if firms engage in intra-firm financing arrangements to shift profits—a practice known as earnings stripping. In a report to Congress, the U.S. Treasury Department (2007) concludes that U.S. MNEs are less inclined to engage in earnings stripping than foreign MNEs operating in the United States because U.S. firms are subject to anti-deferral rules and passive income rules under U.S. Treasury Regulations that do not apply to foreign firms. BEA's published statistics on direct investment seem to support this conclusion. In 2014, U.S. affiliates' payments of interest to foreign parents were $30.0 billion on $945.8 billion of debt—an implied interest rate of 3.2 percent—and U.S. affiliates' interest receipts were $4.6 billion on $384.7 billion of debt—an implied interest rate of 1.2 percent—which suggests U.S. affiliates incurred a higher interest expense per dollar of debt. In contrast, U.S. parents' payments of interest to foreign affiliates were $5.7 billion on $528.0 billion of debt—an implied interest rate of 1.1 percent—and U.S. parents' interest receipts were $14.7 billion on $764.6 billion of debt—an implied interest rate of 1.9 percent—which suggests U.S. parents incurred lower interest expense per dollar of debt.

est paid by US parents to their foreign affiliates.[18] The decrease in measured income receivable from non-residents is 34.9 percent. We do not calculate any measured effects in the secondary income account.

The positive effects of the operating surplus adjustment in the goods and services account are more than offset by the larger negative adjustments for earnings and net interest received on USDIA in the primary income account. Thus, the net effect on the current account balance (row 1) in table 5.1 is a $26.4 billion decrease—7.1 percent. Measured US net borrowing (row 35) increases as a result of changes in the preceding accounts. The only change in the financial account in table 5.2 is on measured equity (rows 5 and 6) as a result of the previous adjustment transactions, which also increases net borrowing in the financial account. The increases in measured US net borrowing in both the current and capital accounts and the financial account are 7.1 percent and 8.1 percent, respectively, the difference of which is a result of the statistical discrepancy between the two accounts.

The *BPM* international investment position for 2014 is presented in table 5.3. Since the international investment position reflects stocks of assets and liabilities, we include accumulations for each of our adjustment measures in the financial account for 1973–2014 using annual estimates from Guvenen et al. (2017). The cumulative adjustments for operating surplus, earnings on USDIA, and net interest received on USDIA (row 3) from the financial account are $3.457 trillion, $3.587 trillion, and $145.4 billion, respectively. The decrease in measured international investment position assets is 1.1 percent because the increases in services exports are less than the decreases in reinvested earnings and net interest receivable on USDIA over time. Thus, the decrease in the measured net international investment position is 4.0 percent.

The *BPM* beginning and ending direct investment positions for 2014 are presented in table 5.4, which provides further detail on rows 2 to 4 in table 5.3. The difference between the international investment position at the beginning and end of the year results from two sources: financial transactions and other changes. Given the modest size of the net adjustments for financial transactions—a decrease of $26.4 billion—we do not make an adjustment for other changes. For the beginning net direct investment position (column 5), the cumulative adjustments decrease the US net direct investment position by 15.4 percent. For the ending net direct investment position (column 8), the cumulative adjustments decrease the US net direct investment position by 27.8 percent because the increases in services exports are less than the decreases in reinvested earnings and net interest receivable on USDIA over time.

---

18. The $8.7 billion decrease reduces net interest received by U.S. parents published for 2014 to almost nothing and could generate a negative net interest received in some years. Since net interest received includes interest received from foreign affiliates less interest paid to foreign affiliates, net interest received can be positive, negative, or zero.

Table 5.2 *BPM* balance of payments financial account for the United States

Line	Net acquisition of financial assets — Published (1)	Adjustments: Operating surplus (2)	Adjustments: Earnings (3)	Adjustments: Net interest (4)	Adjusted (5)	BPM Code	SNA Code		Net incurrence of liabilities — Published (6)	Adjustments: Operating surplus (7)	Adjustments: Earnings (8)	Adjustments: Net interest (9)	Adjusted (10)
1								Stat. disc. (current and capital-financial account)	−47.0				−47.0
2	313.5	255.5	−273.1	−8.7	287.2		B9	Net lending / borrowing (financial account)	−326.8	255.5	−273.1	−8.7	−353.2
3	330.4	255.5	−273.1	−8.7	304.0	3.1	FD	Direct investment	212.3				212.3
4	18.8	255.5		−8.7	265.5	3.1.1	F5D	Equity	146.4				146.4
5	311.6		−273.1		38.5	3.1.1.1		Equity other than reinvestment of earnings	51.6				51.6
6	−16.8				−16.8	3.1.1.2		Reinvestment of earnings	94.8				94.8
7	582.7				582.7	3.1.2	F3D	Debt instruments	65.9				65.9
8	431.6				431.6	3.2	FP	Portfolio investment	703.5				703.5
9	151.1				151.1	3.2.1	F5P	Equity	154.3				154.3
10						3.2.2	F3P	Debt securities	549.2				549.2
11	−99.2				−99.2	3.3	F7F	Financial derivatives	54.3				54.3
12	−161.8				−161.8	3.4	FO	Other investment	150.2				150.2
13	68.4				68.4	3.4.2	F2O	Currency and deposits	59.7				59.7
14	−5.8				−5.8	3.4.3	F4O	Loans	77.9				77.9
15						3.4.4-6		Other	12.6				12.6
16	−3.6				−3.6	3.5	FR	Reserves					
17	0.0				0.0	3.5.1	F11	Monetary gold					
18	0.0				0.0	3.5.2	F12	Special drawing rights					
19	−3.8				−3.8	3.5.3		Reserve position in the IMF					
20	0.2				0.2	3.5.4		Other					
21	793.5	255.5	−273.1	−8.7	767.1	3	F	Totals	1,120.3				1,120.3

Table 5.3 BPM international investment position for the United States

Line	Assets						BPM code	SNA code	Liabilities				
	Published	Operating surplus	Earnings	Net interest	Adjusted				Published	Operating surplus	Earnings	Net interest	Adjusted
	(1)	(2)	(3)	(4)	(5)				(6)	(7)	(8)	(9)	(10)
1		3,451.5	−3,587.0	−145.4		Net position		B90	−6,980.2	3,451.5	−3,587.0	−145.4	−7,261.2
2	7,189.4	3,451.5	−3,587.0	−145.4	6,908.5	Direct investment	1	AFD	6,369.5				6,369.5
3	6,040.1	3,451.5	−3,587.0	−145.4	5,759.2	Equity	1.1	AF5D	4,895.8				4,895.8
4	1,149.3				1,149.3	Debt instruments	1.2	AF3D	1,473.8				1,473.8
5	9,704.2				9,704.2	Portfolio investment	2	AFP	16,921.4				16,921.4
6	6,770.6				6,770.6	Equity	2.1	AF5P	6,642.5				6,642.5
7	2,933.6				2,933.6	Debt securities	2.2	AF3P	10,278.9				10,278.9
8	3,252.3				3,252.3	Financial derivatives	3	AF7F	3,166.8				3,166.8
9	4,252.4				4,252.4	Other investment	4	AFO	5,355.1				5,355.1
10	1,807.1				1,807.1	Currency and deposits	4.2	AF2O	2,890.0				2,890.0
11	2,398.2				2,398.2	Loans	4.3	AF4O	2,253.7				2,253.7
12	47.0				47.0	Other	4.4–7		211.5				211.5
13	434.3				434.3	Reserves	5	AFR					
14	315.4				315.4	Monetary gold	5.1	AF11					
15	51.9				51.9	Special drawing rights	5.2	AF12					
16	25.2				25.2	Reserve position in the IMF	5.3						
17	41.8				41.8	Other	5.4						
18	24,832.6	3,451.5	−3,587.0	−145.4	24,551.7	Totals		AF	31,812.8	3,451.5	−3,587.0	−145.4	31,812.8

Table 5.4   BPM direct investment position for the United States

	Line	Assets Beginning of year (1)	Changes Financial transactions (2)	Changes Other changes (3)	End of year (4)	BPM code	SNA code		Liabilities Beginning of year (5)	Changes Financial transactions (6)	Changes Other changes (7)	End of year (8)
Published	1							Net position	1,305.8	101.2	−587.1	819.8
Published	2	7,120.7	338.9	−270.2	7,189.4	1	AFD	Direct investment	5,814.9	237.7	316.9	6,369.5
Published	3	6,054.2	330.4	344.5	6,040.1	1.1	AF5D	Equity	4,443.2	146.4	306.1	4,895.7
Published	4	1,066.5	8.5	74.3	1,149.3	1.2	AF3D	Debt instruments	1,371.7	91.2	10.8	1,473.8
Adjustments	5							Net position	−201.7	−26.4		−228.0
Adjustments	6	−201.7	−26.4		−228.0	1	AFD	Direct investment				
Adjustments	7	−201.7	−26.4		−228.0	1.1	AF5D	Equity				
Adjustments	8					1.2	AF3D	Debt instruments				
Adjusted	9							Net position	1,104.1	74.8	−587.1	591.8
Adjusted	10	6,919.0	312.5	−270.2	6,961.3	1	AFD	Direct investment	5,814.9	237.7	316.9	6,369.5
Adjusted	11	5,852.6	304.0	−344.5	5,812.1	1.1	AF5D	Equity	4,443.2	146.4	306.1	4,895.7
Adjusted	12	1,066.5	8.5	74.3	1,149.2	1.2	AF3D	Debt instruments	1,371.7	91.2	10.8	1,473.8

5.5.2   SNA Measures

The *SNA* current accounts are presented in tables 5.5 and 5.6. The $255.5 billion adjustment for operating surplus in 2014 is a net reattribution of measured operating surplus from foreign affiliates to US parents, which we apply in the production account as an implied increase in output (row 3) and in the goods and services account as an implied increase in exports (row 2) to account for the increase in receipts on the use of intellectual property, which was presented in the discussion of the *BPM* balance of payments in section 5.5.1. Thus, the supply-use identity is maintained, and the statistical discrepancy is unaffected. The increase in GDP is 1.5 percent, and the percentage increase in operating surplus is 3.5 percent.

The $273.1 billion adjustment for earnings on USDIA is also a net reattribution of measured earnings from foreign affiliates to US parents, which we apply in the allocation of primary income account as a decrease in reinvested earnings on foreign direct investment (row 20). Likewise, the $8.7 billion adjustment for net interest received on USDIA reflects a reduction in measured net interest received by US parents from their foreign affiliates, which we also apply in the primary income account as a decrease in interest flows (row 18). The decrease in income receivable from the rest of world for both adjustments is 33.5 percent, which is a bit lower than the BPM measures as a result of the difference in the scope of rest of world transactions between the two sets of accounts.[19]

From an accounting perspective, the adjustment for operating surplus in the production and generation of income accounts may be expected to exactly offset the adjustments for earnings and net interest received on USDIA in the allocation of primary income account. However, the effect of the operating surplus adjustment is more than offset by the effect for earnings and net interest received because of the differences in concepts outlined in section 5.3.3. Thus, the net effect on measured GNI is a $26.4 billion decrease—about 0.1 percent—which we demonstrated is also the change in the current account balance. Absent any related changes in the secondary distribution of income account, the decrease in measured disposable income is also about 0.1 percent. However, measured gross saving in the use of disposable income account decreases by 0.8 percent, and measured net saving decreases by 4.3 percent. The $26.4 billion decrease in GNI, disposable income, and saving is a contrast to the increase in operating surplus and GDP. However, the $26.4 billion decrease is small relative to the effects on operating surplus and income on USDIA. In addition, all adjustments—operating surplus, earnings on USDIA, income on USDIA—are of similar magnitudes.

The *SNA* accumulation accounts are presented in tables 5.7 and 5.8. The

19. In the U.S. NIPAs, U.S. territories, Puerto Rico, and the Northern Mariana Islands are included in the rest of world. In the U.S. ITAs, they are treated as part of the United States.

Table 5.5 SNA current accounts for the United States: Uses

Line	SNA code		Rest of world					Total economy				
				Adjustments					Adjustments			
			Published	Operating surplus	Earnings	Net interest	Adjusted	Published	Operating surplus	Earnings	Net interest	Adjusted
			(1)	(2)	(3)	(4)	(5)	(6)	(7)	(8)	(9)	(10)
		Production Account										
1	P7	Imports of goods and services	2,373.6				2,629.1					
2	P6	Exports of goods and services		255.5								
3	P1	Output										
4	P2	Intermediate consumption						13,606.4				13,606.4
5	B1	GDP (expenditure-based)	509.5					17,427.6	255.5			17,683.1
6	B11	External balance of goods and services		-255.5			254.0					
		Generation of Income Account										
7		Statistical discrepancy ($GDP^I - GDP^E$)										
8	B1	GDP (income-based)										
9	D1	Compensation of employees						9,267.0				9,267.0
10	D2	Taxes on production and imports						1,221.6				1,221.6
11	D3	Subsidies (−)						-58.1				-58.1
12	B2	Operating surplus, gross						7,227.0	255.5			7,482.5
		Allocation of Primary Income Account										
13	B2	Operating surplus, gross										
14	D1	Compensation of employees	6.5				6.5					

Line	Code	Item	(1)	(2)	(3)	(4)	(5)	(6)	(7)	(8)
15	D2	Taxes on production								
16	D3	Subsides on production (−)								
17	D4	Property income	840.7	−273.1	558.9					6,236.3
18	D41	Interest	154.4	−8.7	145.7					3,228.9
19	D42	Distributed income of corporations	341.7		341.7					2,888.9
20	D43	Reinvested earnings on FDI	344.6	−273.1	71.5					95.0
21	D4	Rent								23.5
22	B5	Gross national income				17,892.1	255.5	−273.1	−8.7	17,865.7
		Secondary Distrib. of Income Account								
23	B5	Gross national income								
24	D5	Current transfers	145.3		145.3	6,827.2				6,827.2
25	D5	Current taxes on income, wealth, etc.				2,290.9				2,290.9
26	D61	Net social contributions				1,155.3				1,155.3
27	D62	Social benefits other than STiK				2,518.1				2,518.1
28	D7	Other current transfers				862.9				862.9
29	B6	Disposable income, gross				17,783.1	255.5	−273.1	−8.7	17,756.7
		Use of Disposable Income Account								
30	B6	Disposable income, gross								
31	P3	Final consumption expenditure				14,426.4				14,426.4
32	B8g	Saving, gross				3,356.7	255.5	−273.1	−8.7	3,330.3
33	P51c	Consumption of fixed capital				−2,748.0				−2,748.0
34	B8n	Saving, net				608.7	255.5	−273.1	−8.7	582.3
35	B12	Current external balance	384.0				−255.5	273.1	8.7	410.4

Table 5.6   *SNA* current accounts for the United States: Resources

			Rest of world					Total economy				
				Adjustments					Adjustments			
Line	*SNA* code		Published	Operating surplus	Earnings	Net interest	Adjusted	Published	Operating surplus	Earnings	Net interest	Adjusted
			(1)	(2)	(3)	(4)	(5)	(6)	(7)	(8)	(9)	(10)
		Production Account										
1	P7	Imports of goods and services	2,883.1									
2	P6	Exports of goods and services					2,883.1					
3	P1	Output						31,034.0	255.5			31,289.5
4	P2	Intermediate consumption										
5	B1	GDP (expenditure-based)										
6	B11	External balance of goods and services										
		Generation of Income Account										
7		Statistical discrepancy (GDP^I − GDP^E)						229.9				229.9
8	B1	GDP (income-based)						17,657.5	255.5			17,913.0
9	D1	Compensation of employees										
10	D2	Taxes on production and imports										
11	D3	Subsidies (-)										
12	B2	Operating surplus, gross							255.5			
		Allocation of Primary Income Account										
13	B2	Operating surplus, gross						7,227.0	255.5			7,482.5
14	D1	Compensation of employees	17.1				17.1	9,256.5				9,256.5

No.	Code	Item						
15	D2	Taxes on production		1,221.6				1,221.6
16	D3	Subsides on production (-)		-58.1				-58.1
17	D4	Property income	595.5	6,481.4		-273.1	-8.7	6,199.6
18	D41	Interest	306.6	3,076.5				3,067.8
19	D42	Distributed income of corporations	193.9	3,036.3				3,036.8
20	D43	Reinvested earnings on FDI	95.0	344.6		-273.1	-8.7	71.5
21	D4	Rent		23.5				23.5
22	B5	Gross national income						
		Secondary Distrib. of Income Account						
23	B5	Gross national income		17,892.1	255.5	-273.1	-8.7	17,865.7
24		Current transfers	254.4	6,718.2				6,718.2
25	D5	Current taxes on income, wealth, etc.		2,300.5				2,300.5
26	D61	Net social contributions		1,160.5				1,160.5
27	D62	Social benefits other than STiK		2,498.8				2,498.8
28	D7	Other current transfers		758.4				758.4
29	B6	Disposable income, gross						
		Use of Disposable Income Account						
30	B6	Disposable income, gross		17,785.1	255.5	-273.1	-8.7	17,756.7
31	P3	Final consumption expenditure						
32	B8g	Saving, gross						
33	P51c	Consumption of fixed capital						
34	B8n	Saving, net						
35	B12	Current external balance						

Table 5.7 SNA accumulation accounts for the United States: Changes in assets

			Rest of world					Total economy				
				Adjustments					Adjustments			
Line	SNA code		Published	Operating surplus	Earnings	Net interest	Adjusted	Published	Operating surplus	Earnings	Net interest	Adjusted
			(1)	(2)	(3)	(4)	(5)	(6)	(7)	(8)	(9)	(10)
		Capital Account										
36	B8	Saving, net										
37	B12	Current external balance										
38	P5g	Gross capital formation						3,510.8				3,510.8
39	P5n	Net capital formation						762.8				762.8
40	P51g	Gross fixed capital formation						3,432.8				3,432.8
41	P52	Changes in inventories						78.0				78.0
42	P51c	Consumption of fixed capital						−2,748.0				−2,748.0
43	D9r	Capital transfers, receivable										
44	D9p	Capital transfers, payable										
45	B101	Changes in net worth due to saving and capital transfers										
46		Reverse stat. disc. (GDP^I − GDP^E)										
47	B9	Net lending / borrowing (capital account)	384.4	−255.5	273.1	8.7	410.8	−384.4	255.5	−273.1	−8.7	−410.8
		Financial Account										
48		Stat. disc. (capital-financial account)										
49	B9	Net lending / borrowing (financial account)										

#	Code	Item						
50		Net acquisition of financial assets/liabilities	1,150.6	5,465.5	255.5	−273.1	−8.7	5,439.1
51	F1	Monetary gold and SDRs	0.0	0.0				0.0
52	F2	Currency and deposits	101.1	843.7				843.7
53	F3	Debt securities	533.6	802.5				802.5
54	F4	Loans	136.7	964.3				964.3
55	F51	Equity	331.9	805.0	255.5	−273.1	−8.7	778.6
56	F52	Investment fund shares	34.7	282.0				282.0
57	F6	Insurance, pension and stand. guar. sch.	0.0	651.4				651.4
58	F8	Other receivables/payables	12.6	1,116.6				1,116.6
		Other Changes in Vol. of Assets Account						
59	B102	Changes in net worth due to OCVA						
		Revaluation Account						
60	AN	Non-financial assets		3,064.5				3,064.5
61	AF	Financial assets/liabilities	680.7	4,183.5				4,183.5
62	AF1	Monetary gold and SDRs	−3.2	−3.3				−3.3
63	AF2	Currency and deposits	−0.2	−1.7				−1.7
64	AF3	Debt securities	53.3	311.7				311.7
65	AF4	Loans	0.0	0.0				0.0
66	AF5	Equity	608.0	3,308.7				3,308.7
67	AF5	Investment fund shares	23.1	480.2				480.2
68	AF6	Insurance, pension and stand. guar. sch.	0.0	87.9				87.9
69	AF8	Other receivables/payables	−0.3	0.0				0.0
70	B103	Changes in net worth due to nominal holding gains and losses						

Table 5.8   SNA accumulation accounts for the United States: Changes in liabilities or net worth

			Rest of world					Total economy				
				Adjustments					Adjustments			
Line	SNA code		Published	Operating surplus	Earnings	Net interest	Adjusted	Published	Operating surplus	Earnings	Net interest	Adjusted
			(1)	(2)	(3)	(4)	(5)	(6)	(7)	(8)	(9)	(10)
		Capital Account										
36	B8	Saving, net						608.7	255.5	−273.1	−8.7	582.3
37	B12	Current external balance	384.0	−255.5	273.1	8.7	410.4					
38	P5g	Gross capital formation										
39	P5n	Net capital formation										
40	P51g	Gross fixed capital formation										
41	P52	Changes in inventories										
42	P51c	Consumption of fixed capital										
43	D9r	Capital transfers, receivable	0.4				0.4	110.6				110.6
44	D9p	Capital transfers, payable	0.0				0.0	−111.0				−111.0
45	B101	Changes in net worth due to saving and capital transfers	384.4	−255.5	273.1	8.7	410.8	608.3	255.5	−273.1	−8.7	581.9
46		Reverse stat. disc. (GDP^I − GDP^E)						−229.9				−229.9
47	B9	Net lending / borrowing (capital account)										
		Financial Account										
48		Stat. disc. (capital-financial account)	50.3				50.3	−45.4				−45.4
49	B9	Net lending / borrowing (financial account)	334.1	−255.5	273.1	8.7	360.5	−339.0	255.5	−273.1	−8.7	−365.4

50		Net acquisition of financial assets/liabilities	816.5	255.5	−273.1	−8.7	790.1	5,804.5
51	F1	Monetary gold and SDRs	0.0				0.0	0.0
52	F2	Currency and deposits	−122.6				−122.6	924.9
53	F3	Debt securities	162.8				162.8	1,173.3
54	F4	Loans	49.2				49.2	946.6
55	F51	Equity	732.9	255.5	−273.1	−8.7	706.5	404.1
56	F52	Investment fund shares	0.0				0.0	316.5
57	F6	Insurance, pension and stand. guar. sch.	0.0				0.0	651.3
58	F8	Other receivables/payables	−5.8				−5.8	1,387.8
		Other Changes in Vol. of Assets Account						
59	B102	Changes in net worth due to OCVA	−50.2				−50.2	339.6
		Revaluation Account						
60	AN	Non-financial assets						
61	AF	Financial assets/liabilities	−72.8				−72.8	3,837.7
62	AF1	Monetary gold and SDRs	−3.3				−3.3	−3.2
63	AF2	Currency and deposits	−12.9				−12.9	0.0
64	AF3	Debt securities	54.6				54.6	0.0
65	AF4	Loans	0.0				0.0	0.0
66	AF5	Equity	−110.7				−110.7	3,245.2
67	AF5	Investment fund shares	0.0				0.0	507.9
68	AF6	Insurance, pension and stand. guar. sch.	0.0				0.0	244.5
69	AF8	Other receivables/payables	−0.5				−0.5	−156.7
70	B103	Changes in net worth due to nominal holding gains and losses	753.5				753.5	3,410.3

only change we include in the capital account is the amount carried forward with the saving measure (row 36) from the use of disposable income account. We do not reallocate capital formation in intellectual property products.[20] Likewise, the only change we include in the financial account is in equity (row 55) as a result of the previous adjustment transactions—we assume the additional exports that result from the operating surplus adjustment are financed with equity rather than debt. The balancing items in the capital account and the financial account—net lending/borrowing—are also affected by the net decrease of $26.4 billion in external transactions. The increase in measured US net borrowing in the capital account is 6.9 percent, and the increase in the financial account is 7.8 percent—the difference between the percentages is a result of the statistical discrepancy between the two accounts. There are no measured effects in the other changes in the volume of assets account or the revaluation account at the bottom of table 5.8.

The *SNA* balance sheets are presented in tables 5.9 and 5.10. Just like the *BPM* international investment position, the *SNA* balance sheets reflect stocks of assets and liabilities, which requires an accumulation of each of our adjustment measures using annual estimates from Guvenen et al. (2017). The opening balance sheet at the top of table 5.9 presents the cumulative adjustments for operating surplus, earnings on USDIA, and net interest received on USDIA for the period 1973–2013. The closing balance sheet at the bottom of table 5.10 presents the cumulative adjustments for the period 1973–2014. Retaining our assumption that the additional exports that result from the operating surplus adjustment are financed with equity rather than debt, the cumulative adjustments decrease measured US equity assets by 0.5—0.6 percent for both the opening balance of equity (row 77) and the closing balance of equity (row 102) because the increases in operating surplus are less than the decreases in income receivable from rest of world over time. Thus, measured US net worth in both the opening balance sheet and the closing balance sheet decreases by 0.3 percent.

5.5.3   Analytic Uses

We consider implications for five common analytic uses of the US economic accounts: labor share of income, national saving rates, returns on domestic nonfinancial business, returns on foreign direct investment, and

---

20. We do not make an effort to reallocate flows and stocks of intellectual property products for three reasons. First, the income measures that we reallocate reflect returns to all intangible capital, but intellectual property products are only a subset of intangible capital. Second, intellectual property products in the U.S. national accounts are measured as a sum of costs and any reallocation under formulary apportionment would, thus, be reduced by the extent to which costs incurred consist of payments to unrelated parties and to labor. Third, to the extent that intellectual property products consist of R&D expenditures, very little reallocation would likely result because the majority of R&D expenditures by U.S. MNEs are incurred by U.S. parents and consist largely of payments to unrelated parties and to labor. Of the $330.8 billion spent on R&D by U.S. MNEs in 2014, $275.5 billion—83.3 percent—was incurred by U.S. parents.

Table 5.9   SNA balance sheets for the United States: Stocks and changes in assets

Line	SNA code		Rest of world					Total economy				
			Published	Adjustments			Adjusted	Published	Adjustments			Adjusted
				Operating surplus	Earnings	Net interest			Operating surplus	Earnings	Net interest	
			(1)	(2)	(3)	(4)	(5)	(6)	(7)	(8)	(9)	(10)
		Opening balance sheet										
71	AN	Non-financial assets						70,352.4				70,352.4
72	AF	Financial assets/liabilities	21,238.9				21,238.9	173,474.4	3,196.0	−3,313.9	−136.7	173,219.8
73	AF1	Monetary gold and SDRs	54.4				54.4	66.2				66.2
74	AF2	Currency and deposits	1,418.9				1,418.9	14,694.2				14,694.2
75	AF3	Debt securities	9,586.9				9,586.9	27,793.4				27,793.4
76	AF4	Loans	845.1				845.1	24,570.9				24,570.9
77	AF5	Equity	8,526.3				8,526.3	46,778.3	3,196.0	−3,313.9	−136.7	46,523.7
78	AF5	Investment fund shares	659.3				659.3	14,391.5				14,391.5
79	AF6	Insurance, pension and stand. guar. sch.	0.0				0.0	26,914.4				26,914.4
80	AF8	Other receivables/payables	148.0				148.0	18,265.5				18,265.5
81	B90	Net worth										
		Total changes in assets/liabilities										
82	AN	Non-financial assets						4,014.8				4,014.8
83	AF	Financial assets/liabilities	1,831.2				1,831.2	9,426.5	255.5	−273.1	−8.7	9,398.1
84	AF1	Monetary gold and SDRs	−3.2				−3.2	−3.3				−3.3
85	AF2	Currency and deposits	100.9				100.9	901.8				901.8
86	AF3	Debt securities	586.9				586.9	776.1				776.1

(continued)

Table 5.9 (continued)

Line	SNA code		Rest of world					Total economy				
				Adjustments					Adjustments			
			Published	Operating surplus	Earnings	Net interest	Adjusted	Published	Operating surplus	Earnings	Net interest	Adjusted
87	AF4	Loans	136.7				136.7	924.8				924.8
88	AF5	Equity	939.9				939.9	4,111.8	255.5	−273.1	−8.7	4,085.4
89	AF5	Investment fund shares	57.7				57.7	766.5				766.5
90	AF6	Insurance, pension and stand. guar. sch.	0.0				0.0	834.7				834.7
91	AF8	Other receivables/payables	12.3				12.3	1,112.1				1,112.1
92	B10	Changes in net worth										
93	B101	Saving and capital transfers										
94	B102	Other changes in the volume of assets										
95	B103	Nominal holding gains and losses										
		Closing balance sheet										
96	AN	Non-financial assets						74,367.2				74,367.2
97	AF	Financial assets/liabilities	23,070.1				23,070.1	182,898.9	3,451.5	−3,587.0	−145.4	182,618.0
98	AF1	Monetary gold and SDRs	51.2				51.2	62.9				62.9
99	AF2	Currency and deposits	1,519.8				1,519.8	15,596.0				15,596.0
100	AF3	Debt securities	10,173.8				10,173.8	28,569.5				28,569.5
101	AF4	Loans	981.8				981.8	25,495.7				25,495.7
102	AF5	Equity	9,466.2				9,466.2	50,890.1	3,451.5	−3,587.0	−145.4	50,609.2
103	AF5	Investment fund shares	717.0				717.0	15,158.0				15,158.0
104	AF6	Insurance, pension and stand. guar. sch.	0.0				0.0	27,749.1				27,749.1
105	AF8	Other receivables/payables	160.3				160.3	19,377.6				19,377.6
106	B90	Net worth										

Table 5.10   SNA balance sheets for the United States: Stocks and changes in liabilities and net worth

Line	SNA code		Rest of world					Total economy				
			Published	Adjustments			Adjusted	Published	Adjustments			Adjusted
				Operating surplus	Earnings	Net interest			Operating surplus	Earnings	Net interest	
			(1)	(2)	(3)	(4)	(5)	(6)	(7)	(8)	(9)	(10)
		Opening balance sheet										
71	AN	Non-financial assets										
72	AF	Financial assets/liabilities	16,717.5	3,196.0	−3,313.9	−136.7	16,462.9	161,476.5				161,476.6
73	AF1	Monetary gold and SDRs	55.2				55.2	54.4				54.4
74	AF2	Currency and deposits	1,031.4				1,031.4	15,929.6				15,929.6
75	AF3	Debt securities	2,649.5				2,649.5	34,730.8				34,730.8
76	AF4	Loans	1,000.8				1,000.8	24,737.1				24,737.1
77	AF5	Equity	11,927.2	3,196.0	−3,313.9	−136.7	11,672.6	34,208.8				34,208.8
78	AF5	Investment fund shares	0.0				0.0	15,050.8				15,050.8
79	AF6	Insurance, pension and stand. guar. sch.	0.0				0.0	26,914.3				26,914.3
80	AF8	Other receivables/payables	53.4				53.4	9,850.8				9,850.8
81	B90	Net worth	4,521.4	−3,196.0	3,313.9	136.7	4,776.0	82,350.2	3,196.0	−3,313.9	−136.7	82,095.6
		Total changes in assets/liabilities										
82	AN	Non-financial assets										
83	AF	Financial assets/liabilities	743.5	255.5	−273.1	−8.7	717.1	9,081.7				9,081.7
84	AF1	Monetary gold and SDRs	−3.3				−3.3	−3.2				−3.2
85	AF2	Currency and deposits	−135.5				−135.5	924.8				924.8
86	AF3	Debt securities	217.4				217.4	1,145.9				1,145.9
87	AF4	Loans	49.1				49.1	907.2				907.2

(continued)

Table 5.10   (continued)

Line	SNA code		Rest of world					Total economy				
				Adjustments					Adjustments			
			Published	Operating surplus	Earnings	Net interest	Adjusted	Published	Operating surplus	Earnings	Net interest	Adjusted
88	AF5	Equity	622.2	255.5	−273.1	−8.7	595.8	3,508.3				3,508.3
89	AF5	Investment fund shares	0.0				0.0	824.4				824.4
90	AF6	Insurance, pension and stand. guar. sch.	0.0				0.0	834.7				834.7
91	AF8	Other receivables/payables	−6.4				−6.4	939.6				939.6
92	B10	Changes in net worth	1,087.7	−255.5	273.1	8.7	1,114.1	4,357.6	255.5	−273.1	−8.7	4,331.2
93	B101	Saving and capital transfers	384.4	−255.5	273.1	8.7	410.8	608.3	255.5	−273.1	−8.7	581.9
94	B102	Other changes in the volume of assets	−50.2				−50.2	339.6				339.6
95	B103	Nominal holding gains and losses	753.5				753.5	3,410.3				3,410.3
		Closing balance sheet										
96	AN	Non-financial assets										
97	AF	Financial assets/liabilities	17,461.0	3,451.5	−3,587.0	−145.4	17,180.1	170,558.3				170,558.3
98	AF1	Monetary gold and SDRs	51.9				51.9	51.2				51.2
99	AF2	Currency and deposits	895.9				895.9	16,854.4				16,854.4
100	AF3	Debt securities	2,866.9				2,866.9	35,876.7				35,876.7
101	AF4	Loans	1,049.9				1,049.9	25,644.3				25,644.3
102	AF5	Equity	12,549.4	3,451.5	−3,587.0	−145.4	12,268.5	37,717.1				37,717.1
103	AF5	Investment fund shares	0.0				0.0	15,875.2				15,875.2
104	AF6	Insurance, pension and stand. guar. sch.	0.0				0.0	27,749.0				27,749.0
105	AF8	Other receivables/payables	47.0				47.0	10,790.4				10,790.4
106	B90	Net worth	5,609.1	−3,451.5	3,587.0	145.4	5,890.0	86,707.8	3,451.5	−3,587.0	−145.4	86,426.9

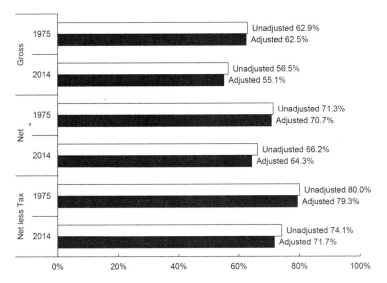

Figure 5.2   US labor share of income for 1975 and 2014
Note: Shares are calculated as a percentage of value added for corporate business. *Gross* refers to gross value added in the denominator, *net* refers to net value added in the denominator, and *net less tax* refers to net value added minus taxes less subsidies on production and imports in the denominator. See appendix A for a description of calculations.

external balances. We provide additional details on calculations for each of the analytic uses in appendix A.

Karabarbounis and Neiman (2014) and Bridgman (2018) each report declines in the labor share of income since 1975. Following the previous authors, we calculate the labor share for the US corporate business sector by dividing compensation by value added with and without our operating surplus adjustment for 1975 and 2014. Since compensation in the numerator is unchanged, the results yield declines in the labor share. The shares are reported in figure 5.2 for three alternative denominators used in Bridgman (2018): gross value added, net value added, and net value added minus taxes less subsidies on production and imports. The adjusted shares reported in figure 5.2 for 2014 demonstrate a decline of 1.4 percentage points, 1.9 percentage points, and 2.4 percentage points for gross value added, net value added, and net value added minus taxes less subsidies on production and imports, respectively. In addition, the adjusted shares demonstrate a larger decline in the labor share from 1975 to 2014 under each alternative denominator—15.6 percent for gross value added, 25.5 percent for net value added, and 28.8 percent for net value added minus taxes less subsidies on production and imports.

Reinsdorf (2004) presents measures of US personal saving, business saving, and national saving as a percentage of national income. In addition, BEA publishes quarterly and annual measures of net national saving and

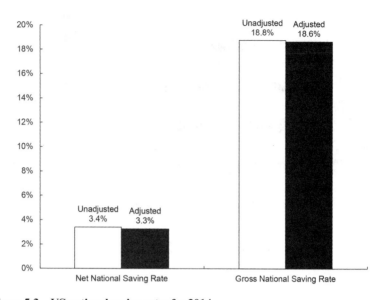

Figure 5.3   US national saving rates for 2014

Note: Saving rates are calculated as a percentage of GNI. See appendix A for a description of calculations.

gross national saving as a percentage of GNI. We present net and gross national saving rates for 2014 in figure 5.3. We calculate the rates by dividing the national saving measures by GNI, and we apply our formulary adjustments from tables 5.5 and 5.6 to both the numerator and the denominator. The rates in figure 5.3 show relatively small declines of 0.1 and 0.2 percentage point for the net and gross saving measures, respectively, which is a result of the same downward adjustment of $26.4 billion that affects both the numerator and the denominator in the calculation.

Osborne and Retus (2017) report rates of return for US domestic nonfinancial business. The returns are calculated by dividing net operating surplus by the net stock of produced assets for nonfinancial business. We use the unadjusted rate of return for 2014 directly from Osborne and Retus (2017) and add our formulary adjustments on operating surplus for nonfinancial industries—an amount of $217.4 billion—to the numerator in their calculation to derive an adjusted rate of return for 2014. As we explained in section 5.5.2, we do not adjust the stock of intellectual property products in the denominator. The result is reported in figure 5.4, which shows a 1.3 percentage point increase in the rate of return after our adjustments are applied.

McGrattan and Prescott (2010) and Bridgman (2014) document a persistent gap since 1982 between rates of return on direct investment abroad by US MNEs and foreign direct investment in the United States (FDIUS) by foreign MNEs. Rates of return are calculated by dividing income on foreign direct investment by the direct investment component of the interna-

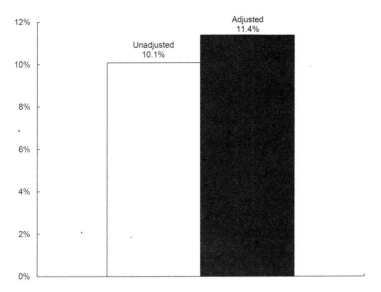

Figure 5.4   Return on US domestic nonfinancial business for 2014
Note: Returns are calculated by dividing net operating surplus by the net stock of produced assets. See appendix A for a description of calculations.

tional investment position. In 2014, the rate of return on USDIA at current cost was 8.5 percent, and the rate of return on FDIUS at current cost was 5.5 percent (United States Bureau of Economic Analysis 2017a, 2017b). McGrattan and Prescott (2010) focus on the exclusion of intangible assets in the denominator as a source of the gap. Bridgman (2014) focuses on the exclusion of intangible assets and repatriation taxes as a source of the gap. Both studies find a much narrower gap when they make adjustments for the exclusions. Following calculations in table 1 of United States Bureau of Economic Analysis (2017a), we calculate an adjusted rate of return on USDIA at current cost using the adjusted income on USDIA reported in table 5.1 and the adjusted beginning and ending direct investment position assets reported in appendix table 5A.1. The adjusted and unadjusted returns are presented in figure 5.5. Since our formulary adjustments decrease the numerator of the calculation by a larger percentage than the denominator, the adjusted rate of return on USDIA of 3.5 percent is less than half of the unadjusted rate of 8.5 percent. In addition, the adjusted rate of return on USDIA is closer to the rate of return on FDIUS for the year.[21]

21. The unadjusted rate of return of 8.5 percent is closer to the long-run rate of return on an investment portfolio of listed stocks such as the S&P 500. Given the resources that MNEs devote to actively managing their operations abroad, management and owners are unlikely to accept a rate of return that falls significantly short of a return on a passive portfolio over the long run. Drawing a reliable conclusion regarding the accuracy of the unadjusted rate of return over the adjusted rate of return would require an analysis over a much longer period of time than the single year we present here.

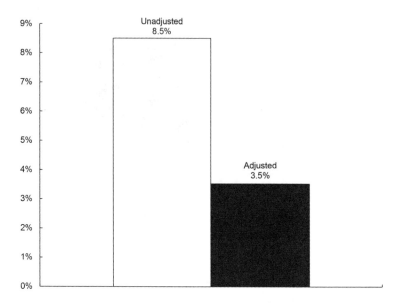

Figure 5.5   Return on US direct investment abroad for 2014

Note: Returns are calculated by dividing direct investment income at current cost by the average of beginning and ending direct investment asset positions at current cost. See appendix A for a description of calculations.

Figure 5.6 presents adjusted and unadjusted external balances from the current account of the US balance of payments presented in table 5.1. Balances are presented as a percentage of expenditure-based GDP or GNI presented in tables 5.5 and 5.6. Since we treat our adjustments as an implied increase in exports of services, there is no effect on the measured goods balance. However, the goods balance as a percentage of GDP declines slightly because of the implied increase in services exports and the resulting increase in GDP. As a percentage of GDP, the services balance almost doubles from 1.5 percent to 2.9 percent, which increases the trade balance from negative 2.8 percent to negative 1.3 percent. As a percentage of GNI, the primary income balance decreases from 1.2 percent to negative 0.4 percent. The only effect our adjustments have on the current account balance is the decline of $26.4 billion, which reduces the current account balance from negative 2.1 percent of GNI to negative 2.2 percent of GNI.

5.6   Conclusions

Offshore profit shifting accomplished through complex global structuring that includes holding companies and special purpose entities imposes challenges for the treatment of MNEs in the *SNA* and *BPM* frameworks. The international guidelines recommend that transactions and other flows with a holding company or special purpose entity be recognized in economic

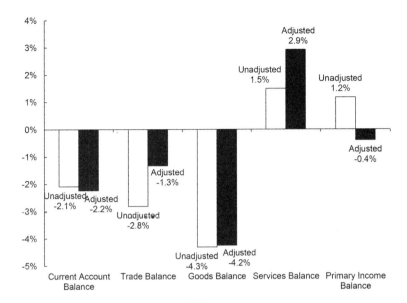

Figure 5.6   US external balances for 2014

Note: Trade balances are shown as a percentage of expenditure-based GDP. Current account and primary income balances are shown as a percentage of GNI. See appendix A for a description of calculations.

accounts if the holding company or special purpose entity is resident in an economy other than its parent. Using results from Guvenen et al. (2017), this chapter empirically demonstrates the effects on the US economic accounts in 2014 of using a method of formulary apportionment in lieu of separate accounting, which results in a reattribution of operating surplus and income on USDIA from foreign affiliates to US parents.

For 2014, we find notable changes in key economic accounting measures throughout the US economic accounts, which may have significant implications for their analytic uses. Our adjustments yield a 3.5 percent increase in US operating surplus, which generates a 1.5 percent increase in US GDP as a result of an implied increase in output that is used as services exports. We find a 33.5 percent decrease in US income receivable from the rest of world, which is overwhelmingly attributable to a decrease in earnings on USDIA with a small amount attributable to net interest receivable on USDIA. In dollar amounts, the increase in operating surplus is offset by a larger decrease in income receivable from the rest of world. As a result of these offsetting effects, US GNI and gross national disposable income decrease by 0.1 percent, while gross national saving decreases by 0.8 percent and national borrowing increases by 6.9 percent. Finally, net worth in the balance sheet decreases by 0.3 percent.

The results for analytic uses include a decrease for the labor share of income of 1.4 to 2.4 percentage points and a decrease for the return on

USDIA of 5.0 percentage points. The results for analytic uses also include an increase for the trade in services balance as a percentage of GDP of 1.4 percentage points and an increase for the return on domestic nonfinancial business of 1.3 percentage points. Changes for the national saving rate and the current account balance as a percentage of GDP are negligible.

Appendix A
Calculations for Analytic Uses

This appendix provides details on calculations for each of the five analytic uses of the US economic accounts presented in section 5.5.3.

Labor Share of Income

Calculations are based on data from NIPA tables 1.14 and 7.5 for corporate business. We calculate the 2014 unadjusted gross labor share by dividing compensation by gross value added (GVA) as follows:

$$(A1) \quad Unadjusted\ Gross\ Labor\ Share = \frac{Compensation}{GVA}$$

$$= \frac{5,647.8}{10,000.2} = 56.5\%.$$

Gross value added is the sum of compensation, taxes less subsidies on production and imports, net operating surplus, and consumption of fixed capital. We calculate the 2014 unadjusted net labor share by dividing compensation by net value added (NVA) as follows:

$$(A2) \quad Unadjusted\ Net\ Labor\ Share = \frac{Compensation}{NVA}$$

$$= \frac{5,647.8}{8,534.5} = 66.2\%.$$

Net value added excludes consumption of fixed capital. We calculate the 2014 unadjusted net labor share less taxes by dividing compensation by net value added minus taxes less subsidies on production and imports minus current business transfer payments (NVAT) as follows:

$$(A3) \quad Unadjusted\ Net\ Labor\ Share\ less\ Taxes = \frac{Compensation}{NVAT}$$

$$= \frac{5,647.8}{7,622.8} = 74.1\%.$$

We calculate the adjusted shares by adding the \$255.5 billion adjustment for operating surplus (OS) to the denominator in each calculation as follows:

$$(A4) \quad Adjusted\ Gross\ Labor\ Share = \frac{Compensation}{GVA + OS\ Adjustment}$$

$$= \frac{5,647.8}{10,000.2 + 255.5} = 55.1\%,$$

$$(A5) \quad Adjusted\ Net\ Labor\ Share = \frac{Compensation}{NVA + OS\ Adjustment}$$

$$= \frac{5,647.8}{8,534.5 + 255.5} = 64.3\%,$$

and

$$(A6) \quad Adjusted\ Net\ Labor\ Share\ less\ Taxes = \frac{Compensation}{NVAT + OS\ Adjustment}$$

$$= \frac{5,647.8}{7,622.8 + 255.5} = 71.7\%.$$

We calculate the 1975 shares in the same manner. Capital shares of income can also be calculated and would be equal to one minus the labor share.

National Saving Rates

Calculations are based on data from tables 5.5 and 5.6. We calculate the 2014 unadjusted net national saving rate by dividing net national saving (line 34) by GNI (line 22) as follows:

$$(A7) \quad Unadjusted\ Net\ Rate = \frac{Net\ National\ Saving}{GNI}$$

$$= \frac{608.7}{17,892.1} = 3.4\%.$$

We calculate the unadjusted gross national saving rate by dividing gross national saving (line 32) by GNI (line 22) as follows:

$$(A8) \quad Unadjusted\ Gross\ Rate = \frac{Gross\ National\ Saving}{GNI}$$

$$= \frac{3,356.7}{17,892.1} = 18.8\%.$$

We calculate the adjusted rates by substituting the adjusted measures from tables 5.5 and 5.6 as follows:

(A9) $Adjusted\ Net\ Rate = \dfrac{Adjusted\ Net\ National\ Saving}{Adjusted\ \text{GNI}}$

$$= \frac{582.3}{17,865.7} = 3.3\%$$

and

(A10) $Adjusted\ Gross\ Rate = \dfrac{Adjusted\ Gross\ National\ Saving}{Adjusted\ \text{GNI}}$

$$= \frac{3,330.3}{17,865.7} = 18.6\%.$$

Return on US Domestic Nonfinancial Business

Calculations are based on data from Osborne and Retus (2017). We calculate the 2014 unadjusted return by dividing net operating surplus (NOS) for nonfinancial business available in the US NIPAs by the net stock of produced assets for nonfinancial business available in the US Fixed Assets Accounts as follows:

(A11) $Unadjusted\ Return = \dfrac{\text{NOS}}{Net\ Stock\ of\ Produced\ Assets}$

$$= \frac{1,680.4}{16,670.4} = 10.1\%.$$

We calculate the adjusted return by adding the adjustment of $255.5 billion (less $38.1 billion for financial industries) on operating surplus (OS) for nonfinancial industries to the numerator as follows:

(A12) $Adjusted\ Return = \dfrac{\text{NOS} + \text{OS}\ Adjustment}{Net\ Stock\ of\ Produced\ Assets}$

$$= \frac{1,680.4 + 255.5 - 38.1}{16,670.4} = 11.4\%.$$

The denominator includes capital measures of intellectual property products, which we do not adjust, as explained in section 5.5.2.

Return on US Direct Investment Abroad

Calculations are based on data from table 5.1 and appendix table 5A.1. We calculate the 2014 unadjusted return by dividing income on USDIA at current cost presented in table 5.1 (line 22) by the average of beginning and ending direct investment asset positions at current cost presented in appendix table 5A.1 (lines 2 and 14) as follows:

$$\text{(A13)}\quad Unadj.\ Return = \frac{Unadjusted\ Income\ on\ \text{USDIA}}{(Unadj.\ Beg.\ Assets + Unadj.\ End.\ Assets) \div 2}$$

$$= \frac{464.6}{(5,296.4 + 5,633.1) \div 2} = 8.5\%.$$

We calculate the adjusted return using the income on USDIA reported in table 5.1 (line 22) and the adjusted beginning and ending direct investment asset positions reported in appendix table 5A.1 (lines 10 and 22) as follows:

$$\text{(A14)}\quad Adj.\ Return = \frac{Adjusted\ Income\ on\ \text{USDIA}}{(Adj.\ Beg.\ Assets + Adj.\ End.\ Assets) \div 2}$$

$$= \frac{182.7}{(5,032.8 + 5,343.2) \div 2} = 3.5\%.$$

US External Balances

Calculations are based on data from tables 5.1, 5.5, and 5.6. We calculate the 2014 unadjusted balances from table 5.1 as a percentage of unadjusted expenditure-based GDP or GNI from tables 5.5 and 5.6 as follows:

$$\text{(A15)}\quad Unadjusted\ Current\ Account = \frac{Unadjusted\ \text{CA}\ Balance}{Unadjusted\ \text{GNI}}$$

$$= \frac{-373.8}{17,892.1} = -2.1\%,$$

$$\text{(A16)}\quad Unadjusted\ Trade = \frac{Unadjusted\ Trade\ Balance}{Unadjusted\ \text{GDP}}$$

$$= \frac{-490.3}{17,427.6} = -2.8\%,$$

$$\text{(A17)}\quad Unadjusted\ Goods = \frac{Unadjusted\ Goods\ Balance}{Unadjusted\ \text{GDP}}$$

$$= \frac{-751.5}{17,427.6} = -4.3\%,$$

$$\text{(A18)}\quad Unadjusted\ Services = \frac{Unadjusted\ Services\ Balance}{Unadjusted\ \text{GDP}}$$

$$= \frac{261.2}{17,427.6} = 1.5\%$$

and

(A19) $\quad Unadjusted\ Primary\ Income = \dfrac{Unadjusted\ Primary\ Income\ Balance}{Unadjusted\ \text{GNI}}$

$$= \frac{210.8}{17,892.1} = 1.2\%.$$

We calculate the adjusted balances from table 5.1 as a percentage of adjusted expenditure-based GDP or GNI from tables 5.5 and 5.6 as follows:

(A20) $\qquad Adjusted\ Current\ Account = \dfrac{Adjusted\ CA\ Balance}{Adjusted\ \text{GNI}}$

$$= \frac{-400.2}{17,865.7} = -2.2\%,$$

(A21) $\qquad\qquad Adjusted\ Trade = \dfrac{Adjusted\ Trade\ Balance}{Adjusted\ \text{GDP}}$

$$= \frac{-234.9}{17,683.1} = -1.3\%,$$

(A22) $\qquad\qquad Adjusted\ Goods = \dfrac{Adjusted\ Goods\ Balance}{Adjusted\ \text{GDP}}$

$$= \frac{-751.5}{17,683.1} = -4.2\%,$$

(A23) $\qquad\qquad Adjusted\ Services = \dfrac{Adjusted\ Services\ Balance}{Adjusted\ \text{GDP}}$

$$= \frac{516.6}{17,683.1} = 2.9\%$$

and

(A24) $\qquad Adjusted\ Primary\ Income = \dfrac{Adjusted\ Primary\ Income\ Balance}{Adjusted\ \text{GNI}}$

$$= \frac{-71.1}{17,865.7} = -0.4\%.$$

Table 5A.1 **BPM direct investment position reconciliation for the United States**

	Line	Assets — Current cost directional basis (1)	Adjustment to market value (2)	Adjustment to asset-liability basis (3)	Asset-liability basis at market value (4)	BPM code	SNA code		Liabilities — Current cost directional basis (5)	Adjustment to market value (6)	Adjustment to asset-liability basis (7)	Asset-liability basis at market value (8)
Beginning of Year — Published	1							Net position	1,975.5	−669.8		1,305.8
	2	5,296.4	957.8	866.5	7,120.7	1	AFD	Direct investment	3,320.9	1,627.6	866.5	5,814.9
	3	5,096.4	957.8	866.5	6,054.2	1.1	AF5D	Equity	2,815.7	1,627.6	866.5	4,443.2
	4	199.9			1,066.5	1.2	AF3D	Debt instruments	505.2			1,371.7
Adjustments	5							Net position	−263.6			−263.6
	6	−263.6			−263.6	1	AFD	Direct investment				
	7	−263.6				1.1	AF5D	Equity				
	8				−263.6	1.2	AF3D	Debt instruments				
Adjusted	9							Net position	1,711.9	−669.8		1,042.1
	10	5,032.8	957.8	866.5	6,857.1	1	AFD	Direct investment	3,320.9	1,627.6	866.5	5,814.9
	11	4,832.8	957.8	866.5	5,790.6	1.1	AF5D	Equity	2,815.7	1,627.6	866.5	4,443.2
	12	199.9			1,066.5	1.2	AF3D	Debt instruments	505.2			1,371.7

(continued)

Table 5A.1   (continued)

	Line	Assets				BPM code	SNA code		Liabilities			
		Current cost directional basis	Adjustment to market value	Adjustment to asset-liability basis	Asset-liability basis at market value				Current cost directional basis	Adjustment to market value	Adjustment to asset-liability basis	Asset-liability basis at market value
Published	13							Net position	2,092.5	−1,272.6		819.9
	14	5,633.1	643.7	912.6	7,189.4	1	AFD	Direct investment	3,540.7	1,916.2	912.6	6,369.5
	15	5,396.5	643.7		6,040.1	1.1	AF5D	Equity	2,979.5	1,916.2		4,895.8
	16	236.7		912.6	1,149.3	1.2	AF3D	Debt instruments	561.1		912.6	1,473.8
Adjustments	17	−290.0			−290.0			Net position	−290.0			−290.0
	18	−290.0			−290.0	1	AFD	Direct investment				
	19					1.1	AF5D	Equity				
	20					1.2	AF3D	Debt instruments				
Adjusted	21							Net position	1,802.5	−1,272.6		529.9
	22	5,343.2	643.7	912.6	6,899.4	1	AFD	Direct investment	3,540.7	1,916.2	912.6	6,369.5
	23	5,106.5	643.7		5,750.2	1.1	AF5D	Equity	2,979.5	1,916.2		4,895.8
	24	236.7		912.6	1,149.3	1.2	AF3D	Debt instruments	561.1		912.6	1,473.8

(Left margin: the groups Published, Adjustments, and Adjusted together comprise "End of Year.")

Note: BEA presents direct investment statistics on two bases: the directional basis and the asset-liability basis. On a directional basis, direct investment claims and liabilities are classified according to whether the direct investor is a US resident or a foreign resident. On this basis, US direct investment abroad is the net claims of a US parent on its foreign affiliates. On the asset-liability basis, direct investment claims and liabilities are classified according to whether the direct investment enterprise that receives the funds is resident in the United States or abroad. A direct investment asset is created when a US parent or a US affiliate establishes a claim on a related foreign person. Similarly, a direct investment liability is established when a foreign person establishes a claim on a related direct investment enterprise in the United States. Furthermore, BEA publishes direct investment statistics based on three valuation methods: historical cost, current cost, and market value. Historical cost is the basis on which BEA's direct investment surveys collect direct investment position data because that is the primary valuation method used in company accounting records. Current cost estimates revalue parents' historical cost equity claims in their affiliates' plant and equipment, land, and inventory stocks to a replacement value of tangible assets. The market value estimates are featured in BEA's international investment position accounts because market valuation is used for other functional categories in these accounts.

References

Altshuler, Rosanne, and Harry Grubert. 2010. "Formula Apportionment: Is It Better Than the Current System and Are There Better Alternatives?" *National Tax Journal* 63 (4): 1145–84.

Avi-Yonah, Reuven S. 2010. "Between Formulary Apportionment and the OECD Guidelines: A Proposal for Reconciliation." *World Tax Journal* 2 (1): 3–18.

Baldwin, Robert E., and Fukunari Kimura. 1998. "Measuring U.S. International Goods and Services Transactions." In *Geography and Ownership Bases for Economic Accounting*, edited by Robert E. Baldwin, Robert E. Lipsey, and J. David Richardson, 9–48. Chicago, IL: The University of Chicago Press.

Bridgman, Benjamin. 2018. "Is Labor's Loss Capital's Gain? Gross versus Net Labor Shares." *Macroeconomic Dynamics* 22 (8): 1–18.

Bridgman, Benjamin. 2014. "Do Intangible Assets Explain High U.S. Foreign Direct Investment Returns?" *Journal of Macroeconomics* 40 (A): 159–71.

Brynjolfsson, Erik, and Andrew McAfee. 2011. *Race against the Machine: How the Digital Revolution is Accelerating Innovation, Driving Productivity, and Irreversibly Transforming Employment and the Economy*. Lexington, MA: Digital Frontier Press.

Byrne, David M., John G. Fernald, and Marshall B. Reinsdorf. 2016. "Does the United States Have a Productivity Slowdown or a Measurement Problem?" Brookings Paper on Economic Activity, March 10–11.

Byrne, David M., Stephen D. Oliner, and Daniel E. Sichel. 2015. "How Fast Are Semiconductor Prices Falling?" NBER Working Paper No. 21074. Cambridge, MA: National Bureau of Economic Research.

Clausing, Kimberly A. 2016. "The Effect of Profit Shifting on the Corporate Tax Base in the United States and Beyond." *National Tax Journal* 69 (4): 905–34.

Clausing, Kimberly A., and Reuven Avi-Yonah. 2007. Reforming Corporate Taxation in a Global Economy: A Proposal to Adopt Formulary Apportionment. The Hamilton Project Discussion Paper 2007-08.

Cooper, Michael, John McClelland, James Pearce, Richard Prisinzano, Joseph Sullivan, Dany Yagan, Owen Zidar, and Eric Zwick. 2015. "Business Income in the United States: Who Owns It and How Much Tax Do They Pay?" NBER Working Paper No. 21651. Cambridge, MA: National Bureau of Economic Research.

Corrado, Carol, Charles Hulten, and Daniel Sichel. 2009. "Intangible Capital and U.S. Economic Growth." *Review of Income and Wealth* 55 (3): 661–85.

DeBacker, Jason M., and Richard Prisinzano. 2015. "The Rise of Partnerships." *Tax Notes* 147 (13): 1563–75.

Dharmapala, Dhammika. 2014. "What Do We Know about Base Erosion and Profit Shifting? A Review of the Empirical Literature." *Fiscal Studies* 35 (4): 421–48.

Dowd, Tim, Paul Landefeld, and Anne Moore. 2017. "Profit Shifting of U.S. Multinationals." *Journal of Public Economics* 148: 1–13.

Eisfeldt, Andrea L., and Dimitris Papanikolaou. 2013. "Organization Capital and the Cross- Section of Expected Returns." *Journal of Finance* 68 (4): 1365–1406.

European Commission, International Monetary Fund, Organisation for Economic Co-operation and Development, United Nations, and World Bank. 2009. System of National Accounts. 2008. New York, NY: United Nations.

Fernald, John. 2014. "Productivity and Potential Output before, during, and after the Great Recession." NBER Working Paper No. 20248. Cambridge, MA: National Bureau of Economic Research.

Fuest, Clemens, Thomas Hemmelgarn, and Fred Ramb. 2007. "How Would the Introduction of an EU-Wide Formula Apportionment Affect the Distribution and Size of the Corporate Tax Base?" *International Tax and Public Finance* 14 (5): 605–26.

Gordon, Roger, and John D. Wilson. 1986. "An Examination of Multi-jurisdictional Corporate Income Taxation under Formulary Apportionment." *Econometrica* 54 (6): 1357–73.

Gresik, Thomas A. 2001. "The Taxing Task of Taxing Transnationals." *Journal of Economic Literature* 39 (3): 800–38.

Guvenen, Fatih, Raymond J. Mataloni Jr., Dylan G. Rassier, and Kim J. Ruhl. 2017. "Offshore Profit Shifting and Domestic Productivity Measurement." NBER Working Paper No. 23324. Cambridge, MA: National Bureau of Economic Research.

Hines, James R. 2010. "Income Misattribution under Formula Apportionment." *European Economic Review* 54 (1): 108–20.

Hines, Jr., James R., and Eric M. Rice. 1994. "Fiscal Paradise: Foreign Tax Havens and American Business." *Quarterly Journal of Economics* 109 (1): 149–82.

International Monetary Fund. 2009. Balance of Payments and International Investment Position Manual. 6th edition. Washington, DC: International Monetary Fund.

Karabarbounis, Loukas, and Brent Neiman. 2014. "The Global Decline of the Labor Share." *Quarterly Journal of Economics* 129 (1): 61–103.

Kimura, Fukunari, and Robert E. Baldwin. 1998. "Application of a Nationality-Adjusted Net Sales and Value-Added Framework: The Case of Japan." In *Geography and Ownership Bases for Economic Accounting*, edited by Robert E. Baldwin, Robert E. Lipsey, and J. David Richardson, 49–82. Chicago, IL: The University of Chicago Press.

Landefeld, J. Steven, Obie G. Wichard, and Jeff H. Lowe. 1993. "Alternative Frameworks for U.S. International Transactions." *Survey of Current Business* 73 (12): 50–61.

Lipsey, Robert E. 2010. "Measuring the Location of Production in a World of Intangible Productive Assets, FDI, and Intrafirm Trade." *Review of Income and Wealth* 56 (1): S99–S110.

McGrattan, Ellen R., and Edward C. Prescott. 2010. "Technology Capital and the U.S. Current Account." *American Economic Review* 100 (4): 1493–1522.

Mokyr, Joel. 2014. "Secular Stagnation? Not in Your Life" In *Secular Stagnation: Facts, Causes and Cures*, edited by Coen Teulings and Richard Baldwin. London: CEPR Press.

Moulton, Brent R., and Peter van de Ven. 2018. "Addressing the Challenges of Globalization in National Accounts." Paper prepared for the NBER-CRIW conference on The Challenges of Globalization in the Measurement of National Accounts.

Organisation for Economic Co-operation and Development. 2015a. *Measuring and Monitoring BEPS, Action 11—2015 Final Report*. Paris: OECD Publishing.

Organisation for Economic Co-operation and Development. 2015b. *Transfer Pricing Documentation and Country-by-Country Reporting, Action 13—2015 Final Report*. Paris: OECD Publishing.

Osborne, Sarah, and Bonnie A. Retus. 2017. "Returns for Domestic Nonfinancial Business." *Survey of Current Business* 97 (12): 1–6.

Rassier, Dylan G. 2017. "Improving the *SNA* Treatment of Multinational Enterprises." *Review of Income and Wealth* 63 (s2): S287–S320.

Rassier, Dylan G., and Jennifer Koncz-Bruner. 2015. "A Formulary Approach for Attributing Measured Production to Foreign Affiliates of U.S. Parents." In *Measuring Globalization: Better Trade Statistics for Better Policy*, edited by Susan N.

Houseman and Michael Mandel. Kalamazoo, MI: W. E. Upjohn Institute for Employment Research.

Reinsdorf, Marshall B. 2004. "Alternative Measures of Personal Saving." *Survey of Current Business* 84 (9): 17–7.

Runkel, Marco, and Guttorm Schjelderup. 2011. "The Choice of Apportionment Factors under Formula Apportionment." *International Economic Review* 52 (3): 913–34.

Sanchirico, Chris William. 2015. "As American as Apple Inc.: International Tax and Ownership Nationality." *Tax Law Review* 68 (2): 207–74.

Syverson, Chad. 2017. "Challenges to Mismeasurement Explanations for the U.S. Productivity Slowdown." *Journal of Economic Perspectives* 31 (2): 165–86.

United Nations; Eurostat; and Organisation for Economic Co-operation and Development. 2011. *The Impact of Globalization on National Accounts*. New York and Geneva: United Nations.

United States Bureau of Economic Analysis. 2017a. "U.S. Direct Investment Abroad for 2014–2016: Detailed Historical Cost Positions and Related Financial Transactions and Income Flows." *Survey of Current Business* 97 (9).

United States Bureau of Economic Analysis. 2017b. "Foreign Direct Investment in the United States for 2014–2016: Detailed Historical Cost Positions and Related Financial Transactions and Income Flows." *Survey of Current Business*, 97 (9).

United States Department of the Treasury. 2007. Report to the Congress on Earnings Stripping, Transfer Pricing, and U.S. Income Tax Treaties.

Comment   Stephen J. Redding

I am delighted to discuss this chapter. Reading it made me think of the following quote from Ben Bernanke: "In many spheres of human endeavor, from science to business to education to economic policy, good decisions depend on good measurement." In my view, this chapter provides an excellent example of good measurement, and not simply for its own sake but also for deepening our understanding of a range of substantive economic issues.

The research question addressed in the chapter is, How should the economic activity of multinational enterprises (MNEs) be apportioned across countries? A distinction is drawn between two main approaches. First, there is "separate accounting," as used in the System of National Accounts (SNA) and Balance of Payments and International Investment Position Manual (BPM). According to this approach, the economic activity of multination-

Stephen J. Redding is the Harold T. Shapiro '64 Professor in Economics at Princeton University, a research fellow of the Centre for Economic Policy Research, and a research associate and director of the International Trade and Investment Program at the National Bureau of Economic Research.

For acknowledgments, sources of research support, and disclosure of the author's material financial relationships, if any, please see https://www.nber.org/books-and-chapters/challenges-globalization-measurement-national-accounts/comment-multinational-profit-shifting-and-measures-throughout-economic-accounts-redding.

als is allocated to locations based on the residences of transacting entities, where residence may be the economy of legal incorporation or registration of a holding company or special purpose entity. Second, there is "formulary apportionment," as used in this chapter and the related work in Guvenen et al. (2017). According to this methodology, the transactions of multinationals are attributed across the various locations in which they operate based on apportionment factors that reflect their relative levels of economic activity in those locations.

This is an important research question, because multinationals have access to countries that vary widely in corporate tax rates, which creates both incentives and opportunities to shift profits from high to low tax countries. This profit shifting can occur through a variety of means, including transfer pricing and holding companies that are resident in an economy of legal incorporation or registration that can differ from a multinational's main centers of operations. As a result, the measured distribution of economic activity of multinational corporations across locations can appear quite different under separate accounting versus formulary apportionment.

To provide evidence on the empirical relevance of this issue, this chapter recomputes key economic accounting measures in the US national accounts and balance of payments for 2014 using formulary apportionment. The impact of offshore profit shifting is measured using the differences between the values of these measures under formulary apportionment versus separate accounting. The chapter then goes beyond measurement to examine the economic implications for common analytic uses of the US national accounts and balance of payments including: (i) the labor share of income; (ii) national saving rates; (iii) returns on domestic financial business; (iv) returns on foreign direct investment; and (v) external balances.

The resulting empirical findings connect with a series of recent economic debates about the role of measurement in understanding key trends in economic performance, including the productivity slowdown and the decline in the labor share. It is clear that there is the potential for profit shifting under separate accounting, and formulary apportionment provides a natural and intuitive benchmark for comparison that has the potential to be more widely used in future research.

One of my main comments on the chapter relates to what are the right weights. Although the chapter provides an intuitive economic motivation for formulary apportionment, I found the text unclear, and I thought that this discussion could be tightened to think more carefully about the implicit assumptions on production technology and market structure. For each location n in the set Ω in which a given multinational has operations, we start by constructing an apportionment weight ω_n for that multinational based on the arithmetic average of location n's share in the wage bill and revenue of the multinational:

(1)
$$\omega_n = \left(\frac{1}{2} \times \frac{w_n L_n}{\sum_{i \in \Omega} w_i L_i} \right) + \left(\frac{1}{2} \times \frac{p_n y_n}{\sum_{i \in \Omega} p_i y_i} \right).$$

We next consider a particular economic variable of interest (ψ_i), such as employment or profits, for this multinational in each location i. Summing this variable across the set of locations (Ω), we obtain a measure of multinational's total scale of operations for that variable ($\sum_{i \in \Omega} \psi_i$). Finally, we use the apportionment weights (ω_n) to allocate this total amount across the individual locations and generate a predicted value of the economic variable ($\bar{\psi}_n$) in each location under formulary apportionment:

(2)
$$\bar{\psi}_n = \psi_n \sum_{i \in \Omega} \psi_i.$$

This procedure immediately suggests a number of questions. Why do we use the arithmetic mean of the wage bill and sales shares as the weights rather than some other weights, such as wage bill or sales shares by themselves? Could we derive the appropriate weights from an underlying economic model based on assumptions on the production technology and market structure? For example, if we assume a Cobb-Douglas production technology, the wage bill in each location is proportional to the total production cost in that location. Additionally, if we assume monopolistic competition and no transfer pricing, markups are constant and the same for all locations, which implies that the share of each location in the multinational's costs equals its share in revenues. Therefore, these two assumptions together seem to imply that wage bill shares should equal revenue shares, and hence either measure or both measures together could be used to construct the apportionment weights. Is this the right way to think about microfoundations for these apportionment weights? How large is the class of economic models for which these apportionment weights would provide a good approximation to the underlying distribution of multinational activity in the model? Although there are some robustness checks in the chapter, it would be helpful to provide more evidence on the sensitivity of the results to alternative assumptions about these weights. Are the circumstances under which the appropriate weight could depend on the economic question at hand?

Another of my comments relates to overidentification checks on the predicted distribution of economic activity under formulary apportionment. Notably, the chapter finds that around 75 percent of the adjustments to the measured distribution of economic activity are foreign affiliates classified as holding companies, which is consistent with profit shifting through the use of such companies and special purpose entities. By itself, this is a powerful overidentification check that the adjustments under formulary apportionment are capturing what we would expect them to capture. As already discussed to some extent in the chapter and related research by the authors, these overidentification checks could be pushed further, using variation across countries and industries where relevant. For example, are the countries and industries where the biggest differences between formulary apportionment and separate accounting those where we expect to find the greatest incentive and opportunity for profit shifting?

Another question suggested by the results is, What is the right metric for assessing the economic magnitude and statistical significance for the adjustments? Many of the findings exceed commonsense notions for what is large in economic magnitude, such as percentage points of GDP. But what is the right formal metric for assessing the economic magnitude of the results? What about statistical inference? Should we think of the apportionment weights as estimates from an underlying distribution? If so, can the authors provide evidence on the statistical significance of the various adjustments to the distribution of economic activity under formulary apportionment?

I found the implications of the measures for analytic uses of the US national accounts and balance of payments to be particularly interesting. I would encourage the authors to push further in terms of these economic implications. In particular, what are the economic questions for which formulary apportionment changes the answer in quantitatively relevant ways? Are there questions to which we get the answer wrong if we use separate accounting rather than formulary apportionment? Would we obtain substantially different estimates of key model parameters if we used data based on separate accounting instead of formulary apportionment? What are the implications of these findings for public policy?

Taken together, this is an excellent chapter with important measurement contributions and important substantive economic insights for a host of issues of great contemporary relevance. I look forward to following the authors' ongoing research in this area.

References

Bruner, Jennifer, Dylan G. Rassier, and Kim J. Ruhl. 2018. "Multinational Profit Shifting and Measures throughout Economic Accounts." Paper prepared for NBER-CRIW conference on The Challenges of Globalization in the Measurement of National Accounts. March, Bethesda, MD.
Guvenen, Fatih, Raymond J. Mataloni Jr., Dylan G. Rassier, and Kim J. Ruhl. 2017. "Offshore Profit Shifting and Domestic Productivity Measurement." NBER Working Paper No. 23324. Cambridge, MA: National Bureau of Economic Research.

6

Strategic Movement of Intellectual Property within US Multinational Enterprises

Derrick Jenniges, Raymond Mataloni Jr., Sarah Atkinson, and Erin (Yiran) Xin

6.1 Introduction

The shifting of profits abroad by US multinational enterprises (Mnes) through the movement of intellectual property (IP) has been widely documented. Profit shifting can occur through the use of internal transactions such as licensing agreements and research and development (R&D) cost sharing agreements (CSAs). These arrangements, which can be written to take advantage of ambiguities in tax laws, allow Mnes to legally shift the location of ownership of IP assets within the firm at a reduced price. This activity, also known as transfer pricing, was documented in a Credit Suisse report (Credit Suisse 2015, 35):

> Transfer pricing determines where profits on intercompany transactions are booked for tax purposes . . . By entering into transactions with them-

Derrick Jenniges is a senior economist at the Internal Revenue Service and was an economist at the Bureau of Economic Analysis when this chapter was written.

Raymond Mataloni Jr. was chief of the Research and Methodology Group at the Bureau of Economic Analysis before his death in 2021.

Sarah Atkinson is an economist at the Farm Production and Conservation Business Center of the US Department of Agriculture.

Erin (Yiran) Xin was an economist at the Bureau of Economic Analysis when this chapter was written.

This chapter benefited from comments received from Sally Thompson and other colleagues at the US Bureau of Economic Analysis, J. Brad Jensen and other participants at the March 2018 NBER CRIW conference on The Challenges of Globalization in the Measurement of National Accounts, and Tom Neubig. The views expressed in this paper are solely those of the authors and not necessarily those of the US Bureau of Economic Analysis or the US Department of Commerce. For acknowledgments, sources of research support, and disclosure of the authors' material financial relationships, if any, please see https://www.nber.org/books-and-chapters /challenges-globalization-measurement-national-accounts/strategic-movement-intellectual -property-within-us-multinational-enterprises.

selves . . . , using transfer pricing to price them, a dose of intercompany finance and a few loopholes, companies can move profits to low tax countries and costs to high tax countries.

Although the ultimate effects of the 2017 changes to US tax law remain to be seen, there is reason to believe that the incentives for this behavior have not disappeared. The behavior may continue due to the growing importance of intangibles in the production of goods and services, the difficulty in obtaining comparable market prices for these transactions, and the ability to sell ownership of intangible assets, like any other asset, within the firm.

Business entities that span multiple tax jurisdictions, such as multinational enterprises, present a challenge for tax authorities. To parse these expansive business entities into separate units that fit within the boundaries of tax jurisdictions, tax authorities have adopted the notion of separate accounting. However, as Seidman (2003, p. 541) notes, a business, which is primarily concerned with its overall results, has an incentive to manipulate these separate accounts.

> Group organization of corporations, all owned ultimately by the same stockholders, has been developed by modern businesses for perfectly legitimate reasons, among them being separate accounting for the various parts of an enterprise and the desirability, and frequently the necessity, of creating an independent corporation for the purpose of carrying on a particular part of the business, both at home and abroad. The mere fact that by a legal fiction these are separate entities should not obscure the fact that they are in reality one and the same business, owned by the same individuals, and run as a unit.

Businesses with operations that span multiple tax jurisdictions have an incentive to minimize the profits of their entities located in high-tax jurisdictions and to maximize the profits of their entities located in low-tax jurisdictions. Therefore, to the extent that it is permissible by the tax authorities, or to the extent that the business can avoid detection, the business has an incentive to shift expenses toward entities in high-tax jurisdictions and to shift revenues toward entities in low-tax jurisdictions. To prevent opportunistic behavior, tax authorities have applied the notion of the *arm's length standard*, which requires that intra-firm transactions in goods, services, or assets be priced at a comparable price to what the business would charge to an unrelated party. When businesses fail to adhere to this standard to minimize taxes, the activity is known as *transfer pricing*.

In the United States, concern about transfer pricing between the domestic and foreign units of US multinationals goes back to at least the 1920s. A 1921 report of the House Ways and Means Committee noted that:[1]

---

1. House of Representatives Report No. 350, 67th cong., 1st Sess., 14(1921).

Subsidiary corporations, particularly foreign subsidiaries, are sometimes employed to "milk" the parent corporation, or otherwise improperly manipulate the financial accounts of the parent company.

In 1928, Congress established Section 45 of the tax code to provide guidelines on transfer pricing within US MNEs. These laws held for decades, but the post–World War II expansion of US multinationals into Europe in the 1950s and 1960s created renewed interest in the topic, and in 1968, US transfer pricing law was updated under Section 482 of the US tax code. Picciotto (1992, p. 186) maintains that the 1968 guidelines "provided the basis for the monitoring of transfer pricing by the US Internal Revenue Service (IRS) for two decades without substantial changes." In the mid-2000s, an abrupt slowdown in the growth of corporate profits brought renewed scrutiny to transfer pricing practices. In 2006 congressional testimony, the commissioner of the US IRS stated that:

> Taxpayers shift significant profits offshore by manipulating the price of related party transactions so that the income of an economic group is earned in low-tax or no-tax jurisdictions, rather than the U.S., thus reducing the enterprise's worldwide tax liability . . . The levels of aggressiveness vary from one taxpayer to another . . . high technology and pharmaceutical industries are shifting profits offshore through a variety of intangibles to related foreign entities for inadequate consideration. Cost sharing arrangements are often the method of choice for this activity.[2]

Concerns over tax base erosion have led the US government to investigate this behavior. In 2012, the US Senate Permanent Subcommittee on Investigations questioned Microsoft's use of an intra-firm CSA, suggesting that aggressive transfer pricing was used to shift its IP assets from the US headquarters to subsidiaries in Puerto Rico, Ireland, and Singapore in an effort to avoid or reduce its US taxes (US Congress Senate Committee on Homeland Security and Governmental Affairs 2012). According to the Senate testimony, the majority of Microsoft's R&D was conducted in the United States. However, using a CSA, Microsoft Singapore and Microsoft Ireland reimbursed its US parent for some R&D costs in exchange for the right to collect royalties on the resulting IP in certain geographic markets. The Senate testimony indicates that Microsoft Singapore and Microsoft Ireland then marked up and relicensed these IP assets to other subsidiaries, paying 2.74 percent and 5.76 percent effective tax rates, respectively, to their host governments on income earned in 2011; these tax rates are significantly lower than the statutory US corporate tax rate of 35 percent, which prevailed at the time. Similarly, in 2013 the US Senate subcommittee concluded that

2. Mark Everson testimony to Senate Committee on Homeland Security and Governmental Affairs Permanent Subcommittee on Investigations hearing on Offshore Abuses: The Enablers, the Tools, and Offshore Secrecy, August 1, 2006. Quotation from page 17 of Sikka and Willmott (2010).

Apple used a CSA, a variety of offshore structures, and favorable transfer pricing to shift billions of dollars of profits to Ireland from the United States (US Congress Senate Committee on Homeland Security and Governmental Affairs, 2013). The subcommittee found that over the period of 2009–2011, Apple Sales International (ASI), the subsidiary that holds most of Apple's IP abroad, earned $38 billion in profits but paid only $21 million in taxes for an effective tax rate of 0.06 percent.

In this study, we explore profit shifting behavior of US MNEs through the use of CSAs. We expect that having a CSA is associated with lower profits for the US parent and higher profits for its foreign affiliates. We test this hypothesis on a sample of R&D-intensive MNEs over the 2006–2015 period and find support for our hypothesis. Specifically, foreign affiliates of parents with CSAs tend to be more profitable relative to their US parent compared with affiliates of parents without CSAs. Our study also offers an explanation for the small amount of research on this topic. It is very difficult to find public information identifying US MNEs with CSAs, and efforts by the US government to collect and publish this information have not been successful.

6.2   Literature review

Most of the academic studies of transfer pricing by US multinationals offer indirect evidence of strategic transfer pricing. In a seminal study, Grubert and Mutti (1991) use tabular data from the 1982 Benchmark Survey of US Direct Investment Abroad to show that the profitability of foreign manufacturing affiliates of US multinational enterprises is negatively related to the host country statutory tax rate, even after controlling for other economic factors in the host country. The authors also find a higher propensity for the US parent to export to their manufacturing affiliates in low tax countries, suggesting that at least part of the transfer pricing activity occurs by manipulating the prices for intra-firm trade in goods. In Grubert and Mutti (2009), the authors turn their attention to intra-firm pricing of IP. The paper is motivated by anecdotal cases of US multinational enterprises that have moved valuable IP created in the United States to entities in low tax countries. The authors focus on the specific tax management strategy of CSAs. Riedel (2014, p. 15) maintains that studies such as this one that focus on a specific strategy provide the strongest evidence of transfer pricing.

The most convincing empirical evidence has been presented by academic studies that investigate specific profit shifting channels, as their empirical tests are more direct and offer less room for results being driven by mechanisms unrelated to income shifting.

Under CSAs, a unit in a low tax country shares in the cost of developing IP through R&D in return for the right to earn royalties on those assets in certain geographic areas (typically in all non-US markets). Using tabular data on foreign affiliates of US MNEs from the US IRS and from the US

Bureau of Economic Analysis (BEA), Grubert and Mutti find that evidence of rising payments by affiliates to their US parents under CSAs is associated with a reduction in royalty payments by affiliates to their parents, which is consistent with a rise in transfer pricing under CSAs by US MNEs. In a related study, Bridgman (2014) shows how strategic movement of IP assets affects the location of profits of US MNEs by demonstrating how excluding intangible assets from the calculation of foreign direct investment (FDI) returns impacts US returns from the rest of the world compared with domestic returns.

In addition to these studies, a few studies employ firm-by-transaction-level data to provide direct evidence of transfer pricing. Bernard, Jensen, and Schott (2006) examine export transactions of US-based firms at the 10-digit Harmonized System level over the period 1993–2000. They find that when host country statutory tax rates are low, US multinationals tend to charge related parties lower prices than they charge unrelated parties for the same goods, which is consistent with tax-motivated profit shifting behavior. Other papers examining European multinationals employ a similar method and find similar results for Danish and French multinationals (Cristea and Nguyen 2013; Vicard 2015). This chapter is the first effort, to our knowledge, to employ firm-level data to examine profit shifting through the pricing of intangible assets under a specific tax strategy.

6.3   Challenges of Measuring IP Asset Movement within MNEs

6.3.1   Definition of IP Assets

The 2008 System of National Accounts (SNA) defines five types of IP assets: R&D; mineral exploration and evaluation; computer software and databases; entertainment, literary, and artistic originals; and other IP assets. The ownership of IP assets can be retained, in whole or in part, by the developer of these assets or transferred between entities within an MNE. Transferring the ownership of these rights occurs either through selling the rights outright or leasing them, and is governed by licensing agreements. US tax law on transfers of IP within an MNE are based on the arm's length standard, which requires that the price paid for the IP asset be commensurate with the expected income flows from that asset. Receipts and payments for the use of IP assets between US MNEs and foreign entities are recorded by BEA in the US International Transactions Accounts (ITAs) as exports and imports of services.

6.3.2   IP Assets Have an Important Role in US Trade in Services

IP assets play an important role in US trade in services, especially within MNEs. In 2016, US exports of services were $752.4 billion, up from $271.3 billion in 1999. Of this amount in 2016, $124.5 billion (17 percent) was accounted for by charges for the use of IP (sometimes referred to as licensing). Moreover, $69.4 billion (56 percent) of these exports occurred within US MNEs; that is, trade between US parents and their foreign affiliates. Charges for the use of IP are a return to the final output generated by R&D and other innovative activities. Firms also receive payments to fund in-process R&D on behalf of others, including affiliated customers. These charges are recorded under R&D services. In 2016, the United States had exports of R&D services of $37.2 billion, of which $20.6 billion (55 percent) occurred within US MNEs.

6.3.3   Movement of IP Assets within MNEs and Its Effects on Measures of Production

For tax purposes, and for economic accounting purposes, an IP asset is taxed based on the geographic location of its owner. This convention creates an incentive for MNEs to transfer ownership of IP that has been generated in their home country to affiliates in countries with lower tax rates at a price less than an arm's length price to reduce global income taxes. When successful, this practice can lead to large discrepancies between the location of productive economic activity generated through the use of IP assets and the location of legal ownership of these same IP assets. Under the SNA guidelines, many economic statistics, including stocks of IP assets, should be collected and presented based on the concept of economic ownership. Economic ownership is said to accrue to the entity that bears the risks and reaps the rewards of using the IP. As a practical convenience, economic ownership is often ascribed to the legal owner or paying user of the IP and is therefore attributed to that entity's place of legal incorporation or registration. In MNEs, legal and economic ownership of IP assets is sometimes transferred between units at less-than-arm's-length prices. This strategic movement of IP causes official economic statistics to not fully represent where the economic benefits of production associated with the IP are realized. The incidence of creating IP assets in a higher tax country and transferring ownership of them to a related entity in a lower tax countries at an artificially reduced price leads to increased exports of services and higher gross domestic product (GDP) estimates in low tax countries, and reduced exports of services and lower GDP estimates in higher tax countries.

6.4   CSAs

6.4.1   Description of CSAs

CSAs are defined under Section 482 of the US tax code regulations as an agreement under which the parties agree to share the costs of developing one or more intangibles in proportion to the share of reasonably anticipated benefits from exploiting the intangibles assigned to them under the arrangement. By sharing in the costs, the parties agree to share in the associated revenue if the outcome of the R&D has value. The most common method for assigning the division of revenue is based on territory (Bose 2002, 10), often with the US parent retaining rights to earn income from sales in the United States and the affiliate receiving rights to earn income from sales to the rest of the world. CSAs do not involve a full transfer of ownership. Instead, through joint funding of the development of these assets, the firms jointly share in the ownership of these assets. Under the agreements, each party is assigned a portion of the worldwide territory in which it can sell goods or services produced using these IP assets and/or to which they can license these IP assets to other affiliates and third parties. Each party separately earns income from sales to affiliates and to third parties.

6.4.2 Impacts of CSAs on Official Statistics

Transfer pricing through receipts under a CSA by US parents from foreign affiliates in low tax regions will impact the National Income and Product Accounts (NIPAs), as well as the trade in services and the primary income components of the current account of the US International Transactions Accounts (ITAs). These impacts will carry through to key economic aggregates, including GDP. Specifically, these impacts will affect the value of exports of services from the parent to the affiliate. Cross-border payments by foreign affiliates to US parents under CSAs are recorded as R&D services exports in the ITAs and the NIPAs. If the parent charges the affiliate less than the true costs of developing the IP asset, the parent's exports of R&D services and the affiliate's imports of R&D services will be understated. If the affiliate earns revenue from the IP abroad commensurate with the true value of these underlying assets, then its earnings will be increased by the transfer pricing. This will lead to an undervaluation of US GDP and an overvaluation of GDP in the affiliate's country (United Nations 2011, 113).

The US parent's share of the income earned by the foreign affiliate from the sale of goods or services embodying these IP assets is recorded in the ITAs under direct investment income. Because the undervaluation of the IP assets provided to the affiliate lowers the affiliate's costs, the parent's direct investment income receipts are increased. Assuming that the affiliate is fully owned by the parent, the effects of the parent's reduced exports of R&D services are effectively offset by increased direct investment income, so that the current account of the ITAs and GNP, which both take into account the trade in R&D services and investment income, are not affected. However, the GDP of the host country of the affiliate is raised by the earnings on the IP assets.

6.4.3 Example of a CSA and Its Impacts on National Statistics

The following hypothetical example details the sequence of events when a multinational enterprise utilizes a CSA. *The effects of the CSA on official statistics are indented and shown in italics.*

1. Suppose a US parent invests $100 million in R&D costs for a new product that will be sold both domestically and internationally.
2. The US parent enters into an intercompany CSA with its Irish affiliate. The two parties agree that the US parent retains the rights to sell the product in the United States (domestic sales) and the Irish affiliate obtains the rights to sell the product in all other countries.
3. Under the agreement, domestic sales are expected to be one-fourth of all total worldwide sales, implying the Irish affiliate will pay three-fourths of the R&D costs, or $75 million.

- *The $75 million payment to the US parent would be recorded as US exports of $75 million in R&D services to Ireland.*

4. Suppose that the product is developed successfully and generates $1 billion in worldwide revenues. Also suppose that the US parent earns $200 million in revenues in the domestic market and the Irish affiliate earns $800 million in revenues from sales to the rest of the world.

- *US FDI income receipts are $800 million, assuming, for simplicity, that the Irish affiliate's costs are zero.*
- *US exports of R&D services are zero.*
- *US exports of charges for the use of IP are zero.*
- *Had the parent not engaged in a CSA with its Irish affiliate and had retained all rights, US exports of charges for the use of IP would have been $1 billion.*

6.4.4   Methods Explored but Not Used to Identify MNEs with CSAs

Information on CSA activity is collected by the IRS, but firm-level information is not publicly available. Under Subsection 26 of Section 482 of the US tax code governing CSAs, taxpayers participating in a qualified CSA must attach to their US tax returns (or to a Schedule M of forms 5471 or 5472 for firms that pay foreign taxes) a statement indicating that they participate in a qualified cost-sharing arrangement. They must also provide names and information of the other participants, the method to determine the share of each participant's intangible development costs, any prior research and buy-in payments, and any allocations for stock-based compensation for plans filed after 2003. We ultimately hope to obtain access to this information to improve the data underlying our study, but we were not able to make these arrangements in time to incorporate the data into this chapter. Obtaining these records would allow us to construct an accurate and precise measure of firms with CSAs for each year. It would also improve on our current measure of CSAs by providing affiliate and country-level detail.

Some relevant firm-level information is provided by US Patent and Trademark Office (USPTO) records. However, it is difficult to link patent data to specific US MNEs, and it is even more difficult to match foreign patent data with foreign affiliates of US MNEs. Patent data provide information only on the patent titleholder and generally not on other participants, and the data are often not updated to reflect the transfer of IP assets to different entities within the MNEs. Because of these difficulties, in January 2014, the USPTO proposed updating its rules "to facilitate the examination of patent applications and to provide greater transparency concerning the ownership of patent applications and patents."[3] However, based on the public comments it received, the USPTO decided not to implement this proposal.[4]

We also explored using micro-data collected on BEA's benchmark (BE-120) and quarterly (BE-125) surveys of transactions in selected services and IP with foreign persons (henceforth, services surveys). US firms engaging in CSAs with foreign persons, including foreign affiliates, are required by law to report exports of R&D services on these surveys. One difficulty of using this information is that the surveys do not separately identify transactions related to CSAs. When possible, we linked the micro-data from these surveys to BEA's Activities of Multinational Enterprises (AMNEs) surveys, the BE-10 benchmark and BE-11 annual surveys, but differences in reporter names, coverage, and reporting thresholds on the services and AMNE surveys limited this approach.[5]

6.4.5   Method Used to Identify US MNEs with a CSA

We identify US MNEs with CSAs based on information in Securities and Exchange Commission (SEC) 10-K filings. We linked the firm-level BEA data on US MNEs to the firm-level corporate 10-K records using clerical name matching. We found evidence of intra-firm CSAs by conducting text searches of the 10-Ks. We limit our analysis to R&D-intensive US MNEs because of the resource-intensive nature of the exercise and because these firms are more likely to create and transfer valuable IP assets to foreign affiliates. We define R&D-intensive US MNEs as those having domestic R&D expenditures to sales ratios greater than or equal to 10 percent. To help avoid arbitrary exclusions, any US MNE meeting this criterion in any of four selected years (2006, 2009, 2012, or 2015) was included in our study. Applying this definition resulted in a list of 237 R&D-intensive US MNEs from BEA's AMNE surveys.

The text searches of 10-K filings were done primarily using the SEC Edgar online search engine. Using a keyword search for "cost sharing" or

3. Changes To Require Identification of Attributable Owner, Volume 79, No. 16, *Federal Register* (January 24, 2014).
4. https://www.uspto.gov/patent/initiatives/attributable-ownership.
5. Reporters to the BE-120 services survey data used in this study, covering 2006 and 2011, were required to report receipts from (sales to) affiliated or unaffiliated foreign persons of a particular type of service or IP greater than $2 million by country and by type of service. For the BE-125 services survey data used in this study, covering the other years, the cutoffs were $6 million for receipts and $4 million for payments, respectively. For the BE-10 benchmark AMNE survey data used in this study, covering 2009 and 2014, affiliates with assets, sales, or net income (±) of at least $80 million were required to report all of the data items used in this study. For the BE-11 annual AMNE survey data used in this study, covering the other years, the cutoff was $150 million for 2006–2008 and $60 million for 2010–2013 and 2015.

"cost-sharing," we looked for evidence that the company had an intra-firm CSA in place. This search was done by company and by year for the period 2006–2015. Using the Edgar search engine, we also attempted to search for intra-company CSA references by firm across all documents filed with the SEC. However, the option to search across all documents for a given year in Edgar is limited to filings during the past four years. Expanding our search in this way resulted in the identification of only a few additional CSAs, and their inclusion did not have a significant impact on our analysis. In addition to the Edgar search engine, we searched for CSA references within company filings and other documents using the commercial SEC document search engine BamSEC. This commercial search platform allowed us to search for CSA references across all SEC filings, news releases, and transcripts of earnings calls for a given US MNE. As with the comprehensive Edgar text search, utilizing this commercial search engine identified only a small number of additional US MNEs with CSA references, and their inclusion did not have a significant impact on our results. Nevertheless, comparing our results across these different methods gave us confidence that the main strategy of focusing on 10-K reports was robust and that the 10-K reports provide a systematic and reliable way to identify most of the large firms with intra-firm CSAs.

There are limitations to the 10-K search approach. Only US MNEs listed on a US stock exchange are required to file 10-Ks. As a result, we excluded from our analysis firms that did not file a 10-K record. Most importantly, the 10-K reports do not indicate the years in which the firm participated in a CSA or the level of CSA payments. Timing is important because during the time in which an affiliate is making its cost sharing installment payments to its US parent, its profits will be depressed. After it has completed those payments, its profits will be boosted by the favorable return on investment from those assets. The 10-K reports also do not necessarily indicate the country of the affiliate with whom the parent company enters into a CSA.[6] Additionally, the absence of country information requires that the CSA variable used in the regression analysis be applied at the parent level and to all affiliates of the given parent, whereas in reality, innovation and cost sharing activity is usually concentrated among a few affiliates (Bilir and Morales 2016) and in one or two specific countries. We partly overcome this limitation by employing country fixed effects in our regression analysis.

We linked our list of MNEs engaging in CSAs with profits and other

---

6. While supplementing our search using the Edgar SEC database with commercially available databases, such as BamSEC and Bloomberg, can provide additional firm-level information on CSAs, these databases do not solve the root issues with using 10-K reports to identify firms with CSAs. These include the danger of false negatives. That is, just because we do not find a CSA reference is not a complete guarantee that the company does not have a CSA. In addition, the information in these datasets is generally based on corporate 10-K information collected by the SEC so the dataset is restricted to listed firms. Moreover, it may also be biased toward firms that have been listed for a longer time and, as a result, filed more documents with the SEC, and larger MNEs, which are likely to have filed more detailed financial documents with the SEC.

Table 6.1   **R&D-intensive[a] US MNEs by CSA reference, 2006–2015**

Cost sharing reference	Number of US parents	Percent of total
Yes	42	18%
No and listed[b]	152	64%
No and private or not listed	43	18%
Total	237	100%

[a] R&D intensive = R&D expenditures-to-sales ratio >= 10 percent in any of the following years: 2006, 2009, 2012, or 2015.
[b] Listed means the corporation was listed on a US stock exchange and filed a 10-K in at least one of the years in the sample period.

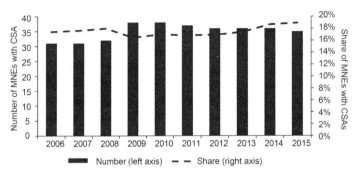

Figure 6.1   **Number and share of US MNEs having a CSA reference, 2006–2015**

data from BEA's AMNE surveys and with data on the level of cost sharing payments, as indicated by R&D services exports from parents to affiliates reported on BEA's services surveys.

6.4.6   Characteristics of US MNEs with CSAs

From our list of 237 R&D-intensive US MNEs reporting on the AMNE surveys, we identified 42 as having an intra-firm CSA at some time during our period of study, 2006–2015. The remaining MNEs without a CSA reference were split into public corporations that filed a 10-K during the 2006–2015 sample period (152 MNEs) and private and other corporations that did not file a 10-K during the same period (43 MNEs). These results are summarized in table 6.1 and figure 6.1.

US MNEs with CSAs are concentrated in a few key industry sectors. The majority of US MNEs with CSAs are classified in the following North American Industry Classification System (NAICS) industry sectors: metals and machinery manufacturing, excluding chemicals (NAICS sector 33); information (NAICS sector 51); and professional, scientific, and technical services (NAICS sector 54). Figure 6.2 presents counts of MNEs in the four-digit NAICS industries in these industry sectors, for all MNEs and for those

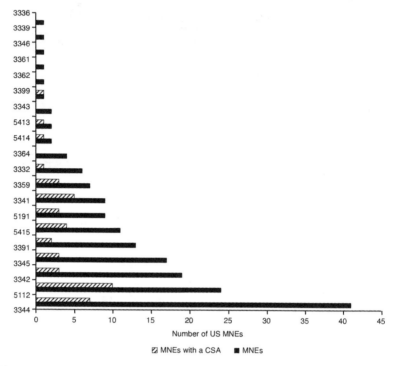

Figure 6.2   R&D-intensive US MNEs by industry of US parent, 2006–2015
Note: A description of the NAICS codes is provided in appendix A.

having a CSA. These industry sectors could be considered "high-tech" and R&D intensive. Firms within the information and professional, scientific, and technical services industry sectors tend to have a relatively large portion of their total assets in intangible capital. Previous research (such as Grubert 2012) has found stronger links between parents in high-tech industries, the establishment of subsidiaries in low tax countries, and the movement of IP for profit shifting activities.

6.5   Model, Data, and Empirical Results

6.5.1   Methodology and Model

Our model is motivated by a basic return on assets framework for parents and affiliates, which measures the profitability of an operating unit within an MNE as generated by its stock of tangible and intangible assets. Denoting i as the operating unit (US parent or foreign affiliate), the rate of return is given by profit-type return (PTR) scaled by a firm's stock of assets, which consists of physical assets, such as building structures, land, and equipment, as well as intangible assets, such as IP.[7]

$$Rate\ of\ Return_i = \frac{PTR_i}{Physical\ assets_i + Intangible\ assets_i}$$

A unit's profitability is a function of its physical asset stock and its intangible asset stock, which can be either created in house or purchased. We use the value of net property, plant, and equipment as the measure of the stock of physical assets. As a measure of the stock of intangible assets, we utilize data on R&D performed by the unit for its own use, R&D services payments and receipts, and affiliated IP royalty payments. The R&D stock is calculated using the perpetual inventory method where the flows equal R&D performed for own account, minus R&D services exports, plus R&D services imports. In the model, we also include affiliated royalty payments, since they represent compensation for shared R&D assets within an MNE; royalty payments represent period-specific leasing of R&D assets rather than an accumulation of R&D assets over time, so they are simply added to the denominator rather than being included in the perpetual inventory calculation. This approach acknowledges that the stock of intangible assets within a unit of an MNE may be either created in house or purchased from outside. Both intangible and tangible assets are expected to generate a return for the unit, resulting in the following profit equation for US parents:

$$(1) \quad PTR_{USP,t} = \beta_0 + \beta_1 PPE_{USP,t} + \beta_2 R\&D\ Stock_{USP,t}$$

$$+ \beta_3 Royalty\ Payments_{USP,t} + \beta_4 Cost\ Sharing_{USP,t}$$

$$+ \varepsilon_{USP,t}.$$

The inclusion of the parent PPE accounts for firm size, and we limit the analysis to R&D-intensive parents. Equation 1, which is estimated with panel data for US parents (USP), is also estimated with industry fixed effects.

Conceptually one might imagine a similar equation for individual foreign affiliates because, just like US parents, both their tangible and intangible assets are expected to generate a return. However, two data limitations prevent the estimation of such an equation for affiliates. First, our data do not identify specific foreign affiliates with which US parents had CSAs. As a result, the binary variable denoting a CSA is a firm-level variable. The second limitation is that the services surveys (the surveys that collect data for royalty payments and R&D exports and imports) are collected only at the country

---

7. Profit-type return is BEA's measure of profits from current production based on its AMNE surveys. It is derived from financial accounting data and is calculated as net income before taxes minus capital gains and losses, depletion, and income from equity investment. For details, see the technical note to Mataloni and Goldberg (1994).

level, not at the foreign affiliate level, which becomes an issue when an MNE has more than one foreign affiliate in a particular country.

As a result of these data limitations, we aggregate foreign affiliate data to the country of the affiliate and construct an equation that compares the profitability of the parent and the country-aggregated foreign affiliate units of a US MNE to uncover evidence that is consistent with US parents shifting profits abroad through the use of CSAs. We begin with an equation similar to equation 1 except instead of variables representing the data for US parents, they represent the sum of that data item for all affiliates of a given parent in a given country:

$$(2) \quad PTR_{C,t} = \beta_0 + \beta_1 PPE_{C,t} + \beta_2 R\&D\ Stock_{C,t}$$

$$+ \beta_3 Royalty\ Payments_{C,t} + \beta_4 Tax\ rate_C + \varepsilon_{C,t}.$$

We add a variable denoting the median effective tax rate faced by affiliates in a country in 2006–2015. Then, we subtract equation (1) from equation (2) to examine the difference in the profitability of affiliates and parents. The resulting equation is given by:

$$(3)\ (PTR_C - PTR_{USP})_t = \alpha_0 + \alpha_1(PPE_C - PPE_{USP})_t$$

$$+ \alpha_2(R\&D\ Stock_C - R\&D\ Stock_{USP})_t$$

$$+ \alpha_3(Royalty\ Payments_C - Royalty\ Payments_{USP})_t$$

$$+ \alpha_4 Cost\ Sharing_{USP,t} + \alpha_5 Tax\ Rate_C + \eta_t.$$

In equation 3, variables with the subscript C denote the sum of the data for all foreign affiliates of a particular MNE in a particular country. For example, if a US parent has three affiliates in Belgium, then the R&D stock for each of these three affiliates would be aggregated into a single R&D stock in Belgium for that US parent. The tax rate variable captures the effect of host country tax rates. Following similar studies of profit shifting by MNEs, we explored different tax rate variable specifications. First, we explored using the inverse of the tax rate, which would acknowledge that the impact of a change in tax rates on profits may be larger for affiliates in low tax countries than for affiliates in high tax countries or, likewise, for those having a CSA with their parents compared to those without a CSA with their parents. Other explorations of a nonlinear relationship between tax rates and affiliate profitability included interacting the tax rate with the cost sharing fixed effect, using the square of the median effective tax rate, and using the natural log of the median effective tax rate. None of these alternative specifications are reported here because they did not have a significant impact on the results. To isolate the main industries that are driving our results, we estimate equation 3 with industry fixed effects. To isolate the main host countries that are driving our results, we also estimate equation 3 with country fixed effects.

Table 6.2   **Variable definitions and sources**

Variable	Definition	Unit of measure	Source
PTR	Profit-type return; equals net income + host country income taxes – capital gains/losses – income on equity.	Fractional decimal	BEA BE-10/11 surveys
PPE	Net property, plant, and equipment.	Millions of dollars	BEA BE-10/11 surveys
R&D Stock	R&D performed for own account – R&D services exports + R&D services imports, where flow data are converted to a stock using perpetual inventory method.	Millions of dollars	BEA BE-10/11 and BE-120/125 surveys
Royalty Payments	Royalty payments paid by the US parent (foreign affiliates) to the foreign affiliates (US parent).	Millions of dollars	BEA BE-120/125 surveys
Cost Sharing	A binary variable that equals 1 if US parent has a CSA with its foreign affiliates; equals zero otherwise.	Binary 0/1	SEC 10-K text searches
Tax Rate	The median tax rate faced by foreign affiliates in the host country in 2006-2015	Fractional decimal	BEA BE-10/11 surveys

6.5.2   Variable Definitions and Sources

Details about the definitions and data sources used to construct the variables in equations 1 and 3 are provided in table 6.2.

6.5.3   Results

Our econometric results are consistent with the use of CSAs between US parent companies and their foreign affiliates to shift profits to lower tax jurisdictions. The first stage of our analysis is to examine the profitability of US parents with and without CSAs. All else equal, we would expect those with CSAs to be less profitable. Using panel analysis to estimate equation 1, the results in table 6.3 show that, in general, there is not a statistically significant relationship between the profitability of US parents with CSAs and parents without CSAs. This result holds whether examining all industries (column 1) or whether the analysis is limited to the industries where CSAs are concentrated (column 2). However, the lack of significance partly reflects differences in the importance of having a CSA across industries (column 3). In three of the ten NAICS industries in which CSAs are concentrated, there is a significant negative relationship between the profitability of US parents and engaging in CSAs with their foreign affiliates. For example, parents in software publishing (NAICS industry 5112) with CSAs had average profits that were $114 million lower than similarly endowed parents in that industry without CSAs. In one of the ten industries, there is a significant positive relationship between parent profits and engaging in CSAs. In six of the ten NAICS industries, there is not a statistically significant relationship. Although the evidence is mixed, on balance, there is more evidence for our hypothesis than against it. The mixed nature of these results is not surprising given our crude measure of CSA activity and the volatility of our profit measure.

6.5.3.1   Parent Results

Although US parent results are generally consistent with our hypothesis, they provide only a partial understanding of the relationship between CSAs and the location of MNE profits. The US parent estimates provide information about the relative profitability of those with CSAs and those without CSAs, but they do not explain why we observe this relationship. Is it because parents with CSAs are truly less able to generate profits than those without CSAs, or is it the case that parents with CSAs appear less profitable because they shift profits to foreign affiliates in lower tax countries? To help answer this question, we turn to equation 3, which estimates the impact of CSAs on the difference between profitability of foreign affiliates and profitability of their US parent. The results of estimating equation 3 using panel analysis are provided in tables 6.4a and 6.4b.[8]

Overall, affiliates engaging in CSAs with their parents tend to be more profitable than their parents. As illustrated in table 6.4a, in all industries, profits of affiliates with CSAs are $63 million higher on average than similarly endowed US parents. In the three NAICS sectors in which CSAs are concentrated, the difference is $105 million. Across the more detailed NAICS industries, the results are mixed but, overall, tend to support our hypothesis. In six of the ten NAICS industries in which CSAs are concentrated, there are significant positive relationships between the profitability of affiliates relative to their US parents and the existence of a CSA. For example, affiliates in software publishing (NAICS industry 5112) had average profits that were $106 million higher than similarly endowed parents in that industry when a CSA was present. In three of the ten industries, there is a significant negative relationship between the relative profitability of foreign affiliates and the existence of a CSA. In one of the ten NAICS industries, there is not a statistically significant relationship.

We also examine country-level differences by including country of affiliate fixed effects. The results are shown in table 6.4b. Including these country-

---

8. Similar to the parent-level regressions, we eliminated outliers in the data by trimming the five percent tails in the dependent and independent variables for the regressions reported in tables 6.4a and 6.4b.

Table 6.3   US parent results, 2006–2015

Variable	All industries	Key CSA industry sectors[a]	Key CSA industry sectors[b]	Number of parents
Constant	51.930	22.340	53.562	
	(196.343)	(51.699)	(49.480)	
PPE_{USP}	0.139	0.227*	0.226*	
	(0.086)	(0.889)	(0.089)	
$R\&D\ Stock_{USP}$	0.068***	0.055**	0.053*	
	(0.0178)	(0.021)	(0.021)	
Royalty Payments$_{USP}$	2.14**	6.600	6.762*	
	(0.678)	(5.497)	(3.380)	
Cost Sharing Agreement$_{USP}$ (CSA)	−3.83	−13.100		
	(42.612)	(37.688)		
$CSA*NAICS\ 3332_{USP}$			212.466**	6
(Industrial Machinery Manufacturing)			(45.000)	
$CSA*NAICS\ 3341_{USP}$			53.943	9
(Computer and Peripheral Equipment Manufacturing)			(85.161)	
$CSA*NAICS\ 3342_{USP}$			111.905	18
(Communications Equipment Manufacturing)			(135.960)	
$CSA*NAICS\ 3344_{USP}$			−1.586	40
(Semiconductor and Other Electronic Component Manufacturing)			(45.464)	
$CSA*NAICS\ 3345_{USP}$			432.870	17
(Navigational, Measuring, Electromedical and Control Instruments Manufacturing)			(225.264)	
$CSA*NAICS\ 3359_{USP}$			39.656	6
(Other Electrical Equipment and Component Manufacturing)			(32.942)	

(*continued*)

Table 6.3 (continued)

Variable	All industries	Key CSA industry sectors[a]	Key CSA industry sectors[b]	Number of parents
CSA*NAICS 3391$_{USP}$ (Medical Equipment and Supplies Manufacturing)			-109.885** (37.685)	13
CSA*NAICS 5112$_{USP}$ (Software Publishers)			-114.485* (50.613)	23
CSA*NAICS 5191$_{USP}$ (Other Information Services)			-149.912*** (53.354)	8
CSA*NAICS 5415$_{USP}$ (Computer Systems Design and Related Services)			-101.049 (95.354)	9
Year fixed effects	Yes	Yes	Yes	
Two-digit NAICS fixed effects	Yes	Yes	No	
Number of observations	1,303	1,124	1,124	
Number of US parents	187	164	164	
R squared	0.383	0.371	0.372	

Note: Outliers, defined as observations at or below the 5th percentile and those at or above the 95th percentile, were excluded from the analysis.

Dollar denominated flow data are adjusted for inflation using the GDP implicit price deflator from BEA's NIPA table 1.1.9. Dollar denominated stock data are first adjusted from historical cost to current cost using current-cost to historical-cost ratios from BEA's fixed asset by industry accounts (tables 3.1ESI and 3.3ESI) and are then adjusted for inflation.

Coefficient estimates with heteroscedasticity-robust standard errors in parentheses. Significant coefficients are denoted by ***, **, * at the 1, 5, and 10 percent significance levels, respectively.

[a] Column 2 includes US MNEs classified in the two-digit NAICS sectors 33, 51, and 54.

[b] Column 3 includes US MNEs classified in the two-digit NAICS sectors 33, 51, and 54 and estimates cost sharing fixed effects for all four-digit US parent NAICS codes where MNEs with CSA were identified within these two-digit NAICS sectors and the number of MNEs was greater than one.

Table 6.4a   Affiliate-parent difference results (without country fixed effects), 2006–2015

Variable	All industries	Key CSA industry sectors[a]	Key CSA industry sectors[b]
Constant	209.790	32.660	-149.089***
	(80.088)	(45.017)	(46.457)
$PPE_C - PPE_{USP}$	-0.012	0.111***	0.093***
	(0.015)	(0.018)	(0.018)
$R\&D\ Stock_C - R\&D\ Stock_{USP}$	0.079***	0.078***	0.086***
	(0.003)	(0.004)	(0.004)
$Royalty\ Payments_C - Royalty\ Payments_{USP}$	-0.588**	0.058	0.005
	(0.206)	(0.127)	(0.125)
$Cost\ Sharing\ Agreement_{USP}$ (CSA)	63.350*	104.810***	
	(24.363)	(24.623)	
$Tax\ Rate_C$	-289.388	-273.505	-323.225
	(212.994)	(193.314)	(203.401)
$CSA*NAICS\ 3332USP$			-163.002***
(Industrial Machinery Manufacturing)			(18.046)
$CSA*NAICS\ 3341USP$			-161.272**
(Computer and Peripheral Equipment Manufacturing)			(61.450)
$CSA*NAICS\ 3342USP$			920.760***
(Communications Equipment Manufacturing)			(108.229)
$CSA*NAICS\ 3344USP$			-28.298
(Semiconductor and Other Electronic Component Manufacturing)			(16.833)
$CSA*NAICS\ 3345USP$			-589.176***
(Navigational, Measuring, Electromedical and Control Instruments Manufacturing)			(60.406)
$CSA*NAICS\ 3359USP$			166.792***
(Other Electrical Equipment and Component Manufacturing)			(19.138)
			(continued)

Table 6.4a   (continued)

Variable	All industries	Key CSA industry sectors[a]	Key CSA industry sectors[b]
$CSA*NAICS\ 3391USP$ (Medical Equipment and Supplies Manufacturing)			92.549*** (21.635)
$CSA*NAICS\ 5112USP$ (Software Publishers)			105.620*** (18.617)
$CSA*NAICS\ 5191USP$ (Other Information Services)			615.167*** (119.880)
$CSA*NAICS\ 5415USP$ (Computer Systems Design and Related Services)			40.323* (18.231)
Year fixed effects	Yes	Yes	Yes
Two-digit NAICS fixed effects	Yes	Yes	No
Number of observations	21,251	17,799	17,799
Number of parent-country pairs	3,851	3,281	3,281
R squared	0.448	0.593	0.567

Note: Outliers, defined as observations at or below the 5th percentile and those at or above the 95th percentile, were excluded from the analysis.

Dollar denominated flow data are adjusted for inflation using the GDP implicit price deflator from BEA's NIPA table 1.1.9. Dollar denominated stock data are first adjusted from historical cost to current cost using current-cost to historical-cost ratios from BEA's fixed asset by industry accounts (tables 3.1ESI and 3.3ESI) and are then adjusted for inflation.

The dependent variable is the difference between the country-level aggregates of foreign affiliate profit-type return and the profit-type return of the corresponding affiliate's US parent.

Coefficient estimates with heteroscedasticity-robust standard errors in parentheses. Significant coefficients are denoted by ***, **, *, at the one, five, and ten percent significance levels, respectively.

[a] Column 2 includes US MNEs classified in the two-digit NAICS sectors 33, 51, and 54

[b] Column 3 includes US MNEs classified in the two-digit NAICS sectors 33, 51, and 54 and estimates cost sharing fixed effects for all four-digit US parent NAICS codes where MNEs with CSA were identified within these two-digit NAICS sectors and the number of MNEs was greater than one.

Table 6.4b Affiliate-parent difference results with country fixed effects,[a] 2006–2015

Variable	All industries	Key CSA industry sectors[b]	Key CSA industry sectors[c]
Constant	-133.613	69.246	-162.356*
	(116.397)	(83.518)	(83.610)
$PPE_C{-}PPE_{USP}$	-0.025	0.093***	0.073***
	(0.014)	(0.017)	(0.017)
$R\&D\ Stock_C{-}R\&D\ Stock_{USP}$	0.081***	0.083***)	0.084***
	(0.003)	(0.004	(0.004)
$Royalty\ Payments_C{-}Royalty\ Payments_{USP}$	-0.561**	-0.104	-0.138
	(0.174)	(0.128)	(0.126)
Cost Sharing Agreement$_{USP}$ (CSA)	59.8*	105.590***	
	(24.417)	(24.537)	
$CSA*NAICS\ 3332_{USP}$			-181.133***
(Industrial Machinery Manufacturing)			(20.458)
$CSA*NAICS\ 3341_{USP}$			-182.687**
(Computer and Peripheral Equipment Manufacturing)			(61.862)
$CSA*NAICS\ 3342_{USP}$			943.320***
(Communications Equipment Manufacturing)			(105.658)
$CSA*NAICS\ 3344_{USP}$			-42.956*
(Semiconductor and Other Electronic Component Manufacturing)			(17.489)
$CSA*NAICS\ 3345_{USP}$			-570.638***
(Navigational, Measuring, Electromedical and Control Instruments Manufacturing)			(60.076)
$CSA*NAICS\ 3359_{USP}$			152.231***
(Other Electrical Equipment and Component Manufacturing)			(21.300)
$CSA*NAICS\ 3391_{USP}$			98.008***
(Medical Equipment and Supplies Manufacturing)			(28.149)
$CSA*NAICS\ 5112_{USP}$			95.784***
(Software Publishers)			(18.992)
$CSA*NAICS\ 5191_{USP}$			552.441***
(Other Information Services)			(109.556)
			(*continued*)

Table 6.4b (continued)

Variable	All industries	Key CSA industry sectors[b]	Key CSA industry sectors[c]
CSA*NAICS 5415_USP (Computer Systems Design and Related Services)			
Bahamas 250			39.485
			(20.191)
Ireland 313	1,136.212*	1,1057***	964.532***
	(633.570)	(150.443)	(156.136)
	193.543	236*	184.180
	(126.777)	(109.476)	(109.456)
Year fixed effects	Yes	Yes	Yes
Two-digit NAICS fixed effects	Yes	Yes	No
Number of observations	22,970	19,178	19,178
Number of parent-country pairs	4,285	3,636	3,636
R squared	0.469	0.613	0.588

[a] Country coefficients are reported for large countries with statistically significant coefficients at the 10 percent or higher level of significance for at least one of the regression specifications presented in the table. Large countries are defined as those having an outward foreign direct investment position of greater than $20 billion in 2015. Large countries with statistically insignificant coefficients for all regression specifications at the 10 percent level and higher in order of position size (largest to smallest) are: Netherlands, United Kingdom, Luxembourg, United Kingdom Islands- Caribbean, Bermuda, Singapore, Switzerland, Australia, Germany, Japan, Mexico, China, France, Hong Kong, Brazil, Belgium, Korea, Spain, India, Norway, Sweden, Italy, Chile, and Gibraltar. Outliers, defined as observations at or below the 5th percentile and those at or above the 95th percentile, were excluded from the analysis.

The dependent variable is the difference between the country-level aggregates of foreign affiliate profit-type return and the profit-type return of the corresponding affiliate's US parent.

Dollar denominated flow data are adjusted for inflation using the GDP implicit price deflator from BEA's NIPA table 1.1.9. Dollar denominated stock data are first adjusted from historical cost to current cost using current-cost to historical-cost ratios from BEA's fixed asset by industry accounts (tables 3.1ESI and 3.3ESI) and are then adjusted for inflation.

Coefficient estimates with heteroscedasticity-robust standard errors in parentheses. Significant coefficients are denoted by ***, **, * at the 1, 5, and 10 percent significance levels, respectively.

[b] Column 2 includes US MNEs classified in the two-digit NAICS sectors 33, 51, and 54.

[c] Column 3 includes US MNEs classified in the two-digit NAICS sectors 33, 51, and 54 and estimates cost sharing fixed effects for all four- digit US parent NAICS codes where MNEs with CSA were identified within these two-digit NAICS sectors and the number of MNEs was greater than one.

level fixed effects does not change the overall results, but they do highlight the countries that are contributing most to the overall results. At the country level, affiliates in the Bahamas had average profits that were $965 million higher than a similarly endowed US parent. This finding is consistent with the use of the "Double Irish Dutch Sandwich" tax strategy, which is explained in appendix B.

6.6   Conclusions and Next Steps

The relationship between tax law and the real activities of MNEs has generated widespread interest. This study builds on Guvenen et al. (2017), which shows, at the aggregate level, how strategic movement of IP by MNEs can have important effects on key economic aggregates such as GDP and the trade balance. The apportionment technique used in that paper was mainly designed to answer "how large" the effect of profit shifting by MNEs has been. With our research, we begin to address "how they did" by identifying MNEs that have engaged in CSAs with their foreign affiliates and how those arrangements appear to have affected the geographic allocation of MNE profits.

We explore profit shifting behavior by US MNEs through the use of CSAs. Using a sample of R&D-intensive MNEs from BEA surveys, we use text searches of 10-K documents to identify which of these US MNEs had CSAs between US parents and their foreign affiliates in the 2006–2015 period. We test our hypothesis that having a CSA is associated with relatively lower profits for the US parent and relatively higher profits for foreign affiliates. The initial findings generally support our hypothesis that CSA activity between parents and affiliates is associated with profit shifting. Specifically, while evidence using data for parents alone is inconclusive, when we combine data for parents and affiliates, we find that affiliates of parents with a CSA are more profitable relative to their parents than those without a CSA. In addition, through our use of country fixed effects in the regressions, we can associate this activity with the use of a Dutch Sandwich tax strategy.

Our ability to draw strong conclusions on the use of CSA to facilitate profit shifting among US MNEs was negatively impacted by data limitations. Obtaining information on CSAs and linking the data from the two sets of surveys were two of the greatest challenges in this project. Future research will include exploring potential additional sources for data on CSAs and continuing to improve the links between the BEA AMNE and services surveys. Despite these limitations, we feel that this chapter makes a contribution by using firm-level data to explore how a specific tax can be used to shift profits across units of US MNEs in different countries and affect the measurement of national and international economic accounts in those countries.

Appendix A
Description of Selected NAICS Industry Codes

Table 6A.1   Description of selected NAICS industry codes

NAICS industry code	Description
3332	Industrial Machinery Manufacturing
3336	Engine, Turbine, and Power Transmission Equipment Manufacturing
3339	Other General Purpose Machinery Manufacturing
3341	Computer and Peripheral Equipment Manufacturing
3342	Communications Equipment Manufacturing
3343	Audio and Video Equipment Manufacturing
3344	Semiconductor and Other Electronic Component Manufacturing
3345	Navigational, Measuring, Electromedical and Control Instruments Manufacturing
3346	Manufacturing and Reproducing Magnetic and Optical Media
3359	Other Electrical Equipment and Component Manufacturing
3361	Motor Vehicle Manufacturing
3362	Motor Vehicle Body and Trailer Manufacturing
3364	Aerospace Product and Parts Manufacturing
3391	Medical Equipment and Supplies Manufacturing
3399	Other Miscellaneous Manufacturing
5112	Software Publishers
5191	Other Information Services
5413	Architectural, Engineering, and Related Services
5414	Specialized Design Services
5415	Computer Systems Design and Related Services

Appendix B
Double Irish Dutch Sandwich Tax Strategy

One tax strategy that has been used by US multinational enterprises (MNEs) to reduce (or eliminate) taxes on their IP is known as a "Double Irish Dutch Sandwich." Under this arrangement, IP is held by an affiliated entity in a low tax location such as a Caribbean tax haven country like the Bahamas, where corporate profits are not taxed (Entity B in the diagram). This Caribbean entity is often a brass plate entity having no employees and little, if any, physical presence. Although a resident in a Caribbean Island, it is incorporated in Ireland.

The Caribbean entity, in turn, owns Entity C, an Irish resident and Irish incorporated operating affiliate, and Entity D, a Netherlands resident and Netherlands incorporated affiliate that serves as an intermediary between

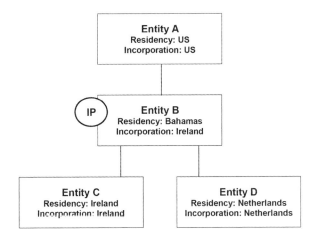

Figure 6B.1   Double Irish Dutch Sandwich Tax Strategy

Entities B and C. Entity B in the Bahamas licenses the IP to Entity D in the Netherlands, which, in turn, licenses the IP to Entity C in Ireland. As the Ireland resident affiliate (Entity C) earns income on the IP, it could pay royalties to the Netherlands resident affiliate (Entity D) without incurring a withholding tax penalty because both countries are members of the European Union. Entity D could then pay royalties to its parent, Entity B, in the Caribbean free of withholding taxes because the Netherlands does not impose withholding taxes on royalties. The Netherlands resident affiliate will undoubtedly charge a small fee for serving as an intermediary, which will be taxed at the Netherlands corporate tax rate of 25 percent. Thus, very little of the income on the IP is subject to taxation and overall the MNE will enjoy a very low effective tax rate on that income. The MNE could avoid US taxation on income because Entities B and C are regarded as a single consolidated entity by the US tax authority and, until 2018, foreign profits generally were not taxed until they were repatriated to the United States. The MNE would be exempt from Irish taxation on income generated by the IP because Irish entities are taxed based on where central management and control is located, which is the brass plate affiliate (Entity B) in the Caribbean.

References

Bernard, A. B., J. B. Jensen, and P. K. Schott. 2006. "Transfer Pricing by US-based Multinational Firms." NBER Working Paper No. 12493. Cambridge, MA: National Bureau of Economic Research.

Bilir, L. K., and E. Morales. 2016. "Innovation in the Global Firm." NBER Working Paper No. 22160. Cambridge, MA: National Bureau of Economic Research.

Bose, A. K. 2002. "The Effectiveness of Using Cost Sharing Arrangements as a Mechanism to Avoid Intercompany Transfer Pricing Issues with Respect to IP." *Virginia Tax Review* 21 (4): 553–649.

Bridgman, B. 2014. "Do Intangible Assets Explain High US Foreign Direct Investment Returns?" *Journal of Macroeconomics* 40: 159–171.

Credit Suisse Securities Research and Analytics. 2015. *Foreign Tax Risk.*

Cristea, A. D., and D. X. Nguyen. 2013. "Transfer Pricing by Multinational Firms: New Evidence from Foreign Firm Ownerships." *American Economic Journal: Economic Policy* 8 (3): 170–202.

Grubert, H. 2012. "Foreign Taxes and the Growing Share of US Multinational Company Income Abroad: Profits, Not Sales, Are Being Globalized." *National Tax Journal* 65 (2): 247–81.

Grubert, H., and J. Mutti. 1991. "Taxes, Tariffs and Transfer Pricing in Multinational Corporate Decision Making." *The Review of Economics and Statistics* 73 (2): 285–93.

Grubert, H., and J. Mutti. 2009. "The Effect of Taxes on Royalties and the Migration of Intangible Assets Abroad." In *International Trade in Services and Intangibles in the Era of Globalization,* edited by M. Reinsdorf and M. J. Slaughter, 111–37. Chicago, IL: University of Chicago Press.

Guvenen, F., R. J. Mataloni Jr, D. G. Rassier, and K. J. Ruhl. 2017. "Offshore Profit Shifting and Domestic Productivity Measurement." NBER Working Paper No. 23324. Cambridge, MA: National Bureau of Economic Research.

Mataloni, R., and L. Goldberg. 1994. "Gross Product of U.S. Multinational Companies, 1977–91." *Survey of Current Business* 74 (2): 42–63.

Picciotto, S. 1992. *International Business Taxation.* London: Weidenfeld and Nicolson.

Riedel, N. 2014. "Quantifying International Tax Avoidance: A Review of the Academic Literature." ETPF Policy Paper, 2.

Seidman, J. S. 2003. *Seidman's Legislative History of Federal Income Tax Laws, 1938–1861.* New York: The Lawbook Exchange, Ltd.

Sikka, P., and H. Willmott. 2010. "The Dark Side of Transfer Pricing: Its Role in Tax Avoidance and Wealth Retentiveness." *Critical Perspectives on Accounting* 21 (4): 342–356.

United Nations. 2011. *The Impact of Globalization on National Accounts.* New York.

United States. Congressional Senate Committee on Homeland Security and Government Affairs. 2012. *Offshore Profit Shifting and the U.S. Tax Code—Part 1 (Microsoft and Hewlett Packard),* Hearings, September 20, 2012. 112th Cong. 2nd sess. Washington: GPO.

United States. Cong. Senate. Committee on Homeland Security and Government Affairs. 2013. *Offshore Profit Shifting and the U.S. Tax Code—Part 2 (Apple).* Hearings, May 21, 2013. 113th Cong. 1st sess. Washington: GPO.

Vicard, V. 2015. Profit Shifting through Transfer Pricing: Evidence from French Firm Level Trade Data.

Comment   J. Bradford Jensen

I would like to start my comments with the observation that intangibles are an increasingly important component of aggregate investment. Corrado, Hulten, Sichel (2009) report that including intangibles investment nearly doubles investment's share of GDP. So, intangibles are important. Second, the location of intangibles is also important—particularly for NIPAs. Other chapters in this volume describe the impact on NIPAs of the relocation of intellectual property to countries like Ireland. This chapter is addressing important questions in the literature.

The lengthy existing literature into which this chapter fits generally finds suggestive evidence that multinationals use intra-firm payments to reduce taxes. For example, intra-firm transfer pricing (broader than transfer pricing within the firm's CSAs) is another arguably important device. In research done with co-authors (Bernard, Jensen, and Schott 2006), we find that within multinationals, "related-party" unit values (for cross-border product trade within the firm) differ on average from "arm's length" counterparts by factors approaching 2, a huge difference. We find that attempts to refine the comparison by controlling for country, product homogeneity, and/or transport mode still leave differences of 10–20 percent or more. With our paper's empirical results in mind, it seems plausible that generalized intra-firm transfer pricing is an important way that multinationals reduce taxes and shift profits.

This chapter adds confirming evidence to the existing literature. This chapter finds that multinationals that are especially dependent on R&D inputs (often intangible capital) use parent-affiliate cost-sharing agreements (CSAs), along with associated licensing and cost-benefit-profit accounting within the firm, to minimize their tax burden. This is useful; however, I wonder whether the chapter is too narrowly framed by the authors.

The first concern is restricting their empirical sample of multinationals to firms that are R&D-intensive. Corrado, Hulten, and Sichel (2009) report that formal R&D is a relatively small share of firm investments in intangibles. Could these other intangible investment intensive firms also be using CSAs? If there are few or no CSAs among multinationals that don't meet the authors' R&D standard, it would be helpful to show that to the reader (their mere "count" of CSAs seems to wander strangely between the 5 firms involved in IRS litigation and the 42 identified by SEC (Securities

J. Bradford Jensen is McCrane/Shaker Chair in international business and professor of economics and international business at the McDonough School of Business at Georgetown University, and a research associate of the National Bureau of Economic Research.

For acknowledgments, sources of research support, and disclosure of the author's material financial relationships, if any, please see https://www.nber.org/books-and-chapters/challenges -globalization-measurement-national-accounts/comment-strategic-movement-intellectual -property-within-us-multinational-enterprises-jensen.

and Exchange Commission) text mining. If CSAs do exist for other purposes than R&D (e.g., for marketing strategy, for brand building, for administrative costs . . .), are their empirical effects small? Are they comparable to those for CSAs among R&D-intensive firms? What about other "footloose" assets (e.g., aircraft leasing in Ireland discussed in another chapter in the volume)?

In this regard, it would be helpful if the authors included more descriptive statistics across industries, countries, firms. For example, it would be useful to show that CSAs are more prevalent in R&D-intensive firms and industries, and by how much. Another important fact to document is whether low tax affiliate jurisdictions are more intensive in MNCs with CSAs than others and, if so, by how much. Last, it would be very helpful to show that the large multinationals with large R&D stocks but with *no* CSAs are, somehow, unusual outliers.

A second concern about the narrow scope is that the chapter does not provide an estimate of the aggregate size or impact of CSAs. Could this be estimated? Other important questions regarding size and scope include: by how much are multinationals' taxes reduced and profits enhanced by CSAs? Do tax collections in affiliates' countries change, and by how much? What are the statistical confidence intervals around such estimates? A potentially useful suggestion in this direction is for the authors to use an interaction variable that would allow their CSA coefficients to vary with the affiliate country's tax rate.

Even more important than these calculations in the context of this volume would be estimates of the effects of CSAs on national income and product. Would such calculations reflect the authors' findings that affiliates in the Bahamas and Ireland stand out (table 6.4b), and therefore also contribute to the infamous surge in Ireland's 2015 GDP growth? And if so, by how much? And what are comparable calculations for the Bahamas?

References

Bernard, A. B., J. B. Jensen, and P. K. Schott. 2006. "Transfer Pricing by U.S. Based Multinational Firms." NBER Working Paper No. 12493. Cambridge, MA: National Bureau of Economic Research.
Corrado, Carol, Charles Hulten, and Daniel Sichel. 2009. "Intangible Capital and U.S. Economic Growth." *Review of Income and Wealth* 55 (3): 661–85.

7

The Relationship between Tax Payments and MNE's Patenting Activities and Implications for Real Economic Activity
Evidence from the Netherlands

Mark Vancauteren, Michael Polder, and Marcel van den Berg

7.1 Introduction

It is well known that in a globalized economy, intellectual property (IP), such as patents, trademarks, and copyrights, is a key driver of international competitive success. Many governments worldwide have indeed put innovation as a stimulus to growth at the forefront of their industrial policy agenda providing fiscal incentives, such as R&D tax credits and patent boxes, to firms investing in R&D.

A sizable literature on the effectiveness of innovation-related tax incentives exists. However, the use of such tax incentives raises the concern of policy makers about yet another tax device that can be employed by firms for tax structuring purposes in the sense that IP-related profits of multinational enterprises (MNEs) can be segregated from ordinary profits across borders. These concerns have been a driver of discussions in the context of the OECD Base Erosion and Profit Shifting (BEPS) and of the EU code of conduct on business taxation with the aim to align taxation with substantial research activity. Because of the opportunity of tax structuring, one should be cautious when interpreting the evidence of the effectiveness of innovation-related tax incentives, as this may be driven by a shift in inno-

Mark Vancauteren is an associate professor of econometrics at Hasselt University, and a senior researcher at Statistics Netherlands.

Michael Polder is a senior researcher at Statistics Netherlands.

Marcel van den Berg is a program manager at Statistics Netherlands.

For acknowledgments, sources of research support, and disclosure of the authors' material financial relationships, if any, please see https://www.nber.org/books-and-chapters/challenges-globalization-measurement-national-accounts/relationship-between-tax-payments-and-mnes-patenting-activities-and-implications-real-economic.

vation efforts from one country to the other rather than an increase in net investment in innovation.

The chapter's focus on the Netherlands provides an interesting case for several reasons. First, MNEs are important in the Netherlands. We define an MNE either as a firm with a foreign mother firm or a Dutch firm with daughter firms abroad. A recent report issued by Statistics Netherlands (CBS 2018) finds, among other issues, that turnover of MNEs amounts to one-quarter of the total turnover and has increased by more than 37 percent between 2010 and 2016. On the other hand, the employment share of MNEs is much lower and amounted to 11 percent in 2016. In addition, it has also been found that MNEs do more R&D and innovate more in comparison to non-MNEs. Second, Netherlands has put several tax instruments in place to lower taxes on R&D and IP-related innovation activities. Under the so-called Dutch innovation box (originally introduced as patent box), income derived from innovations is subject to lower effective tax rates. This benefit can be utilized by any MNEs, that is, foreign companies with operations in the Netherlands as well as by Dutch firms with income derived from various types of intangible assets abroad. This accentuates the globalization issue as well as the key concern that a particular tax scheme must be tied to real economic activity.

The focus of our chapter is to empirically investigate the relationship between tax payments and firms' innovation activities. In particular, we are interested in finding out to what extent innovative firms pay lower taxes and whether they take advantage of tax credits in their real economic activity and how this differs between domestic firms and MNEs. The key methodological challenge in this relationship is to separate the tax structuring motive from the technological motive, which concerns real economic activity rather than fiscal activity. To investigate the existence of a direct channel between innovation efforts and tax payment, we employ different measures of R&D efforts. We consider firm-level patent count applications, R&D expenditures (investments and labor input), as well as R&D-related tax reductions, taking also into account other determinants of firm-level taxation. A major advantage of using patent applications is that the time of filing or applying for a patent coincides very closely with the time that innovative activities take place within a firm (Nagaoka, Motohashi, and Goto 2010).

Our empirical results show that firm-level patenting activities lead to lower tax payments. Indeed, this may be an indication that MNEs shift their IP and R&D related assets, usually at relatively low costs, to countries with a beneficial innovation tax regime. This finding is in line with (the small body of) existing evidence. However, several factors may weaken the relationship between tax payments and innovation efforts. For instance, MNEs usually arrange protection of intellectual property rights in all countries in which they are active. In addition, tax schemes not specifically targeting R&D

and innovation may also affect the decision to locate activities in a certain country. Therefore, we also investigate to what extent R&D investments per employee induce lower tax payments, putting the hypothesis of real economic activities to the test. Our evidence confirms the existence of a positive relationship between R&D success (measured by R&D investments per employee and the number of patents) and reduced tax payments. When we consider several subsamples, our results show that the negative relationship between firm-level patenting activities can only be ascertained by domestic firms and not by the part of MNEs that have foreign headquarters. This all leads us to infer that the Dutch tax regime provides a stimulus to a conducive environment for innovation.

In the next part of the chapter, we zoom in on a specific tax measure to stimulate innovation, which is the innovation box, and study whether firms that take advantage of the innovation box regime also increase their real economic activities. The benefits of the innovation box regime are tied to a minimum requirement of R&D personnel that are subject to pay taxes in the Netherlands. We hypothesize that the labor productivity of firms that utilize the innovation box and R&D related tax credits is higher than the productivity of firms that are not engaged in any of these tax policies. Using a decomposition analysis, we find evidence supporting our hypothesis: firms utilizing the innovation box regime have a higher labor productivity than firms that do not. Furthermore, we find that while the productivity premiums vary across industries, it does not vary systematically between the services sector and manufacturing. We augment our hypothesis by linking labor productivity to profits. Therefore, we also consider a firm's profit as a share of wages, which relates more directly to employment. Our results show that firms that receive an innovation box also report higher profit-wage ratios in comparison to all other firms within a particular sector; however we do not find any convincing evidence across sectors of a situation of high profit-wage ratios and low labor productivity premiums.

Our data consist of an unbalanced panel of patenting firms. The firms in our sample are enterprise groups (the highest national aggregate of the firm) located in the Netherlands, but not necessarily the ultimate parent firm, since foreign control is possible (and controlled for in the analyses). The statistical unit "enterprise group" is essential in the construction of data sets concerning patent data, because firms may register patents (and R&D) under different firm names. Generally speaking, the ownership of a patent applies at the level of the enterprise, and it is practically impossible to link ownership to affiliate or plant level.

We consider two data sets. First, when looking at the relationship between innovation activities and tax payments using regression analysis, we consider a panel covering the period 2000–2010. We work with data including financial information, R&D expenditures, patent application counts, forward citations of these counts, and the utilization of the innovation box regime. A second data set covers the period 2011–2015, which matches population data on the innovation box and the R&D tax credit regime, enabling us to verify to what extent R&D- related tax deductions are related to productivity in conjunction with profits and hence real economic activity.

Profit shifting across borders has implications for the measurement of economic activity in the national accounts, the conceptual scope of which is by definition confined by national borders. Such profit shifting can be the result of differences in tax rates and policies between countries. Distortions in the measurement of national aggregates arise when income from abroad is shifted to a lower tax jurisdiction, without a contribution to actual economic activity. For example, an innovation can be developed outside the Netherlands, but its intellectual property can be allocated here to profit from the tax benefits. This leads to additional income in the Netherlands, without any actual economic activity, and vice versa leads to lower income in the country where the development has taken place. Our analysis sheds light on whether, and to what extent, national tax incentives around innovation lead to a distortion in the national accounts of the Netherlands.

The remainder of the chapter is organized as follows. Section 7.2 presents a review of literature dealing with the relationship between innovation, tax payment, and real economic activity. Section 7.3 outlines our hypotheses. Section 7.4 describes the data. Section 7.5 presents the empirical model. In section 7.6 we present the estimation results of the model. Section 7.7 looks at real economic implications, while section 7.8 discusses implications for the national accounts and concludes.

7.2   Background and Related Literature

A compelling body of empirical literature shows that MNEs tend to shift income across borders (see Hines and Rice 1994, and Desai and Dharmapala 2009, among others, for an overview of the literature). The consensus is that MNEs face a significantly lower tax burden compared to domestic firms which do not have access to international tax strategies. For instance, Egger, Eggert, and Winner (2010) estimate that foreign ownership reduces the tax burden by about 56 percent. Firms can shift income across borders in two ways. First, they can locate the economic activities that generate income in the most beneficial location. For instance, a firm can choose to locate its R&D center in a country that provides the most stimulating environment or the most R&D friendly tax regime. This offers firms the opportunity to minimize tax payments on the income generated from these activities. The OECD (2008) provides some evidence on the estimated impact of tax rate differences on location choice and note that on average a reduction of the effective tax rate of 1 percentage point in one country leads to an investment increase of 3.7 percent in that specific country. Second, firms can also strategically price intra-firm transactions of goods and services (transfer pricing) to minimize the total tax burden by directing profit margins to the most tax-optimal location.[1]

In order to minimize tax payments, firms need to decide strategically where to locate tangible investments, human capital, and IP investments. De Simone, Mills, and Stomberg (2019), using IRS data on cross-border intra-firm transactions of US firms, show that the likelihood of US firms shifting income out of the country is positively related to subsidiaries in tax havens, high-tech operations, income tax incentives, R&D investment and foreign profitability, and negatively related to foreign sales, gross profits, and capital expenditures.[2] Grubert (2003) estimates that about 50 percent of US MNEs' shifting of income to low tax countries can be accounted for by income from intangibles linked to R&D and IP activities. Intangible assets create opportunities for income shifting because it is less costly for intangible assets–intensive firms to relocate their assets in comparison to capital-intensive firms (De Simone, Mills, and Stomberg 2019). One of the attractive features of IP is that ownership can be separated from the innovative activity, implying that firms can strategically claim ownership in favorable locations in term of taxation. This leads to a tax strategy in which firms shift income by locating their patent activities in a country with a favorable tax rate and selling the right to use the patent (licensing) to affiliates in high tax countries.

7.2.1   Innovation Box Regimes

Innovation is considered to be an important determinant of firm growth (Hall and Sena 2017). Therefore, many governments provide incentives for firms to innovate and to attract and retain MNEs by, for instance, providing tax credits on R&D or IP. Over the last decade, so-called patent boxes were introduced, referring to the introduction of reduced tax rates on revenues derived from IP and patent royalties. Comparing across countries, these patent boxes are very heterogeneous in their design. For instance, in the Netherlands, the patent box applies to intangible assets that are self-developed and also covers intangible assets resulting from the efforts of

---

1. Note that intra-firm transactions are required to be settled against market prices according to the Dutch corporate tax law. However, as noted by OECD (2015), "there is room to manoeuvre, especially in the case [. . .] of knowledge content and/or brand reputation, or in [other cases where] products [. . .] are not marketable [and therefore] it is not possible to apply a true market-equivalent price," (op. cit. p. 492).

2. De Simone, Mills, and Stomberg (2019) use several proxies for intangible intensity. These include R&D, advertising (AD), "intangible assets" from the balance sheet, and selling, general & administrative costs (SG&A). AD expenses are a proxy to capture the investments such as self-created IP and brand value that are not capitalized; SG&A is a proxy for intangible assets so to capture investments related to administrative support, such as legal costs associated with patent and trademark expenses.

R&D labor. Alternatively, under the Belgian patent box regime, the patent must have been developed by the firm in an R&D center that qualifies as a branch of activity.[3]

A relevant strand of literature focuses on the way innovation is affected after an innovation box is implemented using patent data. For instance, Karkinsky and Riedel (2012), using data for European MNEs during the period 1995–2003, find a negative relationship between the difference in the relevant corporate tax rate imposed on an affiliate and other firms in the multinational enterprise group and the number of patent applications filed by the MNE affiliate. In particular, the authors find that a 1 percentage point increase in the corporate tax rate reduces patent applications filed in that location by around 3.5 percent. Alstadsaeter et al. (2015) employ a rich firm-level data set concerning the top 2,000 corporate R&D investors worldwide covering the period 2000–2011. The authors show that offering a patent box regime is positively and significantly associated with attracting patents. Interestingly, a similar conclusion can be drawn for high-quality patents, which the authors consider as proxy for innovation with high earning potential. Related studies investigating to what extent innovation box regimes affect the location of firms' IP assets (Ernst and Spengel 2011; Bradley, Dauchy, and Robinson 2015; Gao, Yang, and Zhang 2016; Hassbring and Edwall 2013; and Koethenbuerger, Liberini, and Stimmelmayr 2016) come to similar conclusions.[4]

7.2.2   Implications for the Real Economy

The empirical evidence discussed so far does suggest that, generally speaking, tax rate reductions have strong effects on attracting patents. However, firms' patenting strategies may be heterogeneous when linked to the geographical dimension. Patent applications are affected not only by corporate tax rates in the host country but also by factors such as market size, competition intensity, the quality of the regulatory system, protection of IP rights, as well as firm internal characteristics (quality of R&D personnel). For example, in an online survey asking why firms remain in the Netherlands, den Hertog et al. (2015) report the following location determinants in order of importance: availability of qualified personnel, geographic location, personal preference, availability of knowledge centers, R&D know-how, and policy related innovation incentives.

For several reasons, the link between location, tax payments, and the innovation remains an empirical question which provides the central tenet of this

---

3. Patent box regimes were initially designed as an incentive to boost European R&D activity. Currently, there are seventeen countries in the world that have adopted innovation box regimes. Patent boxes have larger scopes than just patents and may additionally include trademarks, model designs, copyrights, domain names, trade secrets (see Alstadsaeter et al. 2015).
4. The empirical setups for analyzing how tax deductions may impact patent activities are different in some of these papers.

chapter. First, as pointed out by Chen et al. (2016), firms generally file for patent protection in all countries in which they are operatively active. Therefore, the association between IP related tax reductions and income shifting in a particular jurisdiction is unclear ex ante. Second, there is the threat of a crowding out effect. For instance, Evers, Miller, and Spengel (2014) note, in the context of patent box regimes, that firms may already take advantage of alternative tax incentives available to them, watering down the importance of patent box related tax advantages. In addition, firms may relocate their IP income related activities but not their real economic activities. Third, the effective tax payments resulting from the patent box are also influenced by the design of the tax facility. In some countries, like the Netherlands, tax deductions are on the basis of net incomes after R&D cost deductions, to ensure that at least some real activity is associated with the patent box tax credit. In addition, the so-called nexus approach, recently introduced by the OECD and the G20, is also a tax policy design aimed at ensuring that firms establish a clear link between real costs and benefits before taking advantage of relief tax facility. Consequently, the difference in effective tax payments between patenting firms that do not qualify for this type of tax policy and non-patenting firms may disappear.

A primary reason firms invest in, for instance R&D, is to increase their ability to innovate, which in turn provides opportunities for differentiation, organizational renewal, growth, and profitability. Indeed, one of the primary intents of introducing lower tax rates tied up to IP profits is also to encourage domestic innovation, which in return may lead to IP related spillovers that are beneficial to growth, and hence the real economy.[5] In some countries, including the Netherlands since 2008, the patent box regime modified its scope and also covers provisions specifying the link with the underlying research activity, in addition, small and medium sized firms are now also included in the eligibility process.[6]

There is some interesting empirical evidence on the economic effects of R&D related tax credits. For example, Alstadsaeter et al. (2015) look at cross-country mobility of inventors. They investigate whether patent applications lead to an increase in the number of inventors located in the country of patent registration and whether this occurs at the expense of the number

5. For instance, to ensure such aims is the discussion in the context of the OECD Base Erosion and Profit Shifting (BEPS) and at the EU code of conduct on business taxation with the aim to align taxation with substantial research activity. This in turn enforces high tax countries' policy to restrict the outflow of patents and other intangible assets from the host county to low tax economies. Policy measures to circumvent such practices are for instance, tightened legislation which makes foreign income taxable at the parent location. Another instrument was introduced in Germany in 2008, which allowed German tax authorities to tax a fraction of the future income generated from patents and other (intangible) assets developed in Germany even after the relocation to a foreign income.

6. See Evers, Miller, and Spengel (2014) for a detailed overview on innovation boxes in an international perspective. In the appendix we provide a short discussion on the patent box initiatives in the Netherlands.

of inventors located at the parent company.[7] The results show that locational shift of patents due to the existence of patent box regimes does not induce a corresponding shift in the base of inventors. Chen et al. (2016), using data of US and EU multinationals' subsidiaries from 2006 to 2014, find evidence that the introduction of innovation box regimes is associated with labor increases but do not result in significant increases in fixed asset investments. Using US located firm-level data for the period 1987–2010, Gao, Yang, and Zhang (2016) regress multiple measures of firm-level tax payments on the number of patents as well as variables intended to capture patent counts and R&D success measured by patent application and citation counts per R&D dollar, with the premise that R&D investments lead to higher productivity of the innovation process.[8] They find robust evidence that patenting activities are strongly related to lower levels of taxation and this relationship is more pronounced for innovative firms located in states that have R&D tax credits. However, R&D success (i.e., filing of a patent) is not related to lower levels of taxation. Hence, these results suggest that firms are not inclined to allocate part of their income savings in higher R&D investments. Koethenbuerger, Liberini, and Stimmelmayr (2016), using data of European subsidiaries for the period 2007–2013, find that firms directly or indirectly owning patents (within the enterprise group) before patent box regimes were introduced, report on average 2.5–3.9 percent higher pre-tax profits compared to firms not owning patents. However, if the patent box regime only applies to newly created patents requiring a certain amount of R&D activity, the difference in profits between the two groups disappears. The results indicate that the nexus approach seems to be an effective instrument to prevent profit shifting and to encourage real R&D activity.

7.3   Hypotheses

Empirically, the focus of the chapter is to investigate the relationship between various measures of tax payment and firms' innovation activities. The central premise of this chapter is that innovating firms pay less taxes. Among other countries, the Netherlands has implemented the innovation box regime, which, by design, creates a tax-wise favorable environment regarding income generated from intangible activities (patents, R&D). We use historical data on patents, as well as R&D efforts and financial performance measures, as extra controls to isolate the impact of innovation efforts on tax payments. Taking heterogeneity in patent citations into account

7. CEC (2014) points out that for EPO patent applications, the country of the inventor is not a reliable source, as applications are not legally required to inform the EPO about the addresses of the inventors.
8. R&D investments are usually regarded as the input side of innovation generating innovation output in the form of patents, new products, and/or processes, and hence, is therefore an important control for explaining patents (see Vancauteren et al. 2017).

enables us to separate the quantity and the quality component of patenting. That is, whereas a simple unweighted yearly sum of a firm's total patent counts is indicative of its volume, using information on the forward citations of these patents, we are capturing the quality effect of these patents. Higher patent quality implies a higher value of the innovation. According to the literature, important determinants of patent quality are firm efficiency (Nagaoka, Motohashi, and Goto 2010), the willingness to take risks and accept uncertainty (Harhoff et al. 1999), and the investment in seeking network technological externalities (Capaldo and Petruzzelli 2011).

In order to separate purely tax motivated patenting activities from patenting activity derived from real economic activity stemming from local R&D efforts, we also investigate the role of (local) R&D investments. A primary reason for firms to engage in R&D is to increase their ability to innovate, which in turn provides opportunities for productivity growth. However, R&D investments are risky, since firms must incur (considerable) costs in the present period with uncertain gains in the future (Roberts and Van Anh 2013).[9] These anticipated gains and the necessity to invest in R&D in order to spur firm growth are more likely to be realized if they are evaluated over a longer time period. This indicates that R&D activities may be perceived as a way to achieve long-term goals, suggesting that not only patent activities but also R&D investments are an important driver of firm growth. Specifically, if the Dutch taxation climate is actually conducive to the knowledge economy as a driver of economic growth in the sense that it stimulates firms to invest in R&D locally, we should not find a significant difference between R&D efforts (input) and innovative output (i.e., patents) in the relationship with taxation.

These considerations can be operationalized into the following first set of hypotheses:

H1: The number of patents filed by firms is positively associated with lower tax payments.

H2: Innovation success measured by the number of patents and R&D investment per employee is positively associated with lower tax payments.

The proposed analysis should yield an empirical answer to the question of how tax credits relate to innovation among patenting firms. By incorporating R&D investments, we also put (to some degree) the hypothesis of real economic effects to the test. Further, if firms locate their innovation activities (both R&D and patenting activities) in a particular country merely to take advantage of tax benefits, this would have real economic implications. We dig into this issue by investigating to what extent innovation translates

---

9. The paper of de Haan and Haynes (2018) discusses dynamic R&D externalities and how this impacts national accounting measurement.

into higher productivity in terms of a more efficient allocation of resources, even though empirical evidence shows that tax incentives simultaneously provoke misallocation of resources.[10] To sort this out we use a standard (productivity) decomposition approach to discern productivity differentials across sectors between firms that utilize these tax policies and firms that do not. In line with hypothesis 1 and 2, the third hypothesis states:

H3: The productivity contribution of firms utilizing innovation related tax credits is higher than the employment-weighted productivity of firms that are not engaged in this type of tax scheme.

We augment our hypothesis by linking labor productivity to profits. Therefore, we also consider a firm's profit as a share of wages, which relates more directly to employment.

7.4   Data

We compile a panel data set derived from various data sources for our analyses. First, we employ a data set that consists of an unbalanced panel of over 2,700 firms situated in the Netherlands, representing the entire population of firms that has applied for at least one patent during the years 2000–2010. The level of analysis is the enterprise group (the highest national aggregate of the firm) located in the Netherlands. We match the patent data to financial information using the general business register (GBR, the backbone of the firm-level statistics process in the Netherlands) and the database for nonfinancial enterprises in order to be able to connect tax payments and patent related activities. Second, we utilize a data set consisting of an unbalanced panel of 343,025 enterprise groups, which we match with the firm-level population data on the utilization of two tax instruments for the stimulation of innovation: the innovation box and the WBSO covering the period 2011–2015. WBSO is a Dutch acronym for Promotion of Research and Development Act.[11] Earlier data on the innovation box and the WBSO are not available.

7.4.1   Patents and Firm-Level Data

To collect information about the firms that applied for at least one patent, we used the database of the total population of filed patents in Europe (of the European Patent Office, EPO). The patent data give us information about the application number, the patent owner (name of the firm), patent title, name of the inventor, year of publication, and location. Since firms may register patents under different firm names, we retrieve information regarding the firms' complete ownership structure to match the names of

10. Pioneered in Restuccia and Rogerson (2008), the literature has looked at factors in explaining misallocation. These include among others labor and capital tax exemptions, but also institutional differences as well as input and output market imperfections.
11. In Dutch: Wet Bevordering Speur- en Ontwikkelingswerk.

patents with the direct ownership of the enterprise group of all their sub-sidiaries, holding units, and their shareholders. This yields a data set with patents matched to enterprise groups from the GBR.[12] With this database, of all the EPO patent applications, 98 percent were matched with a firm (enterprise groups) from the GBR. The matching procedure linking firms to patent applicant is based upon name and address matching, which for some few cases resulted in name inconsistencies. Applicants that involved private persons were not taken into account.

We match consolidated financial information and foreign ownership information of MNEs located in the Netherlands to our entirely patent firm-level data set. These full population data cover the years 2000–2010 to arrive at a sample of 14,981 firm-year observations of 2,704 firms. These firms are in turn matched to a subsample of firms reporting R&D activities. We extract R&D data from the Community Innovation Surveys (CIS waves) and R&D surveys that are collected by Statistics Netherlands. The R&D surveys report R&D expenditures in the odd years while each of the CIS waves measures R&D expenditures in the even years of our sample period 2000–2010. R&D responding firms that are included in either the R&D and CIS waves are representative of the total firm population in the Netherlands (GBR population defined in December of each year). Firms are stratified according to their economic activity (two-digit NACE) and size class of the firm.

We retain 3,598 firm-year observations distributed over 1,053 firms. To get an idea of their relevance, we note that a total of 36,000 patents applications are retained in the sample, while around 50,000 patents were filed in the total population of the patenting firms before the R&D match was made. This amounts to 75 percent of the total number of patent applications. Possible bias in our estimation due to sample selection, that is, only considering firms that are both engaged in R&D and patenting activities, is examined in our analysis.

Summary statistics of our key variables (transformed to fit our analysis) are shown in table 7A.1. The statistics are based on the sample of firms concerning the period 2000–2010. The unweighted average firm in our sample applies for approximately 1.6 patent counts a year and spends on average 4.8 thousands of euros of R&D per employee. The average annual tax payment as a percentage of pre-tax financial income is equal to 24.3, which is very close to the Dutch corporate tax rate of 25 percent.[13] We also note that the distribution of the patent variables is quite skewed, while the other vari-

---

12. We refer to Vancauteren et al. (2017) for a more detailed description of the data. The paper applies a firm-level analysis using EPO patents for the period 2000–2006. For the purpose of this paper, we extended the database to the most recent year (2010) that can be retrieved from the PATSTAT database within Statistics Netherlands.

13. During our sample period, the taxation rate was much higher. For instance, till 2003 the highest possible rate was 35 percent; this can be reconciled with the overall distribution of our sample taxation rate.

ables are generally more evenly spread. In the specification of the regression equations we account for multiple number of firm financial and innovation characteristics. Along with their conclusions, they might potentially generate multicollinearity problems. The correlation matrix of the variables is presented in table 7B.2. Generally, we observe low correlation coefficients for most of the variables. Low correlation coefficients indicate that multicollinearity is not a problem.

7.4.2   WBSO Tax Credit and Innovation Box

Firms have to supply information on the number of hours of labor invested in R&D and the associated wage costs on an annual basis to be eligible for the WBSO. The WBSO only considers a credit for real R&D activities; R&D management is not taken into consideration. The match between the WBSO data (registered on the Chamber of Commerce number of the firm) with the GBR is set at the consolidated enterprise group level. The WBSO data are available for the period 2011–2015.

The innovation box data are registered at the level of fiscal units, which are the legal entities used by the Dutch tax authority. These units can be matched to the enterprise groups of the GBR. It is important to note that the innovation box concerns profits that are derived not only from patents but also from other intangible assets. Under certain circumstances, the patent is the intangible asset itself or the patent constitutes some part of the intangible asset. The innovation box data are available for the period 2011–2015. The data include information on the profits derived from the intangible assets, given they exceed a threshold value, and costs that are associated with it.[14]

7.5   Empirical Implementation

The following section presents our estimation strategy when examining the impact of patenting activities on tax payments. This analysis is based on our panel data set covering the period 2000–2010, which enables us to investigate whether tax payments are correlated with patenting activities and patent quality. Our data also allow us to investigate to what extent the introduction of the innovation box has accentuated this relationship for 2010, the initial period for which we have innovation box data.

We start by estimating the following equation to examine the effects of innovation activity (patenting) on tax payments:

14. We refer to a recent report by Statistics Netherlands (CBS 2017) on its collection of R&D, the innovation box and other dimensions of innovation. See also table 7B.3, which gives an overview of the number of firms that applied for the innovation box and that have applied for a WBSO tax credit during the period 2011–2015. The table indicates that there is complementarity between R&D input and innovation output: out of the 5,343 innovation box users, 3,312 firms have also applied for the WBSO. Notice that there are also still a significant number of firms that are granted a WBSO tax credit but that do not apply for the innovation box. Or in other terms, a considerable number of firms reports R&D input, but no innovation output.

(1) $TAX\,PAY_{it} = \beta_0 + \beta_1 PAT_{it-k} + \beta_2 X_{it} + Year\,\&\,Industry\,Effects\,+\,\varepsilon_{it}$

where we let a firm be indicated by the subindex i and time by the subindex t and $TAX\,PAY_{it}$ is the firm's effective tax rate. $TAX\,PAY_{it}$ equals the ratio of taxes paid divided by financial income (i.e., profit before taxes). Based on empirical models used in the corporate tax payment literature (Dyreng, Hanlon, and Maydew 2008, 2010; Mills, Nutter, and Schwab 2013; Gao, Yang, and Zhang 2016), a firm's effective tax payment, $TAX\,PAY_{it}$, is a widely used measure not only for evaluating a firm's ability to minimize income tax but also for evaluating a firm's strategy to defer tax payments to later periods (Erickson, Hanlon, and Maydew 2004).

The variable of interest is PAT_{it-k} which expresses a measure that captures a firm's patenting activities[15] (#patents and patent counts per unit R&D), all expressed in logs. We allow for several k time lags as patenting activities and tax payments may not coincide contemporaneously. The vector of independent variables X_{it} represents firm's characteristics, and ε_{it} is a random error with specific clustering at the firm level. We also include year and industry effects to capture additional unobserved heterogeneity.

We include the following independent variables in the vector X_{it} to explain the firm's effective tax rate: total assets ("Assets") measured in logs, the return on assets ("ROA"), the ratio of long-term debt to assets ("Leverage"), the ratio of tangible capital to total assets ("Tangible"), the ratio of intangible income to total assets ("Intangible"), the ratio of inventory to total assets ("Inventory"), R&D investment per employee[16] measured in logs, and a dummy ("Ownership") that takes the value 1 if the firm is foreign owned. The choice of these variables is based on previous studies with respect to explaining firm-level tax payments (see, e.g., Gao, Yang, and Zhang 2016; Dyreng, Hanlon, and Maydew 2008, for a recent review).

The variable Assets, a proxy for the size of a firm, is expected to be negatively correlated with tax payments because it is argued that larger firms are able to work the tax system better than do smaller firms (Mills 1998; Dyreng, Hanlon, and Maydew 2008) and have greater resources to engage in tax planning to reap the benefits from tax shelters (Gao, Yang, and Zhang 2016). We also include firms' profits, ROA, and hypothesize that profits and tax payments are positively correlated (Gupta and Newberry 1997; Mills, Nutter, and Schwab 2013). On the other hand, more profitable firms have a larger incentive to engage in tax structuring due to their greater potential of cost savings (Manzon and Plesko 2002; McGuire, Omer, and Wang 2012). The variables a firm's leverage, its fixed tangible and non-tangible capital capture firm characteristics that may also affect a firm's income tax liability.

---

15. We refer to the data section for further details on these measures. Table 7B.1 in the appendix lists all the variables and its definitions that are considered for this paper.

16. To avoid firms with reported zero investment to drop out of the sample, we use 1+R&D per employee.

Firms with a higher leverage (Leverage) have been found to pay lower taxes (Desai and Dharmapala 2009) and, regarding MNEs, have a greater incentive to locate their leverage in high tax jurisdictions (Gupta and Newberry 1997). Generally, these studies posit a negative relationship between leverage and tax payments. We also control for the ratio of tangible capital to total assets (Tangible) and non-tangible capital to total assets (Intangible), which is expected to be negatively related to tax payments. This is because capital intensive firms have lower tax burdens as a result of legislated tax shields (Gupta and Newberry 1997). Moreover, intangible assets may provide more profit shifting opportunities. In addition, countries often offer tax policies aimed at the promotion of investments, which provides tax planning opportunities (Mills, Nutter, and Schwab 2013). According to Evers, Miller, and Spengel (2014), firms with a greater inventory intensity (Inventory) are restricted in their tax planning activities. Accordingly, we expect a positive relationship between inventory and tax payments. As a final control, we also take into account former ownership to proxy for income shifting opportunities of MNEs (e.g., Mills, Nutter, and Schwab 2013).

7.6   Results

In this section we present our estimation results for the first part of our analysis regarding various specifications of the empirical model, and robustness checks are presented.

7.6.1   Innovation and Tax Payments

We first focus on the regression results explaining tax payments, see table 7A.2. The model is estimated using OLS, and results reported use robust standard errors clustered at the firm level. In the first column (I), we present the results without sector and year dummy effects, using patent counts. Column II shows the results with sector and year dummy effects. First, we notice that the coefficients of the patent count variables are negative and significant ranging between –0.012 (standard error 0.003) and –0.015 (standard error 0.004), after controlling for additional firm characteristics.[17] The magnitude of the results are in line with Gao, Yang, and Zhang (2016). These results indicate that the more patents a firm produces, the lower its effective tax rate, a result that validates hypothesis H1. Second, a robust finding from our regression is that a firm's engagement in R&D activities is consistently and significantly negatively correlated with its effective tax

17. Since we express the # of patents (and citations) as in logs, the interpretation of its corresponding coefficient can be interpreted as follows: a 1 percent change in the # patents is associated with a change in the tax payment ratio of $0.01*(-0.012)$. Is this estimate large or small? From table 7A.1, we may infer that 200 percent increase in patent counts, which moves an average firm from the 25th percentile to the 75th percentile, leads to a tax payment ratio that is 2.4 percentage points lower, which amounts to 10 percent lower tax payment of an average firm.

rate. This suggests that firms pay lower taxes as they increase their R&D expenditures per employee. Indeed, this result can be partially explained by R&D tax incentives that are available to firms, as far as these concern benefits in terms of profit tax. An important result is that the effect of both patenting (innovation output) and R&D activities (innovation input) enter the relationship with tax payments significantly, supporting hypothesis H2 and hence providing some evidence that the Dutch taxation regime is conducive to stimulating innovation.

The additional control variables show that tax payments are positively related to the size of the firm (measured by its total assets), its profit (measured by the return on assets), and its tangible and intangible asset ratios. The leverage of the firm is negatively associated with tax payments. These results partially align with earlier findings. More specifically, based on the literature review in section 7.5.1, we expected that larger and more asset intensive firms would on average pay less taxes. Also important is that we find a positive and significant coefficient on foreign firm dummy (Ownership), which indicates that foreign firms pay on average more taxes.

Columns (III) in table 7A.2 consider again the role of multinational headquarters. We now subgroup our sample where we define a subsample of firms with Dutch headquarters and a subsample of firms that have a foreign parent. We note that a majority of Dutch headquartered firms also fulfill the definition of MNE since they also have foreign subsidiaries. We find that the coefficient of patents is significant for the Dutch firms while the coefficient related to the patent activities of foreign firms is not significant. For R&D, our results show that domestic firms that do more R&D enjoy higher tax benefits while this is not significant for foreign firms. These results indicate heterogeneous behavior between foreign MNEs and firms located in the Netherlands, namely that for those firms that do shift some of their activities to the Netherlands, there is no significant relationship between patenting and tax payments. We also note that only for domestic firms, the result implies that the tax benefit has a positive and significant effect on the real economy, as only actual R&D activities performed locally lower the tax burden.

7.6.2   Some Robustness Checks and Additional Results

7.6.2.1   Sample Selection

In table 7A.3 we present some robustness checks to investigate the sensitivity of our results to various data issues. First, we tackle the issue of selectivity in R&D expenditures. As discussed in detail in section 7.4, the patent population includes all firms that have applied for at least one EPO patent during our sample period while R&D reported figures are extracted from annual survey data. The results so far have been obtained based on a subsample of firms that have reported R&D which may also include true zeros. This gives rise to sample selection. However, firms with missing R&D expenditures, because it is not reported, may also be engaged in patenting activities. The reporting of R&D investment itself may concern a strategic firm decision (Nagaoka, Motohashi, and Goto 2010) or can be due simply to nonresponse. For example, to get an idea on the importance of "missing" R&D, Koh and Reeb (2015) show that firms not reporting R&D have patents that are on average 27 percent more influential (that is, approved and cited) than R&D reporting firms.

Therefore, we run the regression for all firms, that is, R&D reporting and non-R&D reporting firms. From the panel B column of table 7A.3, excluding R&D as a control variable, we can infer that our result concerning the negative effect of patent counts on tax payments becomes even stronger (patent coefficient is -0.022, standard error 0.003). In column panel C, we set the R&D expenditures of firms with missing values to zero. The results are only slightly affected. This implies that the importance of R&D expenditures as an extra control variable does not seem to affect the negative relationship between patent activities and tax payments.

A second robustness check involves adding a control group of non-patenting firms in our sample to the regressions. We match a control group of non-patenting firms with a firm size (in terms of sales revenue) closest to the patenting firm within the same industry (by two-digit SIC classification). We then add an additional dummy variable for non-patenting firms. If the coefficient estimate of the dummy variable has the expected negative sign and is significant, we can conclude that patenting activities do indeed have an effect in terms of tax payments (Gao, Yang, and Zhang 2016). The coefficient on patent counts is -0.021 (standard error 0.003), slightly lower than before. In addition, as expected, the coefficient of the Zero Patent dummy variable is positive and significant (coefficient is 0.012, standard error 0.003). These results thus confirm that patenting firms face a lower effective tax rate relative to non-patenting firms. Thus, besides through the intensive margin, patents are also associated with lower tax payments through the extensive margin.

7.6.2.2   Patents and R&D Success

Table 7A.3, panel E, presents the results regarding an alternative measure of the quality of innovations by looking at patent counts per unit R&D investment. This measure captures the relation between R&D input and innovation success. Because it may take several years to reap the benefits of R&D projects, we try using patent counts with a three-year lag. The results show that the coefficient on the count of lagged patents per R&D is marginally rejected at the 10 percent significance level.

Our results confirm hypotheses 1 and 2 (H1 and H2), confirming to a certain extent that the Dutch taxation regime provides a stimulus to the innovation-based economy. Indeed, on the one hand, patent-active firms are less tax liable, which can be indicative for a favorite tax regime. On the other hand, we also find that the extent of actual innovative activities as measured by R&D investments is also associated with less tax payments.

7.6.2.3 Innovation Box

To get an idea of the effect of the innovation box on the stimulation of innovation, we consider the interaction between the Dutch innovation box and both R&D and patenting activities. We use the Dutch innovation box for the year 2010. This tax device allows firms to enjoy a tax credit of 5 percentage points on profits derived from intangible assets (not only patents) that have resulted from local R&D investments (i.e., R&D personnel) by the firm. As of 2010, firms need to provide proof that the qualified intangible assets derive from the deployment of the firm's own R&D staff. We define the innovation box (IB) as a dummy variable with value 1 if the firm has successfully applied for the IB.

The results, based on the specification of the models reported in table 7A.2, are presented in table 7A.4, columns panels E-F. Fitting the model with data for 2010, we fail to find a significant relationship between patenting and tax payments. The coefficient on the interaction term with patent counts is not significant in addition to the coefficient on the lagged patent measures. Similar results are obtained when we use the aggregated patent counts of year t, $t - 1$ and $t - 2$ or the lagged aggregate ($t - 1$, $t - 2$ and $t - 3$) as an additional robustness test instead, or alternatively, when we express patent counts in four- or five-year averages.[18] We do note that the sample size is now substantially smaller than the sample sizes of the previous regressions, implying that coefficients are less precisely estimated, which may have contributed to a lack of a significant relationship between patenting and tax payments.

7.7 Implications for Local Economy

As already highlighted in section 7.6 of the chapter, our empirical results show that firm-level innovation output is positively related to a lower effective tax rate. In addition, local R&D activities are associated with a lower tax burden. These can be seen as indications that there is no valid reason to justify concerns related to cross-border tax planning concerning innovation tax credits, since patenting firms reaping the benefits of their inventions in terms of lower tax payments also seem to be major R&D players.

A natural question that remains regarding hypothesis H3 is to what extent

---

18. Dynamics are important as we work with patent applications. The European patent grant procedure takes about three to five years from the date your application is filed. It is made up of two main stages. The first comprises a formalities examination, the preparation of the search report and the preliminary opinion on whether the claimed invention and the application meet the requirements of the EPC. The second involves substantive examination.

innovating firms are actually engaged in real economic activity. As a first measure, we consider labor productivity. Labor productivity is decomposed into the contribution of firms that receive tax credits from the innovation box and the WBSO and the contribution of firms that did not. The analysis is conducted at the sector level for the years 2011–2015.

The productivity contribution of firms belonging to category k in a sector j at period t is given by:

(1)
$$P_{jt}^{K_j} = \frac{1}{L_{jt}^{K_j}} \sum_{i \in K_j} L_{ijt} P_{ijt}$$

where L_{ijt} is the employment of firm i in sector j at time t and P_{ijt} is its labor productivity, measured by value added per employee, K_j designates the category type per sector j and $L_{jt}^{K_j}$ measures the total employment at firms in category K_j. We consider two categories. First, we compare a category of firms that utilized the innovation box regardless of whether or not they also received a WBSO tax credit. Second, we define a category of firms that both utilized the innovation box and received WBSO tax credit.

To understand how these firms differ by category from the rest of the sector we compute the weighted average labor productivity in sector j:

(2)
$$\bar{P}_{jt} = \frac{1}{L_{jt}} \sum_i L_{ijt} P_{ijt}.$$

The ratio $P_{jt}^{K_j} / \bar{P}_{jt}$ captures the extent to which productivity in these categories differs.

The ratios expressed in two-digit NACE averages are reported in table 7A.5 with standard deviations (StDev) in parentheses. The first column reports the number of firms that utilized the innovation box, column 2 lists the labor productivity ratio of this subset of firms to that of the total number of firms in the sector, column 3 reports the number of firms that utilized both the innovation box and the WBSO, column 4 reports the ratio of this subset of firms vis-à-vis the total number of firms within the respective sector. We also report the average labor productivity as well as the average employment by sector. Looking at the differences between the two categories, we see that the majority of firms that utilized the innovation box also applied for a WBSO tax credit. For instance, in the IT and IT related service sector (62-63) we see, throughout the period 2011–2015, 1,784 firm-year observations that were granted an innovation box tax credit, of which 1,541 firm-year observations are linked to the WBSO tax credit. This also makes sense because these tax instruments are complementary in nature, one focusing on innovation input, the other on innovation output. A labor productivity ratio larger than one indicates that firms that take advantage of the innovation box are more productive compared to the average weighted labor productivity within a particular sector. We see that for the majority of sectors, this is indeed the case. Sectors with relatively large labor productivity premiums include machinery and equipment (28), textiles and clothing

(13-15), furniture and n.e.c. (31-33). Sectors with a negative productivity premium for firms engaging in R&D and innovation specific tax policies are transportation and storage (49-53) and distribution of natural resources (35-39). Furthermore, we find that these premiums vary by industry, but not systematically between services and manufacturing. In conclusion, the evidence supports the hypothesis that innovation tax credit policies are in general positively associated with higher levels of labor productivity.

To test the existence of possible patent shifting, i.e., where the inventor is located in a different country than the MNE applying for a patent, we also have information on the foreign ownership status of firms that were granted an innovation box tax credit as well as information on whether domestic located firms have affiliates in foreign countries. Table 7A.6 reports the results for selected industries for which we have sufficient observations for doing the analysis. By restricting the above analysis to a sample of either foreign firms or domestic firms with no foreign affiliates, the results are essentially the same, suggesting that firms (whether foreign or domestic with or without foreign affiliates) that utilize the innovation box are more productive compared to their counterparts within a particular sector. In comparison to the other firms within the retail and wholesale sector, we also note a positive labor productivity premium of foreign innovation box firms.

Instead of using labor productivity as a measure of performance, we also consider a firm's profit as a share of wages, which relates more directly to employment and hence is also connected to the domestic economy. For instance, to what extent these firms are willing to be engaged in so-called rent sharing, whereby realized profits, as a result of higher productivity, flow back in the local economy through labor compensation. Results are reported in table 7A.7. We follow the same structure as in table 7A.6 in order to make an interesting comparison. We conjecture that innovation box firms are involved with tax planning activities, and hence participate to a minimum in local economic activities if their income to the Netherlands is high relative to their employment level. This may lead to artificial high labor productivity levels and high profit-wage ratios. On the other hand, if high labor productivity corroborates with a low profit-wage ratio, this may indicate that firms are willing to participate to the local economy (due to, for instance, higher investments, higher wage payments).

Table 7A.7 shows that on average, in comparison to all firms within a particular sector, firms that receive an innovation box report profit-wage premium ratios. For the sector Basic, fabricated metals (24-25) and the food sector (10-12), a profit-wage discount is found for both domestic and foreign firms. By putting our conjecture forward, we do not see any strong evidence of possible profit shifting. Overall, our results show, in comparison with table 7A.6, that firms making use of innovation box incentives have higher labor productivity, but also higher profit-wage ratios. This suggests that any additional income due to increased productivity is not proportionally shared with employees through increased wages. The remaining profit can be used for investment or income for the owner(s). The result is true regardless of ownership, but foreign firms have the highest productivity differential, combined with the highest profit-wage differential. One notable exception is Retail & wholesale (45-47), as it is shown to be the case for domestic firms whereby high profit-wage ratios are associated with low labor productivity. We can infer that these are especially firms that have affiliates abroad. We also note negative profit ratios for the case of foreign firms that belong to IT & related services sector (62-63). This negative profit ratio is due to an unusual low profit-wage ratio of one firm in this relative small subcategory, which makes possible inferences more difficult to make.

7.8   Implications for National Accounts and Concluding Remarks

In July 2016 the Statistical Office of Ireland revised its GDP figure according to the accounting standard framework set by the ESA 2010. The revision implied that the Irish economy had grown by 26.3 percent over 2015. The revision triggered a trail of comments from economists, statisticians, and the media, the bottom line of which was that growth figures of this order of magnitude were hard to take seriously. Paul Krugman referred to the issue as "Leprechaun economics." Referring to James Joyce and Flann O'Brien, *The Financial Times* drew a comparison to the Irish merits regarding works of fiction (*The Financial Times*, July 12, 2016).

For a large part, the growth of Irish GDP was the consequence of inversions related to firms moving assets, intellectual property, or domicile. Being a small open economy, Ireland largely depends on foreign direct investment, and with an attractive corporate tax climate, the country proves to be attractive for big multinational companies.

In response to its publication, Eurostat responded that "[t]his revision can be seen as an effect of increasing globalization. It is primarily due to the relocation to Ireland of a limited number of big economic operators. Based on the preliminary information provided by the CSO, including data, the revision is plausible" (Eurostat 2016). In addition, the pertinent communication warns that this could happen again "if huge multinationals move their business around Europe or the globe."

It is important to reemphasize that the 2015 Irish growth figure was not the product of some evil statistician but the result of applying internationally agreed accounting rules. However, clearly, this example shows the cautions one must be aware of when interpreting GDP figures, as the relation to real economy activity may be tenuous in cases where globalization issues play a big role. In general, the activities of multinational companies may raise concerns for the compilation of national accounts (OECD, 2015). In particular, although there are other considerations to be taken into account, lower tax countries are evidently attractive for businesses to locate. This in itself is not directly a problem, but, as recognized by, for example, the OECD-led initiative against base erosion and profit shifting (BEPS), in practice the locus of production and the location where taxes are paid may get separated, undermining the fairness of tax systems, and indirectly affecting the quality of measuring national economies.

In addition, cross-border intra-firm flows are hard to measure, as a consequence of so-called transfer pricing: firms may strategically price their (intra-firm) exports so as to allocate profits to the location with the most attractive tax regime. Therefore it becomes harder to assess where the actual economic activity is taking place, which affects not only GDP but also the balance of payments. In this context, measurement of intellectual property and flows of R&D are particularly prone to such measurement problems, as market prices are absent and there is no physical flow of products. Because R&D and IP investment have to be capitalized under the SNA 2008 guide lines, this impacts directly upon GDP. The empirical results in this chapter show that in general firms located in the Netherlands that innovate benefit from a relatively lower tax burden. With respect to R&D, this means that the tax incentive seems to stimulate innovative efforts, creating employment for knowledge workers. For patenting activities, especially high-quality patents seem to decrease the tax burden, so that it can be argued that the tax incentive stimulates high-quality innovation.

Our empirical analyses present us with contrasting messages about the consequences for the national accounts. On the one hand, our regression based results suggest that (i) foreign firms do not pay less taxes than other firms, and (ii) tax payments by foreign firms are not significantly correlated with R&D and patenting activity.

Comparing the productivity and profit-wage ratio of firms making use of tax incentives for innovation to those that do not provides some contrasting evidence. Overall, we find that firms making use of these incentives have higher labor productivity, but also higher profit-wage ratios. This suggests that any additional income due to increased productivity is not proportionally shared with employees through increased wages. The remaining profit can be used for investment or income for the owner(s). The result is true regardless of ownership, but foreign firms have the highest productivity differential, combined with the highest profit-wage differential. Unless the excess profits are invested locally, this suggests that the contribution to the local economy of foreign firms with tax benefits from innovation is in fact lower than what one would expect from their relative productivity.

Therefore, in all, we conclude that firms do not seem to use innovation tax incentives to shift profit to the Netherlands, but it does seem that foreign firms making use of these incentives are able to generate relatively large profits, which are not associated with higher wages of local employees.

Appendix
Results

Table 7A.1   Sample means and standard deviations, 2000–2010

Variable	Mean	Std. Dev.	Q1	Median	Q3
Log of patent counts	0.491	0.946	0	0	0.691
Tax payments (ratio)	0.243	0.230	0.054	0.238	0.328
Assets (in thousands)	11.280	2.350	9.651	11.231	12.945
Leverage (ratio)	0.203	0.226	0.001	0.142	0.320
Return on assets (ROA, ratio)	0.099	0.144	0.016	0.066	0.120
Inventory (ratio)	0.136	0.165	0.032	0.107	0.211
Tangibles (ratio)	0.249	0.207	0.085	0.194	0.367
Intangibles (ratio)	0.050	0.114	0	0.002	0.040
Log R&D per employee	1.564	1.290	0.439	1.232	2.251
Origin (Foreign/Dutch, 1/0)	0.344	0.475	0	0	1

Note: Summary statistics of the overall sample consisting of 4,166 panel firm-year observations. Number of firms is 1,192.

Table 7A.2   Corporate tax payments and patents

PANEL A *Indep. Var-s*	(I)	(II)	(III) Foreign	(III) Domestic
Log Assets	0.010***	0.015***	0.013***	0.013***
	(0.001)	(0.002)	(0.005)	(0.002)
Leverage	−0.048**	−0.034**	−0.043	−0.083***
	(0.019)	(0.019)	(0.040)	(0.020)
ROA	0.251***	0.248***	0.184***	0.292***
	(0.040)	(0.037)	(0.063)	(0.045)
Inventory	0.068***	0.028	−0.005	−0.044*
	(0.019)	(0.021)	(0.063)	(0.022)
Tangibles	0.110***	0.129***	0.138***	0.139***
	(0.020)	(0.021)	(0.041)	(0.027)
Intangibles	0.114***	0.120***	0.087	0.132***
	(0.039)	(0.036)	(0.066)	(0.046)
Ownership	0.038***	0.038***		
	(0.009)	(0.009)		
Lag log (1+R&D per employee)	−0.016***	−0.010***	−0.008	−0.010**
	(0.002)	(0.003)	(0.006)	(0.003)
Lag log (1+patent applications)	−0.012***	−0.015***	−0.007	−0.019***
	(0.004)	(0.004)	(0.009)	(0.005)
Sector Effect	No	Yes	Yes	Yes
Year dummies	No	Yes	Yes	Yes
Intercept	0.094***	0.089**	0.158	0.088**
	(0.020)	(0.044)	(0.102)	(0.049)
R^2	0.071	0.142	0.113	0.207

Note: Dependent variable is share of corporate tax payment in total finance. OLS with (robust) standard errors. 3,598 panel firm-year observations. Number of firms is 1,053.
$*p < .1, **p < .05, ***p < .01$

Table 7A.3   Corporate tax payments and patents, alternative panels

	PANEL B Adding R&D Missing firms	PANEL C Adding R&D Missing firms AND setting their R&D expenditure = 0	PANEL D Adding non-patenting firms	PANEL E Innovation quality
Lag log (1+patent applications)	−0.022***	−0.021***	−0.021***	
	(0.003)	(0.002)	(0.003)	
Zero Patent			0.012***	
			(0.003)	
Lag log (1+R&D per employee)		−0.003*		
		(0.001)		
Lag (patents/R&D 3YR)				−2.672
				(1.627)
Sector Effect	Yes	Yes	Yes	Yes
Year dummies	Yes	Yes	Yes	Yes
Observations	13797	13797	31736	1723
R^2	0.170	0.164	0.205	0.136

Note: Dependent variable is corporate tax payment. OLS with (robust) standard errors.
$*p < .1, **p < .05, ***p < .01$

Table 7A.4   Corporate tax payments and patents, innovation box regime, year 2010

	PANEL E Innovation Box (YR 2010)	PANEL F Innovation Box (YR 2010)
Lag log (1+patent applications)	0.004	0.005
	(0.020)	(0.010)
Lag log (1+patent applications)* InnBox		−0.014
		(0.028)
InnBox	−0.020	−0.082*
	(0.026)	(0.045)
Lag log (1+R&D per employee)* InnBox		0.038*
		(0.021)
Lag log (1+R&D per employee)	−0.022**	−0.032**
	(0.010)	(0.013)
Sector Effect	Yes	Yes
Year dummies	Yes	Yes
Observations	259	259
R^2	0.301	0.309

Note: Dependent variable is corporate tax payment. OLS with (robust) standard errors.
$*p < .1, **p < .05, *** p < :01$

Table 7A.5 Average relative labor productivity (LP), 2011–2015

Industry	#Firm-year Inn Box	LP ratio IB firms	#Firm_Inn Box AND WBSO	LP ratio Inn Box& WBSO firms	LP (all firms)	Average Employment (all firms)
Food (10–12)	569	1.032 (0.102)	506	1.033 (0.081)	156.123	28.163
Textiles, clothing (13–15)	36	1.291 (0.125)	32	1.258 (0.106)	65.930	19.446
Wood, paper, printing (16–18)	101	1.124 (0.172)	82	1.122 (0.171)	78.884	23.176
Chemicals, pharmaceuticals (19–21)	320	1.082 (0.115)	270	1.091 (0.122)	161.261	121.988
Plastics, non-metallic minerals (22–23)	286	1.066 (0.094)	254	1.061 (0.093)	80.860	34.120
Basic, fabricated metals (24–25)	507	1.211 (0.057)	438	1.227 (0.061)	78.965	27.859
Computers, electrical equipment (26–27)	391	1.150 (0.308)	363	1.184 (0.328)	130.631	43.584
Machinery, equipment n.e.c. (28)	782	1.302 (0.247)	663	1.334 (0.259)	109.533	40.797
Motor vehicles, other transp. (29–30)	172	1.162 (0.133)	152	0.869 (0.119)	88.971	54.145
Furniture, n.e.c. & recycling (31–33)	306	1.438 (0.144)	262	1.424 (0.187)	56.542	18.960

Distribution natural resources (35–39)	70	0.570 (1.472)	56	0.593 (1.464)	131.920	74.552
Construction (41–43)	263	1.059 (0.070)	240	1.064 (0.071)	66.364	17.914
Retail and wholesale (45–47)	1467	0.820 (0.163)	1229	0.820 (0.163)	53.580	22.834
Transportation and storage (49–53)	56	0.595 (0.083)	43	0.642 (0.122)	69.765	51.046
Publishing & audio (58–60)	45	1.388 (0.628)	26	0.966 (0.732)	74.718	17.911
Telecommunications (61)	62	1.085 (0.021)	24	1.070 (0.060)	218.916	93.406
IT & related services (62–63)	1784	1.131 (0.084)	1541	1.089 (0.139)	84.258	11.050
Financial institutions (64–66)	n.a.					
Consulting & architectural and engineering activities (69–71)	1155	1.116 (0.073)	901	1.189 (0.135)	83.669	5.314
R&D (72)	269	1.403 (0.169)	210	1.477 (0.151)	59.511	16.654
Advertising & other professional activities (73–75)	155	1.463 (0.426)	105	1.492 (0.461)	58.906	8.051
OTHER Services, n.e.c. (77–82)	290	1.655 (0.761)	210	1.185 (0.850)	51.477	60.102

Note: Standard deviations are in parentheses.

Table 7A.6   **Average relative labor productivity (LP) according to ownership status and foreign subsidiaries, selected main sectors, 2011–2015**

Industry	All firms	Only Local firms	Only Foreign MNEs	Local firms AND NO foreign subsidiaries
All firms (all sectors)	1.125	1.133	1.254	1.187
	(0.334)	(0.275)	(1.190)	(0.359)
	[9161]	[8476]	[685]	[3001]
Food (10–12)	1.032	1.025	1.016	1.124
	(0.102)	(0.127)	(0.330)	(0.119)
	[569]	[524]	[45]	[176]
Basic, fabricated metals (24–25)	1.211	1.205	1.103	1.329
	(0.057)	(0.045)	(0.128)	(0.093)
	[507]	[475]	[32]	[132]
Machinery, equipment n.e.c. (28)	1.302	1.348	1.151	1.296
	(0.247)	(0.294)	(0.097)	(0.240)
	[782]	[708]	[74]	[202]
Retail and wholesale (45–47)	0.820	0.858	1.228	0.888
	(0.163)	(0.181)	(0.181)	(0.194)
	[1467]	[1388]	[79]	[463]
IT & related services (62–63)	1.131	1.130	1.162	1.186
	(0.084)	(0.094)	(0.133)	(0.076)
	[1784]	[1704]	[80]	[683]
Consulting & architectural and engineering activities (69–71)	1.116	1.097	1.436	1.147
	(0.073)	(0.065)	(0.218)	(0.074)
	[1155]	[1116]	[39]	[452]

Note: Standard deviations are in parentheses and numbers of firm-year observations are in brackets.

Table 7A.7   Average relative profit-wage ratio according to ownership status and foreign subsidiaries, selected main sectors, 2011–2015

Industry	All firms	Only Local firms	Only Foreign MNEs	Local firms AND NO foreign subsidiaries
All firms (all sectors)	1.279	1.193	1.835	1.167
	(2.492)	(1.195)	(2.133)	(1.706)
.	[9161]	[8476]	[685]	[3001]
Food (10–12)	1.506	1.699	0.910	0.534
	(0.454)	(0.575)	(0.354)	(0.298)
	[569]	[524]	[45]	[176]
Basic, fabricated metals (24–25)	1.298	1.388	0.660	0.830
	(1.258)	(0.525)	(0.849)	(0.414)
	[507]	[475]	[32]	[132]
Machinery, equipment n.e.c. (28)	1.525	1.621	1.348	1.461
	(0.573)	(0.545)	(0.554)	(0.388)
	[782]	[708]	[74]	[202]
Retail and wholesale (45–47)	1.504	1.765	1.876	0.951
	(0.685)	(0.732)	(0.478)	(0.377)
	[1467]	[1388]	[79]	[463]
IT & related services (62–63)	0.308	0.302	−1.252	2.004
	(2.296)	(2.095)	(5.478)	(0.924)
	[1784]	[1704]	[80]	[683]
Consulting & architectural and engineering activities(69–71)	0.420	0.683	0.980	0.263
	(0.410)	(0.564)	(1.102)	(0.980)
	[1155]	[1116]	[39]	[452]

Note: Standard deviations are in parentheses and numbers of firm-year observations are in brackets.

Appendix B
Additional Tables

Table 7B.1   List of variables

Variable	Definition
Basic firm characteristics	
TAX_PAY	MNE's tax payments, defined as the ratio of taxes paid divided by pretax financial income (V14/V13). TAX_PAY values above one (below zero) are set to one (zero). (see also Mills et al. 2013)
Assets	Natural logarithm of assets (D80)
Leverage	Ratio of long-term debt to total assets (C50/D80)
ROA	The ratio of total profitability divided by total assets (V6+V7)/D80
Tangible	Ratio of tangible assets divided by total assets (D20/D80)
Intangible	Ratio of intangible assets divided by total assets (D10/D80)
Inventory	Ratio of inventory to total assets (D50/D80)
Foreign	Ratio of pretax foreign income to total income of subsidiaries (V71/V7)
Firm size	Natural logarithm of average number of employees in each firm of the year, collected in September of that year
Ownership	= 1 if firm is foreign owned; = 0 if firm is in the hands of a Dutch company
Value-added	Turnover (V1) minus intermediate costs (V4)
Profits	On the basis of Net financial results (V17)
Wages	Gross labor costs (V2)
Firm innovative activities	
PATENT	The number of patent applications (counts) recorded by EPO for a firm during the application year, measured as log(1+PATENT) in regression analysis
R&D	R&D intensity, calculated as total R&D expenditures to total employment. R&D missing data were not imputed with 0.

Note: Variable names in brackets refer to items compiled from the Statistics Netherlands financial database on non-financial enterprises (NFO)

Table 7B.2   Correlation matrix

Variables 2000-2010	1	2	3	4	5	6	7	8	9	10
TAX_PAY 1	1.000									
Assets 2	0.052	1.000								
Leverage 3	−0.029	0.032	1.000							
ROA 4	0.123	−0.116	−0.100	1.000						
Inventory 5	0.043	−0.197	−0.051	−0.021	1.000					
Tangible 6	0.084	−0.057	0.164	−0.057	−0.071	1.000				
Intangible 7	0.051	0.162	0.223	−0.076	−0.123	−0.191	1.000			
Origin 8	0.007	0.475	−0.020	−0.075	−0.121	−0.219	0.142	1.000		
R&D 9	−0.093	−0.095	0.004	0.012	−0.036	−0.114	0.016	−0.003	1.000	
PAT 10	−0.075	0.392	0.045	−0.035	−0.099	−0.164	0.082	0.243	0.276	1.000

Table 7B.3   WBSO, innovation box, 2011–2015

	Innovation Box NO	Innovation Box YES	Total
R&D, WBSO NO	320678	2031	322709
R&D, WBSO YES	17004	3312	20316
Total	337682	5343	343025

Note: Table 7B.3 gives an overview of the number of firms that applied for the innovation box and that have applied for a WBSO tax credit during the period 2011–2015. The table indicates that there is complementarity between R&D input and innovation output: out of the 5,343 innovation box users, 3,312 firms have also applied for the WBSO. Notice that there are also still a significant number of firms that are granted a WBSO tax credit, but that does not apply for the innovation box. Or in other terms, a considerable number of firms report R&D input but no innovation output.

Appendix C
Innovation Tax Incentives in the Netherlands

In the Netherlands, there are a number of tax schemes that aim to incentivize firms to innovate. From the perspective of the input side of the innovation process, the so-called WBSO and RDA are tax credit schemes that enable firms to reduce R&D costs. At this stage of the innovation process, firms are rewarded for their innovation efforts regardless of their innovation success. So, at the output side of innovation, the introduction of the innovation box rather focuses on the outcome of R&D whereby profits as the results of successful patenting behavior receive a lower tax rate. In this sense, firms are stimulated to engage in R&D because not only innovation input but also the innovation output as a result of successful R&D merits are subject to lower tax rates.

R&D Tax Credits

Since 1994 the Dutch government introduced the WBSO, which is an acronym for the Wage Tax and Social Insurance Act (in Dutch, Wet Bevordering Speur- en Ontwikkelingswerk, WBSO hereafter) to stimulate firms' R&D activities in the Netherlands. The WBSO is considered an important driver of the ongoing Dutch innovation policy. Its aim is to stimulate R&D expenditures for firms located in the Netherlands. Additionally, there is an extra provision for small and medium sized firms as well as starting firms. The WBSO provides an R&D grant, primarily an R&D wage subsidy that can be granted to any R&D performing firm located in the Netherlands regardless of size. The WBSO adds additional funding under the so-called

RDA (in Dutch, R&D aftrek), which allows firms to deduct an (annually set) fixed amount for R&D on their income tax payment. As of 2016, both the WBSO and the RDA are merged together under the WBSO scheme. The range of R&D projects suitable for assistance include the development of new products, processes and IT software, technical and process oriented scientific research as well as innovation feasibility studies. Concerning the eligibility criteria, R&D development projects must include some degree of technical risks or uncertainties. The most important evaluation criteria that the WBSO consider are the embodied technological novelty in the R&D development project. The technological novelty itself must include a research component whereby technical obstacles as well as possible solutions are defined. R&D projects based on technical scientific research are categorized in domains such as physics, chemistry, biotechnology, production technology, and ICT. Concerning innovation feasibility analysis, the WBSO stipulates that the purpose of the R&D project is already structured and known. Economic and financial aspects surrounding the R&D project is of less importance.

While there have been some changes in the provision of grants over time, the application procedures that make projects eligible for assistance are as follows. The applicant (usually a firm) has to show that he or she is involved with the technical analysis as part of an ongoing R&D project that must take place within the European Union. Additionally, the firm must pay corporate income tax returns as well as wage tax and national insurance contributions for those employees who are involved with R&D. The actual WBSO grant level is calculated on the basis of total R&D working hours multiplied by an average R&D hourly wage.

Innovation Box

An innovation box is a fiscal instrument in the corporate tax regime that can be applied to all firms that have a corporate tax obligation in the Netherlands, that is, local and foreign-owned firms. The point of departure for the application of an innovation box are intangible assets that cover primarily patents and associated patent rights, and to a lesser extent, designs and models, copyrights, and trade secrets.[19] The innovation box entails that the profits that are generated from the eligible intangible assets enjoy a tax deduction. Since 2010, the effective tariff on profits within the innovation box in the Netherlands is 5 percent. Prior to 2010, the official rate was 10 percent.

We note that Evers, Miller, and Spengel (2014) provide a detailed overview across countries. In addition, the authors also calculate a so-called effective tax rate so that non-fiscal country-specificities are netted out. Focusing on

19. We note that the scope of intangible assets to which an innovation box is applicable depends by country. We refer Alstadsaeter et al. (2015) for a cross-country comparison.

the official tax rates, we may conclude that the Netherlands belongs to most favorite tax regime countries, along with Belgium, Luxembourg, Lichtenstein, and Malta.

The effectiveness of an innovation box on tax revenues depends on some additional provisions. In the Netherlands, the innovation box applies to intangible assets that are considered as outcomes from R&D related activities. In that sense, especially, the focus is on technical innovation. Firms that are eligible for WBSO are also eligible for the innovation box; although, the related profits that are generated from the innovation must at least come from patenting activities (den Hertog et al. 2015).

With the innovation box in place, pure fiscal motives may remain. The eligibility criteria make it very attractive for firms that are able to be successful innovators both from the R&D input and the R&D outcome perspective, in terms of patenting. In addition, the so-called 30 percent rule provides an extra stimulus for attracting highly skilled personnel from abroad. In combination with other fiscal incentives (e.g., negotiation with tax authorities is allowed), this makes the Netherlands a fiscally attractive place, apart from the question of whether these firms also play a significant role in the real economy. A recent online survey conducted by the Dutch Ministry of Economic Affairs (den Hertog et al. 2015) concludes that firms do indicate that the favorite fiscal regime as the result of the innovation box does seem to be important.

References

Alstadsaeter, A., S. Barrios, G. Nicodeme, A. Skonieczna, and A. Vezzani. 2015. "Patent Boxes Design, Patents Location, and Location of R&D." Working paper.

Bradley, S., E. Dauchy, and L. Robinson. 2015. "Cross-Country Evidence on the Preliminary Effects of Patent Box Regimes on Patent Activity and Ownership." Mimeo.

Capaldo, A., and M. Petruzzelli. 2011. "In Search of Alliance-Level Relational Capabilities: Balancing Innovation Value Creation and Appropriability in R&D Alliances." *Scandinavian Journal of Management* 27 (3): 273–86.

Chen, S., L. De Simone, M. Hanlon, and R. Lester. 2016. "The Effect of Innovation Box Regimes on Income Shifting and Real Activity." Working paper, Graduate School of Business, Stanford University.

CBS. 2017. Innovatie en Internationalisering: Inventarisatie van bronnen en populatieschets, Report. Heerlen/ Den Haang: Centraal Bureau voor de Statistiek.

CBS. 2018. Multinationals en niet-multinationals in de Nederlandse economie. Heerlen/Den Haang: Centraal Bureau voor de Statistiek.

CEC. 2014. A study on R&D tax incentives: A final report. Brussels: European Commission.

De Haan, M., and J. Haynes. 2018. "R&D Capitalisation: Where Did We Go Wrong?" Paper prepared for the CRIW 2018, Washington DC.

Desai, M., and D. Dharmapala. 2009. "Corporate Tax Avoidance and Firm Value." *Review of Economics and Statistics* 91: 537–46.
De Simone, L., L. F. Mills, and B. Stomberg. 2019. "Using IRS Data to Identify Income Shifting Firms." *Review of Accounting Studies* 24 (2): 694-730.
Den Hertog, P., A. Vankan, B. Verspagen, P. Mohnen, L. Korlaar, B. Eren, M. Janssen, and B. Minne. 2015. Evaluatie innovatiebox 2010–2012. Report prepared for the Ministry of Finance.
Dyreng, S. D., M. Hanlon, and E. L. Maydew. 2008. "Long-Run Corporate Tax Avoidance." *The Accounting Review* 83 (1): 61–82.
Dyreng, S. D., M. Hanlon, and E. L. Maydew. 2010. "The Effects of Executives on Corporate Tax Avoidance." *The Accounting Review* 85 (4): 1163–89.
Egger, P., W. Eggert, and H. Winner. 2010. "Saving Taxes through Foreign Plant Ownership." *Journal of International Economics* 81: 99–108.
Erickson, M., M. Hanlon, and E. Maydew. 2004. "How Much Firms Pay for Earnings That Do Not Exist? Evidence of Taxes Paid on Allegedly Fraudulent Earnings." *The Accounting Review* 29 (2): 387–408.
Ernst, C., and C. Spengel. 2011. "Taxation, R&D Tax Incentives and Patent Application in Europe." ZEW Discussion Papers 11-024.
Eurostat. 2016. Irish GDP revision, Report National Accounts, Reports Directorate C, Luxembourg.
Evers, L., H. Miller, and C. Spengel. 2014. "Intellectual Property Box Regimes: Effective Tax Rates and Tax Policy Considerations." *International Tax and Public Finance* 22 (3): 502–30.
Gao, L., L. Yang, and J. Zhang. 2016. "Corporate Patents, R&D Success, and Tax Avoidance." *Review of Quantitative Finance* 47: 1063–96.
Grubert, H. 2003. "Intangible Income, Intercompany Transactions, Income Shifting, and the Choice of Location." *National Tax Journal* 56 (1): 221–42.
Gupta, S., and K. Newberry. 1997. "Determinants of the Variability in Corporate Effective Tax Rates: Evidence from Longitudinal Data." *Journal of Accounting and Public Policy* 16 (1): 1–34.
Harhoff, D., Narin, F., Scherer, M., Vopel, K. (1999). "Citation frequency and the value of patented inventions." *Review of Economics and Statistics* 81 (3): 511–515.
Hassbring, P., and E. Edwall. 2013. "The Short-Term Effect of Patent Box Regimes." Working paper.
Hall, B., and V. Sena (2017). "Appropriability mechanisms, innovation, and productivity: evidence from the UK." *Economics of Innovation and New Technology* 26: 1–2, 42–62.
Hines, J. R., and E. Rice. 1994. "Fiscal Paradise: Foreign Tax Havens and American Business." *Quarterly Journal of Economics* 109: 149–82.
Karkinsky, T., and N. Riedel. 2012. "Corporate Taxation and the Choice of Patent Location within Multinational Firms." *Journal of International Economics* 88: 176–185.
Koethenbuerger, M., F. Liberini, and M. Stimmelmayr. 2016. "Is It Luring Innovations or Just Profits." Mimeo.
Koh, P. S., and D. Reeb. 2015. "Missing R&D." *Journal of Accounting and Economics* 60: 73–94.
Manzon, G., and G. Plesko. 2002. "The Relation between Financial and Tax Reporting Measures of income." *Tax Law Review* 55: 175–214.
McGuire, S., T. Omer, and D. Wang. 2012. "Tax Avoidance: Does Tax-Specific Industry Expertise Make a Difference?" *The Accounting Review* 87 (3): 975–1003.
Mills, L. 1998. "Book-Tax Differences and Internal Revenue Service Adjustments." *Journal of Accounting Research* 36 (2): 343–56.

Mills, L., S. Nutter, and C. Schwab. 2013. "The Effect of Political Sensitivity and Bargaining Power on Taxes: Evidence from Federal Contractors." *The Accounting Review* 88 (3): 977–1005.

Nagaoka, S., K. Motohashi, and A. Goto. 2010. "Patent Statistics As an Innovation Indicator." In *Handbook of the Economics of Innovation*, edited by B. Hall and N. Rosenberg. North Holland: Elsevier.

OECD. 2008. "Tax Effects on Foreign Direct Investment—Recent Evidence and Policy Analysis." OECD Tax Policy Studies No. 17.

OECD. 2015. "New Standards for Compiling National Accounts: What's the Impact on GDP and Other Macro-economic Indicators?" OECD Statistics Brief.

Restuccia, D., and R. Rogerson. 2008. "Policy Distortions and Aggregate Productivity with Heterogeneous Establishments." *Review of Economic Dynamics* 11 (4): 707–20.

Roberts, M., and V. Van Anh. 2013. "Empirical Modeling of R&D Demand in a Dynamic Framework." *Applied Economic Perspectives and Policy* 35 (2): 185–205.

Vancauteren, M., B. Melenberg, J. Plasmans, and R. Bongard. 2017. "Innovation and Productivity of Dutch Firms: A Panel Data Analysis." Discussion paper, Statistics Netherlands, The Hague/Heerlen: The Netherlands.

Comment   Robert E. Yuskavage

In this chapter, the authors study the behavior of business enterprises located in the Netherlands to determine the extent to which firms engaged in innovative activities are able to reduce their income taxes by taking advantage of related tax incentives, and whether the local economic activity requirements of these incentives prevent a mismatch between where production occurs and where income is reported. This is an important issue for national accounts because the intellectual property (IP)-related profits of multinational enterprises (MNEs) can be shifted to lower tax jurisdictions. It is also important in the context of the Organisation for Economic Co-operation and Development's (OECD) Base Erosion and Profit Shifting (BEPS) initiative, which seeks to align taxation with real economic activity.

The Netherlands has become a favorite location for foreign direct investment by MNEs around the world for many reasons, only some of which are tax related. According to the OECD, foreign firms in the Netherlands account for 15–20 percent of employment and 25–30 percent of private nonfarm business value added. A study of MNE behavior in the Netherlands can thus provide useful insights about how global innovative activity affects national accounts. Two innovation-related tax incentives figure

Robert E. Yuskavage is a retired economist of the Bureau of Economic Analysis.

For acknowledgments, sources of research support, and disclosure of the author's material financial relationships, if any, please see https://www.nber.org/books-and-chapters/challenges-globalization-measurement-national-accounts/comment-relationship-between-tax-payments-and-mnes-patenting-activities-and-implications-real.

prominently in the study. One is an innovation box (IB) that provides for a significantly lower statutory tax rate (5 percent vs. 25 percent) on profits from the use of IP, requiring that the IP be self-produced rather than acquired. The other incentive is a type of research and development (R&D) tax credit known by its Dutch acronym, WBSO. For this provision, firms need to certify the employment and wages of R&D staff.

The chapter offers an interesting perspective on the impact of globalization on national accounts. Whereas most of the conference papers focus on the institutional framework and the accounting concepts underlying aggregate measures of economic activity, this chapter uses a micro-econometric approach to obtain insights into activities that affect national accounts aggregates. Specifically, the authors estimate a reduced form regression equation using the Netherlands effective tax rate (ETR) as the dependent variable to be explained by a variety of indicators related to tax liability, including measures of innovative activity. Three such measures were featured: (1) number of patents filed, (2) number of patent forward citations (proxy for patent quality), and (3) R&D expenditures per employee. Other independent variables suggested by previous studies include total assets, rate of return on assets, tangible capital, intangible capital, leverage, foreign-source income, and foreign ownership.

The sample consists of an unbalanced panel of enterprises located in the Netherlands—both domestic and foreign owned—that applied for a patent at any time during 2000–2010 and that also reported R&D expenditures in selected surveys. Patent data were obtained by matching enterprises from the Netherlands General Business Register (GBR) with a database from the European Patent Office. A total of 1,192 firms yielded 4,166 firm-year observations. These firms were then matched with the GBR to obtain tax and financial data. This work clearly represents an impressive database-building endeavor. However, the construction of the ultimate sample, particularly combining the R&D data with the patent application subsample, was not entirely clear. A better understanding of the relationships among these subgroups and their overall relationship to the larger Netherlands economy would have been helpful.

Under the authors' preferred model with industry and year fixed effects, each of the three lagged innovation-related measures has a significant positive relationship with a reduced Dutch ETR, although the patent forward citation measure is significant only when patent applications are dropped from the equation. However, these patent measures (unlike R&D expenditures) are skewed and highly concentrated among a small number of very large firms. This raises the possibility that the results may be driven by a relatively small subsample. Moreover, in the absence of a structural model, it is difficult to disentangle the various channels for reducing taxes. As a result, the impact on taxes of innovative activities broadly defined may actually be understated. The authors may want to consider using firm fixed effects as a way to account for firm-specific unobservable factors. Another option is to include more measures of firm size, such as sales or employment, to help isolate the impact of very large firms.

In order to tie the performance of tax-reducing innovative activities to local economic activity, the authors compare the labor productivity of firms that utilized the IB or the WBSO tax credit with all other firms over the period 2011–2015. The rationale is that higher labor productivity implies a greater impact on the local economy. Calculated as value added per employee at the two-digit sector level, the authors find that firms that used both tax incentives had higher average labor productivity in 16 of 21 sectors. One possibility, though, is that the results simply reflect the greater capital intensity of these firms, given that they are larger with more assets and most likely have significant intangible assets. Other measures that might be more closely connected to local economic activity include gross output labor productivity, which reflects the use of intermediate inputs in production, and compensation as a share of value added, which relates more directly to employment and household income.

The authors' major conclusion is that the Netherlands' innovation-related tax incentives, while clearly reducing taxes for innovative firms, most likely have little if any impact on national accounts due to the local economic activity requirements and higher labor productivity. This implies no geographic separation of innovative activity and its associated income. However, it is not entirely clear if the direct tax incentives are the only channel for innovative firms to reduce taxes. Tax savings can be achieved either directly via the specific incentives or indirectly by the strategic location of patents and other IP in low tax countries. The indirect channel allows firms that do not qualify for the direct tax benefits to still shift income and reduce taxes, especially if their home tax rates are higher, such as for the affiliates of US MNEs through 2017.

According to the OECD, the Netherlands has a relatively large share (about 40 percent) of shifted patents. These are patents for which the inventor country is the Netherlands but the actual applicant, such as the affiliate of an MNE, is located in a different country. Even if the patent itself is not assigned to a different country, licensing and other rights for use of the patent may be located elsewhere. As a result, firms in the Netherlands that do not necessarily meet the local activity requirements of the direct tax incentives could still pay lower taxes by strategic location of patents and patent rights in countries with lower statutory rates than the Netherlands.

Whether or not this is an issue depends partly on how the foreign affiliates of Dutch MNEs are treated in the business register. If such affiliates are fully consolidated in the enterprise statistics, then shifted patents may be not be an issue. In the United States, for example, foreign affiliate data are not included in enterprise statistics developed from business registers. Fully consolidated statistics for the Netherlands would presumably reflect both foreign affiliate income and the Dutch taxes paid on that income. If not, then the impact on the ETR is uncertain. More information about the Dutch tax system, especially the treatment of MNEs and foreign source income, would be helpful.

Another potentially significant issue is the degree of strictness in the local economic activity requirements of the innovation tax incentives. The WBSO tax credit requires certification of R&D personnel employed on approved projects and their related compensation. The IB requires that the qualifying IP was produced by the taxpayer rather than simply purchased. However, for both provisions it is not clear how much of the underlying R&D was necessarily performed in the Netherlands versus contracted to affiliated parties in other countries. Along these lines, the Netherlands recently revised the criteria for its IB regime to be more consistent with the "nexus" requirements of the OECD's BEPS Action Plan 5, including limitations on outsourcing of R&D to related parties.

One of the robustness checks reported differences in the results for domestic vs. foreign owned firms. For domestic firms, the patent variable—but not the R&D expenditures variable—was significantly negative, while the opposite result was obtained for foreign firms. Given the more stringent local activity requirements for the R&D tax credit, domestic firms may be reducing taxes by locating patents in lower tax countries without necessarily conducting activities in the Netherlands. Foreign firms may be engaged in R&D activities in the Netherlands but their patents and related income may be located in other countries. Because these possibilities have important implications for the national accounts, the authors are encouraged to more closely examine the results for foreign and domestic firms separately.

II

Global Value Chains for Intermediate Products

8

Accounting Frameworks for Global Value Chains
Extended Supply-Use Tables

Nadim Ahmad

8.1 Overview

The increasing international fragmentation of production that has occurred in recent decades, driven by technological progress, reductions in trade costs, improved access to resources and markets, trade policy reforms, and indeed cost factors in emerging economies, has challenged our conventional wisdom on how we look at and interpret globalization. Traditional measures of trade for example, record gross flows of goods and services each and every time they cross borders, leading to what many describe as a "multiple" counting of trade, which may lead to misguided policy measures in a wide range of policy areas. In response to this, the international statistics community began to develop new measures of trade on a value added basis, for example the OECD-WTO Trade in Value-Added (TiVA) database, WIOD, APEC-TIVA, and the European FIGARO initiative.

But important though such initiatives are, they are silent, with the exception of recent exploratory initiatives,[1] on some important aspects of globalization, for example the role of multinationals. Of particular relevance in this context is the ability of multinationals to shift intellectual property products (IPPs) from one economic territory to another, which has generated broader questions on the ability of GDP to accurately describe "meaningful" economic activity, and, by extension, on other macroeconomic sta-

Nadim Ahmad is Deputy Director at the Organisation for Economic Co-operation and Development (OECD) Centre for Entrepreneurship, SMEs, Regions, and Cities.

For acknowledgments, sources of research support, and disclosure of the author's material financial relationships, if any, please see https://www.nber.org/books-and-chapters /challenges-globalization-measurement-national-accounts/accounting-frameworks-global -value-chains-extended-supply-use-tables.

1. http://www.oecd.org/daf/inv/investment-policy/trade-investment-gvc.htm.

tistics, including TiVA. For example, trade in value added measures purport to show how (in which industries) and where (in which territories) value is generated in the production of a good or service, but the simple relocation of an IPP from one economic territory to another[2] can radically alter that view.

In addition, the policy debate in recent years has increasingly focused on what has become referred to in many quarters as "inclusive globalization," referring to the growing realization that the benefits of globalization may not have accrued to all members of society equally, even if only as a process of transition. With traditional macroeconomic statistics, it is not immediately clear, for example, which categories of workers and firms (notably SMEs) in which countries benefit from globalization (and how) and which may have been, even if only temporarily, left behind. This particular issue has gained particular prominence in recent years.

More fundamentally, there is a growing appreciation that the statistical compilation tools and accounting frameworks designed and developed over the last 60 years in various manifestations of the System of National Accounts, despite their significant advances, may reflect a world that no longer exists. These tools were originally designed in a world where production was largely self-contained within an economy, with trade reflecting exports and imports, typically, of finished or primary goods. But today much of global trade is in intermediate parts.

In the early days of the SNA, global value chains showed much lower levels of fragmentation than they do today, and statistical information systems reflected these realities with the Rest of the World (ROW) recorded as a separate institutional sector to and from which goods were sold and bought. Over the years, as global production chains became more fragmented and interconnectedness grew, there was a growing realization that additional information was needed to properly navigate the economic landscape, which resulted in the development of new areas of statistics, such as foreign direct investment measures and data collections focusing on inward and outward activities of foreign affiliates (FATS). More recently, new data collections, or rather compilations, have focused on linking trade and business registers to provide insights on which firms in which sectors engage in imports and exports (referred to as trade by enterprise characteristics).

These more recent innovations have significantly improved our collective understanding of trade, and indeed foreign investment, but they are still, to a large extent, only a partial solution to the statistical challenges presented by globalization and international fragmentation of production: partial in the sense that they remain in many countries the poor relations of the core SNA economic accounting framework, with only limited compilation and collection.

---

2. Albeit a relocation that satisfies the accounting rules regarding economic, as opposed to legal, ownership.

Moreover, the mechanisms for data collection are often outside the conventional framework, meaning that differences may arise between the measures collected within these activities and their implicit equivalents included in the core estimates of GDP. For example FATS data are collected as separate exercises in many countries but information on the same firms is also collected[3] as part of GDP estimation, which may generate different results. And even in cases where the same survey information is used, subsequent adjustments made in the GDP accounting framework (whether reflecting concepts or statistical adjustments) are rarely replicated in the original source data; also resulting in implicit inconsistencies in the eventual published data sets (GDP and FATS).

This largely reflects the stove-pipe approach that has evolved over time to respond to the statistical challenges of globalization.

Arguably a more radical approach is needed that fully reflects the need to have a better articulation of globalization in the core accounting framework: one that doesn't, in extremis, relegate its role to the ROW institutional sector.

Such an approach requires that the role of foreign affiliates in the economic territory and affiliates abroad are captured explicitly (and visibly) in the core accounts. It also requires improved information on the trade relationships of categories of firms (for example exporter and non-exporter), and indeed who those firms trade with. As important is the need to fully articulate income flows in and out of the economy and, in particular, from which category of firms (e.g., industrial sector) these arise.

But this is not all that is needed. The challenges of inclusive globalization require that the view of people (in other words, workers and types of firms in which they work) is also captured in the system. This requires information on skills, occupations, and compensation paid to these categories of workers in different sectors, as well as a more differentiated view of the types of firms. But, again, much of this information is collected in different domains, with different surveys, and so, again, there is a risk that the stove-pipe approach may not be consistent across all domains. For example, labor force survey data on jobs within a sector rarely equal the equivalent measures of jobs in the same sector collected via business surveys or other administrative sources.

Bringing this information together into a coherent and integrated framework not only improves the information content of statistical responses to globalization questions but also improves the quality of that information, including for current TiVA statistics.

TiVA estimates, derived through the construction of a global input-output table, implicitly assume that all firms within a given sector have the same production function (input-output technical coefficients), import intensity, and export intensity. This of course has never been true. We know for

3. Even if only implicitly through sampling and grossing techniques.

example that larger firms will typically have different production functions from smaller firms, because of economies of scale, and also higher labor productivity. And these firms will also typically be more export and, indeed, import orientated than their smaller counterparts (reflecting in part the disproportionate costs of trade faced by smaller firms compared to larger firms). The same generalizations hold true for foreign owned enterprises, or enterprises with affiliates abroad, compared to purely domestic firms. But TiVA estimates, relying as they do on national supply-use and input-output tables, cannot reflect these heterogeneities; meaning that key measures, such as the import content of exports, are typically downward biased, with extensions such as the domestic jobs content of exports,[4] typically being upwards biased.

Moreover, the very process of globalization has increased the scale of these heterogeneities, driving coach and horses through the assumption of homogeneity within sectors. As firms within sectors increasingly specialize in specific tasks in the production process, they also suck in greater imports from the upstream part of the value chain and have greater export orientation. In addition, globalization has itself led to an increased prevalence of (once rare) categories of firms such as *Factoryless Producers* and *Processers*, where recent changes in the accounting system further weaken the case for assumptions of homogeneity in technical coefficients.

For example, all other things being equal, a processing firm in one sector will have significantly less (recorded) imports than a non-processing firm producing the same final product. Similarly, a factoryless producer will be allocated to the distribution sector (with limited intermediate consumption of goods) but the same firm that chooses to buy the material goods used by the processing firms will be allocated to the manufacturing sector (with significant intermediate consumption of goods).

The ability of national (and international) supply-use and input-output tables, based on industrial groupings alone, to describe how demand and supply relationships are related has therefore become more difficult. Typically, in confronting the problem of heterogeneity, the conventional approach has been to provide more detail by aggregating firms at lower levels of the industrial classification system, for example three- or four-digit groupings as opposed to two-digit groupings; subject to confidentiality restrictions being preserved. But this approach may not be optimal, neither in terms of reducing heterogeneity within aggregations (and in a way that best responds to the policy drivers) nor necessarily optimal in terms of processing burdens.

That is not to say that industrial classification systems are completely obsolete. It would serve little purpose for example to devise an optimal sys-

---

4. (i) Because the import content is typically underestimated (meaning that the domestic content and in turn related jobs) are overestimated and (ii) because exporting firms typically have higher labor productivity than non-exporting firms in the same activity.

tem that did not retain some means of classifying firms on the basis of their activity (e.g., manufacturing versus services), if only because these remain the key prisms that users look through when analyzing production. But it does serve to highlight that other approaches to tackling heterogeneity can, and should, be considered.

The tool advocated in the SNA for ensuring coherence across various data sources to assure alignment of GDP estimates created by the income, expenditure, and production approach is supply-use tables; the same underlying core statistical input required for TiVA estimates. As shown in this chapter, through (in principle) simple extensions to conventional supply-use tables, *extended supply-use* tables provide the ideal basis for bringing together these various domains into a single integrated economic accounting framework that puts the measurement of the "global" at the heart of the "national."

8.2   Extended Supply-Use Tables

8.2.1   Extended SUTs in the 2008 SNA

Before beginning, it is perhaps instructive to note that the concept that will be developed here is not radical. Many satellite accounts, for example, work around similar principals to those advocated below. Indeed chapter 14 of the 2008 SNA provides a presentation of supply-use tables that differentiate production on the basis of market output, non-market output, and production for own-final use. Such an approach capitalizes on the readily available nature of data in most countries that can support such a breakdown. Obviously, such a breakdown is superior to conventional tables without a breakdown, as they provide additional information that can support more granular policies, for example with respect to subsistence farming, but they also provide a means for more coherent accounts; for example, imputations of output for own use and corresponding consumption estimates can be more readily aligned.

A few additional "extensions" worth noting that are included in the 2008 SNA (and which provide entry points to analyze impacts on people, while also significantly improving productivity measures) are additional rows showing labor inputs (as hours worked), GFCF, and closing stocks of fixed assets.

That all being said, very few countries currently provide all of the additional information specified above, despite their importance.

8.2.2   Extended SUTs for Globalization

This section considers a range of extensions that could be incorporated in national supply-use tables to improve our understanding of globalization, whilst at the same time recognizing the limitations imposed by confidentiality restrictions.

The section runs through four distinct types of extensions:

- The first looks at very simple extensions that require no additional breakdown of activities into categories or grouping of more homogeneous (or rather less heterogeneous) firms.
- The second looks at extensions that split activities into more homogeneous groupings of firms.
- The third looks at extensions that provide links between the core production accounts and the distribution of income accounts, and also to other important macroeconomic variables (such as employment).
- The final extension—perhaps the most difficult to do, since it may not always be possible to create such breakdowns with existing information without assumptions—is the breakdown of products by distinct category of producer.

8.2.2.1 Simple Extensions

There are a number of relatively simple extensions that can be added to conventional supply-use tables in a way that can greatly improve our ability to analyze and understand globalization.

Perhaps the simplest of these extensions is to separately show estimates of goods for processing transactions (manufacturing services on physical inputs owned by others) and re-exports (if import flow tables are not also provided). Such extensions are important for TiVA calculations, as re-exports typically have only negligible (often zero) domestic content, while information on goods for processing transactions significantly improves the ability to create coherent global supply-use tables.

Such information is even further enhanced if breakdowns of activities also separately differentiate between processing and non-processing production (discussed later). Ideally, for goods for processing transactions, it is also helpful to show the value of those goods that have been imported (but whose ownership has not changed) and the full customs value of goods subsequently exported. Similarly, especially because the process of production is significantly different, it is also useful to show separately the value of merchanting with gross values of exports of goods.

A second set of simple extensions, albeit slightly more complicated, as such information is not always available or collected at the detailed product level available in supply-use tables, concerns the estimates of residents' expenditure abroad and non-residents' expenditure. In many countries these are only shown within conventional supply-use tables as additional separate items added to total imports and total exports respectively (with corresponding adjustments made to household final consumption). Again, for the calculation of global supply-use tables, it is important to have these items broken down by product. Tourism satellite accounts often provide a good basis for creating such breakdowns.

In many countries these items are added as additional rows in national supply-use tables as a single cell, but what is needed are complementary columns showing the expenditure items (imports and exports) broken down by product. It's important to note that separate breakdowns have a variety of applications, first and foremost for a better understanding of the tourism industry, but they also matter greatly for TiVA and trade policy making, as the goods transactions do not (generally) involve tariffs, unlike conventional merchandise trade. This matters because analyses that use TiVA to assess, say, the multiplicative impact of cascading tariffs along a GVC are likely to overestimate these costs if tourism trade in goods is not separated.[5]

A third set of extensions concerns the valuation of imports. Typically, goods transactions are recorded at CIF prices. But global supply-use tables require a common valuation of imports and exports, meaning that import values are also needed at FOB prices. As such, a split of imports of goods into an FOB component and a CIF component is also highly desirable. In addition, in order to analyze the impact of tariffs on GVCs, and indeed to help construct import-flow matrices (particularly those derived using the classic proportionality assumption), complementary information on tariffs/duties paid by product is also highly desirable.

A fourth set of extensions concerns the geographical breakdown of the import flow matrix within the supply-use framework (an essential step needed on the way to producing global input-output tables, but also, even if not widely used, very useful in constructing national supply-use and input-output tables). Countries use a variety of methods to derive their import flow matrices. In some, estimates are based on survey estimates or administrative sources, but in many they are based on the assumption of proportionality.[6] (Ideally these tables could also be broken down by partner, or at least major partners or regional groupings.) In the simplest case, this could be done by also applying a proportionality assumption, but more refined estimates could be derived through linking exercises; in particular through the linking of trade (customs) and statistical business registers at the firm level.

Figure 8.1 describes all of the above extensions in a simple schematic flow

5. Note that this is not unique to tourism expenditures. *De minimis* cross-border trade (below customs thresholds) are also, typically, tariff-free, and so, some consideration could also be given to exploring whether these too should be shown separately in SUTs. In theory this should be realizable, as in practice, in most countries *de minimis* trade is estimated using broader (often macro) approaches. However, and also in practice, these are not typically also estimated with a breakdown by product. For now these are thought to be small-scale transactions and so the working assumption is that they care captured in the balancing process to create the SUT, but digitalization and intermediation platforms (such as Amazon, eBay etc.) have democratized access by households to producers abroad, and so the scale of *de minimis* transactions may be increasing.

6. See UN Handbook on Supply, Use and Input-Output Tables with Extensions and Applications. Ideally the proportionality assumption should be applied at the most detailed product level possible, even if this level is more disaggregated than that used in dissemination, and taking into account end-use—BEC—type classifications.

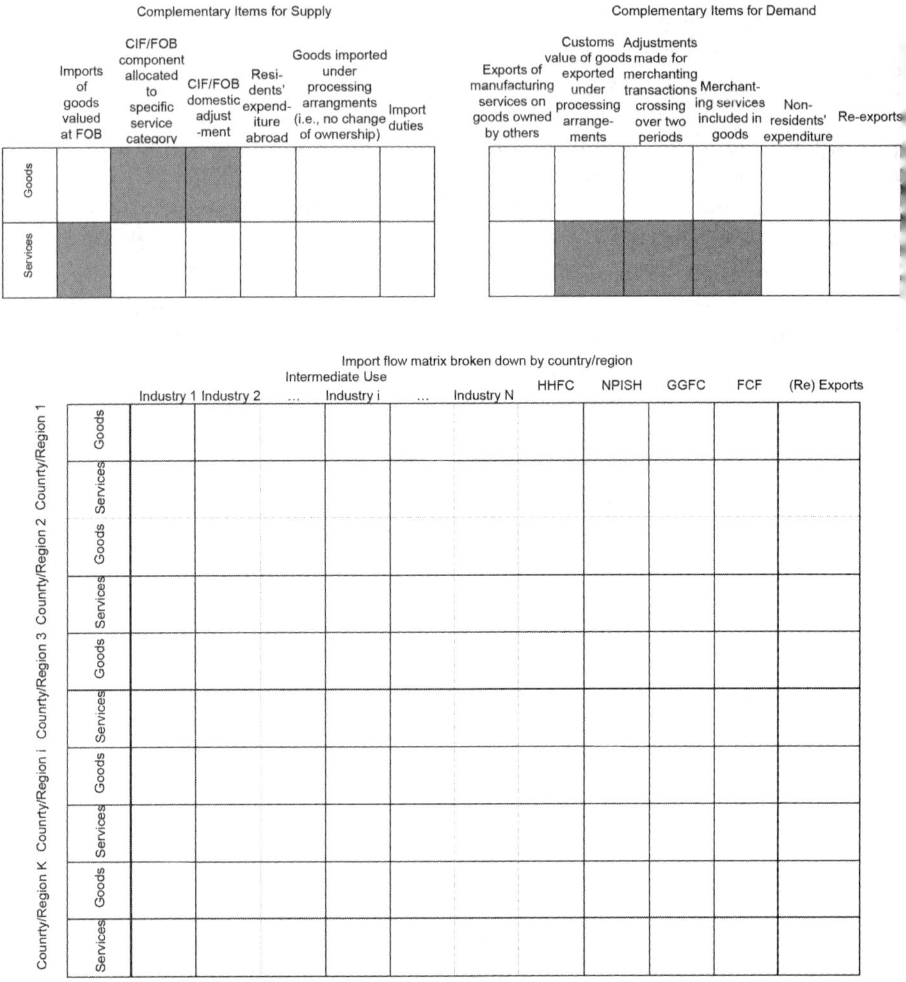

Complementary Items for Supply

	CIF/FOB component allocated to specific service category	CIF/FOB domestic adjust-ment	Resi-dents' expend-iture abroad	Goods imported under processing arrangments (i.e., no change of ownership)	Import duties
Imports of goods valued at FOB					

Complementary Items for Demand

	Exports of manufacturing services on goods owned by others	Customs value of goods made for processing arrange-ments	Adjustments exported merchanting transactions crossing over two periods	Merchant-ing services included in residents' goods	Non-residents' expenditure	Re-exports

Goods

Services

Import flow matrix broken down by country/region

		Intermediate Use					HHFC	NPISH	GGFC	FCF	(Re) Exports
		Industry 1	Industry 2	...	Industry i	...	Industry N					

Country/Region 1 — Goods / Services
Country/Region 2 — Goods / Services
Country/Region 3 — Goods / Services
County/Region i — Goods / Services
Country/Region K — Goods / Services

Figure 8.1 Simple extensions (complements) to SUTs

Note: In the above, the reference to "CIF/FOB domestic adjustment" refers explicitly to the adjustment made in conventional supply-use tables to adjust for the transportation and insurance services provided by resident producers. These expenditures should, in theory, be removed from the total value of imports to ensure that total imports are valued at FOB prices. Typically this adjustment is included as a separate row in most countries' national supply-use tables (with a corresponding adjustment made to exports). The column referred to as CIF/FOB domestic adjustment therefore reflects only the allocation of this component to specific service categories. Note that this is also described in the 2008 SNA, but very few countries provide this information by product.

diagram. For convenience, and also because national practices in the construction and presentation of supply-use tables differ, all items are described as complementary items.

8.2.2.2 Extensions within Activities

As noted above, the concept of breaking down activities into more homogenous or policy relevant groupings is not new. The 2008 SNA for example describes breakdowns between market and non-market activities, and many satellite accounting systems also embody this principle. The approach advocated in this chapter is to develop aggregations of firms (and splits of activities) into those that best respond to the growing demands presented by globalization.

It's important in this respect to note that the approach is deliberately not prescriptive. How countries develop extended SUTs that meet the statistical challenges presented by globalization necessarily depends on national circumstances. These are in the main driven by statistical capacity, but they should also reflect national policy demands.

The OECD Expert Group on Extended Supply-Use tables,[7] created in 2014, focused on three broad approaches that could, in theory, be developed by all countries (with varying degrees of complexity). These three approaches were:

* Breakdowns by size-class of firm (statistical unit)
* Breakdowns by trading status (exporter, two-way trader, importer, non-trader)
* Breakdowns by ownership status (foreign owned affiliates, domestic multinational with affiliates abroad, domestic firm with no foreign affiliates).

Participating countries were also asked to consider variants, including combinations, of the above three breakdowns, for example breakdowns by trading status and size class, and also to consider alternative approaches that better reflected national circumstances. For example Chinese tables were broken down into three categories of firms—exporters operating within the customs processing regime, other exporters, and non-exporters; Mexican tables were developed by grouping firms on the basis of whether they were a global manufacturer or non-global manufacturer; and Costa Rican tables have been broken down into three categories of firms: firms operating within free trade zones, other exporters, and all other firms (and work is ongoing to extend these breakdowns to include an ownership dimension).

Conceptually the breakdown of activities into more distinct groupings of firms (heterogeneous and/or policy relevant) is relatively trivial to illustrate

---

7. https://www.oecd.org/sdd/na/OECD-Expert-Group-on-Extended-Supply-Use-Tables .htm.

Supply

Use

Import Flow

Figure 8.2   Extended supply-use tables (activity breakdown)

(figure 8.2); it merely involves breaking down existing activities into new disaggregations where such disaggregations are meaningful.

For example, it would not be particularly useful, at least with respect to improving homogeneity, to disaggregate a particular activity if the overwhelming majority of output and exports within that activity was conducted by one category of firm. Indeed, in some cases it would not be possible to have disaggregations if the corresponding breakdown resulted in breaches of confidentiality (i.e., statistical disclosure of individual firms). This is another reason why it is preferable not to be prescriptive about the format of extended SUTs.

However, challenges presented by confidentiality do provide an opportunity to consider whether current dissemination strategies are necessarily optimal, from a policy perspective at least. For example, it may be preferable to reduce the degree of industrial activity breakdown presented if this provides scope to provide additional breakdowns by other categorizations of firm.

Figure 8.2 provides a simple illustration of such an extended supply-use table with two categories of firm-type (category 1 and 2). Note the inclusion of additional breakdowns of fixed capital investment, exports and imports by the relevant categories of firms and the additional row under output, showing the value of output that is exported. Note also, for ease of exposition, that the additional extensions described in section 8.2.1 above are not illustrated below. However it follows that it would be preferable to include these extensions with additional breakdowns by category of firm where relevant. This includes, in particular, breakdowns of: *imports of goods under processing arrangements; exports of manufacturing services on goods owned by others; customs value of goods exported under processing arrangements; and adjustments made for merchanting transactions crossing over two periods.*

One additional extension that would be very useful in this context concerns the geographical breakdown of exports. Standard indicators on GVCs, such as those derived via TiVA, are not able to track the true underlying granularity implicit in the value chain. For example, foreign owned affiliates are often more likely to have stronger trade relationships with their parent's resident country than independent firms, both with regards to imports and exports, especially when considering the whole of the value chain. This can make a significant difference to trade relationships derived from TiVA measures where the "averaging" effect tends to weaken the strength of those ties. For example, US firms exporting parts for assembly in Mexico often do so with a view to US markets in mind, but current TiVA estimates are not fully able to capture the granularity of these relationships: a breakdown of the origin of imports by category of firm and, correspondingly, the destination of exports by the same categories of firms would greatly improve the quality of TiVA based estimates, such as the US content of Mexico's exports to the United States, when used to complement breakdowns of activity by firm type. Figure 8.3 provides a schematic of the type of information that would be useful to provide in extended SUTs.

One final complementary extension that would be of considerable use relates to capital flow matrices (figure 8.4). Although many countries are able to produce estimates of gross fixed capital formation by activity, these are typically only available at a relatively aggregated product level, such as "plant and machinery," "intellectual property," etc., and rarely at the level of product detail provided in conventional supply-use tables. This is a significant statistical lacuna. It necessarily hinders the development of high-quality KLEMS type statistics as, by definition, it requires relatively aggregated measures of capital stock (derived typically via the Perpetual Inventory Method), but it also limits extensions in the domain of TiVA-type statistics.

For example, and to illustrate, if Germany only exported capital machinery to China, there would be no German value added embodied in China's

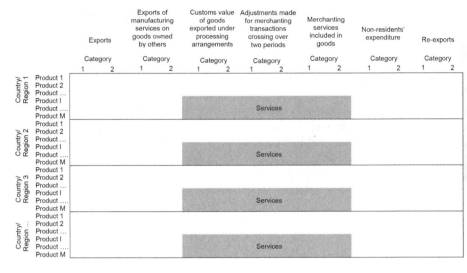

Figure 8.3   Extended supply-use tables (activity breakdown) for exports

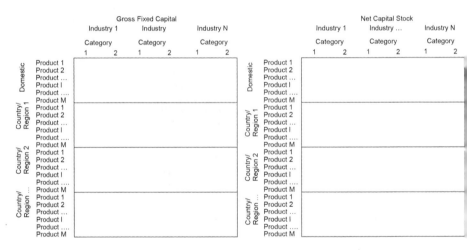

Figure 8.4   Extended supply-use tables (activity breakdown) for investment and capital stock

exports and so Germany's dependencies with consumption in the rest of world (driving production in China and in turn China's demand for German machinery) could appear to be misleadingly limited. However, a time series of capital flow matrices could be used to construct corresponding measures of capital services such that an extended TiVA system could be developed that recorded Germany's exports of capital investment goods as a flow of a series of capital services payments (akin to treating the purchase by China as if it was an operating lease arrangement rather than an acquisition).

It's important to stress that in the same way that all activities do not need to be broken down, neither is it necessary for all of the additional extensions to be provided. For example, breakdowns by category of exports of manufacturing services on goods owned by others can, alone, significantly improve the quality of TiVA indicators. Moreover, and again to labor an important point, how countries define the categories of firms necessarily depends on the quality and availability of complementary information.

8.2.2.2.1   Capitalizing on Customs Registers

One source of information, available in theory in all countries, that provides a rich source of data are registers of exporting firms used for customs purposes. Typically, but not exclusively, these record imports and exports by exporting *enterprises*, and in many countries (for example China and Costa Rica), complementary information is available on the export regime that the enterprises operate within. For example, in China, as is the case in many countries with large processing-based exports, processing firms are able to import parts duty free (as long as the final good is subsequently exported). A similar situation exists for firms operating from free trade zones (FTZs), which forms the basis of firm categorization in Costa Rica's extended SUTs.

But even without this additional granularity available in countries with, for example, large-scale processing sectors and FTZs, customs registers are able to provide an excellent source for extended SUTs because it is, in theory, possible to link the statistical units recorded in customs registers to the corresponding statistical unit recorded in the core statistical business register. Indeed, it is this linking that provides the basis of the Trade by Enterprise Characteristics data sets[8] that have been developed in recent years across many countries. Typically, the following data are available by size class and industry through a simple matching exercise: number of exporting and of importing firms, export values of exporting firms, direct imports by product, direct imports by exporting firms. More recently, a number of countries have also begun to collect information breaking flows down by ownership (foreign/domestic).

Such a linking exercise can provide the building blocks for creating new aggregations of firms within supply-use tables broken down into:

- Firms that have no direct imports and no direct exports
- Firms that have no direct imports but have direct exports
- Firms that have direct imports and exports
- Firms that have direct imports but no direct exports

8. OECD Handbook on Linking Trade and Business Statistics (forthcoming).

Regarding heterogeneity of production functions, with respect to measuring facets of globalization, it is clear that such groupings could significantly improve the quality of estimates as they broadly define firm aggregations on the basis of one of the key target indicators of globalization: *import content of a firm's exports.*

In constructing conventional supply-use tables, national compilers currently produce aggregations based on activity information alone. By using the above additional disaggregations, it is, at least in theory, a trivial exercise to produce extended supply-use tables (broken down by trading status).

There are however a few complicating features that should be borne in mind. The first relates to the statistical unit, which is not always the same in the statistical business register and the customs register, nor indeed necessarily the same as the unit used in constructing conventional national supply-use tables. Customs registers for example often, but not exclusively, capture units in line with (or close to) the enterprise concept but the statistical unit used in statistical business registers is often a legal unit, while in many countries the unit used for conventional SUTs is the establishment.

As such, it is important to ensure that a common unit is used, or that appropriate links and apportionment methods are made to link across the various data sets. That being said, in many countries this is a relatively trivial exercise, as the unit used is the same across all domains. Where the units are not the same, and where the challenges of reliable apportionment are onerous, it seems preferable to select the highest common denominator as the basis for the unit across all three domains, for example the enterprise.[9]

An additional complication with respect to the use of customs registers in compiling extended SUTs relates to the notion of exporting and importing firms. In most countries, for example, a significant share (around half in many countries) of total imports and exports are made by distribution firms (wholesale and retailers).

However, in constructing supply-use tables these firms are only shown as facilitators of imports and exports, in other words the conventional SUTs show the consumption of these imports by other consumers (e.g., firms, government, households, NPISH) and not by the distribution firms themselves, and they also (implicitly) show the exports as having originated in the actual producing sectors, with the contribution of the distribution sector only added as a distribution margin.

If it can be established that the distribution firm is affiliated to an upstream producer, the import and export of the affiliated distribution firm should be allocated to its affiliated consuming or producing partner. If, however, these links cannot be made, and the size of overall exports of a particular

9. By way of a small but relevant digression, it's important to note that, partly because of the challenges presented by globalization, and notably those challenges related to intellectual property, the 2008 SNA research agenda includes an item to investigate whether the establishment should remain the preferred unit for the construction of conventional supply-use tables.

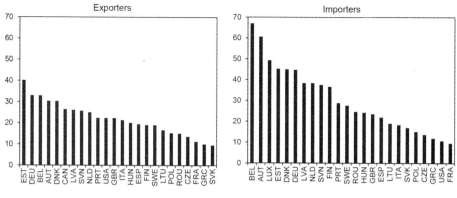

Figure 8.5   Share of all firms (industry, 2014) that are exporters and importers
Source: OECD Trade by Enterprise Characteristics.

product by distributors make up a significant share of overall exports of that particular product, then considerable care is needed in interpretation or at least in terms of terminology. For example, countries should avoid, in these circumstances, referring to firms as being exporters and non-exporters and instead refer to firms as "direct exporters" or "highly export orientated" and "other." The same principals should necessarily be applied for imports, especially because many firms "indirectly" import via distributors.

An additional reason for advocating such precise terminology concerns scale. The shares of firms not engaged in trade are rarely insignificant (figure 8.5), and, moreover, a significant share of these firms exports either very little or indeed only a small percentage of their output.

As such there is a risk that an aggregation of firms purely around the concept of whether they export or import may be too crude an approach to deliver a significant improvement in homogeneity or indeed to deliver meaningful improvements to policy relevant indicators, such as the import content of exports.

A practical approach in this respect is to introduce a size threshold that further differentiates on the basis of the size of the firm or the share of output that is actually exported (for example differentiating between firms that directly export 20 percent of output and less than 20 percent of output, or by only creating aggregations of significant large exporters in the country).

One strength of this approach is that it can significantly reduce compilation burdens that may arise when full linking and full disaggregation of activities is undertaken. For example, in most countries the top 100 exporting enterprises are responsible for around half of all exports (figure 8.6). Clearly some care will necessarily be needed in adopting this approach, as confidentiality issues quickly emerge the higher the threshold for inclusion, but the point is to illustrate that it is possible to introduce significant

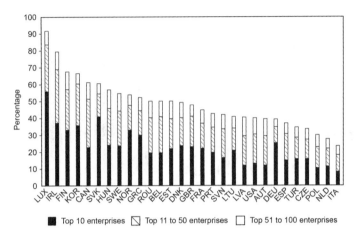

Figure 8.6   Concentration of exports by exporting enterprises, total economy. Percentage of total value of exports, 2015, or latest available year
Source: OECD Trade by Enterprise Characteristics.

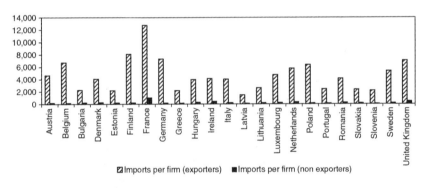

Figure 8.7   Imports per firm, USD 2011
Source: OECD Trade by Enterprise Characteristics.

improvements in homogeneity through looking at only a smaller grouping of firms, and indeed targeted activities. This is perhaps of important note for developing economies where compilation burdens may rapidly become onerous if meaningful thresholds are not introduced. Indeed, such an approach is likely to work particularly effectively in some developing economies where exports are oriented around only a handful of core activities and by a handful of key firms.

Another reason such an approach is worth exploring is the high correlation between direct imports and direct exports (figure 8.7), which is perhaps not surprising given that this is one of the key defining features of GVCs and international fragmentation of production more generally. This means that

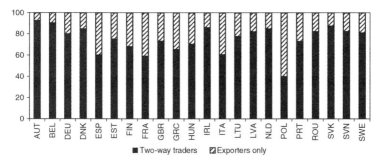

Figure 8.8   Share of two-way traders among trading enterprises (percentage, 2015 or latest available year)
Source: OECD Trade by Enterprise Characteristics.

a simpler approach that focuses on a core set of large exporters and activities is also likely to capture the desired homogeneity that would be obtained through additional aggregations of importers (moreover in most countries most exporters import, figure 8.8).

The approaches used by China and Costa Rica are both examples of this modified "threshold" approach. In the case of China, the approach identifies categories of exporters that differentiate between firms that export under the processing regime, those that export but under the normal regime (both using administrative customs data that identify these firms), and other non-exporting firms. Once identified, the firms are grouped within activities and their respective columns within SUTs can be compiled, using the same data (based on business surveys and other administrative sources) that are used to construct the estimates in conventional SUTs. Costa Rica's approach is similar, except in this case the split is based on those firms operating (exporting from) FTZs.

In both cases the approach ticks two important boxes.

• The first reflects improved homogeneity. It is clear, for example, that processing firms and firms operating from FTZs have very different degrees of global integration than other firms in the same activity. Almost by definition they have higher import content, reflecting in large part their duty-free nature. But they also differ in many other respects too. Processing firms for example are often bywords for assemblers, and even if they are classified to the same activity as firms engaged in producing a good from start to finish, it's also clear that the production function (and so input-output relationships) will differ significantly. The same holds true for firms in FTZs, reflecting a number of factors, including processing, size, degrees of foreign ownership (and, so, access to higher technology, including intellectual property). But this also reflects costs. For example, all other things being equal, the cost structure of a firm in an FTZ, at least with respect to the cost of imports, will by definition (as their imports are tariff free) be lower than for firms outside of FTZs. Section 8.3 presents the results of these exercises and well illustrates the important difference they make to TiVA estimates.

• The second reflects policy. It is clear for example that there is a particular policy and analytical interest in the role of processing firms in China. They have been important drivers of China's integration into GVCs, but their role has been evolving in the last 10 to 15 years, and policy makers are especially interested in motivating their graduation up the value chain to higher skilled activities. The same is true for firms operating from FTZs. Understanding, for example, their integration into GVCs is of particular interest (including in due course how value added generated by foreign owned affiliates is repatriated to parents overseas), but so too is better understanding how they integrate, and therefore how they create upstream spillovers in the domestic economy, not least to assess to what extent FTZs may hinder this (reflecting in part the competitive disadvantages faced by potential domestic upstream providers who have to pay duties on any upstream imports they may require).

8.2.2.2.2   Capitalizing on Structural Business Statistics for a Size Class Dimension

Another area of significant policy interest, but also a long-standing source of heterogeneity, relates to the size of firms. It is a well-known fact that larger firms are typically more capital intensive than smaller firms, and also that they are able to capitalize on economies of scale. But it is also true that these economies of scale also manifest themselves in a trade context. Larger firms for example are more readily able to accommodate any fixed costs (e.g., dealing with regulatory and administrative barriers) involved in international trade, and it is perhaps of no coincidence that in most countries a significantly smaller share of smaller firms is engaged in international trade than larger firms, certainly with respect to exports (figure 8.9).

In practice it is a relatively trivial exercise to create breakdowns of activities into size class dimensions. Statistical business registers nearly always include these dimensions, and together with the activity code, they form one of the most important pillars (stratification variable) of survey sample design. However, considerable interest in respect of globalization concerns the degree of integration of the various categories of firms within GVCs. For those countries where survey or administrative sources reveal the share of output that can be exported, one relatively simple innovation is to include this information as an additional row in SUT.

However, more can be done.

One area that could be explored by countries concerns links at the detailed activity level with merchandise trade customs data. Such a matching exercise could for example reveal that exports of particular detailed six- or eight-digit

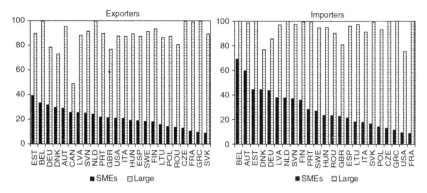

Figure 8.9   Share of all SMEs and large firms (industry, 2014) that are exporters and importers
Source: OECD Trade by Enterprise Characteristics.

HS (Harmonized System) products are only produced by certain categories of firms that can be described as large, medium, or small and only for certain markets. Where more than one category of firm size is responsible for production, proportionality assumptions could be used.[10] This approach provides an ability to split the conventional export column in SUTs into categories of exporters (broken down by size class). It also provides an ability to create a further extension, as shown above, to include a breakdown by destination. This is of particular relevance as the evidence points clearly to smaller firms exporting disproportionately within neighboring countries (and with countries where trade agreements exist) compared to larger firms.

One avenue that could greatly improve the quality of information on imports and exports broken down by size class is to link SBS data to customs registers, by adopting the same linking methods outlined above in section 8.2.2.2.1. Again, however, some care will be needed in compilation as exports and imports included in customs registers are often recorded as being conducted by distributors, but by combining detailed HS data, SBS data, and TEC-type statistics, the quality of this exercise could be greatly enhanced (including through the development of breakdowns that show the origin country of imports and the destination country of exports).

8.2.2.2.3   Capitalizing on FDI and FATs Data, for an Ownership Dimension

Arguably one of the most useful dimensions for constructing Extended SUTs concerns breakdowns by ownership structures—e.g., foreign-owned

10. Although not perfect, not least because there is perhaps a higher probability that larger firms will account for a disproportionate share, when conducted at a relatively detailed product and industry level the impact of the assumption is likely to be lessened.

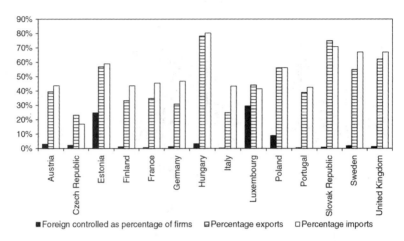

Figure 8.10   Foreign-owned firms across economies (2011)
Source: OECD Trade by Enterprise Characteristics.
Note: Foreign-owned firms are defined according to FATS/AMNE 50 percent thresholds.

affiliates (FA), domestic MNEs (DM) with affiliates abroad, and domestic firms (DF) with no foreign affiliates.

It is clear that foreign-owned firms and multinationals, in general, shape GVCs. It is also clear that foreign-owned affiliates are responsible for considerable shares of overall activity and in particular trade, despite their relatively limited number (figure 8.10), with a much higher orientation toward international than their purely domestic counterparts. A focus on this small number of firms could therefore prove to be a very effective channel for developing extended supply-use tables.

But a focus on ownership dimensions is also crucial for policy reasons. Thus far the TiVA database has been able to provide insights into GVC policy making by creating a narrative around trade. However, to fully understand the nature of GVCs and indeed their drivers, it is important to create a trade-investment story. Multinationals (MNEs) have been important drivers of the growth in GVCs with estimates pointing to around three-quarters of total international trade being driven by the top 500 MNEs.[11] Moreover, the share of value added generated by foreign affiliates approaches around half of all business sector value added in some countries (figure 8.11).

Value added essentially reflects two main components[12]—(i) operating surplus (including mixed income), or compensation for capital, and (ii) compensation for employment. While the latter component largely reflects the direct benefits that accrue and "stick" within the economy through

11. Source: Corpwatch.org.
12. It also includes taxes and subsidies on production.

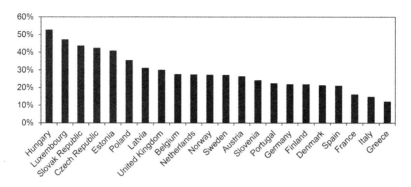

Figure 8.11   Value added at factor cost of foreign affiliates—share of national total, 2014 (ISIC B-N, ex K)
Source: OECD AMNE database.

production,[13] the case is not so clear for the former where foreign affiliates are concerned.

In perfect markets the operating surplus generated by foreign affiliates is equivalent to the return on produced "tangible" and "intangible" capital and also non-produced assets used in production.[14] While the national accounts of countries attribute the ownership of this capital to the affiliated enterprise, the ultimate beneficiary of the operating surplus is not necessarily the affiliate but its parent. This has raised questions—often in emerging economies but also in developed economies—about the actual benefits of foreign MNEs to the host economy. Indeed, more recently it has begun to raise questions about the meaningfulness of GDP itself as a tool for macroecomomic policy making.

Particularly important in this regard are transactions in intangible assets: those recognized as produced in the System of National Accounts (such as research and development, software, etc.), non-produced (such as brands), and also other knowledge-based capital (such as organizational capital, such as management competencies).

Often, in international trade in services statistics, payments for the use of these produced and non-produced assets are recorded as purchases (intermediate consumption) by one affiliated enterprise from another. But often they are not, and instead they are implicitly recorded under primary income payments (such as investment income, or reinvested earnings in the balance of payments). In the former case, the value added of the affiliate using the assets is lower, as the value added generated through ownership of the

13. Not all labor compensation will necessarily stick in the economy; for example, for cross-border workers.
14. Such as land and other intangible assets not recognized as intellectual property products in the SNA.

asset appears on the accounts of the affiliate that owns it. In the latter case, however, the value added of the affiliate using the asset is higher (as there is no intermediate consumption) with the "ultimate" beneficiary (the owning affiliate) recording no value added but instead recieving primary income from the using affiliate. In both cases, however, the ultimate "income" generated by the asset ends up on the books of the owner.[15] Furthermore, the distinction between the two scenarios above is often clouded by (a) the ability of the statistical information system to record the flows and (b) transfer pricing and tax incentives of MNEs. So, while TiVA estimates consistently reflect the way these flows are recorded in a country's national accounts and, so, accurately reflect the share of a country's recorded overall value added that is generated by its exports, they do not necessarily entirely reflect how countries truly benefit from GVCs, since part of the value added that is generated does not remain in the economy but is repatriated to parent enterprises. Indeed, in some countries where foreign affiliates generate significant value added and repatriate significant profits back to parent companies, the policy focus has switched from GDP to GNI, and indeed in some countries, such as Ireland, to new accounting concepts.[16]

This is not however an issue singularly related to knowledge-based assets. Transfer pricing is also prevalent in transactions related to goods. Moreover, notwithstanding these issues, significant income flows generated by an affiliate can be repatratied to parents via other means, for example as interest payments.

Measuring these flows can provide an important narrative on the links between GVCs and foreign direct investment (as well as providing for estimates that overcome differences in statistical practices for recording trade related to knowledge-based assets). This requires more detailed data beyond the current purely industry-level information in the TiVA database. What is required are additional breakdowns of firms classified on the basis of their ownership.

Statistical tools to create these breakdowns do currently exist in many countries, in particular those with good-quality FDI data and also those producing FATS data. Definitional issues are of course of relevance here. FDI data for example capture associate firms (where foreign parents hold between 10–50 percent of the company's capital) and subsidiaries (50 percent and over), while FATS data typically only capture subsidiaries. But, as before, the intention is not to be prescriptive, and countries are encouraged to develop breakdowns in line with national circumstances and data availability. Ideally, however, the breakdowns would follow either FDI or FATS definitions, as this would provide the basis for more coherent and integrated accounting frameworks. In addition, as shown in the section that follows,

---

15. At least in theory, as even the very notion of the ultimate owner is a complex issue.
16. http://www.cso.ie/en/csolatestnews/pressreleases/2017pressreleases/pressstatement macroeconomicreleasesyear2016andquarter12017/.

a breakdown by ownership structures would also provide an ideal basis for integrated and detailed balance of payments and national accounts. The United States (Bureau of Economic Analysis) has already begun to develop extended SUTs on the basis of FATS, with a three-way breakdown between foreign affiliates, domestic firms, and domestic firms with affiliates abroad. Mexico (National Institute of Statistics and Geography) has produced a hybrid variant of the US approach that incorporates the concept of global manufacturers[17] defined to include firms that: a) import the majority of their purchases (imports account for at least two-thirds of their export value); b) produce only for exports; and c) are controlled by a foreign owner. These global firms were responsible for 55 percent of total imported intermediate consumption and for 71 percent of gross exports of the Mexican manufacturing sector in 2008. Details from the results of these initiatives are presented in section 8.3. Costa Rica is also beginning to explore this extension.[18]

8.2.2.3   *Extending the Core Production Accounts to the Distribution of Income Account and Other Macroeconomic Variables*

One of the fundamental drivers behind the development of extended supply-use tables is to provide the accounting framework for coherent and integrated international accounts. Currently, within the SNA and BPM6 there is no requirement to provide an activity breakdown of core economic variables, such as primary income flows. Typically, these transactions, and in particular those relating to the distribution of income, are only compiled on the basis of SNA institutional sectors. This, to a large extent, reflects a current statistical reality concerning the way such data are compiled and, so, in some respects, the recommendations and discussion presented below are more about looking to the future than what can be done in the present. But through an articulation of a potential framework here it is hoped that countries will be motivated to begin to explore these extensions.

One important reflection in this respect concerns the nature of the statistical unit. Although not impossible (through for example assumptions and estimations), it is clear it is likely to be more complicated to produce such extensions when the statistical unit used in constructing SUTs is the establishment as compared to the enterprise, as many of the transactions required for the distribution of income account are less readily available on an establishment basis.

The extensions also include other macroeconomic variables less affected by the choice of statistical unit, and where the feasibility to develop more coherent accounts is higher. These extensions chiefly relate to employment

---

17. http://www3.inegi.org.mx/sistemas/tabuladosbasicos/LeerArchivo.aspx?ct=44462&c=33654&s=est&f=4.
18. See Saborío and Torres (2018).

variables, including headcounts of persons engaged, employees, hours worked, and information on occupations.

Occupational data are a key tool to understanding globalization, providing, as they do, an easily interpretable link to skills and business functions, and, so, providing perhaps one of the most important data mechanisms to analyze heterogeneity across firms and the manner of their integration into GVCs.

International fragmentation of production has significantly hampered the ability of conventional activity-based data to provide this view as firms grouped within certain activities may find themselves engaged in significantly different tasks in the value chain, even if they are allocated to the same sector. Fabless firms for example that purchase material inputs for production by contractors will have a very different set of employees from those firms actually engaged in material production, but such heterogeneity is masked when looking at activity data alone. Occupational data can at least provide some scope to better understand these differences and their implication for growth and employment more generally.

The potential to go further in this regard is significant. It is for example possible to consider additional extensions that partition workers on the basis of wage and salary cohorts, productivity cohorts, or indeed skills, which are also key to understanding the distributional impacts of globalization. However, it is also possible to develop these additional insights in an ad-hoc manner.

The OECD's ANSKILL[19] database for example provides information on employment and skill composition at the industry level. The database matches industry data at the two-digit level (currently classified according to ISIC Rev. 3) to occupations at the two-digit level (classified according to International Standard Classification of Occupations [ISCO]-88). It also includes an additional proxy for skills, in the form of data on the educational attainment of employees (classified on the basis of International Standard Classification of Education [ISCED]-97).[20]

Figure 8.12 presents an overview of the extensions envisaged. As before, it is important to note that not all items are necessarily needed: extensions, in this respect, should not be seen as an "all or nothing" choice. For example,

19. For ANSKILL, the ISCO-88 occupation classification corresponds to high-, medium-, and low-skilled levels, as follows. Categories 1 (legislators, senior officials, managers), 2 (professionals), and 3 (technicians and associate professionals) are regarded as high-skilled; Categories 4 (clerks), 5 (service workers and shop and market sale workers), 6 (skilled agricultural and fishery workers), and 7 (craft and related trade workers) are regarded as medium-skilled; Categories 8 (plant and machine operators and assemblers) and 9 (elementary occupations) are regarded as low-skilled.

20. The ISCED-97 educational classification maps to high-, medium-, and low-skill levels in ANSKILL as follows. Categories 1 (primary education) and 2 (lower secondary/second stage of basic education) are regarded as low-skilled; Categories 3 (upper secondary education) and 4 (post-secondary non-tertiary education) are regarded as medium-skilled; Categories 5 (first stage of tertiary education) and 6 (second stage of tertiary education) are regarded as high-skilled.

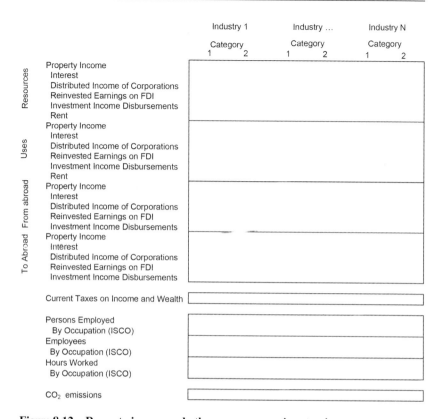

Figure 8.12   Property income and other macroeconomic extensions

in the top half of figure 8.12, the intention is to develop a set of seamless accounts that take users from the production account through to the distribution of income accounts. Doing this at the level of the total economy is needless to say non-trivial but, somewhat fortunately, as this is a key focus, it may be easier to do this for cross-border flows, especially with respect to reinvested earnings and perhaps debt interest.

Of additional note in the set of extensions below are the items on "current taxes on income and wealth" and CO_2 emissions, which are both of significant policy interest. The former, in particular when the breakdown of activities is on the basis of ownership, is of note as there is a long-standing and growing interest in understanding whether multinationals are able to generate significant advantages through fiscal optimization and where there are currently considerable information gaps.

8.2.2.4   Breaking Down SUT Rows by Category of Producer

Perhaps the most complicated feature of full-blown extended supply-use tables is breakdowns of rows (products) by origin producer. It is of course relatively trivial to provide such a breakdown on the supply side, but doing so by category of consumer is significantly more complex, and the complexity necessarily differs depending on the nature of the breakdown used for activities.

For example, breakdowns by size class require that consumers are aware if they purchased their goods and or services from a small, medium, or large enterprise, and this information is rarely collected. In some countries some scope to do this is available from VAT[21] data, but this requires a level of access to firm-level data that is not always forthcoming and entails a not insignificant compilation burden.

For other breakdowns the scope is to some extent less (albeit still) complicated. For example, for the extended supply-use tables produced by Mexico and China, global manufacturers (for Mexico) and processors (for China) produce no output for the domestic market and so the breakdowns by rows are relatively trivial, as the only items where output of these categories of firms is consumed concerns exports (and marginally changes in inventories).

To a lesser extent, this is partially true for any breakdowns that focus on the exporting status of firms. Certainly, the higher the threshold used to determine "exporting firms," the easier the task. For example, if the thresholds used to determine an "exporter" were 90 percent of total output, then, by design, very little of the output would necessarily have to be allocated to other domestic consumers. More generally, irrespective of the type of breakdown used, the higher the export intensity of a category of firms, the lower the impact of assumptions to allocate the residual (non-exported) output to domestic consumers.

Regarding the allocation of residuals (output minus exports) to remaining categories of users, how this is done will necessitate the use of some stylized assumption, not dissimilar to the classic proportionality assumption used in constructing import flow tables. Some refinements are, of course, possible, but these may create circularities that will be important to keep in mind when presenting results. For example, with regards to breakdowns by size class, one could assume that small firms in manufacturing predominantly sell goods and services to larger manufacturers, while their counterparts in certain service activities, such as accounting and legal sectors, predominantly sell to households. But these could ostensibly create self-selecting facts that point to better integration of manufacturing SMEs in domestic value chains than service SMEs; hence the care needed when presenting results to users.

The OECD has used a variety of such approaches in its work to develop information on the scale of integration of SMEs within GVCs,[22] and also regarding the scale of integration of non-trading firms and purely domestic

---

21. Chile, Costa Rica, and Belgium have been exploring the use of such data.
22. https://www.oecd.org/trade/OECD-WBG-g20-gvc-report-2015.pdf.

Supply

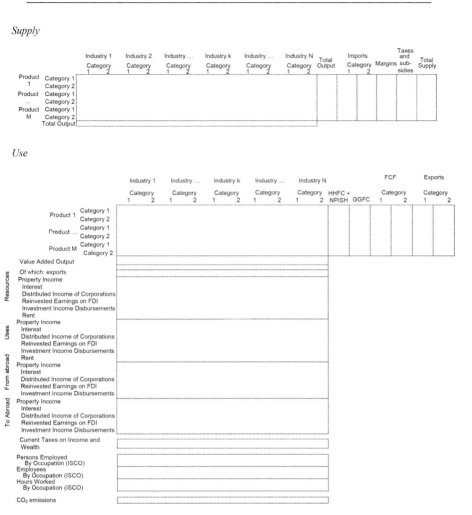

Use

Figure 8.13   Full extended supply-use table

firms.[23] Similar approaches were also used in developing the OECD's Trade and Investment Country Note series, which provides highlights on GVCs using the ownership dimension.[24]

For the US extended supply-use tables, based on ownership breakdowns, the derivation of use relationships was derived using the quadratic programming constrained optimization model adopted in Ma, Wang, and Zhu (2015).

Although relatively easy to conceptualize without a diagram, figure 8.13

23. http://www.oecd.org/std/its/enterprises-in-global-value-chains.htm.
24. http://www.oecd.org/investment/trade-investment-gvc.htm.

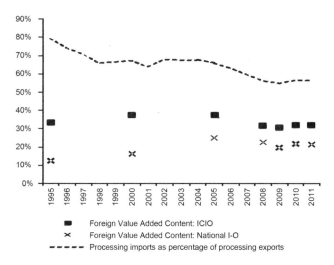

Figure 8.14   Trade in value added estimates for China, with (ICIO) and without (national) a breakdown for heterogeneity

Source: OECD ICIO and Balance of payments database.

presents, for exhaustiveness, a full extended SUT with the requisite product breakdown (again with the two-category example used above). Note that no further breakdowns of import flow tables are required, in addition to those shown in figure 8.2.

8.3   Results from Using Extended Supply-Use Tables

As described above, a number of countries have already begun to develop extended SUTs using a variety of approaches. This section provides a summary of the results of those initiatives and their impact, in particular on trade in value added estimates.

8.3.1   Results for China

Incorporating an extended supply-use table has a significant impact on the quality of TiVA results for China. Figure 8.14, for example, reveals significantly different movements in the trend of the foreign content of China's exports over the last two decades when comparing estimates based on extended SUTs (referred to as ICIO) and pure national tables without a breakdown (referred to as national).

8.3.2   Results for Mexico

Almost by definition the import content of Mexico's global manufacturing firms is significantly higher than comparable firms in the same sector. This can have a significant difference on highly policy-relevant indicators, for

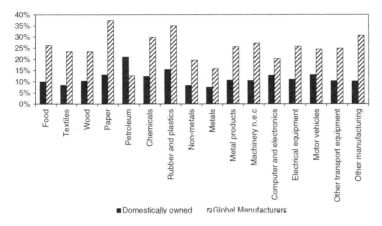

Figure 8.15   US VA content of Mexico's exports %, 2011 (by industry and "owner-ship" of Mexican exporters)
Source: Based on Mexico's extended SUT.

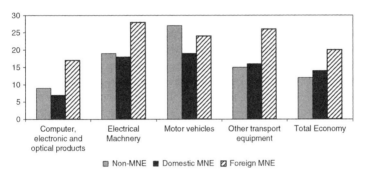

Figure 8.16   Foreign content of US exports, %, 2011 (selected industries)
Source: Based on the US Extended SUT.

example, on measures of the US content of Mexico's exports (figure 8.15), where one-quarter of the exports by GM firms in the motor vehicle sector reflect upstream US contributions, compared to around half that amount for non-GM firms, a relationship seen across most activities.

8.3.3   Results for the United States

Results for the United States also reveal significant differences between the foreign content of exports across categories of firms defined by ownership structure. At the whole economy level, the foreign content of US exports by foreign-owned firms is almost twice that of domestically owned non-MNEs. This partly reflects compositional effects, but the foreign content is higher across nearly all activities (figure 8.16).

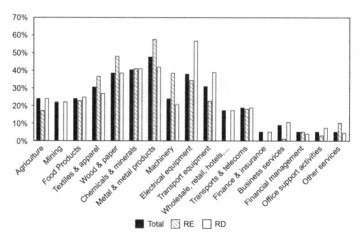

Figure 8.17   Foreign content of Costa Rica's exports, %, 2012
Source: Prepared with data from the Banco Central de Costa Rica.

8.3.4   Results for Costa Rica

A similar picture of strong heterogeneity emerges for Costa Rica, with firms operating from free trade zones (referred to as RE in figure 8.17) displaying a higher import content of exports than firms operating outside of FTZs (referred to as RD) across a range of important export activities.

8.3.5   Results for Canada

Results from a recent collaboration between the OECD and Statistics Canada revealed that the impact of compiling ESUT estimates for the business sector, accounting for either ownership or trading status, was an increase in the overall foreign value added content of Canada's exports of 4 percentage points. Figure 8.18, which shows that foreign-owned firms are responsible for a lower share of exports in value added terms than in gross terms, highlights this higher propensity to import by foreign-owned firms and, of course, the importance of capturing improved firm heterogeneity in national SUTs.

8.3.6   Results for Nordic Countries

In a recent collaboration between five Nordic countries (Denmark, Finland, Iceland, Norway, and Sweden) and the OECD, the OECD developed extended SUTs with three variants of firm breakdown:

- By size class: micro, small, medium, and large, further broken down by whether the micro, small, and medium firms were independent or part of a larger enterprise group
- By trading status: non-traders, two-way traders, importers, and exporters
- By ownership status: non-MNEs, domestic MNEs, and foreign MNEs

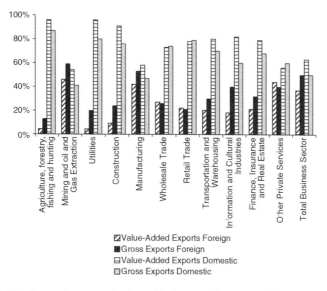

Figure 8.18   Share of gross and value added exports by ownership status, %, 2010 (industries within business sector)

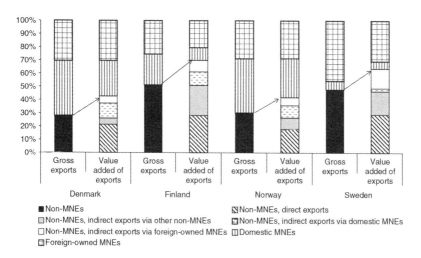

Figure 8.19   Shares of firms in exports in gross and value added terms, %, 2013, by ownership structure

Highlights from this collaboration are presented below as figures 8.19–8.21. Figure 8.19 reveals the significant upstream integration of non-MNEs across all countries, compared to integration seen looking purely at gross trade relationships. Of particular note is the fact that in all countries bar Sweden this integration is primarily channelled via domestic MNEs, but in Sweden the main link is through foreign-owned MNEs, in large part reflect-

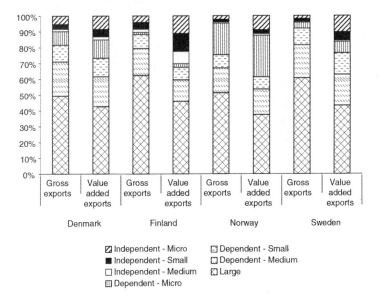

Figure 8.20   Shares of firms in exports in gross and value added terms, %, 2013, by size class

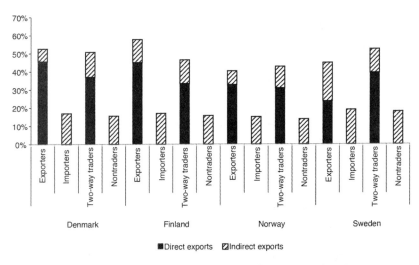

Figure 8.21   Jobs embodied in exports, % of total, 2013, by trading status

ing scale. Figure 8.20 presents a similar picture, showing the higher integration of smaller firms in GVCs when seen in value added terms, through their upstream integration as suppliers to larger exporting firms. Figure 8.21 presents information on jobs sustained through integration in GVCs. A significant insight from this presentation is the fact that even within firms that have no direct exports, around one in six of all jobs in these firms are dependent on foreign markets. It's important to note in this collaborative exercise that the results are unlikely to replicate those that are likely to materialize from national exercises that mainstream the development of extended SUTs in the national statistical information system. The figures produced below, for example, necessarily re-aggregate national data in line with the 34-industry classification used in OECD-WTO TiVA, but national compilers will be able to develop tables with greater granularity.

8.4 Concluding Comments

The statistical challenges of globalization are profound, and it has become increasingly clear in recent years that conventional approaches used to understand how economies work can no longer rely solely on national statistics. Increasingly, in order to understand how economies work, and how to target and create industrial policies focusing on competitiveness, it is necessary to see the whole. National statistics build pictures based on interrelationships between producers and consumers and the rest of world. But these relationships, particularly those with the rest of world, have become increasingly more complex, and, as such, there is an increasing need to consider global production within a global accounting framework. This implies a departure from the traditional role of international organizations as compilers of internationally comparable national statistics, such as national input-output or supply-use tables. Instead, it requires that they bring together these national tables to create a global table.

Although TiVA estimates have been able to shed important light on our understanding of international trade and its relation to activity and competitiveness, in particular the importance of recognizing the importance of imports to exports, and, so, the hitherto hidden costs of protectionism as well as the benefits of trade liberalization, particularly in services, they do not reveal the full picture. With significant shares of exports being driven by foreign affiliates, TiVA estimates (through their current shortcomings) have also revealed the importance of going beyond just value added toward income, in order to capture flows outside conventional international trade statistics, such as the repatriation of profits related to the use of non-produced knowledge-based assets (e.g., brands) and, indeed, the repatriation of profits related to the use of produced knowledge-based assets (e.g., software) that are (often incorrectly) not recorded as receipts from exports of services.

The emergence of global value chains therefore also raises arguably profound questions about the way national statistics are currently compiled. In the same way that international organizations increasingly need to think "national" in the way they present and compile their statistics, where "national" reflects the single economic territory comprising the "world" or large parts of it, national statistics institutions need to think global.

In other words, in the construction of national statistics, greater emphasis is needed on the role of the rest of world, both as a source of demand and supplier of demand but also with regards to the role of multinationals. This requires a rethink of the way that firms are currently aggregated within statistical information systems to move beyond the classic aggregation based almost exclusively on industrial classification systems toward more meaningful aggregations that better reflect today's "global factory."

Such considerations are also essential not only to better understand the way that global production is today organized but also to better understand how investment drives global value chains, and in particular how that very same investment can lead to difficulties in interpreting trade flows as well as GDP.

Extended supply-use tables provide an effective tool to respond to these developments and growing needs. Increasing globalization of production raises challenging questions for national statistics. And fundamental and long-standing axioms regarding the nature of production and the way that statistics are necessarily compiled warrant a rethink. Certainly, the evidence suggests that long-standing assumptions concerning homogeneity of firms within industry classifications should be reviewed. The evidence also suggests, particularly for those countries with FATS and TEC data, that an optimal level of aggregation may be achievable without any significant increase in compilation of reporting burden. But, of course, such reconsiderations need also take into account constraints such as burdens and confidentiality.

Supply-use tables have become the conventional route with which coherent estimates of national accounts, trade, and production are now systematically compiled in many countries and lend themselves as being the ideal way in which to resolve these issues. Extended supply-use tables can play a similar role in responding to questions on globalization.

Four final comments, providing a broader perspective, are worth making in this respect.

The first concerns the quality of national supply-use tables. In many (most) countries, such tables are derived using a series of assumptions at least in some years, reflecting, in part, the often different periodic nature of the large number of data sets needed to construct SUTs. Many of these assumptions are based on some underlying view of stability and homogeneity in production functions. As shown, globalization is increasingly undermining the strength of these assumptions. Looking again at how homogeneity is likely to manifest itself across firms and creating SUTs based around these categorizations of firms can greatly help to mitigate these effects and strengthen these assumptions, which will remain necessary, perhaps indefinitely, across most countries. As such, one important benefit of extended SUTs that should not be overlooked is their ability to improve the quality of the core accounts, and indeed GDP. In the same way, they are also ideally placed to be able to significantly improve the interpretability of the accounts, in particular, when the accounts are affected by phenomena related to globalization, such as relocations.

The second comment concerns the potential momentum extended SUTs could provide to the development and improvement of statistical business surveys. The evidence shows that significant heterogeneity exists across all categories of firms, and that the conventional stratification variables used in survey sampling (typically activity and size) may be sub-optimal. It may for example be necessary to include additional, but readily available, stratification variables, pertaining for example to ownership (e.g., part of a foreign MNE, domestic MNE, an enterprise group, exporter, non-exporter) in designing tomorrow's surveys.

The third comes back to the issue of the statistical unit. The current 2008 SNA preference for the establishment should not be a barrier to developing extended SUTs, if for example these can only be developed using a different statistical unit, then counties are strongly encouraged to consider doing so. There is an increasing recognition that the arguments for the current SNA preference for the establishment have been weakened because of the changing nature of production and indeed because of the changes made in the SNA itself regarding economic ownership. This is further recognized in the 2008 SNA research agenda, where explicit references are made for the need to reconsider the establishment preference, taking into account the "basic source information" and changes in the underlying accounting principles of input-output tables, whose emphasis has moved from a *physical* perspective to an *economic* perspective.

The fourth comment is that the proposals described here should not be seen as the end of the story. Additional challenges around globalization— for example, concerning digitalization— can also be tackled through an extended supply-use framework (Ahmad and Ribarsky 2018). Moreover, other modifications and extensions can be explored to better overcome some of the challenges presented by the constraints of the basic price concept in conventional supply-use tables, which can create difficulties in applications that look at the position of activities in GVCs (particularly distribution activities) (OECD 2019). And yet others can be explored. For example, disaggregations of national data into sub-national components can inform the debate around whether globalization has played a role in geographies of discontent (i.e., significant inequalities within countries).

References

Ahmad, Nadim, and Jennifer Ribarsky. 2018. "Towards a Framework for Measuring the Digital Economy." Paper presented at 16th Conference of IAOS, Paris, France, September 19–21. https://www.oecd.org/iaos2018/programme/IAOS-OECD2018 _Ahmad-Ribarsky.pdf.

Ma, H., Z. Wang, and K. Zhu. 2015. "Domestic Content in China's Exports and Its Distribution by Firm Ownership." *Journal of Comparative Economics* 43 (1): 3–18.

OECD. 2019. "A New Look at Trade in Value-Added and Global Value Chains: A View from the Consumption Perspective." March 6. https://www.oecd.org /officialdocuments/publicdisplaydocumentpdf/?cote=SDD/CSSP/WPTGS (2019)6&docLanguage=En.

OECD. 2017. Handbook on Linking Trade and Business Statistics.

Saborío, Gabriela, and Rigoberto Torres. 2018. *Integrating Foreign Direct Investment Data and Extended Supply and Use Tables into National Accounts.* Paper presented at NBER conference "The Challenges of Globalization in the Measurement of National Accounts," Bethesda, MD, March 9–10, 2018.

UN Handbook on Supply, Use and Input-Output Tables with Extensions and Applications. 2018.

9

Accounting for Firm Heterogeneity within US Industries
Extended Supply-Use Tables and Trade in Value Added Using Enterprise and Establishment Level Data

James J. Fetzer, Tina Highfill, Kassu W. Hossiso,
Thomas F. Howells III, Erich H. Strassner,
and Jeffrey A. Young

9.1 Introduction

There is a growing body of research on improving the measurement of trade in value added (TiVA) statistics and the supply-use tables (SUTs) on which they are based. As noted in Fetzer et al. (2018), this work began with efforts in academia (e.g., Global Trade Analysis Project, GTAP), in government (e.g., US International Trade Commission, USITC, and the

James J. Fetzer is Research Data Center Administrator at the Bureau of Economic Analysis.
Tina Highfill is a senior research economist at the Bureau of Economic Analysis.
Kassu W. Hossiso is an economist at the Bureau of Economic Analysis.
Thomas F. Howells III is chief of the Industry Economics Division at the Bureau of Economic Analysis.
Erich H. Strassner is Associate Director for National Economic Accounts at the Bureau of Economic Analysis.
Jeffrey A. Young is an economist at the Bureau of Economic Analysis.
We would like to thank Shari Allen, John Bockrath, Jeffrey Bogen, Edward Dozier, Andre Garber, Alexis Grimm, C. Omar Kebbeh, Fritz Mayhew, and Dan Yorgason for input in preparing this chapter. We would also like to thank Paul Farello, Susan Houseman, Kristy Howell, Raymond Mataloni, and J. David Richardson for their valuable comments. The statistical analysis of firm-level data on US multinational companies was conducted at the Bureau of Economic Analysis, US Department of Commerce, and the Federal Statistical Research Data Center Network under arrangements that maintain legal confidentiality requirements. The views expressed in this paper are those of the authors and should not be attributed to the Bureau of Economic Analysis, the US Census Bureau, US Department of Commerce, the United States government or the National Bureau of Economic Research. The Census Bureau's Disclosure Review Board and Disclosure Avoidance Officers have reviewed this information product for unauthorized disclosure of confidential information and have approved the disclosure avoidance practices applied to this release. (CMS/Delegated Authority Number 6308). For acknowledgments, sources of research support, and disclosure of the authors' material financial relationships, if any, please see https://www.nber.org/books-and-chapters/challenges-globalization-measurement-national-accounts/accounting-firm-heterogeneity-within-us-industries-extended-supply-use-tables-and-trade-value-added.

World Input-Output Database, WIOD), and in international organizations (e.g., Organisation for Economic Co-operation and Development, OECD, and World Trade Organization, WTO). Research has shown that bilateral trade balances measured using TiVA statistics can be very different from those based on gross trade flows, which is not surprising, since a sizeable share of trade is composed of intermediate goods that have crossed borders multiple times (Johnson and Noguera 2012). TiVA statistics may enhance trade policy and trade theory by revealing differences in competitiveness and comparative advantage that are not apparent from gross bilateral trade flows and by providing other insights about direct and indirect interdependencies among international trading partners.[1]

As noted by Fetzer and Strassner (2015) and others, national statistical offices (NSOs) have found direct measurement of TiVA to be impractical, and their efforts to measure TiVA more accurately have focused on refining national-level SUTs that can be combined into a global SUT to estimate TiVA indirectly. Since this approach to measuring TiVA for a given country depends on the SUTs for the country itself as well as all its major trading partners, NSOs have been engaged in cross-country efforts to build technical knowledge and capacity in the NSOs of partner countries and to reconcile conceptual and measurement asymmetries among national-level SUTs. For example, NSOs from Canada, Mexico, and the United States continue to collaborate to produce regional North American SUTs and associated TiVA statistics. Peluso et al. (2017) outline the conceptual methodology, data requirements, and technical issues associated with construction of these tables and statistics, which will also be used in multilateral efforts by the OECD and Asia-Pacific Economic Cooperation (APEC) countries to produce a consistent set of intercountry input-output tables (IOTs).

In this chapter, we extend work by Fetzer et al. (2018) to estimate experimental extended SUTs for the United States for 2011. Similar to Fetzer et al. (2018), we build on SUTs for the United States published by the US Bureau of Economic Analysis (BEA) (Young et al. 2015). Unlike previous work, we use an unpublished decomposition of the purchaser value use table into basic value, import, tax, trade margin, and transportation matrices in place of the estimated matrices using a quadratic programming approach. We also disaggregate SUTs by firm type based on the methodology of Fetzer and Strassner (2015) using BEA statistics on the activities of multinational enterprises (AMNE). However, in this chapter we rely on establishment-based data from BEA's SUTs rather than relying directly on enterprise-based Internal Revenue Service Statistics of Income data. We also derive symmet-

---

1. See Dervis, Meltzer, and Foda (2013) "Value-Added Trade and Its Implications for Trade Policy" http://www.brookings.edu/research/opinions/2013/04/02-implications-inter national-trade-policy-dervis-meltzer.

ric industry-by-industry extended IOTs from the extended SUTs along with associated TiVA statistics.

TiVA estimates are most rigorously calculated using intercountry IOTs that account for the production of all countries in the world. However, TiVA statistics have also been calculated from single-country IOTs in research such as Ma, Wang, and Zhu (2015) and Tang, Wang, and Wang (2014). Following their approach, we calculate implied domestic value added using the Leontief inverse of the US IOT to calculate single-country TiVA statistics.[2]

For comparison purposes, these statistics include measures based both on standard SUTs as well as extended SUTs that incorporate information on firm-level heterogeneity. The comparative analysis of these two sets of statistics allows us to understand better how firms within industries engage in global value chains and to see more clearly how the incorporation of firm heterogeneity provides a more accurate measure of TiVA.

These tables are a precursor to more precise estimates of extended SUTs that will eventually result from ongoing collaboration between the BEA and the US Census Bureau on a microdata linking project to improve the statistics related to global value chains. Linking the BEA data to census establishment level data will allow us to identify establishments that are part of MNEs and other firm types rather than having to adjust discrepancies that arise when we apportion the components of output based on enterprise-level MNE estimates that have been converted to the establishment level. We also include early results from this project in the form of a case study showing a partial extended SUT for the semiconductor industry. Economy-wide totals for the case study come from establishment-level Census of Manufactures data. Within these totals, we identify firm characteristics of ownership using the AMNE data from BEA, firm size class from enterprise-level aggregations of the Longitudinal Business Database, and data on export intensity from the Economic Census and the Annual Survey of Manufacturers. While we are not able to report the actual extended SUTs for the semiconductor industry due to disclosure restrictions and the need to use data from other industries outside the case study, we are able to show the existence of firm heterogeneity due to characteristics including ownership, firm size class, and export intensity.

9.2   Literature Review

The extended SUTs in this chapter expand on work done by Fetzer et al. (2018) to estimate experimental extended SUTs for the United States for

---

2. The Leontief inverse is a matrix that shows the full requirements (both direct and indirect) of a sector.

2011, which decomposed industry output by firm type, estimated extended IOTs, and estimated TiVA indicators using a single-country IOT model.

A growing literature has found evidence of heterogeneity in value added, trade, and imported intermediates between foreign- and domestic-owned enterprises across a broad group of countries including the United States, Japan, China, and many European countries (Fetzer and Strassner 2015; Piacentini and Fortanier 2015; Ahmad et al. 2013; and Ma, Wang, and Zhu 2015). Also, work by Ito, Deseatnicov, and Fukao (2017) has found heterogeneity in production destined for export versus production destined for domestic consumption. These patterns are consistent with the productivity sorting hypothesis of Melitz (2003) and Helpman, Melitz, and Yeaple (2004), which explains how a firm's level of global engagement tends to be positively associated with its level of productivity. Zeile (1998) also found that valued added as a share of gross output was smaller for US affiliates than US parent firms for most manufacturing industries in 1989 and 1994.

Research that estimates IOTs by type of firm have used a variety of methodologies. Koopman, Wang, and Wei (2012) and Ma, Wang, and Zhu (2015) use constrained optimization to extend IOTs to include both processing and normal trade and to separate foreign-owned enterprises from Chinese-owned enterprises. Ito, Deseatnicov, and Fukao (2017) use matched employer-employee data for Japan to split Japanese output in the OECD Inter-Country IOT into exports and domestic sales. Cadestin et al. (2017) split the WIOD database by firm type using the OECD AMNE database and national source data. Saborío and Torres (2018) create ESUTs for Costa Rica using data on firms operating in free trade zones where over one-half of foreign direct investment in Costa Rica is concentrated. Michel, Hambÿe, and Hertveldt (2018) use firm-level data on exporters to disaggregate manufacturing industries in the Belgian SUTs by exporters and non-exporters. Ahmad (2018) suggests that breaking out ownership by foreign- and domestic-owned MNEs in ESUTs is useful because of their considerable presence in economic activity and trade.

Most researchers, such as Ito, Deseatnicov, and Fukao (2017) and Cadestin et al. (2017), calculate TiVA estimates based on intercountry IOTs, but some generate TiVA estimates using single-country tables, such as Fetzer et al. (2018). As noted by Ma, Wang, and Zhu (2015), single-country models are limited to estimating the domestic content of exports, a measure that excludes domestic value added that has been re-imported. Los, Timmer, and de Vries (2016) indicate that domestic value added in gross exports can be estimated from the difference in reported gross domestic product (GDP) and hypothetical GDP estimated from a single-country IOT assuming the country does not export. However, they indicate that global IOTs are required to decompose domestic value added by end use including the extent to which it is absorbed abroad. Johnson (2018) indicates that single-country IOTs can be used to estimate the domestic value added and import content in exports, but that a multicountry IOT is needed to decompose import content into foreign value added.

9.3 Data

We used data from two main sources: (1) a time series of SUTs published as part of BEA's industry accounts and (2) AMNE data and trade in services data collected and published as part of BEA's international accounts. In addition to these two primary data sets, we also made direct use of several data sets from the Census Bureau. Estimates were prepared for 2005 and 2012 to align with the years chosen by APEC for the ongoing regional APEC TiVA initiative.

9.3.1 Supply-Use Tables

The SUTs for the United States are the foundation on which the experimental extended SUTs were constructed. The supply-use framework comprises two tables. The supply table presents the total domestic supply of goods and services from both domestic and foreign producers that are available for use in the domestic economy. The cells in the main part of the supply table, referred to as the make matrix, show domestic production and indicate the amount of each commodity (row) produced by each industry (column). The make matrix plus an additional column showing the amount of each commodity that was imported give the total supply of each commodity at basic prices (i.e., market prices at the factory door less taxes and subsidies). The remaining columns are valuation adjustments, including trade margins, transportation costs, taxes, and subsidies, that transform total supply for each commodity from basic prices to purchasers' prices.

The use table shows how the supply of each commodity from the supply table is used by domestic industries as intermediate inputs and by final users. The cells in the primary section of the use table indicate the amount of a commodity (row) purchased by an industry (column) as an intermediate input in the industry's production process. The cells in the remaining columns of the table show the flow of each commodity to different components of final demand, including personal consumption, private investment, government consumption and investment, inventory change, and exports. The cells in the remaining rows indicate how the components of value added in an industry are allocated and capture the value of labor and capital inputs used in an industry's production process.[3]

The tables presented here are part of a time series of SUTs, now covering the period 1997–2016, that were first released by BEA in September of

3. Young et al. (2015).

2015.[4] These data are updated and released on an annual basis, consistent with the annual revision of the Industry Economic Accounts.[5] The release of these tables is part of BEA's long-term plan to make US data on output, intermediate inputs, and value added available in a format that is well suited for preparation of TiVA statistics.

Starting with the September 2015 release, data previously presented only in the make-use format were presented in the more internationally recognized supply-use format. Presentation in this format helps to facilitate ongoing efforts to link US data with SUTs from other countries, a step necessary to derive the full suite of TiVA-related statistics. In addition, the SUTs incorporate important valuation changes that bring the tables into better alignment with international standards and enhance the suitability of the tables for use in TiVA analysis.[6]

BEA has recently conducted additional research allowing the breakdown of the use tables valued at purchaser prices into subcomponent matrices necessary for calculating TiVA statistics. This decomposition includes separate matrices for domestically produced inputs valued at basic prices, imported inputs at cost, insurance, and freight (CIF) prices, trade margins, transportation costs, taxes on products, duties on imports, and subsidies on products. Developing these matrices for the use table is more resource intensive than bringing the supply table up to purchasers' prices where only an additional six columns need to be added. In addition to their importance for preparing TiVA statistics, another reason to undertake this task is to facilitate compiling a supply and use table in volume terms. While each of the decomposed matrices is not currently published, these additions were available for purposes of this chapter.[7] The availability of these matrices is a significant improvement as the decomposed component matrices did not need to be approximated as previously using a quadratic programming constrained optimization model on data from the published BEA SUTs.

9.3.2 Activities of Multinational Enterprises

Firm heterogeneity is introduced into the SUTs through the incorporation of BEA AMNE statistics; this addition is partly what distinguishes them as extended SUTs. These statistics cover the financial and operating characteristics of US parent companies (domestic-owned MNEs) and US affiliates that are majority-owned by foreign MNEs (foreign-owned MNEs). They are based on legally mandated surveys conducted by BEA and are used in

4. For a full discussion of the supply-use framework and the methodology followed by BEA to prepare the new tables, see Young et al. (2015).
5. Barefoot, Gilmore, and Nelson (2017).
6. Beginning with the comprehensive update of the industry accounts scheduled for publication on November 1, 2018, BEA will begin featuring supply-use tables as the primary format for publishing input-output data. Make-use tables will continue to be published but will be released as a supplementary product rather than as the featured set of tables.
7. BEA is currently investigating options for making these tables available to the public.

a wide variety of studies to estimate the impact of MNEs on the domestic (US) economy and on foreign host economies. We use data from the inward AMNE surveys to measure the presence of foreign-owned MNEs and data from the outward AMNE surveys for domestic-owned MNEs for 2005 and 2012. The data include components of value added, sales, and trade in goods for both domestic-owned MNEs and foreign-owned MNEs for 31 industries for which the relevant data were published for both surveys. Because AMNE data points are sometimes suppressed to avoid disclosure of firm-level data, we use distributions from nonsuppressed data items as a basis for estimating suppressed values.

For domestic-owned MNEs, we exclude those that are majority foreign owned from the published outward AMNE data. These companies appear in both the inward and the outward AMNE data sets. Because the extent of the overlap is not published for the years covered by this study and because directly removing the overlapping companies could lead to implicit disclosure of firm-level data, we first remove the overlap at the all-industry level and then estimate industry-level overlaps based on distributions of published inward AMNE statistics by industry. That is, we assume that the extent of the overlap is proportional to the size of inward AMNE data by industry. We remove the industry-level estimates of the overlap from the domestic-owned MNE data set, leaving strictly domestic-owned MNEs that can be used to create extended SUTs and calculate TiVA statistics.

We also allocate BEA trade in services data by firm type. Trade in services data collected on BEA's BE-125 (selected services and intellectual property), BE-45 (insurance services), and BE-185 (financial services) surveys for 2012 were matched to the firms' responses on the BEA AMNE surveys to identify services exported and imported by domestic-owned MNEs and foreign-owned MNEs. The matches are made based on firm-level bridges between the three surveys and the AMNE data for 2011. The remaining trade that is not matched with an MNE is assumed to be exported or imported by a non-MNE. Since the trade in services data for 2005 are estimated from a greater number of surveys for which there are no existing ID bridges with the AMNE data, we apply the 2012 allocations by service type to the trade in services data for 2005.[8]

Trade in transport, travel, and government goods and services could not be matched directly to firms in the AMNE data. Transport data could not be matched because there is not currently an ID bridge between BEA's transportation surveys and the AMNE surveys. Travel data could not be matched because the source data are classified based on the buyer, not the seller. Data for firms supplying goods and services to the government could not be

---

8. In addition to the BEA surveys of selected services and intellectual property, insurance services, and financial services, BEA also conducts surveys of trade in services covering air transport and ocean transport.

matched because they are based on data sources that are aggregated above the firm level. The ownership type for these trade in services is based on the types of firms that we believe to be primarily engaged in this type of trade and on data for gross output by ownership type from the extended SUTs. Exports of travel services are allocated based on 2012 data from BEA's Travel and Tourism Satellite Account, 2013 data from the Survey of International Air Travelers, and 2012 data on gross output by ownership type from the extended SUTs. Since imports of travel services and imports of passenger fares for personal travel are typically not made by firms but by individual consumers, we allocated these imports to "final demand" rather than to a firm type.

9.3.3   US Census Bureau Data Sets

For experimental tables, we use BEA's SUTs as a starting point. Construction of the SUTs relies heavily on data from the quinquennial economic census as well as annual and quarterly surveys administered by the Census Bureau. In addition, census employment data at the enterprise and establishment levels from the 2007 and 2012 Economic Censuses are used to convert BEA's multinational data from an enterprise to an establishment basis.

For the microdata linking project covering semiconductor manufacturing, we identify multinational enterprises by linking the establishment level 2012 Census of Manufactures data with the 2012 BEA outward and inward AMNE surveys (BE-11 and BE-12). We identify firm size class for the establishments in the Census of Manufactures by linking that data set with the Census Bureau's Longitudinal Business Database to estimate the number of employees in each firm. We identify export intensity from export and sales data reported in the Economic Census.

9.4   Methodology

Our overall methodology is similar to that of Fetzer et al. (2018) and Fetzer and Strassner (2015). Estimates of value added, sales, trade, employment, and inventories by industry for domestic and foreign-owned MNEs are derived directly from BEA's AMNE data sets as outlined below, and non-MNE activity in these metrics is derived residually as total activity less the MNE data. Previous work by Fetzer et al. (2018) and Fetzer and Strassner (2015) relied on company-based IRS data to derive estimates of total activity. In this chapter, we make direct use of establishment-based data from BEA's published SUTs as our estimates of total activity. BEA's AMNE data are collected on an enterprise-basis and were adjusted to an establishment basis using an enterprise-to-establishment transformation matrix based on census employment data. Once all components were estimated, we constructed an extended SUT by firm ownership and calculated TiVA statistics.

9.4.1 Enterprise-to-Establishment Adjustment

The census employment data are taken from the 2007 and 2012 Economic Censuses. Census provides total employment both by enterprise industry and by establishment industry at the four-digit NAICS level. Census employment data for 2012 were used to convert the AMNE data for 2012, while census data for 2007 were used to convert the AMNE data for 2005.

We first aggregated the data up to the 31 industries estimated for this chapter. At the 31-industry level, we created an enterprise-by-establishment matrix of employment levels, which provided the weights for our conversion matrix. Because the matrix is based on employment levels, a key assumption in creating and using this conversion matrix is that the relationship between employees and the variable to be converted is the same by type of establishment regardless of the industry of the parent enterprise. For example, we assume that employees across all types of retail establishments are equally productive, whether those employees work for a retail establishment that is part of a consumer electronics enterprise or a retail establishment that is part of a furniture enterprise. It is important to note that no output is created or lost in converting from an enterprise to an establishment basis, rather the conversion process is simply one of redistribution.

9.4.2 Decomposing the Purchasers' Price Use Table into Component Matrices

According to the international accounting standards, use table intermediate inputs are valued at purchaser prices. However, a domestic basic price valuation is preferred for purposes of calculating TiVA statistics because it ensures more homogenous valuation across different products, more accurately reflects a country's input-output relationships, and allows separate identification of the effects of import tariffs, production taxes, and subsidies.

The purchaser price reflects the price paid by the buyer to take delivery of the good or service and includes the value of the underlying product plus taxes, wholesale and retail markups, and transportation costs. This is the value that matters for decision making by the buyer. The basic price reflects the price ultimately received by the producer and includes the price at which the underlying good or service is sold plus any subsidies received. In addition, the total value of purchased inputs in a standard use table combines both domestically produced and imported goods and services.

Conceptually, the process of converting use table intermediate inputs from purchaser prices to domestic basic prices involves removing taxes less subsidies, wholesale and retail markups, and transportations costs from each cell and separating imported and domestically produced inputs. Taxes less subsidies are moved to the value added row, while wholesale, retail, and transportation costs are moved to rows that show their purchase explicitly in the table rather than implicitly embedded in the value of goods purchases.

Finally, the resulting basic price values are separated into domestically produced and imported components. This process is often subdivided to provide additional information. For example, it is common to show trade and transportation margins separately rather than grouped as distributive services. Likewise, taxes are often identified separately from subsidies, and within taxes, tariffs and duties are often shown separately from domestic taxes on production. This additional detail can be useful for policy studies using computable general equilibrium models that are based on SUTs. The number of ways in which to subdivide the transformation of purchaser to basic prices ultimately depends on data availability and the needs of the project.

The adjustments to transform use table intermediates from purchasers' prices to basic prices are depicted as matrices. The taxes less subsidies matrix is constructed in such a way that subtracting this matrix from the use table leaves total output by industry unchanged. This matrix shifts taxes collected on purchased intermediate inputs out of intermediate inputs and into value added. Similarly, the matrix shifts subsidies away from value added and into the value of the intermediate inputs purchased. The purpose of this transformation is to have intermediate inputs more accurately reflect production costs.

The distributive services matrix is similarly constructed such that subtracting it from intermediate inputs leaves total intermediate inputs unchanged. The transformation alters the composition of intermediate inputs to reflect lower values in merchandise purchases and larger values in trade and transport purchases. The purpose of this transformation is to show margins being purchased explicitly, as opposed to being purchased implicitly in purchasers' prices. Showing margins explicitly allows for better evaluation of each industry's input structure for TiVA analysis.

The import matrix shows the purchase of imported inputs by industry and final use category. The import matrix allows the partitioning of intermediate inputs between domestically sourced and imported inputs. Imports are estimated in two stages. First, in the development of BEA's conventional SUTs, they are allocated by industry using the import proportionality assumption wherein industries are assumed to use imported intermediate inputs in the proportion to the import share of total domestic supply. Samuels et al. (2015) provide a complete description of the BEA import use methodology. Second, to account for firm heterogeneity in the use of imports, these first approximations are adjusted using imports of goods reported on the AMNE surveys and microdata from BEA's trade in services surveys linked to the AMNE data. This technique, however, could bias downward the import shares of MNEs because the AMNE surveys collect only direct imports by the firm themselves, whereas the import proportionality assumption implicitly captures imports purchased by the firm itself and those purchased through other domestic businesses, such as a broker or a wholesaler.

We mitigated this bias by reallocating imports from MNEs in industries reporting imports that were greater than the imports in our published SUTs. The reallocation was particularly large for reported imports by MNEs in wholesale trade. We expect that the bulk of imports by MNEs in wholesale trade are used as inputs by establishments in different industries. Distinguishing between imported and domestically sourced inputs is necessary for the proper identification of input structures for TiVA analysis.

The use table for the United States is computed such that intermediate inputs can be converted in a straightforward way between purchasers' and basic prices. Most of the components for preparing these two matrices and the transformation matrices that link them are generated in the normal course of statistical production.

Providing trade and transportation matrices for TiVA analysis largely entails aggregating this underlying data to an appropriate level of detail. The underlying US data also include an import use table which allows import-specific prices to be applied during the calculation of inflation-adjusted industry estimates. This import matrix is used to differentiate between changes in relative prices between domestic and foreign inputs. The import use table valuation includes import tariffs and duties, which for multicountry TiVA analysis needs to be shown separately from imports in basic prices. The data underlying the US use tables also allow for an explicit identification of product-related domestic taxes. Subsidies, however, are not easily identified based on the underlying level of detail. Thus, the two main challenges in developing domestic intermediate input estimates at basic prices for the United States are calculating the tariff and duties matrix and the subsidies matrix.

Calculating the tariffs and duties matrix requires coupling the underlying use table import data with customs data to determine appropriate estimates by product category. These product estimates are then apportioned to purchasing industries proportionately and aggregated to the desired level. Subsidies are first estimated by product based on the product mix produced by the industry receiving the subsidies. These estimates of product subsidies are then apportioned to intermediate inputs proportionately.

9.4.3 Estimating Firm Type Shares

Following the decomposition of the purchaser price use table, we break out the industry columns in the resulting component matrices into foreign-owned MNEs, domestic-owned MNEs, and non-MNEs. The MNE components are calculated using the AMNE data, while the non-MNE component is calculated as the residual of the total value less the MNE pieces. The resulting distribution is used to generate firm type shares for each industry.

Shares are prepared by industry for gross output, intermediate inputs, employee compensation, capital compensation (gross operating surplus plus taxes on products), exports, imports, and employment. For each of these variables, an establishment-based industry distribution is drawn from the supply-use framework. The establishment-based distributions for foreign- and domestic-owned multinational enterprises created from the AMNE and census employment data are subtracted from the SUT-based totals to create a residual estimate of non-multinational activity by industry.

In some instances, multinational activity as measured by valued added, sales, and other metrics mentioned above is larger than total activity from the SUTs. These discrepancies are likely the result of limitations in the enterprise-to-establishment adjustment process. We adjusted the data to address these negatives and other implausible values.

Firm type shares are applied to all industry columns of the SUT matrices. The shares are estimated so that the resulting extended SUT remains fully balanced and consistent, so the table does not need to be rebalanced.

9.4.4   Input-Output Tables

We use a similar methodology for estimating the TiVA statistics as Fetzer et al. (2018). Once the extended SUTs are constructed, we derive a symmetric industry-by-industry extended IOT from the extended SUTs. First, we generate a commodity-by-commodity IOT using the industry technology assumption that each industry has its own specific method of production, irrespective of its product mix. We derive an industry-by-industry IOT using the fixed product sales structure approach from this table, in which each product has its own specific sales structure, irrespective of the industry in which it is produced.[9] Dietzenbacher et al. (2013) indicate that this approach is also used to construct the world IOTs for the World Input-Output Database Project. They indicate that practitioners prefer the fixed product sales structure approach to the fixed industry sales structure where each industry has its own sales structure. This is because it is more plausible that products have the same sales structure than industries having the same sales structure. It also does not yield negative values in cells that were not negative in the original SUT.

In the extended SUT, export data appear only on a commodity basis; however, the IOT resulting from the above process includes a distribution of exports by industry and firm type. The shares for exports are applied at this stage of the process, and offsetting adjustments are made to non-export activity to keep totals for each row unchanged. TiVA statistics can then be calculated from this "export adjusted" IOT.

9.4.5   TiVA Estimates

While TiVA estimates are most rigorously calculated using international IOTs that account for the production of all countries in the world, TiVA statistics can be calculated using single-country IOTs. We follow the approach of Ma, Wang, and Zhu (2015) and Tang, Wang, and Wang (2014) and

---

9. See Eurostat (2008) for a more detailed explanation of these approaches.

assume that domestic content in gross exports is the same as value added in gross exports. Because part of domestic content in gross exports is re-imported goods, our measure of domestic value added is overstated.

We calculate TiVA measures using a methodology that is typically used for international IOTs. A key to calculating TiVA statistics is the Leontief inverse of the IOT. The matrix depends on both the direct input require-ments from the same industry and the indirect input requirements from other industries. Domestic value added embodied in gross exports for an industry depends on both these direct and indirect requirements. Following Ma, Wang, and Zhu (2015) and Tang, Wang, and Wang (2014), we calculate domestic value added as the product of the vector of the domestic value added share of output for each industry, the Leontief inverse of the US IOT matrix, and the value of gross exports for each industry. Likewise, the *direct* domestic value added content of gross exports is calculated as the vector of domestic value added shares of output multiplied by the value of gross exports for each industry. *Indirect* domestic content of gross exports is calculated as the difference between total and direct domestic value added. Imported content of gross exports is calculated as the difference between gross exports and domestic value added content of exports. We refer to this as *imported content* instead of the more commonly used term *foreign value added*, since it might also include domestic content that had previously been exported.

9.5 Results

In this section we describe the TiVA indicators that measure the contri-bution of US production in both domestic and global value chains. In our experimental tables, we find that the imported content of exports is concen-trated in a few industries. Despite the dominance that MNEs have over trade transactions, both MNEs and non-MNEs make significant contributions to the content of US exports.[10] Estimates based on our microdata linking project suggest that production patterns by ownership, firm size class, and export intensity each exhibit firm heterogeneity to some extent. Estimates from the microdata linking project suggest that production patterns by own-ership, firm size class, and export intensity each exhibit firm heterogeneity to some extent.

Powers (2012) points out that TiVA indicators typically focus on either a decomposition of the value added content of goods where they are con-

---

10. The content of exports is measured by our TiVA indicators, which mainly depend on the input requirements (including imported inputs) from our extended IOTs and the level of exports from each industry by firm type. The result—that the majority of content of exports in service industries is from non-MNEs—is consistent with the relatively high share of value added contributed by non-MNEs in services industries and the relatively large share that own industry inputs contribute to value added.

sumed or a decomposition of gross trade. He shows that examining trade on a value added basis shows a different picture of bilateral trade balances than gross trade flows. However, the total trade deficit of a country summed across all partner countries is identical for both TiVA and gross trade flows. One core measure of TiVA is decomposing the value added content of gross exports into domestic and foreign components. Other things being equal, the higher the foreign value added share of exports, the more the industry is integrated in global value chains. This could mean that the current level of exports depends on foreign content. It is also possible that the foreign content is substituting for potential additional domestic content.

According to the OECD TiVA database, foreign value added content as a share of exports for the United States has been stable, fluctuating between 9 and 13 percent between 2005 and 2016. The share gradually decreased from 11 percent in 2005 to 9 percent in 2016. Foreign value added is a relatively small share of exports for the United States compared with other major economies. Foreign value added as a share of exports in 2016 for the United States is similar to the share of foreign value added in exports for Australia, Japan, and Russia, but is about 10 percentage points lower than the share for most major European countries, China, and Canada and more than 20 percentage points lower than the share of foreign value in exports for Korea and Mexico.[11]

9.5.1   Imported Content of Exports as a Share of Gross Exports

Using our experimental extended IOT, we calculate the imported content of exports as a share of exports for 2005 and 2012 (figure 9.1). Other things being equal, the higher the imported content share of exports, the more exporters are integrated into global value chains. The import content share across industries has a similar pattern to that observed in data from 2011 by Fetzer et al. (2018). Imported content as a share of exports is largest for petroleum manufacturing, likely due to foreign crude oil and coal used to produce refined petroleum for export. Imported content tends to be a small share of exports of services.

Imported content as a share of exports in 2012 is either higher or very similar to the level in 2005 for most industries (figure 9.1). This is consistent with the trends in the foreign value added share of US exports calculated by the OECD. Notable exceptions are other transportation manufacturing, computers and electronics, and petroleum manufacturing. The annual OECD estimates suggest that most of the decrease in computers and electronics occurred between 2008 and 2009 in the aftermath of the financial crisis. We will analyze this change more thoroughly by decomposing domestic and imported content by firm types.

11. OECD, Principal TiVA indicators, https://stats.oecd.org/Index.aspx?DataSetCode =TIVA_2018_C1, downloaded September 2020. Indicators were derived from the 2018 version of OECD's Inter-Country Input-Output (ICIO) Database.

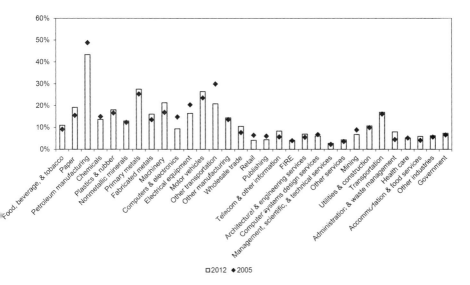

Figure 9.1   Imported content of exports as a share of gross exports, by industry, 2005 and 2012
Source: Authors' calculations based on BEA SUTs.

As noted earlier, our TiVA estimates of imported content might over-state the importance of imported inputs, since they may include domestic content that had previously been exported from the United States. We may also understate imported inputs because some imports in the wholesale trade industry may be used as inputs in other industries. Our estimates of imported content as a share of gross exports across all industries of 14.4 per-cent in 2005 and 15.0 percent in 2012 are larger than the OECD's estimates of foreign value added as a share of gross exports of 10.8 percent in 2005 and 12.4 percent in 2012. As seen in figure 9.2 for 2012, our estimates are larger for most industries that are comparable between the two data sets.

As shown in figures 9.3, 9.4, and 9.5, imported content as a share of exports varies by type of ownership for all industries and for individual industries in both 2005 and 2012. Imported content tends to be a larger share of exports for foreign-owned MNEs during 2012, but non-MNEs have the highest share in several manufacturing industries in 2012 and most manufacturing industries in 2005. However, non-MNEs consistently have the smallest share of imported content in exports from services industries. Imported content as a share of exports in other industries (which are a combination of goods and services) is highest for foreign MNEs.[12] As noted

12. The category Other industries includes agriculture, forestry, fishing, and hunting; non-bank holding companies; educational services; arts, entertainment, and recreation; and miscellaneous services.

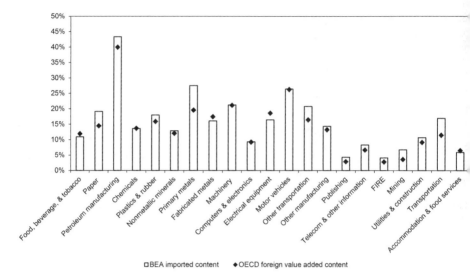

Figure 9.2   BEA import content compared with OECD foreign valued content as a share of gross exports, by selected industries, 2012

Source: Authors' calculations based on BEA SUTs and OECD TiVA database.

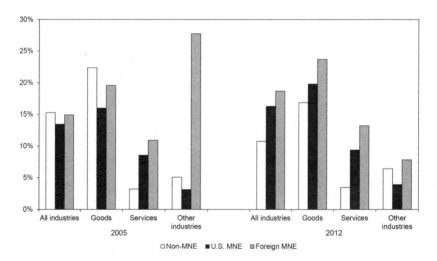

Figure 9.3   Imported content of exports as a share of gross exports, by industry type and firm type, 2005 and 2012

Source: Authors' calculations based on BEA SUTs and BEA AMNE and trade in services microdata.

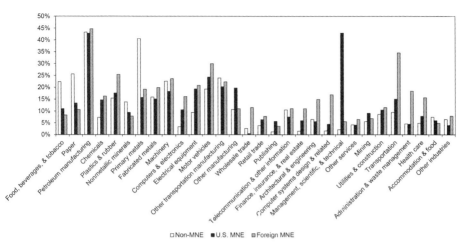

Figure 9.4   Imported content of exports as a share of gross exports, by industry and firm type, 2005

Source: Authors' calculations based on BEA SUTs and BEA AMNE and trade in services microdata.

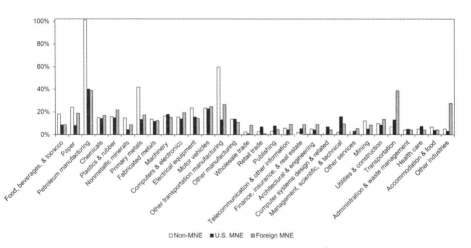

Figure 9.5   Imported content of exports as a share of gross exports, by industry and firm type, 2012

Source: Authors' calculations based on BEA SUTs and BEA AMNE and trade in services microdata.

in section 9.4.2, however, at this stage, the estimates of imports by MNEs may be understated.

Much of imports and exports by both US and foreign MNEs is trade within the MNE. Intra-firm trade in goods is more prevalent for foreign MNEs, comprising more than 80 percent of their imports and more than 60 percent of their exports in 2005 and 2012, while intra-firm trade in goods by US MNEs accounted for close to one-half of their trade in the same periods.[13]

Intra-firm trade in services made up about 20–30 percent of exports and imports of trade in services by all firm types in 2005 and 2012, although this share varies greatly by the type of service.[14] Bruner and Grimm (2019) find that most trade in a selected set of services that is based on survey data collected by BEA was with affiliated parties and that MNEs accounted for over 90 percent of this trade in 2017. These selected services include financial services and charges for the use of intellectual property and make up more than one-half of both exports and imports of services. Intra-firm trade by US parents with their affiliates made up about 80 percent of affiliated exports and about 60 percent of affiliated imports in 2012.[15]

Intra-firm trade in goods by foreign MNEs during 2005 and 2012 was most prevalent among US affiliates in wholesale trade and followed by US affiliates in the transportation equipment industry (mostly motor vehicle affiliates in 2005). More than one-half of US MNE imports from their foreign affiliates are by US MNEs in the motor vehicle, computers and electronics, chemicals, and petroleum manufacturing industries in 2005 and 2012. A slightly smaller share of US MNE exports to their foreign affiliates is by US MNEs in these industries.

9.5.2 Decomposition of Value Added

We also used the experimental tables to decompose domestic value added embodied in exports by ownership type to get a sense of the contribution of different firm types and imported content in exports. Despite the dominance that MNEs have over trade transactions, both MNEs and non-MNEs appear to make significant contributions to the content of US exports. According to our estimates in figure 9.6, non-MNEs contribute close to one-half of the value added content of exports, while US and foreign MNEs together contribute close to 40 percent of the content of exports and the remaining contribution is from imported content. Non-MNEs contribute slightly more

---

13. BEA, Activities of U.S. Affiliates of Foreign Multinational Enterprises, revised data for 2005 and 2012 and BEA, Activities of U.S. Multinational Enterprises, revised data for 2005 and 2012.

14. BEA, U.S. Trade in Services, Table 2.3, U.S. Trade in Services, by Country or Affiliation and by Type of Service, July 10, 2020 release.

15. BEA, U.S. Trade in Services, Table 2.3, U.S. Trade in Services, by Country or Affiliation and by Type of Service, July 10, 2020 release.

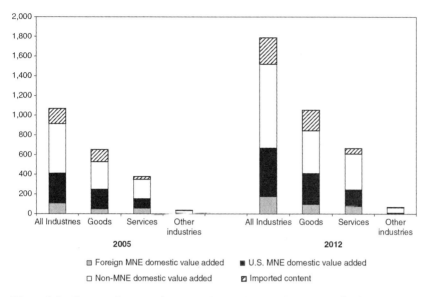

Figure 9.6   Source of content in exports by good producing and service industries, 2005 and 2012 (Billions of $)
Source: Authors' calculations based on BEA SUTs and BEA AMNE and trade in services microdata.

than one-half of the content of exports from services industries, and slightly more content as a share of exports from goods industries than MNEs. However, US and foreign MNEs together contributed more value added content than non-MNEs to exports of seven of the nine largest industries in terms of exports in 2012 and six of the eight largest industries in terms of exports in 2005 (figures 9.7 and 9.8).

Value added content from non-MNEs in exports is spread out across many industries, although close to one-fourth of the content is concentrated in exports from FIRE (finance, insurance, and real estate) and machinery. Almost one-half of the value added content of exports by US MNEs is concentrated in transportation services, computers and electronics, chemicals, and other transportation manufacturing in 2005 and 2012. Two of these industries, computers and electronics and chemicals, are also industries with the largest share of intra-firm trade in goods by US MNEs.

Value added by foreign MNEs as a share of the content in exports is less than the contribution by US MNEs and non-MNEs for all industries except wholesale trade, where it made up 50 percent of the content in exports in 2005 and 35 percent of content in 2012. More than one-half of foreign-owned domestic value added content of exports was in exports from the wholesale trade, motor vehicles, and chemicals industries. A majority of the

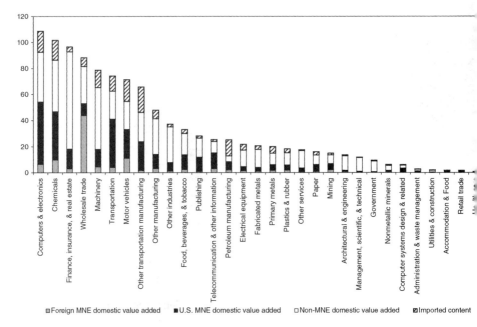

Figure 9.7   Source of content in exports by industry, sorted by value of exports, 2005 (Billions of $)

Source: Authors' calculations based on BEA SUTs and BEA AMNE and trade in services microdata.

intra-firm trade in goods by US affiliates is concentrated in wholesale trade and transportation equipment, which includes motor vehicles.

While these numbers indicate that foreign-owned MNEs contribute significant amounts of domestic value added content of exports for some industries, some foreign-owned MNEs may not be very integrated into a domestic value chain. Estimating the indirect or upstream contribution of foreign-owned MNEs and the other firm types to the domestic value added content of exports helps us understand to what degree value added by foreign-owned MNEs is an input in other US industries. In 2012, about 30 percent of the foreign-owned domestic value added is upstream, although this varies widely by industry.

Turning from exports to domestically consumed goods and services, non-MNEs are the largest source of value added in final domestic demand for both goods and service producing industries in 2012 (figure 9.9). Value added by non-MNEs made up almost three-fourths of final domestic demand for service industries in 2012, while it contributed about one-half of the content of final domestic demand in goods-producing industries. The difference between the contributions to final domestic demand and exports is due to the composition of industries contributing most to final domestic demand

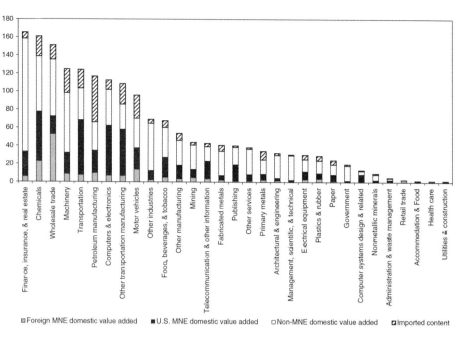

Figure 9.8 Source of content in exports by industry, sorted by value of exports, 2012 (Billions of $)

Source: Authors' calculations based on BEA SUTs and BEA AMNE and trade in services microdata.

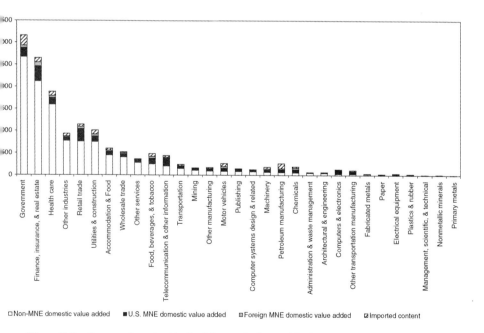

Figure 9.9 Source of content in final domestic demand by industry, sorted by non-MNE domestic value added, 2012 (Billions of $)

Source: Authors' calculations based on BEA SUTs and BEA AMNE and trade in services microdata.

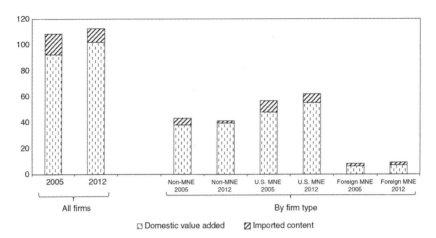

Figure 9.10   Source of content in exports for computers and electronics, 2005 and 2012 (Billions of $)

Source: Authors' calculations based on BEA SUTs and BEA AMNE and trade in services microdata.

compared to exports. Government services, FIRE, and health care are the largest components of final domestic demand, and their value added primarily comes from non-MNEs. Therefore foreign-owned value added only made up about 4 percent of final domestic demand in 2012 compared to 10 percent of exports. The 4 percent share of final domestic demand is slightly less than the share of value added created by non-EU-owned enterprises in the median EU country (Stapel-Weber et al. 2018).

We can also use this decomposition to better understand the decrease in the imported content of exports as a share of exports for the computer and electronics industry. Figure 9.10 shows that we can now see the changes in export content for each firm type. The decline in imported content as a share of exports between 2005 and 2012 is mostly due to an increase in direct domestic value added by US MNEs and there is some substitution of domestic value added for imported content by US MNEs and non-MNEs.

9.5.3   Labor Productivity

Our results also indicate that MNEs are more productive than non-MNEs overall and in many key industries. This is consistent with Bloom, Sadun, and van Reenen (2012), who find that US and other multinationals in the UK were more productive than domestic firms from 1995 to 2003.

Consistent with the productivity sorting hypothesis of Melitz (2003) and Helpman, Melitz, and Yeaple (2004), we find that labor productivity measured by gross output per employee for both US-owned MNEs and foreign-owned MNEs is almost twice as large as that for non-MNEs in both 2005 and 2012. When measuring labor productivity by value added as a share of employment, US-owned MNEs and foreign-MNEs are almost 25 percent more productive than non-MNEs across all industries. However, non-MNEs are more productive on a value added basis than MNEs when the high productivity petroleum manufacturing industry is excluded. It is not surprising that productivity is smaller for MNEs when based on value added rather than gross output because value added doesn't account for productivity associated with utilizing intermediate inputs (Eldridge and Price 2016). Consistent with the framework developed by Bernard et al. (2018) on productivity of global firms, we expect that one source of high productivity of MNEs is that they are more likely to lower their costs by importing inputs from multiple countries and also expand the scale of their operations by exporting a larger number of products to many countries.

Compared to non-MNEs, labor productivity on a gross output basis was higher for foreign-owned MNEs in most industries, and higher for US MNEs in about one-half of our industries. Labor productivity was higher for both foreign-owned and domestic-owned MNEs during 2005 and 2012 in several industries with significant amounts of MNE gross output and employment including food, beverages, and tobacco; machinery; transportation; and utilities and construction.

9.5.4 Analysis of Value Added and Exports for the Semiconductor Industry Using Linked Microdata

The quality of the estimates discussed so far is lessened by the necessity of approximating establishment-level data for MNEs from enterprise-level AMNE data collected by BEA combined with patterns in establishment-level data for all US firms collected by the Census Bureau. BEA is currently conducting research toward building more accurate extended SUTs using linked enterprise-establishment microdata for all firms rather than converting the enterprise-level BEA MNE data to the establishment level and then imposing the MNE data on the published establishment-level SUTs. While the establishment-level conversion is an accepted method of converting the data, it is still necessary to reconcile remaining inconsistencies between the BEA enterprise data and the establishment level census data.

As an initial exercise working with the linked microdata, we constructed these data for US establishments in the semiconductor manufacturing industry. We cannot provide tabular results at this stage due to data disclosure constraints. Using the linked census and BEA AMNE microdata, we measure the components of value added, gross output, and employment for the semiconductor industry by type of ownership, firm size, and export intensity. On an ownership basis, value added as a share of output is highest for US MNEs and lowest for foreign MNEs. The low share for foreign MNEs is consistent with Zeile (1998), who found that, in the electronic components and accessories industry in 1989, foreign-owned US businesses had a domes-

Table 9.1   Components of value added as share of output by ownership, semiconductor industry, 2012

(Share of total output)		Multinational enterprise		Non-multinational enterprise	Exports of goods	Other uses
		US	Foreign			
Multinational enterprise	US				33.1	66.9
	Foreign				34.5	65.5
Non-multinational enterprise					15.0	85.0
Total intermediate inputs		50.2	60.1	57.3		
Value added		49.8	39.9	42.8		
of which:						
Compensation of employees		22.6	22.6	31.2		
Gross operating surplus		26.6	16.7	11.2		
of which:						
Consumption of fixed capital		9.7	8.7	4.9		
Taxes on production and imports		0.6	0.6	0.4		
Total output		100.0	100.0	100.0		

Source: Authors' calculations based on BEA AMNE and US Census Bureau Economic Census microdata.

Table 9.2 Components of value added as share of output by firm size class, semiconductor industry, 2012

(Share of total output)	Small enterprise	Medium enterprise	Large enterprise	Exports of goods	Other uses
Small enterprise				9.5	90.5
Medium enterprise				18.9	81.1
Large enterprise				33.3	66.7
Total intermediate inputs	55.9	49.3	54.3		
Value added	44.1	50.7	45.7		
of which:					
Compensation of employees	32.1	24.3	24.1		
Gross operating surplus	11.6	25.8	21.1		
of which:					
Consumption of fixed capital	4.7	5.5	9.4		
Taxes on production and imports	0.4	0.6	0.5		
Total output	100.0	100.0	100.0		

Source: Authors' calculations based on BEA AMNE and US Census Bureau Economic Census microdata.

Table 9.3   **Components of value added as share of output by export orientation, semiconductor industry, 2012**

(Share of total output)	Enterprise exports	Enterprise doesn't export	Exports of goods	Other uses
Enterprise exports			43.8	56.2
Enterprise doesn't export			0.0	100.0
Total intermediate inputs	51.3	57.9		
Value added	48.7	42.1		
of which: Compensation of employees	23.9	26.9		
Gross operating surplus	24.3	14.6		
of which: Consumption of fixed capital	8.8	7.3		
Taxes on production and imports	0.5	0.6		
Total output	100.0	100.0		

Source: Authors' calculations based on BEA AMNE and US Census Bureau Economic Census microdata.

tic content of 72 percent, compared with 87 percent for domestic-owned businesses. On a firm size class basis, value added as a share of output is highest for medium-sized enterprises and is lowest for small enterprises. On an export intensity basis, value added as a share of gross output is higher for exporting firms than for non-exporters.

All else equal, we would have expected value added as a share of gross output to be smaller for large firms and exporters, since they are more likely to be part of global value chains than medium firms. This intuition is supported by Bernard, Jensen, and Schott (2009). However, it may be that the commodity mix of exports and imports differs among the different firm types so that what we are interpreting as a quantity effect is really a price effect. We will be better able to understand these patterns at a later stage when we have integrated product-level goods trade data, including imported goods data, into our analysis. The ratio of exports to gross output follows a more expected pattern with exports as a share of gross output highest for MNEs and for larger firms.

An important purpose of an extended supply and use table is to illustrate how production patterns can vary by firm characteristic, within an industry. Ideally, the characteristics chosen will be those that are conceptually linked to the differences in production patterns. While we offer some descriptive comparisons of heterogeneity illustrated by the various criteria, we do not attempt to determine which criterion is conceptually most valid for extended supply and use tables. The choice of the most appropriate characteristics will require further research.

The ownership criterion identifies more heterogeneity in value added

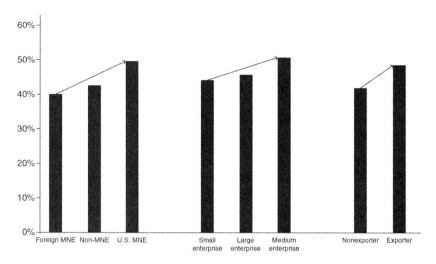

Figure 9.11   Value added as a share of gross output, semiconductor industry, by firm type, 2012

Source: Authors' calculations based on BEA AMNE and US Census Bureau Economic Census microdata.

and its components than firm size class and export intensity criterion.[16] The range between the smallest and largest value added shares of output is almost 10 percentage points based on ownership compared with a range of less than 7 percentage points for both firm size class and export intensity (see figure 9.11). Also, there is greater variance in the three value added to gross output shares based on ownership than in the three shares based on firm size class.

Firm size class identifies more heterogeneity in exports as a share of gross output than the ownership criterion with a range of 24 percentage points compared to range of 20 percentage points for the ownership criterion (see figure 9.12). This supports our expectation that export intensity of the two types of MNEs are similar, and the difference between export intensities of small and large firms capture a great degree of heterogeneity.

Direct comparisons between the experimental ESUT and the semiconductor estimates are difficult for several reasons. First, we are unable to disaggregate the industries in our experimental ESUT down to the 3344 NAICS semiconductor industry for a direct comparison. Semiconductors are a subset of the computer and electronics industry, making up only about one-fourth of the value added and less than one-third of sales in 2012 for

16. Our objective is not to measure how each criterion contributes to heterogeneity but to evaluate to what extent disaggregating the estimates by a particular criterion illustrates heterogeneity, regardless of the underlying source of the heterogeneity.

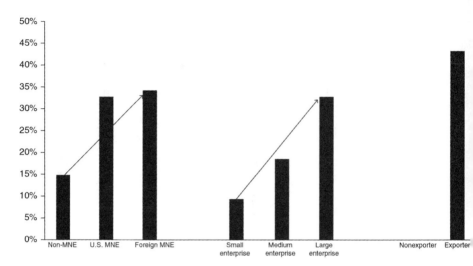

Figure 9.12   Exports as a share of gross output, semiconductor industry, by firm type, 2012

Source: Authors' calculations based on BEA AMNE and US Census Bureau Economic Census microdata.

the industry. Second, due to the preliminary nature of the data linking work we are not able to disclose TiVA measures such as the value added share of exports and final domestic demand due to data needed from other industries outside the scope of our case study. We are limited to estimating metrics that can be calculated using the establishment-level data for the semiconductor industry such as the value added and export shares of output by firm type used in work such as Fetzer and Strassner (2015).

While these results are experimental and only for one industry, they suggest that the three firm types (by ownership, size, and export intensity) all identify heterogeneity in production patterns and that different criteria may better identify heterogeneity for different measures of economic activity. Some unexpected results suggest that more work is needed at the microdata level to ensure that components of output and inputs are being measured and classified properly.

9.6   Conclusion

In this chapter we construct experimental extended SUTs and TiVA estimates for the United States for 2005 and 2012. We find that the imported content of exports is concentrated in a few industries such as petroleum and motor vehicle manufacturing. Despite the dominance that MNEs have over gross trade transactions, both MNEs and non-MNEs make significant contributions to the valued added content of US exports. While non-MNEs contribute more value added content to exports than MNEs on average, MNEs contribute more value added content to exports of at least six of the eight largest industries in terms of exports. We also find that value added to the content by MNEs is concentrated in several industries in which their intra-firm trade in goods is concentrated. More refined estimates for the semiconductor industry based on the Census-BEA microdata linking project suggest that while the ownership criterion identifies the most heterogeneity in the value added share of output, firm size class identifies more heterogeneity in export intensity.

Our results provide further evidence that accounting for firm heterogeneity matters in measuring production. It allows us to better understand the role of global value chains in the US economy. Even though our analysis using a single-country IOT doesn't account for imported content that was originally exported from the United States, we are able to show how US production relies on inputs from both domestic and global supply chains. Our results also inform us about the degree to which foreign ownership contributes to US production.

BEA is participating in statistical initiatives with the OECD and with APEC, where work continues to develop the framework for extended SUTs and APEC regional SUTs and IOTs and associated TiVA estimates. Additionally, BEA and the USITC are collaborating with Statistics Canada and Mexico's Instituto Nacional de Estadística y Geografía to develop North American regional SUTs and associated TiVA statistics.

Lastly, much work remains to improve the statistical infrastructure to support efforts to measure the role of global value chains in the US economy. This work includes enhancing the international comparability of BEA's SUTs and continuing to expand the detail BEA publishes on exports and imports by type of service and by country. In addition, a critical goal is to extend the analysis done on semiconductors to produce official extended SUTs under the microdata linking project with the Census Bureau. This project will link BEA's AMNE and trade in services data with data from Census Bureau economic surveys and census data on trade in goods across all industries. The output of this linking project will identify firm-level heterogeneity tabulations that, ideally, will be made available for use on a recurring basis to construct official statistics.

References

Ahmad, N. 2018. "Accounting for Globalisation: Frameworks for Integrated International Economic Accounts." Prepared for NBER CRIW Conference: The Challenges of Globalization in the Measurement of National Accounts, Bethesda, MD, March 9–10.

Ahmad, N., S. Araujo, A. Lo Turco, and D. Maggioni. 2013. "Using Trade Micro-data to Improve Trade in Value Added Measures: Proof of Concept Using Turk-ish Data." In *Trade in Value Added: Developing New Measures of Cross-Border Trade*, edited by A. Mattoo, Z. Wang, and S. Wei, 187–219. Washington, DC: The World Bank.

Barefoot, K., T. Gilmore, and C. Nelson. 2017. "The 2017 Annual Update of the Industry Economic Accounts: Initial Statistics for the Second Quarter of 2017 and Revised Statistics for 2014–2016 and the First Quarter of 2017." *Survey of Current Business* 97 (12).

Bernard, A. B., J. B. Jensen, and P. K. Schott. 2009. "Importers, Exporters and Multinationals: A Portrait of Firms in the US That Trade Goods." In *Producer Dynamics: New Evidence from Micro Data*, Studies in Income and Wealth, volume 68, edited by T. Dunne, J. B. Jensen, and M. J. Roberts, 513–52. Chicago, IL: University of Chicago Press.

Bernard, A. B., J. B. Jensen, S. J. Redding, and P. K. Schott. 2018. "Global Firms." *Journal of Economic Literature* 56 (2): 565–619.

Bloom, N., R. Sadun, and J. Van Reenen. 2012. "Americans Do IT Better: U.S. Multinationals and the Productivity Miracle." *American Economic Review* 102 (1): 167–201.

Bruner, J., and A. Grimm. 2019. "A Profile of U.S. Exporters and Importers of Services, 2017." *Survey of Current Business* 99 (12).

Cadestin C., K. De Backer, I. Desnoyers-James, S. Miroudot, D. Rigo, and M. Ye. 2017. "An ICIO Split According to Domestic and Foreign Ownership: The OECD TiVA-MNE Project." Paper prepared for the 25th International Input-Output Conference, June 19–23. Atlantic City, New Jersey.

Dervis, K., J. P. Meltzer, and K. Foda. 2013. "Value-Added Trade and Its Impli-cations for International Trade Policy" OP-ED, Brookings Institute. https://www.brookings.edu/opinions/value-added-trade-and-its-implications-for-international-trade-policy/.

Dietzenbacher, E., B. Los, R. Stehrer, M. P. Timmer, and G. J. de Vries. 2013. "The Construction of World Input-Output Tables in the WIOD Project." *Economic Systems Research* 25: 71–98.

Eldridge, L. P., and J. Price. 2016. "Measuring Quarterly Labor Productivity by Industry." *Monthly Labor Review*, June.

Eurostat. 2008. Eurostat Manual of Supply, Use and Input-Output Tables. Eurostat Methodologies and Working Papers. Luxembourg: Office for Official Publications of the European Communities.

Fetzer, J. J., T. F. Howells III, L. Jones, E. H. Strassner, and Z. Wang. 2018. "Estimat-ing Extended Supply-Use Tables in Basic Prices with Firm Heterogeneity for the United States: A Proof of Concept." BEA Working Paper WP2018–12.

Fetzer, J. J., and E. H. Strassner. 2015. "Identifying Heterogeneity in the Production Components of Globally Engaged Business Enterprises in the United States." BEA Working Paper WP2015–13.

Helpman, E., M. J. Melitz, and S. R. Yeaple. 2004. "Export versus FDI with Het-erogeneous Firms." *American Economic Review* 94 (1): 300–16.

Ito, K., I. Deseatnicov, and K. Fukao. 2017. "Japanese Plants' Heterogeneity in Sales, Factor Inputs, and Participation in Global Value Chains." Research Institute of Economy, Trade, and Industry, Discussion Paper Series 17-E-117.

Johnson, R. C. 2018. "Measuring Global Value Chains." *Annual Review of Econom-ics* 10.

Johnson, R. C., and G. Noguera. 2012. "Accounting for Intermediates: Production

Sharing and Trade in Value'Added." *Journal of International Economics* 86 (2): 224–36.

Koopman, R., Z. Wang, and S. Wei. 2012. "Tracing Value-Added and Double Counting in Gross Exports." *American Economic Review* 104 (2): 459–94.

Los, B., M. P. Timmer, and G. J. de Vries. 2016. "Tracing Value-added and Double Counting in Gross Exports: Comment." *American Economic Review* 106 (7): 1958–66.

Ma, H., Z. Wang, and K. Zhu. 2015. "Domestic Content in China's Exports and Its Distribution by Firm Ownership." *Journal of Comparative Economics* 43 (1): 3–18.

Melitz, M. J. 2003. "The impact of trade on intra-industry reallocations and aggregate industry productivity." *Econometrica* 71 (6): 1695–1725.

Michel, B., C. Hambÿe, and B. Hertveldt. 2018. "The Role of Exporters and Domestic Producers in GVCs: Evidence for Belgium Based on Extended National Supply-and-Use Tables Integrated into a Global Multiregional Input-Output Table." Prepared for NBER CRIW Conference: The Challenges of Globalization in the Measurement of National Accounts, Bethesda, MD, March 9–10.

OECD. Principal TiVA indicators. http://stats.oecd.org/Index.aspx?DataSetCode =TIVA_2016_C1.

Piacentini, M., and F. Fortanier. 2015. "Firm heterogeneity and trade in value added." *OECD Working Paper*.

Peluso, A., G. Medeiros, J. Young, R. J. Hallren, L. Jones, R. Nugent, and H. Wickramarachi. "An Overview on the Construction of North American Regional Supply-Use and Input-Output Tables and their Applications in Policy Analysis." USITC, Economics Working Paper Series, 2017–12-A.

Powers, W. 2012. "The Value of Value Added: Measuring Global Engagement with Gross and Value-added Trade." USITC Economics Working Paper Series, 2012–11A.

Samuels, J. D., T. J. Howells III, M. Russell, and E. H. Strassner. 2015. "Import allocations across industries, import prices across countries, and estimates of industry growth and productivity." In *Measuring globalization: better trade statistics for better policy*, eds. S. N. Houseman and M. Mandel. Kalamazoo, MI: W.E. Upjohn Institute for Employment Research.

Saborío, G., and R. Torres. 2018. "Costa Rica: Integrating Foreign Direct Investment Data and Extended Supply and Use Tables into National Accounts." Prepared for NBER CRIW Conference: The Challenges of Globalization in the Measurement of National Accounts, Bethesda, MD, March 9–10.

Stapel-Weber, S., P. Konijn, J. Verrinder, and H. Nijmeijer. 2018. "Meaningful Information for Domestic Economies in the Light of Globalization: Will Additional Macroeconomic Indicators and Different Presentations Shed Light?" Prepared for NBER CRIW Conference: The Challenges of Globalization in the Measurement of National Accounts, Bethesda, MD, March 9–10.

Houseman, S. N., and M. Mandel, eds. *Measuring Globalization: Better Trade Statistics for Better Policy*, 251–89. Kalamazoo, MI: W.E. Upjohn Institute for Employment Research.

Tang, H., F. Wang, and Z. Wang. 2014. "The Domestic Segment of Global Supply Chains in China under State Capitalism." World Bank Policy Research Paper 6960.

Young, J. A., T. F. Howells III, E. H. Strassner, and D. B. Wasshausen. 2015. "BEA Briefing: Supply-Use Tables for the United States." *Survey of Current Business* 95 (9): 1–8.

Zeile, W. 1998. "Imported Inputs and the Domestic Content of Production by

Foreign-Owned Manufacturing Affiliates in the United States." In *Geography and Ownership as Bases for Economic Accounting*, edited by R. E. Baldwin, R. E. Lipsey, and J. D. Richardson, 205–32. Chicago, IL: University of Chicago Press.

Comment   Susan N. Houseman

The international statistical community's embrace of trade in value added (TiVA) statistics is a response to globalization, which has been characterized by international fragmentation of production and the rapid development of global supply chains. In the new global economy, traditional international trade statistics can be misleading. First, measures of exports and imports double count content that is part of a global supply chain as it crosses borders multiple times, inflating the level of trade and, as global production chains expand, its growth. Second, while the gross flows approach to measuring international trade still provides an accurate estimate of a county's overall trade balance, it does not provide accurate estimates of bilateral trade balances because it does not account for the imported content of exports. China's exports, for example, often come from factories engaged in final processing and use inputs produced in other countries. Consequently, exported consumer goods from China embed much value added from other countries. One study finds that trade statistics inflated the US trade deficit with China in the early 2000s by 40 percent (Johnson and Noguera 2012).

In principle, statistics that measure trade in value added resolve these problems. By isolating value added contributed by each country in the production chain, they also can provide better indicators of a country's international competitiveness in various industries. While the national statistical agencies now widely acknowledge the benefits of using a TiVA concept, at least in the short term, it is impractical to directly measure trade in value added. TiVA statistics, therefore, are estimated from existing data collected by national statistical organizations. International efforts, such as those led by OECD, estimate TiVA statistics from intercountry input-output tables that are based on country-level national accounts data and detailed international trade statistics.

The fundamental question addressed in this chapter is whether data already collected as part of the US statistical system can be utilized to generate more accurate TiVA statistics. The work for this chapter is part of an

Susan N. Houseman is Vice-President and Director of Research at the W.E. Upjohn Institute for Employment Research.

For acknowledgments, sources of research support, and disclosure of the author's material financial relationships, if any, please see https://www.nber.org/books-and-chapters/challenges -globalization-measurement-national-accounts/comment-accounting-firm-heterogeneity -within-us-industries-extended-supply-use-tables-and-trade.

ongoing collaboration between the US Bureau of Economic Analysis (BEA) and the Census Bureau to develop better supply and use tables—input-output tables for the US economy—that, with SUTs from other countries, are the basic building blocks in the development of intercountry input-output tables. The chapter provides insights into the challenges in constructing world IO tables and the progress being made in the United States. The exercise also provides some interesting insights into the structure of imports and exports in the United States.

The chapter reports on two technical contributions in the improvement of SUTs for the United States. The first involves breaking out purchasers' prices (the prices purchasers pay for goods and services) into basic prices for domestic inputs and into costs, insurance, and freight (CIF) prices for imported inputs. In so doing, trade margins, transportation costs, taxes, import duties, and subsidies are separately reported.

The second contribution, and the focus of my remarks, involves the introduction of firm heterogeneity into the estimation of SUTs. The underlying issue is that the United States, like other countries, does not track the destination of imports as intermediate inputs or for final use in the economy. Although business surveys collect information on expenditures on intermediates by type of good or service, businesses are not asked to break out these purchases by whether they are sourced domestically or internationally, let alone by the country from which they were sourced. Indeed, particularly if purchased from a wholesaler, businesses may not be able to answer this question. In constructing input-output tables for the US economy, the BEA must estimate imported intermediate inputs used by each industry. To do so, as Fetzer and coauthors explain, the BEA uses the import proportionality assumption: an industry uses imported intermediates in proportion to its overall use of the product in the economy. If, for instance, an industry accounts for 10 percent of the consumption of a product, it is assumed to account for 10 percent of imports of that product. This method implicitly assumes that exporters are no more likely than firms producing solely for domestic consumption to use imported intermediates.

Owing to the growth of globally integrated supply chains, however, it is reasonable to suppose that exporting firms, which at least for merchandise exports are disproportionately multinational enterprises (MNEs), are more likely to also use imported intermediates compared to firms that produce solely for their domestic market. Findings from studies for China and other countries indeed have found this to be the case. To better account for firm heterogeneity, the authors exploit data from the BEA survey on Activities of Multinational Enterprises (AMNE) linked with microdata from BEA trade in services surveys to separately estimate the import content of exports from US-based MNEs, foreign MNEs, and non-MNEs.

Notably, these data only show what is directly imported by MNEs. Fetzer et al. essentially make the conservative assumption that these direct imports account for all imports used by MNEs and that industry import use is fixed at the level given by the import proportionality assumption. After allocating the MNE imports to each of its establishments using census data establishment employment, they compute import use by non-MNEs as a residual— industry-level estimates from the SUT less the estimates of MNE imports based on the AMNE and services import surveys.

Findings and Their Implications for TiVA Statistics

The authors acknowledge that their assumptions bias downward the estimates of import content for MNEs. For industries in which the import values of MNEs based on the AMNE and services import surveys exceed the total estimated import use in the SUT, they reallocate the excess to other industries. These cases, as would be expected, primarily involve industries in the wholesale sector. Such reallocation, the authors point out, helps but does not fully mitigate the downward bias to MNE imports. Nevertheless, their findings indicate, as expected, that on average the import content of exports is higher among MNEs, especially foreign-owned MNEs, than among non-MNEs, though estimates vary across industries and over time (figures 9.3–5). Preliminary estimates from a detailed analysis of the semiconductor industry also show considerable heterogeneity across firm types.

The chapter's analysis yields other interesting insights into the relative importance of MNEs and non-MNEs in accounting for the value of goods and services exports. While their estimates suggest that most of the value of US goods exports comes from the value added of MNEs, particularly the value added of US-based MNEs, about two-thirds of the estimated value of services exports comes from the value added of non-MNEs.

The finding that MNEs on average use relatively more imported inputs than non-MNEs and account for most of the value of goods exports naturally raises the question, Does accounting for heterogeneity between MNEs and non-MNEs in SUTs lead to substantially higher estimates of the imported value of exports? The chapter does not directly answer this question. The authors do report that that their estimates of the imported content of exports across all industries is somewhat *lower* than OECD estimates of foreign imported content for both 2005 and 2012. Because of differences in the way the TiVA statistics were computed, the two sets are not fully comparable, however. The OECD uses intercountry IO tables, whereas Fetzer et al. use the US IO table to compute TiVA, though this method should, all else the same, result in a higher estimate of import content than the OECD's estimate of foreign content. Although they do not discuss the factors underlying this somewhat surprising finding, it may reflect the fact that they report an average for all industries and non-MNEs, which use below average imported intermediates, account for most of exports in the services sector. In addition, the chapter's estimates of import content are to some degree understated for MNEs, which purchase at least some imports from wholesalers.

To directly show the effect of firm heterogeneity on TiVA statistics, it would be helpful in future work to generate comparisons using the same method—first based on the US SUT table and then based on the extended US SUT table that allows for firm heterogeneity. Because the degree to which MNEs account for exports varies considerably across industries, researchers also should show the effect of accounting for firm heterogeneity by sector and industry. Additionally, researchers should test the sensitivity of the effects of firm heterogeneity on TiVA measures under different assumptions about MNE purchases from wholesalers. Currently, they make the very conservative assumption that MNEs import all foreign goods themselves and allocate the residual to non-MNEs (estimated total industry imports based on the import proportionality assumption less MNE direct imports). Instead, they could allocate the residual to both MNEs and non-MNEs under various assumptions about the division, possibly informed by census establishment microdata on expenditures for intermediates. The purpose of such an exercise would be to bound the potential effects of firm heterogeneity on estimates of the imported content of exports.

In other words, it is important to bear in mind that utilizing data on MNE imported intermediates still requires assumptions about how imported intermediates are allocated between different types of firms. If estimates of the imported content of exports are highly sensitive to those assumptions, it would indicate that there are limits to the use of data already collected in the US statistical system to improve TiVA estimates. In this case, new data collection, as discussed by Nadim Ahmad (this volume), would be necessary.

Implications for Labor Productivity

Although not the chapter's focus, Fetzer et al. also use their estimates to compare labor productivity between MNEs and non-MNE establishments. They report that labor productivity among MNEs is nearly double that among non-MNEs when measured as gross output per employee. When measured as value added per employee, MNE labor productivity is only about 25 percent higher, and when the petroleum industry is dropped, labor productivity of MNEs is on average lower than that of non-MNEs. They argue that one source of higher productivity for MNEs is their better ability to source inputs from domestic and foreign firms and that this, in turn, argues for using the gross output concept in computing labor productivity.

The authors should be extremely cautious in making and interpreting such comparisons, however. Cross-establishment labor productivity comparisons implicitly assume that the production functions are homogeneous. Even if they were to control for detailed industry, this assumption would almost certainly be violated. Just as MNEs and non-MNEs systematically differ in their use of imported inputs, they also may systematically differ in the stages of production done within establishments. MNEs have been behind the "slicing up of the value chain" that characterizes globalization. Thus, the greater use of imported inputs by MNEs likely reflects not simply the substitution of imported for domestic inputs but also offshoring—the outsourcing of functions to overseas producers or affiliates. In a case study of the US home furniture industry, Holmes (2011) illustrates the offshoring of processes, which led to wide variation in stages of production performed in domestic factories. In the early 2000s, for instance, some upholstery manufacturers began outsourcing the most labor-intensive stage of the process, the cutting and sewing of the upholstery material, to China; one even outsourced all furniture production to China, retaining only final assembly in the United States.

Such outsourcing will mechanically increase measured labor productivity when labor productivity is measured as gross output per employee; the denominator, employment, will be lower, but the numerator, gross output, all else the same will be unchanged by outsourcing. Because outsourcing lowers both the numerator and the denominator when labor productivity is computed as value added per employee, in general, value added labor productivity measures are less susceptible than gross output labor productivity measures to mechanical changes associated with outsourcing (Dey, Houseman, and Polivka 2012). While firms may reap true productivity gains when they outsource—i.e., the same quantity of output can be produced with fewer inputs—a change in what is produced within the boundary of the firm does not, per se, increase productivity, and labor productivity measures based on gross output measures can be highly misleading.

References

Ahmad, Nadim. 2020. "Accounting Frameworks for Global Value Chains: Extended Supply-Use Tables." In *Challenges of Globalization in the Measurement of National Accounts*, edited by Nadim Ahmad, Brent Moulton, J. David Richardson, and Peter van de Ven. This volume.

Dey, Matthew, Susan N. Houseman, and Anne E. Polivka. 2012. "Manufacturers' Outsourcing to Staffing Services." *ILR Review* 65 (3): 533–59. https://journals.sagepub.com/doi/pdf/10.1177/001979391206500303.

Holmes, Thomas J. 2011. "The Case of the Disappearing Large-Employer Manufacturing Plants: Not Much of a Mystery After All." Economic Policy Paper 11-4. Minneapolis, MN: Federal Reserve Bank of Minneapolis.

Johnson, R. C., and G. Noguera. 2012. "Accounting for Intermediates: Production Sharing and Trade in Value Added." *Journal of International Economics* 86 (2): 224–36.

OECD. 2001. *Measuring Productivity: Measurement of Aggregate and Industry-Level Productivity Growth*. Paris: Organisation for Economic Co-operation and Development. https://www.oecd.org/std/productivity-stats/2352458.pdf.

The Role of Exporters and Domestic Producers in GVCs
Evidence for Belgium Based on Extended National Supply and Use Tables Integrated into a Global Multiregional Input-Output Table

Bernhard Michel, Caroline Hambÿe, and Bart Hertveldt

10.1 Introduction

Trade liberalization and technological developments have largely contributed to increasing global economic integration between the early 1990s and the late 2000s by reducing trade costs (e.g., transport costs, communication costs). This went hand in hand with profound changes in firm organization that still shape production processes today. Firms have reorganized their production processes by dividing them into a growing number of separate stages and by outsourcing more and more of those production stages to domestic and foreign suppliers. Due to these changes, value chains have become increasingly fragmented and international or even global. Input-output tables and models are among the foremost tools for the macroeconomic analysis of value chains because they enable mapping of the full set of upstream and downstream links in the chain. The calculation of multipliers and linkages based on input-output tables yields information on how and to what extent industries are integrated into value chains. Such analyses were traditionally based on national input-output tables and hence restricted to domestic value chains in individual countries. However, the statistical development of global input-output tables over the past decade has

Bernhard Michel is a member of Belgian Federal Planning Bureau and a professor of economics at the University of Mons, Belgium.

Caroline Hambÿe is a member of Belgian Federal Planning Bureau.

Bart Hertveldt is deputy head of the sectoral directorate of the Belgian Federal Planning Bureau.

For acknowledgments, sources of research support, and disclosure of the authors' material financial relationships, if any, please see https://www.nber.org/books-and-chapters/challenges -globalization-measurement-national-accounts/role-exporters-and-domestic-producers -gvcs-evidence-belgium-based-extended-national-supply-and-use.

widened the scope and looks at the integration of countries and industries into global value chains (Koopman et al. 2010; Johnson and Noguera 2012; Inomata 2017; Los 2017).

For input-output-based analyses of value chains, fragmentation also poses a challenge in terms of the granularity of underlying industry-level data. In input-output tables, firms are traditionally grouped into industries according to the type of goods and services they produce. But within fragmented value chains, patterns of specialization are likely to be related to other firm characteristics. Therefore, the analysis of value creation in the context of fragmented value chains can be improved through a breakdown of industries into different types of firms. As suggested in OECD (2015), it is desirable to disaggregate industries in supply-and-use and input-output tables according to firm characteristics such as size, ownership, or exporter status because these characteristics may actually be the source of technological differences between firms within industries that are traditionally defined in terms of product similarity. The same point is made by Los, who argues that "such differences can only be captured in value chain trade indicators if each industry is split in two subindustries" (2017, 317).

This insight has prompted several efforts to account for firm heterogeneity in supply and use tables (SUTs) and input-output tables (IOTs)—that is, to generate so-called heterogeneous or extended tables. This work was initially triggered by the desire to isolate firms engaged in processing trade, as these firms differ from other firms in terms of technology and import patterns. Processing traders were isolated in IOT for China (Koopman, Wang, and Wei 2012; Ma, Wang, and Zhu 2015), and firms operating under special export regimes were separated out in Mexico's IOT (de la Cruz et al., 2011). Both these disaggregations have also been integrated into the OECD's inter-country input-output tables (Yamano and Webb 2018). In a similar vein, firms active in free trade zones have been isolated in tables for Costa Rica (Saborío 2015). Beyond special trade regimes, Ahmad et al. (2013) provide a proof of concept for a micro-data-based split of industries in Turkish IOT into exporters and other firms. Several other initiatives have been gathered in the context of the OECD's Expert Group on Extended Supply and Use Tables: they come, among others, from Austria (disaggregation by exporter status and ownership, see Lais and Kolleritsch, 2017); the Netherlands (disaggregation by size class, see Chong et al. 2017); and the United States (disaggregation by ownership, see Fetzer et al. 2018). Finally, Piacentini and Fortanier (2015), and Cadestin et al. (2018), introduce firm heterogeneity into multicountry input-output tables in terms of firm size and ownership. They do so in a proportional way based on aggregated international firm-level databases.

In this work, we break down manufacturing industries in the 2010 Belgian SUTs and IOT into firms that are export oriented and firms that mainly serve the domestic market. For this purpose, we use the full set of individual firm-level data sources that serve for the construction of Belgium's official SUTs and IOT for 2010. The resulting export-heterogeneous tables allow us to test for differences in input structures and import patterns of export-oriented firms and other firms, and to analyze their respective integration into domestic value chains based on input-output multipliers and linkages as defined in Miller and Blair (2009), and Hambÿe (2012). We also compare our results with those for homogeneous industries derived from the official 2010 Belgian IOT to show that accounting for export heterogeneity in those tables yields important new insights. Moreover, we integrate the export-heterogeneous Belgian IOT into the global tables of the World Input-Output Database (WIOD) to determine how export-oriented and domestic market manufacturing firms contribute to Belgium's participation and position in global value chains. The analysis of contributions to value creation based on data disaggregated along these lines provides a clearer picture of the sources of a country's competitiveness.

The novelty of our approach is twofold: the estimation of the industry-level output, input, and import structures in the exporter heterogeneous SUTs and IOTs are data based rather than just proportional as in most prior contributions, and the integration of the Belgian tables into the global table is such that these Belgian data are not modified. Furthermore, as globalization has become a major challenge in the measurement of national accounts for individual countries, we also see this work as a contribution to determining whether the national accounts—which officially comprise SUTs and IOTs—can accommodate recent findings from the academic literature on international trade. Analyses of the characteristics of exporters based on firm-level data have indeed shown that exporters are different from domestic firms in terms of production technology. Exporters are not only bigger and more productive (Melitz 2003) but they also import more of the intermediates they use (Bas 2009).

This chapter is organized as follows. We start off by providing details on constructing export-heterogeneous supply and use and input-output tables for Belgium in section 10.2. This includes explanations on how we have disaggregated manufacturing industries in Belgian supply and use tables, derived a national heterogeneous input-output table, and integrated it into the global input-output table of the WIOD project. In section 10.3, we analyze differences in input structures between manufacturing exporters and non-exporters and look at their integration into both domestic and global value chains. Finally, we draw conclusions in section 10.4.

10.2   Export Heterogeneity in Supply and Use and Input-Output Tables: Sources and Data Construction

Supply and use tables (SUTs) are an integral part of national accounts (NA) and provide detailed information about economic flows in monetary terms: they describe production processes and income generated through production. As the central balancing tool for the national accounts, they match the supply and use of goods and services. While SUTs are mainly a statistical tool, symmetric input-output tables (IOTs) are an analytical tool derived from SUTs based on assumptions about the relation between output and inputs.[1]

SUTs are product-by-industry tables with domestic production and imports given in the supply table, and intermediate inputs, final uses (final consumption of households and government, gross fixed capital formation, changes in inventories, and exports of goods and services), and value added reported in the use table. Thus, the use table reveals the structure of production costs by industry. The classification of industries in SUTs is such that industries are made up of production units or firms that produce similar goods or services; for instance, all producers of chemicals or financial services are grouped together in one industry. Heterogeneity is traditionally conceived as depending on the detail of the industry classification. The broadly defined chemicals industry will lump together firms that produce different types of chemicals: industrial gases, fertilizers, etc. The standard approach to account for such heterogeneity is further disaggregation of the industry classification along the lines of detailed product categories. However, as emphasized in OECD (2015), there may also be other sources of firm heterogeneity within industries: firms in one industry differ in terms of size and ownership, and they are exporters or serve only the domestic market. Their production cost structure may then differ accordingly. Therefore, it is worthwhile considering alternative disaggregations of industries within SUTs and IOTs.

The focus here is on heterogeneity in terms of export behavior: we disaggregate manufacturing industries into export-oriented firms and firms serving mainly the domestic market. The literature on firm heterogeneity and international trade points to differences between exporters and nonexporters in terms of technology. In particular, exporters are found to have higher productivity levels (and markups), which allows them to cover the fixed cost related to exporting (Melitz 2003). Moreover, the more productive exporters tend to rely more on imported inputs. They have better access to global input markets, which allows them to purchase cheaper and/or higher-quality inputs abroad, thereby further boosting their productivity (Bas 2009). These technological differences may also shape and be shaped by the deeper integration of exporters into global value chains.

We introduce export heterogeneity into Belgian SUTs and IOT for the year 2010 by disaggregating manufacturing industries according to exporter status at the most detailed industry-level breakdown. The official Belgian

---

1. For a more detailed description of the construction of SUTs and IOTs and their role within the system of national accounts, see Beutel (2017).

SUTs for 2010[2] have been constructed according to the rules of the European System of Accounts (ESA 2010).[3] The most detailed unpublished version (workformat) of the SUTs contains a breakdown into 133 industries and 350 product categories, which are respectively based on the European Union industry and product classifications NACE Rev.2 and CPA2008.[4] Manufacturing covers NACE Rev.2 industries 10 to 33, which amounts to 57 industries in the workformat classification. For disaggregating these industries, we rely on most of the firm-level data that are used in the construction of the SUTs. We make sure that our disaggregation is consistent with the official Belgian SUTs, i.e., values for output, intermediate inputs, and value added of the split manufacturing industries sum to the values for the total non-heterogeneous industry.

The stylized supply table and use table shown in tables 10.1 and 10.2 illustrate the SUTs with a disaggregation of manufacturing industries (columns) according to exporter status. Table 10.3 and table 10.4 add a split of the use table according to the origin of the used goods and services, i.e., whether they are imported or purchased from Belgian producers (table 10.3) and, among the latter, whether they are sourced from exporters or non-exporters (table 10.4).

In practice, we proceed in several steps to obtain export-heterogeneous Belgian SUTs for 2010. First, we identify exporters and disaggregate total output and intermediate inputs for the 57 manufacturing industries in the tables. Then, we split the columns of both the supply and the use table that contain the product distribution of output and intermediate inputs for each industry. We also specifically disaggregate the use table to identify the use of imported intermediate inputs and purchases of intermediate inputs from manufacturing exporters and non-exporters. Finally, we derive a symmetric heterogeneous industry-by-industry IOT, which we then integrate into a global multiregional input-output table (GMRIO).

10.2.1   Disaggregating Total Industry-Level Output and Intermediate Inputs

Identifying exporters among manufacturing firms allows us to disaggregate total industry-level output and intermediate consumption for the 57 manufacturing industries in the SUTs based on the exporters' share of turnover and purchases. The results correspond to the dark gray cells in the

2. We will also refer to these as standard SUTs.
3. The 2010 Belgian SUTs at purchasers' prices and at basic prices with a 64 industry and product breakdown (as well as the IOT) can be downloaded for free from the website of the Belgian Federal Planning Bureau (FPB): http://www.plan.be/databases/data-54-en-input +output+tables+2010+esa+2010+december+2015+. Further detail (in French or Dutch) on their construction can be found in FPB (2015).
4. NACE stands for Statistical Classification of Economic Activities in the European Community and CPA for Statistical Classification of Products by Activity in the European Economic Community.

Table 10.1   **Supply table**

	Agriculture	Mining	Manufacturing M1 X	Manufacturing M1 non X	Manufacturing M2 X	Manufacturing M2 non X	Manufacturing ...	Services S1	Services S2	Services ...	Total output by product	Imports	Total supply
Products of agriculture													
Mining products													
Manufactured Products M1													
M2													
M3													
...													
Services S1													
S2													
S3													
...													
Total output by industry													

Table 10.2   Use table (column disaggregation only)

	Agriculture	Mining	Manufacturing						Services			Total intermediate inputs	Final uses	Total use
			M1		M2		…		S1	S2	…			
			X	non X	X	non X	…							
Products of agriculture														
Mining products														
Manufactured Products M1														
M2														
M3														
…														
Services S1														
S2														
S3														
…														
Total use by industry														
Net taxes on products														
Value added														
Output														

Table 10.3   Use table for domestic production and imports

	Agriculture	Mining	Manufacturing M1 (X)	Manufacturing M1 (non X)	Manufacturing M2 (X)	Manufacturing M2 (non X)	... (...)	Services S1	Services S2	...	Total intermediate inputs	Final uses	Total use
Domestic													
Products of agriculture													
Mining products													
Manufactured Products M1													
M2													
...													
Services S1													
S2													
...													
Imports													
Products of agriculture													
Mining products													
Manufactured Products M1													
M2													
...													
Services S1													
S2													
...													
Total use by industry													
Net taxes on products													
Value added													
Output													

Table 10.4   Use table (full disaggregation)

		Agriculture	Mining	Manufacturing						Services			Total intermediate inputs	Final uses	Total use
				M1		M2		…	…	S1	S2	…			
				X	non X	X	non X								
Domestic															
Products of agriculture															
Mining products															
Manufactured Products	X M1														
	M2														
	…														
	non X M1														
	M2														
	…														
Services	S1														
	S2														
	…														
Imports															
Products of agriculture															
Mining products															
Manufactured Products	M1														
	M2														
	…														
Services	S1														
	S2														
	…														
Total use by industry															
Net taxes on products															
Value added															
Output															

bottom row of tables 10.1 and 10.2 and the fourth row from the bottom in table 10.2. Disaggregated value added including net taxes on products is obtained as the difference between total output and intermediate inputs of the heterogeneous manufacturing industries (dark gray cells in the second and third rows from the bottom in table 10.2).

The general business register underlying the 2010 national accounts (NA) and SUTs contains 40 194 manufacturing firms[5] for which data on turnover and total purchases are available based on the following sources: balance sheet data, structural business survey data, and periodical value added tax (VAT) declarations.[6] These are the main data sources used to estimate industry-level NA aggregates for total output and intermediate inputs by industry. The 40 194 manufacturing firms with turnover and total purchases data constitute our *full sample*. Their total turnover sums to €229.7 billion. Merging in merchandise export data, we calculate export to turnover ratios for these firms and consider those with a ratio above 25 percent as export oriented. This yields a sample split for manufacturing firms into 2 430 export-oriented firms, and 37 764 firms that mainly serve the domestic market, which we refer to as domestic market firms. The share of export-oriented firms in turnover amounts to about 75 percent (€171.2 billion). Hence, export-oriented firms are bigger firms: their average turnover is €70.4 million compared to €5.7 million for the entire sample. Due to the 25 percent cut-off ratio for defining export-oriented firms, this category of firms does not account for all exports. Merchandise exports of export-oriented firms amount to €98.2 billion out of a total of €101.3 billion of exports by manufacturing firms (97 percent). All these sample characteristics are summarized in the upper part of table 10.5.

10.2.2   Disaggregating Manufacturing Industries in the Supply and Use Tables

As illustrated by the light gray cells in tables 10.1 and 10.2, the SUTs contain the distribution of industry-level output and use of intermediate inputs over product categories. For the column-wise split of manufacturing industries in the 2010 Belgian SUTs into export-oriented and domestic market firms, we use a *restricted sample* of firms for which we have information on turnover and purchases by product category.

In the Belgian SUTs, the product distribution of output and intermediate inputs is derived from several sources. The main source is two supplementary questionnaires annexed to the structural business survey (SBS): one on the product detail of turnover and the other on the product detail

---

5. Belgian national accounts (NA) are based on legal units, which we refer to as firms.
6. The order of this list of sources reflects the hierarchy in their use. Balance sheet data are the primary source. If balance sheet data are unavailable for a firm, then structural business survey data are used, and if those are not available either, then data from periodical VAT declarations are used.

Table 10.5   Sample characteristics for manufacturing industries, 2010

	Number of firms	Turnover (billion euros)	Average size (million euros)	Exports (billion euros)
Full sample				
All firms	40,194	229.7	5.7	101.3
Export-oriented firms	2,430	171.2	70.4	98.2
	(6.0%)	(74.5%)		(96.9%)
Domestic market firms	37,764	58.5	1.5	3.1
	(94.0%)	(25.5%)		(3.1%)
Restricted sample				
All firms	1,710	181.2	105.9	85.9
Export-oriented firms	980	149.9	153.0	83.9
	(57.3%)	(82.8%)		(97.6%)
Domestic market firms	730	31.2	42.8	2.0
	(42.7%)	(17.2%)		(2.4%)

Note: The *full sample* comprises all firms with data on turnover and total purchases. The *restricted sample* comprises firms with supplementary SBS questionnaires. Export-oriented firms are those with an export to turnover ratio above 25%.

of total purchases. These two questionnaires are sent out jointly every five years to a *restricted sample* of big firms (all firms with at least 50 employees plus smaller firms if necessary to reach a coverage of minimum 50 percent of turnover at the four-digit industry level). For the product detail on output in manufacturing industries, the data from the supplementary SBS questionnaire on turnover are complemented by data from the survey on industrial production (Prodcom). Moreover, the data are compared to firm-level exports by product category to correct inconsistencies. By the same token, the data from the supplementary SBS questionnaire on the product detail of total purchases are cross-checked and corrected for inconsistencies through a comparison with firm-level imports by product category and data on domestic purchases from the VAT transaction data set.[7] The latter comprises all transactions between domestic firms on which VAT is levied. In the construction of the SUTs, the resulting cross-checked data sets are used to distribute total industry-level output and intermediate inputs over product categories.

In 2010, 1 710 manufacturing firms completed the supplementary SBS questionnaires. They form the *restricted sample* for establishing the product distributions. Their turnover amounts to €181.2 billion, which is 79 percent of the total turnover of the 40 194 manufacturing firms in our *full sample*. Among these 1 710 firms, 980 are export oriented (export to turnover ratio above 25 percent). The turnover of these export-oriented firms sums to

7. In the construction of the SUTs, the aim of these corrections is to avoid that the underlying inconsistencies in the firm-level data resurface in the balancing process of the tables.

€149.9 billion (88 percent of the turnover of all 2 430 export-oriented firms in the *full sample*). Within the *restricted sample*, the average size of export-oriented firms also largely exceeds that of firms serving mainly the domestic market (€153.0 against €42.8 million). Finally, exports of export-oriented firms in the *restricted sample* amount to €83.9 billion compared to total exports of €85.9 billion by all firms in the *restricted sample* (98 percent). Again, table 10.5 provides an overview of these sample characteristics.

We split the *restricted sample* into export-oriented and domestic market firms and use the cross-checked data from the supplementary SBS questionnaires on turnover and total purchases to estimate separate product distributions of output and intermediate inputs for both groups of firms in each manufacturing industry. We were able to do so for 47 out of the 57 manufacturing industries. The sample size was insufficient for domestic market firms in eight industries and for export-oriented firms in two industries. In those cases, we had to make a proportionality assumption. Given the aim to investigate differences in production cost structures, we have been striving to determine the product distributions of output and intermediate inputs of heterogeneous industries based on firm-level data rather than just assume proportionality to the non-heterogeneous industries in the official tables. A sample split based on lower export to turnover ratios increases the number of industries where the sample size for non-exporters is insufficient for a data-based estimation of the product distribution of output and inputs. Hence, we faced a trade-off between including exporters with a low export to turnover ratio in the exporter sample and avoiding proportionality in the estimation of the product distributions of the heterogeneous industries.

Finally, we apply a RAS procedure to ensure consistency with respect to the product distribution of output and intermediate inputs of the non-heterogeneous industries in the official SUTs. As a result, we obtain a heterogeneous supply table as shown in table 10.1 and a heterogeneous use table as shown in table 10.2. The heterogeneous use table is still at purchasers' prices. For transformation to basic prices, the valuation matrices for trade and transport margins and for taxes less subsidies on products must be subtracted. As we have no firm-level information that would allow us to disaggregate valuation tables by exporter status, we do so proportionally to values of intermediate inputs at purchasers' prices.

10.2.3   Disaggregating the Use Table according to the Origin of the Products

The disaggregation of the use table at basic prices according to the origin of the products is done in two steps: first a split into imported and domestic goods and services (table 10.3) and then a split of the latter into goods produced by export-oriented manufacturers and by domestic market manufacturers (upper part of table 10.4). The official Belgian use table at

Table 10.6   Heterogeneous supply table for Belgium, 2010, millions of euros

	Export-oriented manufacturers	Domestic market manufacturers	Other industries	Imports	Total supply
Manufactured goods	135,960	47,683	10,767	161,793	356,203
Other goods and services	13,344	4,783	538,571	100,952	657,651
Total output/imports	149,304	52,467	549,338	262,745	1,013,854

basic prices contains a split according to the origin of the goods and services, i.e., a use table for domestic output and a use table for imports. This is necessary for deriving an IOT. Hence, we need to split the heterogeneous use table into heterogeneous use tables for domestic output and imports. This requires specific data work for the columns of manufacturing industries (see table 10.3).[8] To estimate the use of imported intermediate inputs by export-oriented and domestic market manufacturers, we use product-level import data for these firms corrected for re-exports and excluding imports of capital goods. Again, a RAS procedure is applied so that the disaggregation respects the values of imported intermediate inputs in the official use table. The use of domestically produced intermediate inputs by export-oriented and domestic market manufacturers is calculated as the difference between total and imported intermediate inputs.

As shown shaded in light gray in table 10.4, the entire rows for domestically produced manufactured goods in the use table can be further disaggregated according to whether these goods are produced by domestic market manufacturers or by export-oriented manufacturers. To do this, we proceed in two steps. First, we disaggregate exports, which are part of final uses. As illustrated above, export-oriented firms do not account for all exports due to the 25 percent export to turnover cut-off ratio for identifying these firms. Based on the sample split (*full sample*) and firm-level export data by product category, we determine exports by export-oriented and domestic market firms for all categories of manufactured goods. Second, for all other final and intermediate use categories, we disaggregate the rows proportionally for each category of manufactured goods based on shares of export-oriented and domestic market firms in output of these goods that is not exported. These shares are calculated from the data in the heterogeneous supply table.

This completes the column-wise and row-wise disaggregation of Belgium's 2010 SUTs into export-oriented and domestic market firms in manufacturing industries as illustrated in tables 10.1 and 10.4. Tables 10.6 and 10.7 present the resulting heterogeneous SUTs in a very aggregated form.

8. For all other industries and all final demand categories, the split into goods and services of domestic origin and imports is the same as in the official use table.

Table 10.7   Heterogeneous use table for Belgium, 2010, millions of euros

	Export-oriented manufacturers	Domestic market manufacturers	Other industries	Domestic final demand	Commodity exports	Service exports	Total output / imports
Domestic							
Manufactured goods, export-oriented manufacturers	14,816	3,711	9,328	10,058	96,429	1,617	135,960
Manufactured goods, domestic market manufacturers and firms in other industries	8,153	6,650	16,815	13,163	10,891	2,778	58,450
Other goods and services	27,545	12,580	170,954	260,813	21,400	63,404	556,698
Imports							
Manufactured goods	39,416	9,839	15,879	35,285	61,374	0	161,793
Other goods and services	26,526	3,558	49,175	7,382	14,312	0	100,952
Total use	116,456	36,338	262,151	326,702	204,407	67,799	1,013,853
Value added	32,848	16,128	287,187				
Total output	149,304	52,467	549,338				

Table 10.8   **Heterogeneous input-output table for Belgium, 2010, millions of euros**

	Export-oriented manufacturers	Domestic market manufacturers	Other industries	Domestic final demand	Commodity exports	Service exports	Total output
Export-oriented manufacturers	15,335	3,866	11,482	12,446	101,566	4,609	149,304
Domestic market manufacturers	6,900	5,697	14,730	13,278	8,975	2,888	52,467
Other industries	28,279	13,379	170,886	258,311	18,180	60,303	549,337
Imports	65,941	13,397	65,053	42,667	75,686	0	
Value added	32,848	16,128	287,186				
Total output	149,304	52,467	549,337				

10.2.4 Deriving the Export-Heterogeneous Industry-by-Industry Input-Output Table

For the transformation of SUTs at basic prices into symmetric industry-by-industry IOT, we choose the commonly used fixed product sales structure assumption (Model D in Eurostat, 2008). According to this assumption, "each product has its own specific sales structure irrespective of the industry where it is produced" (Beutel 2017, 119). This comes down to assuming that an industry's output of a product is delivered to users in the same proportion as total economy-wide output of that product.[9]

The heterogeneous industry-by-industry IOT that we derive from the heterogeneous SUTs is given in very aggregated form in table 10.8. The rows of this industry-by-industry IOT show the values of deliveries of an industry's output to the different users. The columns for industries indicate where they purchase their inputs from, and their value added, i.e., they describe the industries' cost structures.

10.2.5 Integrating the Export-Heterogeneous IOT for Belgium into a Global Table

The last step of our statistical work is to integrate the 2010 heterogeneous IOT for Belgium into a global multiregional input-output table (GMRIO) for the same year. Among the available GMRIOs, we have chosen the global table from the 2016 release of the World Input-Output Database (WIOD).[10] This 2010 World Input-Output Table (WIOT) is consistent with the 2008 System of National Accounts (SNA 2008) and covers 43 countries (includ-

---

9. See Eurostat (2008) for the mathematical expressions of the derivation of industry-by-industry IOT from SUT under the fixed product sales structure assumption.

10. These tables can be downloaded for free from the website of the WIOD project: http://www.wiod.org/. Timmer et al. (2015) provides an introduction to WIOD data, and Timmer et al. (2016) contains a detailed description of the sources and methodology for constructing the world input-output tables (WIOT).

ing Belgium) and 56 industries in a classification that is compatible with NACE Rev.2.[11] All values are in current dollars.

In a nutshell, the construction of a WIOT starts from publicly available national SUTs, which are complemented with international trade data from COMTRADE and combined into world SUTs. The industry-by-industry WIOT is derived from these world SUTs based on the standard fixed product sales structure assumption. The WIOT respects countries' published national accounts aggregates (output and value added by industry as well as totals of final demand by category), but the inner structure of the tables is not consistent with published SUTs or IOTs of individual countries due to necessary transformations in the course of the construction process (Dietzenbacher et al. 2013). This is problematic for our analysis as we want to keep the structure of our export-heterogeneous Belgian table as it is when integrating it into the WIOT. Edens et al. (2015) have developed a methodology for introducing a national table for the Netherlands into the WIOT without changing these national data: they replace the input data for the Netherlands with more detailed national data, which are actually a firm-level-data-based extension of the most detailed official national SUTs, and they replicate the construction process of the WIOT keeping data for the Netherlands constant. A similar methodology has been applied for Belgium for the years 1995–2007 in Hambÿe, Hertveldt, and Michel (2018). Here, we have opted for a shortcut compared to this thorough method: we directly integrate the Belgian IOT into the 2010 WIOT. This is less cumbersome than the method of Edens et al. (2015). As shown in Hambÿe, Hertveldt, and Michel (2018) for the years 1995–2007, the main difference between official national data and WIOT data for Belgium is in re-exports. This also holds true for the year 2010.

We start off by converting our Belgian IOT into dollars based on the exchange rate used in WIOD (1.3257$/€). As a second step, we use the Belgian firm-level data on exports and imports by partner country to distribute imports and exports in our national tables over countries of origin and destination. This includes determining the specific country distribution of exports and imports of export-oriented manufacturers. For the distribution of Belgian exports over use categories in the destination countries, we rely on data from WIOD on the use of imports from Belgium in these countries. In a third step, we replace all domestic transactions, imports and exports for Belgium in the WIOT by data based on our heterogeneous national IOT (including imports and exports distributed over countries and country-user pairs obtained in the previous step). Then, we adjust the data for all other countries in the WIOT with a RAS procedure. This yields a 2010 WIOT

11. There are 19 manufacturing industries among those 56 industries, which are identical to the 19 manufacturing industries in the A64 breakdown of the NACE Rev.2 of our national tables (see list in the appendix).

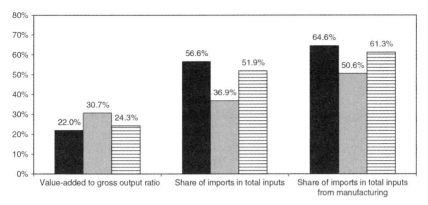

Figure 10.1   Direct production cost structures in manufacturing, heterogenous and standard IOT, 2010, percentages

entirely consistent with national data for Belgium—we also refer to this as the adapted WIOT—with a disaggregation of Belgian manufacturing industries into export-oriented firms and domestic market firms.

10.3   Export Heterogeneity in Input-Output Tables: Analysis

Input-output tables enable the analysis of production structures and value chains. With heterogeneous tables, this analysis can be specifically focused on certain types of firms. In this section, we first compare the direct cost structures of export-oriented and domestic market firms in Belgian manufacturing industries. Then, we proceed to the analysis of their integration into domestic value chains based on the national heterogeneous IOT and standard input-output models taking into account the full indirect cost structures. Finally, we use the GMRIO tables with export heterogeneity for Belgian manufacturing to look at the integration of export-oriented and domestic market firms into global value chains (GVC).

10.3.1   Differences in Direct Production Cost Structures

The IOT with exporter heterogeneity in table 10.8 reveals that export-oriented firms account for almost three-quarters of total output of manufacturing industries but only two-thirds of total manufacturing value added. In other words, export-oriented manufacturers have a lower value added to gross output ratio than manufacturing firms that mainly serve the domestic market (figure 10.1). Moreover, export-oriented manufacturing firms do not only purchase more intermediate inputs compared to their gross output, they also purchase proportionally more of their intermediate inputs from abroad.

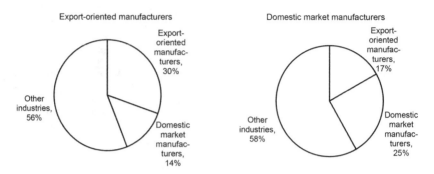

Figure 10.2   Origin of domestically sourced intermediate inputs of export-oriented and domestic market manufacturers, 2010, percentages

Indeed, as illustrated in figure 10.1, imports make for almost 57 percent of total intermediate inputs of export-oriented firms, while this share is just below 37 percent for firms mainly serving the domestic market. Hence, in line with prior findings in the literature on firm heterogeneity and international trade, export-oriented manufacturing firms in Belgium tend to rely more on imported intermediate inputs. Narrowing things down to inputs from manufacturing, this import share becomes 65 percent for export-oriented firms and 51 percent for firms that mainly serve the domestic market (figure 10.1). This corresponds to offshoring of manufactured goods as originally defined in Feenstra and Hanson (1996). Export-oriented manufacturing firms engage more into offshoring, which reflects the greater cross-border fragmentation of their production processes. Figure 10.1 also reports values for these three indicators (value added to gross output ratio, share of imports in total inputs and share of imports in total inputs from manufacturing) for the whole of manufacturing based on the standard IOT for 2010. They turn out to be closer to the values for export-oriented manufacturing firms due to the higher shares of this group of firms in the industry totals.

Based on the heterogeneous IOT and looking at intermediate input structures, figure 10.2 illustrates differences between export-oriented and domestic market manufacturers in terms of their purchases from domestic suppliers. More than half comes from other (service) industries for both groups. But domestic market firms purchase relatively more of their intermediate inputs from other domestic market firms, while export-oriented firms purchase relatively more from other export-oriented firms.

Finally, we also test for similarity of intermediate input structures at a more detailed level by calculating the correlation between technical coefficients of export-oriented and domestic market firms in each manufacturing industry. Technical coefficients are the result of a normalization of an industry's input structure by its output, i.e., they indicate the amount of the dif-

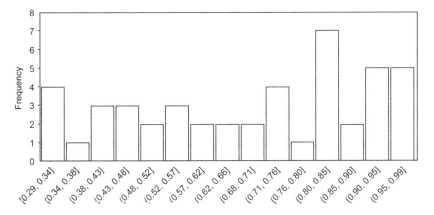

Figure 10.3   Distribution of the industry-level correlation between technical coefficients of export-oriented and domestic market manufacturers

ferent types of intermediate inputs required per unit of output. The average correlation between intermediate input structures of export-oriented and domestic market firms in the same industry is 0.707. This excludes industries for which we had to rely on proportionality when determining the respective product distributions of inputs for export-oriented and domestic market firms. The histogram in figure 10.3 shows the distribution of the correlation coefficients. Among industries for which the input structure is not split proportionally, Printing and Manufacture of motor vehicles have the highest correlation coefficients (0.99) and Manufacture of air and spacecraft and parts thereof and Manufacture of leather and related products the lowest (0.29), i.e., export-oriented and domestic market firms have very similar intermediate input structures in the former and relatively different ones in the latter.

10.3.2   Integration into Domestic Value Chains

Input-output analysis goes one step further by taking into account the (indirect) intermediate input requirements of suppliers. The underlying idea is to determine the effect of a final demand shock (domestic final demand or exports) on economy-wide output or value added. The final demand shock prompts a firm to expand the scale of its production process. The firm purchases more inputs from its suppliers, and, as a consequence, the firm's suppliers also produce more output, for which they purchase additional inputs from their suppliers. In turn, the suppliers' suppliers produce more output and purchase extra inputs, and so on. This gives rise to an upstream effect on output, i.e., through the increase in purchases of intermediate inputs. Standard input-output analysis models the effect of such a demand shock on the entire domestic production chain in terms of output, value added, and employment generated in the chain. Here, we focus on output and value added of export-oriented and domestic market firms.

In the input-output model, the total effect on output is measured by multiplying the shock by the Leontief inverse matrix. This accounts for the magnitude of the shock and all extra output generated in domestic supplying (upstream) industries. In a national IOT framework, the Leontief inverse matrix L^d, which is also called total domestic requirements matrix, is calculated as follows:

(1) $$L^d = (I - A^d)^{-1}$$

where A^d is an industry-by-industry matrix of domestic technical coefficients and I is an identity matrix of the same dimensions as A^d. For any industry, domestic technical coefficients represent the shares of inputs purchased from domestic supplying industries in its total output. The matrix A^d is calculated as $Z^d * \hat{y}^{-1}$ where Z^d is the matrix of domestically produced intermediate inputs and $\hat{y}$ a diagonalized vector of output by industry. Any element l_{ij}^d of the L^d-matrix represents domestic output by industry i generated (directly or indirectly) by a one-euro final demand shock for output of industry j. The sum over all i (producing industries) is called the output multiplier for industry j ($\sum_i l_{ij}^d$). It indicates how many extra euros of domestic output are generated (in all industries) through domestic intermediate input purchases by a one-euro increase in final demand for output of industry j. The output multiplier is an indicator of an industry's backward integration into a country's economy.[12]

Effects can also be calculated in terms of value added. Multiplying l_{ij}^d by industry i's value added in output share v_i yields the amount of value added generated in industry i by this shock to industry j's final demand. The value added multiplier corresponds to the sum over the producing industries ($\sum_i v_i l_{ij}^d$). It indicates how many extra euros of domestic value added are generated (in all industries) through intermediate input purchases by a one-euro increase in final demand for output of industry j.

Based on the 2010 heterogeneous national IOT for Belgium, we calculate output and value added multipliers for export-oriented and domestic market firms in manufacturing industries. Overall results are reported in figure 10.4, including those for total manufacturing based on the standard IOT. The average output multiplier is substantially higher for domestic market firms than for export-oriented firms, i.e., export-oriented manufacturers are less backward integrated into the Belgian economy. This finding reflects the international fragmentation of their production process. They use more intermediate inputs than domestic market manufacturers, but most of these

---

12. Note that, in this national framework, imported intermediate inputs are not taken into account, as they do not generate domestic output. Thus, industries that use relatively more domestically produced intermediate inputs tend to have higher output multipliers.

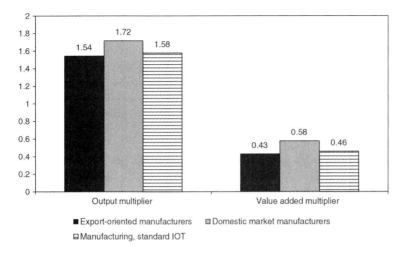

Figure 10.4   Output and value added multipliers in manufacturing, heterogenous and standard IOT, 2010. Millions of euros (per €1 million final demand shock)

inputs are imported, which implies that their (domestic) output multiplier is lower. The value added multiplier for domestic market manufacturers is also higher (0.58 against 0.43 for export-oriented manufacturers). Two underlying differences between export-oriented and domestic market manufacturers drive this result. First, a one-euro final demand shock to the output of export-oriented manufacturers generates less direct value added than an equivalent shock to the output of domestic market manufacturers since the value added in output share is lower for export-oriented manufacturers. Second, it also generates proportionally less output in domestic upstream industries and hence also less value added. The output and value added multipliers for manufacturing overall shown in figure 10.4 are closer to the multipliers for export-oriented firms. This is again due to the higher weight of export-oriented firms in manufacturing industries.

Figures 10.5 and 10.6 report output and value added multipliers by NACE Rev.2 A64 industry for export-oriented and domestic market manufacturers (see list in the appendix). The output multiplier of export-oriented manufacturers is lower for all but five manufacturing industries. Moreover, there is a large spread in the values of output multipliers: between 1.32 and 1.91 for domestic market firms, and between 1.26 and 1.83 for export-oriented firms. The value added multiplier is lower for export-oriented firms than for domestic market firms in all industries except for the pharmaceutical and the other transport equipment industries (codes 21 and 30).

Finally, in input-output analysis, an industry's integration into the domestic economy is considered not only in terms of its purchases of domestically produced intermediate inputs (upstream) but also in terms of its deliveries

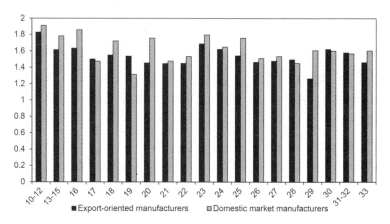

Figure 10.5   Output multipliers of export-oriented and domestic market manufacturers, by industry, 2010. Millions of euros (per €1 million final demand shock)

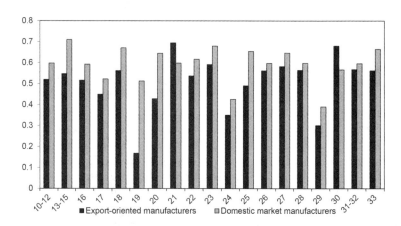

Figure 10.6   Value added multipliers of export-oriented and domestic market manufacturers, by industry, 2010. Millions of euros (per €1 million final demand shock)

of goods and services to other domestic (downstream) industries that use them as intermediates. The former is referred to as backward integration or backward linkages of an industry and, as mentioned above, can be measured by the output multiplier. The latter is referred to as forward integration or forward linkages of an industry. Their calculation is based on the Ghosh inverse matrix:

$$(2) \qquad G^d = (I - B^d)^{-1}$$

where $B^d = \hat{y}^{-1} * Z^d$ is a matrix containing the shares of the (domestic) purchasing industries in the output of the producing industry. Total forward linkages of industry i correspond to the sum of its row in the Ghosh inverse

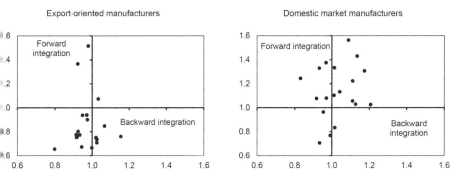

Figure 10.7   Forward and backward integration into the domestic economy, export-oriented and domestic market manufacturers, 2010

matrix ($\sum_j g_{ij}^d$) and measure how a value added shock to industry i (directly and indirectly) affects economy-wide output through the sales of industry i's output as intermediate inputs to other domestic industries. Hence, an industry with high total forward linkages "supplies a significant part of its output as intermediate inputs to other industries" (Miller and Temurshoev 2013, 9).

Our calculations of this forward linkage indicator show that it is generally much lower for export-oriented manufacturers than for domestic market manufacturers, i.e., forward integration into the domestic economy is higher for domestic market firms. Export-oriented firms deliver relatively less of their output to other domestic industries. However, exports may be used as intermediate inputs abroad. Hence, export-oriented firms are likely to be integrated forward into global value chains rather than domestic value chains. This cannot be identified based on a national IOT, which does not provide information on how exports are used in destination countries, but requires a GMRIO.

Integration of export-oriented and domestic market manufacturers into Belgian domestic value chains is summarized in the scatterplots of figure 10.7. Backward integration is shown on the horizontal axis and forward integration on the vertical axis. Both are normalized with respect to the average for all manufacturing industries. The scatterplot for manufacturing firms serving mainly the domestic market is skewed more toward the top and right, indicating a stronger integration into domestic value chains.

10.3.3   Foreign and Domestic Value Added in Exports

As production processes have become increasingly fragmented at the international level, a growing share of international trade is trade in intermediate goods and services (Miroudot, Lanz, and Ragoussis 2009). Moreover, greater fragmentation implies that many goods are shipped back and forth in the course of the production process before being delivered to final consumers. Due to multiple border crossings, gross export flows have increased faster than the underlying value added. These trends in international trade and production have prompted researchers to look at the domestic and foreign value added shares in a countries' exports (Hummels, Ishii, and Yi 2001; Koopman, Wang, and Wei 2014). The vertical specialization in trade (VS) share measure defined by Hummels, Ishii, and Yi represents "the value of imported inputs embodied in goods that are exported" (2001, 76–77) as a share of gross exports. It is a widely used indicator of the extent of the international fragmentation of production processes and reveals how much foreign value added is contained in a country's exports. The VS share is calculated as $i'A^m L^d e / i'e$ where A^m is the matrix of imported intermediate input coefficients, e the vector of gross exports and i a summation vector. Its complement is the domestic value added in exports (DVAX) share (Koopman, Wang, and Wei 2014), calculated as $v'L^d e / i'e$ where v is a vector of industry-level value added in output shares.[13] Belgium's VS share of exports computed with the standard 2010 IOT amounts to 43.7 percent. In manufacturing, Belgium's VS share stands at the much higher level of 55.2 percent.

As emphasized in Piacentini and Fortanier, "the use of homogeneous input-output tables . . . assumes that imported inputs are used evenly in production for domestic sales and exports. If domestic production is different from production for exports, i.e., the input-output structure of exporters is different from the one of non-exporters, then the measure based on standard (IOT) is biased. The direction of the bias is clear: as exporters make a more intensive use of intermediate imports than non-exporters, the standard measure under-estimates vertical specialization" (2015, 16). Based on our export heterogeneous IOT the overall VS share for Belgium amounts to 44.1 percent and for manufacturing to 56.0 percent.[14] Hence, the downward bias of computing the VS share with the standard table is rather small. Nonetheless, computing separate VS shares for export-oriented and domestic market firms reveals a large difference, which is indeed driven by the difference in the intensity in the use of imported intermediates. The VS share is 57.2 percent for export-oriented manufacturers and 45.1 percent for domestic market manufacturers.[15]

Three main factors have an influence on the VS share: (a) the share of exports in total output; (b) the value added to output ratio; and (c) the share of imports in total use of intermediate inputs (Piacentini and Fortanier 2015). By definition, export-oriented manufacturers have a higher share of exports in total output. But the other two factors also play a role. Export-oriented manufacturers have lower value added to output ratios, i.e., use

---

13. The term $i'A^m$ measures the foreign share of output. In the context of calculations with a national IOT, it is taken to measure foreign value added in output. This ignores potential feedback effects that can only be taken into account with a global table (see section 10.3.4).

14. Tables 10.10 and 10.11 give an overview of the VS shares that we have calculated.

15. Appendix figure 10A.1 reports industry-level VS shares for export-oriented and domestic market manufacturers.

Table 10.9   Domestic value added in exports for Belgium, 2010, millions of euros

Value added\exports	Export-oriented manufacturers	Domestic market manufacturers	Other industries	Total
Export-oriented manufacturers	25,992	248	603	26,843
Domestic market manufacturers	2,364	3,900	981	7,245
Other industries	17,069	2,368	56,340	75,776
Total	45,425	6,515	57,923	109,863
Gross exports	106,175	11,862	78,483	196,520

proportionally more intermediates in their production process, and they rely to a larger extent on imports when sourcing these intermediates.[16]

As mentioned above, the complement of the VS share is the domestic value added in exports (DVAX) share. Total domestic value added generated in Belgium in 2010 by exports amounts to €109.9 billion, which corresponds to 55.9 percent of Belgium's total gross exports (€196.5 billion). We use the heterogenous IOT to specifically decompose the domestic (Belgian) value added embodied in exports by industry and firm types. Results are reported in table 10.9 with value added by types of firms in the rows and exports by types of firms in the columns. As an example of how to read this table, take the cell corresponding to the second row in the first column: it contains the value added of domestic market manufacturers generated by exports of export-oriented manufacturers. The table reveals several interesting results. First, the exports of export-oriented manufacturers generate a total domestic value added of €45.4 billion, of which more than half is value added of this group of firms. But their exports also generate a substantial amount of value added in the rest of the Belgian economy: €17.1 billion in other industries, which are mainly service industries, and €2.4 billion for domestic market firms in manufacturing industries. Hence, Belgian service industries do actually participate in GVCs through their deliveries to export-oriented manufacturers. Second, the exports of domestic market manufacturers and firms in the other industries generate only very little value added for export-oriented manufacturers. Again, this is related to the lesser integration of export-oriented manufacturers into the domestic economy. Third, the exports of the other industries, mostly service exports, generate comparatively less value added in manufacturing (for both export-oriented and domestic market firms). Two characteristics of service industries contribute to this finding: they have a higher value added to output ratio, and services make for a larger share of the intermediates they purchase. The comparison of column and row totals of table 10.9 shows, for export-oriented manufacturers, that the value added generated in Belgium by their exports (45.4) is much higher than their value added due to total Belgian exports (26.8).

16. See figures 10A.2 and 10A.3 in the appendix.

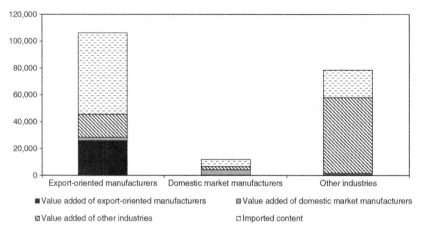

Figure 10.8   Source of content in gross exports by industry and firm type, 2010 (millions of euros)

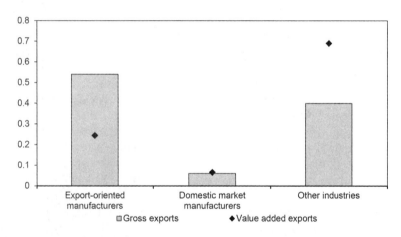

Figure 10.9   Shares in domestic value added in exports and in gross exports by firm type, 2010, percentages

The opposite holds for domestic market manufacturers and firms in other industries. Adding the imported content of exports, figure 10.8 sums up the sources of content in gross exports by types of firms.

Figure 10.9 provides a comparison of shares in gross exports and in domestic value added in exports and reveals striking differences between groups of firms. Export-oriented manufacturers account for more than half of Belgium's total gross exports (54 percent) but only for a quarter of domestic value added generated by exports (24 percent). Most of domestic value added in exports is generated in other industries, i.e., service industries (69 percent), while the share of these industries in gross exports is only 40 percent. For domestic market manufacturers, shares in gross exports and domestic value added in exports are similar and low.[17]

10.3.4 Integration into Global Value Chains

Incorporating the Belgian export-heterogeneous IOT into the 2010 WIOT allows us to look at how Belgian export-oriented and domestic market manufacturers are integrated into and positioned within global value chains. Such an analysis relies on a multiregional input-output model. In essence, the multiregional model works the same way as the national model, but the scope of the effects is extended: the multiregional model takes into account not only purchases and sales of domestically produced intermediates but also purchases of intermediate inputs from abroad as well as deliveries to foreign intermediate and final demand. In the standard Leontief model, all upstream effects are captured by the elements of the multiregional Leontief inverse matrix L_{MRIO}, which is calculated based on the multiregional matrix of technical coefficients A_{MRIO}:

$$(3) \qquad L_{MRIO} = (I - A_{MRIO})^{-1}$$

Any element in this matrix represents the output of a country-industry pair that is generated by a one-dollar[18] final demand shock to output of another country-industry pair. In this multiregional setup, a final demand shock to the output of an industry in a country gives rise to domestic effects and effects in other countries through imports of intermediates (spillover effects). Moreover, it may lead to feedback effects for the country when the industry purchases intermediate inputs from foreign suppliers and these foreign suppliers, in turn, purchase intermediate inputs from the country where the shock has occurred.

10.3.4.1 Vertical Specialization

In a multiregional setting, the VS share is a measure of backward integration into GVCs. Its computation is based on the VBE industry-country by industry-country matrix of value added embodied in exports.

$$(4) \qquad VBE = \hat{v}_{MRIO} * L_{MRIO} * \hat{e}_{MRIO}$$

Here, $\hat{v}_{MRIO}$ is a diagonalized vector of value added in output shares and $\hat{e}_{MRIO}$ a diagonalized vector of gross exports for all country-industry pairs con-

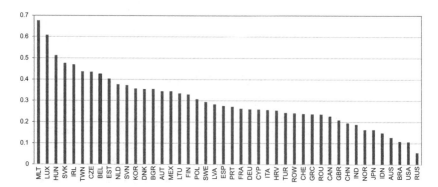

Figure 10.10   Vertical specialization shares (imported content of exports as a share of gross exports), 2010

tained in the GMRIO table. The VBE matrix can be divided into a domestic part VBE^d (on the block diagonal) and a foreign part VBE^{nd} (off the block diagonal). The column sum of the domestic part yields domestic value added in exports by country-industry pair ($i' * VBE^d$) and the column sum of the foreign part yields foreign value added in exports by country-industry pair ($i' * VBE^{nd}$). By summing over industries for each country and dividing by country-level gross exports, we obtain country-level DVAX and VS shares.

A comparison of VS shares for all 43 countries in the adapted WIOT reveals that Belgium is among the countries with the highest shares, i.e., it is highly backward integrated into GVCs. This is illustrated in figure 10.10. As reported earlier, Belgium's VS share stands at 43.7 percent based on the standard (homogeneous) national IOT and at 44.1 percent based on the heterogeneous national IOT. When recalculating VS shares with the adapted 2010 WIOT, i.e., into which we have integrated our national IOT for Belgium, we obtain a VS share of 43.2 percent without export heterogeneity and of 43.7 percent with export heterogeneity.[19] Table 10.10 summarizes VS share results from different types of tables. In our setting where data for Belgium in the GMRIO tables are entirely consistent with the national IOT, VS shares based on multiregional tables are by definition lower than VS shares based on national tables. This is due to the feedback effects in the multiregional model, which increase the domestic value added in exports and hence reduce the VS share.[20] In practice, the difference between VS shares based on multiregional tables and VS shares based on national tables

19. Belgium's VS share calculated with the original 2010 WIOT amounts to 42.7 percent. Note also that Los (2017) reports a VS share of 46 percent for Belgium based on the 2011 WIOT.
20. The consistency of Belgian data in the adapted WIOT with data from the national IOT for Belgium implies that industry-level value added coefficients and gross exports for Belgium are identical in both tables. Hence, differences in national IOT-based and WIOT-based DVAX shares (and also VS shares) originate from differences between L^d and the Belgian domestic part of L_{MRIO}. As the national setting cannot account for feedback effects, the elements of L^d are always smaller than the elements of the Belgian domestic part of L_{MRIO} (see Round 2001, and

Table 10.10   Differences in vertical specialization shares for Belgium between national tables and WIOT, 2010, percentages

	Total economy		Manufacturing industries	
	National IOT	WIOT	National IOT	WIOT
Heterogeneous tables	44.1	43.7	56.0	55.5
Homogeneous tables	43.7	43.2	55.2	54.7

Table 10.11   Differences in vertical specialization shares for Belgium between national tables and WIOT by firm type, 2010, percentages

	National IOT	WIOT
Export-oriented firms	57.2	56.7
Domestic market firms	45.1	44.6

is small because feedback effects are small. Table 10.10 also highlights again that the downward bias due to the use of standard rather than heterogeneous tables is rather small. But export-oriented and domestic market manufacturers have very different VS shares as illustrated in table 10.11.

10.3.4.2   Global Value Chain Participation

The VS share indicates how a country's firms participate backward in GVCs, i.e., through purchases of intermediates from abroad for producing exports. But they may also participate in GVCs by exporting intermediate inputs that are then used (directly and indirectly) in the production of third country exports. This alternative way of participating in GVCs was already identified in Hummels, Ishii, and Yi (2001). These authors suggested measuring such forward integration into GVCs by the VS1 share. In their definition, it is calculated as the value of a country's exports embodied in foreign countries' exports divided by the country's gross exports.[21] In our setup, a country-industry pair's exports embodied in third country exports corresponds to the row sum of the foreign part (off the block diagonal) of the VBE matrix ($VBE^{nd} * i$). A country's VS1 share is then obtained by summing over all industries for that country and dividing by the country's gross exports.[22]

Both VS and VS1 shares for a country depend on its average position

---

Koopman et al., 2010). Therefore, Belgium's national IOT-based DVAX share is smaller than its WIOT-based DVAX share, and the opposite holds for Belgium's VS share (see table 10.10).

21. Computing this VS1 share requires information about the use of exports in the destination country, which is only available in GMRIO tables. Hence, it cannot be done with national IOT. This is why Hummels, Ishii, and Yi (2001) were not able to compute the VS1 share they had defined.

22. There is a slight methodological difference between the forward linkages that we have calculated with the national IOT and the forward integration into GVCs that we calculate with

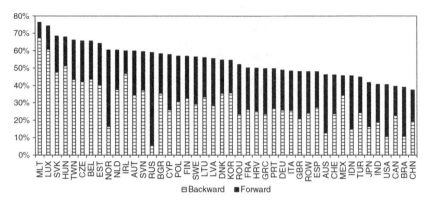

Figure 10.11   Global value chain participation index, 2010, shares in gross exports

in GVCs: countries with a greater share of downstream activities tend to have higher VS shares and lower VS1 shares, and vice-versa for countries with more upstream activities. For a more comprehensive assessment of countries' participation in GVCs, Koopman et al. (2010) define the *GVC participation index* that sums the VS and VS1 measures and is normalized by total country-level exports.[23]

Figure 10.11 shows a comparison of the GVC participation index for all countries in the 2010 WIOT with a split into the contributions of backward and forward integration. Again, Belgium is among the countries with the highest values for this index, i.e., Belgium is highly integrated into global value chains, both backward and forward. This result is in line with the results reported by De Backer and Miroudot (2014) based on data from the OECD's 2009 intercountry input-output (ICIO) table. Forward participation is especially high for countries producing raw materials such as Australia, Norway, and Russia. As a consequence, these countries are higher ranked in terms of GVC participation than in terms of the VS share. Overall, country size does seem to matter for these indicators, with smaller countries having a higher GVC participation index on average.

The integration of the export-heterogeneous IOT for Belgium into the 2010 WIOT allows us to determine contributions of export-oriented manufacturers, domestic market manufacturers, and other industries to Belgium's participation in global value chains as shown in figure 10.12. The third

---

the adapted WIOT: the former is based on a Ghosh inverse matrix, while the latter is based on a (multiregional) Leontief inverse matrix.

23. De Backer and Miroudot highlight an issue of double counting for the GVC participation index: "[a]s domestically produced inputs can incorporate some of the foreign inputs, there is an overlap and potentially some double counting. . . . Likewise, some foreign inputs can incorporate domestic value added exported in an earlier stage of the value chain" (2014, 10).

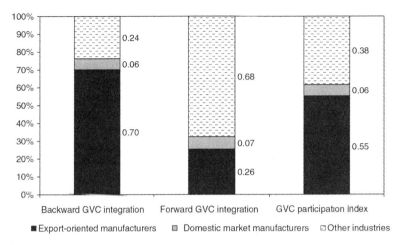

Figure 10.12   Contributions to Belgium's global value chain participation, 2010, shares in total

stacked bar in the figure indicates that Belgium's participation in GVCs is due for 55 percent to export-oriented manufacturing firms, for 38 percent to the firms in other industries and for the remaining 6 percent to domestic market manufacturing firms. The first and second stacked bars illustrate the difference in how export-oriented manufacturers and firms in other industries participate in GVCs. There is a clear distribution of the roles: export-oriented manufacturers essentially participate in GVCs through their purchases of imported intermediate inputs for producing exports (backward integration), while firms in other industries participate in GVCs mainly through exports of intermediates for export production abroad (forward integration).

10.3.4.3   *Position in Global Value Chains*

The set of GVC indicators is completed by two measures of the position of an industry or country in global value chains: the *number of embodied production stages* and the *distance to final demand*. For any industry in a country, the former indicates the average number of production stages up to the point where the industry's production activity takes place, while the latter indicates the average number of production stages until its output becomes embodied in a good or service delivered to final demand. These indicators of position are complementary with respect to vertical specialization and GVC participation, which measure how value chains are fragmented in terms of value added contributions. Our main aim is to compare Belgian export-oriented and domestic market manufacturers in terms of value chain position based on these two indicators. Accounting for export heterogeneity in manufacturing does not significantly alter overall results for Belgium for these position indicators.[24]

The number of embodied production stages indicator was initially proposed in Fally (2012). Its original definition is recursive based on a weighted count of the number of embodied intermediates, i.e., it is a measure of the length of the input chain of an industry's production.[25] It can be shown that the calculation boils down to computing the industry's total backward linkages (Miller and Temurshoev 2013).[26] Thus, with a GMRIO table, it is computed as $(i' * L_{MRIO})$. If the production of an industry does not require intermediate inputs, then the indicator is equal to one. Its value then increases with the number of intermediate inputs used in an industry's production process and their importance in that process (share of intermediates in output). The use of GMRIO tables for calculating the measure allows us to distinguish between the domestic and foreign embodied production stages. In terms of interpretation, De Backer and Miroudot (2014) emphasize that with plant-level information the indicator would represent the actual number of production stages. Given the relatively high level of aggregation of industries in GMRIO tables, and in the WIOT in particular, the indicator calculated with such tables should rather be interpreted as an ordinal measure for comparing countries or industries.

Averaging over industries with output weights, we find a slightly higher number of embodied production stages for export-oriented manufacturers (2.89) than for domestic market manufacturers (2.72) as shown in table 10.12. This also holds for most individual manufacturing industries (figure 10.13) and is consistent with our earlier finding that export-oriented manufacturers purchase more intermediates per unit of output, i.e., outsource more. Moreover, export-oriented manufacturers have, on average, more foreign embodied production stages than domestic market manufacturers (1.33 against 0.99) and less domestic embodied production stages (1.56 against 1.73) as could be expected based on their respective import shares. Figure 10.13 shows that this is also the case for almost all individual manufacturing industries. Finally, the number of embodied production stages of the other industries (mostly services) is lower (2.07), and most of their embodied pro-

24. Computing the number of embodied production stages and the distance to final demand for Belgium with the homogeneous or heterogeneous adapted WIOT makes for a difference of 0.1 percent or less. Values for these position indicators based on the original WIOT differ by approximately 2 percent from values based on the adapted WIOT.
25. The measure is sometimes also referred to as "value chain length" (De Backer and Miroudot 2014), but it should be kept in mind that it is a purely backward-looking indicator, i.e., of the length of the input chain up to the industry's production, and not of the entire value chain up to final demand. Miller and Temurshoev (2013) have independently developed the equivalent measure of "input downstreamness." In an earlier contribution, Dietzenbacher and Romero (2007) proposed the more complex "average propagation length" measure.
26. This is true because "the distance between any two stages of production is assumed to be one" (Miller and Temurshoev 2013, 10).

Table 10.12   **Embodied production stages and distance to final demand for Belgium by industry and firm type, 2010**

	Embodied production stages			Distance to final demand		
	Total	Domestic	Foreign	Total	Domestic	Foreign
Export-oriented manufacturers	2.89	1.56	1.33	2.66	1.33	1.33
Domestic market manufacturers	2.72	1.73	0.99	2.50	1.85	0.65
Other firms	2.07	1.60	0.47	2.12	1.65	0.47
Belgium	2.28	1.60	0.68	2.25	1.60	0.65

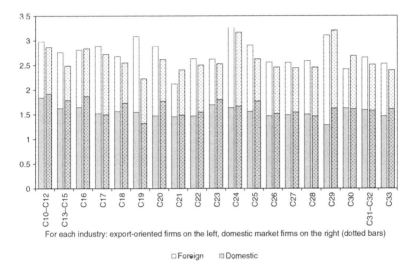

Figure 10.13   Number of embodied production stages of export-oriented and domestic market manufacturers, by industry, 2010

duction stages are domestic (1.60 against 0.47 for the foreign ones). In terms of country ranking, figure 10.14 shows that, in international comparison, Belgium has an above average number of embodied production stages.

The distance to final demand indicator was originally suggested by Fally (2012) and Antràs et al. (2012).[27] It is the forward-looking complement of the number of embodied production stages indicator. Its calculation is a weighted count of the number of production stages until an industry's output (initially often sold for intermediate consumption) becomes embodied in a good or service delivered to final demand. It turns out that it is equivalent to an industry's total forward linkages (Miller and Temurshoev 2013).

27. Note that it has also been referred to as an indicator of "upstreamness" by these authors and as "output upstreamness" by Miller and Temurshoev (2013).

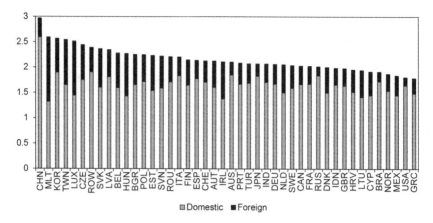

Figure 10.14   Average number of embodied production stages, 2010

In a GMRIO setup, it is thus calculated for any industry by taking the row sum of the multiregional Ghosh inverse matrix ($G_{MRIO} * i$ where $G_{MRIO} = (I - B_{MRIO})^{-1}$). The indicator takes a value of 1 if all of an industry's output is delivered to final demand, and it increases with the share of the industry's output that is delivered to other industries (i.e., intermediate demand) and with the number of production stages (i.e., industries) involved until the output becomes embodied in a good or service delivered to final demand. Industries with a higher distance value are also said to be more upstream and industries with a lower value are said to be more downstream.[28] Again, values should be interpreted as ordinal, i.e., for comparing countries or industries. Moreover, the use of GMRIO tables allows for a distinction between a domestic distance to final demand and a foreign distance to final demand.

According to our results with industry distance values aggregated with output weights, manufacturing industries in Belgium are on average more upstream with a distance value of 2.62 against 2.12 for the other—mainly service—industries. This is consistent with the idea that, for example, basic metal products are transformed in a greater number of production stages before reaching final customers than personal services. Within manufacturing, export-oriented firms have a slightly higher distance to final demand than domestic market firms (2.66 against 2.50, see table 10.12). For the former, the domestic and foreign distance are identical (1.33), while for the

28. As a caveat, Los (2017) points out that "the upstreamness of an industry (defined at a relatively aggregated level as in most global IO databases) can vary substantially across countries, due to the fact that an industry in a country can be specialized in the production of components, while the same industry in a different country can be specialized in assembly activities (which are downstream). . . . The apparently rather different activities carried out in these industries show that international fragmentation of production processes makes comparisons of industries with identical labels or codes increasingly difficult" (307).

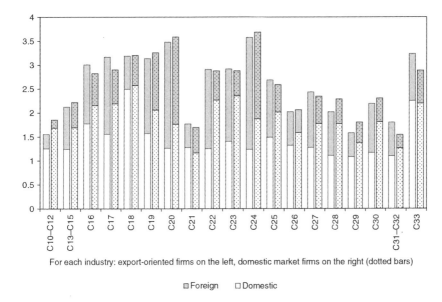

For each industry: export-oriented firms on the left, domestic market firms on the right (dotted bars)

□ Foreign   □ Domestic

Figure 10.15   Distance to final demand of export-oriented and domestic market manufacturers, by industry, 2010

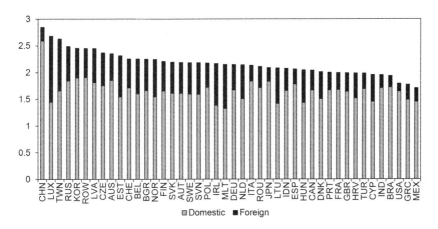

□ Domestic   ■ Foreign

Figure 10.16   Average distance to final demand, 2010

latter domestic distance dominates (1.85 against 0.65). Figure 10.15 shows a large spread in distance to final demand across manufacturing industries in Belgium but only small differences between export-oriented and domestic market firms. Finally, in terms of the country ranking for distance to final demand, Belgium is slightly more specialized in upstream activities than the world average (distance value of 2.25 against 2.20, see figure 10.16).

10.4. Conclusions

The disaggregation of industries in SUTs and IOTs according to exporter status is considered as highly desirable, since it may actually reveal technological differences between firms within an industry defined in terms of product similarity (OECD 2015; Los 2017). In this chapter, we describe the statistical methodology for obtaining export-heterogeneous SUTs and IOT for Belgium for 2010 and their integration into a GMRIO table, and we present results from analyses based on these tables.

From a statistical point of view, our data-based split of manufacturing industries into export-oriented and domestic market firms represents a clear improvement with respect to the proportionality assumptions that most prior contributions in this field have relied on. This is true in particular for the product structures of output and intermediate inputs of these two types of firms. Our work also illustrates a statistical limitation in this respect: for a small country like Belgium, sample sizes may prove insufficient at the most detailed industry level for such a data-based split of output and input structures. In our case, we faced a trade-off between including minor exporters in the category of export-oriented firms and avoiding proportionality in the estimation of product distributions for heterogeneous industries. Although this may be less of an issue for larger countries, it represents a serious constraint for combined disaggregations of SUTs and IOTs, e.g., for firm size and ownership.

The analyses based on the resulting national export-heterogeneous IOT reveal differences between export-oriented and domestic market firms in manufacturing industries in terms of input structures and import patterns. Export-oriented manufacturers have lower value added in output shares, and they import proportionally more of the intermediates they use, i.e., their production processes are more fragmented, in particular internationally. These results, obtained in a setting that is consistent with the national accounts, confirm findings in prior analyses on firm heterogeneity in international trade (Melitz 2003; Bas 2009). Furthermore, our input-output analyses show that export-oriented manufacturing firms are less integrated upstream and downstream into the Belgian economy than domestic market firms, and that the exports of export-oriented manufacturers generate a substantial amount of value added in other Belgian firms, in particular providers of services.

With the heterogeneous Belgian table incorporated into the WIOT, we obtain further insights on the roles of the different types of firms in Belgium's integration into global value chains. Export-oriented manufacturers are the drivers of Belgium's backward GVC participation, i.e., through imports of intermediates for export-production, while the other firms push Belgium's forward GVC participation, i.e., by producing intermediates for other countries' exports. Moreover, export-oriented manufacturers participate in value chains that comprise, on average, a greater number of upstream and downstream production stages and of which a greater share is located abroad.

The value chain analysis based on the heterogeneous IOT highlights that the external competitiveness of Belgian manufacturing depends not only on export-oriented manufacturing firms but also on manufacturing firms that mainly serve the domestic market and supplier firms in service industries. Export-oriented manufacturers need to be competitive on foreign markets and domestic suppliers have to be competitive in the production of the inputs delivered to those export-oriented firms (internal competitiveness). Hence, it is not sufficient to focus only on export-oriented firms. They are the spearhead of participation in GVCs, but domestic upstream suppliers must also be taken into account. Overall, for Belgium to reap the full benefits from exports, the entire value chains must be considered.

Appendix

Table 10A.1   **Manufacturing industries in the A64 breakdown of the NACE Rev.2 classification**

10–12	Manufacture of food products, beverages and tobacco products
13–15	Manufacture of textiles, wearing apparel and leather products
16	Manufacture of wood and of products of wood and cork, except furniture
17	Manufacture of paper and paper products
18	Printing and reproduction of recorded media
19	Manufacture of coke and refined petroleum products
20	Chemical industry
21	Manufacture of pharmaceutical products
22	Manufacture of rubber and plastic products
23	Manufacture of other non-metallic mineral products
24	Manufacture of basic metals
25	Manufacture of fabricated metal products, except machinery and equipment
26	Manufacture of computer, electronic and optical products
27	Manufacture of electrical equipment
28	Manufacture of machinery and equipment n.e.c.
29	Manufacture of motor vehicles, trailers and semi-trailers
30	Manufacture of other transport equipment
31–32	Manufacture of furniture; Other manufacturing
33	Repair and installation of machinery and equipment

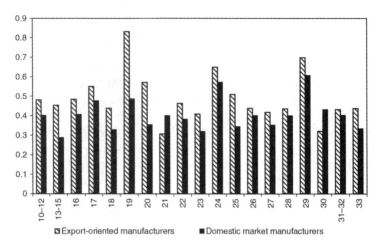

Figure 10A.1   Imported content of exports as a share of gross exports (VS share), export-oriented and domestic market manufacturers, by industry, 2010

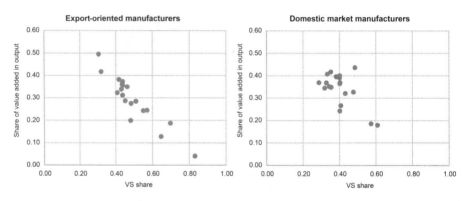

Figure 10A.2   VS share and value added to output ratio, export-oriented and domestic market manufacturers, 2010

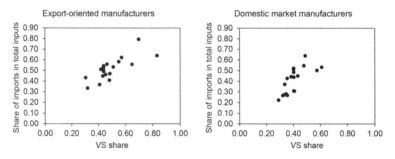

Figure 10A.3   VS share and share of imports in total inputs, export-oriented and domestic market manufacturers, 2010

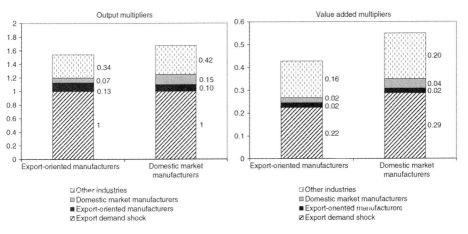

Figure 10A.4   Output and value added multipliers of a €1 million export shock, 2010 (millions of euros)

References

Ahmad N., S. Araújo, A. Lo Turco, and D. Maggioni. 2013. "Using Trade Microdata to Improve Trade in Value-Added Measures: Proof of Concept Using Turkish Data." In *Trade in Value Added: Developing New Measures of Cross-Border Trade*, edited by A. Mattoo, Z. Wang, and S.-J. Wei, 187–220. World Bank.

Antràs, P., D. Chor, T. Fally, and R. Hillberry. 2012. "Measuring the Upstreamness of Production and Trade Flows." *American Economic Review* 102 (3): 412–16.

Bas, M. 2009. "Trade, Foreign Inputs and Firms' Decisions: Theory and Evidence." CEPII Working Paper N°2009–35, December.

Beutel, J. 2017. "The Supply and Use Framework of National Accounts." In *Handbook of Input-Output Analysis*, edited by T. Ten Raa. Cheltenham: Edward Elgar.

Cadestin, C., K. De Backer, I. Desnoyers-James, S. Miroudot, D. Rigo, and M. Ye. 2018. "Multinational Enterprises and Global Value Chains: The OECD Analytical AMNE Database." OECD Trade Policy Papers, No. 211. Paris; OECD Publishing.

Chong, S., R. Hooekstra, O. Lemmers, I. Van Beveren, M. Van den Berg, R. Van Der Wal, and P. Verbiest. 2017. "The Role of Small and Medium Enterprises in the Dutch Economy: An Analysis Using an Extended Supply and Use Table." Unpublished, transmitted by the authors.

De la Cruz, J., R. Koopman, Z. Wang, and S.-J. Wei. 2011. "Estimating Foreign Value-Added in Mexico's Manufacturing Exports." Office of Economics Working Paper N° 2011–04A, US International Trade Commission.

De Backer, K., and S. Miroudot. 2014. "Mapping Global Value Chains." European Central Bank Working Paper n° 1677. Frankfurt.

Dietzenbacher, E., and I. Romero. 2007. "Production chains in an interregional framework: Identification by means of average propagation lengths." *International Regional Science Review* 30 (4): 362–83.

Dietzenbacher E., B. Los, R. Stehrer, M. Timmer, and G. de Vries. 2013. "The Construction of World Input-Output Tables in the WIOD Project." *Economic Systems Research* 25 (1): 71–98.

Edens B., R. Hoekstra, D. Zult, O. Lemmers, H. Wilting, and R. Wu. 2015. "A method to create carbon footprint estimates consistent with national accounts." *Economic Systems Research* 27 (4): 440–57.

Eurostat. 2008. Eurostat Manual of Supply, Use and Input-Output Tables. Luxembourg.

Fally, T. 2012. "Production staging: Measurement and facts." Discussion Paper, University of Colorado-Boulder.

Feenstra, R., and G. Hanson. 1996. "Globalisation, Outsourcing, and Wage Inequality." *American Economic Review* 86 (2): 240–45.

FPB. 2015. "Tableaux Entrées-Sorties 2010." Federal Planning Bureau. Brussels.

Fetzer, J. J., T. Highfill, K. Hossiso, T. F. Howells III, E. H. Strassner, and J. A. Young. 2018. "Accounting for Firm Heterogeneity within U.S. Industries: Extended Supply-Use Tables and Trade in Value Added using Enterprise and Establishment Level Data." Paper presented at the CRIW Conference on the Challenges of Globalization in the Measurement of National Accounts, Bethesda, MD, March 9–10.

Hambÿe, C. 2012. "Analyse entrées-sorties: modèles, multiplicateurs, linkages." Working Paper 12–12, September. Bureau fédéral du Plan.

Hambÿe, C., B. Hertveldt, and B. Michel. 2018. "Does consistency with detailed national data matter for calculating carbon footprints with global multi-regional input–output tables? A comparative analysis for Belgium based on a structural decomposition." *Journal of Economic Structures* 7 (11) https://doi.org/10.1186/s40008-018-0110-6.

Hummels, D., J. Ishii, and K.-M. Yi. 2001. "The nature and growth of vertical specialization in world trade." *Journal of International Economics* 54: 75–96.

Inomata, S. 2017. "Analytical frameworks for global value chains: An overview." In *Global Value Chain Development Report 2017: Measuring and analyzing the impact of GVCs on economic development*. International Bank for Reconstruction and Development/The World Bank.

Johnson, R. C., and G. Noguera. 2012. "Fragmentation and Trade in Value Added Over Four Decades." NBER Working Paper No. 18186. Cambridge, MA: National Bureau of Economic Research.

Koopman, R., W. Powers, Z. Wang, and S.-J. Wei. 2010. "Give credit where credit is due: Tracing value added in global production chains." NBER Working Paper No. 16426. Cambridge, MA: National Bureau of Economic Research.

Koopman, R., Z. Wang, and S.-J. Wei. 2012. "Estimating domestic content in exports when processing trade is pervasive." *Journal of Development Economics* 99: 178–89.

Koopman, R., Z. Wang, and S.-J. Wei. 2014. "Tracing Value added and Double Counting in Gross Exports." *American Economic Review* 104 (2): 459–94.

Lais, K., and E. Kolleritsch. 2017. "OECD Expert Group on Extended SUTs: Final Report Austria." Unpublished, transmitted by the authors.

Los, B. 2017. "Input-output analysis of international trade." In *Handbook of Input-Output Analysis*, edited by T. Ten Raa. Cheltenham: Edward Elgar.

Ma, H., Z. Wang, and K. Zhu. 2015. "Domestic content in China's exports and its distribution by firm ownership." *Journal of Comparative Economics* 43: 3–18.

Melitz, M. J. 2003. "The Impact of Trade on Intra-Industry Reallocations and Aggregate Industry Productivity." *Econometrica* 71 (6): 1695–1725.

Miller, R. E., and P. D. Blair. 2009. *Input-output analysis: foundations and extensions*, second edition. Cambridge: Cambridge University Press.

Miller, R. E., and U. Temurshoev. 2013. "Output upstreamness and input downstreamness of industries/countries in world production." GCDC Working Papers, Vol. GD-133. University of Groningen.

Miroudot, S., R. Lanz, and A. Ragoussis. 2009. "Trade in Intermediate Goods and Services." OECD Trade Policy Working Paper, no. 93. Paris: OECD.

OECD. 2015. Terms of Reference, Expert Group on Extended Supply and Use Tables. Paris.

Piacentini, M., and F. Fortanier. 2015. "Firm heterogeneity and trade in value added." STD/CSSP/WPTGS(2015)231. OECD Publishing.

Round, J. 2001. "Feedback Effects in Interregional Input-Output Models: What have we learned?" In *Input-Output Analysis: Frontiers and Extensions*, edited by M. Lahr and E. Dietzenbacher, 54–70. New York: Palgrave Macmillan.

Saborío, G. 2015. "Costa Rica: An Extended Supply-Use Table." Paper prepared for 23rd IIOA Conference, Mexico City.

Timmer, M. P., E. Dietzenbacher, B. Los, R. Stehrer, and G. J. de Vries. 2015. "An Illustrated User Guide to the World Input–Output Database: The Case of Global Automotive Production." *Review of International Economics* 23: 575–605.

Timmer, M. P., B. Los, R. Stehrer, and G. J. de Vries. 2016. "An Anatomy of the Global Trade Slowdown based on the WIOD 2016 Release." GGDC research memorandum number 162. University of Groningen.

Yamano, N., and C. Webb. 2018. "Future Development of the Inter-Country Input-Output (ICIO) Database for Global Value Chain (GVC) and Environmental Analyses." *Journal of Industrial Ecology* 22 (3): 487–88.

Measuring Bilateral Exports
of Value Added
A Unified Framework

Bart Los and Marcel P. Timmer

11.1 Introduction

Which countries are most important in demanding value added of a country? This is a pressing question for policy makers seeking for example to (re)negotiate trade agreements or assessing the domestic consequences of foreign demand shocks. If trade in intermediate products would be absent, the answer to this question would be simple and could be derived from bilateral gross export statistics. However, with international fragmentation of production processes, trade flows need to be measured in value added terms as countries will be exporting and importing intermediates (Hummels, Ishii, and Yi 2001).[1] The main aim of this chapter is to offer an integrated discussion on measures of value added in *bilateral* trade flows. We provide a unified framework based on an application of the hypothetical extraction method in global input-output tables, along the lines of Los, Timmer, and

Bart Los is professor of Economics of Technological Progress and Structural Change at the University of Groningen, and a member of the Groningen Growth and Development Centre.

Marcel P. Timmer is professor of Economic Growth and Development at the University of Groningen, and a member of the Groningen Growth and Development Centre.

Financial support from the UK Economic Statistics Centre of Excellence (ESCoE) for Bart Los and from the Dutch Science Foundation (NWO) for Marcel Timmer (grant number 453–14–012) is gratefully acknowledged. The authors thank Wen Chen for research assistance. They also thank Robert Johnson, Helena Loiola, and participants at the NBER-CRIW Conference on The Challenges of Globalization in the Measurement of National Accounts, (March 9–10, 2018, Washington DC, USA) and the 26th International Input-Output Conference (June 25–29, 2018, Juiz de Fora, Brazil) for useful comments. For acknowledgments, sources of research support, and disclosure of the authors' material financial relationships, if any, please see https://www.nber.org/books-and-chapters/challenges-globalization-measurement-national-accounts/measuring-bilateral-exports-value-added-unified-framework.

1. Trade in value added measurement has quickly expanded and broadened into a wider set of so-called global value chain (GVC) measures. See Johnson (2017) for a general overview. By now, these statistics are part of the toolkit for trade policy analysis. For example, they are published on a regular basis by the OECD/WTO Trade in value added (TiVA) initiative and in the WITS (World Integrated Trade Solution) database.

de Vries (2016). We believe that this is helpful in cleaning up terminology, standardizing concepts, and more generally providing clear guidelines about which measure to use for what type of questions.

In particular, we show that the bilateral trade measures introduced by Johnson and Noguera (2012) (value added consumed abroad) and Los, Timmer, and de Vries (2016) (value added in exports) are special cases of a general class of VAX measures. We will therefore refer to these as VAX-C and VAX-D, respectively. In addition we suggest a novel third measure, VAX-P, which indicates the value added used abroad in the final stage of production. This is another relevant measure as it is at this final stage where demand shocks are transmitted to production and associated intermediates trade flows, as in Bems, Johnson, and Yi (2011, 2013). As for VAX-C, there can be flows of VAX-P between pairs of countries that do not directly trade with each other.

We show that all VAX measures can be derived with the method of hypothetical extraction in a general input-output model. In addition, the framework will also help to elucidate the relationship between aggregate and bilateral measures.[2] This is important as currently there are two alternative definitions of bilateral VAX-D: one suggested by Los, Timmer, and de Vries (2016) and another by Wang, Wei, and Zhu (2018). We will argue that the first is more suitable for trade analysis as it does not impose that the sum of VAX-D to all destinations is equal to VAX-D in aggregate exports. We show that the difference is small empirically (at current levels of international fragmentation of production processes) but outline the fundamental conceptual difference which potentially can cause major confusion for users.

The remainder of the chapter is organized as follows. We will lay out concepts and terminology through some simple examples in section 11.2. This is to develop intuition. The actual computational formulas are given in section 11.3. Empirical examples for a few large countries based on data from the World Input-Output Database are discussed in section 11.4.[3] Section 11.5 defends our choice for a bilateral VAX-D measure. Section 11.6 concludes.

11.2 Concepts and Terminology

In this section we will lay out our concepts and terminology, and illustrate these with an example of a simple sequential production chain (a "snake"). The general insights do not depend on the example, however, and as shown

---

2. We use the term *aggregate exports* to refer to the total exports of a country, irrespective of the partner country. This is to be distinguished from *bilateral exports* that are for a specific destination.

3. A full annual time series (2000–2014) of bilateral measures for 43 countries has been made available to the research community, via https://www.rug.nl/ggdc/valuechain/gvc-research/2018-nber.

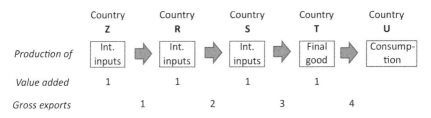

Figure 11.1. Example of sequential production chain

| | | Intermediate use | | | | | Final use | | | | | Total |
		Z	R	S	T	U	Z	R	S	T	U	use
Produced by	Z	0	1	0	0	0	0	0	0	0	0	1
	R	0	0	2	0	0	0	0	0	0	0	2
	S	0	0	0	3	0	0	0	0	0	0	3
	T	0	0	0	0	0	0	0	0	0	4	4
	U	0	0	0	0	0	0	0	0	0	0	0
	value added	1	1	1	1	0						
	gross output	1	2	3	4	0						

Figure 11.2   Input-output table corresponding to figure 11.1

algebraically in section 11.3, they are generally applicable in any constellation of the production network.[4]

Figure 11.1 depicts a simple production process in which there are four stages of production, each taking place in a different country. We opt for the most simple constellation through which we can still illustrate our concepts. Country Z produces an intermediate input (from scratch), used by country R to produce intermediates, which are subsequently used by country S to produce an intermediate for country T. Country T is what we call the country-of-completion. This is the country where the final stage of production takes place. Country U is importing the final good from Country T and consumes it.[5] In each stage of production 1 unit of value is added to the product, such that the price paid for the final product is 4.

In Figure 11.2 we show the input-output table that corresponds to this production chain. The intermediate use block has the very simple structure of a sequential production chain.[6] Note that gross output of each product

4. It can consist of snakes, spiders, or any combination of these (see Baldwin and Venables 2013 for a discussion of the differences).

5. Throughout the paper we will refer to consumption, for ease of exposition. In the empirical analysis, we consider final use, which does not only include household and government consumption, but also private and public gross fixed capital formation and changes in inventories.

6. More formally, a snake is a production chain that can be represented (with suitable permutation) in the intermediate use matrix by a single non-main diagonal of positive transaction values and zeros elsewhere.

Table 11.1   Measures of bilateral exports

	From R to			From S to		From T to U
	S	T	U	T	U	
Gross exports	2	0	0	3	0	4
Domestic value added exports (VAX)						
for direct use (VAX-D)	1	0	0	1	0	1
for final stage production (VAX-P)	0	1	0	1	0	0
for consumption (VAX-C)	0	0	1	0	1	1

Note: based on Figure 11.1.

(in the bottom row) is equal to its total use (indicated in the last column) as required to have a closed system such that use is equal to supply for all products.[7] In the next section, we will use this IO table to discuss the complications arising from "loops."

With this setup we next introduce the family of bilateral export measures. These are shown in table 11.1. We only report on those country pairs for which there is a non-zero export flow for at least one of the measures (so we do not report, for instance, on bilateral exports from U to any other country). We also do not report on Z, as this is not needed for making our main points. The numbers should be clear from the example, and can be checked using the information in table 11.1 with the formulas to be presented in section 11.3. The first row indicates the traditional gross flows. The next rows show three different variants of value added exports (VAX): for direct use (VAX-D), for final stage production (VAX-P) and for consumption (VAX-C).

Various alternative indices of bilateral VAX-D have been suggested, e.g., by Hummels, Ishii, and Yi (2001); Los, Timmer, and de Vries (2016); and Wang, Wei, and Zhu (2018). We prefer to use the one suggested by Los, Timmer, and de Vries (2016) as will be explained in section 11.5. VAX-D is equal to gross exports when all activities needed to produce the exported good are performed within the exporting country. The share of VAX-D in gross exports is declining in the amount of intermediates imported by the country in any domestic stage of production. For R, the share of VAX-D in gross exports is 0.5. Note that VAX-D includes value added in the export of intermediates (as in exports from S to T) as well as of final goods (as in exports from T to U).

Johnson and Noguera (2012) introduced the concept of VAX-C at both the aggregate and bilateral level. Johnson (2014) provides an overview of stylized facts. It is defined as the value added that is generated in a country but consumed abroad.[8] We refer to it as VAX-C. Unlike VAX-C, VAX-D

7. The input-output tables presented throughout the paper are expressed in monetary units.
8. Johnson and Noguera (2012, 2017) refer to it as "value added absorbed abroad." In the context of VAX-P and VAX-C, "absorbed by" is ambiguous (as it could be absorbed in the final product, or by the consumer) and we therefore say "consumed abroad" instead.

includes all value added that crosses the border, irrespective of where it is ultimately consumed. Considered for the aggregate set of other countries, it is therefore always at least as large as VAX-C, and strictly larger if some VAX-D is consumed domestically (as shown in Koopman, Wang, and Wei 2014). This is not true when considering bilateral flows, however. It is here that the conceptual difference between VAX-D and VAX-C is most visible. There can be a bilateral flow of VAX-C between a pair of countries without a direct flow of exports, as in the case of R to U, or S to U, as indicated in table 11.1.

This characteristic of VAX-C has major implications for its use in trade analysis. VAX-C is a popular measure and used for example by Aichele, Felbermayr, and Heiland (2014); Johnson and Noguera (2017); Kaplan, Kohl, and Martinez-Zarzoso (2018); and Brakman, Garretsen, and Kohl (2018) in studies of the effects of trade agreements. They relate bilateral VAX-C flows to trade agreements between the two countries involved, using a gravity equation framework. Using trade flows in value added terms rather than gross exports is needed indeed. Yet, such analyses should ideally be based on VAX-D rather than VAX-C flows.[9] This can be explained by referring to the stylized production chain in figure 11.1. A reduction of trade barriers between R and S is commonly supposed to have positive effects on the bilateral value added exports between these two countries, which is captured by VAX-D. The effects of a trade agreement between R and U are less obvious, however. Such an agreement will not reduce trade barriers at borders that are crossed by R's exported value added, which are the borders between R and S, between S and T, and between T and U. The first order effect of a trade agreement between R and U on the value added exported from R to U is therefore expected to be nil. Trade barriers at other borders are likely to be much more relevant and should be modeled as well in the gravity setup, even when one is only interested in the effects of trade agreements on VAX-C.[10]

We introduce a third measure of VAX, namely VAX for final stage production (VAX-P). It is the domestic value added in exports that is used abroad in the production of a final good. This is another relevant measure, as it is at this final stage where consumption and investment demand shocks for specific products are transmitted to production and associated intermediates trade flows, as in Bems, Johnson, and Yi (2011, 2013), who studied the causes of the global trade collapse in 2008–2009. There might also be idiosyncratic shocks to the final-stage country, which will percolate to its trading partners further up the chain. Blanchard, Bown, and Johnson (2017), for example,

9. This might not be surprising, given the fact that VAX-C was the only value added based trade measure defined at the bilateral level for quite a while. More recently, Dhingra, Freeman, and Mavroeidi (2018), and Laget et al. (2018) studied trade policies using VAX-D measures. Unfortunately, they use the measure proposed by Wang, Wei, and Zhu (2018), about which we argue that it has an undesirable property (see section 11.5).
10. This point is also made in Noguera (2012).

			Use by country-industries						Final use by countries			Total use
			Country 1		...	Country M			Country 1	...	Country M	
			Industry 1	Industry N	...	Industry 1	...	Industry N				
Supply from country-industries	Country 1	Industry 1										
		...										
		Industry N										
	...	...										
	Country M	Industry 1										
		...										
		Industry N										
Value added by labor and capital												
Gross output												

Figure 11.3   The structure of a global input-output table

Note: Global IO tables do not have country detail for all countries in the world. Hence, Country M often refers to a region labeled "Rest of World."

Source: Timmer et al. (2015).

analyze the relationships between tariffs on final products sold by specific countries and the origins of value added contained in these.

As a final comment, it should be noted that in principle an unlimited number of related measures could be introduced, only bounded by the number of stages in the chain. We view VAX-P as the most relevant, however (in addition to VAX-D and VAX-C), as it clearly delineates between trade in intermediate and in final products. After this stage there is only trade in final goods, and before this stage there is only trade in intermediates in the chain. As for VAX-C, there can be flows of VAX-P between a pair of countries without a flow of direct exports, as from R to T.

11.3   A Unified Framework for Bilateral Value Added Export Measures

11.3.1   Preliminaries and Notation

In this section, we show how the three indicators of bilateral exports of domestic value added can be computed if a global input-output table is available. The general structure of such a table is given by figure 11.3.

In what follows, we will assume that the countries in a global input-output table can be grouped into three groups: (i) the country (or group of countries) for which we want to compute VAX-indicators, indicated by r; (ii) the country (or group of countries) that acts as the destination of the VAX, indicated by s; and (iii) the other countries in the world, indicated by t. In matrix notation, the input-output structure of figure 11.3 can in this context be represented by a limited number of matrices and vectors:[11]

---

11. Matrices are indicated by bold capitals, column vectors by bold lowercases, and scalars by italics. Primes denote transposition, and hats stand for diagonal matrices.

$$\mathbf{Z} \equiv \begin{bmatrix} \mathbf{Z}_{rr} & \mathbf{Z}_{rs} & \mathbf{Z}_{rt} \\ \mathbf{Z}_{sr} & \mathbf{Z}_{ss} & \mathbf{Z}_{st} \\ \mathbf{Z}_{tr} & \mathbf{Z}_{ts} & \mathbf{Z}_{tt} \end{bmatrix}; \mathbf{Y} \equiv \begin{bmatrix} \mathbf{Y}_{rr} & \mathbf{Y}_{rs} & \mathbf{Y}_{rt} \\ \mathbf{Y}_{sr} & \mathbf{Y}_{ss} & \mathbf{Y}_{st} \\ \mathbf{Y}_{tr} & \mathbf{Y}_{ts} & \mathbf{Y}_{tt} \end{bmatrix}; \mathbf{w} \equiv \begin{bmatrix} \mathbf{w}_r \\ \mathbf{w}_s \\ \mathbf{w}_t \end{bmatrix}; \mathbf{x} \equiv \begin{bmatrix} \mathbf{x}_r \\ \mathbf{x}_s \\ \mathbf{x}_t \end{bmatrix}.$$

There are M countries, each with N industries. $\mathbf{Z}$ is the $NM \times NM$ matrix of which the elements indicate the transaction values of sales among industries in the accounting period, usually a year. The rows refer to the supplying industries, the columns to using industries. Both transactions within a country (in the diagonal submatrices) and cross-border transactions (in the off-diagonal submatrices) are included in this matrix. It should be noted that the submatrices generally do not have the same dimensions. In order to avoid aggregation biases (Morimoto 1970), all industry and country detail should be retained in the computations. If r is a single country, $\mathbf{Z}^{rr}$ has N rows and columns. If s is a group of M_s countries, $\mathbf{Z}^{ss}$ has NM_s rows and columns.

$\mathbf{Y}$ is the rectangular matrix of which the elements give the transaction values of sales by industries to final users. Like in $\mathbf{Z}$, both domestic and international transactions are contained in this matrix. Since we treat all final use categories (household consumption, gross fixed capital formation, etc.) in the same way, $\mathbf{Y}$ contains M columns (one column for each country). Since all industries in all countries can sell to final users, the number of rows is NM. The dimensions of the submatrices vary, depending on the numbers of countries included in r, s, and t.

Value added in each of the industries in each country is contained in the NM-vector $\mathbf{w}$, and gross output levels in the NM-vector $\mathbf{x}$. The well-known input-output identities apply. The sum of intermediate sales and sales to final users (both summed over countries of destination) equals gross output, $\mathbf{x} = \mathbf{Zi} + \mathbf{Yi}$, in which $\mathbf{i}$ denotes a summation vector (of appropriate length) containing ones; the sum of purchases of intermediate inputs and payments for production factors (value added) also add up to these values, $\mathbf{x} = \mathbf{i'Z} + \mathbf{w}$.

The production requirements *per unit of output* are given by the $NM \times NM$ matrix $\mathbf{A}$ (for intermediate inputs) and the NM-vector $\mathbf{v}$ (for factor payments):

(1) $$\mathbf{A} = \mathbf{Z}\hat{\mathbf{x}}^{-1} = \begin{bmatrix} \mathbf{A}_{rr} & \mathbf{A}_{rs} & \mathbf{A}_{rt} \\ \mathbf{A}_{sr} & \mathbf{A}_{ss} & \mathbf{A}_{st} \\ \mathbf{A}_{tr} & \mathbf{A}_{ts} & \mathbf{A}_{tt} \end{bmatrix}; \mathbf{v} = \hat{\mathbf{x}}^{-1}\mathbf{w} \equiv \begin{bmatrix} \mathbf{v}_r \\ \mathbf{v}_s \\ \mathbf{v}_t \end{bmatrix}.$$

Country r's GDP can now be obtained by linking value added generation to the final demand levels in $\mathbf{Y}$ by means of Leontief's demand-driven input-output model:

(2) $$GDP_r = \tilde{\mathbf{v}}_r'(\mathbf{I} - \mathbf{A})^{-1}\mathbf{Yi}$$

in which $\tilde{\mathbf{v}}_r$ denotes the NM-vector that is identical to $\mathbf{v}$ as defined in (1) with respect to the part $\mathbf{v}_r$, but in which all other elements are set equal to zero.[12] The matrix $(\mathbf{I} - \mathbf{A})^{-1}$ is known as the Leontief inverse. The industry that is producing the final product often uses its own production factors, as well as intermediate inputs from first-tier suppliers. These can be located in the same country, but also elsewhere. First-tier suppliers generate value added themselves, but might also use intermediate inputs for their activities. The same goes for second-tier suppliers producing these, and so on.[13]

In their comment on Koopman, Wang, and Wei (2014), Los, Timmer, and de Vries (2016) showed that using a particular type of the "Hypothetical Extraction Method" (HEM) as pioneered by Paelinck, de Caevel, and Joseph Degueldre (1965) and Strassert (1968) can be used to derive VAX-D.[14] The main part of Los, Timmer, and de Vries (2016) dealt with the aggregate case, in which domestic value added in the exports of country r to all other countries is considered at once. They also proposed a bilateral extension, to which we will turn now.

11.3.2   The Hypothetical Extraction Method (HEM)

HEM-applications usually "extract" industries or countries from input-output structures by setting corresponding parts of matrices that are involved in the computations to zero. Equation (2) is then recomputed for the modified matrices: the result is called the hypothetical GDP level. The difference between the actual and the hypothetical GDP levels is a measure of the importance of the extracted industry. In computing VAX-D, we do not extract entire industries (or countries) from the system, but just some transactions. If we are interested in VAX-D between r and s, we set all elements of $\mathbf{A}_{rs}$ and $\mathbf{Y}_{rs}$ to zero, assuming that s does not use any imports of intermediate and final products from r. One might think of this as a situation in which s sets import tariffs on goods from r that are prohibitively high. We indicate the modified matrices with a *:

$$(3) \qquad \mathbf{A}_r^{*s} \equiv \begin{bmatrix} \mathbf{A}_{rr} & \mathbf{0} & \mathbf{A}_{rt} \\ \mathbf{A}_{sr} & \mathbf{A}_{ss} & \mathbf{A}_{st} \\ \mathbf{A}_{tr} & \mathbf{A}_{ts} & \mathbf{A}_{tt} \end{bmatrix}; \mathbf{Y}_r^{*s} \equiv \begin{bmatrix} \mathbf{Y}_{rr} & \mathbf{0} & \mathbf{Y}_{rt} \\ \mathbf{Y}_{sr} & \mathbf{Y}_{ss} & \mathbf{Y}_{st} \\ \mathbf{Y}_{tr} & \mathbf{Y}_{ts} & \mathbf{Y}_{tt} \end{bmatrix}.$$

Next, we compute the GDP level in r for the situation in which these matrices would have represented the global production structure and final demand levels:

---

12. If the vector $\mathbf{v}$ would be used instead, we would obtain world GDP rather than GDP of r.
13. See, e.g., the appendix of Los, Timmer, and de Vries (2015) for a more extensive exposition.
14. See Miller and Lahr (2001) for a comprehensive overview of HEM-based input-output analyses, and Dietzenbacher, van der Linden, and Steenge (1993) for an application involving multiple countries.

(4) $$GDP_r^{*s} = \tilde{\mathbf{v}}_r'(\mathbf{I} - \mathbf{A}_r^{*s})^{-1}\mathbf{Y}_r^{*s}\mathbf{i}.$$

The value added of r contained in direct exports to s is now given by the difference between r's actual GDP level and its hypothetical GDP level:

(5) $$VAXD_{rs} = GDP_r - GDP_r^{*s}.$$

We would like to emphasize that GDP_r^{*s} should not be seen as the GDP level that would result if exports to s would be prohibitive. In a general setting with more flexible production and demand functions, substitution effects will occur. As a consequence, the global production structure and final demand levels will change and the global production structure after the tariff shock will not be represented by $\mathbf{A}_r^{*s}$ and $\mathbf{Y}_r^{*s}$. $VAXD_{rs}$ should therefore be regarded as an upper limit to the loss in GDP_r and is most meaningful if compared to other scenarios of extracted transactions. Put otherwise, it is a measure of the relative importance of country s for exports of value added by r.[15]

We now show how VAX-P can be computed in a similar framework by setting elements of one or more matrices in (2) to zero (see below for a simpler computational formula). VAX-P is the amount of value added used abroad for final production. If we hypothetically extract all final demand for output produced by industries in country s, we have

(6) $$\mathbf{Y}_r^{\#s} \equiv \begin{bmatrix} \mathbf{Y}_{rr} & \mathbf{Y}_{rs} & \mathbf{Y}_{rt} \\ \mathbf{0} & \mathbf{0} & \mathbf{0} \\ \mathbf{Y}_{tr} & \mathbf{Y}_{ts} & \mathbf{Y}_{tt} \end{bmatrix}$$

and hypothetical GDP in r is given by

(7) $$GDP_r^{\#s} = \tilde{\mathbf{v}}_r'(\mathbf{I} - \mathbf{A})^{-1}\mathbf{Y}_r^{\#s}\mathbf{i}.$$

For VAX-P, we now have the expression

(8) $$VAXP_{rs} = GDP_r - GDP_r^{\#s}.$$

Johnson and Noguera's (2012) VAX-C indicator can also easily be considered within this HEM-approach (see below for a simpler computational formula for VAX-C). If we hypothetically extract all demand by final users in country s, we have

(9) $$\mathbf{Y}_r^{\&s} \equiv \begin{bmatrix} \mathbf{Y}_{rr} & \mathbf{0} & \mathbf{Y}_{rt} \\ \mathbf{Y}_{sr} & \mathbf{0} & \mathbf{Y}_{st} \\ \mathbf{Y}_{tr} & \mathbf{0} & \mathbf{Y}_{tt} \end{bmatrix}.$$

15. See, for example, Chen et al. (2018), who measure regional GDP-shares "at risk" to Brexit using this HEM-approach, but argue that substitution effects will most probably lead to smaller actual GDP losses.

The hypothetical GDP-level associated with this extraction reads

(10) $$GDP_r^{\&s} = \tilde{\mathbf{v}}_r'(\mathbf{I} - \mathbf{A})^{-1}\mathbf{Y}_r^{\&s}\mathbf{i}$$

and we obtain the following expression for VAX-C:

(11) $$VAXC_{rs} = GDP_r - GDP_r^{\&s}.$$

This completes the discussion of the unified framework in which the three measures of bilateral exports of value added can be presented. The aggregate indicator of VAX-D can be computed by means of slightly modified versions of (3), (4) and (5). $\mathbf{A}_r^{*st}$ and $\mathbf{Y}_r^{*st}$ are obtained by simultaneously setting $\mathbf{A}_{rs}$, $\mathbf{A}_{rt}$, $\mathbf{Y}_{rs}$ and $\mathbf{Y}_{rt}$ equal to zero, after which they are substituted for $\mathbf{A}_r^{*s}$ and $\mathbf{Y}_r^{*s}$ in (4). The result (GDP_r^{*st}) is then subtracted from actual GDP, as in (5). The aggregate counterpart of VAX-P is computed by not only setting the row associated with final demand for output from country s but also the row for output from country t equal to zero in (6). Finally, setting both columns for consumption in s and in t in (9) to zero, (10) and (11) yield the aggregate VAX-C.

11.3.3   Simplified Expressions for Calculation of VAX

So far, we derived VAX measures using the HEM approach. We did this to stress the relationships between the three VAX indicators. Yet, VAX-P and VAX-C can also be computed in a simpler way given the fact that it only involves the tracing of parts of the final demand matrix. Following the exposition by Los, Timmer, and de Vries (2015), VAX-P from r to s can be expressed as a simple multiplication with demand for products finalized in s (by any country in the world, including r):

(12) $$VAXP_{rs} = \tilde{\mathbf{v}}_r'(\mathbf{I} - \mathbf{A})^{-1} \begin{bmatrix} \mathbf{Y}_{sr} & \mathbf{Y}_{ss} & \mathbf{Y}_{st} \end{bmatrix} \mathbf{i}.$$

Likewise, Johnson and Noguera's (2012) bilateral VAX-C from r to s is usually written as:

(13) $$VAXC_{rs} = \tilde{\mathbf{v}}_r'(\mathbf{I} - \mathbf{A})^{-1} \begin{bmatrix} \mathbf{Y}_{rs} \\ \mathbf{Y}_{ss} \\ \mathbf{Y}_{ts} \end{bmatrix},$$

involving only the demand of s for products finalized in any country, including country r itself.

11.4   Empirical Illustrations

In this section we provide some empirical illustrations of the measures we introduced using the 2016 release of the World Input-Output Database (Timmer et al. 2015). We study the VAX of some major countries in the world (China, Japan, Germany, United Kingdom, and United States), as

Table 11.2   Various aggregate VAX measures, 2014

	VAX-D/GX	VAX-C/VAX-D	VAX-P/VAX-D
China	82.4%	96.3%	47.1%
United States	87.0%	92.1%	61.1%
Germany	70.2%	95.4%	53.8%
Japan	74.7%	98.4%	56.8%
United Kingdom	77.4%	97.9%	63.1%
Australia	83.9%	99.1%	83.7%
Brazil	77.1%	99.4%	74.6%

Note: Authors' calculations based on WIOD, 2016 release.

well as some global suppliers of raw materials (Australia and Brazil).[16] We show that bilateral measures can vary widely across the various measures and provide some intuitive interpretation. All results are for the year 2014 and values are expressed in million US$. For background, we first provide a comparison of aggregate measures of GX, VAX-D, VAX-P and VAX-C in table 11.2. Tables 11A.1 to 11A.7 provide for each country the bilateral GX and VAX flows to each of the 42 partner countries (and the rest-of-the-world region), the share of each partner in total flows as well as the ranking based on these shares. We highlight some interesting results.

11.4.1   VAX-D Compared to GX

Column 1 in table 11.2 confirms the finding of Koopman, Wang, and Wei (2014) that aggregate VAX-D is smaller than gross exports (GX). Ratios vary from 70 percent for Germany to 87 percent for the United States, reflecting the difference in the import content of their exports as stressed by Hummels, Ishii, and Yi (2001). As argued by Koopman, Wang, and Wei (2012), these ratios are likely to be overestimations if firm heterogeneity is such that more export-intensive firms have lower VAX-D ratios. They showed that this was the case for China, using data that distinguish between processing exports and other firms.[17]

Appendix tables 11A.1 through 11A.7 provide information on the bilateral VAX-D values. In general, the rankings of export destinations are similar for the gross exports and the VAX-D measures. This is not surprising given the nature of the available data. Information on input requirements generally does not vary across export partners. As a consequence, the representation of production technologies of exporting industries is not destination specific, and the WIOD data are no exception. Hence, the VAX-D to GX ratio

---

16. The measures for all 43 countries included in the 2016 release of WIOD have been made available at the WIOD website (www.wiod.org/gvc#nber).
17. The OECD Trade in Value Added database makes this distinction for China and Mexico.

for a given product is the same across all partners. The variation in results across bilateral partners thus comes from variation in the product mixes of exports bundles toward the various destinations. For example, Canada and Mexico become less important as export partners for the United States in terms of VAX-D compared to gross exports. This is because the US exports to these countries is skewed toward products with a low VAX-D ratio. On the other hand, China becomes more important for Brazil as an export destination in terms of VAX-D, because Brazilian exports to China mainly consist of raw materials, which have a very high VAX-D ratio.

11.4.2   VAX-C Compared to VAX-D

VAX-D includes all value added that crosses the border, irrespective of where it is ultimately consumed. From an aggregate perspective, it is therefore always at least as large as VAX-C, as VAX-C only considers value added that is also ultimately consumed abroad (Johnson and Noguera 2012). Koopman, Wang, and Wei (2014) showed that the empirical differences are small, and we confirm this in the second column of table 11.2. This is not true when considering bilateral flows, however, and it is here that the conceptual and empirical differences are clearly visible. First of all, bilateral VAX-C can be higher than GX, and we find many examples of this, in particular in exports toward major consumer markets such as China, Japan, and the United States. Countries export directly toward these destinations, but also indirectly through other countries (as also found by Johnson and Noguera 2012).

Second, for individual countries, the importance of various destinations do change compared to VAX-D. For example, South Korea and Taiwan are less important for Japan as consumers of its value added than as direct export markets, while the United States is more important as a consumer than as a direct export destination. Similarly, Canada and Mexico are less important for the United States, and continental Europe is less important for Germany as consumers than as direct export destination. These findings confirm the well-documented existence of regional production networks (see, e.g., Los, Timmer, and de Vries 2015).

11.4.3   VAX-P Compared to VAX-D

The last column of table 11.2 provides a comparison of aggregate VAX-P with VAX-D. It reveals interesting variation across countries. VAX-P must be lower than VAX-D by definition, as it only captures exports of value added that are used in final production abroad. Hence VAX-P will not include exports of final goods, and the ratio of VAX-P to VAX-D will thus be mainly influenced by the share of intermediate products (including natural resources) in a country's exports. Not surprisingly, the ratio varies from 47 percent for China, which exports relatively little intermediates, to as much as 84 percent for Australia, which mainly exports primary intermediates.

The bilateral measures shown in the appendix tables reveal additional

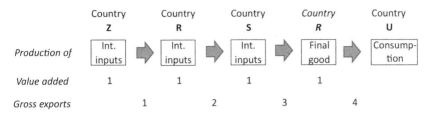

Figure 11.4   Example of production chain (with loop)

patterns. The share of VAX-P going to China is typically (much) higher than the share of VAX-D or VAX-C going there, confirming its important role as a final assembler using intermediates produced elsewhere. For example, 15.3 percent of direct VAX from Japan goes to China, vs. 19.6 percent of VAX-P. Similarly, 5.7 percent of US VAX-D goes to China, while 8.1 percent of VAX-P. Interestingly, Chinese VAX-P goes more to less advanced countries (such as India, Indonesia, and Mexico) and South Korea (relative to VAX-D or VAX-C shares). Yet the United States and Japan are still the largest receivers of Chinese VAX-P.

11.5   Which Bilateral VAX-D Measure to Use?

The *aggregate* concept of value added exports for direct use (VAX-D) has been introduced by Hummels, Ishii, and Yi (2001), and Koopman, Wang, and Wei (2012), and there is unanimous agreement on how to measure it.[18] This is not true for the *bilateral* VAX-D measure. Various alternative indices have been suggested, including those by Hummels, Ishii, and Yi (2001); Los, Timmer, and de Vries (2016); and Wang, Wei, and Zhu (2018). We prefer to use the one suggested by Los, Timmer, and de Vries (2016) because it is the only one which allows for a situation in which the sum of the bilateral measures across all destinations is not equal to the aggregate measure. This is so in cases in which an exporting country is involved in a specific type of "feedback loop" (Miller 1966). This situation arises if a country is importing its own value added (embodied in intermediate inputs) from one country to produce its exports to another country.[19]

An example is easily created by replacing country T in figure 11.1 by country R, see figure 11.4. In this case, R is importing its own value added

18. In fact, Hummels, Ishii, and Yi (2001) suggested the complement to VAX-D: the import content of exports, and referred to it as VS ("vertical specialization"). Koopman, Wang, and Wei (2012) showed that VAX-D is equal to gross exports minus VS (see also Los, Timmer, and de Vries, 2016).

19. Value added exported to the final stage, or the final consumer, can obviously never be exported by the exporting country again. Hence bilateral VAX always sums to aggregate VAX in the case of VAX-P and VAX-C.

		Intermediate use				Final use				Total Use
		Z	R	S	U	Z	R	S	U	
Produced by	Z	0	1	0	0	0	0	0	0	1
	R	0	0	2	0	0	0	0	4	6
	S	0	3	0	0	0	0	0	0	3
	U	0	0	0	0	0	0	0	0	0
	value added	1	2	1	0					
	gross output	1	6	3	0					

Figure 11.5   Input-output table corresponding to figure 11.4

Table 11.3   Measures of bilateral exports

	From R to			From S to		
	S	U	*All*	R	U	*All*
Gross exports	2	4	*6*	3	0	*3*
Domestic value added exports (VAX)						
for direct use (VAX-D)	1	2	*2*	1	0	*1*
for final stage production (VAX-P)	0	0	*0*	1	0	*1*
for consumption (VAX-C)	0	2	*2*	0	1	*1*

Note: based on Figure 11.4

that was generated in an earlier stage when producing its exports to S. The corresponding input-output table is shown in figure 11.5. Mathematically, an input-output table has a loop if none of all possible permutations of the intermediate use matrix yields a *triangular matrix*, defined as a matrix with exclusively zeros below the main diagonal. Such permutations must involve simultaneous changes in the order of the columns and corresponding rows, otherwise the equality of row (use) and column sum (supply) is violated.[20] In the example of figure 11.4, it is clear that there is a loop, as S delivers intermediates to R and vice versa, hence there is always a positive value below the diagonal block, irrespective of how the countries are ordered in the table.

In table 11.3 we report on the bilateral VAX measures, as well as the aggregate (in the columns headed by All). Again, we only report on pairs of countries for which there is a non-zero flow for at least one of the VAX measures. The measures for S are not surprising and basically repeat those for T in the snake example presented in section 11.2 (see table 11.1). R is the country of interest. It carries out two stages of production, and exports

20. Chenery and Watanabe (1958) discuss triangularization of input-output matrices in order to make matrix manipulations computationally less cumbersome (which at that time was of course an important topic). Simpson and Tsukui (1956) discuss the economic meaning of (block)triangular input-output tables.

directly to two countries: S and U. Its gross exports are 6, while it generates only 2 units of value added in the chain. This is clear from VAX-C: both units are ultimately consumed in U and the sum of the bilateral measures is equal to the aggregate measure. This is also true for VAX-P, which in this case is not so insightful, as R is the country of completion so VAX-P is zero by definition, for all bilateral pairs as well as in the aggregate sense.

The interesting case arises for VAX-D. R exports 1 unit of value added to S, and R exports 2 units of its value added to U: the value added in the second stage of the chain and in the fourth stage. Yet, the aggregate VAX-D is also 2. This is obvious as R adds only 2 units of value added to the chain. We now have a case where the sum of the bilateral measures is higher (3) than the aggregate one (2). The reason is that R exports the value added it generates in the second stage of the chain twice: first directly to S, and again embodied in exports to U. We therefore refer to the difference between the sum of the bilateral VAX-Ds and the aggregate VAX-D as the *double count of domestic value added in summing bilateral measures*.

In a recently revised paper, Wang, Wei, and Zhu (2018)—WWZ from hereon—provide an alternative measure of bilateral VAX-D, which rules out this type of double counts by design. The authors wish to develop an accounting system in which the overall value added (GDP) of a country is assigned to (bilateral) export flows in a mutually exclusive way. From that perspective, it is only natural to impose an aggregation restriction upfront. But there is a cost involved regarding the measurement of trade relationships. In the WWZ accounting framework, the value added in exports from R to U would be only 1 unit, not 2. In that way the bilateral measures sum to the aggregate. This might be justified when accounting for GDP, but it is counterintuitive from a trade perspective. If U would no longer demand the final good from R, value added in R will decline by 2 units, as both stages of production are no longer needed. The hypothetical extraction method introduced in the previous section provides a mathematical underpinning for this intuition.

One could argue (as in WWZ) that by tracing the exports and contributions *of different industries in a country* this double counting would be eliminated. Assume that the first task carried out by R is done in industry R1 (which exports to S), and the second task by industry R2 (which exports to U). When considering the exports to U one could say that the exports *from R2* contain 1 unit of value added *by R2*. Yet, it remains true that the aggregate exports from R contain 2 units of R's value added. Having more detailed input-output tables will thus not resolve this as long as one wishes to study aggregate exports of a country, rather than of separate industries in a country.

To be clear, we do not claim that the WWZ decomposition is mathematically "wrong." As long as the accounting restrictions are obeyed, an accounting framework is correct. But we do claim that the decomposition

Table 11.4   **VAX-D double counts, selected countries, 2014**

	VAX-D double count
Germany	1.8%
China	0.8%
United States	0.7%
Japan	0.3%
United Kingdom	0.3%
Australia	0.1%
Brazil	0.1%

Note: VAX-D double count is the sum of the bilateral VAX-D to all partners minus the aggregate VAX-D. It is expressed as a percentage of aggregate VAX-D. Authors' calculations based on WIOD 2016 release.

is essentially arbitrary as one can come up with many alternatives that are equally valid. Without an economic model, it is impossible to defend any choice among these. This point is also made by Nagengast and Stehrer (2016), and they propose to identify the trade flow in which value added is actually recorded for the first time in international trade statistics to allocate value added. Actually, there is a deep and fundamental problem in trying to allocate value added to gross trade flows. Note that the elements in an IO table are summations of transactions within a particular time frame, typically a year. It does not record the sequence of the transactions. This is important to emphasize, because it implies that it is generally impossible to retrieve the underlying production chain, except in very simple cases such as a snake (as stressed by Nomaler and Verspagen, 2014). If loops are present, many different networks can underlie the same IO table. Hence, it is impossible to allocate value added to gross flows, and any "solution" is essentially arbitrary.

Fortunately in empirical terms, the double counts have (so far) been minor. Table 11.4 provides information on the double count in VAX-D. It is defined as the sum of the bilateral VAX-D to all export partners minus the aggregate VAX-D, expressed as a percentage of the latter. It follows that this term is not large, and typically less than 1 percent. The maximum (1.8 percent) is found for the case of Germany, signifying that this country has sizeable back-and-forth trade that is bigger than for other countries. The lowest double counts are found for Australia and Brazil, countries that specialize in exporting natural resources. The value added generated in mining for exports is generally not returning to these countries in the form of intermediate inputs.

11.6   Concluding Remarks

In this chapter we provided an integrated discussion of three useful measures of value added exports at the bilateral level: VAX-D as introduced by

Los, Timmer, and de Vries (2016); VAX-C as introduced by Johnson and Noguera (2012); and VAX-P, a novel measure that indicates the value added used abroad in the final stage of production. We showed that the measures have different interpretations, while they belong to the same class of indicators. All can be derived with the method of hypothetical extraction in a general input-output model. In addition we show that the sum of bilateral measures for VAX-D might differ from the corresponding aggregate measure (as opposed to VAX-P and VAX-C). This happens if the country of interest is involved in feedback loops within production networks, i.e., if the production of exports of a country requires imported intermediates to which the country contributed value added in upstream stages of production. This is an inherent feature of intricate production networks. We illustrate all measures with some numerical examples using the World Input-Output Database and show that they do not differ only conceptually but also empirically.

Many extensions are possible, in particular using economic indicators other than value added, such as labor income or hours worked (see, e.g., Chen et al. 2018). Progress will depend on the further availability of new and improved data sources. The popularity of VAX measures in the policy arena is not (yet) properly matched by the quality of the available data, as many gaps and inconsistencies in primary data collection remain. Harmonizing national and international data collection efforts and institutionalizing their production in regular statistical programs is a major challenge, see, e.g., Landefeld (2015). Ongoing efforts in the international statistical community toward this goal are therefore very welcome and deserve full support.

Appendix

Table 11A.1 Bilateral exports by China, 2014

	Million US$				Shares in total				Ranking of countries			
	GX	VAX-D	VAX-P	VAX-C	GX	VAX-D	VAX-P	VAX-C	GX	VAX-D	VAX-P	VAX-C
United States	347,311	280,320	123,637	320,289	14.3%	14.0%	13.1%	16.7%	1	1	1	1
Japan	172,861	140,285	55,341	137,386	7.1%	7.0%	5.9%	7.1%	2	2	2	2
South Korea	101,924	81,605	46,955	56,392	4.2%	4.1%	5.0%	2.9%	3	3	3	5
Germany	88,465	72,334	35,614	71,375	3.6%	3.6%	3.8%	3.7%	4	4	4	3
Russian Federation	65,198	56,474	14,834	62,062	2.7%	2.8%	1.6%	3.2%	5	5	13	4
United Kingdom	51,850	42,270	21,216	49,968	2.1%	2.1%	2.3%	2.6%	6	6	8	6
Canada	49,636	40,763	21,667	43,000	2.0%	2.0%	2.3%	2.2%	7	7	7	8
Australia	48,459	39,568	19,714	43,198	2.0%	2.0%	2.1%	2.2%	8	8	10	7
India	44,869	36,269	24,407	39,846	1.8%	1.8%	2.6%	2.1%	9	9	5	9
Taiwan	43,622	34,210	14,413	20,401	1.8%	1.7%	1.5%	1.1%	10	11	14	16
Netherlands	42,640	34,215	13,863	26,891	1.8%	1.7%	1.5%	1.4%	11	10	15	13
France	41,291	34,061	21,759	38,267	1.7%	1.7%	2.3%	2.0%	12	12	6	10
Brazil	38,988	31,703	19,966	36,926	1.6%	1.6%	2.1%	1.9%	13	13	9	11
Mexico	38,330	30,554	17,932	25,082	1.6%	1.5%	1.9%	1.3%	14	14	12	15
Indonesia	34,969	28,644	19,225	29,300	1.4%	1.4%	2.0%	1.5%	15	15	11	12
Italy	28,865	23,873	13,690	25,699	1.2%	1.2%	1.5%	1.3%	16	16	16	14
Turkey	23,149	18,558	10,112	18,765	1.0%	0.9%	1.1%	1.0%	17	17	17	18
Spain	21,496	17,849	9,595	19,998	0.9%	0.9%	1.0%	1.0%	18	18	18	17
Poland	14,316	11,541	5,868	11,771	0.6%	0.6%	0.6%	0.6%	19	19	20	19
Belgium	11,804	9,862	6,303	9,490	0.5%	0.5%	0.7%	0.5%	20	20	19	20
Sweden	11,173	9,445	5,849	9,005	0.5%	0.5%	0.6%	0.5%	21	21	21	21
Czech Republic	8,898	6,855	3,952	4,800	0.4%	0.3%	0.4%	0.2%	22	22	22	27

Switzerland	7,293	5,911	3,944	7,879	0.3%	0.3%	0.4%	0.4%	23	23	23	23	22
Finland	6,870	5,644	3,781	5,056	0.3%	0.3%	0.4%	0.3%	24	24	24	24	25
Denmark	6,199	5,215	3,553	5,101	0.3%	0.3%	0.4%	0.3%	25	25	25	25	24
Hungary	5,396	4,135	3,035	2,342	0.2%	0.2%	0.3%	0.1%	26	26	26	26	32
Norway	4,563	3,786	2,270	5,183	0.2%	0.2%	0.2%	0.3%	27	27	27	29	23
Austria	4,242	3,500	2,493	4,875	0.2%	0.2%	0.3%	0.3%	28	28	28	27	26
Greece	4,190	3,436	1,246	4,399	0.2%	0.1%	0.1%	0.2%	29	29	29	32	28
Ireland	3,471	2,816	2,342	3,204	0.1%	0.1%	0.2%	0.2%	30	30	30	28	29
Romania	2,614	2,089	1,573	2,850	0.1%	0.1%	0.2%	0.1%	31	31	31	31	30
Portugal	2,251	1,844	1,219	2,620	0.1%	0.1%	0.1%	0.1%	32	32	32	33	31
Slovak Republic	2,002	1,596	1,711	1,700	0.1%	0.1%	0.1%	0.1%	33	33	33	30	33
Slovenia	1,369	1,137	482	1,167	0.1%	0.1%	0.0%	0.1%	34	34	34	35	34
Estonia	1,073	862	457	683	0.0%	0.0%	0.1%	0.0%	35	35	35	37	39
Bulgaria	1,029	847	536	1,150	0.0%	0.0%	0.0%	0.1%	36	36	36	34	35
Lithuania	947	780	381	948	0.0%	0.0%	0.1%	0.0%	37	37	37	38	36
Luxembourg	911	711	458	920	0.0%	0.0%	0.0%	0.0%	38	38	38	36	37
Croatia	714	586	344	832	0.0%	0.0%	0.0%	0.0%	39	39	39	39	38
Latvia	654	544	269	646	0.0%	0.0%	0.0%	0.0%	40	40	40	40	40
Cyprus	583	487	189	569	0.0%	0.0%	0.0%	0.0%	41	41	42	42	41
Malta	455	376	211	350	0.0%	0.0%	0.0%	0.0%	42	42	41	41	42
Rest of world	1,038,525	870,577	385,318	771,233	42.8%	43.6%	40.9%	40.1%					
Sum of bilaterals	2,425,464	1,998,134	941,724	1,923,618	57%	56%	59%	60%					
Aggregate	2,425,464	1,981,364	941,724	1,923,618									

Note: Authors' calculations based on WIOD, 2016 release.

Table 11A.2   Bilateral exports by United States, 2014

	Million US$				Shares in total				Ranking of countries			
	GX	VAX-D	VAX-P	VAX-C	GX	VAX-D	VAX-P	VAX-C	GX	VAX-D	VAX-P	VAX-C
Canada	291,930	242,458	120,217	185,228	15.1%	14.5%	11.7%	12.0%	1	1	1	1
Mexico	178,587	146,127	91,872	99,465	9.3%	8.7%	9.0%	6.4%	2	2	2	3
China	112,051	95,421	83,364	120,552	5.8%	5.7%	8.1%	7.8%	3	3	3	2
Germany	79,939	70,486	46,817	69,805	4.1%	4.2%	4.6%	4.5%	4	4	4	5
United Kingdom	73,796	62,847	35,678	69,873	3.8%	3.7%	3.5%	4.5%	5	5	7	4
Japan	63,598	54,682	40,820	61,562	3.3%	3.3%	4.0%	4.0%	6	6	5	6
Ireland	61,756	58,371	29,031	16,962	3.2%	3.5%	2.8%	1.1%	7	7	8	15
France	57,720	49,924	37,565	49,212	3.0%	3.0%	3.7%	3.2%	8	8	6	7
Netherlands	47,920	42,699	20,478	26,914	2.5%	2.5%	2.0%	1.7%	9	9	11	11
South Korea	43,887	38,138	24,817	32,619	2.3%	2.3%	2.4%	2.1%	10	10	10	9
Brazil	40,464	33,572	25,773	36,374	2.1%	2.0%	2.5%	2.4%	11	11	9	8
Belgium	29,823	26,553	15,603	19,119	1.5%	1.6%	1.5%	1.2%	12	12	13	13
Australia	26,813	23,109	13,636	27,004	1.4%	1.4%	1.3%	1.7%	13	13	15	10
Luxembourg	20,862	19,896	7,786	2,130	1.1%	1.2%	0.8%	0.1%	14	14	18	32
Italy	19,655	17,071	16,581	22,286	1.0%	1.0%	1.6%	1.4%	15	15	12	12
Taiwan	16,415	13,934	7,661	10,924	0.9%	0.8%	0.7%	0.7%	16	17	20	20
India	16,233	13,937	14,511	18,889	0.8%	0.8%	1.4%	1.2%	17	16	14	14
Sweden	13,598	12,437	7,675	12,559	0.7%	0.7%	0.7%	0.8%	18	18	19	17
Switzerland	13,415	11,797	9,671	12,484	0.7%	0.7%	0.9%	0.8%	19	19	16	19
Spain	10,955	9,312	9,049	13,821	0.6%	0.6%	0.9%	0.9%	20	20	17	16
Turkey	8,302	6,855	6,944	9,032	0.4%	0.4%	0.7%	0.6%	21	21	21	21

Russian Federation	7,081	5,811	4,984	12,557	0.4%	0.3%	0.5%	0.8%	22	23	24	18
Denmark	6,837	6,209	5,103	5,223	0.4%	0.4%	0.5%	0.3%	23	22	23	27
Norway	6,564	5,726	4,271	6,797	0.3%	0.3%	0.4%	0.2%	24	24	25	23
Finland	6,197	5,612	3,917	5,314	0.3%	0.3%	0.4%	0.3%	25	25	27	26
Indonesia	5,864	5,069	6,458	8,331	0.3%	0.3%	0.6%	0.5%	26	26	22	22
Poland	4,602	3,999	4,189	6,351	0.2%	0.2%	0.4%	0.4%	27	28	26	24
Austria	4,581	4,031	3,834	5,504	0.2%	0.2%	0.4%	0.4%	28	27	28	25
Hungary	3,402	3,093	2,582	2,523	0.2%	0.2%	0.3%	0.2%	29	29	27	30
Czech Republic	2,746	2,439	2,570	2,985	0.1%	0.1%	0.3%	0.2%	30	30	29	29
Greece	2,274	2,062	1,931	3,084	0.1%	0.1%	0.2%	0.2%	31	31	31	28
Portugal	1,566	1,383	1,595	2,429	0.1%	0.1%	0.2%	0.2%	32	32	32	31
Romania	1,223	1,042	1,376	2,000	0.1%	0.1%	0.1%	0.1%	33	33	33	33
Slovak Republic	763	687	1,111	1,159	0.0%	0.0%	0.1%	0.1%	34	34	34	34
Bulgaria	546	484	526	829	0.0%	0.0%	0.1%	0.1%	35	35	35	35
Croatia	480	437	436	625	0.0%	0.0%	0.0%	0.0%	36	36	37	37
Lithuania	435	368	269	659	0.0%	0.0%	0.0%	0.0%	37	37	39	36
Slovenia	372	327	327	596	0.0%	0.0%	0.0%	0.0%	38	38	38	38
Malta	356	313	491	285	0.0%	0.0%	0.0%	0.0%	39	39	36	42
Estonia	252	221	227	360	0.0%	0.0%	0.0%	0.0%	40	40	40	40
Latvia	233	207	213	394	0.0%	0.0%	0.0%	0.0%	41	41	41	39
Cyprus	146	130	181	341	0.0%	0.0%	0.0%	0.0%	42	42	42	41
Rest of world	642,853	577,983	312,213	559,590	33.4%	34.5%	30.5%	36.2%				
Sum of bilaterals	1,927,091	1,677,256	1,024,353	1,544,752	67%	66%	70%	64%				
Aggregate	1,927,091	1,666,117	1,024,353	1,544,752								

Note: Authors' calculations based on WIOD, 2016 release.

Table 11A.3   Bilateral exports by Germany, 2014

	Million US$				Shares in total				Ranking of countries			
	GX	VAX-D	VAX-P	VAX-C	GX	VAX-D	VAX-P	VAX-C	GX	VAX-D	VAX-P	VAX-C
United States	135,642	95,970	58,466	117,597	8.1%	8.1%	9.2%	10.4%	1	1	1	1
France	133,788	92,097	49,683	82,206	8.0%	7.8%	7.8%	7.3%	2	2	3	3
China	122,900	87,554	50,447	97,226	7.3%	7.4%	7.9%	8.6%	3	3	2	2
United Kingdom	103,347	73,161	39,573	74,075	6.1%	6.2%	6.2%	6.6%	4	4	4	4
Italy	84,740	58,590	33,124	49,916	5.0%	5.0%	5.2%	4.4%	5	5	5	5
Austria	77,551	52,540	21,284	35,208	4.6%	4.4%	3.4%	3.1%	6	6	6	8
Netherlands	72,853	48,837	19,555	32,708	4.3%	4.1%	3.1%	2.9%	7	7	9	9
Switzerland	63,955	45,823	20,935	35,731	3.8%	3.9%	3.3%	3.2%	8	8	7	7
Poland	61,604	41,328	20,485	31,549	3.7%	3.5%	3.2%	2.8%	9	9	8	11
Spain	50,542	35,337	19,104	32,109	3.0%	3.0%	3.0%	2.9%	10	10	10	10
Russian Federation	49,265	33,299	17,645	36,857	2.9%	2.8%	2.8%	3.3%	11	11	11	6
Czech Republic	42,855	29,056	14,061	15,467	2.5%	2.5%	2.2%	1.4%	12	12	12	17
Belgium	41,918	28,491	14,032	19,838	2.5%	2.4%	2.2%	1.8%	13	13	13	14
Sweden	32,584	22,950	10,117	20,040	1.9%	1.9%	1.6%	1.8%	14	14	16	13
Turkey	28,860	19,362	10,744	18,239	1.7%	1.6%	1.7%	1.6%	15	15	15	15
Hungary	27,183	19,047	10,099	8,425	1.6%	1.6%	1.6%	0.7%	16	16	17	27
South Korea	25,415	17,721	9,823	16,690	1.5%	1.5%	1.5%	1.5%	17	17	18	16
Japan	24,757	17,315	12,309	22,324	1.5%	1.5%	1.9%	2.0%	18	18	14	12
Denmark	24,165	16,554	9,784	11,677	1.4%	1.4%	1.5%	1.0%	19	19	19	21
Brazil	17,775	12,327	9,248	15,288	1.1%	1.0%	1.5%	1.4%	20	20	20	18
Canada	17,148	12,039	7,501	14,709	1.0%	1.0%	1.2%	1.3%	21	21	22	19

Finland	15,078	10,670	5,867	8,688	0.9%	0.9%	0.9%	0.8%	22	22	22	25	25
Mexico	14,849	10,388	7,519	10,197	0.9%	0.9%	1.2%	0.9%	23	23	23	21	23
Slovak Republic	14,645	10,062	5,918	5,840	0.9%	0.9%	0.9%	0.5%	24	24	24	24	31
Romania	13,071	9,083	5,177	8,676	0.8%	0.8%	0.8%	0.8%	25	25	25	26	26
India	13,025	8,964	7,302	11,778	0.8%	0.8%	1.1%	1.0%	26	26	26	23	20
Norway	12,835	8,880	4,694	9,832	0.8%	0.7%	0.7%	0.9%	27	27	27	28	24
Australia	12,143	8,540	4,795	11,568	0.7%	0.6%	0.8%	1.0%	28	28	28	27	22
Taiwan	10,385	7,129	3,086	6,073	0.6%	0.6%	0.5%	0.5%	29	30	30	31	30
Luxembourg	10,284	7,548	2,671	3,816	0.6%	0.6%	0.4%	0.3%	30	29	29	33	34
Portugal	9,998	6,895	3,358	6,489	0.6%	0.6%	0.5%	0.6%	31	32	32	30	28
Ireland	9,475	7,077	4,238	5,174	0.6%	0.6%	0.7%	0.5%	32	31	31	29	32
Greece	7,710	5,514	1,975	6,266	0.5%	0.5%	0.3%	0.6%	33	33	33	34	29
Slovenia	4,664	3,232	1,416	2,506	0.3%	0.3%	0.2%	0.2%	34	34	34	35	36
Indonesia	4,215	2,916	2,820	4,492	0.3%	0.2%	0.4%	0.4%	35	35	35	32	33
Bulgaria	4,150	2,852	1,303	2,877	0.2%	0.2%	0.2%	0.3%	36	36	36	36	35
Croatia	3,231	2,268	1,138	2,369	0.2%	0.2%	0.2%	0.2%	37	37	37	37	37
Lithuania	2,752	1,882	705	1,888	0.2%	0.2%	0.1%	0.2%	38	38	38	38	38
Estonia	2,139	1,427	652	1,166	0.1%	0.1%	0.1%	0.1%	39	39	39	39	39
Latvia	1,396	964	459	1,085	0.1%	0.1%	0.1%	0.1%	40	40	40	40	40
Cyprus	924	668	231	735	0.0%	0.1%	0.0%	0.1%	41	41	41	42	41
Malta	442	320	246	307	0.0%	0.0%	0.0%	0.0%	42	42	42	41	42
Rest of world	275,991	204,172	111,575	226,516	16.4%	17.3%	17.6%	20.1%					
Sum of bilaterals	1,682,253	1,180,849	635,165	1,126,218	84%	83%	82%	80%					
Aggregate	1,682,253	1,159,581	635,165	1,126,218									

Note: Authors' calculations based on WIOD, 2016 release.

Table 11A.4   Bilateral exports by Japan, 2014

	Million US$				Shares in total				Ranking of countries			
	GX	VAX-D	VAX-P	VAX-C	GX	VAX-D	VAX-P	VAX-C	GX	VAX-D	VAX-P	VAX-C
China	129,230	93,215	67,837	95,238	15.8%	15.3%	19.6%	15.9%	1	1	1	2
United States	121,144	89,546	50,727	104,210	14.8%	14.7%	14.6%	17.4%	2	2	2	1
South Korea	56,449	37,847	23,791	22,927	6.9%	6.2%	6.9%	3.8%	3	3	3	3
Taiwan	44,809	31,139	12,680	16,457	5.5%	5.1%	3.7%	2.7%	4	4	4	4
Germany	20,383	15,187	9,546	15,068	2.5%	2.5%	2.8%	2.5%	5	5	5	5
Indonesia	16,155	11,296	9,496	11,389	2.0%	1.9%	2.7%	1.9%	6	6	6	8
Mexico	14,993	11,081	8,487	9,028	1.8%	1.8%	2.4%	1.5%	7	7	7	11
Australia	14,950	10,140	4,710	11,992	1.8%	1.7%	1.4%	2.0%	8	9	12	7
Russian Federation	14,597	11,026	3,506	13,274	1.8%	1.8%	1.0%	2.2%	9	8	14	6
Canada	11,500	8,678	6,272	10,190	1.4%	1.4%	1.8%	1.7%	10	10	8	9
United Kingdom	9,647	7,403	5,970	10,143	1.2%	1.2%	1.7%	1.7%	11	11	9	10
India	8,031	5,347	5,889	7,615	1.0%	0.9%	1.7%	1.3%	12	13	10	12
Netherlands	7,893	5,888	3,107	5,041	1.0%	1.0%	0.9%	0.8%	13	12	15	15
France	6,978	5,232	4,768	7,393	0.9%	0.9%	1.4%	1.2%	14	14	11	13
Brazil	5,558	4,082	4,380	6,676	0.7%	0.7%	1.3%	1.1%	15	15	13	14
Belgium	3,808	2,838	1,885	2,562	0.5%	0.5%	0.5%	0.4%	16	16	17	19
Italy	3,135	2,369	2,709	3,981	0.4%	0.4%	0.8%	0.7%	17	17	16	16
Spain	2,794	2,121	1,807	3,450	0.3%	0.3%	0.5%	0.6%	18	18	19	17
Turkey	2,587	1,853	1,846	2,873	0.3%	0.3%	0.5%	0.5%	19	21	18	18
Switzerland	2,495	1,958	1,290	2,335	0.3%	0.3%	0.4%	0.4%	20	20	21	20
Ireland	2,485	2,040	1,302	1,374	0.3%	0.3%	0.4%	0.2%	21	19	20	24

Poland	2,017	1,497	1,097	2,219	0.2%	0.2%	0.3%	0.4%	22	22	22	21
Sweden	1,524	1,152	738	1,695	0.2%	0.2%	0.2%	0.3%	23	23	25	22
Norway	1,476	1,071	598	1,412	0.2%	0.2%	0.2%	0.2%	24	24	27	23
Czech Republic	1,396	1,041	873	911	0.2%	0.2%	0.3%	0.2%	25	25	23	26
Austria	1,245	904	646	1,260	0.2%	0.1%	0.2%	0.2%	26	26	26	25
Hungary	1,146	873	773	532	0.1%	0.1%	0.2%	0.1%	27	27	24	30
Finland	546	409	432	647	0.1%	0.1%	0.1%	0.1%	28	28	30	28
Denmark	512	403	552	694	0.1%	0.2%	0.1%	0.1%	29	29	28	27
Slovak Republic	367	277	495	367	0.0%	0.1%	0.1%	0.1%	30	30	29	33
Portugal	342	256	310	482	0.0%	0.1%	0.1%	0.1%	31	31	32	31
Luxembourg	325	274	192	267	0.0%	0.1%	0.1%	0.0%	32	32	34	34
Greece	241	183	200	585	0.0%	0.1%	0.1%	0.1%	33	33	33	29
Romania	233	168	320	465	0.0%	0.0%	0.1%	0.1%	34	34	31	32
Cyprus	150	115	21	158	0.0%	0.0%	0.0%	0.0%	35	35	42	37
Estonia	128	95	58	134	0.0%	0.0%	0.0%	0.0%	36	36	37	38
Slovenia	101	74	84	162	0.0%	0.0%	0.0%	0.0%	37	37	36	36
Bulgaria	84	62	103	180	0.0%	0.0%	0.0%	0.0%	38	38	35	35
Malta	41	29	36	48	0.0%	0.0%	0.0%	0.0%	39	39	41	42
Lithuania	33	25	57	116	0.0%	0.0%	0.0%	0.0%	40	40	39	39
Croatia	27	21	57	114	0.0%	0.0%	0.0%	0.0%	41	41	38	40
Latvia	25	18	36	68	0.0%	0.0%	0.0%	0.0%	42	42	40	41
Rest of world	305,935	241,127	107,149	224,819	37.4%	39.5%	30.9%	37.4%				
Sum of bilaterals	817,514	610,362	346,832	600,551	63%	60%	69%	63%				
Aggregate	817,514	608,320	346,832	600,551								

Note: Authors' calculations based on **WIOD**, 2016 release.

Table 11A.5   **Bilateral exports by United Kingdom, 2014**

	Million US$				Shares in total				Ranking of countries			
	GX	VAX-D	VAX-P	VAX-C	GX	VAX-D	VAX-P	VAX-C	GX	VAX-D	VAX-P	VAX-C
United States	85,559	64,519	47,428	77,249	11.4%	11.1%	12.9%	13.6%	1	1	1	1
Germany	54,147	40,702	25,403	36,615	7.2%	7.0%	6.9%	6.4%	2	2	3	2
France	46,573	36,845	25,954	34,209	6.2%	6.3%	7.1%	6.0%	3	3	2	3
Ireland	34,477	27,275	13,478	14,828	4.6%	4.7%	3.7%	2.6%	4	4	5	6
China	27,405	19,194	18,140	29,480	3.6%	3.3%	4.9%	5.2%	5	6	4	4
Luxembourg	23,757	20,654	8,153	2,404	3.2%	3.6%	2.2%	0.4%	6	5	8	29
Netherlands	23,602	17,874	8,065	12,956	3.1%	3.1%	2.2%	2.3%	7	7	10	8
Italy	21,798	17,132	11,863	17,953	2.9%	2.9%	3.2%	3.2%	8	8	6	5
Belgium	21,045	16,017	8,138	11,526	2.8%	2.8%	2.2%	2.0%	9	9	9	11
Switzerland	19,449	15,218	7,844	13,332	2.6%	2.6%	2.1%	2.3%	10	10	12	7
Canada	17,523	13,282	9,360	12,365	2.3%	2.3%	2.5%	2.2%	11	11	7	10
Russian Federation	14,236	10,309	3,625	12,742	1.9%	1.8%	1.0%	2.2%	12	12	20	9
Spain	12,959	9,666	5,975	10,234	1.7%	1.7%	1.6%	1.8%	13	13	13	13
Sweden	11,769	9,048	4,627	7,796	1.6%	1.6%	1.3%	1.4%	14	14	17	15
Norway	11,426	8,671	5,017	7,679	1.5%	1.5%	1.4%	1.3%	15	15	16	16
Japan	9,919	7,414	8,036	11,280	1.3%	1.3%	2.2%	2.0%	16	16	11	12
South Korea	9,694	7,405	5,808	7,148	1.3%	1.3%	1.6%	1.3%	17	17	14	17
Australia	8,990	6,920	3,998	8,393	1.2%	1.2%	1.1%	1.5%	18	18	19	14
Denmark	8,101	6,271	4,354	4,900	1.1%	1.1%	1.2%	0.9%	19	19	18	21
India	7,260	4,781	5,528	6,261	1.0%	0.8%	1.5%	·1.1%	20	21	15	18
Poland	7,153	5,509	3,281	5,880	1.0%	0.9%	0.9%	1.0%	21	20	22	20

Turkey	6,082	4,262	3,042	4,662	0.8%	0.7%	0.8%	0.8%	22	22	23	22
Brazil	5,091	3,838	3,439	5,885	0.7%	0.7%	0.9%	1.0%	23	23	21	19
Finland	3,784	2,940	1,957	2,810	0.5%	0.5%	0.5%	0.5%	24	24	26	25
Austria	3,486	2,658	2,061	3,342	0.5%	0.4%	0.6%	0.6%	25	25	25	24
Czech Republic	3,060	2,313	1,654	2,051	0.4%	0.4%	0.5%	0.4%	26	26	27	30
Portugal	3,050	2,372	1,433	2,606	0.4%	0.4%	0.4%	0.5%	27	27	28	26
Mexico	2,784	2,134	2,616	3,705	0.4%	0.4%	0.7%	0.7%	28	28	24	23
Greece	2,627	2,097	1,131	2,588	0.3%	0.4%	0.3%	0.5%	29	29	33	27
Taiwan	2,228	1,705	1,403	2,453	0.3%	0.3%	0.4%	0.4%	30	30	30	28
Hungary	2,122	1,657	1,249	1,339	0.3%	0.3%	0.3%	0.2%	31	31	31	33
Malta	1,983	1,717	1,175	653	0.3%	0.3%	0.3%	0.1%	32	32	32	37
Romania	1,567	1,204	988	1,547	0.2%	0.2%	0.3%	0.3%	33	33	34	32
Cyprus	1,080	853	303	836	0.1%	0.1%	0.1%	0.1%	34	34	37	34
Indonesia	972	722	1,415	1,993	0.1%	0.1%	0.4%	0.4%	35	35	29	31
Slovak Republic	810	605	608	730	0.1%	0.1%	0.2%	0.1%	36	36	35	35
Bulgaria	754	577	349	676	0.1%	0.1%	0.1%	0.1%	37	37	36	36
Lithuania	544	409	191	499	0.1%	0.1%	0.1%	0.1%	38	38	41	39
Croatia	521	420	294	519	0.1%	0.1%	0.1%	0.1%	39	39	38	38
Estonia	476	364	177	393	0.1%	0.1%	0.0%	0.1%	40	40	42	41
Latvia	465	359	194	416	0.1%	0.1%	0.1%	0.1%	41	41	40	40
Slovenia	421	315	225	376	0.1%	0.1%	0.1%	0.1%	42	42	39	42
Rest of world	230,852	183,150	107,091	184,102	30.7%	31.5%	29.2%	32.3%				
Sum of bilaterals	751,599	581,373	367,067	569,411	69%	68%	71%	68%				
Aggregate	751,599	579,453	367,067	569,411								

Note: Authors' calculations based on WIOD, 2016 release.

Table 11A.6   Bilateral exports by Australia, 2014

	Million US$				Shares in total				Ranking of countries			
	GX	VAX-D	VAX-P	VAX-C	GX	VAX-D	VAX-P	VAX-C	GX	VAX-D	VAX-P	VAX-C
China	76,645	64,395	59,484	59,182	26.7%	26.7%	29.5%	24.8%	1	1	1	1
Japan	46,272	39,248	30,752	32,570	16.1%	16.3%	15.3%	13.6%	2	2	2	2
South Korea	16,058	13,436	9,498	8,734	5.6%	5.6%	4.7%	3.7%	3	3	4	4
Taiwan	11,409	9,636	5,196	4,717	4.0%	4.0%	2.6%	2.0%	4	4	6	7
United States	10,161	8,294	9,546	17,430	3.5%	3.4%	4.7%	7.3%	5	5	3	3
India	7,844	6,305	6,625	6,661	2.7%	2.6%	3.3%	2.8%	6	6	5	5
Indonesia	6,361	5,294	5,010	5,962	2.2%	2.2%	2.5%	2.5%	7	7	7	6
United Kingdom	3,736	3,134	2,517	4,267	1.3%	1.3%	1.2%	1.8%	8	8	8	8
Brazil	1,952	1,683	2,149	2,873	0.7%	0.7%	1.1%	1.2%	9	9	9	10
Canada	1,807	1,506	1,275	2,482	0.6%	0.6%	0.6%	1.0%	10	10	12	11
Germany	1,602	1,346	2,056	3,046	0.6%	0.6%	1.0%	1.3%	11	11	10	9
France	1,271	1,084	1,670	2,232	0.4%	0.4%	0.8%	0.9%	12	12	11	12
Switzerland	1,086	954	741	1,032	0.4%	0.4%	0.4%	0.4%	13	13	18	18
Netherlands	941	785	771	1,147	0.3%	0.3%	0.4%	0.5%	14	14	17	15
Italy	887	745	1,220	1,519	0.3%	0.3%	0.6%	0.6%	15	15	13	14
Turkey	677	482	952	973	0.2%	0.2%	0.5%	0.4%	16	18	15	19
Spain	674	566	851	1,131	0.2%	0.2%	0.4%	0.5%	17	17	16	16
Belgium	672	569	640	638	0.2%	0.2%	0.3%	0.3%	18	16	19	20
Poland	475	408	472	626	0.2%	0.2%	0.2%	0.3%	19	19	21	21
Mexico	475	387	990	1,110	0.2%	0.2%	0.5%	0.5%	20	20	14	17
Sweden	389	331	306	451	0.1%	0.1%	0.2%	0.2%	21	21	22	22

Russian Federation	360	292	623	1,631	0.1%	0.1%	0.3%	0.7%	22	22	22	20	13
Denmark	329	287	285	312	0.1%	0.1%	0.1%	0.1%	23	23	23	23	24
Ireland	230	202	254	259	0.1%	0.1%	0.1%	0.1%	24	24	24	24	26
Norway	205	170	188	328	0.1%	0.1%	0.1%	0.1%	25	25	25	27	23
Austria	197	166	228	310	0.1%	0.1%	0.1%	0.1%	26	27	26	25	25
Bulgaria	192	167	128	127	0.1%	0.1%	0.1%	0.1%	27	26	27	29	32
Czech Republic	143	123	225	214	0.0%	0.1%	0.1%	0.1%	28	28	28	26	28
Finland	108	88	147	198	0.0%	0.1%	0.1%	0.1%	29	29	29	28	30
Romania	73	62	120	203	0.0%	0.1%	0.1%	0.1%	30	30	30	33	29
Luxembourg	66	61	60	59	0.0%	0.0%	0.0%	0.0%	31	31	31	35	36
Slovak Republic	47	40	122	116	0.0%	0.1%	0.1%	0.0%	32	32	32	31	33
Greece	41	36	121	222	0.0%	0.1%	0.1%	0.1%	33	33	33	32	27
Slovenia	34	28	41	60	0.0%	0.0%	0.0%	0.0%	34	34	34	36	35
Hungary	25	21	126	110	0.0%	0.1%	0.1%	0.0%	35	35	35	30	34
Portugal	22	18	117	157	0.0%	0.1%	0.1%	0.1%	36	36	36	34	31
Estonia	9	8	20	29	0.0%	0.0%	0.0%	0.0%	37	37	37	39	41
Lithuania	8	6	32	51	0.0%	0.0%	0.0%	0.0%	38	38	38	37	37
Croatia	7	6	31	48	0.0%	0.0%	0.0%	0.0%	39	39	39	38	38
Latvia	7	6	17	29	0.0%	0.0%	0.0%	0.0%	40	41	41	40	40
Cyprus	7	6	13	31	0.0%	0.0%	0.0%	0.0%	41	40	40	41	39
Malta	5	4	12	15	0.0%	0.0%	0.0%	0.0%	42	42	42	42	42
Rest of world	93,652	78,402	55,886	75,384	32.6%	32.6%	27.7%	31.6%					
Sum of bilaterals	287,162	240,786	201,516	238,674	67%	67%	72%	68%					
Aggregate	287,162	240,468	201,516	238,674									

Note: Authors' calculations based on **WIOD**, 2016 release.

Table 11A.7   Bilateral exports by Brazil, 2014

	Million US$				Shares in total				Ranking of countries			
	GX	VAX-D	VAX-P	VAX-C	GX	VAX-D	VAX-P	VAX-C	GX	VAX-D	VAX-P	VAX-C
China	41,012	33,493	32,027	32,570	15.2%	16.1%	20.6%	15.7%	1	1	1	1
United States	29,552	20,999	18,184	25,488	10.9%	10.1%	11.7%	12.3%	2	2	2	2
Japan	9,054	7,084	6,202	8,508	3.4%	3.4%	4.0%	4.1%	3	3	3	3
Netherlands	8,682	6,497	3,385	3,828	3.2%	3.1%	2.2%	1.8%	4	4	8	9
Germany	7,025	5,359	4,938	6,015	2.6%	2.6%	3.2%	2.9%	5	6	5	4
India	6,891	5,654	5,695	5,804	2.5%	2.7%	3.7%	2.8%	6	5	4	5
France	4,871	3,879	3,771	4,737	1.8%	1.9%	2.4%	2.3%	7	7	6	7
Mexico	4,856	3,388	2,419	3,193	1.8%	1.6%	1.6%	1.5%	8	10	12	13
United Kingdom	4,779	3,840	3,047	5,107	1.8%	1.8%	2.0%	2.5%	9	8	9	6
South Korea	4,341	3,416	3,407	3,471	1.6%	1.6%	2.2%	1.7%	10	9	7	10
Italy	4,090	3,169	2,908	3,290	1.5%	1.5%	1.9%	1.6%	11	11	10	11
Russian Federation	3,656	2,833	1,125	4,055	1.4%	1.4%	0.7%	2.0%	12	12	18	8
Canada	3,495	2,600	2,300	2,949	1.3%	1.2%	1.5%	1.4%	13	15	14	14
Indonesia	3,476	2,736	2,851	3,209	1.3%	1.3%	1.8%	1.5%	14	13	11	12
Spain	3,302	2,601	2,418	2,632	1.2%	1.2%	1.6%	1.3%	15	14	13	15
Belgium	3,121	2,408	1,296	2,013	1.2%	1.2%	0.8%	1.0%	16	16	17	16
Taiwan	2,572	2,058	1,637	1,723	1.0%	1.0%	1.1%	0.8%	17	17	15	18
Norway	1,708	1,362	855	1,095	0.6%	0.7%	0.5%	0.5%	18	18	20	20
Turkey	1,677	1,280	1,509	1,504	0.6%	0.6%	1.0%	0.7%	19	19	16	19
Portugal	1,185	940	720	849	0.4%	0.5%	0.5%	0.4%	20	21	21	21
Australia	1,164	942	1,086	1,943	0.4%	0.5%	0.7%	0.9%	21	20	19	17

Denmark	908	744	556	531	0.3%	0.4%	0.4%	0.3%	22	22	23	26
Ireland	832	606	293	654	0.3%	0.3%	0.2%	0.3%	23	23	29	25
Sweden	697	546	498	712	0.3%	0.3%	0.3%	0.3%	24	24	24	24
Poland	646	510	589	760	0.2%	0.4%	0.2%	0.4%	25	25	22	22
Switzerland	561	424	413	740	0.2%	0.3%	0.2%	0.4%	26	27	25	23
Finland	560	435	362	397	0.1%	0.2%	0.2%	0.2%	27	26	26	28
Romania	347	273	328	383	0.1%	0.2%	0.2%	0.2%	28	28	27	29
Austria	341	265	319	491	0.1%	0.2%	0.2%	0.2%	29	29	28	27
Slovenia	323	254	243	251	0.1%	0.2%	0.1%	0.1%	30	30	30	32
Bulgaria	195	163	137	147	0.1%	0.1%	0.1%	0.1%	31	31	34	34
Hungary	187	142	189	169	0.1%	0.1%	0.1%	0.1%	32	33	32	33
Greece	183	148	202	330	0.1%	0.1%	0.1%	0.2%	33	32	31	30
Czech Republic	143	110	182	271	0.1%	0.1%	0.1%	0.1%	34	34	33	31
Slovak Republic	65	48	121	128	0.0%	0.1%	0.1%	0.1%	35	35	36	35
Croatia	61	49	65	91	0.0%	0.0%	0.0%	0.0%	36	36	35	36
Estonia	50	34	30	50	0.0%	0.0%	0.0%	0.0%	37	37	38	40
Lithuania	46	36	50	88	0.0%	0.0%	0.0%	0.0%	38	38	37	37
Cyprus	42	31	20	56	0.0%	0.0%	0.0%	0.0%	39	39	39	39
Latvia	30	23	28	46	0.0%	0.0%	0.0%	0.0%	40	40	41	41
Luxembourg	29	24	54	77	0.0%	0.0%	0.0%	0.0%	41	41	40	38
Malta	22	15	13	26	0.0%	0.0%	0.0%	0.0%	42	42	42	42
Rest of world	113,484	87,038	49,074	76,775	42.0%	41.8%	31.5%	37.1%				
Sum of bilaterals	270,263	208,455	155,545	207,157	58%	58%	68%	63%				
Aggregate	270,263	208,346	155,545	207,157								

Note: Authors' calculations based on WIOD, 2016 release.

References

Aichele, Rahel, Gabriel Felbermayr, and Inga Heiland. 2014. "Going Deep: The Trade and Welfare Effects of TTIP." CESifo Working Paper 5150, CESifo Munich.

Baldwin, Richard, and Anthony J. Venables (2013). "Spiders and Snakes: Offshoring and Agglomeration in the Global Economy." *Journal of International Economics* 90 (2): 245–254.

Bems, Rudolfs, Robert C. Johnson, and Kei-Mu Yi. 2011. "Vertical Linkages and the Collapse of Global Trade." *American Economic Review (Papers and Proceedings)*: 101 (3): 308–12.

Bems, Rudolfs, Robert C. Johnson, and Kei-Mu Yi. 2013. "The Great Trade Collapse." *Annual Review of Economics* 5 (1): 375–400.

Blanchard, Emily, Chad P. Bown, and Robert C. Johnson. 2017. *Global Value Chains and Trade Policy*. Mimeo, August.

Brakman, Steven, Harry Garretsen, and Tristan Kohl. 2018. "Consequences of Brexit and Options for a 'Global Britain.'" *Papers in Regional Science* 97 (1): 55–72.

Chen, Wen, Bart Los, Philip McCann, Raquel Ortega-Argilés, Mark Thissen, and Frank van Oort. 2018. "The Continental Divide? Economic Exposure to Brexit in Regions and Countries on Both Sides of the Channel." *Papers in Regional Science* 97 (1): 25–54.

Chenery, Hollis B., and Tsunehiko Watanabe. 1958. "International Comparisons of the Structure of Production." *Econometrica* 26 (4): 487–521.

Dhingra, Swati, Rebecca Freeman, and Eleonora Mavroeidi. 2018. "Beyond Tariff Reductions: What Extra Boost from Trade Agreement Provisions?" CEP Discussion Paper 1532. London School of Economics.

Dietzenbacher, Erik, Jan A. van der Linden, and Albert E. Steenge. 1993. "The Regional Extraction Method: EC Input-Output Comparisons." *Economic Systems Research* 5 (2): 185–206.

Hummels, D., J. Ishii, and K.-M. Yi. 2001. "The Nature and Growth of Vertical Specialization in World Trade." *Journal of International Economics* 54 (1): 75–96.

Johnson, Robert C. 2014. "Five Facts about Value-Added Exports and Implications for Macroeconomics and Trade Research." *Journal of Economic Perspectives* 28 (2): 119–42.

Johnson, Robert C. 2017. "Measuring Global Value Chains." NBER Working Paper No. 24027. Cambridge, MA: National Bureau of Economic Research. Forthcoming in *Annual Review of Economics*.

Johnson, Robert C., and Guillermo Noguera. 2012. "Accounting for Intermediates: Production Sharing and Trade in Value Added." *Journal of International Economics* 86 (2): 224–36.

Johnson, Robert C., and Guillermo Noguera. 2017. "A Portrait of Trade in Value Added over Four Decades." *Review of Economics and Statistics* 99 (5): 896–911.

Kaplan, Lennart C., Tristan Kohl, and Inmaculada Martinez-Zarzoso. 2018. "Supply-Chain Trade and Labor Market Outcomes: The Case of the 2004 European Union Enlargement." *Review of International Economics* 26 (2): 481–506.

Koopman, Robert, Zhi Wang, and Shang-Jin Wei. 2012. "Estimating Domestic Content in Exports When Processing Trade Is Pervasive." *Journal of Development Economics* 99 (1): 178–89.

Koopman, Robert, Zhi Wang, and Shang-Jin Wei. 2014. "Tracing Value-Added and Double Counting in Gross Exports." *American Economic Review* 104 (2): 459–94.

Laget, Edith, Alberto Osnago, Nadia Rocha, and Michele Ruta. 2018. "Deep Trade

Agreements and Global Value Chains." Policy Research Working Paper 8491. World Bank.

Landefeld, J. Steven. 2015. *Handbook for a System of Extended International and Global Accounts (SEIGA) Overview of Major Issues.* Draft November 23 for United Nations Statistical Division.

Los, Bart, Marcel P. Timmer, and Gaaitzen J. de Vries. 2015. "How Global Are Global Value Chains? A New Approach to Measure International Fragmentation." *Journal of Regional Science* 55 (1): 66–92.

Los, Bart, Marcel P. Timmer, and Gaaitzen J. de Vries. 2016. "Tracing Value-Added and Double Counting in Gross Exports: Comment." *American Economic Review* 106 (7): 1958–66.

Miller, Ronald E. 1966. "Interregional Feedback Effects in Input-Output Models: Some Preliminary Results." *Papers in Regional Science* 17 (1): 105–25.

Miller, Ronald F., and Michael L. Lahr. 2001. "A Taxonomy of Extractions." In *Regional Science Perspectives in Economic Analysis*, edited by Michael L. Lahr and Ronald E. Miller, 407–41. Amsterdam: Elsevier Science.

Morimoto, Yoshinori. 1970. "On Aggregation Problems in Input-Output Analysis." *Review of Economic Studies* 37 (1): 119–26.

Nagengast, Arne J., and Robert Stehrer. 2016. "Accounting for the Differences Between Gross and Value Added Trade Balances." *The World Economy* 39 (9): 1276–1306.

Noguera, Guillermo. 2012. "Trade Costs and Gravity for Gross and Value Added Trade." University of California at Berkeley and Columbia University, mimeo.

Nomaler, Z. Onder, and Bart Verspagen. 2014. *Analysing Global Value Chains Using Input-Output Economics: Proceed with Care.* UNU-MERIT Working Papers Series, No. 2014–070. Maastricht: UNU-MERIT.

Paelinck, Jean, Jean de Caevel, and Joseph Degueldre. 1965. "Analyse Quantitative de Certaines Phénomènes du Développement Régional Polarisé: Essai de Simulation Statique d'Itéraires de Propagation." In *Problèmes de Conversion Économique: Analyses Théoriques et Études Appliquées*, Bibliothèque de l'Institut de Science Économique, No. 7, 341–87. Paris: M.-Th. Génin.

Simpson, David, and Jinkichi Tsukui. 1965. "The Fundamental Structure of Input-Output Tables, An International Comparison." *Review of Economics and Statistics* 47 (4): 434–46.

Strassert, Günter. 1968. "Zur Bestimmung strategischer Sektoren mit Hilfe von Input-Output-Modellen." *Jahrbücher für Nationalökonomie und Statistik* 182 (3): 211–15.

Timmer, Marcel P., Erik Dietzenbacher, Bart Los, Robert Stehrer, and Gaaitzen J. de Vries. 2015. "An Illustrated User Guide to the World Input-Output Database: The Case of Global Automotive Production." *Review of International Economics* 23 (3): 575–605.

Wang, Zhi, Shang-Jin Wei, and Kunfu Zhu. 2018. "Quantifying International Production Sharing at the Bilateral And Sector Levels." NBER Working Paper No. 19677, revised version. Cambridge, MA: National Bureau of Economic Research.

III

Globally Intangible Capital

12

A Portrait of US Factoryless
Goods Producers

Fariha Kamal

12.1 Introduction

Goods production is increasingly vertically disintegrated (Johnson and Noguera, 2012). An extreme form of fragmentation of the goods production process entails outsourcing the processing and manufacturing activities while retaining ownership of the intellectual property and controlling sales to customers, giving rise to the so-called factoryless goods producers (FGPs). Firms may choose to outsource the physical transformation process both within and across firm as well as national borders. Firm organization decisions that give rise to complex global production chains have been linked to the simultaneous ascent of China as the world's factory and the decline in US manufacturing (Feenstra and Wei 2010; Autor, Dorn, and Hanson 2013; Pierce and Schott 2016). The fragmented nature of economic activity has reshaped the global production landscape and subsequently poses challenges for producing meaningful national statistics.

The Office of Management and Budget (OMB) mandated US statistical agencies to classify FGPs within the existing data collection system to bet-

Fariha Kamal is a principal research economist at the US Census Bureau.

Any opinions and conclusions expressed herein are those of the authors and do not represent the views of the US Census Bureau or the Bureau of Economic Analysis. All results have been reviewed to ensure that no confidential information is disclosed. I thank James Boohaker for outstanding research assistance. I thank Emek Basker, Teresa Fort, Brent Moulton, John Murphy, and seminar participants at the Census Bureau Economic Research seminar for valuable comments, and Nikolas Zolas for generously sharing data on firm ownership of intellectual property. Jim Fetzer and William Wisinewski provided timely disclosure assistance. For acknowledgments, sources of research support, and disclosure of the author's material financial relationships, if any, please see https://www.nber.org/books-and-chapters/challenges-globalization-measurement-national-accounts/portrait-us-factoryless-goods-producers.

425

ter reflect the changes in modern production arrangements.[1] The Census Bureau's efforts to isolate goods producers that do not perform physical transformation of goods led to data collection, through a special inquiry, on the purchase of contract manufacturing services (CMS). Purchase of CMS indicates if an establishment outsources part or all of its production transformation activities to another establishment either under common ownership or at arm's length, within or outside the United States. However, post-collection interviews with responding establishments revealed inconsistencies in how respondents understood the CMS purchase question as intended (Murphy 2015). OMB concluded that the special inquiry failed "to yield responses that provide accurate and reliable identification and classification of FGPs" at the establishment level and resulted in the latest recommendation to further evaluate "the feasibility of developing methods for the consistent identification and classification of Factoryless Goods Producers that are accurate and reliable" (80 FR 46479–6484).[2]

This chapter explores the feasibility of identifying FGP *firms*. Recognizing that establishment responses to purchase of CMS alone may yield unreliable classification of FGPs, this chapter augments establishment responses (in the 2012 Economic Census) with firm responses to purchase of CMS (in the 2012 Company Organization Survey) and information on firms' manufacturing activities (measured as employment in the manufacturing sector).[3] Although OMB's Economic Classification Policy Committee (ECPC) recommends measuring FGPs at the establishment level, a number of characteristics essential to identifying FGPs have historically not been collected at the establishment level. Research and design activities at the establishment level are collected on a yes/no basis and only for the wholesale sector, but real measures are available at the firm level in all sectors. Merchandise imports (more likely associated with FGP firms when production is not only outsourced but also offshored) are available at the firm level only. Moreover, company headquarters, which possess comprehensive knowledge of the firm's operations, may be better suited to respond to the special inquiry intended to measure FGP activity.

The focus on identifying factoryless activity as a firm level concept is further motivated by the view of the firm as the central decision maker that controls and coordinates the key economic activities of design, production, and sales, with each of its establishments specializing in a given activity. This view accords well with the empirical reality of within-firm realloca-

---

1. See the first federal register notice, issued on May 12, 2010, 75 FR 26856–26869, for more details.

2. See http://www.census.gov/eos/www/naics/federal_register_notices/fedregister.html for a comprehensive list of federal register notices pertaining to the North American Industrial Classification System.

3. Murphy (2015) reports results from the 2012 Economic Census. Responding firms to the special inquiry in the 2012 Company Organization Survey were not interviewed as extensively as responding establishments to the special inquiry in the 2012 Economic Census.

tions as well as the general importance of firms in shaping a range of economic outcomes. Fort, Pierce, and Schott (2018) document that plant exits at incumbent firms accounted for three-quarters of the total decline in US manufacturing between 1977 and 2012. A small number of "superstar" firms are responsible for the growing concentration of employment and output in US industries (Autor et al. 2017) and even comparative advantage of a country (Freund and Pierola 2015).

The classification of FGP firms in the existing data collection system faces two main challenges. First, goods-producing firms that outsource all production transformation activities are currently classified outside the manufacturing sector with other services-producing firms. Second, goods-producing firms that outsource only a part of the production transformation process are currently classified in the manufacturing sector with all other goods-producing firms. An instructive comparison of FGPs to other goods producers requires distinguishing the extent of factoryless production arrangements among manufacturing firms. The special inquiry on purchase of CMS was sent to both manufacturing and non-manufacturing establishments in an effort to identify all possible goods producers in the economy separately from services-producing firms.

This chapter begins by identifying three types of goods producers distinct from firms that provide services: FGP firms that outsource all production activities and do not have any domestic manufacturing activity; hybrid manufacturers that outsource some production activities but also own domestic manufacturing plants; traditional manufacturers that do not outsource any production and perform all production-related activities at own domestic plants; and distinct from goods producers are service providers that do not undertake any manufacturing activity—neither outsourcing nor owning any domestic manufacturing plants.[4]

The chapter then performs two sets of comparisons—FGP firms to service providers and hybrid manufacturers to traditional manufacturers—of characteristics guided by the conceptual definition of factoryless production. The ECPC's definition of FGPs states that the FGP "outsources all transformation steps that traditionally have been considered manufacturing, but undertakes all of the entrepreneurial steps and arranges for all required capital, labor, and material inputs required to make a good" (OMB, 2010). The conceptual definition of factoryless production can then be summarized along three main attributes: ownership of intellectual property, ownership and control of finished products, and outsourcing transformation activities (Doherty 2015). The characteristics studied, therefore, include ownership

---

4. I thank John Murphy for suggesting the terminology for the distinct firm types. Traditional manufacturers include both integrated manufacturers and firms that provide CMS. Hybrid and traditional manufacturers represent firms with primary activity in the manufacturing sector (NAICS 31–33). Service providers represent firms with primary activities outside the manufacturing sector.

of intellectual property (measured as research and development expenditures, number of patents, number of trademarks); ownership and sales of finished goods (measured as revenue); incidence of borderless production arrangements (measured as imports); incidence of "headquarter" activity encompassing strategic or organizational planning and decision-making activities (measured as employment in NAICS 54 and 55). These variables capture features hypothesized to be more prevalent at firms that outsource production. This approach, thus, combines two distinct strategies for identifying FGPs—self-identification by companies and their establishments on statistical surveys and implementation of a profiling method based on conceptual definitions.

The comparison of employment mix across sectors, ownership of intellectual property, and foreign imports between FGPs and service providers yields correlations consistent with the conceptual definition of factoryless production. I find that FGP firms tend to have higher shares of workers engaged in the provision of "headquarter" services, greater ownership of intellectual property, and higher propensities to import from abroad than service providers. FGPs tend to be smaller and younger than service providers. I also find that hybrid manufacturers tend to have higher shares of nonproduction workers, lower shares of production workers, greater ownership of intellectual property, and higher propensities to import from abroad than traditional manufacturers. Hybrid manufacturers tend to be larger than and similarly aged as traditional manufacturers.

The analyses in this chapter offer three main insights to guide identification of FGP firms within existing data collection systems. First, disagreements in responses to purchase of CMS between respondents in the Economic Census and the Company Organization Survey provide an instructive set of cases to select for cognitive interviews to help inform the feasibility of identifying FGPs at the establishment or firm level. Second, combining responses to the special inquiry with firm-level information on ownership of intellectual property, imports, and employment mix across sectors yields a picture consistent with the conceptual definition of factoryless production arrangements. Comparison of FGPs with service providers highlights differences in characteristics between two distinct entities currently classified outside the manufacturing sector. Comparison of hybrid manufacturers with traditional manufacturers highlights differences in characteristics between goods producers that outsource some production and those that perform all production and are currently classified together in the manufacturing sector. The results suggest a profiling method based not only on responses to special inquiries but one that also harnesses existing sources of data, hence, reducing respondent burden. Third, the meaningful correlations uncovered in this chapter between variables identified based on conceptual definitions and outsourcing status indicate a possible path toward developing a model-based approach to identify FGP firms.

This chapter relates closely to a set of studies examining responses to the special inquiry on purchase of CMS to characterize the extent and nature of FGP activity in the US economy. Kamal, Moulton, and Ribarsky (2015) evaluate data collection efforts on enterprises' purchase of CMS by the Census Bureau on the 2011 Company Organization Survey and the Bureau of Economic Analysis on the 2009 Benchmark Survey of US Direct Investment Abroad. The authors find that CMS purchasing firms tend to be larger and older. Bernard and Fort (2013), using the 2002 and 2007 Census of Wholesale Trade, find that firms with manufacturing activity that also have a FGP establishment in the wholesale sector are significantly larger compared to firms with a FGP establishment in the wholesale sector and wholesale activity only. Bernard and Fort (2015), using the 2007 Census of Wholesale Trade, document that FGP firms tend to be larger but younger than traditional wholesalers. Tracing employment back in time, they also document that FGPs include former manufacturing firms, new firms born as FGPs, and other firms that became FGPs. Bayard, Byrne, and Smith (2015) identify FGP firms engaged in semiconductor production in the 2007 Economic Census using external company directories and document that FGP firms are larger than non-FGP firms. Previous studies characterizing factoryless production arrangements have relied on a single source of data, or on data for a narrowly focused sector, and applied varying definitions of factoryless status, making it difficult to compare and draw inferences for the whole economy. This chapter implements a consistent definition of factoryless status across all sectors and draws from multiple data sources to provide a comprehensive picture of FGP firms as distinct from other goods- and services-producing firms in the US economy.

Developing reliable methods to classify FGP firms accurately in US data not only fulfills the Census Bureau's mandate to implement OMB's recommendation but also provides the foundation to conduct careful analyses of the economic consequences of extreme production fragmentation. Factoryless goods production divorces research and design from physical production. This has potentially significant implications for occupational structures, innovation, and international trade. Papers studying the impact of offshoring, an arrangement where goods production is located abroad, offer partial glimpses on the economic consequences along these dimensions.[5] Offshoring is associated with higher relative wages and demand for skilled labor in the home country, consistent with the concentration of design and R&D activities in the home country, while lower skilled production activities shift abroad (Bernard et al. 2017; Hummels et al. 2014; Mion and Zhu 2013). Offshoring is also associated with increases in product development and R&D expenditures (Bernard et al. 2017). Vertical specialization, an out-

---

5. Fort (2017), using the 2007 Census of Manufactures, documents that domestic outsourcing is more prevalent than offshoring but offshoring firms are almost twice as large.

come under extreme production fragmentation, changes the composition of international trade as it entails increases in imported intermediate inputs to produce goods for export (Hummels, Ishii, and Yi 2001).

The rest of the chapter proceeds as follows. Section 12.2 describes the data sources used to identify outsourcing of the physical transformation process and firm level inputs, output, ownership of intellectual property and imports. Section 12.3 identifies FGP firms currently classified outside the manufacturing sector and systematically documents the extent and characteristics of these firms in relation to service providers. Section 12.4 identifies hybrid manufacturers, manufacturing firms that outsource a part of the production process, and systematically documents the extent and characteristics of these firms in relation to traditional manufacturers. The final section concludes with discussion for future work.

12.2   Data

There does not exist a single data source that contains the ideal set of information to identify FGPs. Therefore, I utilize a host of confidential microdata sourced from the Census Bureau for the most recent year, 2012, of comprehensive data collection efforts. Responses to the special inquiry about purchase of CMS in the Economic Census and the Company Organization Survey are used as a first step toward identifying FGP firms.[6,7] Establishment responses in the Economic Census are aggregated at the firm level to enable comparison to responses in the Company Organization Survey.

The Economic Census, conducted in years ending in 2 and 7, cover the universe of private, non-farm establishments active in the economy. The annual Company Organization Survey is designed chiefly to maintain the Business Register. The Business Register is a current list of business establishments in the US and used as a survey frame to conduct the Economic Census every five years. The Company Organization Survey covers all multiunit companies with 250 or more employees and a selection of smaller companies. Smaller companies are only selected when administrative records indicate that the company may be undergoing organizational change and is expanding (adding establishments) or shrinking (dropping establishments).

The responses to the special inquiry are further combined with additional

6. In the context of this study, the Economic Census refers to the Census of Manufactures, Census of Wholesale Trade, and Census of Services. Establishments in every six-digit industry within manufacturing (NAICS 31–32), wholesale (NAICS 42), and Professional Scientific, and Technical Services (NAICS 54) and establishments in Corporate, Subsidiary, and Regional Managing Offices (NAICS 551114) were legally required to respond to the special inquiry on the use of CMS.

7. The Bureau of Economic Analysis also included a question about CMS on the BE-120 (Benchmark Survey of Transactions in Selected Services and Intellectual Property with Foreign Persons) and BE-10 (Benchmark Survey of U.S. Direct Investment Abroad) surveys. These data are not used in this paper.

firm-level variables. Employment by sector, number of establishments under common ownership, and payroll are aggregated to the firm level using the Longitudinal Business Database (LBD). The LBD contains information on employment, payroll, ownership, sector, and geography of the universe of establishments operating in the US private, non-farm sector with at least one employee (Jarmin and Miranda 2002). Firm age is equivalent to the age of its oldest establishment. The LBD also provides total revenue for the firm (Haltiwanger et al. 2017).[8]

Firm-level imports are sourced from the Longitudinal Firm Trade Transactions Database (LFTTD) that links the universe of individual customs transaction records to the firms that carry out these transactions (Bernard, Jensen, and Schott 2009).[9] Information on firm ownership of intellectual property—patents, trademarks, and R&D expenditures—is obtained from Dinlersoz, Goldschlag, Myers, and Zolas (forthcoming). The authors combine survey data on research and design expenditures sourced from the Business R&D and Innovation Survey (BRDIS) with administrative data sourced from the US Patent and Trademark Office on number of granted patents and trademarks. The statistics on R&D expenditures used in this chapter only include firms surveyed in the BRDIS.[10] US multinational firms and US affiliates of foreign multinational firms are identified using the mandatory surveys—US Direct Investment Abroad (USDIA) and Foreign Direct Investment in the United States (FDIUS)—conducted by the Bureau of Economic Analysis.[11]

12.2.1 Special Inquiry on Contract Manufacturing Services

The purchase of CMS identifies whether an establishment or firm outsources the fabrication of products. Appendix figures 12A.1 and 12A.2 display excerpts of the specific question about purchase of CMS from the Economic Census and Company Organization Survey, respectively.[12] The Economic Census and Company Organization Survey ask whether the establishment and firm, respectively, purchase CMS. The Economic Census also asks for the costs incurred to purchase these services, while the Company Organization Survey asks for the CMS cost as a percent of all expenses. The Company Organization Survey further asks whether the company pur-

8. See http://www.nber.org/data-appendix/c13492/appendix.pdf for details on construction of firm-level revenue.
9. LFTTD contains the universe of import transactions valued over $2,000.
10. Patent and trademark data are available for all firms in the LBD, but R&D data are only available for firms sampled in the BRDIS. The BRDIS sample constitutes firms that are known to have some R&D activity.
11. The Center for Economic Studies, in a joint project with the Bureau of Economic Analysis, has linked the 2012 USDIA and FDIUS to the Census Bureau's Business Register. The resulting crosswalks identify multinational firms in the LBD.
12. The Company Organization Survey and the Census of Manufactures also ask about providing CMS. The focus of this paper is CMS purchasers, not CMS providers.

chased these services inside or outside the United States and whether own affiliates abroad provided CMS.

A firm purchases CMS if at least one of its establishments in the Economic Census responded yes or it responded yes in the Company Organization Survey. An establishment in the Economic Census is identified as purchasing CMS if it answers affirmatively to the question of purchasing CMS or if it reports a non-zero value for either costs incurred to purchase CMS or sales generated from products whose purchases were reported as CMS costs. A firm in the Company Organization Survey purchases CMS if it answers affirmatively to the question of purchasing CMS, or it provides a non-zero percent of the cost of sales from expenses for CMS, or it answers affirmatively to using a third-party contractor either inside or outside the United States. A firm does not purchase CMS if all its establishments respond no to purchasing CMS in the Economic Census or it responded no in the Company Organization Survey.

The choice to utilize responses in the Economic Census aggregated at the firm level in addition to firm-level responses to the Company Organization Survey ensures the broadest coverage of likely FGP firms. The unweighted response rates for purchasing CMS are 61.4 percent for the Census of Wholesale Trade, 57.7 percent for the Census of Manufacture, and 47.9 percent for the Census of Services (Murphy 2015). Over 95 percent of firms provided a response (yes or no) to purchasing CMS in the Company Organization Survey.[13] There is a high degree of disagreement in responses across the two data sources. Table 12A.1 shows the distribution of firms by their response status (yes/no/missing) to purchasing CMS in the Economic Census and the Company Organization Survey. The total number of firms represent the analysis sample of FGP and other goods- and services-producing firms considered in this study. About 40 percent of firms that provided a non-missing response in both data sets disagreed in their responses. Most of the disagreements are due to firms that respond no to purchasing CMS in the Company Organization Survey but one of their establishments responded yes to purchasing CMS in the Economic Census.[14]

I apply a broad and restricted definition of CMS purchase status to balance between the goal of comprehensively identifying outsourcing firms in the economy and accounting for the high incidence of disagreement in firm responses to purchase of CMS across the two data sources. Under the broad

13. The Economic Census and Company Organization Survey data from the special inquiry are not adjusted for non-response.

14. The high incidence of disagreement might be driven by differences in survey questionnaires. The Company Organization Survey specifies use of "company's patents, trade secrets, or proprietary technology" in purchase of CMS while the Economic Census does not (see figures 12A.1 and 12A.2). The 2017 Economic Census asks establishments if it determined "the design or specifications for any of the products that were manufactured on its behalf." For example, see https://bhs.econ.census.gov/ombpdfs/export/MC-32312_mu.pdf (accessed September 30, 2018). An assessment of responses to the newly designed questions offers a potentially fruitful avenue for evaluating the disagreements.

definition, an outsourcing firm responds yes to purchasing CMS in either data source.[15] Under the restricted definition, an outsourcing firm responds yes to purchasing CMS in both data sources. Firms that do not outsource are similarly categorized except the firm responds no to purchasing CMS. Thus, firms under the restricted definition are necessarily a subset of firms under the broad definition. Analyses in the chapter only include firms that can be classified as purchasing or not purchasing CMS. Respondents that did not provide a response and respondents that did not receive the special inquiry are excluded. An assumption maintained in the discussion of descriptive results in this chapter is that non-respondents are not systematically different from respondents.

Under the broad definition, the analyses sample contains 16,500 FGPs and 112,000 service providers; and 11,000 hybrid manufacturers and 10,000 traditional manufacturers. Under the restricted definition, the analyses sample contains 400 FGP and 1,300 service providers; and 750 hybrid manufacturers and 400 traditional manufacturers.[16] The identified firms are not nationally representative, but they provide the opportunity to assess the potential scope and challenges associated with the task of measuring factoryless activities in the existing data collection system.

For ease of exposition, each section discusses results based on the broad definition unless statistics differ markedly between the broad and restricted definitions.

12.3 Factoryless Activity outside the Manufacturing Sector

The goal in this section is to identify FGPs among firms that are currently classified outside manufacturing sector. A FGP is defined as a firm that purchases CMS and does not have any manufacturing employment. However, this definition does not explicitly capture performance of design activities, a key FGP characteristic. Nonetheless, in contrast to prior studies, it offers the advantage of enabling consistent classification of FGP firms in both the wholesale and services sectors. For example, Bernard and Fort (2015) define an FGP firm as having at least one establishment in the wholesale sector that performs design/engineering/R&D activity, purchases CMS, and has no manufacturing establishments. This definition cannot be applied to the services sector where comparable measures of design/engineering/R&D

15. Under the broad definition, a firm purchases CMS if it meets any of the following four criteria: (i) responds yes to purchasing CMS in the Company Organization Survey but one of its establishments responded no in the Economic Census; (ii) responds no to purchasing CMS in the Company Organization Survey but one of its establishments responded yes in the Economic Census; (iii) missing response in Company Organization Survey but one of its establishments responded yes in the Economic Census; or (iv) missing response in Economic Census but responded yes to purchasing CMS in the Company Organization Survey.

16. The final analyses samples only include firms for which we are able to obtain information on basic characteristics from the LBD. Over 90 percent of identified firms were linked to the LBD. Firm counts are rounded to comply with Census Bureau rules on disclosure avoidance.

Table 12.1   **Firm employment shares of goods producers outside the manufacturing sector, 2012**

		Services		
	Wholesale	All	% Share in headquarter services	Other
Broad Definition				
FGP	0.92	0.04	63%	0.03
Service Provider	0.16	0.40	35%	0.45
Restricted Definition				
FGP	0.75	0.16	80%	0.09
Service Provider	0.46	0.26	65%	0.28

Note: This table displays firms' average share of sectoral employment. FGP: firms that purchase CMS and do not have manufacturing employment. Service Provider: firms that do not purchase CMS and do not have manufacturing employment. See text for "broad" and "restricted" definitions. Headquarter Services refers to employment in NAICS 54 (Professional, Scientific, and Technical Services) and NAICS 55 (Management of Companies and Enterprises). Other refers to employment in retail, agriculture, transportation, warehousing and utilities, construction, and public administration.

activities at the establishment level do not exist. To test whether this definition is capable of capturing FGPs as suggested by the conceptual definition of factoryless production arrangements, I compare the sectoral employment distribution, ownership of intellectual property, and foreign imports at identified FGPs with those at identified service providers.

12.3.1   Employment Shares

The conceptual definition of FGPs—entities that outsource all transformation activities and retain control of research and design and final sales to customers—suggests three implications for the employment mix at an FGP firm. First, the FGP firm should have little to no manufacturing employment. Second, FGP firms should be more active than service providers in the wholesale sector that encompasses delivery, warehousing, order fulfillment, and logistics. Third, services employment at an FGP firm should be relatively concentrated in "headquarter" services, which includes R&D personnel. The focus on FGP firms currently classified outside the manufacturing sector already excludes manufacturing activity and, thus, by construction is concentrated in the wholesale and services sectors. We should then expect to observe FGP firms with relatively higher shares of employment in wholesale and services than service providers.

Table 12.1 presents the average shares of employment in wholesale, services, and all other sectors at FGP and service-providing firms.[17] Employment in the services sector is further decomposed into employment in pro-

17. "Other" sectors include retail, agriculture, transportation, warehousing, and utilities, construction, and public administration but exclude manufacturing.

Table 12.2   **Innovative activity by goods producers outside the manufacturing sector, 2012**

	R&D Spending	Number of patents	Number of trademarks
Broad Definition			
FGP	3,039	0.32	0.30
Service Provider	862	0.09	0.12
Restricted Definition			
FGP	13,630	1.43	2.20
Service Provider	198	0.19	0.13

Note: This table displays firms' average R&D expenditures, ownership of the number of granted patents and trademarks. FGP: firms that purchase CMS and do not have manufacturing employment. Service Provider: firms that do not purchase CMS and do not have manufacturing employment. See text for "broad" and "restricted" definitions. R&D spending based only on firms surveyed in the Business R&D and Innovation Survey. R&D spending in US$1,000.

fessional, scientific, and technical services (NAICS 54) and management of companies and enterprises (NAICS 55). Employment in NAICS 54 includes workers providing scientific research and development services. Based on the definition of FGP activities, we would expect FGP firms to specialize in providing "headquarter" services.

FGP firms, on average, have most of their employment in wholesale and the remaining almost evenly divided between services and other sectors of the economy. FGP firms with employment in the services sector have the majority of their workers engaged in provision of "headquarter" services. Service providers, in contrast, have most of their employment housed in other sectors of the economy, and only a third of their services workers are engaged in the provision of "headquarter" services. Using the restricted definition, service providers display higher shares of employment in wholesale and "headquarter" services, although these shares do not reach the levels of FGP firms.

12.3.2   Innovative Activity

A key feature of FGPs is control of the research and design processes, so we expect to observe higher shares of employment in R&D activities as found in table 12.1. We also expect FGP firms to own intellectual property defined here as R&D expenditures, ownership of granted patents, and trademarks. Table 12.2 presents average values of the ownership of intellectual property. FGP firms have substantially higher average values of R&D expenditures and counts of granted patents and trademarks than service providers.

The differences in average innovative outcomes between FGPs and service providers are magnified when we use the restricted definition. For instance, FGP firms display almost seventy times more R&D expenditures than ser-

Table 12.3   **Importing activity by goods producers outside the manufacturing sector, 2012**

	Importer share	Imports		Imports/ revenue
		All	Low-income country % share	
Broad Definition				
FGP	0.59	10,150	0.47%	0.46
Service Provider	0.19	9,078	0.29%	0.14
Restricted Definition				
FGP	0.84	33,430	0.78%	0.26
Service Provider	0.42	23,600	0.32%	0.08

Note: This table displays firms' average importing characteristics. FGP: firms that purchase CMS and do not have manufacturing employment. Service Provider: firms that do not purchase CMS and do not have manufacturing employment. See text for "broad" and "restricted" definitions. Importer share is the fraction of firms that report positive imports. Imports/ Revenue is the ratio of imports to total firm revenue. Low-income countries defined using United Nations' country classification. Imports in US$1,000.

vice providers under the restricted definition. This difference is only about four times under the broad definition. The patterns in ownership of intellectual property in this table demonstrate that FGPs have a higher likelihood of controlling the research and design process than service providers.

12.3.3   Importing Activity

FGP firms may use factories located in foreign countries to manufacture the goods they control. This implies that FGP firms are likely to import the foreign-produced goods back to the United States for domestic sale or further processing. Table 12.3 shows that, indeed, FGP firms are more likely to be importers relative to service providers. The vast majority of FGP firms engage in importing, while less than half of service providers import. Average import values are also larger at FGP firms.

Table 12.3 also provides the average share of firm imports sourced from low-wage countries. Lower-income countries are more likely to be low-wage countries (Bernard, Jensen, and Schott 2006). If lower labor costs motivate FGP firms to use foreign factories, we would expect to see higher shares of imports from low-wage countries at FGP firms. Imports from low-income countries are a very small share of total firm imports (less than 1 percent) at both FGP and service-providing firms. However, the average share of imports from low-wage countries is about twice as high at FGP firms. Finally, imports as a share of firm revenue are more than three times higher at FGP firms. Together, these results suggest that FGP firms are more likely to utilize borderless-production arrangements than service providers.

A striking 80 percent of global trade takes place in production networks administered by multinational firms (UNCTAD 2013). We may expect that

Table 12.4 **Firm characteristics of goods producers outside the manufacturing sector, 2012**

	Revenue	Employment	Revenue per worker	Payroll	Payroll per worker	Number of establishments	Age
Broad Definition							
FGP	31,290	102	564	6,026	65	3	14
Service Provider	48,760	284	240	14,000	51	9	22
Restricted Definition							
FGP	147,000	404	568	28,920	78	9	20
Service Provider	292,700	1,320	404	55,780	49	44	25

Note: This table displays average firm characteristics. FGP: firms that purchase CMS and do not have manufacturing employment. Service Provider: firms that do not purchase CMS and do not have manufacturing employment. See text for "broad" and "restricted" definitions. Revenue and payroll in US$1,000.

FGPs are more likely to also be multinational firms than service providers. For example, Kamal et al. (2015) document that over half the firms that purchase CMS outside the United States do so from their affiliates. Using the USDIA and FDIUS linked to the Business Register and using the broad definition only, FGP firms that are currently classified outside the manufacturing sector account for 3 percent of all multinational firms operating in the United States; 5 percent of all US multinational parent firms; and 3 percent of all US affiliates of foreign parent firms. These shares are considerably higher for service providers. Service providers account for 14 percent of all multinational firms operating in the United States; 25 percent of all US multinational parent firms; and 10 percent of all US affiliates of foreign parent firms. These statistics, although not meant to be nationally representative, suggest a more nuanced relationship between multinational status and factoryless activity of firms outside the manufacturing sector.

12.3.4 Firm Characteristics

The descriptive analyses in the previous sections establish meaningful correlations between the definition of FGP firms and observable outcomes implied by factoryless activity. FGPs are associated with higher concentration of employment in "headquarter" services, greater ownership of intellectual property, and higher import shares than service providers. This section presents characteristics—revenue, employment, revenue per worker, payroll, payroll per worker, number of establishments, and age—of an average FGP classified outside the manufacturing sector and an average service provider.

Table 12.4 shows that FGP firms earn lower average revenue than service providers. FGP firms also employ almost three times fewer workers, have smaller payroll, and own fewer establishments than service providers. These findings are in contrast to Bernard and Fort (2015), who find that FGP firms tend to be larger than traditional wholesalers using the Census of Wholesale only. However, there is no obvious prediction for firm size and factoryless status. Outside the manufacturing sector, FGP firms may employ fewer workers at fewer numbers of establishments than service providers if non-production activities focused on managing production transformation tasks require fewer workers and physical facilities. FGP firms may display lower sales if they are more likely than service providers to locate production and sales abroad.

Prior research has found a close and generally positive relationship between firm size and productivity (Haltiwanger, Lane, and Spletzer 1999). This may lead us to expect that smaller FGP firms are less productive than the larger service providers. However, table 12.4 shows that FGP firms display higher average revenue and payroll per worker (the difference is more pronounced using the broad definition of FGP firms). Finally, FGP firms tend to be younger, a finding consistent with that in Bernard and Fort (2015), by an average of five to six years.

12.4   Factoryless Activity in the Manufacturing Sector

The goal in this section is to separately identify goods producers that outsource a part of the production process (hybrid manufacturers) and goods producers that do not outsource any production (traditional manufacturers), both currently classified in the manufacturing sector. Although the ECPC's conceptual definition of FGPs precludes any production transformation activities, existing evidence shows the growing prevalence of outsourcing by firms with manufacturing activity (Bayard, Byrne and Smith 2015). The authors find that only 30 percent of firms with some manufacturing activity in the United States engaged in factoryless manufacturing in 2002 but by 2012 this share had increased to half. Thus, an additional challenge faced by the statistical system is to distinguish between the extent of factoryless activities at a firm. A hybrid manufacturer is defined as purchasing CMS and having employment in the manufacturing sector. A traditional manufacturer is defined as not purchasing CMS and having employment in the manufacturing sector. The goal, as in section 12.3, is to compare hybrid manufacturers and traditional manufacturers along dimensions suggested by the conceptual definition of factoryless production and test whether the implied correlations exist for hybrid manufacturers that outsource only a part of the production process. The broad and restricted definitions used are as described in section 12.2.1.

12.4.1   Employment Shares

The focus on hybrid manufacturers currently classified within the manufacturing sector implies that these firms will have a larger share of their employment in the manufacturing sector. Table 12.5 confirms that the average share of manufacturing employment at both types of goods-producing

Table 12.5   **Firm employment shares of goods producers in the manufacturing sector, 2012**

			Manufacturing		
	Wholesale	Services	All	Share production workers	Share non-production workers
Broad Definition					
Hybrid Manufacturer	0.03	0.03	0.94	66%	34%
Traditional Manufacturer	0.06	0.06	0.88	71%	29%
Restricted Definition					
Hybrid Manufacturer	0.09	0.11	0.80	63%	37%
Traditional Manufacturer	0.11	0.07	0.82	69%	31%

Note: This table displays firms' average share of sectoral employment. Hybrid Manufacturer: firms that purchase CMS and have manufacturing employment. Traditional Manufacturer: firms that do not purchase CMS and have manufacturing employment. See text for "broad" and "restricted" definitions.

firms is over 80 percent. The table presents the share of production and non-production workers in lieu of comparing the share of employment in "headquarter" services at hybrid and traditional manufacturing firms. We expect hybrid manufacturers to have fewer production workers than traditional manufacturers, since part of production at hybrid manufacturing firms is outsourced. Concurrently, we expect hybrid manufacturers to have more non-production workers than traditional manufacturers. Table 12.5 shows that, in comparison to traditional manufacturers, the average share of production workers is lower at hybrid manufacturing firms, while the average share of non-production workers is higher.

12.4.2   Innovative Activity

Table 12.6 presents average R&D expenditures and ownership of intellectual property for hybrid and traditional manufacturing firms. Hybrid manufacturers have higher average R&D expenditures than traditional manufacturers. Hybrid manufacturers also have higher numbers of patents and trademarks than traditional manufacturers. These patterns suggest that even hybrid manufacturers that outsource only a part of the production transformation process display patterns in ownership of intellectual property that are consistent with the conceptual definition of factoryless production.

12.4.3   Importing Activity

Average trade characteristics displayed in table 12.7 yield three sets of correlations that are consistent with the idea that hybrid manufacturers may use foreign factories to manufacture goods more intensively than traditional manufacturers. First, both types of manufacturers are almost equally likely

Table 12.6   Innovative activity by goods producers in the manufacturing sector, 2012

	R&D spending	Number of patents	Number of trademarks
Broad Definition			
Hybrid Manufacturer	23,270	0.45	2.69
Traditional Manufacturer	2,969	0.33	0.53
Restricted Definition			
Hybrid Manufacturer	48,890	1.34	11.4
Traditional Manufacturer	2,410	0.45	0.36

Note: This table displays firms' average R&D expenditures, ownership of the number of granted patents and trademarks. Hybrid Manufacturer: firms that purchase CMS and have manufacturing employment. Traditional Manufacturer: firms that do not purchase CMS and have manufacturing employment. See text for "broad" and "restricted" definitions. R&D spending based only on firms surveyed in the Business R&D and Innovation Survey. R&D spending in US$1,000.

Table 12.7   Importing activity by goods producers in the manufacturing sector, 2012

	Importer share	Imports		
		All	Low-income country % share	Imports/ revenue
Broad Definition				
Hybrid Manufacturer	0.63	104,900	0.14	0.23
Traditional Manufacturer	0.64	47,440	0.11	0.19
Restricted Definition				
Hybrid Manufacturer	0.92	188,000	0.32	0.30
Traditional Manufacturer	0.72	73,050	0.30	0.12

Note: This table displays firms' average importing characteristics. Hybrid Manufacturer: firms that purchase CMS and have manufacturing employment. Traditional Manufacturer: firms that do not purchase CMS and have manufacturing employment. See text for "broad" and "restricted" definitions. Importer share is the fraction of firms that report positive imports. Imports/Revenue is the ratio of imports to total firm revenue. Low-income countries defined using United Nations' country classification. Imports in US$1,000.

to import (under the broad definition), but imports make up 23 percent of total revenue at hybrid, compared to 19 percent at traditional manufacturing firms. Under the restricted definition, 92 percent of hybrid manufacturers and 72 percent of traditional manufacturers import, and the share of imports in total revenue is 30 and 12 percent, respectively. Together, these statistics suggest that hybrid manufacturers are more likely to import than traditional manufacturers. Second, average import values are almost three times larger at hybrid manufacturing firms. Finally, hybrid manufacturers have higher shares of imports from low-wage countries than traditional manufacturers.

Since multinational firms mediate a large share of world trade, we may expect there to be a correlation between propensity to engage in factoryless production and multinational status of a firm. Using the USDIA and

Table 12.8   Firm characteristics of goods producers in the manufacturing sector, 2012

	Revenue	Employment	Revenue per worker	Payroll	Payroll per worker	Number of establishments	Age
Broad Definition							
Hybrid Manufacturer	363,400	831	257	60,190	56	11	24
Traditional Manufacturer	194,000	515	299	26,060	50	12	27
Restricted Definition							
Hybrid Manufacturer	978,200	1,744	427	153,600	67	16	29
Traditional Manufacturer	567,900	1,052	366	53,020	51	28	29

Note: This table displays average firm characteristics. Hybrid Manufacturer: firms that purchase CMS and have manufacturing employment. Traditional Manufacturer: firms that do not purchase CMS and have manufacturing employment. See text for "broad" and "restricted" definitions. Revenue and payroll in US$1,000.

FDIUS linked to the Business Register and the broad definition only, hybrid manufacturers account for 8 percent of all multinational firms operating in the United States; 22 percent of all US multinational parent firms; and 3 percent of all US affiliates of foreign parent firms. These shares are lower for traditional manufacturers. Traditional manufacturers account for 7 percent of all multinational firms operating in the United States; 14 percent of all US multinational parent firms; and 5 percent of all US affiliates of foreign parent firms. These preliminary share statistics suggest that hybrid manufacturers are more likely to be multinational firms than traditional manufacturers.

12.4.4   Firm Characteristics

The descriptive analyses in the previous sections demonstrate that factoryless activity in the manufacturing sector is associated with lower shares of production workers, higher shares of non-production workers, greater ownership of intellectual property, and higher import shares. Thus, meaningful correlations between factoryless status and observable outcomes implied by ECPC's conceptual definition also hold for firms that outsource only a part of production. This section presents characteristics—revenue, employment, revenue per worker, payroll, payroll per worker, number of establishments, and age—of an average hybrid manufacturer and an average traditional manufacturer.

Table 12.8 shows that hybrid manufacturers are larger than traditional manufacturers in terms of average revenue, employment, and payroll. However, hybrid manufacturers own fewer numbers of establishments consistent with the idea that firms require fewer physical plants when part of the production is outsourced. Hybrid manufacturers have higher average payroll per worker (under both definitions) and higher average revenue per worker (under the restricted definition only). Both types of manufacturers display similar ages, averaging over twenty-four years.

12.5   Conclusion

The rise of complex production arrangements in recent decades demands the need for statistical agencies to better reflect these activities in economic statistics. This chapter evaluates 2012 data collection efforts by the US Census Bureau to identify factoryless goods producers that outsource physical transformation activities while retaining control of designing and marketing a product. All establishments in the manufacturing and wholesale sectors and a select set of establishments in the services sector were legally required to respond to a special inquiry that captures a key element of this extreme form of production fragmentation—decision to outsource the physical transformation activities to other domestic firms or offshored to foreign firms and/or own affiliates. Headquarter locations of a select set of large firms across a broad range of sectors were also required to respond to the special inquiry. The goal of this study is to evaluate the feasibility of identifying factoryless activity at the firm level in a departure from official guidelines that has mandated identification of FGP establishments. The firm as the focal unit of analysis is motivated not only by the availability of key data elements required to identify factoryless status but also a firm's role as the central decision-making unit that ultimately controls the activities at individual establishments. In this study, FGP firms that have no manufacturing employment are separately analyzed from firms providing services and other goods producers that may or may not outsource some part of the production process.

The chapter starts by documenting a high degree of disagreement in establishment and firm responses to self-identifying as an outsourcer, thereby highlighting challenges in relying on survey responses alone for classification of FGPs. Characteristics implied by the definition of factoryless production arrangements are then explored to reveal meaningful correlations between factoryless status and variables identified based on conceptual definitions: employment mix, innovation, and importing activities. These correlations are presented separately for firms currently classified outside the manufacturing sector from firms currently classified in the manufacturing sector. The unconditional correlations merit further study building toward developing a model-based algorithm to identify FGPs. A model-based approach would capture salient features of factoryless production using existing data sources and reducing sole reliance on survey responses.

There are three practical dimensions along which the identification exercise may be augmented. First, outsourcing status of a firm identified using only the Economic Census requires that one establishment of the firm reports purchasing CMS. I utilize responses to the economic value of activities related to the purchase of CMS to create a binary CMS purchase status indicator. However, this categorization does not explicitly consider the intensity of outsourcing activities. The intensity of activities could indicate how prevalent outsourcing is for FGP firms and suggest thresholds to assign likelihoods of being an FGP firm. This may be more relevant for hybrid manufacturers that outsource only a part of production. Second, more than one establishment of a multi-unit firm may have received the special inquiry on purchase of CMS. The firm is assigned a positive CMS purchase status if at least one establishment responds in the affirmative. However, when multiple establishments respond, analyzing the share that say yes versus no may allow an alternative method of classification, for instance, assigning the firm a positive CMS purchases status if a majority of its establishments outsource production. Third, the Bureau of Economic Analysis added questions about purchase of CMS in two of their mandatory surveys. One of these surveys, the 2009 USDIA, was separately analyzed in Kamal, Moulton, and Ribarsky (2015) but was not linked to Census data. Linking the BEA surveys to Census data used in this study would permit further validation of responses by the same firm and a focus on FGP firms that are also multinationals.

Concerted efforts to collect data on outsourcing activities at the firm level could further complement the above extensions. Sole reliance on surveys of multinational firms and the Company Organization Survey, which is intended primarily to update the Census Bureau's Business Register and accordingly surveys a select set of firms, limits our ability to systematically measure production fragmentation in the US economy. I offer three other potential sources of data collection opportunities at the firm level to augment our discussions of how best to measure factoryless production. First, the Annual Business Survey, covering non-farm businesses with paid employees, may offer a more comprehensive coverage of firms in the US economy.[18] Cognitive testing results from the 2017 Economic Census special inquiry could inform candidate questions. Second, the Services Annual Survey may also offer an additional survey instrument to collect relevant information on a firm's foreign outsourcing activities.[19] The survey currently collects data on firms' exports of services only. Including questions related to services imports could shed light on purchases of foreign manufacturing services. Finally, including questions on customs forms would provide the ability to distinguish between products of a firm that are directly manufactured from those that are processed abroad. Leveraging existing data sources and evaluating the advantages and challenges associated with new data collection opportunities, together, paves a path forward to gaining a deeper understanding of, and the ability to measure, factoryless goods production arrangements in the US economy.

---

18. The Annual Business Survey is the successor of the Annual Survey of Entrepreneurs (Foster and Norman 2017).

19. See https://www.census.gov/programs-surveys/sas/technical-documentation /methodology.html (accessed September 30, 2018).

Appendix

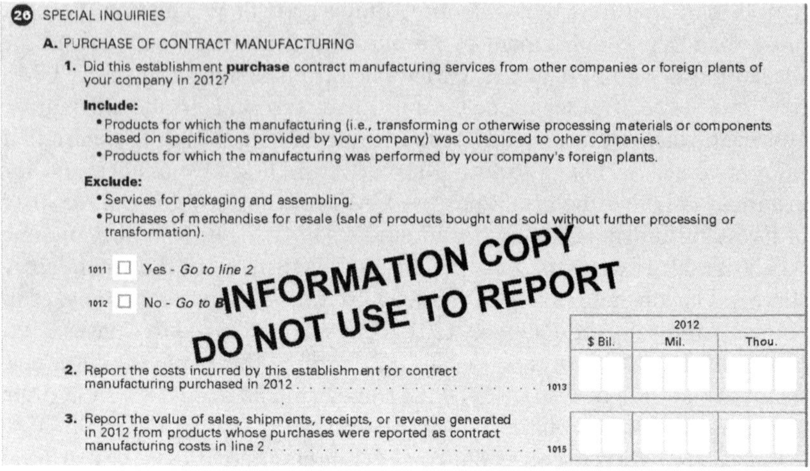

Figure 12A.1   CMS special inquiry, Economic Census, 2012.
Source: US Census Bureau.

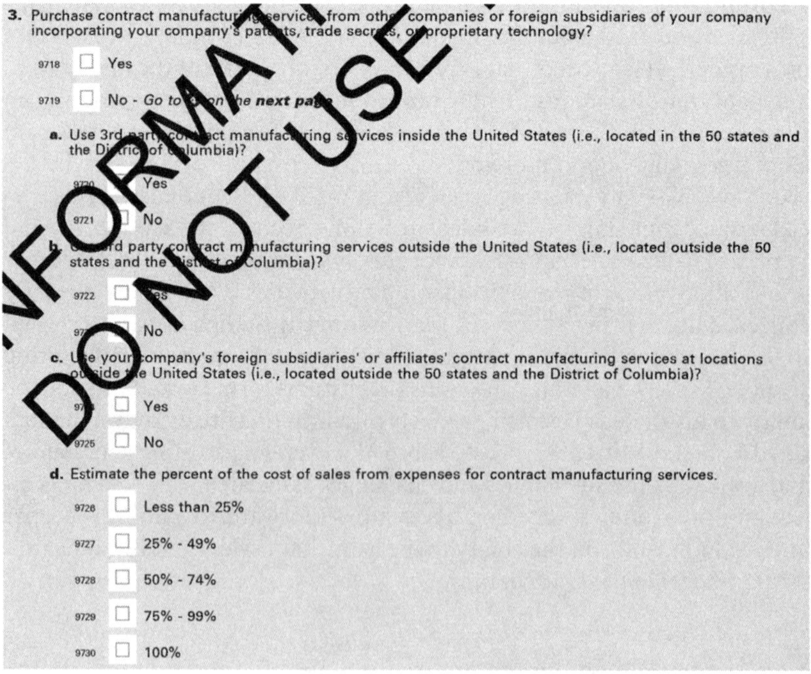

Figure 12A.2   CMS special inquiry, Company Organization Survey, 2012
Source: US Census Bureau.

Table 12A.1   **Firm responses to CMS purchase in Economic Census and Company Organization Survey, 2012**

	Company Organization Survey			
	Yes	No	Missing	Not in company organization survey
Economic Census				
Yes	1,200	1,900	150	23,000
No	80	1,700	100	9,600
Missing	950	27,000	—	—
Not in Economic Census	800	83,000	—	—

Note: This table displays the number of firms (both with and without manufacturing employment) that have been identified as purchasing CMS, not purchasing CMS, or missing a response in the Economic Census and Company Organization Survey. Firm counts are rounded to comply with Census Bureau rules on disclosure avoidance and may not sum to totals.

References

Autor, David, David Dorn, and Gordon H. Hanson. 2013. "The China Syndrome: Local Labor Market Effects of Import Competition in the United States." *American Economic Review* 103 (6): 2121–68.

Autor, David, David Dorn, Lawrence F. Katz, Christina Patterson, and John Van Reenen. 2017. "The Fall of the Labor Share and the Rise of Superstar Firms." NBER Working Paper No. 23396. Cambridge, MA: National Bureau of Economic Research.

Bayard, Kimberly, David Byrne, and Dominic Smith. 2015. "The Scope of U.S. Factoryless Manufacturing." In *Measuring Globalization: Better Trade Statistics for Better Trade Policy*, Volume 2, edited by Susan Houseman and Michael Mandel, 81–120.

Bernard, Andrew A., J. Bradford Jensen, and Peter K. Schott. 2006. "Survival of the Best Fit: Exposure to Low-Wage Countries and the (Uneven) Growth of U.S. Manufacturing Plants." *Journal of International Economics* 68: 219–37.

Bernard, Andrew B., J. Bradford Jensen, and Peter K. Schott. 2009. "Importers, Exporters, and Multinationals: A Portrait of Firms in the U.S. That Trade Goods." In *Producer Dynamics: New Evidence from Micro Data*, Studies in Income and Wealth Volume 68, edited by Timothy Dunne, J. Bradford Jensen, and Mark J. Roberts, 513–52. Chicago: University of Chicago Press.

Bernard, Andrew B., and Teresa C. Fort. 2013. "Factoryless Goods Producers in the U.S." NBER Working Paper No. 19396. Cambridge, MA: National Bureau of Economic Research.

Bernard, Andrew B., and Teresa C. Fort. 2015. "Factoryless Goods Producing Firms." *American Economic Review Papers and Proceedings* 105 (5): 518–23.

Bernard, Andrew B., Teresa C. Fort, Valerie Smeets, and Frederic Warzynski. 2017. "Offshoring and Reorganization." Mimeo.

Dinlersoz, Emin, Nathan Goldschlag, Amanda Myers, and Nikolas Zolas. Forthcoming. "The Anatomy of Trademarking by Firms in the United States." In *Measuring and Accounting for Innovation in the 21st Century*, edited by Carol Corrado, Javier Miranda, Jonathan Haskel, and Daniel Sichel.

Doherty, Maureen. 2015. "Reflecting Factoryless Goods Production in the U.S. Statistical System." In *Measuring Globalization: Better Trade Statistics for Better Trade Policy*, Volume 2, edited by Susan Houseman and Michael Mandel, 13–43.

Feenstra, Robert C., and Shang-Jin Wei. 2010. "Introduction to 'China's Growing Role in World Trade.'" In *China's Growing Role in World Trade*, edited by Robert C. Feenstra and Shang-Jin Wei, 1–31. Chicago: University of Chicago Press.

Fort, Teresa C. 2017. "Technology and Production Fragmentation: Domestic versus Foreign Sourcing." *Review of Economic Studies* 84 (2): 650–87.

Fort, Teresa, Justin Pierce, and Peter K. Schott. 2018. "New Perspectives on the Decline of U.S. Manufacturing Employment." *Journal of Economic Perspectives* 32 (2): 47–72.

Foster, Lucia, and Patrice Norman. 2017. "The Annual Survey of Entrepreneurs." *Journal of Economic and Social Measurement* 3 (4): 199–224.

Freund, Caroline, and Martha Denisse Pierola. 2015. "Export Superstars." *Review of Economics and Statistics* 97 (5): 1023–32.

Haltiwanger, John, Julia Lane, and James Spletzer. 1999. "Productivity Differences Across Employers: The Roles of Employer Size, Age, and Human Capital." *American Economic Review Papers and Proceedings*: 94–98.

Haltiwanger, John, Ron S. Jarmin, Robert Kulick, and Javier Miranda. 2017. "High Growth Young Firms: Contribution to Job, Output, and Productivity Growth." In *Measuring Entrepreneurial Businesses: Current Knowledge and Challenges*, Studies in Income and Wealth volume 75, edited by John Haltiwanger, Erika Hurst, Javier Miranda, and Antoinette Schoar, 11–62. Chicago, IL: University of Chicago Press.

Hummels, David, Jun Ishii, and Kei-Mu Yi. 2001. "The Nature and Growth of Vertical Specialization in World Trade." *Journal of International Economics* 54 (1): 75–96.

Hummels, David, Rasmus Jørgensen, Jakob Munch, and Chong Xiang. 2014. "The Wage Effects of Offshoring: Evidence from Danish Matched Worker-Firm Data." *American Economic Review* 104 (6): 1597–1629.

Jarmin, Ron S., and Javier Miranda. 2002. "The Longitudinal Business Database." Center for Economic Studies Discussion Paper No. CES-WP-02–17. Suitland, MD: U.S. Census Bureau, Center for Economic Studies.

Johnson, Robert C., and Guillermo Noguera. 2012. "Accounting for Intermediates: Production Sharing and Trade in Value Added." *Journal of International Economics* 86: 224–36.

Kamal, Fariha, Brent Moulton, and Jennifer Ribarsky. 2015. "Measuring 'Factoryless' Manufacturing: Evidence from U.S. Surveys." In *Measuring Globalization: Better Trade Statistics for Better Trade Policy*, Volume 2, edited by Susan Houseman and Michael Mandel, 151–94.

Mion, Giordano, and Linke Zhu. 2013. "Import Competition from and Offshoring to China: A Curse or Blessing for Firms?" *Journal of International Economics* 89: 202–15.

Murphy, John. 2015. "Identifying Factoryless Goods Producers (FGPs)—Efforts to Date." Accessed January 27, 2018. https://unstats.un.org/unsd/class/intercop/tsg/16-05/ac315-9.PDF.

Office of Management and Budget (OMB). 2010. "Economic Classification Policy Committee Recommendation for Classification of Outsourcing in North American Industry Classification System (NAICS) Revisions for 2012." Accessed February 14, 2018. https://www.census.gov/eos/www/naics/fr2010/ECPC_Recommendation_for_Classification_of_Outsourcing.pdf.

Pierce, Justin, and Peter K. Schott. 2016. "The Surprisingly Swift Decline of U.S. Manufacturing Employment." *American Economic Review* 106 (7): 1632–62.

UNCTAD. 2013. *World Investment Report*. Accessed December 15, 2016. http://unctad.org/en/pages/PressRelease.aspx?OriginalVersionID=113. Accessed December 15, 2016. http://unctad.org/en/PublicationChapters/wir2013ch4_en.pdf.

Comment   Teresa C. Fort

Overview and Contribution

"A Portrait of US Factoryless Goods Producers" by Fariha Kamal makes an interesting contribution to the growing body of evidence on firms that do not perform physical transformation activities but are nevertheless broadly involved in the manufacturing of goods. These firms are important to understand because they show how traditional measures of manufacturing activity based on production workers may miss important parts of the overall production process. Moreover, factoryless goods producers (FGPs) seem to be innovation intensive when compared to other firms, which suggests that their activities are likely to have important implications for growth and productivity.

Kamal (forthcoming) adds to existing work on FGPs by combining a number of micro-level data sets on employment, R&D, patenting, and trademarking with new data sources for identifying FGPs. This work leads to two significant contributions. First, she assesses the extent of FGP firms outside manufacturing and wholesale. Second, she can measure the extent to which FGP activity is tied to standard measures of innovation, such as patenting and R&D expenditure.

There are two particularly interesting results in Kamal (forthcoming). First, Kamal finds that FGPs' workforce composition is skewed toward workers in headquarter establishments. This is similar to Bernard and Fort (2015), who find that FGP wholesale firms have an average of three times as much management and professional and technical services employment as non-FGP wholesale firms. Finding these results outside the wholesale sector is suggestive of an important role for FGPs in the growth of pro-

Teresa C. Fort is an associate professor of business administration at Tuck School of Business, Dartmouth College, and a faculty research fellow of the National Bureau of Economic Research.

The research in this paper was conducted while the author was a Special Sworn Status researcher of the US Census Bureau at the Boston Research Data Center and the Center for Economic Studies. Any opinions and conclusions expressed herein are those of the authors and do not necessarily reflect the views of the Census Bureau, the NBER, or any other institution to which the authors are affiliated. All results have been reviewed to ensure that no confidential information is disclosed. For acknowledgments, sources of research support, and disclosure of the author's material financial relationships, if any, please see https://www.nber.org/books-and-chapters/challenges-globalization-measurement-national-accounts/comment-portrait-us-factoryless-goods-producers-fort.

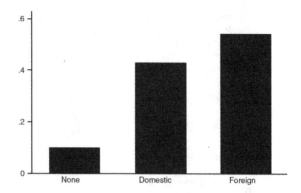

Figure 12C.1   2007 share of wholesales establishments that design their products, by contract manufacturing purchase status.
Source: 2007 Census of Wholesale trade.

fessional and technical services employment in the United States. It also raises a number of potentially interesting venues for future work. Do FGP firms have foreign production facilities with which these professional and technical services employees interact? Are FGPs associated with growth of outsourcing of manufacturing as firms specialize in the innovation part of the production process?

Second, Kamal finds that FGPs perform considerably more innovation than non-FGP firms. For instance, her results show that FGP firms spend four to seven times more on R&D expenditures compared to non-FGP firms. FGPs also patent and trademark more than non-FGP firms. Given the importance of innovation for long-term growth, these results are particularly interesting. They resonate with findings in Bernard and Fort (2013), where we find that wholesale firms that purchase contract manufacturing services (CMS) are more likely to design the goods they sell. Figure 12C.1 shows that while less than 10 percent of wholesale plants that do not purchase CMS design their products, about 40 percent of plants that purchase domestic CMS design their own products, and over 50 percent of plants that purchase CMS from foreign countries design their goods. An interesting and related question for future work is to assess the extent to which the ability to leverage low-cost production opportunities in foreign countries has increased US innovation. Kamal's work on FGPs provides strong evidence that any answer to this question must examine the innovative decisions of not only US manufacturers but also non-manufacturing FGP firms.

Comments

In this section, I describe two important considerations for interpreting the results of the chapter. First, I discuss the likely role of industry compo-

Table 12C.1   **Plant shares and characteristics by response status**

	Participation Shares			Means		
	Plants	Sales	Emp	Sales (000s)	Emp	ln(VAP)
In CMS Sample	0.54	0.75	0.71	**36,778**	**86**	**4.56**
Out of CMS Sample Not Answered	0.21	0.23	0.24	**29,548**	**77**	**4.61**
Not Asked	0.25	0.02	0.05	2,314	13	4.25
No Info	0.00	0.00	0.00	21,147	61	4.75
All Manufactures	1.00	1.00	1.00	26,638	66	4.50

Note. 2007 Special inquiries data for the Census of Manufactures. Excludes administrative records. CMS questions only asked on CMF long form.

sitional differences. Second, I describe the role of sample selection. Finally, I conclude by discussing interesting potential avenues for future work raised by this chapter.

Industry compositional differences may drive the results. For instance, if FGPs are concentrated in semiconductor manufacturing-related activities, as studied by Bayard, Byrne, and Smith (2015), then it is likely not meaningful to compare them to firms in other sectors, such as Walmart.

These compositional differences are likely quite important. For example, Bernard and Fort (2015) find that wholesale FGP firms' imports are highly concentrated in two sectors: electrical machinery and equipment and machinery (HS2 product codes 84 and 85). These two sectors comprise 40 percent of wholesale FGP firms imports but only 30 percent of non-FGP wholesale firms' imports. While this comparison is limited to wholesale, the possibility of compositional factors driving results becomes more severe when comparing wholesale FGP firms to retail or other sector non-FGP firms. This is highlighted by the fact that Kamal finds that the share of imports over sales is three times higher at FGP firms compared to non-FGPs. In contrast, Bernard and Fort (2015) find that within the wholesale sector, FGP firms import just 38 percent of sales compared to non-FGPs that import 86 percent. Kamal's finding that FGP firms are smaller than non-FGPs is also reversed when comparing FGP wholesale firms to non-FGP wholesale firms. Bernard and Fort (2015) find that FGPs are about twice the size of non-FGPs. In additional results, we found these differences persisted when controlling for industry differences.

Another important consideration when analyzing the results from this chapter is the role of selection into the sample. In Fort (2017), I show that there is considerable selection into the special inquiries data, both in terms of which establishments were asked the question, and conditional on being asked, which establishments responded to the question. Table 12C.1 shows that establishments in the 2007 Census of Manufactures (CM) that responded to the special inquiry question had an average of 86 employees and $37 million in sales, while plants that were asked but did not answer the question had 77 employees and only $30 million in sales. A further 25 percent of plants were not asked the question at all, and these plants are considerably different. The non-asked establishments had just 13 employees and $2 million in sales.

The role of selection will be even more severe when analyzing the Company Organization Survey, as that survey is geared toward large, multi-establishment firms. Specifically, it covers all large firms (multi-establishment firms with 250 or more employees) and smaller companies that appear to be expanding to multiple establishments. Assessments about the relative size or other activities of FGP versus non-FGP firms may thus be different when considering the universe of US firms instead of the selected sample of large firms for which CMS data are available. It is also possible that the share of aggregate FGP activity will be overstated if larger firms are more likely to be FGPs and those are disproportionately represented in the samples.

Overall, this is an interesting new chapter on factoryless goods producers that takes a first stab at expanding the analysis beyond the manufacturing and wholesale sectors. By exploiting the new data constructed by Kamal, we can hope to learn more about the sectoral composition of FGP firms, and about how FGPs differ from other firms in their industry.

References

Bayard, Kimberly, David Byrne, and Dominic Smith. 2015. "The Scope of US Factoryless Manufacturing." In *Measuring Globalization: Better Trade Statistics for Better Trade Policy*, Volume 2, edited by Susan Houseman and Michael Mandel, 81–120. Upjohn Institute.

Bernard, Andrew B., and Teresa C. Fort. 2013. "Factorlyess Goods Producers in the US." NBER Working Paper No. 19396. Cambridge, MA: National Bureau of Economic Research.

———. 2015. "Factoryless Goods Producing Firms." *American Economic Review: Papers and Proceedings* 105 (5): 518–23.

Fort, Teresa C. 2017. "Technology and Production Fragmentation: Domestic versus Foreign Sourcing." *Review of Economic Studies* 84 (2): 650–87.

Kamal, Fariha. 2018. "A Portrait of US Factoryless Goods Producers." In *Challenges of Globalization in the Measurement of National Accounts*, edited by Nadim Ahmad, Brent Moulton, J. David Richardson, and Peter van de Ven. Chicago, IL: University of Chicago Press. This volume.

13
R&D Capitalization
Where Did We Go Wrong?

Mark de Haan and Joseph Haynes

13.1 Introduction

A significant innovation in the latest SNA update (2008 SNA) was the capitalization of expenditure on research and development (R&D). In the process of the SNA update, Statistics Netherlands produced several papers on this issue (de Haan and van Rooijen-Horsten 2004; van Rooijen-Horsten, Tanriseven, and de Haan 2007). These papers highlighted several data issues, such as the translation of Frascati-based R&D statistics to National Accounts data; assessing service lives of R&D assets; and dealing with possible overlaps between R&D and computer software. This kind of guidance was later formalized in the OECD Handbook on deriving capital measures of intellectual property products (OECD 2009). While the 1993 SNA implementation included the introduction of computer software capitalization for which the first country results showed a disparity of applied methods and results, the introduction of R&D capitalization was "managed" in a more careful way. Unfortunately, we cannot conclude that R&D capitalization in the national accounts has been totally successful.

Mark de Haan is currently a senior economist in the real sector divisions at the International Monetary Fund, and was head of the integration of government finance statistics unit at Statistics Netherlands when this chapter was written.

Joseph Haynes is an economist working in the national accounts and public sector finances division at Statistics Netherlands.

The authors would like to thank Dirk van den Bergen, Tihomira Dimova, Henk Nijmeijer, Paul Konijn Rami Peltola, Peter van de Ven, Piet Verbiest, and two anonymous referees for their excellent comments. For acknowledgments, sources of research support, and disclosure of the author's or authors' material financial relationships, if any, please see https://www.nber.org/books-and-chapters/challenges-globalization-measurement-national-accounts/rd-capitalisation-where-did-we-go-wrong.

In the papers produced by Statistics Netherlands, two conceptual concerns were brought to attention:

1. R&D in the public domain does not necessarily comply with the general definition of an asset in the SNA sense. Economic ownership of public knowledge cannot be claimed by one particular economic agent;

2. Guidance on how to account for R&D flows and stocks inside the multinational enterprise (MNE) is totally lacking.

Supporters of the first proposition (e.g., representatives from Statistics Denmark, Statistics Netherlands, and the UK Office for National Statistics) "lost the battle." Ultimately it was decided that R&D expenditure, both public and private, should be treated equally as fixed assets in the 2008 SNA. The arguments supporting this choice were pragmatic rather than conceptual. Our impression is still that publicly available knowledge contrasts with the general SNA definition of an economic asset.[1] This broad demarcation of R&D assets is also ambiguous and creates implausible outcomes. Therefore we revisit this issue in the subsequent section of this chapter before moving on to the issue of globalization.

In recent years, the second issue on R&D within MNE groups and globalization has received increasing attention. For national accountants, one of the key challenges of economic globalization is explaining how capital services of intellectual property enter the globally organized production chains. Several developments are complicating this globalization puzzle. Firstly, the international fragmentation of production chains, inside or outside MNE structures, may imply that business functions such as R&D and software development (i.e., product development and design, development of software inputs) are being separated and (spatially) disconnected from the process of physical transformation (the actual manufacturing of the good embedding the intellectual property). Secondly, production chain fragmentation may also enter the stages of physical transformation. Examples of highly fractured and specialized manufacturing webs are those found in the automobile or aircraft industry.

Nowadays some manufacturers entirely offshore the physical transformation stages of production; such production arrangers are also called factoryless goods producers (FGPs). The issue of FGPs was intensively discussed in the UNECE task force on global production (UNECE, 2015). Questions about their economic classification and the kinds of transaction these companies are generally engaged in were, unfortunately, not brought to a final conclusion. Both issues are closely linked to recording R&D or, more generally, intellectual property (IP) flows and stocks.

R&D capitalization suggests that intellectual products can be accounted

---

1. The misplaced *conceptual* argument in which public R&D is compared to public infrastructure is discussed later in this paper.

for like any other fixed asset in the national accounts. Our view on globalization is that this is not the case. This point is picked up in section 13.3 of this chapter.

An additional complicating factor is that IP, or intangible assets more broadly, may become a vehicle for tax planning. MNE groups may locate their IP and report related IP revenues (i.e., royalties) in low tax jurisdictions and subsequently charge affiliated companies, which report substantive shares of the group's turnover, for the use of the IP. Such tax planning arrangements may involve a range of special purpose entities (SPEs) located in a variety of countries. A national accountant is usually able to observe only fragments of the tax planning arrangement and is easily misled by the information being obtained at the level of individual SPEs, or other entities in a tax planning arrangement. Judgements on substance or divergences in legal vis-à-vis economic ownership are extremely difficult. This is the main issue in section 13.4.

Section 13.5 winds up with (tentative) conclusions and suggestions for future work.

13.2   The Wheel of Knowledge and IP Creation

Knowledge cannot be valued in money terms. Any attempt to do so is doomed to fail, as the importance of knowledge to society cannot be comprehensively evaluated in terms of all capital services obtained by society from our common knowledge base. One crucial characteristic of knowledge is its use for purely scientific reasons, i.e., building up new knowledge. Knowledge creation inherently depends on existing knowledge. We call this the *wheel of knowledge* (which also happens to be a video game).

Another important problem to confront is that knowledge itself does not depreciate. Codified knowledge may get lost in the course of catastrophic losses (library fire or computer crash), which is according to the SNA not the same as depreciation. Crucial too in the process of knowledge creation is that the complementary tacit knowledge, or human capital, is being maintained, or even expanded, by our educational systems.

In the process of developing an electric automobile in the twenty-first century, one cannot say that the required knowledge obtained in ancient times, say the invention of a wheel millennia ago, is less significant to the car than more recent inventions, e.g., the development of powerful batteries. As such we cannot argue that the invention of the wheel is at this point in time (partly or fully) depreciated. We are still enjoying, as ever, the fine properties of a wheel.

Equally, we cannot say that contributions from ancient philosophers like Pythagoras or Socrates to contemporary thinking have become less relevant and should therefore be depreciated. But if knowledge does not depreciate, then the wheel of knowledge becomes larger and larger, year after year.

How does this thinking contribute to national accounting? The last two versions (1993, 2008) of the SNA underscored rightfully the increasing significance of knowledge as a production factor. Business value and profits increasingly rely on tacit knowledge (human capital) and codified knowledge (intellectual property products). This is why computer software, artistic originals, mineral exploration, and research and development were included in the SNA list of fixed assets (not human capital, which is another story).

This issue of whether intellectual property products have equal properties as other (tangible) fixed assets is picked up in the subsequent sections of this chapter. The minimum requirement is that intellectual property products should comply with the general definition of an asset: they are subject to economic ownership and provide future benefits to its owner. In addition, a *fixed* asset must be the outcome of production.

With respect to intangible assets, these conditions should be given careful consideration. In relation to R&D performed by businesses, we can safely assume that companies are able to claim the benefits from the R&D they fund or carry out themselves. As high-tech companies may spend up to 10 percent of their turnover on R&D, it is quite likely that these companies will be receiving a reasonable return on R&D capital and are capable of claiming R&D ownership by patenting or other ways of limiting access.

In the context of globalization, this chapter explains that at the level of a multinational company the concepts of ownership and obtaining related benefits are conceptually sound and applicable. When stepping down at the level of individual member companies, or when assessing ownership and R&D returns at country level where these member companies are resident, both concepts become fuzzy and less easily applicable.

We think this is a serious issue. If national accountants are not able to explain how R&D is linked to production and output, they are not capable of accounting properly for R&D flows and stocks. These concerns are picked up in the subsequent sections of this chapter.

De Haan et al. (2004) raised the question, What are the conditions under which R&D complies with the general SNA asset definition (at least at the level of a multinational enterprise)? They concluded that due to the exclusive access to knowledge acquired from R&D, the owner may exert a certain level of market power which has a clear and distinct market value. This knowledge may be translated into products with, in the eyes of the consumer, unique and well-appreciated properties, not found in the products offered by rival suppliers. The service obtained from knowledge assets will decay in correspondence with the loss in monopolistic power the owner will inevitably experience over time. Competitors will eventually be able to copy the invention or may develop themselves, by way of new R&D projects, product properties that outperform previous product innovations.

This loss in market power causes the knowledge asset to depreciate over time. This depreciation is by definition the outcome of obsolescence, as

R&D or intellectual property generally will not be subject to wear and tear. The knowledge itself will not disappear, it may generate a positive contribution to society for many years, yet its commercial value will inevitably decline. This distinction between knowledge and its possible commercial value is of crucial importance. The knowledge as obtained from R&D will not depreciate. However, access exclusiveness and its potential commercial value will depreciate. Depreciation refers to the fact that a patent (or exclusive user rights more generally) is time limited and the progression of technology inevitably implies advancing obsolescence.

As a thought experiment it may be worth considering the (part fictional) story of the discovery of penicillin by Alexander Fleming and his refusal to take out a patent, believing that the discovery was too important to limit its use. As national accountants the question we should be asking is whether the discovery of penicillin therefore led to a fixed asset. If neither Fleming nor anyone else could claim economic ownership and accrue future benefits due to the knowledge being freely available and usable, then there is no fixed asset. Instead there is only knowledge. However had Fleming opted to obtain a patent, then there would have been an economic owner and a fixed asset. This example shows that it is the patent, or more generally obtaining exclusive ownership, that gives rise to the fixed asset and not the knowledge or discovery itself. Where knowledge is not protected by any means, such as a patent or secrecy, a fixed asset cannot be recognized.

Sharing profitable knowledge incurs a cost, as it may delimit the monopolistic power of the initial owner. One should be aware that commercial success is often the combination of codified knowledge (the R&D asset) and tacit knowledge (the complementary human capital required to translate knowledge into successful product blueprints). Copying tacit knowledge may be harder than copying R&D assets. This means that exclusive ownership of scientific knowledge is not necessarily safeguarded by patenting but can equally be obtained by way of secrecy or by the exclusive access to the complementary tacit knowledge.

The service lives of patents in the various scientific areas (e.g., pharmaceutics, electronic appliances, IT) may be a reasonable proxy for assessing service lives of patented and non-patented R&D projects. This is how many national statistical institutes go about assessing service lives of R&D assets. As unsuccessful projects are unavoidable in the process of seeking commercial success, capitalizing expenditure on both successful and unsuccessful projects is defendable in the attempt to approximate the overall market value of business R&D capital.

The 2008 SNA recommends the capitalization of all R&D; for example, business research and noncommercial research (e.g., university research). The argument used in the 2008 SNA for also capitalizing the latter type of research is that university R&D is a public good which is beneficial to society for a longer time period, similar to public roads or bridges. The arguments below speak against this analogy. The 2008 SNA (paragraph 10.98) explains that "the knowledge remains an asset as long as its use can create some form of monopoly profit for its owners. When it is no longer protected . . . it ceases to be an asset." Yet this wording could be read as the 2008 SNA itself already rejecting the idea of publicly shared knowledge as an asset in the SNA sense.

First, looking at the resemblance between public research and public bridges or roads, there is generally no confusion about economic ownership of the latter (we leave aside the complexity of public-private operations, which is not germane to this discussion). The government is responsible for maintaining the road and may even be liable for damages to users caused by deficiencies. The government has decision power. It may, for example, decide to sell the road to a private operator or put the underlying land to another (public) use. In this sense public infrastructure meets the definition of a fixed asset. This may not always be the case for R&D in the public domain. Once in the public domain the R&D asset has become a pure public good. To consider this more fully we first break down, non-exhaustively, the kinds of research projects carried out in the public domain.

Government bodies may conduct scientific research for various reasons. Some of this research may be linked to commercial purposes and may even be patented (e.g., supporting agriculture or enhancing the circular economy, or, more generally, improving the environmental performance of businesses). This type of research is quite comparable to business R&D. When businesses are able to claim the (commercial) revenues of this public research, one may argue that this R&D has been transferred to them. This exclusivity gives rise to economic ownership and therefore is an indicator that such public R&D should be recorded as a fixed asset. Given its purpose this dedicated R&D is likely subject to obsolescence as newer techniques may replace old ones. So, this R&D depreciates in an economically meaningful way. Crucial in this context is whether or not the government unconditionally grants all parties access to this knowledge. If so, the knowledge is in fact a public good and cannot be an economic asset in the SNA sense.

Another example is defense-related research. This research may be performed either by commercial or government institutes. One may expect that this research is conducted under strict secrecy, since its key purpose is obtaining a military advantage over (potential) enemy states. In relation to dedicated military research there will generally be no misunderstanding about ownership and the beneficiaries of this research. By not publicizing such research, the government maintains a quasi-monopoly position and is the economic owner of a fixed asset. In the arms race equal steps taken by potential enemy states will inevitably lead to diminishing the defensive advantages of research projects over time, again implying this research can be depreciated in a meaningful way, even though the purpose of this R&D may be (partly) non-commercial.

Another part of R&D performed in the public domain is purely noncommercial scientific university research. Obviously the origin of scientific research is being claimed by their authors in scientific journals. This is not the same as claiming economic ownership. The main purpose of this research is extending science, which requires among other things allowing full access to scientific results, for verification purposes or for allowing other scholars to extend on published findings. The main purpose of university research is feeding scientific debate. In the strict context of university research, notions such as economic ownership and economic revenue become meaningless. Scientific results are shared and applied by others for the sake of conducting new research. Once academic research has been published, the revealed knowledge immediately becomes not only a pure *public* but also a *free* good.[2] A pure public good cannot be a fixed asset, as no single owner exists who can claim economic ownership and earn any future benefits. Therefore this element of public R&D does not meet the definition of a fixed asset, as it is not subject to economic ownership.

This chapter has already argued that the depreciation of business R&D is the outcome of two factors. First, competitors in the market may catch up (dispersion or sharing of knowledge). Second, new research and innovations may outperform previous innovations, which will inevitably lead to its obsolescence. Following this line of thinking one may argue that eventually the R&D assets as owned by companies will be transformed into R&D in the public domain. At that moment the R&D ceases to be an asset in the SNA sense, as it has become public knowledge.

This leads to the following conclusions. The main purpose of most academic research is generating public knowledge over which ownership cannot be claimed by one economic agent, not even a government. The outcome (we hesitate to call this revenue) of research is commonly shared by academia. Therefore academic research, once published, does not meet the definition of an asset. Furthermore, academic research, and knowledge in general, is not subject to economic depreciation, as service lives are, in principle, indefinite. Depreciation functions applied to academic research lack any conceptual underpinning.

The intrinsic inconsistency of such calculations can be underscored by the following representation of a production function of academic research (in ISIC Rev.4 code 85). In case of public education and research, the SNA convention is to value output (X) as the sum of costs. Let us assume a purely scientific research institute (perhaps allied to a university). Its main current costs are the salaries of researchers (L). According to the 2008 SNA the output of this research institute is R&D, which is recorded as gross fixed capital formation. Its depreciation feeds back in the production account of

2. A public good means that individuals cannot be effectively excluded from use. The use by one individual does not reduce availability to others. Public R&D is also a *free* good, as its use is principally unlimited and not subject to depreciation.

the research institute. We assume that the salaries and labor input are constant in time. We also assume geometric depreciation (d). The production function is represented by equation (1). The capital accumulation function is represented by equation (2).

(1) $$X_t = L + d \times R\&D_t$$

(2) $$R\&D_t = (1 - d) \times R\&D_{t-1} + X_{t-1}$$

(3) $$X_t - X_{t-1} = d \times L.$$

So the remarkable outcome of the SNA convention is that while labor input (L) remains constant over time, each year the R&D output of this research institute will linearly increase by $d \times L$ while the R&D capital stock will annually expand by L.

What is modeled by equations (1) and (2) is the expanding wheel of knowledge, which has nothing to do with economic accounting. According to equations 1 and 2, government consumption would annually increase by $d \times L$ according to the SNA convention of non-market output valued at sum of costs and ignoring labor productivity changes, while intuitively one would agree that given constant labor input the research institute would generate constant output.

In other words the R&D output of this research institute should be recorded directly as government consumption and not as gross fixed capital formation. It should be emphasized that either the consumption or investment option will have a similar impact on GDP. Though the investment option leads to the undesirable disturbance of recursive GPD additions as the consumption of fixed capital will additionally add to the output of the government sector, measured as the sum of costs.

13.3   Corporate R&D Property and Global R&D Networks

13.3.1   Introduction

At least two complicating factors limit our understanding of how the services of R&D capital enter the global production chain. The first one is the global fragmentation of production and, within the global value chain, the disconnected supply of physical and intangible inputs. The second is that R&D creation itself can be subject to interlinked global research networks. Both issues are considered in this section.

13.3.2   Globally Fragmented Value Chains

Global production contrasts with the idea of "national" accounting, and this is why so much effort has recently been put into developing guidance supplementing the 2008 SNA (UNECE 2011, 2015; Eurostat 2014). As explained by the OECD, international production, trade, and investments are increasingly organized within so-called global value chains (GVCs), where the different stages of the entire production process, from product design all the way to product distribution and after sales services, are located across different countries.[3]

Intellectual property and information technologies play a fundamental enabling role in the global value chain. For example, communication networks enable product development and design to be geographically disconnected from goods fabrication.

The well-known value added breakdown of an iPhone indicates that the physical parts and assembling costs represent roughly half the iPhone retail price.[4] All other value added generated by the iPhone output is connected to the intangible inputs such as R&D, design, marketing, and presumably activities such as supply-chain management. The income is generated in different regions of the world.

Graphic presentations of global supply chains nicely show the geographic distribution and clustering of manufactured parts and assembling making up the iPhone, an automobile, or an airplane.[5] How R&D feeds into the global value chain is harder to explain. This issue is often ignored as analyses of global production networks often limit themselves to the physical transformation segments of global production.

However, if according to the 2008 SNA R&D is a fixed asset, like any other (tangible) fixed asset, the national accounts should be able to explain which entities inside the MNE structure are actually investing in R&D and consuming the concomitant R&D services. In other words, we should be able to explain which (affiliated) entity (in which country) owns the R&D asset and is accountable for its depreciation or more generally the costs of using the R&D asset. Similarly, the accounts should be able to explain how R&D and intellectual property (IP) contribute to output and multifactor productivity on a country-by-country basis.

There are several reasons why these questions are difficult to answer:

1. Basic and applied research provides capacity-enhancing technologies that facilitate product innovation but will not directly result in blueprints of new products.[6] In other words, in contrast to product development, basic research misses a direct link to the goods and services outputs. This being the case, the head office of an MNE seems the most obvious candidate for economic owner of this truly corporate R&D property. It is quite likely that head offices take the (funding) decisions on basic research investments in line with the overall corporate innovation strategy. The latest Frascati handbook

3. http://www.oecd.org/sti/ind/global-value-chains.htm.

4. https://www.digitaltrends.com/mobile/IPPhone-cost-what-apple-is-paying/.

5. http://www.aeronewstv.com/en/industry/commercial-aviation/3707-boeing-787-dream liner-structure-parts-from-around-the-globe.html.

6. Basic and applied research represents 20 percent of total business R&D in the United States: https://www.nsf.gov/statistics/2017/nsf17320/.

(OECD 2015, par. 3.11) confirms this view: "In large and complex organisations, decisions concerning the strategic direction and financing of R&D activities units tend to occur at a higher organisational level than does the day-to-day management of R&D operations. . . . These decisions can cut across national borders, thus raising a challenge for the statistical authorities and agencies, whose responsibility is often limited to gathering information from resident units." In other words, allocation of basic and applied research or allocating its capital services to the goods manufacturers inside the MNE is inherently without economic meaning.

2. R&D is different from most activities performed by a corporation in the process of its operation. Research is typically not performed with the expectation of immediate profit. Instead, it is focused on the long-term profitability of a company. As such the way in which R&D feeds into the production function is unlike other fixed asset categories. Even for computer software, its presence in a local computer or in the cloud is needed in the course of the transformation process in order to deliver its capital services. Obviously, a similar presence is also required for tangible capital items. In contrast, once a potentially successful recipe for a new medical drug, or the technical design of a new automobile, has been developed, the production process will be set up according to this new blueprint, after which the R&D capital has delivered its contribution to output. This does not imply there is no return to R&D capital involved in the course of producing the medical drug or automobile. However, this different mechanism by which R&D contributes to output implies that the R&D asset is not necessarily found in the balance sheet of the entity engaged in the transformation, i.e., the actual fabrication of the drug or automobile. Instead the R&D asset may be on the balance sheet of an affiliated company (in a low tax jurisdiction) or may not feature on any balance sheet at all, as corporate accounting rules are generally quite restrictive in capitalizing R&D.

3. Inside or outside the MNE group's scope, a production network is not just the sum of its component parts. Product development and design are typically carried out by the arrangers or principal entities inside global production networks. So these entities are often the main R&D investors inside the global value chain. This is also according to the explanation of factoryless goods producers (FGPs) in the *Guide to Measuring Global Production* (UNECE 2015). In this regard FGPs and head offices of MNE groups carry out similar tasks: they both manage global supply chains with the aim of optimizing network synergy. They are both expected to bring together the intangible and physical stages of global production. The main difference is that FGPs have outsourced the physical transformation activities, while inside the MNE these activities are (partly) carried out by affiliated companies. Also different from an FGP, a head office will not necessarily report turnover from sales of goods. Alternatively this turnover is expected to be reported by one or several of the MNE group's affiliated goods producers.

As product and process innovations obtained from R&D may affect several stages in the production network, from a holistic point of view it seems defendable that the FGP or head office is the typical stage where R&D enters the global production chain. It does not seem feasible to assign R&D inputs to the separate transformation stages in the production chain. One R&D asset, or one piece of knowledge, may lead to multiple product innovations and the enhancing of profits of several business units inside the MNE group.

4. In the context of an FGP arrangement, R&D may lead to innovations of products assembled and supplied by non-affiliated contract producers in various parts of the world. The value added and profits generated by these contract producers will typically omit the return to R&D assets, as their production costs, and thus their output prices, will not include R&D costs. The R&D returns are directly captured by the principal of the global production arrangement. Discussions in the global production taskforce (UNECE 2015) showed that in the case of an FGP, national accountants have great difficulties in explaining the nature of the transaction between the contract manufacturer and the principal: the purchase of a good or the purchase of a (manufacturing) service. Our conclusion is that in economic terms the good purchased from the contractor differs fundamentally from the good sold to consumers, even though in physical terms no distinction can be made. This may have implications for the commodity classification in the national accounts and the balance of payments. In the classifications of goods not only are the physical characteristics of the product relevant, but also the conditions under which the product is transferred from one economic owner to another.

5. In the context of an MNE the output price of the affiliated contract producer may indeed include the return to R&D capital, as its output may be directly distributed to the end consumers. However, the required R&D assets may, or may not, be found on the balance sheet of the affiliated manufacturer. It is still possible that headquarters, in their role as global production arrangers, provide the R&D inputs, possibly without any intracompany flows of R&D services being observed. In such a situation the R&D profits will be repatriated to the headquarters via property income (dividends or retained earnings).

6. The latter point shows that corporate funding of R&D is not necessarily linked to how and where the R&D is translated into commercial success. Ignoring tax planning for a moment, from the MNE group's perspective a spatial allocation of generated R&D income is irrelevant, as this income will eventually reach the MNE's shareholders wherever generated. Discussions with a number of R&D managers of Dutch multinational companies led to the conclusion that cost redistribution is not common practice (de Haan and van Rooijen-Horsten 2004).

7. Ironically R&D cost accounting (IP-related royalty payments) within the MNE is particularly observed in the context of tax planning arrange-

ments. Fair competition authorities, tax authorities, and statisticians alike have to evaluate to what extent IP cost accounting arrangements have economic substance. Looking at recent events one must conclude that tax planning arrangements of MNE groups may place national accountants in a very difficult position. This issue is further discussed in section 13.4 of this chapter.

To conclude, (national) IP economic ownership in the context of global production is still not a well-understood concept. The arguments above indicate that IP economic ownership seems to usually coincide with the decision-making entities in the global value chain. These are the entities that are expected to manage overall the intangible and tangible inputs of production. However such a view has several implications that require further examination:

- Assigning economic R&D ownership to headquarters on behalf of the MNE requires, among other things, a careful examination of cross-border R&D flows as they are reported in the international trade in services statistics. R&D conducted by foreign affiliated entities may, or may not, be (partly) funded by headquarters (or by sister companies) or may even have been purchased. This means that the practicalities of such an approach need to be carefully thought through. Some guidance is already provided by Frascati in showing a data collection scheme for R&D expenditure at the MNE level (Figure 11.2 in OECD 2015).
- The commodity (CPC) classification should be further examined to address the economic characteristics of the output of contract producers and FGP arrangements.

13.3.3 Global R&D Networks

R&D (Frascati) statistics provide information on R&D expenditure. This is without any doubt crucial information for the purpose of measuring R&D investment. The assumption that R&D expenditure is overall a reasonable approximation of its commercial benefits is not likely to be replaced by an alternative measurement method. The costs of carrying out R&D and maintaining global R&D networks can be statistically observed in a meaningful way on a country-by-country basis. The allocation of (economic ownership of) investments of R&D networks on a country-by-country basis is a less clear concept. Of course we can assume that the allocation of costs is representative for the allocation of investments, but this seems to be a rather shaky assumption.

Global R&D networks within MNE groups are best illustrated with the help of a few real-life examples. The technology firm Samsung has over 50,000 employees working in collaboration on R&D spread across multiple R&D centers in South Korea as well as others in Russia, India, China, Israel,

Table 13.1   **The Samsung R&D network**

	Research institute	Country	Type of R&D activities
1	Beijing Samsung Telecommunication	China	Mobile telecommunications standardization and commercialization for China
2	Samsung Semiconductor Chine R&D	China	Semiconductor packages and solutions
3	Samsung R&D Institute India	India	System software for digital products, protocals for wired/wireless networks, application and graphic design
4	Samsung Telecom Research Israel	Israel	Hebrew software for mobile phones
5	Samsung Yokohama Research Institute	Japan	Core next-generation parts and components, digital technologies
6	Samsung Poland R&D Center	Poland	STB SW platform development, EU STB/DTV commercialization
7	Moscow Samsung Research Centre	Russia	Optics, software algorithms and other new technologies
8	Samsung Electronics Research Institute	UK	Mobile phones and digital TV software
9	Dallas Telecom Laboratory	US	Technologies and products for next-generation telecommunication systems
10	Samsung Information Systems America	US	Strategic parts and components, core technologies

Japan, Poland, the United States, and the United Kingdom.[7] Table 13.1 details some of the R&D activities undertaken by Samsung outside South Korea.

Another example is Philips, which is a leading technology company operating in the healthcare and consumer electronics sector and one of the largest Dutch MNE groups with its technology headquarters located in the Netherlands. However Philips also conducts R&D activities across the world, as shown in table 13.2.[8]

Although we did not undertake a full investigation, the literature on R&D management seems to confirm that regional R&D facilities may support local product development as well as the overall MNE's longer-term research strategy. For example Papanastassiou and Pearce (2005) find that local R&D laboratories in the UK are mostly funded by the parent company of the MNE group. This is considered as being powerfully indicative of the manner in which such decentralized operations are now integral to the ways in which these companies seek to apply existing core technologies and to regenerate and broaden the scope of these crucial knowledge com-

7. http://www.samsung.com/semiconductor/about-us/research-development/.
8. https://www.philips.com/a-w/research/locations.html.

Table 13.2   The Philips R&D network

Research institute	Country	Type of R&D activities
1 Philips Research Shanghai	China	Imaging systems
2 Philips Research Suresnes	France	Healthcare
3 Philips Research Aachen	Germany	Healthcare
4 Philips Research Hamburg	Germany	Imaging systems, biological modelling, computer assisted detection
5 Philips Research Asia	India	Healthcare
6 Philips Research Africa	Kenya	Healthcare, design, user interface
7 Philips Research Eindhoven	Netherlands	Healthcare and global headquarters for all R&D
8 Philips Research Cambridge	UK	Healthcare
9 Philips Research North America	US	Healthcare, artificial intelligence

petences. It depicts a process of refocusing decentralized R&D away from the short-term objective of assisting particular subsidiaries to apply existing technologies to their specific competitive situation, toward positions integral to the more sustained technological and competitive development of the MNE group. In contrast to independently operating R&D facilities, close cooperation between the regional R&D units within an MNE is expected to provide substantial externalities, in the form of systematic group-level spillover benefits. Central financial participation in the funding of laboratories can be seen as crucial in developing the necessary interdependencies between decentralized R&D units, and in securing the cohesive growth of intra-group knowledge flows.

Some MNE groups like Apple follow quite aggressive strategies in obtaining the knowledge required for strengthening global competitiveness. Recently Apple opened R&D units in Berlin, the French Alps, and New Zealand, all in the close neighborhood of companies with a strong record in certain scientific areas (e.g., mapping or augmented reality). In several cases these companies lost employees to Apple soon after Apple opened its new R&D unit.[9] This shows that the choice of location of newly established R&D units is on occasion solely driven by knowledge acquisition, the availability of human capital/tacit knowledge and not by locating the R&D unit close to those MNE affiliates that are supposed to transform the R&D to product innovation, output, and commercial success.

The existence of R&D networks within the MNE structure appears to

9. https://www.bloomberg.com/news/articles/2017-09-21/apple-s-global-web-of-r-d-labs -doubles-as-poaching-operation.

have similar implications for the national accounts as the existence of fragmented production chains. While the geographical distribution of R&D costs within the MNE structure as reflected by Frascati-based statistics is likely to be reasonably well measured, the distribution of (the economic ownership of) the created R&D assets inside the MNE is not well understood. For smaller national firms, there will likely be a strong geographical correlation between R&D activities and the obtained commercial gains. In those cases it is reasonable to assume that the location of R&D activity coincides with R&D asset ownership. However, within the MNE framework this assumption cannot generally be made on solid grounds. As R&D strategies and R&D funding are expected to result from the overall corporate strategy, the choice of considering R&D as genuine corporate property appears attractive. However, as mentioned, the practicalities of such a choice should be carefully considered.

When assigning R&D ownership to the head offices one should assure that the production accounts for each of the MNE group's entities represent meaningfully the various fragments of production encountered inside the MNE group. For example, each of the accounts should sufficiently support productivity measurement (Schreyer 2018). This implies that together with R&D ownership, the R&D revenues need to be recorded in the accounts of the head office. Equally, the R&D costs need to be assigned to the MNE groups' affiliates. This is not a new phenomenon, as head offices will more broadly provide all sorts of intra-group services to its affiliates i.e., supply chain management services, financial services, marketing activities, and so on.

One way to allocate all of these costs is using allocation mechanisms such as the formulary apportionment techniques used by Guvenen et al. (2017). The main goal of Guvenen et al. is to allocate the generated income over those entities in the MNE that are carrying out the actual production activities. This as an attempt to overcome the disturbances caused by tax planning arrangements. In this chapter we suggest allocating the sum of "overhead costs," or in other words all intra-group services provided by head offices, to those affiliated companies that carry out part of the genuine economic activities. Obviously such allocation requires a concerted action of all the NSIs involved. The outcome of this exercise should be an economically sound allocation of the MNE group's value added and gross operating surplus leading to meaningful productivity statistics at the level of individual enterprises or establishments inside the MNE group. This goal corresponds closely to formulary apportionment allocation of profits as carried out by Guvenen et al. Please be aware that the proposed exercise may also help to overcome some of the substantive bilateral asymmetries in the trade in services statistics today. Perhaps a concerted cost allocation of head offices could also overcome some of the disturbances of transfer pricing.

The example presented in the appendix to this chapter is quite simple, as all R&D costs are assigned to one single affiliated company. But in essence it illustrates the cost reallocation proposed in this chapter.

13.4   Intellectual Property and Tax Planning

One may argue that R&D capitalization in the 2008 SNA revealed (but not necessarily caused!) the national accounts' vulnerability to problems arising from globalization, as MNE groups may use IP assets as vehicles for tax planning. The goal of such tax planning is to shift revenue to units within the MNE structure that are tax resident in low tax jurisdictions, a consequence of which MNE groups can minimize their global tax liability. This is often achieved through the use of royalty and license agreements linked to IP assets. Units of an MNE will typically be required to pay a royalty charge to another unit within the MNE for the right to use assets intrinsic to the production process. In doing so profit from sales in higher tax jurisdictions can be transferred to units in lower tax jurisdictions, minimizing the global tax liability for an MNE. Such constructions are often used by MNE groups in the technology industry where R&D and other forms of intellectual property play a crucial role. The lack of a physical presence of IP assets lends themselves to such constructions, as they can be easily located and relocated around the world at little cost. Under such conditions, the observable global value chain of MNE groups reflects an artificial, tax-driven reality rather than what could be considered the true production process reflecting economic substance. We should also note that movable tangible assets such as transportation equipment may also be subject to tax planning arrangements, as their (legal) ownership can be assigned to a leasing company resident in a low tax jurisdiction.

The two real-life examples of Google and Nike explored in this section highlight the expected consequences of following, as a national accountant, the legal reality as revealed in source statistics, rather than looking through the legal reality and depicting the MNE group's real economic substance, which can only be seen once the entire "elephant" has been observed.

It should again be emphasized that all information on both cases has been obtained from public sources that have previously been published, such as news articles and business reports and does not disclose information from official statistics as collected for individual companies.

13.4.1   The Double Irish with a Dutch Sandwich[10]

13.4.1.1   Explaining the Case

The double Irish with a Dutch sandwich is a name given to a legal business arrangement designed to minimize the MNE's global tax liability. This technique has most prominently been used by technology companies, because

---

10. A detailed legal explanation of the Double Irish with a Dutch Sandwich is given in "From the Double Irish to the Bermuda Triangle," J. Brothers, November 2014, Tax Analysis.

these firms can easily shift large portions of profits to other countries by assigning intellectual property rights to subsidiaries abroad. From 2015 onwards Irish tax legislation does not allow companies to use the Double Irish Dutch Sandwich for new tax plans. Existing plans can be continued until 2020. The latter may have severe repercussions for national statistics as in response MNE groups may restructure their business and set up alternative tax planning schemes. Business restructurings may also be the response to the recent US tax reforms.

One of the MNE groups using the Double Irish Dutch Sandwich construction was Google.[11] The main ingredients, which are typical for the Double Irish Dutch Sandwich recipe, are as follows.

The parent company at the top of the corporate hierarchy is Alphabet Inc. This company is based in Mountain View, California, USA. Although most of the ultimate parents of MNE groups using the Double Irish Dutch Sandwich structure are resident in the United States, this is not necessarily the case. Google Inc. sits below Alphabet Inc. in the hierarchy and is the top of the structure for what can best be described as the everyday Google internet functions such as search, maps, email. A large number of companies operating across the world sit below Google Inc. in the hierarchy.

One of these is Google Ireland Holdings Unlimited, which is an Irish incorporated entity managed and controlled from Bermuda—a common choice. This is an SPE registered in Ireland but not liable for tax in Ireland. Rather it is tax liable in Bermuda, from where it is officially managed and controlled.[12] This type of holding company with only holding activities has no physical presence and zero employees, or only sufficient employment to fulfill a strict legal requirement, i.e., the only employees are directors or shareholders who are normally non-Irish residents.

Google Netherlands Holding B.V. is a Dutch resident company. It is an SPE-type unit with no employees and no activities other than "financing and participating in affiliated companies."[13] This Dutch SPE receives royalty payments from Google units in Ireland and Singapore, which are directly transferred to Google Ireland Holdings Unlimited, minus a small amount of administrative costs.

Google Ireland Limited is an Irish registered company that undertakes real economic activities in Ireland. It also has a wider role outside Ireland of being the company that closes all deals for Google AdWords across Europe. AdWords represents a large portion of Google's revenue. It has been estimated that as much as 88 percent of Google non-US revenue is recorded by Google Ireland Limited.[14] Together these Google affiliates, representing the Double Irish Dutch Sandwich, operate as follows.

11. https://fd.nl/ondernemen/1180304/google-sluisde-vorig-jaar-15-mrd-royalties-door-nederland.
12. Idem.
13. Google Netherlands Holdings B.V. Annual Report 2016.
14. Van Geest, van Kleef, and Smits (2015, 64).

Google Ireland Holdings Unlimited Company owns various IP rights, which it licenses to Google Netherlands Holding B.V., which in turn sublicenses these rights to Google Ireland Limited. Google Ireland Limited uses the sublicenses in its production process and generates revenue. In doing so it is liable to pay royalty fees to Google Netherlands Holding B.V. as a result of using the IP.

Google Netherlands Holdings B.V. is also liable to pay royalty fees to Google Ireland Holdings Unlimited Company on account of the licensing agreement between the two. As such the royalty payments make their way from Ireland via the Netherlands back to an Irish registered company, which is however controlled, managed, and liable to pay corporation tax in Bermuda. Google Netherlands Holdings B.V. acts only to channel cash flows between units. In comparison with the value of the royalty flows, little profit remains in the Netherlands.

The Dutch SPE is not an essential hub in the tax planning arrangement. Rather it is an additional insurance layer against potential withholding tax liabilities arising on direct royalty payments. The zero rate of withholding taxes on incoming and outgoing royalty payments between Ireland and the Netherlands allows this royalty flow to be seen as being taxed already (though at a zero rate) meaning the potential tax liability is therefore removed. Typically the Dutch SPE will pay on virtually identical royalty payments to the Irish Holding unit as it receives. In 2015 over 99.9 percent of the royalties received by Google Netherlands Holdings B.V. were repaid to Google Ireland Holdings.[15] An overview of the Google structure is presented in Figure 13.1.

13.4.1.2   National Accounts Implications

There are several concerns when translating the information obtained from each of these entities to national accounts statistics.

- The arrangement requires that IP ownership is transferred from the ultimate parent (in the United States) to the royalty and license company in a low tax jurisdiction (Bermuda); in the Google case this is Google Ireland Holdings. This apparent IP transfer raises several questions. For example, would this be an IP purchase/sale, and if so, what would be a representative market value of such an intra-company transaction? But perhaps an even more fundamental issue is whether or not this transaction has economic substance at all. Is Google Ireland Holdings, besides the legal owner, also the economic owner of this IP? One may expect that despite this arrangement, strategic decisions about IP creation and allocation continue to be made in the United States, even in cases where

15. As calculated based on data from Google Netherlands Holding B.V. annual report 2015, publicly available at www.kvk.nl. Royalties received €14,963 billion, royalties repaid €14,951 billion.

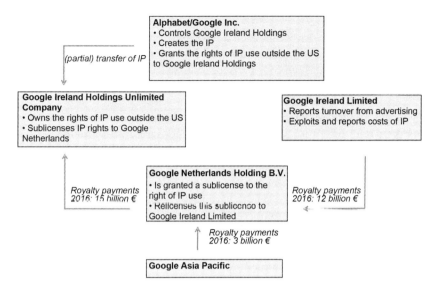

Figure 13.1   A double Irish Dutch sandwich: the Google case

part of its IP ownership is transferred to an affiliated company abroad. A practical question is whether such international intra-group IP transactions will be recorded in all the countries involved in a symmetrical way. In other words, will the value representing the export of the IP from the United States equal the import value as reported in Bermuda/ Ireland?

- Another question is the country of residence of Google Ireland Holdings Unlimited, as this company is registered in Ireland but managed and controlled in Bermuda and also tax liable in Bermuda. Which country should conceptually be recording this unit in their national accounts, and which country is actually doing this?

- Google Netherlands Holding B.V. is registered in the Netherlands, files annual returns to the Dutch Chamber of Commerce, and is liable for tax in the Netherlands. As Google Netherlands Holding B.V. lacks a domestic parent, it must be considered an independent resident institutional unit in the Netherlands. Google Netherlands Holding B.V. is granted a sub-license for the IP assets, but no information of its value is shown in business reports. Google Netherlands Holding B.V. does not carry out significant economic activity from a national accounts perspective, has no employees, and appears to do no more than channel financial flows from one country to another. In doing so it fully acts on behalf of its foreign parent. The inflow of funds equals outflows with a small margin covering local costs. From the point of view of the Netherlands, it is defendable that these in- and outflows are recorded as financial transactions and not as IP related services imports and exports. But from the point of view of Ireland, such a recording would create an asymmetry as Google Ireland Limited is expected to report an import of IP services from the Netherlands. Or perhaps directly from Bermuda?

13.4.1.3   The Bermuda Triangle

Given the residency issue of Google Ireland Holdings Unlimited, it is not unlikely that this entity will show up in neither Irish nor Bermudan statistics. In other words, in the world of statistics the Bermuda triangle appears a real threat. This view is strengthened by simply comparing the value of the royalty transactions involved to the annual GDP figure for Bermuda. In 2015 Bermudan GDP was US$5.9 billion.[16] This amount is far less than the €14.9 billion that Google's Dutch subsidiary paid in 2016 to its Bermudan subsidiary. The tentative conclusion is that earnings of Google Ireland Holdings Unlimited Company are not included in Bermudan measures of GDP. The compilers of Bermudan GDP may not view this unit as being resident in Bermuda, or otherwise may not conceive Google Ireland Holdings Unlimited as the producer of IP services with a €14.9 billion turnover.

The Double Irish with a Dutch Sandwich strategy is known to be used, or has been used, by large companies other than Google. Attempting to extrapolate from this one case study to quantify with any degree of accuracy what might be the total of unrecorded GDP is nearly impossible without vast amounts of time and resources. Even then the wall of corporate secrecy would act as a serious impediment to obtaining good estimates of globally unrecorded output.

Research undertaken in other areas does allow some attempt to be made to come to a ballpark estimate for this global issue. For instance Garcia-Bernardo et al. (2017) analyze global corporate ownership structures from a network analysis approach and in doing so designate certain countries as either sink or conduit financial centers. The authors identify Bermuda as one of the largest sink offshore financial centers in that it is the net recipient of far more foreign capital than would be expected given Bermuda's level of GDP. The question remains whether this lost income should be recorded in Bermuda's GDP at all.

Guvenen et al. (2017) attempt to reattribute foreign earnings of US-led MNE groups to study what impact this has on measures of U.S output and industry productivity. In doing so, they reattribute earnings from Bermuda to the United States of US$35 billion, which represents the equivalent of almost six times Bermudan GDP. The authors conclude that current US measures of output suffer from measurement errors as a result of earnings by US corporations being shifted to countries with relatively low tax rates. The authors also indicate that repatriated earnings from the United King-

---

16. Official estimate of Bermudan government, https://www.gov.bm/bermuda-economic-statistics.

dom Islands in the Caribbean, including the British Virgin Islands, Cayman Islands, and Turks and Caicos Islands, as equal to 4.8 times the GDP of these lands. The largest repatriation, 28 percent of the total, is actually from the Netherlands. This shows that the problem of profit shifting does not necessarily have to involve what could be termed the traditional tax paradises.

This chapter makes no attempt to put a value on the total of global unreported value added. Rather it concludes that this total is expected to be substantial. If the coverage of just one MNE in the national accounts alone is responsible for US$15 billion of missed output, then the total of all MNE groups could easily exceed US$100 billion. Zucman (2015) indicates that profit shifting to low tax jurisdictions outside the United States represents an amount of US$130 billion. One may expect that most of this capital income will not be reported in any country's GDP. Compared to global GDP of around US$75 trillion, this unobserved income may still seem small. But as indicated by Guvenen et al., tax planning arrangements may have significant and undesirable effects on the macroeconomic indicators at national level.

13.4.2   The Case of Nike

A so-called closed Dutch limited partnership (in Dutch, a *commanditaire vennootschap,* or C.V.) is used by several American MNE groups such as Nike, General Electric, Heinz, Caterpillar, Time Warner, and Foot Locker.[17] The C.V. tax planning route has brought the Netherlands under accusation of being a tax haven for American companies similar to places like the Cayman Islands, Switzerland, and Bermuda. How the C.V. construction works is explained with the help of the Nike example.

Also in this case IP assets are a key element in the tax planning arrangement. As explained in the UNECE Global Production Guide (paragraph 2.17), the value of sports brands such as Nike may partly originate from R&D, i.e., the development of "the midsole, the most important part of an athletic shoe, that cushions and protects the foot." However, it is quite clear that sports brands such as Nike are also the outcome of intensive marketing, which is in the strict 2008 SNA sense a non-produced asset. When observing the profit and loss accounts and balance sheets of royalty and licenses companies, the distinction between produced and non-produced intangible assets, also in terms of related capital services or royalty receipts, is not easily made. This point is addressed later in this section.

From a national accounts perspective the case of Nike looks similar to that of Google in that specific units within the MNE own IP assets intrinsic to the production process for which they are reimbursed by other units within the MNE group's global value chain for the use of those IP assets. However Nike does not use Irish registered units but rather a specific type of Dutch legal construction, Nike Innovate C.V., which is a subsidiary of the

17. https://thecorrespondent.com/6942/bermuda-guess-again-turns-out-holland-is-the
-tax-haven-of-choice-for-us-companies/417639737658-b85252de.

Nike Group. It is registered with the Dutch Chamber of Commerce, though with its official address recorded as being in Oregon in the United States. The activities of the business are recorded by the Dutch Chamber of Commerce as "holding IPP rights, financing R&D and buying-out third party licences." As reported in the international media, Nike Innovate C.V. is the legal owner of IP assets including trademarks and designs belonging to the Nike Group.[18] It is useful to emphasize that purchased marketing assets and goodwill are also assets in the SNA sense, however they are classified as non-produced and therefore not considered as intellectual property products.

According to the Dutch tax law, C.V.s are not themselves liable to pay Dutch corporate income tax. It is assumed that the sponsor or owner of the C.V. is liable to pay corporate income tax. However under US tax law the C.V. is seen as liable for tax in the Netherlands. This misclassification can result in certain C.V.s being liable for corporate income tax in neither the Netherlands nor the United States. In effect such C.V.s become stateless.[19]

If Nike Innovate C.V. is not liable to pay corporation tax in the Netherlands, it will also not appear in tax data used by Statistics Netherlands for compiling economic statistics. Also, as Nike Innovate C.V. is not registered with an address in the Netherlands, this entity is not surveyed for official statistics. As a result, Nike Innovate C.V. remains uncovered by the official statistics for the Netherlands. Nor should it be expected that this entity will show up in the statistics of any other country.

The Netherlands also hosts Nike Europe Holding B.V., which is a holding company for other Nike units within Europe, including Nike Europe Operations Netherlands B.V. This unit is the European headquarters of Nike, with around 2,000 employees in the Netherlands. Nike Europe Holding B.V. has a branch located in Belgium, where the Nike customer service center is located. The customer service center provides central warehousing activities to its subsidiary Nike Europe Operations Netherlands B.V., which is the owner of the inventory held at the warehouse and the main commercial entity of the Nike group in Europe and the Middle East. As explained in the financial report[20] the warehousing activities involve all supply-chain-related activities, including receipt, storage, order handling, and shipment of Nike products.

The principal business activity of Nike European Operations Netherlands B.V. is given as the marketing and selling of athletic footwear, apparel, equipment, accessories, and services.[21] For the year June 2015 to June 2016 the unit recorded revenues of €8.4 billion, the majority of which were generated

18. https://www.irishtimes.com/business/how-nike-slashes-its-tax-bill-between-the-netherlands-and-bermuda-1.3281665.
19. http://leidenlawblog.nl/articles/what-about-cv-bv-structures-and-state-aid.
20. Nike Europe Holding B.V. financial report for year ending May 2016, publically available from www.kvk.nl.
21. Nike European Operations Netherlands B.V. financial report for year ending May 2016, publically available from www.kvk.nl.

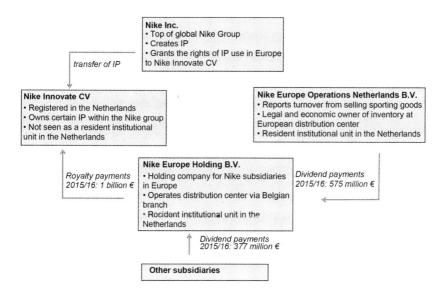

Figure 13.2   The Nike case

outside the Netherlands by its subsidiaries. Nike Europe Operations Netherlands B.V. and its subsidiaries generate revenue by selling goods across Europe and beyond, either directly to consumers, or via independent distributors and licensees.

Revenue of Nike Europe Holding B.V. is solely limited to the services provided by the customer service center to Nike Europe Operations Netherlands B.V. for which they are reimbursed on a cost plus markup basis. For the year from June 2015 to June 2016 this revenue is recorded as €262 million. However Nike Europe Holding B.V. recorded for the same period general and administrative expenses of €1.268 billion. Of this €1.017 billion is recorded as trademark royalties, "in connection with the distribution and commercial exploitation of Nike Intangible Property and Nike marks."[22] The result of making a royalty payment far in excess of revenue is that Nike Europe Holding B.V. records an operating loss which is then financed by dividends from its subsidiaries and principally from Nike Europe Operations Netherlands B.V. This description of Nike's operations in the Netherlands has been the case since November 2012 when Nike Europe Holding B.V entered into "a certain agreement in connection with the distribution and commercial exploitation of Nike intangible property and Nike marks."[23]

Figure 13.2 details the transactions that take place between the units

22. Ibid.
23. Nike Europe Holding B.V. financial report for year ending May 2013, publicly available from www.kvk.nl.

under discussion with additional details taken from the publicly available annual reports filed at the Dutch Chamber of Commerce.

The case of a sports shoes manufacturer was also a prominently used example in the UNECE *Guide to Measuring Global Production* (UNECE 2015). The example was used to discuss the production arrangements between a principal and contracted foreign suppliers including the more specific issues of merchanting and FGPs. However the particular issue of IP assets being held in a stateless entity, as far as national accounts measures were concerned, was not discussed. Before the information revealed by the Paradise Papers, such an example was simply too bizarre to imagine.

As a *commanditaire vennootschap*, Nike Innovate C.V. is not required to file annual accounts with the Dutch Chamber of Commerce. Obtaining details on any of this entity's transactions is therefore difficult. The accounts of Nike Europe Holding B.V. do not reveal the names of the recipients of the royalty payments within the Nike Group. Media reports have identified Nike Innovate C.V. as being the recipient of royalty payments from Nike's European headquarters in the Netherlands.[24]

From a conceptual viewpoint, it is not clear how the income flows related to non-produced intangible assets such as brand names should be recorded in the national accounts. Marketing assets, trademarks, and designs fall outside the fixed assets boundary. As explained by BMP6 (par. 10.140), trademark revenue, payments for use of brand names, and so forth include aspects of property income (i.e., putting a nonfinancial non-produced asset at the disposal of another unit) as well as aspects of services (such as the active processes of technical support, product research, marketing, and quality control). The recording of income flows obtained from non-produced intangible assets such as trademarks and brand names is not explicitly addressed in the 2008 SNA.

13.4.2.1   National Accounts Implications

- It is expected that the revenues of the above C.V.s will not be accounted for in either the GDP of the United States or the Netherlands. This is due to the peculiar tax status of these C.V.s. The repercussion for statistical measurement is that Nike Innovate C.V. has no resident status. This would imply that the more benign-sounding Dutch Polder is equally as dangerous to global GDP as the Bermuda Triangle. Both places function as royalty income sinks. Looking at the substance of the arrangement, one would probably argue that the actual economic ownership of the Nike brand name is still in the hands of Nike headquarters in Beaverton, Oregon, United States.
- At the same time, one may expect that the service charges for using the Nike brand will be (implicitly) recorded in business surveys as production costs of Nike European Operations Netherlands and perhaps of

24. https://www.theguardian.com/news/2017/nov/06/nike-tax-paradise-papers.

other affiliated companies. Whether these cost charges are "at arm's length" cannot be assessed.

- Also, the 2008 SNA is not particularly clear on whether these expenses should be part of the current cost of production, i.e., intermediate consumption, at all. The Nike case shows that non-produced assets can be put at the disposal of other units for use in their production process. If done so the owner of the assets may receive royalty or license payments in exchange. This can be the case with marketing assets such as trademarks, logos, or brand names. Royalty payments in exchange for the use of marketing assets would differ from those for produced assets, as marketing assets are classified in the SNA as non-produced assets. This raises the question of how royalty payments for the use of non-produced assets should be recorded.

Besides loopholes caused by differences in tax policies, the national accounts seem to suffer from a similar kind of mismatch. Entities such as Google Ireland Holdings and Nike Innovate CV appear to be stateless in the eyes of the national accountant. This may partly result from differences in how national accountants put in practice the SNA guidelines on, for instance, the residency principle of statistical units.

13.5 Conclusion

Unlike Lynch and Thage (2017) we generally support the choice of capitalizing R&D expenditure in the national accounts. It is beyond doubt that knowledge investments are crucial for the competitiveness of firms. As successful knowledge investments will generate returns over a range of years, it is difficult to ignore the concept of knowledge capital in the national accounts. Doing so would inevitably diminish the relevance of national accounting.

At the same time we argue that the 2008 SNA approach of R&D capitalization has gone too far. The 2008 SNA is insufficiently clear in explaining under which conditions knowledge truly represents an economic asset in the SNA sense. As argued in this chapter, knowledge becomes an economic asset under the following conditions:

1. The economic owner has *exclusive* ownership over the knowledge;
2. This exclusive ownership is expected to generate for its owner an economic (competitive) advantage and a return on investment.

Exclusive ownership enforced by a patent, secrecy, or by other means (having access to the complementary tacit knowledge) is, in our opinion, a. precondition for the existence of a knowledge asset. As a consequence, capitalization of freely accessible academic research as recommended in the 2008 SNA should be reconsidered.

Also within the enterprise group the concept of knowledge (R&D) ownership is insufficiently understood. The national accounts methodology does not acknowledge that decisions on R&D programs and funding are often made by headquarters and affect the entire MNE structure. As such the international guidelines do not adequately explain how knowledge capital is linked to the MNE and international value chains. For example the SNA should provide guidance on whether knowledge capital ownership should be identified at the level of the establishments, enterprises, or enterprise groups. Additional guidance on these general principles is highly needed. This chapter shows that R&D ownership is most easily identified at the level of the enterprise group. Assigning its ownership to lower levels in the MNE structure such as establishments, as is done for other fixed capital asset categories, is not straightforward.

In the national accounts, production is described at the level of establishments or kind of activity units. Their classification is according to ISIC. Similarly, a multifactor-type productivity analysis usually requires that inputs and outputs of production can be statistically described at the level of establishments. Our impression is that R&D is different from other fixed assets. Particularly within the global value chain R&D asset ownership is not easily linked to the individual fragments of the global value chain and cannot be assigned to individual ISIC establishment classes. The Frascati Manual (OECD 2015) recommends collecting R&D statistics at the level of the institutional unit (i.e., the enterprise) and not the kind of activity unit. Vancauteren, Polder, and van den Berg (2018) show that for the analysis of patent ownership the enterprise is essential in the construction of patent data sets, as firms tend to register patents (and R&D) under separate firm names.

Additionally, the 2008 SNA should provide much more guidance on how to treat R&D (or IP) ownership in the context of tax planning. The UNECE global production guide suggests following legal ownership as a second-best alternative. This chapter shows that this solution is unsatisfactory from an analytical point of view. Following legal ownership seems to imply that portions of IP-related income are not accounted for at all, neither from a national nor global viewpoint.

Finally this chapter shows that official statistics as collected at national level will not necessarily reveal the tax planning arrangements MNE groups are undertaking. Official statistics can only fulfill their key task of informing the public about macroeconomic developments if national accountants combine their efforts in making sense of the data collected from internationally operating companies. The work on data sharing that is currently being undertaken is therefore very welcome. Also, one may hope that the OECD Base Erosion and Profit Shifting (BEPS) initiative will provide improved data sources on the activities of MNE groups.

Our recommendations to improve the recording of R&D and IP in national accounts are the following:

- The definition of (R&D) knowledge assets in the SNA requires refinement to explain that freely shared knowledge is not an asset in the SNA sense.
- The issue of R&D asset ownership inside the MNE requires continued investigation. As a starting point it is worth investigating whether R&D ownership could and should be assigned to the enterprise group or its headquarters. This is where decision making on R&D programs and budgets often take place. However, from a statistical measurement point of view this proposal has undoubtedly several practical implications. For example:
  - As explained in section 13.3, this would require modifications in the accounts and close cooperation between all national statistical institutes involved. A rerouting of a more limited scope would address the IP transactions of artificial brass plate type royalty and licenses companies. A worked example is presented in the appendix. The operation increases in complexity once several affiliates or business units inside the MNE group may generate profits which partly originate from the MNE group's intellectual property. The option of applying cost retribution methods in the national accounts, not only for IP costs but generally for all sorts of intra-group services provided by head offices, should be investigated.
  - Another proposed step is assigning the R&D from regional R&D units to headquarters (cf. tables 13.1 and 13.2). From the perspective of the country (A) in which this R&D facility is resident, the recording of its output would be export rather than gross fixed capital formation. The accounts of country (B) domiciling the headquarters would show the R&D gross fixed capital formation which originates from import. The R&D would subsequently be depreciated in country (B).
  - The extent to which MNE group activities can impact macroeconomic statistics may require the need for more radical solutions that go beyond rerouting within the current SNA framework. For example Rassier (2017) has raised the question of whether MNE group activities would be better recorded in an SNA framework that offers dual presentation measures rather than single measures that conflate operating entities with special purpose entities.

  Obviously, all such options require a concerted action of all the countries involved. Such accounting solutions can only work when national statistical offices start working closely together. In the current information society this should work, particularly when NSIs are able to overcome legal constraints when strictly cooperating within multinational official statistics networks.
- Throughout the world, and of course on a confidential basis, national

accountants could share their data and knowledge on MNE groups with the main goal of improving the common understanding of MNE group structures and the recording of MNE group activities on a country-by-country basis. Recent experiences show that accounting for MNE groups is no longer achievable on an individual country basis. The accurate recording of IP transactions and ownership inside the MNE groups requires international statistical coordination to avoid the existence of GDP sinks such as the Bermuda Triangle and the Dutch Polder. International organizations could facilitate such data sharing initiatives. Some of them—Eurostat, UNECE, and OECD—have already started doing so.

- Statisticians and national accounts compilers could inform the public that tax planning is not only an issue for government revenue but also for official statistics. This may sound naïve as tax base erosion is of course primarily an issue of social fairness in terms of fair tax bill sharing between citizens and companies and in terms of fair corporate competition. However, one of the undesired consequences of non-published arrangements between MNE groups and tax authorities is that statisticians are seriously hampered in their task to inform the public properly on the actual state of economic affairs and the nature of activities companies are undertaking in their countries.
- National accountants could emphasize the need of a country-by-country company reporting as recommended in the OECD's Base Erosion and Profit Shifting prevention initiative as a way to ensure an improved monitoring of national and global economic developments.[25]
- Future updates of SNA could consider the recording of non-produced nonfinancial assets (marketing assets) and royalties earned on them particularly in the context of tax planning strategies within MNE groups. The 2008 SNA should as a minimum elaborate on the advice of BPM6 for how to deal with income (rent) obtained from the ownership of non-produced assets (i.e., trademark and marketing assets).

Appendix
Google Case: Rerouting of IP Transactions

The concerted accounting treatment of Google, as proposed in this chapter, would be to identify Alphabet as the genuine producer of the IP services as consumed by Google Ireland Limited (and of course as consumed by any other non-US Google affiliate). This coincides with the economic ownership

25. http://www.oecd.org/tax/beps/country-by-country-reporting.htm.

of the IP being assigned to Alphabet in the United States (in contrast with legal ownership). Of course this would imply that Google Ireland Holding is no longer identified as a royalty and licenses firm. In fact both Google Ireland and Google Netherlands holdings would be classified as purely financial vehicles, "Other financial intermediaries" (S.127), with no output. Their main purpose seems to be managing the international cash flows on behalf of the mother company.

Figure 13A.1   **Legal representation**

Figure 13A.2   **Economic interpretation**

References

Brothers, J. 2014. "From the Double Irish to the Bermuda Triangle." *Tax Analysis*, November.

De Haan, M., and M. van Rooijen-Horsten (2004). "Measuring R&D Output and Knowledge Capital Formation in Open Economies." Paper prepared for the 28th General Conference of the International Association for Research in Income and Wealth, Cork.

Eurostat. 2014. "Manual on goods sent abroad for processing."

Garcia-Bernardo, J., J. Fichtner, F. W. Takes, and Eelke M. Heemskerk. 2017. "Uncovering Offshore Financial Centers: Conduits and Sinks in the Global Corporate Ownership IPP

Geest, M. van, J. van Kleef, and H. Smits. 2015. *Het belastingparadijs: waarom niemand hier belasting betaalt; behalve u*: van Kleef, Joost, Smits, Henk Willem, van Geest, Martin: Business Contact.

Guvenen, F., Raymond J. Mataloni Jr., Dylan G. Rassier, and Kim J. Ruhl. 2017. "Offshore Profit Shifting and Aggregate Measurement: Balance of Payments, Foreign Investment, Productivity, and the Labor Share." NBER Working Paper No. 23324. http://www.nber.org/papers/w23324. Cambridge, MA: National Bureau of Economic Research.

Haan, M. de, and M. van Rooijen-Horsten. 2004. "Measuring R&D Output and Knowledge Capital Formation in Open Economies." Paper Prepared for the 28th

General Conference of The International Association for Research in Income and Wealth, Cork, Ireland, August 22–28.

Haan, M. de, P. H. van Mulligen, P. van de Ven, and K. Zeelenberg. 2004. "National accounting in the knowledge and information society." Paper prepared for the 28th General Conference of The International Association for Research in Income and Wealth, Cork, Ireland, August 22–28.

European Commission, IMF, OECD, UN & World Bank. 2008. *System of National Accounts 2008*.

Lynch, R., and B. Thage. 2017. "Maintaining the National Accounts as official statistics." *Review of Income and Wealth* 63 (2): 411–36.

OECD. 2009. *Handbook on deriving Capital Measures of Intellectual Property Products*.

OECD. 2015. *Frascati Manual*.

Papanastassiou, M., and R. Pearce. 2005. "Funding sources and the strategic roles of decentralised R&D in multinationals." *R&D Management* 35 (1), January.

Rassier, D. 2017. "Improving the SNA treatment of multinational enterprises." *Review of Income and Wealth* 63 (2).

Rooijen-Horsten, M. van, M. Tanriseven, and M. de Haan. 2007. "R&D Satellite accounts in the Netherlands, a progress report." Paper prepared for the OECD Working Party on National Accounts, Paris, October 3–5. Session: Measuring capital stock, capital services and productivity.

Schreyer, P. 2018. "Globalization, Intellectual Property Products and Measurement of GDP: Issues and Some Proposals." Back paper for the CSSP Informal Reflection Group.

UNECE. 2011. *The impact of globalization on the National Accounts*.

UNECE. 2015. *A guide to measuring global production*.

Vancauteren, M., M. Polder, and M. van den Berg. 2018. "The relationship between tax payments and MNEs patenting activities and implications for real economic activity: Evidence from the Netherlands." Paper for Conference on Research in Income and Wealth, The Challenges of Globalization in the Measurement of National Accounts, March 9–10, Bethesda, MD.

Zucman, G. 2015. *The hidden wealth of nations*. Chicago: University of Chicago Press.

Comment   Michael Connolly

This is a very interesting and stimulating chapter, particularly in light of globalization events in the recent past. It is a good addition to the literature on the subject of economic ownership, and research and development (R&D). The conceptual debate in the first half of the chapter concerning R&D in the public domain is particularly interesting, as are the case studies in the final section of the chapter.

Michael Connolly is a senior statistician at the Central Statistics Office, Ireland.

For acknowledgments, sources of research support, and disclosure of the author's material financial relationships, if any, please see https://www.nber.org/books-and-chapters/challenges -globalization-measurement-national-accounts/comment-rd-capitalisation-where-did-we -go-wrong-connolly.

R&D in the Public Domain

One of the debates that took place in the lead into the 2008 SNA and ESA 2010 dealt with the treatment of R&D in the public domain. Three different examples are presented in the chapter as the authors revisit the decisions taken and the associated recommendations included in the 2008 SNA for capitalizing government or public domain R&D activities.

At the outset the authors outline the challenges in applying the concepts of a tangible capital asset to intangible assets, such as the nature of depreciation, which is not related to wear and tear but instead to obsolescence. Also a clear distinction is made between tacit knowledge related to human capital, which is not considered an asset in the current SNA, and codified knowledge, such as a patent or an intellectual property product, which is to be considered as an asset.

In this context the authors define the characteristics of an R&D asset in order to determine if it should be capitalized:

- The asset is subject to economic ownership and the owner receives a stream of future benefits.
- There is a degree of exclusivity, and the asset is protected through a patent or otherwise kept secret.

The three examples of government or public domain R&D are then considered to see if they really meet these requirements to be considered assets and be capitalized:

1. Areas where R&D could be capitalized and the recommended approach supported are government scientific research that can have an impact either in improving crop yields or environmentally, where a cleaner approach to agricultural production is developed. In these cases, a stream of future income would result from the research, and this R&D asset could potentially be sold by government.

2. Where a government carries out research into defense, the activity takes place in secret and the outcomes of this R&D are not available to the general public. On account of the limited access to the research, the authors support the decision to capitalize this type of R&D.

3. When the authors get to assess the 2008 SNA recommendations on scientific research that is reported in academic journals, there is not a meeting of minds. This activity is considered to lead to the creation of R&D assets in the 2008 SNA and is capitalized. In the authors' opinion this is a pure public good accessible to all and without any tangible evidence of an owner or a future stream of benefits as a basis for capitalizing the activity.

The guidance in SNA 2008 is that publicly available R&D is to be considered as a capital asset because it generates benefits for society as a whole. Nevertheless, the authors' position, as outlined above, is justified, as there is no clear benefit that can be measured or imputed in relation to this particular example of the creation of a public good, and therefore no basis for estimating the value of this R&D asset in terms of the future income stream or asset life. Ultimately, it appears as if these particular recommendations in 2008 SNA really represent a pragmatic solution; in reality, distinguishing the time spent by postdoctoral students on university campus working for companies where assets are regularly created from R&D activities from the time spent writing academic articles is practically impossible. The nature of these calculations are that the specifics of every student cannot be individually considered, and it is practically impossible to allocate time between research activities leading to the creation of R&D assets and other research leading to the creation of public goods. In reality certain generalizations are applied with the result that this particular aspect of public research is included within what is considered the creation of R&D assets, most likely because to exclude them would be a difficult task in practice. In this respect, it must be clear to the reader that this is a concept paper, so the practical difficulties associated with the implementation of the authors' recommendations are not fully explored. In reality, we cannot overlook such implementation challenges.

R&D in Multinational Enterprises (MNEs)

Following on from the public domain R&D discussion the authors then consider the ownership of R&D assets that are the result of research and development in an MNE group. The main argument of the authors is that on account of globalization and the fragmentation of the physical transformation process, it is difficult to assess where the value of the intellectual property (IP) enters the production cycle and also who in the MNE is the economic owner of the IP. This dislocation between the development and use of intellectual property products (IPPs) is to be expected and is probably inevitable in MNEs, given their size and global reach, which is illustrated with the Samsung example in the chapter.

National accountants need to answer the following questions:

- Which entities in the MNE are investing in R&D?
- Which entities are consuming these R&D services?
- In which country production account are the R&D assets being depreciated?
- How do R&D activities and IP assets contribute to output and KLEMS productivity on a country-by-country basis?

However, as the authors explain, these can be difficult questions to answer.

Economic ownership of IP assets in MNE groups receives considerable attention. The recommendations of the Task Force on Global Production in relation to economic ownership of IP are referenced. In fact the UNECE

Guide to Measuring Global Production (UNECE 2015) contains the following decision-tree-style recommendations:

- IPP producers are also the owners of IPP,
  - unless a sale of the original to parent or subsidiary has occurred;
  - unless no IP-related turnover is generated—control by parent.
- Without conclusive evidence, assign ownership to the IP producer.
- Rerouting of ownership away from SPE /royalty companies is not recommended:
  - assign economic ownership to these units;
  - recognize a separate institutional unit that de facto becomes the owner of the IP assets—case of non-resident SPE;
  - record these SPE-related transactions separately.

However, the authors argue that these recommendations are not complete and require further consideration. In fact, assigning ownership of IP to the parent or the enterprise group is recommended as the only viable solution after having considered the consequences of the status quo where there is no clear association between the production and the benefits accruing from R&D investment. They maintain that in effect R&D activities are centrally controlled in an MNE group and accordingly the R&D assets should be also assigned to a central position. The alternatives for the location of economic ownership in the MNE group of R&D assets are either at the headquarters, at the level of enterprise group, or simply across the group in line with the current treatment. The authors favor the former alternative. Significantly, they say that *"assigning economic ownership to headquarters on behalf of the MNE requires . . . a careful examination of cross-border R&D flows as they are reported in the international trade in services statistics. R&D conducted by foreign affiliated entities may or may not be (partly) funded by headquarters (or by sister companies) or may even have been purchased. This means that the practicalities of such an approach need to be carefully thought through. . . ."* In the concluding part of this section the authors say, *"The choice of considering R&D as genuine corporate property seems attractive. However . . . the practicalities of such a choice should be carefully considered."*

Although the chapter is a conceptual one, it is clear that the authors are aware of the practical difficulties that result from imputing ownership of R&D to the center or headquarters of an MNE, away from the point of observation. Or in other words moving away from the "follow the money" approach. This approach which is recommended by the authors requires a high degree of international coordination and of course data exchange between the statistical compilers of all the countries involved and may even ultimately involve the central collection of MNE data either regionally (EU, OECD, etc.) or internationally.

The proposals, in addressing one set of challenges and managing existing risks in the compilation system, do have the potential to introduce another series of risks. One risk is that a type of "spaghetti junction" is created with all of the rerouting and imputations of transactions associated with the IP viz. restated balance sheet positions in equity, intercompany loans and other balance sheet items, rerouted profits, services, IP assets, etc. from compiling countries where the transactions are reported to the headquarters of the MNE and so on. The opportunity to verify economic transactions through the actual accounts of the entities in the MNE would be lost in this scenario, and the continuity over time of balanced balance sheet positions would also be lost. This is before considering the impact of these imputations on the balance of payments and other key statistics. The symmetrical treatment by all national compilers involved is critical for the authors' proposals to work in practice. Indeed there is always the risk of some of these MNE entities not being observed at all by one of the national statistical compilers involved— for these proposals to work the level of international coordination required to avoid such scenarios would need to be comprehensive.

Tax Planning Case Studies

The final part of the chapter deals with two case studies relating to the location of intellectual property (IP) and tax planning in MNE groups. The case studies relate to particular structures established in Google and Nike. In these cases the authors use publicly sourced information to develop their understanding of tax planning, thus avoiding any confidentiality constraints.

The first case study illustrates how revenues are shifted from high to low tax locations through the charging for royalties against turnover or sales in affiliates in a high tax country. The corresponding income from the royalty or license charges is earned by an affiliate in a low tax economy, in this case Bermuda. This is described as *"creating an artificial reality as opposed to the true production linked economic reality"* by the authors. The authors explain that these scenarios could apply also to highly mobile tangible assets such as aircraft, in addition to R&D-type intangible assets.

In the case of Google, the so-called double Irish with a Dutch sandwich structure is discussed. The key question relating to this arrangement is the following: who is the economic owner of the intellectual property that the royalties and licenses are leveraged on:

- The unit in the Netherlands is little more than a conduit—and an SPE-type structure.
- The unit in Bermuda is an SPE-type structure.
- As with all MNEs, the "real" ultimate owner and beneficiary is the parent in the United States.

It is also interesting that the authors say it is defendable that Statistics Netherlands record these royalty flows in the financial accounts. Clearly, if other countries involved as counterparts to these transactions record the royalties as imports of services, there will be significant asymmetries at EU level in addition to the country asymmetries.

The discussion in the case study argues that the royalty income earned in Bermuda doesn't appear to be included in reported Bermuda GDP and is therefore lost to the international system of measurement and world GDP, although the profits earned in Bermuda of course do return to the United States as reinvested earnings and are thus recorded in US GNI.

The second case study relates to Nike Innovate C.V. in Netherlands. These C.V. companies are "fiscally transparent entities,"[1] meaning that the entity is considered a US resident from the Netherlands perspective and considered a Netherlands resident from the US perspective. This setup is quite similar to the double Irish sandwich, where the Google entity is considered a Bermudan resident by the Irish authorities and considered an Irish resident by the US authorities. However Nike Innovate C.V. is effectively a stateless entity, whereas the Google Ireland Unlimited is a Bermudan resident.

The consequence of these arrangements from a national accounts point of view is that GDP being generated by these activities is being lost to world GDP. The authors have investigated the level and trends in Bermudan GDP and also the counterpart recording of value added between Netherlands and the United States for Nike, and in both cases there are gaps in the recording of these activities. To remedy this situation the authors consider stricter implementation of economic ownership as it applies to IP. A consequence of this arrangement would be that IP located in Bermuda and the Dutch C.V. company would be attributed directly to the parent in the United States. However this would entail a considerable number of imputations as outlined earlier. The SNA however discourages imputation, and additionally the UNECE *Guide to Measuring Global Production* in paragraph 4.44 encourages compilers to remain close to statistical observation, even in clear cases where legal ownership does not match with the SNA principles of economic ownership. The consequence of the level of imputation or rerouting of transactions suggested by the authors would be that the risk of asymmetries becomes substantial.

There are of course other issues to consider. Firstly, following the adoption by most OECD countries of the recommendations of the OECD Base Erosion and Profit Shifting (BEPS), many of the tax optimization arrangements are being ceased. For example, the Double Irish sandwich

---

1. Fiscally transparent entities (FTEs) are entities wherein the owners and investors are taxed for the income earned by the entities and not the entities themselves. The income flows through to the investors and owners of the entities. These entities are considered as non-entities for tax purposes, because all the burden of taxation is borne by owners and investors. Common forms of FTEs are partnerships, Limited Partnerships, and LLPs.

is being completely phased out in 2020, and stateless entities in Ireland are now assigned Irish residency (taxation and registration) if such a scenario arises after 2015. There are also many similar legal changes to the national tax codes that may well end the C.V. preferential arrangements in Netherlands and elsewhere. In this case it seems best to await the outcome of these changes before making radical changes to the SNA.

Of course in the meantime the MNE accountants and tax advisers will probably devise other ways of structuring their activities that will be BEPS compliant but still pose other measurement challenges for national accountants and statisticians.

14

Capturing International R&D Trade and Financing Flows
What Do Available Sources Reveal about the Structure of Knowledge-Based Global Production?

Daniel Ker, Fernando Galindo-Rueda, Francisco Moris, and John Jankowski

14.1 Introduction

Globalization is usually described as a multifaceted process of structural, economic, and social change characterized by the opening of national economies to trade, foreign capital, and workers, as well as the integration (and dis-integration) of activities across national borders. Measuring the magnitude and intensity of this process across its many different dimensions is a key activity of statistical agencies in response to growing demand from policy makers. The fragmentation of production processes across different global sites is one of the most distinctive features of the recent wave of globalization and has profound implications for countries' economic and financial interdependence. In turn, research and development (R&D) activities have also become fragmented, with a combination of demand factors, incentivizing the dispersal of production into global value chains (GVCs), as well as being driven from the supply side as knowledge creation requires inputs from dispersed technological inputs across and within companies.

Daniel Ker is an economist-statistician at the United Nations Conference on Trade and Development (UNCTAD). He was an economist at the OECD Directorate for Science, Technology and Innovation when this work was originally carried out.

Fernando Galindo-Rueda is the senior economist in charge of the S&T indicators unit within the Science and Technology Policy Division at the OECD Directorate for Science, Technology and Innovation.

Francisco Moris is Senior Science Resource Analyst at the National Science Foundation.

John Jankowski is Senior Economic Advisor in the National Center for Science & Engineering Statistics at the National Science Foundation.

The opinions expressed and arguments employed herein are solely those of the authors and do not necessarily reflect the official views of the US National Science Foundation, the OECD, or its member countries. For acknowledgments, sources of research support, and disclosure of the authors' material financial relationships, if any, please see https://www.nber.org/books-and-chapters/challenges-globalization-measurement-national-accounts/capturing-international-rd-trade-and-financing-flows-what-do-available-sources-reveal-about.

Thus, a better understanding of the processes driving the creation, funding, diffusion, and exploitation of knowledge-based assets can contribute to furthering our understanding of global production.

This chapter emphasizes the importance of compiling and contrasting various statistics about knowledge-based assets, incorporating sources that are specifically designed to map the creation and funding of R&D. R&D, as defined by the OECD Frascati Manual (OECD 2015), comprises *"creative and systematic work undertaken in order to increase the stock of knowledge—including knowledge of humankind, culture and society—and to devise new applications of available knowledge."* R&D covers three types of activity: basic research, applied research, and experimental development.[2] For over 50 years, Frascati R&D statistics have kept track of investment in this very important type of knowledge both within and across countries. It is only with the 2008 revision of the System of National Accounts (SNA 2008) (EC et al. SNA 2008, 2009) that expenditures on R&D were formally recognized as investment, thus as assets that can be used by their owner(s) for their own internal use or for a range of possible commercialization activities, including with affiliates, that may span beyond a country's national boundaries.

The main focus of this chapter is on R&D globalization in the business sector,[3] examining new and existing international statistical evidence in this area. R&D activities are important factors in variations in productivity and innovation performance among multinational enterprises (MNEs) and other companies engaged in cross-border trade and/or foreign direct investment (FDI) (Berry 2014; Castellani et al. 2016; Kylaheiko et al. 2011). In terms of the structure of global production, increased production fragmentation by MNEs in the form of vertical FDI and global value chains (GVCs) (Baldwin 2006; Sturgeon 2013; UNECE, OECD 2015) have resulted in dispersed R&D activities that require exchanges of R&D inputs and outputs (Cantwell 2017; Moris 2017; Dachs, Stehrer, and Zahradnik 2014). These trends are apparent in official data such as trade in R&D services statistics, which represent transactions in knowledge-based intermediaries, as well as business R&D statistics, which capture the complex international

---

2. Basic research is experimental or theoretical work undertaken primarily to acquire new knowledge of the underlying foundation of phenomena and observable facts, without any particular application or use in view. Applied research is original investigation undertaken in order to acquire new knowledge. It is, however, directed primarily toward a specific, practical aim or objective. Experimental development is systematic work, drawing on knowledge gained from research and practical experience, and producing additional knowledge, which is directed to producing new products or processes or to improving existing products or processes.

3. It is nonetheless important to note the importance of other actors in the globalization of R&D, including the role of international organizations as performers of R&D—especially of large collaborative undertakings requiring shared infrastructure, cross-border bilateral and multilateral government R&D funding. Private nonprofit organizations also fund and undertake R&D across different locations globally. In many economies, these non-business-related flows can be significant. It is therefore important that these are correctly identified in line with current SNA rules on R&D capitalization.

R&D funding flows associated with outsourcing, contracting with external partners, and with cost sharing agreements within MNEs.

The 2015 Frascati Manual incorporated recommendations for tracking R&D globalization that are still in the process of being implemented by countries. This chapter aims to promote further work in this area by demonstrating the relevance of the additional evidence to a wide range of current statistical and policy discussions that span areas such as output, income and productivity measurement, international trade, investment, intellectual property, taxation, and the migration of highly qualified individuals, as well as the importance of collaboration across national statistical organizations (NSOs) in delivering new data and insights. This chapter presents, to our knowledge, the first attempt to bring together a comprehensive range of R&D statistics relevant to the analysis of globalization following the revision to the various statistical manuals that underpin their conceptualization and collection. In this respect, this document provides an updated view to previous OECD work (OECD 2008).

This chapter is organized as follows: Section 14.2 discusses the rationale and approach to measurement of R&D globalization, and the implications of treating R&D as a produced asset in the SNA, going on to introduce the main three types of interrelated sources that support measurement, namely those relating to international trade, R&D performance, and the activities of MNEs. Section 14.3 examines evidence from trade statistics. This is followed by section 14.4, an assessment of the evidence provided by Frascati-based R&D performance and funding statistics, and comparison with the findings from trade statistics. Section 14.5 investigates the R&D funding and performance of multinational enterprises (MNEs), adopting both inward and outward perspectives when data are available. Section 14.6 concludes with the main findings and proposals for further analysis, including links to other complementary data sources.

14.2   Measuring R&D Globalization

14.2.1   Why Measure R&D Globalization?

Economic globalization presents opportunities to decouple where, and under whose responsibility, innovation activities take place. This runs from who funds R&D to where and how it gets used, along various dimensions. This decoupling can be in itself a major driver of economic globalization. Innovation practices that generate knowledge flows crossing organizational boundaries trade off control for benefits from specialization. Furthermore, organizations can distribute their internal innovation activities across different locations, with knowledge and related financial flows within them resulting from a range of possible considerations, such as the availability of human resources and infrastructures to draw upon to generate new knowledge, synergies with other activities, and other objectives including the ability to control knowledge outputs and minimize global tax obligations. The combination of these elements lies behind the interconnectedness of cross-boundary material flows for both intermediate and final goods that is associated with GVCs and the networks underpinning knowledge flows across organizations and countries in pursuit of innovation—often referred to as global innovation networks (GINs) (OECD 2017a).

In the business context, innovation refers to the introduction to the market of new or significantly improved products and processes (OECD, Eurostat 2005). It is closely related to, but distinct from, R&D. R&D is a key component of the innovation activities and strategies of a large number of firms, including those in more traditional industries (OECD 2009a). The Frascati Manual defines R&D globalization as the subset of global activities involving the funding, performance, transfer, and use of R&D (OECD 2015).

Having a global perspective on business R&D and innovation more broadly is of particular importance across several research and policy domains. For economic policy management purposes, as well as for productivity analysis, it is important to base decisions on R&D asset stocks and services that are aligned with measures of economic output. Cross-country R&D knowledge flows also matter when assessing the sustainability of a country's trade and financial position with respect to the rest of the world. Understanding the link between GINs and GVCs can add to a more nuanced assessment of the impact of barriers to trade and investment. This can also inform the allocation of government support for R&D as well as help in mapping global processes of value creation, key factors for international tax policy standards.

14.2.2   R&D Capitalization as a Test Case for Measuring and Understanding R&D Globalization

The capitalization of R&D in the 2008 SNA—i.e., the treatment of R&D as a production activity that generates assets (capital formation)—had a series of implications for the compilation of national accounts. A key factor in the capitalization decision was the availability of R&D data gathered under the OECD Frascati Manual guidelines for collecting and reporting data on R&D (OECD 2015). These record, among other things, spending on inputs used for R&D within national economies and are thus used to estimate domestic production of R&D by summing R&D production costs and import data in accordance with the method laid out in the 2008 SNA and related international manuals drafted or revised thereafter.

Building upon this, both conceptual and practical data considerations were considered in preparing the OECD Handbook on Deriving Capital Measures of Intellectual Property Products (OECD 2010a), an explanatory manual on how to measure R&D, software and databases, and other intellectual property products (IPPs) as capital formation for national accounting purposes, including IPP trade. In the course of this work, various globalization-related issues were highlighted, including:

- *Imports of R&D services* add to total supply (domestic production plus imports) of R&D and represent capital formation of the purchasing country (OECD 2010a). Unlike the no-capitalization scenario, under the 2008 SNA imports of R&D assets have no impact on the measure of GDP as they increase capital formation by the same amount as they reduce net exports.
- *Patented entities* and related assets are no longer treated as non-produced assets in the 2008 SNA. Transactions in the outright ownership of these legal rights, which are now presumed to come into existence through production, cease to be represented as acquisitions less disposals of non-produced assets and are therefore included in exports and imports.[4] To the extent that these transactions can be large and infrequent, this can in turn generate lumpy shocks to IPP trade and capital formation, and GDP statistics in small economies.
- *Unconditional transfers* of R&D. The provision across boundaries of R&D knowledge (or R&D financing) without receiving in return from the recipient any good, service, or asset represents a capital transfer. Such transactions would previously have been recorded as current transfers and would not necessarily have been identified as R&D related.

Notwithstanding practical differences across R&D performance measures and SNA IPP investment statistics (notably, the recognition of R&D relating to software development as *software* investment),[5] the globalization of R&D appears to be, as expected, a first order factor underpinning observed differences between Frascati-based statistics on R&D performance and the SNA view of how much countries invest in R&D (figures 14.1 and 14.2). In most countries, the value of R&D assets capitalized annually has been fairly similar to the value of domestic R&D performance, with the ratio of R&D investment to performance sitting in a band between roughly 80 percent and 110 percent in many cases and being relatively stable over time. However, divergence has been more marked in countries characterized by large international R&D-related flows. In Ireland, R&D investment

---

4. The 1993 SNA, by convention, included patent licensing related services in output, and, therefore, royalty and similar payments in respect of patent licenses were considered payment for services and not property income as in the 1968 SNA (1993 SNA, page 660). https://unstats.un.org/unsd/nationalaccount/docs/1993sna.pdf. In spite of this, some licensing flows related to R&D knowledge continued to be reported or recorded as property income.

5. According to OECD (2010a) guidance, R&D relating to software development is to be included under software investment, not R&D investment. Cross-country R&D GFCF data used in this paper were compiled in late 2017 and reflect this guidance. For the United States, starting with the 2018 Comprehensive Update of the NIPAs (released by the Bureau of Economic Analysis July 27, 2018), software R&D investment appears under R&D GFCF. See Chute, McCulla, and Smith 2018.

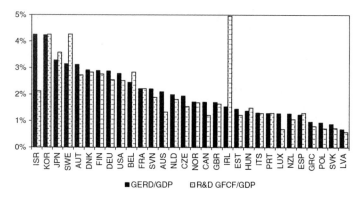

Figure 14.1   Comparison between R&D performance within countries and national accounts measures of R&D capital formation, 2015, as a percentage of GDP

Note: 2014 for DNK, EST, DEU, IRL, LVA, NOR, POL, PRT, SVK, ESP, SWE. 2013 for AUS, ITA.

Source: OECD National Accounts Database (oe.cd/1Fb), OECD R&D Statistics (RDS) database (oe.cd/rds), US Bureau of Economic Analysis, fixed assets accounts. (http://www.bea.gov/iTable/iTable.cfm?ReqID=10&step=1#reqid=10&step=1&isuri=1). October 2017.

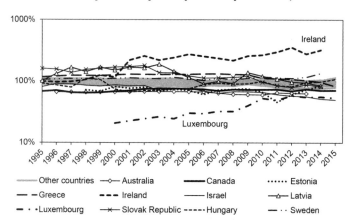

Figure 14.2   Evolution of R&D capital formation as ratio to R&D performance, 1995–2015, ratio as percentage in log scale

Note: "Other countries": AUT, BEL, CZE, DNK, FIN, FRA, DEU, ITA, JPN, KOR, NLD, NZL, NOR, POL, SVN, POL, PRT, SVN, ESP, GBR, USA.

Source: OECD National Accounts Database (oe.cd/1Fb), OECD R&D Statistics database (oe.cd/rds), US BEA, www.bea.gov/iTable/iTable.cfm?ReqID=10&step=1#reqid=10&step=1&isuri=1). October 2017.

has grown much more quickly than GERD (gross domestic expenditure on R&D)[6] since around 1997. This difference is driven by large imports of R&D assets as noted in OECD (2016) and has led Ireland's R&D stock to increase more than ninefold, from US$9.6 billion PPP in 2000 to US$88 bil-

---

6. GERD is total intramural expenditure on R&D performed in the national territory.

lion PPP in 2014 (latest available). By contrast, R&D investment in Israel[7] is estimated to be less than half of R&D performance in 2014, having declined from nearer 100 percent in the 1990s.

14.2.2.1   The Concept of R&D Ownership and the Market for Intellectual Property

A fundamental foundation of the national accounts approach to measuring assets (including R&D assets) is that they should be recorded in the national balance sheets of the country where the "*institutional unit entitled to claim the benefits associated with the use of the [assets] in question in the course of an economic activity by virtue of accepting the associated risks*" is considered to be resident (2008 SNA). However, identifying the economic owners of knowledge products such as the results of R&D is challenging (United Nations Economic Commission for Europe 2015). This is in large part because of the intangible nature of those products, characteristics of which are relative ease to codify and transfer the information and a lack of rivalry in use of knowledge (Lipsey 2010; Rassier 2017).

One "knowledge item" can combine with several others and give rise to multiple entities and associated flows, including those applying to the effective and legal right to use and exclude others from the knowledge for a wide range of possible uses. Economic ownership over R&D assets and related asset bundles can be exerted at different operational levels which need not neatly fit within jurisdictional boundaries. Furthermore, control over R&D and derived assets can also be used to exert ownership over broader operations in cases where most of the value added can be accounted for by the capital services generated by intellectual assets.

Evidence from R&D and innovation surveys and administrative data suggests that a wide range of intellectual property rights (IPRs), especially patents, are of importance for R&D performers and funders but indicate that maintaining secrecy is especially key (OECD 2013). This is relevant when examining trade in R&D and derived assets within and across international boundaries. IPRs other than patents are also used to protect outcomes of R&D. Explicit IPRs facilitate the existence of markets for protected knowledge assets that incorporate outcomes of R&D, facilitating their transferability (as well as their use as collateral for financing purposes), but these markets are underdeveloped for a number of reasons, including the idiosyncratic features of knowledge (OECD 2013). Knowledge that is protected in principle by trade secrets can be exchanged by means of confidentiality agreements.

Use of R&D outcomes is not systematically associated to separately identifiable transactions. Companies may acquire financial interests in other

---

7. The statistical data for Israel are supplied by and under the responsibility of the relevant Israeli authorities. The use of such data by the OECD is without prejudice to the status of the Golan Heights, East Jerusalem, and Israeli settlements in the West Bank under the terms of international law.

companies in order to gain access to or ownership of IP assets. In the case of IP assets, true economic ownership may not stop at the entity that makes effective use of knowledge in production (e.g., of goods or services for the market) but on the ultimate controlling financial owner of that entity. Therefore, similar levels of control over R&D outcomes can be exerted by using a range of very different administrative arrangements. These create various records that statistics can draw upon. In some cases, international mergers and acquisitions (M&A) may be considered as implying automatic transfers of R&D to the buying company, but this can be difficult to establish if the acquired entity maintains its activities.

The M&A example also helps highlight that R&D capitalization has implications not only for production and accumulation accounts but also for income distribution. A case in point is the treatment of R&D ownership within MNEs. While the R&D costs incurred by a foreign-controlled firm developing knowledge for its own internal use ("own-account R&D") generate assets that add to the domestic stock of knowledge and to gross operating surplus, the resulting notional earnings, ultimately, represent property (investment) income of the foreign owner of the affiliate, which it may "reinvest" or transfer; raising questions about who in fact is the ultimate owner of the R&D asset and indeed where (in which country) the value added generated by the asset should be recorded. Property income accrues when the owners of financial assets and natural resources put them at the disposal of other institutional units. The income payable for the use of financial assets is called investment income. Operating surplus associated to own account R&D capital formation represents a source of investment income for the unit with equity on the economic owner of the R&D asset (Yorgason 2007).

National income includes all income earned by a country's resident persons and businesses including property income from intellectual property abroad—while excluding domestically generated property income flowing to residents of other countries. This implies a need for detailed and coordinated understanding of where in the world decisions over intellectual property assets are being taken, what production processes rely on them, the incomes they generate, and where and who those revenues accrue to.

The distinction between economic ownership and financial (or legal) ownership has implications for measurement. Practical challenges for global measurement of flows arise when complex ownership structures are put in place and involve entities located in jurisdictions in which statistical coverage is limited. The existence, economic meaningfulness, and measurability of R&D-related flows are shaped by a wide range of economic factors and government and business policies. In particular, businesses may choose between keeping R&D performance and intellectual property activities "in house"—at their head office or in their home country—or distribute them across the globe for reasons including access to labor with the required skills, proximity to local markets abroad, and incentives relating to government policies such as tax and contract law relating to intellectual property. Some firms find incentives to establish holding companies in jurisdictions abroad to hold and manage their intellectual property or even to act as the ultimate owning company of the business as a whole. Economic ownership is, therefore, especially challenging to identify in the case of MNEs (United Nations Economic Commission for Europe 2015).

It can become unclear which economic entity ultimately makes decisions about the use of the knowledge and the financial results so that identifying ownership and/or control over the asset—that is, identifying the economic owner (or perhaps even the legal owner)—can be challenging, as can be establishing whether a cross-border financial flow (e.g., license payment) relates to R&D assets owned and recorded in the capital stock of the recipient country or elsewhere. Since functionally equivalent production activities can yield different arrays of recorded transactions reflected in statistics, this poses crucial challenges for presentations and analyses focused on "economic" (rather than legal) reality, including national accounts.

14.2.3   Sources of Empirical Evidence on R&D Globalization

Data limitations have been a long-standing obstacle to developing an accurate picture of R&D globalization (OECD 1998). The protection of confidentiality can be at odds with mapping out in sufficient detail different flows, by partner and for detailed industry groups. The complexity and commercial sensitivity of the information requested is therefore seen to present challenges to eliciting responses from businesses if surveyed. Furthermore, targeted respondents may have restricted awareness about decisions that span multiple jurisdictions. As a result, it may be the case that information about certain aspects of R&D globalization can be more accurately reported at a local level while others require a higher-level view of the organization, especially in the case of MNEs.

The remainder of this document reviews evidence from three main families of statistical sources that have been used to track R&D globalization from different perspectives and are consistent with the new "Measurement of R&D Globalization," chapter 11 in the OECD Frascati Manual:

- Trade statistics contain information on the flow of services as implied by related payments across different economies. This allows tracking not only the provision of custom R&D services but also payments for the right to use or control the outcomes of past R&D efforts.
- R&D performance and funding statistics enumerate financial and human resources dedicated to R&D by resident units within an economy, including funding from external and/or foreign sources. These statistics often also provide information on funding given to third parties.
- Statistics on the activities of multinational enterprises (AMNE), which

include their affiliates abroad, measure MNE operations related to inward and outward investments, including R&D. Information about ultimate cross-border ownership over a company's assets (and liabilities) is another important source of information about R&D globalization.

These three main frameworks are very closely related. These frameworks use similar concepts and definitions for R&D, effectively consistent with the Frascati Manual concepts. On the other hand, R&D services trade and MNE R&D performance statistics emerged as part of broader international economic statistics on trade and MNE activities. For the purposes of analyzing R&D globalization, they offer significant complementarities that help offset the limitations of each individual framework. These complementarities may be exploited by linking R&D and MNE or services trade statistics (Moris and Zeile 2016). The following sections examine the evidence available from these different sources and potential connections across them.

14.3   R&D in Services Trade Statistics

14.3.1   What Is Captured in R&D Trade Statistics?

Transactions in R&D services, as defined in the Manual on Statistics of International Trade in Services 2010 (MSITS) (UN et al. 2010) refer to cross-border transactions in R&D services (part of "Other business services"), where R&D itself is defined by reference to the Frascati Manual. These services trade data are typically collected in international trade surveys and valued at market prices (MSITS 3.32). They may include details for affiliated (intra-MNE) and unaffiliated transactions.

Statistics on R&D services transactions collected on the basis of MSITS are currently used by countries to account for R&D "exports and imports" in national economic accounts.

The hierarchy for these data is set out in the Extended Balance of Payments Services (EBOPS) classification reproduced in table 14.1. Data are most often available for the overarching "R&D services" heading (SJ1), which comprises both two sub-categories: "*Work undertaken on a systematic basis to increase the stock of knowledge*" (SJ11) and "*Other research and development services*" (SJ12). The wording of the former is closely aligned with the R&D definition in the Frascati Manual, however further subdivision into "*Provision of customized and non-customized research and development services*" (SJ111) and "*Sale of proprietary rights arising from R&D*" (SJ112) reveals that there is not full alignment. While the former is compatible with the Frascati Manual definition of R&D, the latter covers payments related to the transfer of intellectual property, namely rights applying to the outright sale of R&D-based IP. This may include outright sales of property rights

Table 14.1   **EBOPS trade categories directly related to R&D**

EBOPs descriptor	EBOPS item code	Commentary
Other business services	SJ	
Research and development services	SJ1	
Work undertaken on a systematic basis to increase the stock of knowledge	SJ11	Aligned to FM definition, but combines provision of R&D produced in the period and produced in the past.
Provision of customized and non-customized research and development services	SJ111	Closest alignment to Frascati R&D performance. R&D is produced within period, contemporary to trade.
Sale of proprietary rights arising from research and development	SJ112	Covers change of economic ownership of the whole of the IPR- seller no longer has rights or obligations with IP. Includes second hand outright sales of IPRs. Computed in SNA93 as capital account transaction.
Other research and development services	SJ12	Not exactly R&D (the R&D definition used in MSITS 2010 includes the rather speculative concept of "other testing and other product development that may give rise to patents").
Charges for the use of intellectual property n.i.e.	SH	Includes charges for "non- produced" assets, not treated as property income since SNA93
Licences for the use of outcomes of research and development	SH2	Relates to R&D produced in previous periods. May or may not represent capital formation on the part of the buyer. Rarely reported in full - combined into SH.

Note: Government services in the CPC classification include the category of Government services to R&D (9114), which might be reported under MSITS category 12.3 "Other government goods and services."

Source: Extended Balance of Payments Services classification, 2010.

relating not only to the outcomes of R&D conducted in the period (current output) but also property rights over R&D conducted in previous periods.[8] This differs from the strict "current period" recording of Frascati Manual R&D data and national accounts R&D output. Additionally, the "*Other research and development services*" (SJ12) category is defined on a residual basis, as activities related to patents, and its scope is somewhat less clear.

An examination of cross-institutional transactions reveals the challenges in aligning business practice with SNA and BOP recording conventions, which add to those already captured in UNECE (UNECE 2011):

8. Licenses for the use of such IP are recorded under a separate category (SH2) under "charges for the use of intellectual property."

- R&D transactions from services trade statistics can relate to R&D produced either in the current period (and hence also covered by statistics from Frascati-based surveys for the same year) or in prior years.
- License agreements for IP may include R&D assets in combination with other related intangible assets, such as—in the technical domain— a range of technology sharing agreements, unpatented proprietary technology, technology development rights, engineering drawings and designs, schematics and technical documentation, regulatory approvals and licenses, as well as computer software (object code and source code), databases, brands, advertising programs, brochures and marketing materials, name-related goodwill. Agreements may apply to individual assets or entire IP portfolios.
- In the case of multiyear licensing contracts, accounting practices indicate that if the provider of the IP is engaged in upgrading its "functionality" over time, then the expenses/income have to be recognized over time rather than as one-off.
- The provision of R&D services or licenses to use outcomes of R&D is often embedded in the price of other goods and services. In such instances, these fees are missed by both services trade and R&D surveys.
- Exchanges corresponding to multiyear exclusive licenses to use outcomes of R&D represent, in principle, a requirement to compute negative capital formation on the part of the seller and positive capital formation on the part of the buyer. This includes exclusive rights in a given territory or market.
- Payments of damages for IPR infringement may be granted by courts or agreed by affected parties. While these may function as ex-post licensing of outcomes of R&D, the recording convention in national accounts appears to be to record them as *current* transfers.
- It is possible for firms originating IP to retain sole exclusive licenses while giving away ownership. The distinctive feature of IP ownership is the ability to bring action against alleged IPR infringement (OECD 2013). The geographic location of this form of residual ownership can be influenced by market size and value as well knowledge of which courts tend to be more favorable toward plaintiffs.
- Cross-licensing is a common, barter-like practice across firms. This means that the gross value of transactions cannot be recorded—only the net money balance that is transferred across organizations (OECD 2013).

14.3.2   A Global Picture of Trade in R&D Services

Figure 14.3 presents net imports (imports *minus* exports) of total R&D services for countries in the OECD EBOPS databases. This margin represents the main adjustment to R&D output required to arrive at a measure of R&D capital formation for any economy (OECD 2010a). As would be expected from the foregoing analysis, this shows a high volume of R&D—

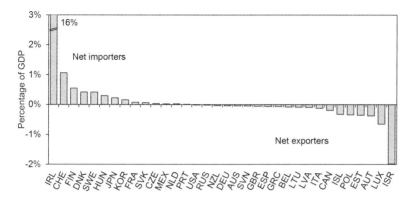

Figure 14.3   Net imports (imports minus exports) of all R&D services (SJ1), 2016, as a percentage of GDP

Note: This chart presents EBOPS 2010 class SJ1 "Research and Development Services."

Source: OECD Trade in Services by Partner Country database (http://oe.cd/2dm), OECD National Accounts database (http://oe.cd/1Fb), Office for National Statistics; February 2018.

equivalent to 16 percent of GDP—being *imported* to Ireland, while Israel sees R&D exports equivalent to 2 percent of GDP. Switzerland is also a significant net R&D importer at 1.1 percent of GDP, while Luxembourg is a net exporter of R&D (0.7 percent of GDP). The United States achieved a near perfect R&D trade balance in 2016, with a net position very close to zero.

The United States, Germany, and France account for over half (52 percent) of the US$138 billion value of R&D exports from these countries. The United States exports the most R&D services, with sales of over US$37 billion in 2016—equivalent to 0.2 percent of GDP. In contrast, R&D services are worth 3.3 percent of GDP in Luxembourg, 2.2 percent in Israel, 1.5 percent in Ireland (though if sales of proprietary rights related to R&D are discounted, the ratio in Ireland falls to 0.7 percent), and 1.1 percent in Belgium. In all other countries the proportion is less than 1 percent (figure 14.4).

Decomposing R&D services exports wherever possible (not the case for the United States using OECD EBOPS data), figure 14.4 shows that sales of rights arising from R&D are generally a relatively small share of total R&D services exports, though in Ireland they comprise over half the total and around a quarter in the Czech Republic and Sweden.

R&D imports are more concentrated, with Ireland, the United States, and Germany receiving 56 percent of the US$190 billion R&D services imported by the countries for which data are available (which, it should be noted, do not include China).

As seen in figure 14.5, in 2016 R&D services imports were equivalent to almost 18 percent of Ireland's GDP—the greatest share in the available data. Changes in tax provisions applying to intangible assets have been linked to this trend (OECD 2016). Imports of R&D services have the second-greatest

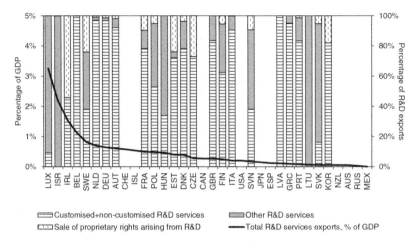

Figure 14.4   Exports of R&D services, 2016 or latest. Total R&D services exports as a share of GDP (left scale), breakdown of total R&D exports (right scale)

Note: Absence of columns indicates that only total exports are available. Netherlands, Lithuania: 2015 data.

Source: OECD Trade in Services by Partner Country database (http://oe.cd/2dm), OECD National Accounts database (http://oe.cd/1Fb), UK Office for National Statistics; February 2018.

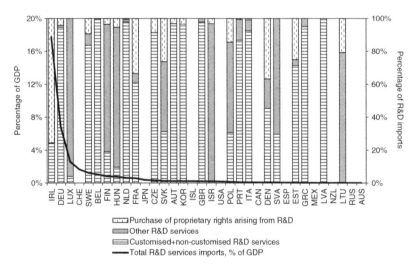

Figure 14.5   Imports of R&D services, 2016 or latest. Total R&D services imports as a share of GDP (left scale), breakdown of total R&D imports (right scale)

Note: Netherlands: 2015 data. Absence of bars indicates that only total exports are available.

Source: OECD Trade in Services by Partner Country database (http://oe.cd/2dm), OECD National Accounts database (http://oe.cd/1Fb), UK Office for National Statistics; February 2018.

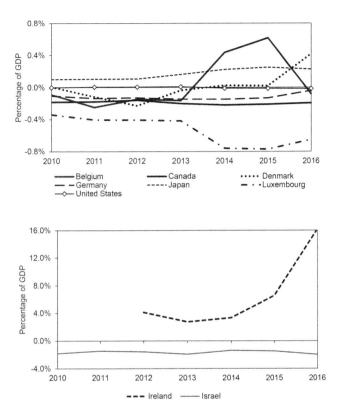

Figure 14.6 **Net imports (imports minus exports) of total R&D services, 2010–2016, selected countries, as a percentage of GDP**

Note: Chart presents EBOPS 2010 class SJ1 "Research and Development Services." In those countries for which further detail is available, this parent class primarily comprises classes SJ111 "provision of customised and non-customised research and development" and SJ12 "other research and development services" but also includes SJ112 "sale of proprietary rights arising from Research and Development."

Source: OECD Trade in Services by Partner Country database (http://oe.cd/2dm), OECD National Accounts database (http://oe.cd/1Fb); February 2018.

ratio to GDP, 6.8 percent, in Germany, while Luxembourg has the third-greatest ratio at 2.6 percent—though the data show none of these imports being purchases of intellectual property, suggesting that such purchases, if in reality there are any, are perhaps recorded in the other categories or have been excluded altogether.

14.3.2.1 R&D Trade Trends

Time series for these detailed data are very limited, only going back to when methodological changes to the SNA and Balance of Payments guidelines were introduced in 2010. It is nevertheless possible to observe in figure 14.6 that the United States has maintained a near zero R&D trade

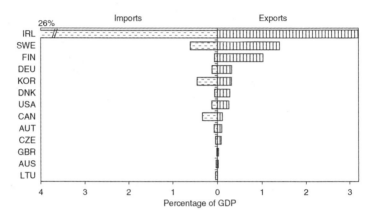

Figure 14.7   International trade in licenses for the use of outcomes of R&D, 2016, as a share of GDP

Source: OECD Trade in Services by Partner Country database. http://oe.cd/2dm, OECD National Accounts database http://oe.cd/1Fb, UK Office for National Statistics; February 2018.

balance over the period, Canada and Germany have been stable net R&D exporters, and Japan is a stable R&D services importer. Denmark has moved from being a net exporter to a net importer, while Belgium's position oscillated sharply to become a net R&D services importer in 2014 but back to a near balance in 2016. Luxembourg's net R&D exporter position has become more accentuated over the period.

Ireland and Israel are shown separately, as they are far outside the range of R&D net import intensities observed in the other presented countries. Israel has been relatively stable as a strong net exporter, averaging 1.7 percent of GDP from 2010 to 2016. Meanwhile, net imports of R&D services to Ireland increased from around 3 to 4 percent of GDP over 2012–2014 to 6.6 percent in 2015 and 16 percent in 2016. Examining the underlying data, this appears to be driven mainly by imports of proprietary rights relating to the outcomes of R&D.

14.3.2.2   R&D Licensing Trade Flows

A further R&D globalization-related component is captured in trade statistics: cross-border payments for the use of intellectual property. As noted earlier, these differ from the "sale of proprietary rights arising from Research and Development." Figure 14.7 presents the value of imports and exports of licenses for the use of outcomes of R&D as a share of GDP. These data are available for a very small set of countries. Exports range from US$0.2 million, worth a minute fraction of GDP in Lithuania, to US$9.5 billion, equivalent to just over 3 percent of GDP in Ireland. This would be generally consistent with there being a relatively large volume of R&D assets owned by resident units in Ireland and these being licensed out for use abroad.

The United States and Germany have the greatest nominal R&D licensing exports—US$47 billion and US$11 billion respectively, though this equates to just 0.3 percent of GDP in both cases.

Ireland also has by far the greatest imports of licenses for the use of outcomes of R&D, at US$80 billion in 2016—equivalent to over a quarter of GDP and more than three times the US$23 billion of licenses flowing to the United States. This suggests that companies in Ireland also engage in holding licenses for the use of intellectual property owned by other parties.

14.3.3   Bilateral Trade in R&D

Table 14.2 details R&D services and licensing exports and imports on a bilateral basis, breaking down total trade figures for selected countries according to the shares going to their five most important trading partners as reported by the published OECD EBOPS data. This shows that the United States is a key hub in global R&D-related trade and the main recipient of R&D services exports from all other countries presented (DEU, FRA, ISR, IRL, CAN), accounting for as much as 62 percent of R&D services exports from Canada and 76 percent from Israel.

Switzerland, Ireland, Singapore, and Bermuda (BMU) also rank highly based on the volume of R&D services they receive from the United States. Meanwhile the United Kingdom and Germany are key partners for almost all the countries presented. For Israel, the British Virgin Islands (VGB) is one of the top five destinations for R&D services exports. The VGB figure is unavailable for the other countries (e.g., due to confidentiality) and therefore is included in the right-hand "other*" column.

Germany and the United Kingdom are also key suppliers of R&D services imports for these selected countries; nevertheless the United States is the source for a greater overall share of R&D services imports than Germany and the United Kingdom combined. India and China rank highly on the basis of their shares in R&D imports to the United States (10.2 percent and 7.6 percent, respectively). France is not a top-five partner for the United States on either R&D imports or exports; its key relationships are with Germany, Ireland, and Canada.

Information on bilateral imports and exports of licenses for the use of outcomes of R&D is only reported by three of these countries: the United States, Germany, and Ireland. Over 18 percent of US license exports flow to Ireland, with a measured export value of around US$8.7 billion (second panel in table 14.2). Switzerland, China, and Korea are other key recipients of license exports. Germany appears particularly closely linked with China, which receives 30 percent of R&D-related licenses exported by Germany. Judging from importers' reports, Japan is a key supplier of R&D licenses, accounting for 44 percent of licenses imported by the United States; Switzerland again features as a key source of licenses.

Table 14.2 Bilateral R&D imports and exports, selected countries, 2016

Exports

Exports of R&D Services, % of total

Exporting country	Total USD PPP	Recipient partner														
		USA	CHE	IRL	SGP	BMU	JPN	DEU	GBR	BEL	ESP	FRA	CHN	ITA	VGB	Other*
USA	37,176	n/a	17.0	21.1	13.3	6.1	8.3	3.2	2.5	X	0.2	1.4	0.4	0.2	X	26.3
DEU	22,290	35.8	11.4	1.1	1.1	X	3.4	n/a	4.8	3.7	1.3	5.3	5.2	2.5	X	24.6
FRA	12,267	15.9	10.9	0.8	0.3	X	3.5	12.8	13.1	3.0	13.3	n/a	1.0	1.3	X	24.2
ISR	6,960	76.2	0.3	-	0.2	X	-	4.1	8.7	-	-	0.2	-	1.5	0.7	8.1
IRL	4,542	18.4	0.6	n/a	-	X	-	7.1	0.1	-	-	0.2	-	-	X	73.6
CAN	4,541	62.3	5.9	1.3	1.3	X	1.4	6.8	1.8	2.6	0.0	1.9	0.0	0.1	X	14.5
Average		*41.7*	*7.7*	*4.9*	*2.7*	*6.1*	*2.8*	*6.8*	*5.2*	*1.9*	*2.5*	*1.8*	*1.1*	*0.9*	*0.7*	*28.5*
Weighted average		*37.3*	*12.0*	*10.8*	*6.4*	*6.1*	*5.7*	*5.6*	*4.9*	*3.3*	*2.6*	*2.4*	*1.9*	*1.1*	*0.7*	*26.0*

Exports of Licences for the use of outcomes of R&D, % of total

Exporting country	Total USD PPP	Recipient partner													
		USA	IRL	GBR	CHE	DEU	CHN	FRA	NLD	SGP	KOR	BEL	AUS	Other*
USA	47,512	X	18.4	3.6	17.8	5.8	8.8	2.2	5.6	4.4	7.0	1.0	0.9	24.5
DEU	11,078	29.1	0.2	2.9	5.4	-	19.9	7.0	3.7	0.6	1.8	0.7	0.5	28.1
IRL	9,540	X	n/a	9.9	1.6	X	0.2	X	1.1	2.2	0.3	2.5	2.0	80.2
Average		*29.1*	*9.3*	*5.5*	*8.3*	*5.8*	*9.6*	*4.6*	*3.5*	*2.4*	*3.0*	*1.4*	*1.1*	*44.3*
Weighted average		*29.1*	*12.3*	*7.2*	*6.7*	*5.8*	*5.4*	*3.8*	*2.8*	*2.6*	*2.4*	*1.8*	*1.5*	*57.2*

Imports   **Imports of R&D Services, % of total**

Imports Importing country	Total USD PPP	Supplier partner											
		USA	DEU	IND	ISR	CHN	GBR	FRA	BEL	ITA	AUT	ESP	Other*
IRL	52,150	34.8	0.1	X	X	X	0.4	0.2	X	X	X	0.2	64.3
USA	34,243	n/a	10.7	10.2	6.5	7.6	7.0	2.7	3.5	1.6	0.2	X	53.3
DEU	20,923	27.7	n/a	4.5	–	6.2	9.1	10.0	1.0	2.7	6.9	1.9	24.0
FRA	14,216	17.6	26.7	2.4	–	2.4	15.0	–	2.6	3.9	0.2	5.5	26.1
CAN	1,184	67.2	X	X	X	X	X	X	X	X	X	X	32.8
ISR	635	41.5	5.6	1.1	–	0.1	6.4	5.6	4.7	0.3	–	2.7	36.7
Average		*37.8*	*10.8*	*4.5*	*6.5*	*4.1*	*7.6*	*4.6*	*3.0*	*2.1*	*1.8*	*2.6*	*39.5*
Weighted average		*30.9*	*7.5*	*6.8*	*6.5*	*6.1*	*5.5*	*2.9*	*2.6*	*2.4*	*2.2*	*1.5*	*49.5*

Imports of Licences for the use of outcomes of R&D, % of total

Imports Importing country	Total USD PPP	Supplier partner									
		USA	JPN	CHE	DEU	FRA	GBR	BEL	MLT	ESP	Other*
IRL	79,820	X	0.7	X	X	0.1	0.8	0.5	0.5	0.2	97.2
USA	23,200	n/a	44.9	14.4	9.0	7.4	4.8	1.1	–	0.1	18.2
DEU	4,126	20.4	5.2	9.9	n/a	5.8	4.0	1.2	X	0.6	52.9
Average		*20.4*	*16.9*	*12.1*	*9.0*	*4.4*	*3.2*	*0.9*	*0.3*	*0.3*	*56.1*
Weighted average		*20.4*	*20.0*	*12.0*	*9.0*	*5.5*	*3.8*	*1.0*	*0.5*	*0.3*	*46.6*

Note: Other* category includes shares relating to partners if unavailable (gray cells). Canada: 2015 data. Shares of total R&D services (SJI) imports to/exports from country; bold and underlined indicates partner in top 5 for one or more reporting country. X: Data unavailable (e.g., due to confidentiality), n.a.: not applicable.

Source: OECD Trade in Services by Partner Country database (http://oe.cd/2dm).

14.3.3.1   Consistency of Bilateral R&D Trade Statistics

Table 14.3 compares the bilateral trade in R&D services reported by different economies in relation to the United States. This involves comparing what the United States reports exporting to any given economy with what that economy reports having imported from the United States—and vice versa for US R&D imports.

Looking at the left-hand "exports from the United States" panel, reported R&D exports from the United States appear to be relatively understated compared to the counterpart R&D imports reported by partner countries.

The right-hand "exports to the United States" panel presents a more mixed picture. With regard to large R&D performers such as France, Germany, and Canada, declared imports from the US side are relatively lower than the amounts that these countries declare exporting as R&D services to the United States. This appears to suggest that smaller amounts are systematically reported by the United States than by its counterparts. In the cases of Canada and Germany, the bilateral trade balance is not significantly impacted by the reporting perspective, but for Israel, Sweden, and France there is a US$3 billion, US$1 billion, and US$1 billion gap, respectively.

In the case of US R&D imports from Ireland, the largest in value from a US perspective, it is US-reported imports that are relatively higher than exports reported by Ireland. Thus, from a US viewpoint, the trade balance is close to US$2 billion, while from an Irish perspective, it is close to US$18 billion. This gap may be affected by the comparison being based on older 2013 trade data from Ireland, however.

There are several potential reasons for the lack of balancing in R&D trade data: they may stem from differences in data collection and use of standards, differences in valuation, as well as potentially from re-exporting, which is a factor known to distort bilateral trade comparisons for all goods and services. In the case of R&D services, this may be related to subcontracting or R&D services being embedded into other goods and services. While it is recognized that these are important issues, it is beyond the scope of this chapter to attempt to provide an explanation. The OECD working party on trade in goods and services has an ongoing initiative that brings together trading partners to discuss the large discrepancies and try to determine what is causing them and if they can be resolved.[9]

14.3.4   R&D Trade between Affiliates

Multinationals play a first-order role in the global trade of R&D. However, the amounts reported for such transactions may be distorted for various reasons, including as a means to transfer profits from one country to

---

9. The OECD and WTO have developed a balanced bilateral trade in services database based on EBOPS 2002 data. For more info see: http://www.oecd.org/sdd/its/balanced-trade-in-services.htm.

Table 14.3　**Comparison of R&D services bilateral trade figures involving the United States, 2016 (millions of US dollars, annual average exchange rates)**

	Exports from the United States				Exports to the United States			
	US R&D services exports	R&D services imports from USA	Ratio (%)	Year (if not 2016)	US R&D services imports	R&D services exports to USA	Ratio (%)	Year (if not 2016)
	A	B	B/A		A	B	B/A	
Total	37,176				34,243			
Australia	291				297			
Austria	10	60	600		67	76	113	
Belgium	1,094	1,264	116	2015	1,198			
Canada	391	796	204		2,025	2,601	128	
Chile	6				68			
Czech Republic	13	9	67		140	97	69	
Denmark	395	335	85	2015	185			
Estonia	2	1	60		44			
Finland	337	384	114	2015	279	115	41	
France	517	2,498	483		919	1,949	212	
Germany	1,206	5,805	481		3,674	7,979	217	
Greece	0	3			22	9	41	
Hungary	6			2013	63			
Ireland	7,842	18,172	232		5,387	420	8	2013
Israel	153	264	172		2,242	5,306	237	
Italy	91	161	177		537	834	155	
Japan	3,100				1,253			
Korea	304				268			
Latvia	0	0			5	3	60	
Luxembourg	288				19			
Mexico	89				695			
Netherlands	2,009	1,258	63		1,371	1,466	107	
New Zealand	5				33			
Norway	64				184			
Poland	30	22	74		194	474	244	
Portugal	7				19			
Slovak Republic	5	5	102		16	7	44	
Slovenia	0	2			3	6	200	
Spain	60				183			2015
Sweden	1,194	2,407	202		287	292	102	
Switzerland	6,326				1,072			
Turkey	2			2015	29			
United Kingdom	919				2,406			
Reporting Source	USA	Partner			USA	Partner		

Source: OECD Trade in Services by Partner Country database (http://oe.cd/2dm); February 2018.

another for tax reasons or because the country where the ultimate owner enterprise is domiciled imposes restrictions on the repatriation of income. Transfer prices are the prices at which an enterprise provides physical goods, services, or intangible property to affiliated enterprises.

The OECD Transfer Pricing Guidelines (OECD 2017b) stipulate the application—for MNE and tax administration purposes—of the arm's length principle, whereby individual group members must be attributed profits and taxed on the basis that they act at arm's length in their transactions with each other, i.e., applying comparable prices to those that would transpire in transactions with non-affiliated parties. Intangibles may have special characteristics that complicate the search for such comparators, and in some cases make pricing difficult to determine at the time of the transaction. Key factors to take into consideration are the exclusivity, extent, and duration of legal protection; the geographic scope; expected useful life; stage of development; rights to enhancements, revisions, or updates; and expectations of future benefit associated to the assets subject to transaction.

There are few published data sources that break down R&D trade between affiliates from the total. The valuation of intra-MNE transactions of any type is challenging, given concerns over transfer prices (UN et al. 2011; IMF 2009). Further, some desirable information such as industry detail and the type of R&D being transmitted are not available, while guidance to distinguish sales vs. licensing of IP resulting from R&D has yet to be implemented across countries (see Moris and Zeile 2016).

Figure 14.8 presents evidence for the United States that the affiliate share of R&D trade is very significant, accounting for more than 90 percent of R&D exports from the United States. Nearly two-thirds corresponds to trade between US parents with their foreign affiliates, while the remainder corresponds to services provided by US-based affiliates with their parents abroad. For comparison, the affiliate share for all services is 30 percent.

Affiliated trade is nearly as important for US R&D imports, though with a less significant role for groups owned abroad. Thus, behind the US net export position for R&D, the figures indicate that arms' length trade exhibits a US$1 billion deficit, US parents show a deficit in excess of US$6 billion, while the overall net exporting position is accounted for by affiliated trade within foreign groups, which has a net export position in 2016 in excess of US$10 billion.

In the case of licenses for the use of R&D outcomes, these are approximated in the affiliate trade statistics by figures on licenses on industrial processes. Non-affiliated trade is slightly more important but still a minority at 30 percent for exports and is 20 percent for imports. US parents account for most of license exports but only a fraction of imports, suggesting that licensing financial flows go toward the parent which is in principle holding the asset. What is not possible to establish from the data is the extent to which there is trade with other affiliates of the same parent company.

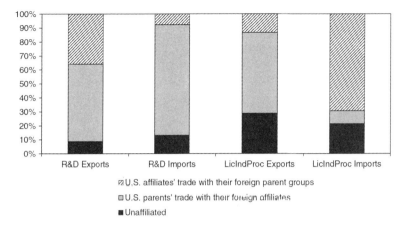

Figure 14.8   Affiliate and non-affiliate R&D-based trade, United States, 2016, shares of total trade

Note: LicIndProc: "Licensing of Industrial Processes"; considered a proxy for licenses to use R&D outcomes.

Source: Bureau of Economic Analysis. US Trade in Services, by Type of Service and by Country or Affiliation, 2017.

Given the difficulties in tracing and pricing R&D flows, developing a clear view of R&D globalization requires building up evidence on where substantive R&D production activities are taking place in order to follow on and assess related flows. The next section discusses the relevant evidence.

14.4   Statistics on R&D Performance and Sources of Funding

14.4.1   R&D Performance and Flows of Funds

Frascati Manual–based business surveys focus on current-year domestic R&D activity, which is conceptually close to the SNA concept of R&D output when measured as the sum of production costs. The business sector is the main R&D performer in most countries, undertaking around 70 percent of R&D on average across the OECD area.

Frascati surveys can help inform a better understanding of R&D globalization along different dimensions:

- They help identify the location of substantive R&D activity on a performance basis, including the location of human resources dedicated to R&D.
- Information on sources of funding for such R&D helps identify the engagement of other parties based abroad.
- They also gather data on payments made to other units outside the

country for R&D performance, referred to as "funding for extramurally performed R&D."

- Data on R&D performance and funding can be further complemented with enterprise ownership data to provide a view of the role of MNEs in R&D performance and funding (Moris 2016).

A fundamental principle behind R&D performers' reporting of the sources of funding for their R&D activities is that amounts received are only reported as external R&D funds if they were specifically earmarked or intended for R&D. Internal R&D funds are defined as "the amount of money spent on R&D that originates within the control of, and are used for R&D at the discretion of, a reporting statistical unit. Internal R&D funds do not include R&D funds received from other statistical units explicitly for intramural R&D" (OECD 2015). If external funding is received without explicitly being for R&D but the receiving unit internally makes the decision to use them for R&D, this expenditure is recorded as based on an *internal* source of R&D funds. Loans received from other units that the recipient may use for R&D but must repay under normal market terms are also treated as internal R&D funds for the same reason. A reporting convention for international comparisons is that funds from other units in the same business group should be treated as external funds but separately itemized whenever possible, especially in the case of international funding flows.

14.4.2   Business R&D Funded by the Rest of the World

Figure 14.9 presents business enterprise expenditure on R&D (BERD) and the shares thereof funded by different sectors including the Rest of the World (RoW) sector.[10] Businesses in OECD countries spent US$0.86 trillion PPP on R&D in 2015, with United States businesses accounting for almost 42 percent of that amount. Funding from abroad is greatest in Israel, which appears to be consistent with Israel having the lowest net R&D imports (i.e., greatest net exports) as shown in figure 14.3. Likewise, a relatively large share of R&D performed in Iceland is also funded from abroad. Ireland ranks fifth for the share of business R&D funded by the RoW but first in terms of R&D exports.

Figure 14.10 presents changes in the share of BERD funded by the Rest of the World in selected countries over the period 2000–2015. The general trend has been upward—consistent with R&D becoming a more globalized activity. The United Kingdom and China are exceptions to this trend (as are Australia, Austria, and Canada; not presented). Even so, the share of BERD funded from overseas remains relatively high in the United Kingdom at almost 30 percent. In China it has declined from 4 percent in 2000 to less

---

10. In what follows, the terms *Rest of the World (RoW)*, *abroad*, *overseas*, and *outside the country* are used as equivalents.

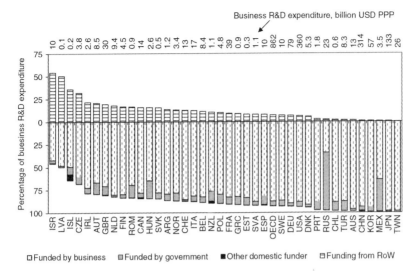

Figure 14.9   Business R&D expenditure by sector providing funding for R&D, 2015
Note: IRL, ISR, ITS, FRA, PRT: data relate to 2014; AUS, AUT, BEL, SWE: 2013.
Source: OECD Main Science and Technology Indicators database (http://oe.cs/msti); January 2018.

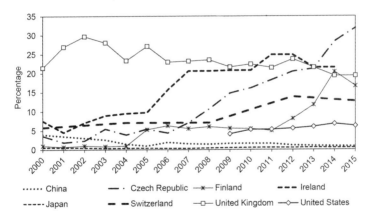

Figure 14.10   Share of BERD funded by the rest of the world, selected countries, 2000–2015
Source: OECD Main Science and Technology Indicators database (http://oe.cs/msti); January 2018.

than 1 percent in 2015 despite the value of R&D funding from abroad more than doubling in real terms as domestic funding has grown rapidly.

The Czech Republic is representative of the strong upward trend seen in various Eastern European countries, including Poland and the Slovak Republic (not shown). Overseas funding of business R&D has been persis-

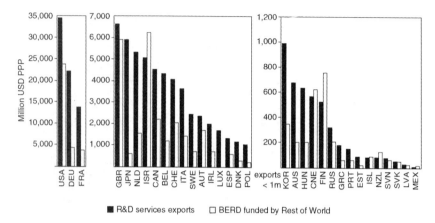

Figure 14.11a   R&D services exports and BERD funded by rest of the world, 2015 or latest

tently low in Japan and also in Korea (not shown), indicative of a relatively low level of integration by businesses in these countries in the international R&D environment. The share of business R&D performed in Ireland that is funded from abroad increased markedly from less than 9 percent in 2003, the year a business R&D tax credit was introduced (OECD 2017c), to reach 25 percent in 2012.

14.4.3   Comparing R&D Funding from the Rest of the World and Trade Statistics

Services trade and Frascati Manual–based business R&D sources have complementary strengths relative to other sources for capturing international flows of R&D funding and outputs (Moris 2009). Trade surveys collect transactions on R&D services based on either current or prior R&D, and also collect data on R&D services imports even if the respondent company is not an R&D performer or funder of current-year R&D (or historically). These transactions are valued at market prices (MSITS 3.32), while Frascati data are on a factor cost basis and capture current R&D production only.

Figures 14.11a and 14.11b compare R&D services exports recorded by trade statistics with BERD funded by the Rest of the World. In about three-quarters of countries, R&D services exports exceed R&D reported as being funded from abroad. Large differences are found in many countries; for example, Japan's R&D services export revenues are seven times greater than the funding businesses receive from overseas for R&D. As noted earlier, differences should be expected for many reasons, notably:

- BERD funding is constrained to equal businesses' total expenditure on R&D (i.e., input costs) while exports include any **profit** made on the

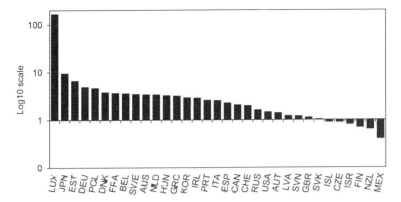

Figure 14.11b   R&D services exports relative to BERD funded by the rest of the world, 2015. R&D services exports/BERD funded by the rest of the world, Log10 scale

Note: When multiple is 1, R&D services exports = BERD funded by the rest of the world. Latest year for which both export and R&D expenditure data are available: data for France 2014, Sweden 2013.

Source: OECD Trade Statistics database, OECD R&D statistics database (http://oe.cs/rds); February 2018.

transaction. On this basis, exports will tend to be larger than funding from abroad because of margins missing from the latter.

- R&D services exports use a broader definition of R&D, including "other product development that may give rise to patents."
- BERD funding relates specifically to **R&D performed in the period** while the category of R&D services exports (SJ1) includes "sales of proprietary rights arising from R&D," which may sometimes relate to R&D conducted in earlier periods. A comparison should focus in principle on trade category SJ111 *"Provision of customized and non-customized research and development services"* though data availability limits this. This also contributes to R&D exports being larger, and potentially more volatile, than funds from abroad.
- R&D export statistics apply to the **entire economy**. There are no readily available statistics that break down exports by institutional sector to allow a like-for-like comparison with R&D funds received by businesses only. This effect is expected to be small for a majority of countries due to limited R&D export activity of units in other sectors.
- Funding of R&D from the Rest of the World includes not only payments for purchases of R&D services but also **unrequited payments made to support R&D performance**. Under current SNA and balance of payments manual (International Monetary Fund 2009) rules these would, in theory, be recorded as capital transfers—reflecting the recommendation in the 2008 SNA that expenditures on R&D are recorded as

investment when they occur, as long as the expenditures satisfy investment criteria (formerly current transfers under the 1993 SNA).[11] Therefore, these payments do not imply a stake in or economic ownership over any results.

This last point is crucial; R&D funding from the RoW is not a measure of international trade in R&D but of a construct that combines trade and transfer elements. Cash and in-kind transfers are contemplated in the balance of payment manuals but not as part of trade statistics. On that basis, R&D funding from RoW may provide an upper bound of the share of current-year business R&D performance which might result in outputs that are de facto owned by the RoW. The gap is likely to be larger in the case of countries whose businesses rely more on R&D grants and related contributions from supranational agencies and international donors. This is fairly consistent with the results in figures 14.11a and 14.11b.

The Frascati Manual 2015 explicitly acknowledges the need to distinguish funding transactions by introducing a recommendation to undertake a new disaggregation of R&D funding into:

- **exchange** funds—funds paid in exchange for the provision of R&D services—which imply a sale of R&D, and;
- **transfer** funds—which are paid toward the business's R&D performance but with no expectation that the funder will directly own or access the results; as such economic ownership remains (at least initially) with the R&D performer. In the international arena, an example would be R&D grants provided by the European Union through any of its R&D funding programs.

This breakdown promises further insight into the economic *nature* of the transaction taking place—a commercial sale or an unrequited transfer—and this can provide an indication of whether the resulting R&D assets will be owned in the producing country or elsewhere.[12]

National statistical authorities are still in the process of implementing the 2015 Frascati Manual, including data on R&D globalization. As a result, the data currently available are very limited, especially when it comes to funds from the RoW. However, new, not yet published data provided to the OECD by Statistics Finland and the Federal Statistical Office of Switzerland suggest that over 80 percent of R&D funds received by businesses from the Rest of the World are exchange funds, and that the precise share is likely to vary between countries—being 97 percent in Finland, 82 percent in Switzerland.

11. In practice, this may still be the case, especially in cases where it is not clear that the funding is for the creation of an asset—in cases of uncertainty the 2008 SNA advocates recording transactions as current and not capital transfers.

12. It is worth noting that exchange funds may still entail a transfer component if the buyer relinquishes its IP rights in part or in full, for example if the buyer only secures rights for its own use.

In the case of Switzerland, the amount of exchange-based funding from abroad (82 percent) is less than the total amount of R&D funding originating from business abroad (93 percent). This implies that some funding from businesses abroad is being reported as transfer funding. This gap may perhaps be explained by contributions or subscriptions to R&D performing non-profit institutions classified in the business sector, such as industry association bodies, though the details needed to make this assessment are unavailable.

While these data suggest a strong correlation between the provision of R&D funding and ownership as indicated by exchange funding, there is at this point not enough exchange and transfer data available to draw firm conclusions. Nevertheless, this indicates that firms, including MNEs, can use a diverse range of arrangements to fund their R&D activities, and how this may be translated into reporting, notwithstanding measurement guidelines. Key considerations are whether funds are internal or external to the unit, whether they are explicitly aimed for R&D or not, and what mechanism the funder has in place to get a return on the funding allocation. The ultimate equity on the outcomes of R&D is, in principle, an asset that can represent a counterpart to the funds provided, but the uncertainty about the final outcome may plausibly entice respondents to record the funding on a transfer basis. This requires further investigation; box 14.1 briefly presents data on revenues from sales of R&D collected through Frascati Manual–based sources.

14.4.4 Sources of R&D Funds from the Rest of the World

While relatively little information is currently available about the precise "exchange" or "transfer" nature of R&D funding from the RoW, for many countries there is information available on the foreign funders themselves. Figure 14.12 presents the shares of BERD funding coming from businesses located outside the reporting country, the European Commission, and other funders abroad, including foreign governments and higher education institutions abroad. It can immediately be seen that foreign affiliates of the R&D performing business are key funders, accounting for more than half of funds from the RoW in all but seven of the countries presented. In those countries, EU funding tends to make up a large share, though unaffiliated businesses account for almost 70 percent of foreign BERD funding in Slovenia, the greatest share of any country.

While transactions between unaffiliated enterprises might reasonably be assumed to be economically meaningful market transactions (i.e., with a price reflecting demand and supply), the economic substance of transactions between affiliates is harder to ascertain. Nevertheless, MNEs are clearly important actors in the international R&D ecosystem and are the focus of section 14.5.

Table 14.4 shows time series data on the distribution funding sources for

Box 14.1   Data on Business Sales of R&D

Several countries have implemented a Frascati Manual 2015 recommendation to gather data on R&D performers' revenues from sales of R&D in the period. The available data show that businesses in Norway and the Czech Republic made similar amounts of R&D sales in 2015. In the Czech Republic, 80 percent of businesses' R&D sales were to customers abroad, while for businesses in Norway a majority (59 percent) of sales was also to customers outside the country.

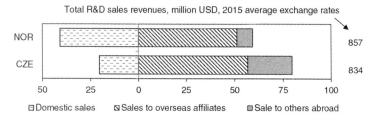

Total R&D sales revenues, million USD, 2015 average exchange rates

NOR 857
CZE 834

50   25   0   25   50   75   100

□ Domestic sales   ◪ Sales to overseas affiliates   ▨ Sale to others abroad

R&D sales revenues by customer location & relationship to R&D performing business, 2015
Source: Czech Statistical Office, Statistics Norway.

The importance of foreign affiliates can immediately be seen. In both cases a similar share of R&D sales are to related businesses abroad (a little over 50 percent) with sales to unaffiliated businesses being greater for R&D performers in the Czech Republic.

R&D performed by businesses in the United States from its Business R&D and Innovation Survey. This long-standing survey takes as its reporting unit the domestic consolidated business group, which includes individual enterprises or groups that are ultimately owned by foreign companies. Over 90 percent of annual business R&D performed in the United States was domestically funded, though foreign sources increased marginally over the period. Within foreign funding, the majority of the funding was intra-MNE.

Funds explicitly aimed to fund R&D from foreign parents of these units only account directly for 3 percent of US BERD, well below the 15 percent of US BERD that is accounted for by majority-owned affiliates of foreign MNEs (see next section). Part of this gap may be due to a combination of other external sources (e.g., government funds) but also to the fact that domestic groups are in some cases given some degree of discretion on how to use their financial resources including how much to dedicate to R&D.

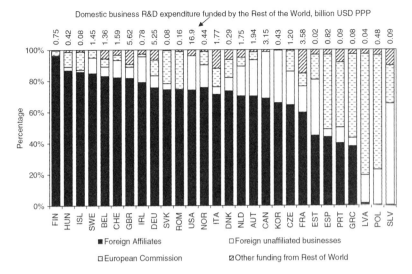

Figure 14.12   Funding of business R&D by non-resident sources, 2015, shares of total BERD funding from abroad, 2015

Notes: Estonia, France: 2014 data.

Source: OECD R&D statistics database (http://oe.cs/rds); pre-release data.

14.4.5   Business Funding of R&D Performed Abroad

The Frascati Manual framework also recommends collecting information on *extramurally performed R&D*; that is, information on the amounts paid out by R&D funders for the performance of R&D by others. This serves a practical role in helping R&D survey respondents delineate their own R&D from that which they have paid others to do, but it is also a source of information on the outsourcing of R&D. The Frascati Manual 2015 also proposes several breakdowns of funds for extramural R&D provided by businesses including distinguishing exchange and transfer funding provided and recipient type (e.g., business, government, higher education, nonprofit and whether they are domestic or abroad).

Although the OECD maintains a facility to collect data on funds for extramural R&D, very few countries provide these at present. The fact that, due to survey design, the data often represent only funds provided by businesses which themselves perform R&D (omitting firms which fund but do not perform R&D) and the resultant scope for user misinterpretation of the figures have been cited as concerns. This difference in scope implies that the reported amounts are less directly comparable to R&D import figures than funds from abroad are when compared with exports. Nevertheless, these data may provide some additional insight into international R&D linkages.

The US Business Research and Development and Innovation Survey

Table 14.4   Source of funds for R&D performed by business in the United States, 2010–2015 (millions of current dollars)

	2010	2011	2012	2013	2014	2015
R&D performed by business	278,977	294,093	302,250	322,528	340,728	355,821
Domestic funding	264,332	278,551	285,409	303,176	317,714	332,093
Funds from within the company's US-located units[a]	218,187	235,426	242,674	259,908	277,272	289,892
Other US-located companies	11,013	11,124	11,624	13,450	13,227	14,595
Federal government	34,199	31,309	30,621	29,362	26,554	26,990
All other domestic organisations[b]	933	692	490	456	661	616
Foreign funding	14,645	15,541	16,841	19,353	23,014	23,728
Funds from parent or subsidiary companies abroad	10,621	10,780	13,092	15,450	18,705	19,364
Foreign parent companies of US subsidiaries	7,102	7,438	8,486	10,445	13,407	12,579
Subsidiaries of US located companies[a]	3,519	3,342	4,606	5,005	5,298	6,785
Other companies abroad[b]	3,913	4,569	3,607	3,346	3,839	3,738
Other organisations abroad[c]	111	192	142	557	470	626

Note: In the US R&D survey, the reporting unit is the US-based company, including all subsidiaries and divisions where there is more than 50% ownership. In the case of companies owned by a foreign parent, the reporting unit for the survey is the US-located company, including all majority-owned subsidiaries and divisions regardless of location. For reporting purposes, foreign parents and any foreign affiliates not owned by the US company are treated as any business partner, customer, or supplier that it does not own.

[a] US-located companies include companies owned by foreign enterprises.

[b] Other organizations abroad include foreign governments and all other non-business organizations outside the United States. All other domestic organizations include households and nonprofit organizations.

[c] This category may include affiliated companies that are neither parents nor majority owned subsidiaries of the US-located company.

Source: National Science Foundation, National Center for Science and Engineering Statistics, Business R&D and Innovation Survey (annual series). Science and Engineering Indicators 2018.

(BRDIS) collects rich information on funds for extramural R&D, including whether the recipient is: in the United States or abroad; a majority-owned subsidiary or a separate business (defined as including foreign parents and affiliates which aren't direct subsidiaries); and the country where those subsidiaries are domiciled. The R&D paid for with funds provided to the company by others is also reported.

Table 14.5 presents these data, which show US$83.5 billion paid to companies abroad, of which US$73.7 billion went to majority-owned subsidiaries of the US-located unit. It should be noted that while the responding units are US located, they may be ultimately owned elsewhere.

The greatest individual share of this R&D funding, US$8.5billion, flows to subsidiaries in the United Kingdom, while those in Germany receive nearly as much— US$8.2 billion. Businesses in China and India also receive

Table 14.5   **R&D performed abroad funded by businesses active in the United States, 2015. Selected countries with greatest US business-funded R&D performance, USD million**

Location	Total	Paid for by the company	Paid for by others	Share paid for by others
Total R&D performed abroad	83,501	76,985	6,515	8%
Performed by other companies abroad	9,810	9,163	647	7%
Performed by foreign subsidiaries of US-based companies[a]	73,691	67,822	5,868	8%
United Kingdom	8,565	7,368	1,197	14%
Germany	8,157	7,770	387	5%
China	6,265	6,000	266	4%
India	5,534	5,325	209	4%
Canada	4,381	4,172	209	5%
Israel	3,530	3,457	73	2%
Switzerland	2,926	2,489	437	15%
France	2,772	2,496	276	10%
Japan	2,684	2,307	378	14%
Ireland	2,317	2,268	49	2%
Belgium	2,058	1,911	148	7%
Singapore	1,707	1,520	186	11%
Brazil	1,413	1,323	90	6%
Australia	1,305	1,194	111	9%
Finland	1,255	1,241	14	1%
Netherlands	1,237	1,127	109	9%
Korea	1,148	1,087	61	5%
Italy	1,027	935	92	9%

[a] Includes companies ultimately owned by foreign MNEs.

Source: 2015 Business Research and Development and Innovation Survey (BRDIS). National Science Foundation, National Center for Science and Engineering Statistics, Business R&D and Innovation Survey.

considerable R&D funding from US-located parents—US$6.3 billion and US$5.5 billion, respectively. The 18 selected countries presented account for 79 percent of all R&D funding flowing from US located to subsidiaries abroad.

Of these flows between US-located parents and their subsidiaries, 92 percent are funded by the US parent itself and 8 percent by others—including other businesses in the United States and abroad and the US government. This split varies by the country of the recipient however, from 15 percent of funds flowing to Switzerland-located subsidiaries and 14 percent of funds flowing to United Kingdom-located subsidiaries, to just 2 percent of flows to Israel-located subsidiaries and 1 percent of flows to Finland-located subsidiaries. This may suggest the extent to which US-based companies engage in joint R&D activities abroad.

14.5   R&D Performance by MNEs

The growth in the importance of foreign affiliates as sources of funding for R&D points to the major role, already alluded to, of MNEs as conduits for R&D globalization. This should be expected as firms can, and increasingly do, engage in offshoring R&D out of the country where they are based/ headquartered (UNCTAD 2005; Maftei 2007).

Though data on business R&D funding from the Rest of the World *by country of origin* (i.e., where the unit providing the funds is located) are not available, some countries detail domestic R&D performed by foreign-controlled affiliates. In some cases this R&D total is also available distributed by the *country of residence* of foreign parent companies (either immediate parent company or ultimate controlling business). This chapter examines statistical evidence on R&D performed by domestic units that are foreign controlled, as well as R&D performed by foreign affiliates of domestic R&D performers. Data used in this section originate from either Frascati Manual–based business R&D surveys or R&D-related questions included in surveys specifically aimed at collecting information on the inward and outward activities of MNEs.[13]

14.5.1   R&D Performance by Foreign-Controlled Affiliates

Foreign-controlled affiliates (FCAs) can account for a considerable share of business R&D performance. Around 60 percent of all business R&D in Ireland, Belgium, the Czech Republic, and the Slovak Republic takes place within businesses majority owned by firms abroad. In the United Kingdom and Austria, the share is over 50 percent, and out of the countries for which data are available—presented in figure 14.13—the FCA share of business R&D is only below 10 percent in Japan.

Despite this, in many cases the share of business R&D funded from abroad is strikingly low. For example, in Belgium FCAs perform 62 percent of business R&D but only 10 percent is reported as being funded from abroad. In Ireland, FCAs account for 64 percent of R&D performed by businesses but 27 percent of BERD is funded by overseas businesses. Large differences are also seen in the Slovak Republic, Poland, Sweden, Spain, Slovenia, Estonia, and Germany. In the United States, FCAs account for an estimated 16 percent of BERD, while 5 percent of BERD funding comes from abroad.

There is no definitive evidence on the precise causes of these disparities, but some potential drivers can be considered and contrasted with well-documented business practices which are also acknowledged in the revised Frascati Manual (OECD 2015). Some FCA R&D costs are likely covered

---

13. For example, U.S. reported FCA data originate from the MNE surveys conducted by the Bureau of Economic Analysis, whereas U.S. BERD totals, including that of FCAs in the United States, originate from R&D surveys conducted by NSF/NCSES and the U.S. Census Bureau. Consequently, R&D totals for a similar set of companies may differ in the two sets of surveys.

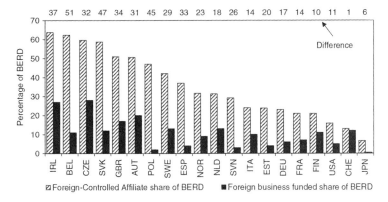

Figure 14.13   BERD performed by FCAs and BERD funded by foreign businesses, as a percentage of BERD, 2015 or latest

Note: For NLD, POL, SVN, ESP only sections B to F of ISIC Revision 4 are covered. For EST and FIN only sections B to E are covered. SVN figures refer to 2011. NOR figures refer to 2012. AUS, AUT, BEL, EST, FIN, POL, ESP figures refer to 2013. FRA, ITA, JPN, NLD, USA figures refer to 2014.

Source: OECD, Activity of Multinational Enterprises Database (http://oe.cd/amne); OECD Research and Development Statistics Database (http://oe.cd/rds); Eurostat, Inward FATS Database; national sources, July 2017, US Bureau of Economic Analysis, January 2018.

with locally generated funds, e.g., from domestic sales of the company's main products. However, domestic firms may receive funds—from group companies abroad—which are not specifically earmarked for R&D but nevertheless are eventually used to cover the costs of R&D performance. As explained in the previous section, these would be recorded as FCAs' "internal funds." This would understate the importance of funds from outside the unit but internal to the global group. As an example, an MNE parent outside Belgium may provide a lump sum to a Belgium-based FCA to cover marketing, design, and R&D activities. The parent sets the key outputs and performance indicators for these activities but does not prescribe how the sum is to be allocated to deliver those activities, leaving this to the FCA to decide. The funds used for R&D would likely be recorded as internal in the FCA's R&D survey response even though it is explicit that a (non-prescribed) portion of the money received is for the conduct of R&D.

The portion of R&D conducted using internal funds is one indicator currently used by national accountants to identify "own account" R&D, which, by definition, is owned by the producing unit and hence recorded in the balance sheet of the company, industry, sector, and country which produced it. While the party identified as performing and directly funding the R&D *may* be the economic owner, it is possible that the MNE group could be paying or authorizing the FCA to conduct R&D in the expectation that some or all of the other companies within the global group could have access to and benefit from the results.

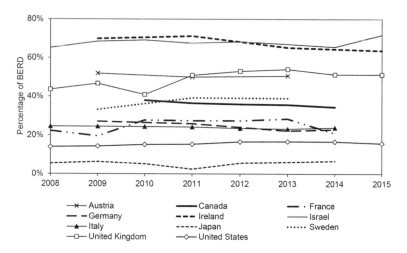

Figure 14.14   Recent trends in business R&D performed by FCAs, 2008–2015, share of business R&D performed by FCAs

Note: Data cover the "business sector" defined in the AMNE database as International Standard Industrial Classification sections B to S excluding O.

Source: OECD AMNE database (http://oe.cd/amne), UK Office for National Statistics, US Bureau of Economic Analysis, Statistics Canada, Stifterverband Germany, Central Bureau of Statistics Israel.

Available statistics indicate that the share of business R&D performed by FCAs has been relatively stable over the time period available, 2008–2015 (figure 14.14). The share of BERD performed by FCAs in Israel and Ireland is consistently greater than the other countries for which data are available. In the United States, the FCA share of business R&D has increased slightly, from 14 percent in 2009 to 16 percent in 2015.

Table 14.6 explores the ownership distribution over domestic R&D performing units. It presents total R&D expenditure by FCAs in the United States, Germany, United Kingdom, France, Canada, and Switzerland broken down by the place of residence of the ultimate owner of the FCA. For FCAs located in the United States, the countries with ownership over FCAs performing the greatest shares of BERD echo some of the key R&D services exporting partners identified in table 14.2—with Switzerland and Japan being home to the parents of FCAs performing the greatest share of total FCA R&D. However, FCA ownership does not appear to align too closely with R&D services exports in other cases as Ireland ranks relatively low, with US$3.9 billion of FCA R&D, behind the Netherlands (US$4.6 billion), France (US$5.3 billion), Germany (US$7.2 billion), and the United Kingdom (US$7.9 billion), as well as Japan (US$8 billion) and Switzerland (US$9.6 billion).

Germany-owned FCAs undertake around 8 percent of all FCA-performed

Table 14.6   Domestic R&D expenditures by foreign-controlled affiliate firms, by location of ultimate majority ownership. Selected countries, latest available year, million USD PPP.

Country of ultimate majority owner	Country of business R&D performance (reporting country)					
Total	**56,344**	**16,934**	**15,983**	**8,112**	**5,164**	**1,624**
USA	n/a	6,338	5,664	2,216	3,216	396
CAN	864			47	n/a	
Europe	40,707	9,136	5,596	5,476	1,571	
AUT	28			48	–	17
BEL	375			301	17	
CHE	9,670			1,514	183	n/a
CZE	–			–	7	
DEU	7,176	n/a	1,246	1,127	136	391
DNK	433			80		
ESP	114			123		
FIN	119			48		
FRA	5,317		960	n/a	334	108
GBR	7,943		n/a	440	423	32
IRL	3,943				8	
ISL	9					
ITA	179			188		28
LUX	22			281		107
NLD	4,645			790	67	
NOR	26			9		
PRT	3					
SWE	639			410	307	
Other Europe	69		3,390	118	90	
Caribbean	751				2	
BRA	27					
BHR	11					
CHN	545					
IND	114				50	
ISR	1,043				85	
JPN	8,019		959	235		57
KOR	1,034					
SGP	380					
THA	5					
TWN	106					
AUS	179					
Africa	14					
Residual	2,542	1,489	3,765	138	241	490

Source: US Bureau of Economic Analysis, UK Office for National Statistics, Stifterverband Germany, Statistics Canada, Ministère de l'Enseignement supérieur, de la Recherche et de l'Innovation France, Federal Statistical Office Switzerland.

R&D in the United Kingdom but almost double that (14 percent) in France and match US FCAs' 25 percent share in Switzerland.

For Canada, the United Kingdom, and France, the greatest share of BERD performed by foreign-controlled affiliates is by businesses owned in the United States. The relationship is reciprocated somewhat in the case of the United Kingdom, which is one of the most likely headquarter countries for R&D-performing FCAs in the United States alongside Germany and Japan.

However, US-owned FCAs spent US$5.7billion PPP on R&D in the United Kingdom in 2017, while UK-owned companies in the United States spent almost a third more—US$8 billion. This asymmetry is echoed for Germany, France, and especially Switzerland, where US-owned FCAs performed US$0.4billion PPP of R&D in 2015, while Switzerland-owned FCAs in the United States spent S$9.7 billion PPP.

This indicates that in absolute levels, more European MNEs carry out R&D in the United States than US MNEs conduct research in Europe. A markedly different relationship exists between the United States and Canada, with US-owned FCAs in Canada spending US$3.2 billion PPP on R&D in 2014, almost four times more than the US$0.86 billion than Canada-owned FCAs spent on R&D in the United States in 2015.

These figures provide a partial indication of the extent of global ownership linkages concerning businesses that conduct R&D and suggest that this may, to some extent, translate into flows of R&D services and licensing exports.

One key finding is the relative importance of US MNEs for R&D performance within European economies. US-owned FCAs account for around a third of FCA-performed R&D in Germany and the United Kingdom, and around a quarter of FCA R&D in France and Switzerland, but account for 62 percent of FCA-performed R&D in Canada. Figure 14.15 visualizes the ownership links in table 14.6 between R&D-performing FCAs in the United States, United Kingdom, and Canada and the countries where the FCAs' majority owners are domiciled. While these are not necessarily either transfers of R&D services or funds paid for R&D, they give an indication of the extent to which the knowledge gained might benefit MNE parents (and their other affiliates) abroad.

14.5.2   R&D Performed by Foreign Affiliates of Domestic MNEs— The Outward Perspective

The inward perspective of MNE R&D activities can be complemented with an outward perspective looking at R&D performed abroad by affiliates of domestically owned MNEs. The combination of inward and outward perspectives is necessary in order to properly identify the net balance of R&D performance ultimately controlled by resident units and so to underpin the measurement of national income.

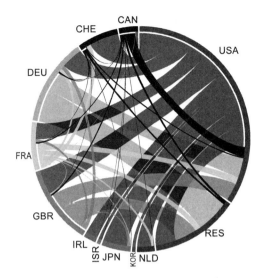

Figure 14.15   FCAs' R&D expenditure by country of FCA majority owner. Ribbons indicate FCA location (country of R&D performance)

Note: "RES" indicates "residual countries" i.e., the portion of FCA-performed R&D for which the country of ownership is not presented or not available. For example, in Germany only R&D performed by FCAs majority owned in the United States is available separately; the ownership countries of all other FCAs are therefore not known and so the majority of R&D-performing FCAs in Germany are shown as being owned by "residual countries" even though some or all of these FCAs may in reality be owned by businesses in other countries presented such as France and Switzerland. Due to data availability, IRL, ISR, JPN, KOR, NLD, RES are presented only as FCA-ownership countries; the R&D performed by FCAs in those countries is not presented.

Source: US Bureau of Economic Analysis, UK Office for National Statistics, Germany's Stifterverband, Statistics Canada, Ministère de l'Enseignement supérieur, de la Recherche et de l'Innovation France, Federal Statistical Office Switzerland.

Germany's business R&D statistics for 2015 indicate that German companies undertake US$89 billion PPP worth of R&D worldwide, of which US$ 58 billion is carried out domestically and US$31 billion abroad (Stifterverband 2017), nearly double[14] the US$16.9 billion reported in table 14.6 as being performed in Germany by FCAs. This information, combined with the trade statistics in section 14.3, allows some simplistic calculations for the potential impact of R&D globalization on the GDP and GNI aggregates for Germany:

- Germany has a net R&D export balance of US$1.4 billion. Since R&D capital formation is likely to be close to the level of R&D per-

14. The difference between what German companies report spending on R&D in the United States and what U.S.-based affiliates of German companies report is smaller but still quite significant if current exchange rates at the time are used instead of using USD PPPs (US$26 billion vs US$31 billion).

Table 14.7   **Intramural R&D expenditure of affiliates located abroad vs R&D by affiliates of foreign-owned companies, 2014 or most recent year available**

Reporting country	Outward activity of reporting country	Year	Inward activity in reporting country	Year	Unit
Germany	17,274	2013	11,925	2013	Million EUR
Israel	3,717	2011	18,913	2011	Million NIS
Japan	834,001	2014	902,529	2014	Million YEN
Slovenia	15	2014	134	2011	Million EUR
Sweden	33,825	2013	Not available		Million SEK
United States	52,174	2014	56,904	2014	Million USD

Note: Data cover the "business sector" defined in the AMNE database as International Standard Industrial Classification sections B to S excluding O.

Source: OECD AMNE Database (http://oe.cd/amne). MNE inward & outward activity by country of location.

formance indicated by Frascati Manual R&D expenditure data *minus* this balance, more R&D can be used by units abroad than is secured by domestic units from units abroad and therefore, keeping everything else constant, R&D capital formation will be lower than R&D output.

- German MNEs appear to have an excess of financial claims on R&D carried out abroad over the claims of foreign MNEs on R&D carried out in Germany amounting to US$14.1 billion PPP (US$31 billion outward minus US$16.9 billion inward). This would be expected to represent a positive net property income flow to Germany, thus raising GNI relative to GDP. However, it should be noted that in order to carry out a more precise calculation, it would be necessary to identify the extent to which foreign or domestic MNEs are involved in R&D trade.

The OECD database on the activities of MNEs includes statistics on the outward activity of MNEs by location including R&D. However, this database is sparsely populated and allows for few comparisons with R&D expenditure by affiliates of foreign-owned companies (table 14.7).

With the exception of Germany, inward R&D expenditures are greater than their outward counterparts; Japan, Israel, and the United States appear to attract more MNE R&D spending than they create abroad. Outward R&D activity can still be considerable and is equivalent to 39 percent of domestic business R&D expenditure in Sweden, 32 percent in Germany, 15 percent in the United States, 12 percent in Israel, 6 percent in Japan, and 2 percent in Slovenia.

In the case of the United States, figures show that US$52 billion of R&D is carried out by majority-owned subsidiaries of US companies abroad versus US$57 billion of R&D by subsidiaries of foreign-owned MNEs in the United States.

Available US Bureau of Economic Analysis (BEA) statistics also make

Table 14.8   Business R&D performed by affiliates of US companies abroad, 2014

Country of R&D performance	R&D performed by majority owned subsidiaries of US companies	BERD performed by FCAs ultimately owned by US companies
Total	52,174	
Germany	8,344	5,305[a]
United Kingdom	6,306	6,412
Switzerland	4,140	515[a]
Canada	3,418	3,593
China	3,036	
India	2,906	
Israel	2,695	
Japan	2,521	
Ireland	2,415	
France	2,395	2,363
Netherlands	1,226	
Brazil	1,221	
Australia	1,185	
Belgium	1,151	
Korea	946	
Italy	800	
Singapore	767	
Sweden	711	
Reporting source	United States	Partner country

Note: The figures reporting on the right column are the exchange rate converted equivalent figures of those presented in Table 14.6 in USD PPPs. US and partner country data sources, million USD (exchange rate).

Source. Column 1: US Bureau of Economic Analysis, Activities of US Multinational Enterprises: US Parent Companies and Their Foreign Affiliates: US MNE Activities: Preliminary 2014 Statistics (https://faq.bea.gov/international/xls/usdia2014p/Part%20II%20I1-I5.xls). Column 2: UK Office for National Statistics, Stifterverband Germany, Statistics Canada, Federal Statistical Office Switzerland.

[a] Germany, Switzerland: 2015 data.

it possible to provide a geographic breakdown for the US$52 billion of R&D performed abroad by majority-owned subsidiaries of US companies. Table 14.8 shows that Germany is a major location chosen by US companies to carry out R&D abroad, followed by the United Kingdom, Switzerland, Canada, and China. Comparing the US-reported data to BERD in the country of R&D performance, US-owned FCAs appear to be of particular importance in Israel (27 percent) and especially Ireland (94 percent).

The availability of R&D performance statistics from an outward perspective also opens up the opportunity for comparison with available counterpart inward reports as presented in the third column of table 14.7. The gap between US-reported outward estimates and inward estimates by the countries where R&D takes place is particularly pronounced in the case of

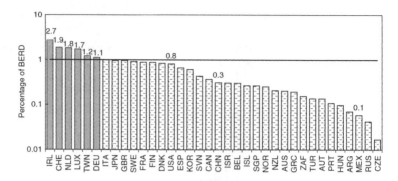

Figure 14.16   R&D expenses reported by highest R&D reporting by headquarters country, 2015. Ratio of R&D expenses by 2 500 companies in EU R&D Scoreboard to BERD, log scale

Note: Data for IRL, RUS, SGP relate to 2014; AUS, ZAF to 2013.

Source: OECD Research and Development Statistics http://oe.cd/rds, February 2018, and 2017 EU Industrial R&D Investment Scoreboard. http://iri.jrc.ec.europa.eu/scoreboard17 .html.

US MNEs' R&D performance in Switzerland, where the difference is an entire order of magnitude—Swiss-reported statistics record US$515 million of R&D performed by affiliates of US MNEs while more than US$4 billion is reported by US parents. This raises the question of whether a material share of US-located parents are ultimately owned outside the United States. Differences are also pronounced for German-owned firms.

Statistics on "outward" R&D performance are rarely available—the authors are only aware of the US data being broken down by country—and as a result it is not possible to derive a more complete figure, limiting the scope for a full analysis of the net balance between outward and inward R&D performance within MNEs. Published company reports and accounts including details on R&D activities might in principle allow for a comparative exercise, but these provide only limited and self-selected information which cannot be readily compared with official R&D statistics due to variations in R&D reporting requirements, consolidation practices, and the use of a different "net" approach from the intramural R&D concept in the Frascati Manual.

Nevertheless, with these limitations in mind, figure 14.16 compares the total R&D expenses reported by the 2 500 companies (consolidated to include all subsidiaries) with the greatest reported R&D expenses worldwide as presented in the EU R&D scoreboard (EU Joint Research Centre 2017) against national BERD. It shows that, in their business accounts, these business groups headquartered in Ireland, Switzerland, the Netherlands, and Luxembourg reported global R&D expenses significantly greater than the total business R&D expenditure performed in those countries. Indeed, the total R&D reported by "Irish" companies was three times domestic BERD in Ireland. The opposite was true 10 years ago.

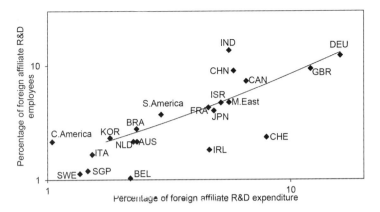

Figure 14.17   US majority-owned foreign affiliates R&D expenditure and personnel, 2014. Shares of economy over total affiliate values, log scale
Source: US Bureau of Economic Analysis, Activities of US Multinational Enterprises: US Parent Companies and Their Foreign Affiliates: US MNE Activities: Preliminary 2014 Statistics (https://faq.bea.gov/international/xls/usdia2014p/Part%20II%20I1-I5.xls).

This finding is consistent with the foregoing analysis, which has found that Ireland and Switzerland are particularly integrated, alongside the United States, in the international R&D production, trade, and ownership ecosystem. This is also true of the United Kingdom and Germany, where the R&D reported by business groups ultimately owned in those countries is equal to domestic business expenditure on R&D.

14.5.3   Identifying Substantive R&D Activity

One takeaway from the previous sections is the difficulty in integrating expenditures reported under different frameworks. The concept of expenditure associated with R&D performance aims to identify the cost of substantive R&D activity within statistical units and economies, but this requires engaging companies in a process to separate out elements that incorporate R&D carried out elsewhere in order to avoid double counting. Where this translation is not explicit, it is particularly difficult to assure that it is R&D *performance* and not another concept that is being captured because companies are more likely to refer to what is readily available in their accounts.

One mechanism for assessing the potential misalignment between reported R&D expenditures and substantive activity is to examine the link with other indicators of resources used for R&D activity. Human resources devoted to R&D are an ideal candidate because they account for a bulk of R&D expenditures across most industries and are more easily attributable to a particular location.

Figure 14.17 compares different locations' shares in the total R&D personnel and expenditures of US majority-owned affiliates abroad using BEA data for MNEs. The results, presented on a log scale, indicate a close proportional relationship between the two measures of resources (financial and human) devoted to R&D. Some outliers may be explained by differences in wage rates (e.g., India's and China's relatively high share of human resources to expenditures) and possibly also sector composition. A more in-depth analysis should take these into consideration. It is also worth noting that Switzerland, Ireland, and Belgium, to a lesser extent, have relatively low R&D employment levels in comparison to the amounts of R&D expenditures reported. This suggests that such R&D expenditures may include payments for R&D carried out elsewhere, including the United States.

Another important message is that tracking transactions may not suffice to achieve the various intended uses of R&D globalization data. Additional measurement sources and instruments may need to be deployed in order to assess where R&D assets are being used (see box 14.2).

14.6   Conclusions

This chapter has investigated available statistical evidence for OECD countries on the extent and nature of R&D globalization based on three interrelated domains: services trade, MNE activities, and R&D performance. It has made extensive use of US data owing to the greater availability and detail for this country, but it has also used a wide range of OECD and national sources to provide a complementary picture for other countries and their mutual linkages whenever possible.

On this basis, this chapter has presented what appears to be the first broad-ranging view on R&D globalization measurement based on new or recently updated international statistics manuals across the three statistical domains. Once fully implemented across countries, updated guidance may inform a better understanding of the role of R&D funding, performance, exchange, and use decisions in global production and innovation networks.

The concept of economic ownership of R&D assets across international boundaries plays a central role in making sense of the data. MNE activities represent the largest share of international R&D transactions, either trade based or funding related.

Official statistics at the level of MNE groups as a whole (business ownership–based frameworks) might often better reflect the true economic owner of R&D assets. For example, undertaking productivity analysis requires allocating inputs and outputs, including R&D, across the units to which it delivers capital services in production.

Based on the evidence examined in this chapter, it is possible to conclude with a number of recommendations for future statistical efforts:

- Various relevant data sources exist, but variations in their conceptual frameworks and perspectives need understanding and bridging. Therefore triangulation across different sources can shed useful insights. It is

Box 14.2 Patent statistics and R&D globalization

Patent statistics are based on administrative data and provide a rich source of evidence on R&D globalization (OECD 2009b; OECD 2010b). They contain information among other things on the registered ownership of patented inventions—i.e., to whom the patent is assigned. Patent data can be combined with company data to establish the characteristics of the registered "assignees," i.e., their "owners," which may be individuals or legal entities, as well as the entities that own the latter. Due to registration conventions, patent data also record information on the identity and characteristics of inventors, the individuals who are credited with developing the patented invention. The comparison between the location of inventors and ownership provides a useful source of evidence on the extent of R&D-related globalization for R&D activities more likely to be subject to this type of IP protection, as shown in the figure below.

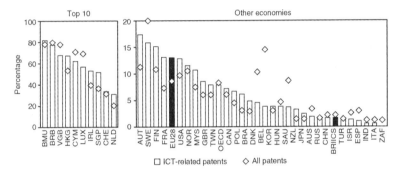

Domestic-owned patents invented abroad, as a percentage of economies' owned total IP5 patent families

Note: Foreign inventions owned by an economy relate to the number of IP5 patent families owned by a resident of an economy for which none of the inventors reside in that economy, presented as a share of total IP5 patent families owned by that economy. Data refer to IP5 families, by filing date, according to applicant residence using fractional counts.

Source: OECD, Science, Technology and Industry Scoreboard 2017, based on STI Micro-data Lab: Intellectual Property Database, http://oe.cd/ipstats, June 2017. http://dx.doi.org/10.1787/888933619049.

Patent administrative data can also leave a trace of ownership changes over time. Registering ownership with IP offices is generally not compulsory and can be costly, but owners have incentives to register such changes in order to assert their IPRs relative to third parties (OECD 2013). Such data have been used for example to track patent relocation in response to policy incentives in the form of regimes that provide a favorable treatment of incomes arising from IPRs. For example, Ciaramella (2017) shows that Ireland witnessed the highest ratio among EU countries of EPO (European Patent Office) patents gained to lost (5 times), followed by Luxembourg, Malta, and Portugal. These data can be in principle compared with trade on proprietary rights arising from R&D.

also important to understand what records companies have access to and use as the basis of their responses when they complete statistical survey questionnaires.

- It appears increasingly important to consider and understand the role of exchanges between affiliated companies. Cases of direct parent/subsidiary relationships, as have been a main focus in this chapter, are a first step, though other forms of relationship, such as affiliated enterprises related between a mutual parent (i.e., sister companies), also need to be captured in data sources in order to achieve a comprehensive and consistent statistical representation of the world.

- Within countries, coordinating or benchmarking data collection on MNEs, as well as data linking across different statistical domains, may facilitate policy making and research on intangibles and knowledge as business assets.

- Analysis of microdata can help provide a more detailed understanding of the dynamics and compositional patterns associated with R&D globalization. For example, it appears from ongoing OECD distributed R&D microdata work (http://oe.cd/microberd) that in spite of increasing concentration of economic activity on large players, R&D performance itself is becoming less concentrated within countries, pointing at a potential growing decoupling of R&D performance and use.

- Greater coordination across countries' statistical offices could help ensure a more robust and comprehensive view of R&D globalization. New tools and standards may allow for this to take place without breaching confidentiality.

- Administrative data on intangibles have yet to be integrated in the analysis of R&D and innovation globalization.

- The analysis of R&D globalization needs to be better integrated in the broader analysis of global innovation networks. This is a major area for dedicated innovation surveys to attempt to develop further, including within the ongoing revision of the Oslo Manual innovation measurement framework (OECD, Eurostat 2005).

References

Baldwin, R. 2006. *Globalization: The Great Unbundling(s)*. Economic Council of Finland.

Berry, H. 2014. "Global Integration and Innovation: Multicountry Knowledge Generation within MNCs." *Strategic Management Journal* 35 (6): 869–90.

Cantwell, J. A. 2017. "Innovation and international business." *Industry and Innovation* 24 (1): 41–60. https://doi.org/10.1080/13662716.2016.1257422.

Castellani, D., S. Montresor, T. Schubert, and A. Vezzani. 2016. "Multinationality,

R&D and productivity: Evidence from the top R&D investors worldwide." *International Business Review* 26 (3): 405–16.

Chute, J. W., S. H. McCulla, and S. Smith. 2018. "Preview of the 2018 Comprehensive Update of the National Income and Product Accounts Changes in Methods, Definitions, and Presentations." *Survey of Current Business* 98 (4).

Ciaramella, L. 2017. "Patent Boxes and the Relocation of Intellectual Property." https://dx.doi.org/10.2139/ssrn.2943435.

Dachs, B., R. Stehrer, and G. Zahradnik, eds. 2014. *The Internationalisation of Business R&D*. Cheltenham, UK: Edward Elgar.

EU Joint Research Centre. 2017. The 2017 EU Industrial R&D Investment Scoreboard. http://iri.jrc.ec.europa.eu/scoreboard17.html.

European Commission, International Monetary Fund, OECD, United Nations, World Bank. 2009. System of National Accounts 2008. https://unstats.un.org/unsd/nationalaccount/sna2008.asp.

International Monetary Fund. 2009. *Balance of Payments and International Investment Position Manual, Sixth Edition*. International Monetary Fund. https://www.imf.org/external/pubs/ft/bop/2007/pdf/bpm6.pdf.

Kylaheiko, K., A. Jantunen, K. Puumalainen, S. Saarenketo, and A. Tuppura. 2011. "Innovation and internationalization as growth strategies: The role of technological capabilities and appropriability." *International Business Review* 20 (5): 508–20.

Lipsey, R. E. 2010. "Measuring the Location of Production in a World of Intangible Productive Assets, FDI, and Intrafirm Trade." *Review of Income and Wealth* 56 (1): 99–110.

Maftei, V. 2007. "R&D internationalization. An overview of the driving forces." Analele Stiintifice ale Universitatii "Alexandru Ioan Cuza" din Iasi - Stiinte Economice (1954-2015). Alexandru Ioan Cuza University, Faculty of Economics and Business Administration, vol. 54, 138–143. http://anale.feaa.uaic.ro/anale/resurse/20_Maftei_V_-_R&D_internationalization.pdf.

Moris, F. 2009. "R&D exports and imports: new data and methodological issues." In *International Trade in Services and Intangibles in the Era of Globalization*, Studies in Income and Wealth volume 69, edited by M. Reinsdorf and M. J. Slaughter, 175–97. Chicago, IL: University of Chicago Press.

Moris, F. 2016. R&D Performance of US-Located Multinational Companies: Results from Multiagency Survey Linking Project. National Science Foundation.

Moris, F. 2017. "Intangibles Trade and MNEs: Supply-Chain Trade in R&D Services and Innovative Subsidiaries." *Journal of Industry, Competition and Trade* 1–23. https://doi.org/10.1007/s10842-017-0265-0.

Moris, F., and W. Zeile. 2016. "Innovation-Related Services Trade by Multinational Enterprises." *Survey of Current Business* 1–6. doi:10.1007/s10842-017-0265-0.

OECD. 1998. Internationalisation of Industrial R&D: Patterns and Trends. Paris: OECD Publishing. http://dx.doi.org/10.1787/9789264163782-en.

OECD. 2008. Recent trends in the internationalisation of R&D in the enterprise sector. Paris: OECD Publishing.

OECD. 2009a. Innovation in Firms: A Microeconomic Perspective. Paris: OECD Publishing. http://dx.doi.org/10.1787/9789264056213-en.

OECD. 2009b. Patent Statistics Manual. Paris: OECD Publishing. doi:dx.doi.org/10.1787/9789264056442-en.

OECD. 2010a. Handbook on Deriving Capital Measures of Intellectual Property Products. Paris: OECD Publishing. http://www.oecd.org/publications/handbook-on-deriving-capital-measures-of-intellectual-property-products-9789264079205-en.htm.

OECD. 2010b. Measuring Globalization: OECD Economic Globalization Indicators 2010. Paris: OECD Publishing. doi:dx.doi.org/10.1787/9789264084360-en.

OECD. 2013. Knowledge Networks and Markets. Science, Technology, and Innovation Policy Papers. http://dx.doi.org/10.1787/5k44wzw9q5zv-en.

OECD. 2015. Frascati Manual 2015: Guidelines for Collecting and Reporting Data on Research and Experimental Development. Paris: OECD Publishing. http://dx.doi.org/10.1787/9789264239012-en.

OECD. 2016. "Irish GDP up by 26.3% in 2015?" Accessed February 2018. https://www.oecd.org/std/na/Irish-GDP-up-in-2015-OECD.pdf.

OECD. 2017a. "The links between global value chains and global innovation networks." OECD Science, Technology, and Innovation Policy Papers. doi:dx.doi.org/10.1787/76d78fbb-en.

OECD. 2017b. Transfer Pricing Guidelines for Multinational Enterprises and Tax Administrations 2017. Paris: OECD Publishing. doi:dx.doi.org/10.1787/tpg-2017-en.

OECD. 2017c. R&D Tax Incentive Country Profiles: Ireland. http://www.oecd.org/sti/RDTax%20Country%20Profiles%20-%20IRL.pdf.

OECD, Eurostat. 2005. Oslo Manual: Guidelines for Collecting and Interpreting Innovation Data, 3rd Edition. Paris: OECD Publishing. http://www.oecd.org/sti/inno/oslomanualguidelinesforcollectingandinterpretinginnovationdata3rdedition.htm.

Rassier, D. G. 2017. "Improving the SNA Treatment of Multinational Enterprises." *Review of Income and Wealth* 287–320. https://doi.org/10.1111/roiw.12323.

Stifterverband. 2017. ꝺ:R ꝺN 'DI: ANALYSEN 2017. Stifterverband. https://www.stifterverband.org/arendi-analysen_2017.

Sturgeon, T. J. 2013. Global Value Chains and Economic Globalization—Towards a New Measurement Framework; Report to Eurostat. Eurostat. http://globalvaluechains.eu.

UNCTAD. 2005. World Investment Report 2005: Transnational Corporations and the Internationalisation of R&D. http://unctad.org/en/pages/PublicationArchive.aspx?publicationid=693.

UNECE, OECD. 2015. *Guide to Measuring Global Production.* UNECE.

United Nations Economic Commission for Europe. 2011. The Impact of Globalization on National Accounts. Geneva: United Nations. http://www.unece.org/fileadmin/DAM/stats/groups/wggna/Guide_on_Impact_of_globalization_on_national_accounts_FINAL21122011.pdf.

United Nations Economic Commission for Europe. 2015. Ownership of Intellectual Property Products inside global production. In *Guide to Measuring Global Production.* United Nations. http://www.unece.org/fileadmin/DAM/stats/publications/2015/Guide_to_Measuring_Global_Production__2015_.pdf.

United Nations, Eurostat, International Monetary Fund, OECD, United Nations Conference on Trade and Development, World Tourism Organization, World Trade Organization. 2011. Manual on Statistics of International Trade in Services 2010. United Nations. https://unstats.un.org/unsd/publication/seriesm/seriesm_86rev1e.pdf.

Yorgason, D. 2007. "Treatment of International Research and Development as Investment: Issues and Estimates." BEA/NSF R&D Satellite Account Background Paper. Washington, DC: Bureau of Economic Analysis.

Comment   Nune Hovhannisyan

Introduction

The fragmentation of production processes across international borders represents a new aspect of globalization. As part of this phenomenon, research and development (R&D) activities have also become fragmented. This shift has been driven by foreign direct investment (FDI) and global value chains mostly within multinational corporations (MNC), looking at both trade in R&D services and business R&D statistics. As a case in point consider US MNCs. Branstetter, Glennon, and Jensen (2018) report that the foreign R&D landscape of US MNCs changed dramatically from 1989 to 2014, where the importance of the traditional R&D hubs (the UK, Germany, France, and Canada) reduced from 74 percent of all foreign US MNC R&D to 43 percent. That decline mainly resulted from the emergence of new hubs such as Israel, India, and China. Research has shown that R&D is an important component that explains differences in productivity and innovation among MNCs and other firms through international trade and FDI linkages (Bilir and Morales 2019). It is widely known that R&D and innovation are crucial for economic growth and the convergence of countries. Thus, it is imperative to collect and construct various statistics to better understand R&D globalization.

In this chapter, Ker, Galindo-Rueda, Moris, and Jankowski present an excellent collection of R&D statistics from existing and new sources by covering many countries pertinent to R&D globalization, following the revision of statistical guidelines. Their work highlights the importance of this new evidence for statistical and policy discussions in various economic areas, and promotes further work using R&D globalization data. Furthermore, their work compares various frameworks to measure their compatibility and provides excellent explanations of potential disparities.

Previous data limitations and challenges have been an impediment to the measurement of R&D globalization, but recent statistical advances offer improved methods of analysis. Specifically, the chapter refers to the following statistical advances: (1) the System of National Accounts (SNA) revision of 2008 recognized R&D expenditures as a form of investment, (2) the Manual on Statistics in International Trade in Services (MSITS) provided new details for international transactions in R&D services, and (3) the 2015 Frascati Manual presented new guidelines for measuring R&D globalization in business and elsewhere (OECD 2015). The authors note

Nune Hovhannisyan is an associate professor of economics at Loyola University Maryland.
For acknowledgments, sources of research support, and disclosure of the author's material financial relationships, if any, please see https://www.nber.org/books-and-chapters/challenges -globalization-measurement-national-accounts/comment-capturing-international-rd-trade -and-financing-flows-what-do-available-sources-reveal-about.

that the globalization of R&D and international R&D-related flows plays a major role in observed differences between Frascati-based R&D statistics and the SNA view of R&D investment (see figures 14.1 and 14.2 in chapter 14; all references to figures, paragraphs, and tables in this comment apply to the original paper). For example, Ireland presents an interesting case where, driven by large imports of R&D assets, R&D stock has grown more than ninefold from 2000 to 2014.

Using economic ownership as a key organizing concept, the authors present evidence of R&D globalization through three different interrelated data channels:

1. R&D in services trade statistics (who buys and sells R&D);
2. Statistics on R&D performance and sources of funding (who funds R&D);
3. R&D performance by MNCs (who owns the company).

R&D in Services Trade Statistics

The presentation of R&D in services trade statistics in 2016 reveals that Ireland and Switzerland are net importers of R&D services (for Ireland, net imports of R&D services represent a striking 14 percent of its GDP). Israel and Luxembourg are net exporters, while the United States has a nearly zero balance (see figure 14.3). In terms of volume, the main exporters of R&D services are the United States, Germany, and France, while the main importers are Ireland, the United States, and Germany.[1] With regard to bilateral trade statistics, the authors acknowledge the inconsistency of R&D services reported by different countries in relation to the United States (see table 14.3). Specifically, the data show that R&D exports from the United States reported by the United States itself are much smaller than the R&D imports from the United States reported by other countries, with differences ranging from 60 percent for Estonia to 600 percent for Austria. The authors mention several possible reasons for these discrepancies, including different data collection methods and standards, re-exporting, and R&D services subcontracting. However, they defer to another OECD working party that is responsible for investigating these issues further. If we compare the trade in services to trade in goods, imports data generally represent a more reliable source than exports data because tariffs are assessed on the imports side, though the question remains as to which source is more reliable for trade in R&D services.

The data illustrate that multinationals play a leading role within R&D services trade, with affiliated (parent-affiliate) trade being close to 90 percent for both R&D services exports from the United States and R&D services imports to the United States (see figure 14.8). As the authors note,

1. These data are based on the OECD Extended Balance of Payments Services (EBOPS) database, which does not include countries like China or India.

the absence of industry detail and data on trade with other affiliates of the same parent company (affiliate-affiliate) are major limitations. It would be interesting to look for additional evidence in relation to these issues in the Bureau of Economic Analysis (BEA) benchmark surveys, which typically provide more detailed data (including some data listed by both country and industry), as well as utilizing the royalties and licenses data collected by the BEA.

Statistics on R&D Performance and Sources of Funding

The data presented show that business enterprise expenditures on R&D (BERD) in OECD countries in 2015 totaled around US $0.86 trillion, with US businesses representing approximately 42 percent of the total amount. Israel had the largest funding from abroad while having the lowest R&D net imports (greatest net exports). Ireland ranks fifth in R&D funding from abroad but, as noted above, leads in R&D net imports. The authors construct an interesting figure to compare R&D services exports with the BERD funded by the rest of the world (see figure 14.11), highlighting the fact that R&D services exports are much larger than R&D funded from abroad. The authors list multiple reasons for this discrepancy and argue that funding of R&D from abroad is not a measure of international trade in R&D but rather includes both payments for the acquisition of services and unrequited payments to support R&D performance. Good progress in this regard is illustrated by the Frascati Manual 2015, which recommends distinguishing R&D funding transactions between "exchange funds," which imply sales of R&D, and "transfer funds," which are paid toward R&D performance. Preliminary evidence from Switzerland and Finland presented by the authors suggests that less than 20 percent of R&D funding from the rest of the world for these countries are transfer funds. Meanwhile, the data behind who funds R&D from abroad indicate that multinationals play a leading role here as well (see figure 14.12). Indeed, in most of the countries, foreign affiliates are the main funders of R&D.

According to the authors, for many countries there is little data on R&D payments for R&D performed by others or outsourcing of R&D, mainly due to survey designs that make it difficult to distinguish R&D funders from performers. The authors mention that the United States Business R&D and Innovation Survey (BRDIS) collects rich data on the outsourcing of R&D. Indeed, these data shed light on US-based companies engaging in R&D activities abroad and are very useful for studying technology transfer issues. For example, the data show that in 2015 most of the total R&D performed abroad was performed by foreign subsidiaries of US-based companies and was mostly paid for by the companies themselves. It would be beneficial if other OECD countries collected similar data to facilitate similar research on other countries.

R&D Performance by MNC

As mentioned above, the intricacy of multinational firms has a huge impact on globalization of R&D, as foreign affiliates comprise a significant portion of business R&D performance. For example, "around 60 percent of all business R&D in Ireland, Belgium, the Czech Republic, and the Slovak Republic takes place within businesses majority owned by firms abroad" (see chapter 14, section 14.5.1 and figure 14.13). However, the same figure shows that the share of business R&D that is funded from abroad is low. For Belgium, for example, those numbers are 62 percent and 10 percent, respectively. The authors offer a possible explanation involving the distinction between "internal" and "external" funds. Furthermore, the evidence presented shows that foreign-controlled ownership does not match closely with R&D services exports.

The authors present interesting data indicating that more European MNCs engage in R&D in the United States than US MNCs do R&D in Europe (see table 14.6). This provides strong support for the technology sourcing hypothesis that countries can tap into US frontier knowledge by locating R&D in the United States (Griffith, Harrison, and van Reenen 2006) or by sending its business travelers to the United States (Hovhannisyan and Keller 2019). Furthermore, the same table shows that US MNCs account for 25 to 35 percent of R&D in Europe but 62 percent in Canada. This suggests that even in the context of R&D globalization, geographic distance still matters, as there is "gravity of knowledge" (Keller and Yeaple 2013) and that face-to-face communication is preferable for technology transfer and innovation (Hovhannisyan and Keller 2015).

The authors compare R&D performance statistics from an outward perspective to an inward perspective for the United States. They show that there are large discrepancies in R&D reporting by majority-owned foreign controlled affiliates of US MNCs compared to partner countries reporting inward R&D. For example, the case for Switzerland is particularly striking, with figures being $4 billion vs. $4 million, respectively. More data and research are required to explain such discrepancies. In addition, "outward" R&D statistics by countries are only available for US multinationals, and other OECD countries should collect and report similar data. Using the European Union scoreboard for the R&D expenditures of 2,500 companies and comparing it to national business expenditures on R&D, the authors provide some limited findings that show that total company-reported R&D in Ireland is three times the business expenditures on R&D, while it was quite the reverse a decade earlier. The question remains to what extent tax savings and transfer pricing matter for R&D data discrepancies for MNCs. For example, Bilicka (2019) finds that foreign multinational subsidiaries in the UK considerably underreport their taxable profits compared to domestic firms.

Conclusions and Possible Future Directions

The chapter by Ker, Galindo-Rueda, Moris, and Jankowski analyzed available statistical data from OECD countries on R&D globalization, examining services trade, R&D performance, and MNC activities. The chapter did an excellent job of presenting evidence that these three ways of looking at R&D data are intertwined. The authors mention several important takeaways from their chapter. First, various data sources exist but there are considerable differences in their conceptual frameworks. Second, affiliated companies play a major role in R&D globalization, and although parent-affiliate connection data are available, there is a need for more affiliate- affiliate connection data. Third, more coordination between different statistical agencies and more international cooperation is crucial. Fourth, the analysis of micro-data and comparison with macro data are important. An interesting preliminary insight from micro-data shows that R&D performance is becoming less concentrated despite increasing concentration of economic activity between large players. Fifth, R&D and innovation are inextricably linked, and therefore R&D globalization should be viewed within the lens of global innovation frameworks. Finally, data on intangibles are not collected and/or integrated in R&D globalization data, however intangibles might also play a major role in R&D globalization.

Several opportunities to pursue future research in line with the conclusions enumerated by the authors should be noted. For US R&D data, for example, the three-way data linkage project between the BEA, the Census Bureau, and the National Science Foundation allowed further analysis of R&D data. Similar efforts to achieve data standardization and linkage for other OECD countries would be very valuable for the same purposes. Additionally, it is widely known that technological knowledge is hard to codify, and this might drive the underreporting of R&D trade in services, along with other factors such as tax shifting/transfer pricing. Future research in this area would be beneficial.

Additional avenues for future research include:

1. Data by industry, as R&D globalization might impact various industries disproportionally. For example, Branstetter, Glennon, and Jensen (2018) offer a new explanation for the shift in the location of foreign R&D, which involves an increasingly central role of information technology and a global shortage of engineers with basic skills.

2. Data by geographic detail, which would provide additional evidence on R&D globalization. For example, within the United States more disaggregated data at the state or county level could uncover the location of R&D. In our research, we linked several data sources to create US R&D data by state and found that there is a lack of R&D data at a more geographically disaggregated level. Similarly, examining data sources for regional R&D in

Europe, we found that many missing observations inhibit research in this area (Hovhannisyan and Keller 2019).

3. Data on knowledge spillovers. While there are no data on knowledge spillovers per se, it is important to augment the current framework with proxies or indirect measures of knowledge spillovers as research has established the significance of those (Keller 2004).

4. Data on patents. Although the authors offer some initial statistics on patenting, more patenting and patent-citation data are needed. For example, using patenting databases from the United States Patent and Trademark Office (USPTO), it is possible to identify the percentage of US-owned patents invented by foreign inventors. In addition, the USPTO patent inventor database provides rich geographic and assignee details, so it is possible to gauge joint US/foreign innovation to augment data on R&D globalization.

5. Data on royalty and license payments are not linked, which would provide additional insights on the extent of R&D globalization.

To conclude, this is an excellent chapter offering an important contribution to the understanding and measurement of R&D globalization, with helpful implications for further research and policy discussion.

References

Bilicka, K. A. 2019. "Comparing UK Tax Returns of Foreign Multinationals to Matched Domestic Firms." *American Economic Review* 109 (8): 2921–53.

Branstetter, L., B. Glennon, and B. J. Jensen. 2018. "Knowledge Transfer Abroad: The Role of U.S. Inventors within Global R&D Networks." NBER Working Paper No. 24453. Cambridge, MA: National Bureau of Economic Research, Inc.

Bilir, K. L., and E. Morales. 2019. "Innovation in the Global Firm." *Journal of Political Economy* 128 (4): https://doi.org/10.1086/705418.

Griffith, R., R. Harrison, and J. van Reenen. 2006. "How Special Is the Special Relationship? Using the Impact of U.S. R&D Spillovers on UK Firms as a Test of Technology Sourcing." *American Economic Review* 96 (5): 1859–79.

Hovhannisyan, N., and W. Keller. 2015. "International Business Travel: An Engine of Innovation?" *Journal of Economic Growth* 20 (1): 75–104.

Hovhannisyan, N., and W. Keller. 2019. "International Business Travel and Technology Sourcing." NBER Working Paper No. 25862. Cambridge, MA: National Bureau of Economic Research, Inc.

Keller, W. 2004. "International Technology Diffusion." *Journal of Economic Literature* 42 (3): 752–82.

Keller, W., and S. R. Yeaple. 2013. "The Gravity of Knowledge." *American Economic Review* 103 (4): 1414–44.

OECD. 2015. *Frascati Manual 2015: Guidelines for Collecting and Reporting Data on Research and Experimental Development, The Measurement of Scientific, Technological and Innovation Activities.* Paris: OECD Publishing.

Contributors

Nadim Ahmad
OECD
2, rue André Pascal
75016 Paris, France

Sarah Atkinson
US Department of Agriculture
1400 Independence Avenue, SW
Washington, DC 20250

Maria Borga
International Monetary Fund
700 19th Street, NW
Washington, DC 20431

Jennifer Bruner
Bureau of Economic Analysis
4600 Silver Hill Road
Washington, DC 20233

Cecilia Caliandro
Analysis Group
35 boulevard des Capucines
75002 Paris, France

Michael Connolly
Central Statistics Office
Ardee Road
Dublin D06 FX52, Ireland

Mark de Haan
International Monetary Fund
700 19th Street, NW
Washington, DC 20431

James J. Fetzer
Bureau of Economic Analysis
4600 Silver Hill Road
Washington, DC 20233

John FitzGerald
Department of Economics
Trinity College Dublin
Dublin 2, Ireland

Teresa C. Fort
Tuck School of Business
Dartmouth College
100 Tuck Hall
Hanover, NH 03755

Fernando Galindo-Rueda
OECD
2 rue André Pascal
75775 Paris Cedex 16, France

Caroline Hambÿe
Federal Planning Bureau
Rue Belliard 14-18
1040 Brussels, Belgium

Joseph Haynes
CBS/Statistics Netherlands
Henri Faasdreef 312
2492 JP The Hague, the Netherlands

Bart Hertveldt
Federal Planning Bureau
Rue Belliard 14-18
1040 Brussels, Belgium

Tina Highfill
Bureau of Economic Analysis
4600 Silver Hill Road
Washington, DC 20233

Kassu W. Hossiso
Bureau of Economic Analysis
4600 Silver Hill Road
Washington, DC 20233

Susan N. Houseman
W. E. Upjohn Institute for
    Employment Research
300 S. Westnedge Avenue
Kalamazoo, MI 49007

Nune Hovhannisyan
Department of Economics
Loyola University Maryland
4501 North Charles Street
Baltimore, MD 21210

Thomas F. Howells III
Bureau of Economic Analysis
4600 Silver Hill Road
Washington, DC 20233

John Jankowski
National Science Foundation
2415 Eisenhower Avenue
Alexandria, VA 22314

Derrick Jenniges
Internal Revenue Service
77 K Street NE
Washington, DC 20002

J. Bradford Jensen
McDonough School of Business
Georgetown University
Washington, DC 20057

Fariha Kamal
US Census Bureau
4600 Silver Hill Road
Washington, DC 20233

Daniel Ker
UNCTAD, Palais des Nations
8-14, Avenue de la Paix
1211 Geneva 10, Switzerland

Paul Konijn
Eurostat
5, Rue Alphonse Weicker
L-2721, Luxembourg

Bart Los
Faculty of Economics and Business
University of Groningen
9700 AV Groningen, the Netherlands

Raymond Mataloni Jr. (deceased)

Bernhard Michel
Federal Planning Bureau
Rue Belliard 14-18
1040 Brussels, Belgium

Francisco Moris
National Science Foundation
2415 Eisenhower Avenue
Alexandria, VA 22314

Brent R. Moulton
366 Hart Road
Gaithersburg, MD 20878

Henk Nijmeijer
CBS/Statistics Netherlands
Henri Faasdreef 312
2492 JP The Hague, the Netherlands

Michael Polder
CBS/Statistics Netherlands
Henri Faasdreef 312
2492 JP The Hague, the Netherlands

Dylan G. Rassier
Bureau of Economic Analysis
4600 Silver Hill Road
Washington, DC 20233

Stephen J. Redding
Department of Economics and SPIA
Princeton University
Princeton, NJ 08544

J. David Richardson
Department of Economics
110 Eggers Hall
Syracuse University
Syracuse, NY 13244-1090

Kim J. Ruhl
Department of Economics
University of Wisconsin-Madison
7444 Social Science Building
1180 Observatory Drive
Madison, WI 53706

Silke Stapel-Weber
Directorate General Statistics
European Central Bank
60640 Frankfurt am Main, Germany

Erich H. Strassner
Bureau of Economic Analysis
4600 Silver Hill Road
Washington, DC 20233

Marcel P. Timmer
Faculty of Economics and Business
University of Groningen
9700 AV Groningen, the Netherlands

Mark Vancauteren
Hasselt University
Campus Diepenbeek, Agoralaan,
   Gebouw D
B-3590 Diepenbeek, Belgium

Peter van de Ven
Dauw 4
3454 TN De Meern
The Netherlands

Marcel van den Berg
CBS/Statistics Netherlands
Henri Faasdreef 312
2492 JP The Hague, the Netherlands

John Verrinder
Eurostat
5, Rue Alphonse Weicker
L 2721, Luxembourg

Erin (Yiran) Xin
Bureau of Economic Analysis
4600 Silver Hill Road
Washington, DC 20233

Jeffrey A. Young
Bureau of Economic Analysis
4600 Silver Hill Road
Washington, DC 20233

Robert E. Yuskavage
Bureau of Economic Analysis
4600 Silver Hill Road
Washington, DC 20233

Author Index

Subject Index

Page numbers followed by "f" or "t" refer to figures or tables, respectively.